"The Judaism we practice today is, in so many ways, sourced in the theological revolution of the Baal Shem Tov, the founder of Chasidus. Now, Rabbi Burt Jacobson leads us into the profound psycho-spiritual teachings of the Baal Shem, which are centered in the love of God, and shows us how they can become the communal and personal animating principles of our lives. Such brilliant scholarship and depth of soul!" —RABBI WAYNE DOSICK, PhD, author of *Living Judaism* and *Radical Loving*

"Burt has striven his entire life to hand over the legacy of Hasidism and of my father to generations to come. Let us listen to his voice in the pages of this book so that we may be enriched by our Hasidic inheritance and offer that heritage as a great fire of passionate devotion to God, to one another, to our fragile earth to generations to come." —SUSANNAH HESCHEL, Eli M. Black Distinguished Professor of Jewish Studies, Dartmouth College

"Rabbi Burt Jacobson has given us the work of a lifetime—a treasury of stories, practices, and scholarship—bringing to life a Tzadik with the power to awaken our capacity for direct mystical experience. *Living in the Presence* is an important book for all spiritual seekers bearing much needed medicine for our troubled modern souls." —RABBI TIRZAH FIRESTONE, PhD, author of *Wounds into Wisdom: Healing Intergenerational Jewish Trauma*

"We step into the Besht's transformative presence. Rabbi Burt brings us with him on a journey of deep reflection. Though based on a lifetime of dedication to his subject and meticulous scholarship, this is not an academic book but a practical one that speaks to the relevance of the Besht's wisdom to issues that have always been central to the spiritual quest—the meaning of suffering and trauma, the lessons of justice and injustice, and the path to communion with the divine." —KENNETH COHEN, author of *Honoring the Medicine: The Essential Guide to Native American Healing*

"A masterpiece of profound insight, powerful love, and intimate longing. Rabbi Jacobson has opened us to a vast stream of timeless Wisdom, illuminated by his own deeply personal journey into Mystery and ultimate meaning. I am so grateful to Burt for his penetrating honesty, and for connecting me to this lineage of Love." —RABBI SHEFA GOLD, author of *Torah Journeys: The Inner Path to the Promised Land*

"This unique memoir recounts the author's lifelong search for truth, healing, and spiritual awakening. Jacobson shares his intimate struggles with faith and how he eventually found a way to integrate his universal aspirations as a child of the Sixties with the radical wisdom teachings of Hasidism. This is not just another book on Kabbalah and Hasidism, but a masterpiece crafted over many decades of deep contemplation of the mystical teachings and life of the author's spirit guide, the Baal Shem Tov." —ESTELLE FRANKEL, psychotherapist, spiritual director, and teacher of Jewish mysticism; author of *Sacred Therapy* and *The Wisdom of Not Knowing*

"This deeply profound and personal work transcends genres—memoir, history, mystery, theology, text study, spiritual practice—and is an indispensable guidebook for those looking to find modern meaning in ancestral wisdom." —ZVIKA KRIEGER, spiritual leader, Chochmat HaLev; former director of responsible innovation, Facebook/Meta

"Burt Jacobson has had front-row seats if not leadership positions in the hottest epicenters of American neo-Hasidism, from Heschel's classrooms to Havurat Shalom, from the House of Love and Prayer to the Aquarian Minyan and, ultimately, his own revolutionary Kehilla Community Synagogue. At once personal memoir, mystical meditation, and scholarly exploration, *Living in the Presence* illuminates what it can mean to cultivate a relationship with a Rebbe from the past and thereby deepen one's connections to beings in the present." —SAM S.B. SHONKOFF, Taube Family Assistant Professor of Jewish Studies, Graduate Theological Union

"*Living in the Presence* is a great gift to every spiritual seeker." —RABBI EDWARD FELD, author of *The Book of Revolutions*

LIVING
IN THE
PRESENCE

A PERSONAL QUEST
FOR THE BAAL SHEM TOV

A RABBI'S JOURNEY TO DISCOVER THE
ORIGINAL MEANING OF HASIDISM

BURT JACOBSON

FOREWORD BY
SUSANNAH HESCHEL

AFTERWORD BY
RICHARD STONE

Monkfish Book Publishing Company
Rhinebeck, New York

Paperback ISBN 978-1-958972-63-2
Hardcover ISBN 978-1-958972-67-0
eBook ISBN 978-1-958972-64-9

Library of Congress Cataloging-in-Publication Data

Names: Jacobson, Burt, author. | Heschel, Susannah, writer of foreword. |
    Stone, Richard, 1943-2018, writer of afterword.
Title: Living in the presence : a personal quest for the Baal Shem Tov : a
    rabbi's journey to discover the original meaning of Hasidism / Burt
    Jacobson ; foreword by Susannah Heschel ; afterword by Richard Stone.
Description: Rhinebeck, New York : Monkfish Book Publishing Company, 2024.
    | Includes index.
Identifiers: LCCN 2024031999 (print) | LCCN 2024032000 (ebook) | ISBN
    9781958972632 (paperback) | ISBN 9781958972670 (hardcover) | ISBN
    9781958972649 (ebook)
Subjects: LCSH: Ba'al Shem Ṭov, approximately 1700-1760. |
    Rabbis--Ukraine--Biography. | Hasidism.
Classification: LCC BM755.I8 J34 2024 (print) | LCC BM755.I8 (ebook) |
    DDC 296.8/332092 [B]--dc23/eng/20240801
LC record available at https://lccn.loc.gov/2024031999
LC ebook record available at https://lccn.loc.gov/2024032000

Cover painting: "Jews Praying in the Synagogue on Yom Kippur" (1878) by
Maurycy Gottlieb
Book and cover design by Colin Rolfe

Monkfish Book Publishing Company
22 East Market Street, Suite 304
Rhinebeck, New York 12572
(845) 876-4861
monkfishpublishing.com

FOR DIANE

"For love is as strong as death."
SONG OF SONGS 8:6

[W]e must ask to what extent religion is absolute presence, absolute present that can never become past and
must therefore become present and be present in every
time and for every time.

MARTIN BUBER

Hasidism is a movement of the spirit that arises as a
yearning for God and the sacred, and which expresses
itself through acts of lovingkindness and service to the
same. Hasidism is the willingness to make ourselves
transparent to God's grace and will, to live in the authentic Presence of God—*nokhah peney ha-Shem*—as if facing God in every moment, allowing this awareness to
change our behavior, to make sacred acts out of potentially profane and purely secular moments.

REB ZALMAN SCHACHTER-SHALOMI

CONTENTS

PART THREE: EXCAVATING THE BAAL SHEM'S LEGACY

FOREWORD

To have a life partner as a wellspring of inspiration is a precious gift that Burt Jacobson has cultivated as a disciple of the Baal Shem Tov, a gift that he now offers to us in this magnificent memoir of introspection and teaching.

A spiritual seeker, Burt did not fit well into the rigors of Conservative rabbinical training that emphasized Talmudic learning, adherence to halakha, and little nourishment of the inner life. And then he discovered, through his teacher, my father, Rabbi Abraham Joshua Heschel, the Baal Shem Tov, the founder of Hasidism. Burt was a "spiritual seeker" who became a disciple of the Baal Shem Tov, the Besht. What does it mean to be a disciple of the Besht? To be a witness: one who understands through the soul, not only through the mind; one who strives to lead a life like that of the great Hasidic teachers, a life lived in the presence of God, a presence found in the hearts of our fellow human beings, in the words of Torah, in nature, and in prayer.

Having spent his life living in the presence of the Besht, Burt now reflects on the inspiration and guidance he received. He sought to understand the manifold ways of the Besht, his interactions with people as well as his teachings. My father writes that the Besht "brought heaven down to earth." Joy filled the hearts of Jews: to live in God's presence is to live with joy and celebration.

Yes, there is deep pain in our world. Such pain is precisely why we turn to rabbis. Hasidism understands this, and Burt emphasizes the importance for a rabbi to enter the pain of others, to share it, and to try to lift people up. Burt experienced some terrible episodes of adversity that he describes in his book, yet as a disciple of the Besht he knew that adversity does not have to lead to resentment and anger, but rather inspired him with a longing to find ways to soothe other people's troubles, to heal their suffering. That is the obligation—indeed, the privilege—of being a rabbi.

My father was deeply troubled that the great spiritual movement of Hasidism was so badly misunderstood. Too often reduced to psychological or sociological categories, as if this extraordinary religious revolution within Judaism could be attributed to simple-mindedness, ignorance, primitive conditions. Hasidism to my father, as Burt writes, had to be understood on its own terms: "What does it mean to be a Hasid? To be a Hasid is to be in love, to be in love with God and with what God has created. Once you are in love you are a different human being." Hasidism changed the Jewish people.

What are the questions a religious movement seeks to answer? For Hasidism, the questions concerned prayer: how can I pray with greater devotion and intensity? They also concerned our daily life: Hasidic rebbes helped people in need—of a doctor, of money, of a *shidduch* for a child. Most of all, Hasidism was concerned with cultivating the inner life: How can my heart become more sensitive to the needs of my fellow human beings, of nature as God's creation? How can I cultivate my heart so that I can find God's presence when I study Torah, but also when I walk in a forest or talk to my friends?

My father used to say that the most important word that represents Judaism is compassion. It is the compassion we should express to one another, the compassion of God for us, and our compassion for God who suffers pain when we hurt one another.

Burt wisely understands that my father's phenomenology of piety was based on his understanding of the Baal Shem Tov. It was also based on my father's experience of Hasidic rebbes in Poland, where he grew up, surrounded, he wrote, by people of "religious nobility."

Just after the war, when we learned the horrors of the murder of six million Jews and the massive destruction of the Eastern European life that had nurtured Hasidism, my father wrote a eulogy, published as a book, *The Earth Is the Lord's: The Inner World the Jew in East Europe*. This was not a book about the social and historical experiences of Jews in Poland; it was a eulogy for the rich spiritual life cultivated by Hasidism: "In the days of Moses, Israel had had a revelation of God; in the days of the Baal Shem Tov God had a revelation of Israel. Suddenly there was revealed a holiness in Jewish life that had accumulated in the course of many generations."

So much was lost, and it fell upon Burt Jacobson's generation to preserve and revive. With this book, Burt gives us a legacy and a challenge,
reminding us of what my father warned: "We are either the last Jews or
those who will hand over the entire past to generations to come. We will
either forfeit or enrich the legacy of ages." In the introduction is a beautiful teaching of the Besht, who comments on Leviticus 6:6: "A fire shall be
kept burning upon the altar continually; it shall not go out." What is that
altar? The Baal Shem Tov taught:

> Let your heart be that altar, and in everything you do let
> a spark of that holy fire continually glimmer within you.
> And know that if you tend this flame, and never allow
> it to go out, no matter how small it may flicker, you will
> always be able to fan it into a great fire.

Burt's heart is that altar, as all who are his congregants, friends, family, and students attest. He is also offering us the possibility of making our
hearts that altar—indeed, offering us the possibility of becoming, like
him, a disciple of the Besht. Burt has striven his entire life to hand over
the legacy of Hasidism and of my father to generations to come. Let us
listen to his voice in the pages of this book so that we may be enriched by
our Hasidic inheritance and offer that heritage as a great fire of passionate devotion to God, to one another, to our fragile earth to generations to
come.

SUSANNAH HESCHEL
ELI M. BLACK DISTINGUISHED PROFESSOR OF JEWISH STUDIES
DARTMOUTH COLLEGE

INTRODUCTION

It is half a century since Abraham Joshua Heschel's passing, but his courageous public stances and spiritual and prophetic writings continue to stir religious seekers. I had the good fortune to study with him as a student at the Jewish Theological Seminary (JTS) in Manhattan and was enchanted by his assertion that religion is sourced in wonder, mystery, and radical amazement.

Heschel grew up in a Hasidic family in Warsaw. When he escaped from Europe, fleeing to the United States, the Nazi aim of annihilating the Jewish people was well underway. Extremely knowledgeable and erudite, in this country Heschel gradually became a renowned religious teacher, social critic, and activist. He took powerful public stands, aligning himself with the Civil Rights and the anti-war movements.

Underlying all his various activities, however, was a mission that guided him in all of his work. In *The Earth Is the Lord's*, his elegy for the Jews of Europe, he wrote: "A world has vanished. All that remains is a sanctuary hidden in the realm of spirit. We of this generation are still holding the key. Unless we remember, unless we unlock it the holiness of ages will remain a secret of God. We of this generation are still holding the key—the key of the sanctuary which is also the shelter of our own deserted souls. If we mislay the key, we shall elude ourselves."[1] This mission was intimately tied to his relationship with the Baal Shem Tov, the visionary founder of the Hasidic movement in eighteenth-century Poland.

In Heschel's final book, *A Passion for Truth,* published in 1973, which was also the year of his death, Heschel wrote that he saw the Baal Shem as the equal of Moses himself. "In the days of Moses, Israel had had a revelation of God; in the days of the Ba'al Shem Tov God had a revelation of Israel. Suddenly there was revealed a holiness in Jewish life that had accumulated in the course of many generations." Heschel writes that, like Moses, "The Besht left behind a new people.... [He] taught that Jewish life is an occasion for exaltation. Observance of the Law is the basis, but exaltation through observance is the goal."

Heschel was one of my most important teachers during four of the seven years I studied to become a rabbi at JTS. Nonetheless, despite the various classes and seminars I took with him, I cannot recall him ever mentioning the Baal Shem Tov. I later learned that at one time Heschel had been engaged in research for a book about the Besht, a work that he unfortunately never completed because of a major fire that occurred at the seminary in 1966, my senior year. All of Heschel's notes as well as many of the books he was studying were destroyed. So as I read his final book, *A Passion for Truth*, I was both surprised and enticed by his promise: "The Baal Shem made being Jewish a bliss, a continuous adventure. He gave every Jew a ladder to rise above himself and his wretched condition."

It took a number of years, but eventually the Besht (an acronym for Ba'al Shem Tov) became my own religious model and rebbe, and since that time I've been ardently devoted to the study of his life and thought. This book describes the journey that I took in an attempt to learn as much as possible about the founder of Hasidism. In studying what his disciples and the stories and traditions stated about the Baal Shem, I have been drawn to what his teachings reveal about his personality, his psychospiritual development, his mystical experience and thought, and the ways that he effected the transformation of Polish Jewry.

But this book is not only an intellectual journey of discovery. For almost forty years the Baal Shem Tov has served as a model for my spiritual growth and illumination. I've studied his teachings, and the legends about him, as well as historic and phenomenological studies. I've taught generations of rabbinical students and congregants about the Besht's life, shared his teachings, and experimented with his spiritual practices.

My growing understanding of the Besht was not without its challenges. One of these had to do with the clash between two very different and opposing images of him found in Hasidic tradition. Most of the written sources picture him as a fully realized compassionate master, and yet there are a number of early stories that describe him as being crude and mean, subject to anger and other moral failings. A good deal of my original motivation in studying the literature associated with the Besht had to do with reconciling this contradiction. Examining the original sources led me to develop a theory about the Baal Shem's historical identity that varies considerably from the widespread image of the man as a free spirit who never experienced adversity and taught only joy and love.

After decades of study, I came to agree with Heschel's appraisal of the Baal Shem Tov as one of the greatest Jewish spiritual teachers who ever lived, but not exactly for the same reasons Heschel had put forward. The picture of the master's life that gradually emerged for me was far more complicated and more human than the Hasidic legends claim. Given the traumatic experiences the Besht underwent in early life, his transformation into a powerful healer, spiritual teacher, and founder of Hasidism are absolutely remarkable and perhaps unprecedented. It was this radical transformation that drew me to him and led me to take him as my *rebbe*, my spiritual master. And it is because of this that I am able to affirm Heschel's promise, the stirring words that inspired my journey: "He who really wants to be uplifted by communing with a great person whom he can love without reservation, who can enrich his thought and imagination without end, that person can meditate about the life and being of the Besht. There has been no one like him in the last thousand years."[2]

I carry the Baal Shem Tov in my heart and turn to his life and teachings in times of difficulty. A day rarely passes when I don't think about my teacher. Perhaps it is a spiritual insight of his that comes to mind, or the recollection of a story that I read about him sometime in the past. I often reflect on his primary teaching, that God's goodness and love are streaming through the world, permeating every bit of reality, flowing through me and through everything. I may close my eyes and experience the Baal Shem's presence in my awareness as a manifestation of that love. If I am feeling low, the thought of the Besht will often lift my spirits, and his teachings about dealing with adversity continually support me on my path. Entering into the stories about his life and deeds and penetrating his teachings eventually remade me as a Jew, enabling me to learn to love people and expand my understanding of my place in a world of wonder and mystery. Though he passed from this world over 250 years ago, I feel gratitude for his presence in my life now, for his love, his kindness, his generosity, and his encouragement.

* * *

On a fateful Sunday in August 1991, a devastating firestorm swept through the East Bay, destroying many hundreds of homes. As soon as he heard the news about the fire my housemate, Don Goldmacher, left our house in the Rockridge section of Oakland, but because the fire seemed distant from where we lived, I remained at home. Around 1pm Don called from his nephew's home. "Get out, Burt! Get out immediately! The fire has jumped both freeways and is climbing the hillside behind the houses on our street."

What to take? I grabbed a few of my mother's paintings, my personal documents, the files containing my Baal Shem writings, my floppy discs, and the small collection of books related to my Hasidic studies. As I began to drive down the hill, I saw that several of my neighbors were trying to save their homes from the conflagration by saturating them with water from their garden hoses. I stopped briefly, opened all the windows of my car, and as I continued to drive down the street I screamed as loud as I could, "Get out! Get out now! The fire's coming up the side of the hill! You only have a few minutes to escape!"

When I reached the bottom of the hill, I found that the police had put up a barricade. An officer came up to my window and told me to leave my car and walk out of the area by foot. I remembered one road, however, that might not yet be closed off. I backed up, and turned the car around. Sure enough, that road was not guarded. As I drove across the Bay Bridge to San Francisco, I felt a fantastic rush. I am alive! I am alive! I gave thanks to God.

The fact that I had been able to save my Baal Shem research and books from the East Bay Firestorm was a kind of portent to me: I felt that this work was something I was fated to do, a kind of personal destiny. In some very small way, I see this book as a continuation of Heschel's unfinished project.

The last several years have been traumatic for many Californians. What is known as "fire season"—which now extends roughly from May through

November—brings the possibility of major wildfires to those of us who live here. For several years now my wife and I have had to pack suitcases with essentials and leave them next to the door to the garage in case we're suddenly told to evacuate. A number of the essential books from my Baal Shem shelves are marked to take along with my document files.

But there is another kind of fire that is creative rather than destructive. The Baal Shem Tov speaks about the fiery faith that allows individuals and communities to persist even through the most grueling of times. And what is faith? It is, the Besht teaches, the continual awareness of the existence of a living flame that illuminates everything that exists and cannot perish. Here is his teaching:

> The Torah teaches us that *"A fire shall be kept burning upon the alter continually; it shall not go out."* (Leviticus 6:6) The Baal Shem Tov taught, "Let your heart be that altar, and in everything you do let a spark of that holy fire continually glimmer within you. And know that if you tend this flame, and never allow it to go out, no matter how small it may flicker, you will always be able to fan it into a great fire."[3]

This flame is in no way exclusive to Hasidism. Ram Dass, a devotee of Hindu Vedanta, whom I also consider to be one of my teachers, wrote in *Be Here Now*: "In each of us there once was a fire. For some of us it seems as if there are only ashes now. But when we dig in the ashes we find one ember, and very gently we fan that ember, blow on it. It gets brighter. And from that ember we rebuild the fire. The only thing that's important is that ember. That's what we are here to celebrate."

From the Baal Shem I have learned the way to keep the flame alive. How? Through the cultivation of consciousness, the awareness of what is truly real—the sky, the countless stars, the sun lighting up the heavens every morning, generations of tender hearts aching for the light, longing for that elusive mystery we sometimes call God. My "I" cannot last, but there is an eternal Presence that will not disappear even when I am gone. How precious it is then to live in the light of that Presence, to be part of it for these few years of my existence.

My deepest hope is that this book will provide some keys for such a journey to those already on the Jewish path, and direction for seekers considering a way to integrate the vision of the Baal Shem Tov into their own lives.

PART ONE

IMAGES OF A SPIRITUAL MASTER

CHAPTER ONE

SEEKING A JEWISH PATH

"O purify our hearts so that we may serve You in truth!"
THE SIDDUR

"There is no path to the truth. Truth must be discovered, but
there is no formula for its discovery. What is formulated is not
true. You must set out on the uncharted sea, and the uncharted
sea is yourself."
J. KRISHNAMURTI

Jewish religious writers throughout the centuries seldom wrote anything like memoirs or autobiographies. As the great modern pioneer of the study of Jewish mysticism, Gershom Scholem, wrote, "The Kabbalists... are no friends of mystical autobiography.... They glory in an objective description and are deeply averse to letting their own personalities intrude into the picture."[4] And even when they did record their passionate mystical encounters with the Divine, Jewish mystics almost always described them in the third person as if these were objective occurrences.

Why the reticence, one may ask. It seems to me that the Jewish mystics were so taken with the vastness and magnificence of what they were describing that they felt inserting anything personal into their accounts would only draw unnecessary attention to their part in channeling spiritual truth. But this is changing. With the emphasis on individual creativity in our modern world, memoirs and autobiographies are becoming a Jewish religious genre. The most important of these for me was Etty Hillesum's journals and letters, which I first read in the 1990s.

Hillesum (1914-1943) was a young Jewish woman from an assimilated German family that moved to Holland to escape the Nazis. But it wasn't long until the Germans occupied Holland as well. Etty shared her inner life in a candid and intimate way. Her journals revealed the ways in which her mentor helped lead her from self-indulgence to psychological and spiritual maturity. Her reflections about the God she discovered at her own depths are profound. In a short amount of time these discoveries led her to develop a great sense of compassion together with the knowledge that she could be a support to Jews confined at the Westerbork Transit Camp, which was near Amsterdam. Etty entered the camp of her own free will, strengthened and encouraged fellow prisoners, and then accompanied and comforted her family and fellow Jews as they were deported to Auschwitz. She was twenty-nine when she was killed.

Part of what drew me to Hillesum's writings was the way she met the adversity of the Holocaust with great spiritual courage. One of the challenges I faced as a highly sensitive child was my knowledge of what was occurring in Europe, and a large part of my spiritual journey has had to do with the question of how to face such suffering and still retain my faith. As I studied the teachings of the Baal Shem Tov, I discovered that this issue was central to his worldview as well.

It is probably natural to want to be remembered for what one contributed to the world, but my primary objective in sharing my journey is to show how one latter-day disciple of the Baal Shem was able to cultivate a meaningful spiritual life during a highly chaotic and confusing period of history through devotion to a wise spiritual teacher. I also hope that my journey will inspire seekers to study the life and teachings of the Besht so they can deepen their own life journeys.

WOUNDS OF CHILDHOOD

I was born in 1936, the eldest son of Gertrude and Albert Jacobson, in Cleveland, Ohio. As an infant and young child, I was stricken with bouts of bronchial asthma which at times threatened my life with suffocation. My earliest memory was lying in my crib in absolute panic, unable to call for help. Where was my mother? Had I been abandoned? But the attack finally subsided on its own.

Asthma, however, continued all through childhood. I still carry the image of the chiropractor that my mother summoned in the middle of the night. Dr. Greenbaum would set up his table in the living room and adjust my body so I could breathe freely again.

Many years later my mother told me that both I and my younger brother, Stuart, had been sickly children. She apologized because she and my father hadn't had enough energy to care for both of their sons equally, especially when we were both gravely ill at the same time.

In another conversation my mother shared that she had been concerned because as a baby I would sit on the living room floor, immobile. When I did move, I did so unhurriedly. I was two years old before I began to walk. In kindergarten and elementary school, I was passive, slow, and averse to competition. Learning to read and write were major challenges, and arithmetic was nearly impossible. My third-grade teacher suspected I might be mentally disabled. Testing revealed I was dyslexic, but at that time there were no effective remedies for this learning disorder.

I was a highly sensitive child with little inner strength or ability to defend myself. I was the butt of jokes by classmates because of my weight. And disturbances in my family life, such as expressions of strong negative emotions, felt hurtful even if they weren't directed at me. Any sort of personal criticism could be deeply wounding, so I learned to behave as expected. Whatever anger I felt—and there was quite a bit—would be immediately suppressed. One of my earliest memories was being punished by my mother for some infraction by being made to sit for a long time in silence in my chair, facing the living room wall.

Although she cared for me, my mother was distant, angry, and frequently punitive. Nevertheless, I do recall an incident that gave me a sense my mother loved me. It occurred in third grade. At lunchtime, a child in the cafeteria line intentionally shoved me and I fell down on the hard floor. The bruise on my forehead began to swell and the principal called my mother. At home in bed, I cried while she tended my wound with the flat of a knife. "What can I do for you, baby, what can I do?" she said, comfortingly.

My father, Albert Jacobson, was warmer than my mother, but was most often away at work, or indulging in his passion for bowling. I once asked why he didn't spend more time at home with our family. "What do you think I'm doing all day long?" he responded unsympathetically, "I'm earning the money that we need to survive!" And then he needed the relaxation and fun he would get from bowling with his buddies to counterbalance his compulsive overwork. I once accompanied him to the bowling alley and I recall the smiles, banter, and riotous jokes of the men, seasoned with off-color Yiddish humor. He once took me to his bowling alley to teach me to bowl. There was a special lane reserved for children. Both the pins and the balls used were smaller than those on the adult lanes. My father tried his best to guide me but even so, every ball I threw landed in the gutter. My father became more and more annoyed, finally losing his temper and shouting at my ineptitude: "Oh, you're just no good, Burton!" After that I was no longer interested in bowling.

There were times when I experienced happiness, especially when playing outside with the other children in the neighborhood, Saturday evening outings to Chagrin Falls for ice cream, and Thanksgiving and July 4th get-togethers with extended family. And summer vacations to Moss' Farm and Mentor-on-the-Lake with uncles, aunts, and cousins. What I recall of my nuclear family life, however, was rarely serene. I think my parents must have initially loved one another, but their interests and values never meshed, and eventually their married life fell into disarray. Their bickering could easily erupt into explosions of anger. These struggles left me anxious, fearful, and depressed. I so wished to do something to stop the fighting, but was afraid and stayed silent, disappearing into my daydreams and fantasies.

I think about the ways in which my mother blossomed as a person in her middle and later years. She lost her rigidity and expanded her sense of compassion. Her anger subsided. During the last two decades of her life, she developed a great sense of humor and deep interest in spirituality. Just a few years before her death she sent a letter to my brother Stuart and to me which contained a heartfelt apology for the severe and inconsiderate way she had reared us.

Sad to say, though, my father and I never saw eye to eye. I do think he loved us, but he hardly knew how to express it. At his funeral there was little I could remember to tell the rabbi about what I learned from him. I recall mentioning his irreverent humor and his having been a good provider, and the few times he attempted to protect me from my mother's rage. I now recognize that my dad was truly made for his times: an American Jew from a dysfunctional immigrant family, and the first of his family to go to college, earning a degree in law. A man who had suffered through the Great Depression, and whose spirit had remained indomitable despite everything, making it possible for his sensitive wife and two sons to live free of want and strike out on their own in new directions.

IN THE HOLOCAUST'S SHADOW

It was not only the struggles and suffering my mother experienced in confrontations at home and in our extended family gatherings that fueled her fear, anxiety, and anger. During my childhood, Gert Jacobson was the chairperson of the local chapter of the Anti-Defamation League. In that capacity she waged a furious campaign to convince leaders of the Cleveland Jewish community that Adolf Hitler's rise to power in Germany posed a threat to the Jews of Europe. She also traveled to Washington, DC to meet with senators and congressmen, beseeching them to do something before European Jewry met catastrophe. The sense of helplessness she felt left her enraged, bitter, and depressed. Against the onslaught of history and the fate of millions, the needs of her children must have seemed to be an irritant and a distraction. Mother's sighs and her dread about the fate of Europe's Jews entered my soul, contaminating my sense of being Jewish with the misery of victimhood.

One evening—I must have been five or six—my parents took me to the home of friends to welcome a couple who had just arrived from Europe. Many people were present in the living room to greet the Weintraubs, but I was the only child. When the couple entered the living room, everyone became quiet and my father bent down and whispered in my ear, "The Weintraubs were buried alive, but they escaped." What did this mean? Why had they been buried alive? How could they have been buried alive and escape? I didn't ask.

I recall a recurring dream from those years. It was the middle of the night and everyone in the house was asleep. I would rise, go to the dark screened-in porch next to the dining room and wait for a train that would take me away. I did not know where it would take me but that did not matter. The train never came.

Because of my asthma I couldn't trust my body. I often experienced anxiety or melancholy, and at times these feelings were overwhelming. At a young age, however, I sensed a potent truth—that the outer world simply could not be all there was. There had to be something more, something beyond the pain of the present.

All four of my grandparents had immigrated to the U.S. from Eastern or Central Europe and in the process shed their religious and most of their cultural roots. They underwent harsh experiences—antisemitism and poverty in Europe, and bigotry and poverty in America. This left them less than whole, if not traumatized. It was most evident with my grandmothers, but also apparent in the relationships—or lack of—that took place between some of my uncles, aunts, and cousins in my father's family. There was lots of shouting, sometimes accompanied by the dread that little problems were bound to escalate into something major. For instance, my father's refusal to speak with his mother for almost fifteen years. And I remember clearly the screaming match that occurred between one of my cousins and my father's older brother over perceptions or misperceptions of one another's characters. This family atmosphere brought about the tragic suicide of one of my aunts. I've wondered whether these incidents of dysfunction were the legacy of my family's Jewish past in Europe, or the result of the difficulties in adjusting to the conditions of a new country.

GRANDPA GOLDBERG

The Baal Shem Tov saw divinity everywhere. And he taught that God's presence becomes most obvious during moments of mystery, transcendence, and love. As I look back at my formative years, that presence became most tangible in my relationships with men who became both my models and teachers. This began with my maternal grandfather, Rudolf Goldberg.

In retrospect it seems that my grandfather escaped from the harsh experiences of his youth in Romania more intact than my other grandparents. He would take me on outings to the zoo, and to the Cleveland ballpark to see the Indians play, and on July 4th for the fireworks; and he would take me to a theater in downtown Cleveland to watch Blackstone the Magician perform his amazing magical tricks.

Everyone in my family was secular in outlook. The only holidays celebrated in our home were Thanksgiving and Independence Day. But when I was seven, Grandpa Goldberg took me to a synagogue for the first time. The building was cavernous, dark, and old, but it was the eve of Simhat Torah, the holy day of rejoicing, which celebrates the completion of the annual cycle of reading of the Torah and the beginning of a new cycle. We children were given decorated paper flags with apples stuck onto their thin wooden poles, and lit candles set onto the apples. Waving our illuminated flags, we marched happily around the synagogue following the men who were carrying the Torah scrolls. When we had made a complete round of the synagogue, they began to sing and dance joyously with the Torahs. Then another group would take the scrolls and wend their way around the synagogue, and we would follow. What great fun! My grandfather did not take part in the singing, dancing, or marching, but he sat in his pew and smiled warmly each time I passed by.

Romania had been rife with antisemitism that was officially enforced by the government when Ruby Goldberg found a way to emigrate. He was sixteen when arriving in the U.S. I asked him if he had been religious. He told me about his first night in this country. Friends of his family who had immigrated to the U.S. earlier met him at the steamship and brought him to their home in Brooklyn. When he opened his steamer trunk, all of his clothes stank. He hung them on the fire escape to air out. His *tefillin* (prayer phylacteries) and *tallit* (prayer shawl) also smelled bad and he put these on the fire escape with his clothes. The next morning everything was gone. That was the last time he *davened* (prayed), he said with a slight grin on his face.

Grandpa Goldberg never revealed anything about his family or life in the old country. Though profoundly identified with the Jewish people and its history and culture, he became a secular socialist, and always held a strong ambivalence toward religion and Judaism. I never asked him why he'd forsaken traditional Judaism, but I imagine it had something to do with the rigid way the religion was observed in the old country and its irrelevance to his life here.

During my years at the Jewish Theological Seminary (JTS), I spent several summers at home in San Antonio. My grandfather's tailoring shop was located in the storeroom attached to the garage, and throughout the day he would come into the house to use the bathroom or to get a glass of milk to treat his ulcers. I remember the time I was listening to a Hasidic recording on the record player in our family living room.

Grandpa wandered in, lay down on the carpet, and silently cried. Did he come from Hasidic stock? I could have asked, but I didn't.

Ruby Goldberg was a negotiator for the Ladies' Garment Union. My mother once told me that every six months, following negotiations with the employers, he would come home enraged, go to the kitchen, pick up a large carving knife, and beat it against the counter. "Those goddamn bosses!" he would shout, "They won't give us a nickel!"

Then there was a story my mother told me that I have cherished since I first heard it. "Gertie, I've read every word of Karl Marx, and I truly respect his ideas," he told his eldest daughter, "but there's one important thing he left out of his books—*love*." Perhaps it was this perception that underlaid his concern for me. He advised my mother that she go to the public library and read about Jewish history and antisemitism. It was this that led to my mother's work with the Anti-Defamation League.

OTHER MENTORS AND TEACHERS

In San Antonio, my mother decided she wanted me to have a bar mitzvah, and my parents joined Temple Beth El, the local Reform synagogue. At that time, Reform Judaism emphasized the ethical aspects of the religion, rather than the observance of traditional ritual. But Milton Bendiner, the educational director at the temple, was a traditionally observant Jew and he became both my Hebrew teacher and my bar mitzvah mentor.

Mr. Bendiner could be harsh and brittle at times, but he was a man with a passionate love for ideas, and this quality was to help shape my young unformed mind. Yet, his attitude toward ideas alone would not have built the bridge of affection and esteem that I, and many other former students, held for him throughout his life. There was something else as well: his quality of caring. How well I recall the attention and concern he lavished on me—a confused boy with a rather poor self-image. Here was a great man who thought that I mattered, that my life was important.

Mr. Bendiner would conduct Friday evening services at the temple for families with children, and whenever I could I would attend with my mother. But on one Friday night each month, in place of the family service, he would invite two or three of his bar mitzvah students to his apartment, where he and his wife, Anne, would host a charming dinner. I had never seen a home with so many books. And not only in the many bookcases, but also stacked on the coffee table and end tables, and piled high on Milton's baby grand piano.

As always, Milton wore his black suit and black tie, but just before the rituals, he took off his jacket, revealing his crisp white starched shirt. Then Anne lit the two Shabbat candles and recited a Hebrew blessing, and Milton followed by chanting *Kiddush,* the long Hebrew blessing over wine which officially inaugurates the Sabbath. He took a sip and passed the silver cup around so each of us could also taste the wine. Then he lifted the two twisted hallah loaves and chanted the blessing over bread. Throughout the meal Milton told us stories from Jewish tradition, and he talked about ideas—like the meaning of the Sabbath, or why prayer was essential—as if they were really important. And all through the meal he came up with his terrible puns and everyone around the table was chuckling. He also asked us questions about public school and what we were learning, about the books we were reading, and about our hobbies. Toward the end of the evening, he passed out coins and stamps from foreign countries. What an evening that was!

I took the Friday evening ritual home with me. My father, never a person interested in religion, hated this. "How long is this going to take?" he irritably asked. We began the ritual but then, during the blessing over wine, the telephone rang. My father jumped up and took the call. It was a client calling about a proposed real estate deal. My mother, brother, and I sat there in silence, waiting for the loud conversation to end. This scenario repeated itself again and again, despite my father's antagonism. With my mother's support, however, I persisted.

Throughout early adolescence, Milton held Judaism up as a prism through which I might see value, purpose, and meaning. Despite his influence, however, during my teenage years I felt myself to be an outsider, an odd person, not really important. I had a few close friends in high school, but I knew that many of the kids saw me as a nerd, including those who were part of my Jewish high school fraternity, AZA (Aleph Zaddik Aleph). In high school I did what I was told, but due to my inertia and dyslexia I received poor grades. I also had difficulty making decisions and could be passive-aggressive and stubborn.

As an undergraduate at the University of Texas, I began to question the materialistic values that characterized not only my parents' lives, but

American life in general. I also adopted a critical attitude toward capitalism and nationalism and began to read about socialism, whose premises
made a great deal of sense. I understood that my parents had grown up in
immigrant families that were striving to raise themselves out of poverty
and prejudice, and I came to feel that in the process they'd traded in their
Jewish heritage for an assimilated American life, merely colored by the
remnants of old country Jewish ethnicity.

Religion was much more important to me than the subjects I was
studying, and by my second year in Austin I understood clearly that my
road to meaning would be Judaism. I was drawn more to Conservative
Judaism than I had been to the Reform Judaism of my temple in San
Antonio, largely because of the influence that Milton Bendiner had
on my life. I began to teach children in the Hebrew school of the local
Conservative synagogue in Austin, and often attended services there on
the Sabbath. It was at those services where I met Avraham Gottesman, a
rigidly Orthodox Jew and Holocaust survivor who then took me under his
wing. Following services, I would accompany Mr. Gottesman to his home
and he would talk to me about the fundamentals of traditional Judaism.
He never spoke about the Shoah, but his loathing toward Christianity
was intense.

Mr. Gottesman had survived the Holocaust, yet maintained his traditional Jewish faith with a vehemence. When I would share what I was
learning in classes at the university, he'd often counter what my instructors were teaching. He urged me to study the portions of the Five Books of
Moses that were read each Shabbat morning in the synagogue, and gradually I began to learn Torah. I began to see the world through his passionate
eyes and soon Orthodox Judaism became the only truth for me. As a result,
my own observance became more and more fervent and intense.

Another aspect of traditional Judaism which Mr. Gottesman introduced me to was *musar*, an ascetic religious trend that developed among
Jews in Lithuania during the nineteenth century. The Musar movement
sprang out of a specific form of medieval Jewish religious literature that
emphasized the importance of personal piety and ethical behavior as
an indispensable complement to intellectual studies of the Torah and
Talmud. The stories about Rabbi Israel Salanter (1810-1883), who initiated
the movement, impressed me deeply, for he seemed to be a kind and

caring human being. It was during that time when I first encountered the great Catholic saint, Francis of Assisi, in a medieval history class. I was deeply impressed by Francis' humility and love, and it was this, together with what I was learning about Rabbi Salanter, that forged a lifelong infatuation with religious piety. Nevertheless, my character was so psychologically uninformed that I could not discern how to actually embody such piety.

Salanter's approach to religion seemed to offer a remedy for my anxiety and weakness. The rabbi taught that because the urge to engage in evil thoughts and deeds is so powerful, one must be continually on guard to defeat its machinations. Fear of punishment, the negation of worldly pleasure, and striving for moral perfection were at the core of Salanter's spiritual awareness and asceticism. Such discipline involved the continual monitoring of thoughts and deeds with ongoing rigorous self-examination. I followed Rabbi Salanter in his belief that self-denial and self-control would lead to the true affirmation of God, attempting to suppress my desires and appetites, especially my sexual drive. And of course my failure with these practices only reinforced the dismal view of myself they were meant to correct.

I was drawn to the God of Deuteronomy—demanding, absolutist. (A psychologist might say it was a masculine version of, and counterbalance to, my mother's authoritarianism.) Reflecting on the miserable conditions of the world, I felt disgust at the failure of human beings to follow God's will. People were callous, vain, petty, and violent. God had provided humanity with a wondrous opportunity, and we had squandered his gift, failing to live in the divine image. I came to believe that because of my faith and observance, God would lift me out of the chaos and heartaches of my life.

My religious practice was regulated by the stringencies of Jewish law, especially in the areas of the dietary proscriptions, the Sabbath, holy days, and daily prayer. When I would return to San Antonio, I would exasperate my parents with my newfound truths and dietary demands.

BECOMING A RABBI

By junior year of college, I knew that I wanted to become an Orthodox rabbi, but the Yitzhak Elhanan Yeshivah at Yeshiva University wouldn't accept my application because of my lack of Hebrew and ignorance of Jewish religious literature. My mentor Milton Bendiner had graduated from the Conservative Teachers' Institute of the Jewish Theological Seminary of America, also in Manhattan, and so it was there that I finally decided to study, matriculating in 1959.

The assignments were extremely demanding. Hebrew and Talmud were the most challenging, made even more difficult because of my learning disability. In order to keep up, I would often study until 2am, and then get up at 7am for the community prayer service. My anxiety level was extremely high. But I continued on this path because I believed God wanted me to do what I was doing.

I brought my absorption in musar with me to seminary. Will Herberg's *Judaism and Modern Man*, a book I was assigned to read for theology class, placed Israel Salanter's views into a contemporary context. The author, a theologically-inclined sociologist, wrote that "human life is a permanent existential crisis," and that human beings "stand confounded, perplexed, consumed with anxiety." Herberg stressed the unrelenting tension between God and the urge to do that which was sinful, and the unending struggle to end the tyranny of the self-centered ego. This certainly seemed to describe my life. Herberg wrote that the only answer to this existential predicament was a leap of faith. Turning to God in contrition and humility "creates a 'new heart' within us and transforms us in a new self."[5] Herberg's arguments were convincing. Indeed, I had already taken a leap of faith, and was hoping for the personal revolution that he described as inevitable. But that kind of transformation never happened. I remained anxious and fearful. Where was the new heart and the new self that his book promised?

A HASIDIC REBBE

During my first year of rabbinical school, my new best friend, Ira Gordon, invited me to accompany him to Brooklyn to spend a Sabbath with the Lubavitcher/Chabad Hasidim, one of the largest Hasidic communities in the world. I had met two Hasidim from the Lubavitcher community who had been traveling through San Antonio during my college years, but I was not at all prepared for what I was about to experience.

The best time to visit the Lubavitch was *Shabbos M'vorkhin* (the

Sabbath of Blessing), the Sabbath before the week during which the new moon appears in the night sky. It was then that the *Rebbe*—the spiritual leader of the community—whose name was Rabbi Menachem Mendel Schneerson (1902-1994), would conduct what is known in Yiddish as a *Farbrengen,* a festive celebration during which he offered spiritual teachings and led the community in ecstatic song. Ira knew a Hasidic family that would provide us lodging on Friday night and would welcome us to all three Shabbat meals. Of course, I wanted to go. So on Friday afternoon, we took the IRT subway from upper Manhattan to Crown Heights Brooklyn, and that night we attended the Shabbat service in a huge prayer hall filled with men and boys. The services were animated, hundreds of intense Hasidim rapidly shaking their bodies back and forth and gesticulating as they davened and sang. I had been davening in a similar manner for years, but had never seen such intense devotion in a communal setting.

Following the service, we returned to the home of our hosts for the evening meal, religious discussion, and singing. On Saturday morning, we again attended synagogue and returned to our hosts for the afternoon meal. In mid-afternoon we walked to a huge auditorium for the Farbrengen. The great hall, with its remarkably high ceiling, was brimming with Hasidim. Almost all the men were garbed in black coats and fedoras, and had unruly beards. We stood on the rows of bleachers that gradually ascended toward the ceiling. At the rear of the hall near the ceiling, I saw a narrow horizontal window through which some of the women were peering.

There was a hush as the Rebbe entered the hall, dressed in the same garb as his disciples. The dignified man took his place before the lectern, closed his eyes and began to intone a joyous *niggun,* a devotional melody. The mass of men immediately joined in. With fists clenched, the Rebbe thrust his arms toward the ceiling indicating that he desired greater fervor, and the chorus of voices swelled. We sang the jubilant, fast-paced niggun over and over in a hypnotic way, and as we did so we jumped up and down on the bleachers to the incessant beat. The wooden slats beneath our feet were bobbing up and down with our leaping, and I wondered if they would hold our weight. Soon they began to pass bottles of vodka and small paper cups throughout the hall.

Some twenty minutes later the Rebbe stopped singing and lowered his arm. Then we toasted him with our filled cups. *"L'chaim! L'chaim!* To life, to life!" And once again the room became hushed. The Rebbe spoke in a mixture of Yiddish, Hebrew, and Aramaic, and I hardly understood a word or phrase of his long discourse, although I recognized that he was weaving his teachings around the section of the Torah that was chanted in the synagogue that morning. When he finished, he led another long round of singing. So it went on for perhaps three hours. Carried away by the vodka, singing, hypnotic voice of the Rebbe, and joy and enthusiasm of the multitude of men around me, I felt as if a window had opened into a transcendent realm. Month after month, I returned to Lubavitch to lose myself again in the ecstatic currents of this Hasidic path to God.

Soon, the Lubavitchers tried to persuade me to leave the seminary and enter their yeshivah, and I was so fascinated by the community's intensive, all-encompassing joyous spirituality, I considered their appeals. But as time went on, the visits began to put me off. I learned that it was unacceptable to disagree with any of the doctrines espoused by the Hasidim. Whenever I talked about something I had learned at the seminary that contradicted Hasidic belief, or when I ventured a personal opinion that conflicted with the Rebbe's views, I was told I was wrong. Questioning and dispute of any kind were not tolerated. More than once my host said (using my Hebrew name), "Boruch, you ought to leave that place of lies and *apikorsus* (heresy) and come to the Lubavitch Yeshiva. Here you'll find the real truth." I valued freedom of thought, and could not abide what felt like parochialism. So after almost two years of regular visits, I gave up and never visited the community again.

But the time I spent at Lubavitch enabled me to begin to change. I'd been filled with guilt, shame, and low self-esteem, and through my apprenticeship with Avraham Gottesman and Rabbi Israel Salanter I was drawn to a stern and judgmental version of traditional Judaism. My early encounters with Lubavitch, in contrast, offered me a respite from these dark broodings through joy and celebration.

A PIOUS TALMUDIST

I remember a strange figure entering my grandparent's living room when I was a young boy. I was told he was my great uncle Rabbi Maishe Yitzhak, who had just arrived from Lumsa, Poland, my father's ancestral family home, brought over by my grandfather, to save him from the Nazis. The man's beard, his strange black clothing, his Yiddish—all of these features cast a kind of spell over me. My father's family, there to welcome him, seemed uncomfortable in his presence.

During my second year at seminary, I became curious, remembering this, and just before the High Holy Days decided to visit my great uncle Maishe Yitzhak and my aunt Mashi. I'd spent the summer at my parent's home in San Antonio, and just a few weeks before Rosh Hashanah, traveled by rail to Syracuse. I took a cab to my uncle and aunt's home. They welcomed me warmly.

My uncle would rise every morning at 4am to study Talmud. At 6am, he'd walk to the synagogue for *S'li'khot,* the special prayers for forgiveness recited in the days before Rosh Hashanah. I wanted to join him and asked to be woken up so I could accompany him, but he told me I was young and needed the sleep.

Uncle Maishe was revered as the foremost Orthodox rabbi in Syracuse. Other traditional rabbis came to him with their *halakhic* (legal) questions. He was also a kashrut supervisor, in charge of washing and inspecting all of the kosher meat that was traveling through Syracuse by train on its way to New York City. He also taught classes in Talmud.

Unlike my uncle, my Aunt Mashi spoke some English. One day I was talking with her in the kitchen and she surprisingly recited to me an entire passage from the Talmud in the original Aramaic and Hebrew. I knew that Orthodox women did not study Talmud. "How did you learn that?" I asked. Nonchalantly, she answered, "Oh, when I'm in the kitchen I can overhear your uncle teaching his students, and I have heard him reciting that section of the Talmud so many times that I came to know it by heart." She had a twinkle in her eye.

One Friday afternoon, my uncle, with his lame right leg, began to vacuum the living room rug. I thought this was women's work, but my uncle said, "It's important for every Jew to help prepare for Shabbos."

Uncle Maishe Yitzhak and Aunt Mashi lived next door to a Christian clergyman. I was with my uncle one day on the street when he acknowledged the minister with a smile, later telling me that it was important to greet everyone in an openhearted way. This deeply impressed me, for my only other intimate contact with Orthodoxy had been with Mr. Gottesman in college, and he hated Christianity, angrily dismissing missionaries that frequently appeared at his door.

On Rosh Hashanah itself, and ten days later, on Yom Kippur, we walked to the synagogue. As I davened next to my uncle, I heard him quietly uttering the words of the *mahzor* (the High Holy Day prayerbook), heard his plentiful sighs, and felt him disappearing into a higher realm. Once again, ten days later on Yom Kippur I davened next to my uncle in the Young Israel synagogue. I watched as he made a full prostration on the ground, surrendering to God.

My aunt and uncle were not Hasidim. Their forms of devotion were not energetic and boisterous like those I'd witnessed at Lubavitch. Nor did they have a rebbe whom they venerated. Yet, somehow, I could relate to their piety personally, in part because they were my family, the last remnant of an ancestral connection with Jewish Poland. And despite the Holocaust, and the loss of their Jewish life in Poland, and displacement to a land that they never fully accepted, it seemed as though their faith had not wavered.

I wondered what my uncle thought of my attending a non-Orthodox seminary. "It's fine," he assured me. "Learn everything you can. Just remain fully observant." I don't think he knew much about non-Orthodox forms of Judaism, for if he had he would have likely been more critical of the education I was receiving.

A LOSS OF FAITH

But my leap of faith in the God of Judaism began to falter during my fourth year in seminary. I came across two books that shook me to the core, Andre Schwartz-Bart's *The Last of the Just*, and Elie Wiesel's *Night*. The first was a novel about a Jew who suffered the trials of the Holocaust and ultimately died in a concentration camp. *Night* is an autobiographical account of Wiesel's ordeal in Auschwitz, where he watched his father wither away. His father died of a beating while the boy lay silently on the bunk below for fear of being beaten too. Both authors harbored rage toward God and struggled with the question of why God had allowed the Nazis to butcher six million Jews. I wondered where this God had been during the Holocaust. Was he really the Lord of the universe, ruling history? Perhaps God was a mere figment of the human imagination.

These ruminations brought me to feel that my attempt at piety and humility had been a sham, and my subservience to God had been a delusion. How could I have allowed myself to believe in all this traditional garbage? The world is off-kilter, flooded with moral chaos. If there is a God at all, I thought, he must be evil as well as good. And if he is evil, then why worship him? I was caught in ambivalence, for despite my unrest the seminary had become my home. I was no longer sure I could believe in God, and I thought about leaving, but in truth I could imagine nowhere else to go, nothing else to do. I was clearly lost. Was there some way out of this empty wilderness of self-estrangement and alienation?

ABRAHAM JOSHUA HESCHEL

In those years, Abraham Joshua Heschel became a model of Jewish spirituality, a man who combined scholarship, prayer, spiritual searching, and political activism into an integral religious life. He had become a renowned social activist, addressing public issues such as healthcare, juvenile delinquency, the elderly, and racism. He'd given himself to the cause of civil rights, marching alongside the Reverend Dr. Martin Luther King, Jr. in Selma, Alabama, and he'd spoken out on behalf of the oppressed Jews of the Soviet Union.

Heschel had also taken an early and courageous public stance against the war in Vietnam, despite the fact that the seminary and the established Jewish community, like the country at large, favored our government's intervention against communism in southeast Asia. Initially confused about the morality of the war—which the government always called a "police action"—I had been inspired by Heschel's public stance in opposition. Considering the issues more deeply, I finally decided to protest the war. But as the years wore on, and my doubts about Judaism surfaced, Heschel's classes didn't really deal with the questions that were uppermost in my mind, except in the seminar on the biblical prophets that I took with him during my second year. Speaking through the demanding voices of the prophets, my teacher squarely placed the blame for human evil on human beings themselves.

I read Heschel's two works of religious philosophy, *Man Is Not Alone* and *God in Search of Man,* and was enchanted by what he had to say about wonder, mystery, and radical amazement as the roots of religious awakening. And yet he did not deal with the issues that really bothered me. Didn't the Holocaust call into question the fundamental theological premises of Judaism itself? How could one believe in God in a world glutted by so much evil? I only discovered years later that Heschel had been dealing with similar questions at this time. In his final book, *A Passion for Truth,* he confronted the tragedy of the Holocaust:

> Life in our time has been a nightmare for many of us, tranquility an interlude, happiness a fake. Who could breathe at a time when man was engaged in murdering the holy witness to God six million times?[6]

Heschel shared his own anguish through the medium of Menahem Mendl, the Hasidic rebbe of Kotzk: "[T]he Kotzker was tormented by...the awareness that God was ultimately responsible for the hideousness of human mendacity. It was this concern with the paradox of divine responsibility that finally plunged his soul into the dark grief of his last years."[7]

As I think back about my relationship with Rabbi Heschel, I find that my memories are complicated and tangled with regret. Certainly, we never connected in the way that a mentor and a student might. Although I learned a great deal from him in classes and seminars, my private meetings with him were plainly missed opportunities. I was in awe of Dr. Heschel and did not want to waste the time of a great man. I was simply too closed off and ashamed of my inner life to reveal anything to him.

I recall especially the summer afternoon in 1963 at Camp Ramah in New York State, where I was working as a bunk counselor. Rabbi Heschel was serving as the camp's scholar-in-residence. In the city, he was always dressed formally in suit and tie, carrying himself with a dignified bearing. Around the camp, however, he wore a short-sleeved shirt and blue shorts. I found him sitting on his cottage porch without a head covering. I'd come unannounced with what felt like a serious problem. My bunk of fourteen-year-old boys had camped out with a girls' bunk two nights before. In the morning I found one of my campers sleeping in a bedroll with a female camper. I'd become angry, irrational, and had screamed at both of them. "We didn't do anything, Burt! We didn't do anything!" Bobby yelled back.

I was disturbed by the incident and by my reactions to it, but I couldn't bring myself to tell my teacher what happened, nor how I'd reacted. "Dr. Heschel," I blurted out, "I think you ought to write a book on sexuality!" He looked surprised. "No," he said, "I'm afraid not." He told me that if he wrote such a book, he would have to base it on traditional Jewish sexual ethics, and the psychologists would dismiss it. And the traditionalists would also reject it because he would have to depart from many old Jewish certainties about sexuality. Then he told me that he was working on a book that would be titled *Who Is Man?* He hoped to convey to readers his sense of what it meant to be truly human. Even though this book would not contain anything explicit about sexuality, it would explore modes of being which characterize the uniqueness of being human. The reader would be able to apply these insights to many areas of human existence.

Then he told me he was about to go over to the lake to use one of the paddleboats. He invited me to accompany him. Of course, he sensed that the request I'd brought to him had hidden motivations, and as we were walking, he put his arm around my shoulders and asked, "And how is your life going, Burt? What are *your* concerns?" I immediately froze inside and mumbled something superficial. At the first opportunity I thanked him and returned to my bunkhouse. Years later I realized that Bobby, my young camper friend, had spoken the truth. I got to know him and he was a fine and honest person. He told me that despite appearances he and his girlfriend had not engaged in sex. So it had really been my own discomfort with sexuality that had been at the root of my violent reaction. Rabbi Heschel had offered me the opportunity to share my pain, but I hadn't allowed him to learn why I'd come to see him that day.

A SCHOLARLY MYSTIC

Arthur Green entered JTS in 1963 and soon began studying Kabbalah with Heschel. We got to know one another, and Art's presence in my life was a blessing. He opened my consciousness and intellect to new worlds that amazed me, which now enabled me to begin to redirect my life and thought in a radically new direction. For a few years he was my closest friend, confidant, and mentor.

When we met, I knew relatively little about Jewish mysticism. Art spoke about the way in which the sixteenth century kabbalist, Rabbi Isaac Luria, dealt with the problem of evil in the world—that evil had cosmic origins, and wasn't fully the result of human sin. This amazed me. Art also shared what he was learning from the writings of Joseph Gikatilla, a thirteenth century kabbalist who sought to reconcile mysticism with philosophy. And he told me about the bible of the kabbalah, the *Zohar*, composed primarily by the thirteenth century Spanish kabbalist, Moses de Leon.

Although he was a student, Art initiated me into a way of reading Jewish sacred texts more deeply than any of the linguistic or historical approaches I'd been exposed to in seminary classrooms. He sensitized me to the spiritual power of traditional language, revealing how myth and symbol could be windows into spiritual truth. And he introduced me to the field of comparative religion, suggesting I read books by Alan Watts, Mircea Eliade, Joseph Campbell, Hermann Hesse, and Nikos Kazantzakis. Through his guidance I began to sense not only the power of Jewish mysticism, but the universal underpinnings of religion, mythology, and mysticism, and the intrinsic bonds that linked all the great religious paths.

Most importantly, Art shared his sense of the spiritual quest as the central defining characteristic of the religious enterprise. He revealed his personal search, his longing for something beyond the confines of ordinary consciousness, and encouraged me to share my searching with him. In these animated conversations he drew me towards his emerging spiritual worldview, which stressed the centrality of the quest for unity with the Divine. I found myself looking up to Art even though he was younger than I. It was hard to believe that only recently I had thought seriously about leaving seminary, unable to sustain faith in the God of the covenant who had failed to come to the aid of the Jewish people during the Holocaust. I now understood that although God could not necessarily act in the realm of history, this inscrutable presence was very much present in human consciousness, symbol, and myth.

In 1964-65, my junior year, I spent nine months in Israel attending classes at Hebrew University. One course I took was an introduction to the *Zohar*. This fascinating collection of symbolic teachings opened the world of Jewish mysticism to me in a fuller way.

MY FINAL YEAR

My final year at seminary was arduous, especially after having spent that exhilarating academic year in Israel. Most of the senior faculty members with whom I'd studied conducted their classes in a domineering fashion, and the texts they were teaching had no contemporary relevance, at least not in the way they were being taught. It finally dawned on me: I had desired to become a rabbi in order to serve God, but there was no room for God in the classrooms of JTS. My teachers shared nothing of their personal religious or spiritual lives in class. Their entire concern was preparing students to study the classical texts from an academic point of view.

Why was this? A number of my instructors had been educated in the Lithuanian yeshivah tradition with its sole emphasis on the vigorous study and explication of the Talmud. They were, of course, practicing Jews as well, but it seemed to me that it was the analytical scrutiny of traditional texts that really mattered to them. I also suspected that for some—those who had escaped from Europe before or during the Holocaust—there might be something else. I wondered if they'd lost their faith in God and then transferred their religious concerns to the traditional books they studied or wrote about. Whatever it was, their classes held little or no meaning for a young rabbinical student who thought he would soon be leading and teaching in an American synagogue.

When I told my faculty advisor, Rabbi Raphael Posner, about my dissatisfaction with the way that I was being taught, he looked at me with a smile. "The trouble with you, Jacobson," he said, "is that you're *really* religious." But Rabbi Posner understood my issues, because he followed that remark by saying that what was lacking at the seminary were spiritual mentors for students. He himself had such a mentor at the musar-based Gateshead Yeshivah in England, where he was ordained, although the strictness of his education had affected him rather badly.

During that final year I also became angry, in fact, furious. It seemed that I had wasted seven years learning halakhah, philology, and history! Where was religion? Where was God? Did it all have to do with correct observance, with adherence to an archaic past, with learning Jewish texts and history? I began acting out in class, sassing my instructors. And even though I had little idea what I might do as a rabbi, I certainly looked forward to ordination, which would free me from my subservient role as a student. I was shocked then when I was asked to join the faculty of the rabbinical school, to teach Jewish worship, and become the editor of all of the liturgical publications of the Conservative movement. I certainly felt flattered, but Art Green, who knew me well, easily convinced me to decline the offer. You don't want to be stuck for life in this seminary, he argued. He was right. And because of the influence that Milton Bendiner had on me, I made the decision to become a Jewish educator.

* * *

I look back now at all the occurrences of my young life and wonder how much of what happened had been determined by the traumatic events caused by Christian antisemitism in the lives of my grandparents in Europe. After escaping from Europe, my grandparents had also experienced the trials of assimilation into an American culture that saw them as inferior. And perhaps because of the authoritarian character of Orthodox religious life they made conscious or unconscious decisions to put that past behind them and to become secular Jews in this new land, without the baggage of the past. My parents had acceded to this whole set of values, and perhaps this is why I'd been deprived of the riches of traditional Judaism.

The Baal Shem Tov taught that we must have love and compassion even for those who do wrong. But was it even wrong? Hadn't my parents done the best they were able to do given the difficult circumstances of their lives and the great challenges they had to deal with? I came to understand that despite everything my parents had endured, they'd shown stamina, perseverance, and hope for the future.

Another of the Baal Shem's core insights would become a powerful tool for my transformation. He taught that we have the ability to look at suffering as a catalyst for a life of meaning, virtue, and decency. Although the circumstances of my early years had in some ways twisted my psyche and behavior in injurious ways, eventually those disorders became the springboard for the work I took on, transforming and refining my character.

CHAPTER TWO

ENCOUNTERING DR. HESCHEL
IN SAN FRANCISCO

*"The spontaneous movement in all of us is toward connection,
health, and aliveness. No matter how withdrawn and isolated
we have become or how serious the trauma we have experienced, on the deepest level, just as a plant spontaneously moves
toward sunlight, there is in each of us an impulse moving
toward connection and healing."*
LAURENCE HELLER AND ALINE LAPIERRE[8]

Just before my rabbinic ordination, something unexpected and momen-
tous occurred, an experience that would change my self-understanding
and the entire course of my life.

For several months, my friend and fellow student, Arthur Green, was
suggesting I experiment with the psychedelic, lysergic acid diethylamide.
He more than hinted that something profound was likely to occur on the
"trip" that I would take. Finally, on a Friday night in June 1966, two days
before rabbinic ordination, I ingested a sugar cube laced with the drug.

During the next hour the objects in the dorm room began to vibrate
and their colors became amazingly rich and brilliant. I stared into the
palm of my left hand for what seemed like thirty or forty minutes, watching the blood course through my veins and arteries. Then slowly I began
to ascend to a state of consciousness in which all my normal cares and
anxieties simply lifted from my awareness. An incredibly wondrous living energy began to pulsate through my body and mind.

My need for control, in fact, all of my psychological defenses slipped
away. *My* concerns, *my* anxieties, *my* "I"—none of these mattered. I realized that my conscience, too, had disappeared and I was free of all psychological and moral constraints. As my sense of boundaries dissolved, I
became a vast transparent center of awareness, totally open, accepting,

loving, and ecstatic. Being was an entirely blessed and holy state—indeed, the *only* state.

At one point Art stepped into the bathroom. I walked toward the dormitory window. The spaciousness and beauty of the Manhattan skyline with countless tiny lights shining out of the darkness was intense. The desire arose to fly, to soar into the darkness of the infinite sky. As I cried out in exuberance, and lifted my arms, my friend came back into the room, gently took my hand, and led me away from the window.

During the night, we went for a long walk through the West Side on a tree-lined walkway above the Hudson River. Profound and silly insights alternately rushed through my mind and I shared them with my friend. When we returned to the dormitory, my awareness was ascending even further, and my sense of being an "I" dissolved. Now all the dichotomies, polarities, and conflicts of existence flowed together into a molten cosmos both sacred and whole. The center of consciousness simply witnessed the sacred moving in and through everything, sensing and resonating with the ineffable order of a mystery that could never be known. And now this center of awareness was intimately linked with everything, one with the entirety of the Universe, knowing that it was merely a small part of a vast oneness, of what I had always termed "God."

The world was incredibly awesome, beautiful, bountiful, good. There was a transparency and perfection to it all. Each thing was in its right place, as it was meant to be; nothing was lacking. The realization came that what people called evil was really only a slim thread winding through this wholeness that was in its essence perfection. The upward arc continued, and now there were no things at all, nothing to speak of—only the intense rapture of mysterious Is-ness. Consciousness completely merged with cosmos.

THE AFTEREFFECTS OF LSD

After that night, the rabbinic student Burt Jacobson went through with ordination and, almost as if on automatic pilot, became a Conservative rabbi. He then joined the faculty of the Melton Research Center for Jewish Education, which was pioneering new methods of classroom education for children. The Melton Pilot School was located in Columbus,

Ohio, and there he began developing experiential approaches to teaching Jewish prayer to children. Much of what he experimented with in the classroom derived from insights that had come to him following his encounter with LSD.

I lived much of that year in an elevated state of bliss, for the lingering effects of the psychedelic lasted almost six months. Not knowing any better, I imagined that LSD had permanently altered my life. I thought that I had actually become enlightened. As I later found out, I was actually in a state of ego inflation.

One morning I awoke in my apartment in Columbus feeling anxious. It took me a few days to figure out that the effects of the psychedelic had worn off and my old worried and fearful self were back. As I thought about this new state of affairs it seemed that I was being given a message: You now have to take full responsibility for your life! Throughout my years in seminary, I'd been part of a religious academic community. I'd followed the rules and completed my assignments to the best of my ability. That structured existence was now gone and I was on my own. Nor could I depend on the elevated mood induced by LSD. I was facing a new reality, and had to take full responsibility for life, steering my present and future. What had the past six months been? I wondered. It then seemed to me that the experience with LSD had been false, an illusionary interlude that artificially buoyed up my spirit.

TOWARD NEO-HASIDIC COMMUNITY

After two years in Columbus I moved to Cambridge, Massachusetts to take part in the creation of Havurat Shalom, a spiritual community founded by Arthur Green. Havurat Shalom was one of the first Jewish intentional communities that brought about the Jewish counterculture of the 1960s and 70s. Among the teachers on its faculty during the first year were Rabbis Zalman Schachter, Everett Gendler, Al Axelrad, Joe Lukinsky, and Edward Feld, and scholars Michael Fishbane and Stephen Mitchell. Many of us were recent ordainees of JTS, strongly critical of the academic style of learning at that institution as overly academic and spiritually irrelevant. We longed for a more open and egalitarian climate, and wanted to teach classes in a way that would make the subject matter come alive for people.

Yet the havurah was certainly more than a place to study Judaism in a spiritual fashion; we were also searching for community. The strong sense of American individualism had been something we took for granted, but we understood that without genuine community such individualism could be terribly oppressive. We were critical of the loss of authentic community in the established Jewish institutions, especially the synagogue. What we were yearning for were intimate connections with like-minded comrades and with the Divine. Some of us also felt a longing, even nostalgia, for the spiritual depth of an Eastern European Judaism we had never known.

Art provided the guiding vision for Havurat Shalom. He sought to meld the spiritual ideals of the late eighteenth-century Hasidic communities of Eastern Europe with radical democratic and communitarian values then emerging in American counterculture. At the havurah we not only sought interpersonal intimacy and communal experience, we also wanted to revitalize Jewish forms of prayer through creative and joyous worship services. At the same time the Havurah was to be a haven for young Jewish men who opposed the war in Vietnam by giving out draft deferments to those who wished to study to become rabbis. By year two, however, we knew we didn't have the resources to develop a serious rabbinic training program and so dropped the word "seminary" from the name of the community.

Many of the features that had drawn me so strongly to Lubavitch a decade earlier emerged in a radically new way at the havurah: intense hours of blissful meditation and prayer, joyous singing and dancing on Shabbat and holy days, and passionate dedication to sacred study. There was a spirit of openness, creativity, and youthful experimentation that I'd found lacking both at seminary and Lubavitch, and members felt free to express doubts about aspects of the tradition, including traditional notions of God.

Early on during my three years at the Havurah, memories of my first LSD experience resurfaced and I experimented again and again with psychedelics, regaining my assurance that indeed there was a spiritual world that existed beyond the material world. And I began to feel perhaps it was the separateness and brokenness of the physical world that was in some way illusory.

ON THE ROAD

I also served as the educational director of a large suburban synagogue school in the Boston area. The rabbi and synagogue board gave me free rein to create new and experimental approaches to learning with students in the school. I continued to develop the Melton experiential worship curriculum that I had worked on in Columbus. And with the help of two of my buddies from Havurat Shalom, I began to create what I hoped would be an authentic community among older teenagers at the synagogue.

Two years later, however, a decline in the economy caused many congregants to lose their jobs and all of my novel educational programs at the school were terminated. I was more than disappointed and disillusioned. I became angry at the decision of the rabbi and synagogue board in tightening the budget. In my fury I gave up my position and determined to end my career in Jewish education. Why should I give my life to the thankless task of educating children? I wondered. And I began to consider living without the rigid structure of Jewish religious discipline, without the ever-present ghosts of Jewish persecution and the death camps defining my attitude toward possibility. In 1971, just five years after my rabbinic ordination, I made what I thought would be a complete break with Jewish tradition and identity.

What was I seeking? What was calling me? Whatever it was, I had a hunch it might be found in California. With everything of value packed into my beat-up Plymouth Valiant, and with not a little fear, I set off with a hazy image of finding a commune to live in, hoping a trek to the West Coast would provide the freedom necessary for clarity. I wanted more of life, and for this I needed to shed the guise of a traditional Jew, facing the world once again as Burt, rather than Rabbi Jacobson.

Oddly though, I took two Jewish books with me, both related to the life and teachings of Rav Abraham Isaac Kook (1865-1935), the first Chief Rabbi of Jewish Palestine and a profound Jewish mystic. If I was truly longing to escape Judaism, why was I carrying these? What I did not want to admit at that time was how I was still looking for something or someone in Jewish tradition who might help me find a path to reconnect with my heritage. What I sensed in Rav Kook's writings was an awareness of ultimate freedom, mystery, unity, and vastness of the world of the Spirit. His evocative descriptions of inner journeys reminded me of my experiences with psychedelics. But it was beyond my ken to figure out how a mystic like Kook was able to remain an Orthodox Jew. Could he teach me a way to be spiritually Jewish without the anxiety, guilt, and morbidity that I had for so long felt was bundled up in Judaism?

Travelling up and down the coast of California, visiting and spending time in various communes and experimental communities, I didn't find one that really suited me. By 1973 I was living a thoroughly alternative life, residing in the Haight-Ashbury section of San Francisco, sharing an apartment with two friendly hippies. We often hung out, rapping, smoking marijuana, dancing to rock music, or listening to an undergraduate neighbor declaim his ersatz Beat poetry. During the days, I taught literature and other subjects at an experimental high school, which was part of Project One, a radical alternative warehouse community in San Francisco.

For years, I had been studying the depth psychology of Carl Jung, and reading the wisdom texts of India, China, and Japan. Intrigued by the centrality of the personal quest and the non-authoritarian character of these paths to the Spirit, I continued my studies in San Francisco, focusing on mythology and the study of human consciousness. I also continued to delve into Rav Kook's visionary writings, but I did not know where all this was taking me.

Once in a while I found myself drifting into Rabbi Shlomo Carlebach's House of Love and Prayer for a Friday evening service of ecstatic prayer, song, and dance. The House was a spiritual gathering place in San Francisco founded by Carlebach in the late 1960s. Jewish hippies by the dozens hung out there. Shlomo was most often on tour, but every few months he showed up at the House. I felt some ambivalence about being in this world, but Shlomo was a personable and engaging rabbi-troubadour able to reach young Jews of many backgrounds with a message of joy and love derived from Hasidism. Every time Shlomo saw me, he would smile and embrace me even though we had never formally met or had a conversation. And he would remember my name: "How are you, Burt?" he would ask.

A PASSION FOR TRUTH

One day in 1973, while browsing a bookstore on Haight Street, I came across a new book by Abraham Joshua Heschel titled *A Passion for Truth*. The dust jacket told me it was a parallel study of two nineteenth-century spiritual teachers: Polish Hasidic master, Reb Menachem Mendl of Kotzk, and Danish Christian theologian Soren Kierkegaard. I opened the book and began to read the introduction. Immediately I found myself riveted by Heschel's words. He wrote about a lifelong struggle that raged within him, as two radically different spiritual masters—Israel Baal Shem Tov and the Kotzker Rebbe—battled for his soul. Heschel had rarely written in an autobiographical manner and yet here, he was candidly disclosing a struggle that had defined his life.

I knew something about the Baal Shem Tov of Medzhibozh, the founder of Hasidism, and I had dipped into the writings of Soren Kierkegaard, one of the founders of existentialism. But Menachem Mendel of Kotzk was new to me. I was intrigued by Heschel's way of contrasting the Baal Shem Tov and the Kotzker:

> I was taught about inexhaustible mines of meaning by the Baal Shem; from the Kotzker I learned to detect immense mountains of absurdity standing in the way. The one taught me song, the other—silence. The one reminded me that there could be a heaven on earth, the other shocked me into discovering Hell in the alleged Heavenly places in our world.[9]

I knew Heschel had once been engaged in writing a book on the Baal Shem Tov—a work never completed—and I'd wondered about his relation to the founder of Hasidism. Paging through the first chapter, looking for other insights about the Baal Shem's influence on him, I found many: "When millions of our people were still alive in Eastern Europe and their memory and faith vibrated with thought, image and emotion, the mere mention of Reb Israel Baal Shem Tov cast a spell upon them. The moment one uttered his name, one felt as if his lips were blessed and his soul grew wings."[10] Something touched me. I paid the cashier, went back to my apartment, sat down on a large, threadbare cushion, and turned to the first chapter.

> The period of the Baal Shem was one in which poetic imagination was suppressed by Talmudic speculation. Blinders seemed to have been placed on the eyes of the soul. The Besht removed them, hearts opened, and fantasy began to sing. Fountains of joy bubbled forth, followed by passionate insights, intoxicating tunes, exquisite tales. It was as if the world had regained its chastity, and holiness was gazing at itself in the mirror of all things. Faith was at home with beauty.[11]

The words were like a key, opening a long-forgotten place in my heart. What was it—hope, memory, possibility? But Heschel would not stay in this place of joyous holiness. He kept returning to the heaviness of the Kotzker, admitting that his soul was torn between the Besht and the Kotzker. "Years later I realized that, in being guided by both the Baal Shem Tov and the Kotzker, I had allowed two forces to carry on a struggle within me. One was occasionally mightier than the other. But who was to prevail, which was to be my guide?"[12]

The Kotzker recognized that justice, compassion, humility, awe, and spirituality were noble virtues. Yet without truth and integrity, these qualities were merely a sham. And human beings go to great lengths to deceive themselves and others. Therefore, one must dedicate one's entire life to struggling for truth, and such a quest requires the total abandonment of ego. One must continually ferret out conceit, self-satisfaction, and mendacity to attain true closeness to God.

I found myself becoming frightened, even repelled. Part of this had to do with the stark typology Heschel was using. But it was also more than this.

> Wonder and exaltation infused the words of the Baal Shem Tov. His teaching called for fervor, joy and ecstasy. Suffering and torment suffused the maxims of the

Kotzker. His teaching called for earnest reflection and self-inquiry, for sobriety and severity.

> Spiritual tranquility is not found in the thinking of either Kierkegaard or the Kotzker...[T]he religious life is a perpetual struggle, tension and suffering. The last stage in this life is that act of self-annihilation in which the ideal task of being an existing individual and the impossibility of fulfilling it concretely are at war with each other. An awareness of this incompatibility is the root of religious torment.[13]

This was too much like the struggle, tension, and suffering I'd experienced as a traditional practicing Jew. I also had come close to a kind of self-annihilation arising out of such violent spiritual torment—my proximity to suicide during my first year at JTS.

The Kotzker reminded me of Rabbi Israel Salanter, whose writings had so affected me. The two teachers were, of course, different. Salanter fought the power of the evil instinct, while the Kotzker struggled against deceit and inauthenticity. At the time, though, these distinctions didn't seem apparent or important to me. Both teachers favored a somber ascetic approach to life that seemed to be self-deprecating—and both triggered my anxiety and guilt. Wasn't this one of the major reasons I had turned away from Judaism—to rescue myself from seemingly inevitable misery? Who needed such harshness and judgmentalism? There was already too much sadness in being a Jew, too much self-deprecation. Why would Heschel make this a virtue? Why would anyone seek to deepen their sense of wretchedness and self-abasement? I wanted no part of this conversation, yet because of my regard for Heschel I couldn't dismiss the question out of hand.

HIDING FROM THE TRUTH

I thought back about my relationship to Rabbi Heschel. My memories were complicated, tangled with regret. I learned a great deal from him in classes and seminars. The few private meetings we had, however, were missed opportunities. In the main, I was simply too closed off and ashamed of my inner life to reveal anything to him. Now, in the midst of what I thought was my escape from Judaism in San Francisco, here was Heschel, my old Jewish mentor. Through his distinctive portraits of the Baal Shem and the Kotzker he seemed again to question me, to challenge me to face my brokenness.

Since leaving the East Coast I had become accustomed to staying up late into the night. I looked at the clock and saw that it was 3am. I closed Heschel's book, put on a denim jacket, left the apartment, and walked along the Panhandle toward Golden Gate Park. There were wisps of fog in the air and a pervasive quiet, broken only by an occasional car passing. As I entered the park, the darkness and fog thickened. I buttoned my jacket and walked along in the lovely silence.

"You really do need to give up your sadness, you know," said a familiar voice within.

"Yes, I know, I know," I mumbled, "but I don't know how."

"You'll find a way...and I will help you," said the voice in my heart, "but you must learn persistence.... You can't give up."

"I know," I said, as if Heschel—or the Baal Shem Tov—were speaking with me, heart-to-heart.

CHAPTER THREE

OPENING TO THE BAAL SHEM TOV

I was drawn to the Besht, but I couldn't return to Heschel's book. He had written the section on the Baal Shem and the Kotzker in such a way that it was impossible to disentangle the two teachers within the web of his personal experience. At least I could not untangle them in mine. And I did not want to expose myself further to the spiritual ruthlessness of Menachem Mendel of Kotzk.

I shelved the book. But my mind kept going back to Heschel's characterization of the Baal Shem's love, compassion, and joy, and his elevation of the gift of Jewishness. Perhaps it was time to re-enter the Jewish world. I now had the opportunity, for students of Rabbi Zalman Schachter, a Habad-educated neo-Hasidic teacher, had started a New Age spiritual community in Berkeley called the Aquarian Minyan.

I began to drive over the Bay Bridge on Friday afternoons to take part in the Minyan's Shabbat services. Playful experimentation was the norm there, and Jewish tradition was honored for its wisdom, not for its authority. After a few months, while hiding my rabbinic identity, I moved to the East Bay. I found a room in a communal house of Jewish leftists who found a politically radical rabbi interesting, even though none of them had the slightest interest in Judaism. Within a few months I felt safe enough to become a spiritual leader in the Minyan, both teaching and helping to lead services.

A few years after this, I underwent "PsychoGenesis," an intensive psychotherapeutic process that enabled me to understand the roots of my anger, my perfectionistic self-judgment, and the poor self-esteem rooted in my traumatic childhood. I was able to purge myself of much of the fiendish power that my internalized parents had held over me and I began to experience compassion for both myself and them. Having undergone this healing process, I returned once again to *A Passion for Truth*. I was still irritated by the Kotzker rebbe, but I did not let this deter me from experiencing an openness to the immense love for the Baal Shem Tov now stirring in my heart. I was especially moved by Heschel's description of the Baal Shem's experience of the omnipresence of the Spirit:

> He revealed the Divine as present even in our shabby world, in every little thing, and especially in man. He made us realize that there was nothing in man—neither limb nor movement—that did not serve as vessel or vehicle for the Divine force. No place was devoid of the Divine. Furthermore, every man in this world could work deeds that might affect the worlds above. Most important, attachment to God was possible, even while carrying out mundane tasks or making small talk. Thus, unlike the sages of the past, who delivered discourses about God, the Baal Shem brought God to every man.[14]

I read this passage again and again. I also longed to see Divinity everywhere, to feel God surging through my limbs, to witness the Presence in my consciousness. I wanted to be attached to God while carrying out mundane tasks or making small talk.

The image of God that had formed within me while growing up derived from the way I experienced my relationship with my parents. My mother was distant and punitive and my father was absent when I needed him. Thus, the notion of God I developed was of a distant, transcendent, omnipotent Being who held absolute authority over me and judged me. Now the Besht's understanding of the Divine as a compassionate motherly presence *within* the world offered me a potential foundation for self-esteem.

Heschel wrote that to the Baal Shem Tov the physical world consisted of nothing but veils hiding the Oneness of reality. If we can just learn to see through the veils, we will be able to experience the immediacy of the Divine in every event and thing, in ourselves and in all being. "Since the divine was everywhere, one might easily experience the radiance of the Holy in any place at any moment. There is nothing that does not contain a glint of holiness, for without it nothing could possibly exist."[15] Even more important to me was the Baal Shem's conviction that the Divine lives within every individual. And Heschel demonstrated that the Besht himself exemplified these truths in the way that he lived his life: "[He] thought of the holiness and beauty every man's soul contained, and whenever he met the plainest man, he would offer love first and only then ask him to divest himself of the shackles that prevented him from being in love with God. He related to people as if everybody were his equal. The glory in being human, in being a Jew, enchanted him. He could discover jewels in every soul, and wherever he went he sought to foster reconciliation."[16]

"And what does it mean to be a Hasid?" Heschel asked rhetorically. "To be a Hasid is to be in love, to be in love with God and with what God has created. Once you are in love you are a different human being."[17] And because people are divine at their core, loving a human being is equivalent to loving God.

In the eloquent language he used in all of his writing, Heschel goes on to illuminate other virtues and values accentuated by the Besht, spiritual truths which are also ways of living in the world. Foremost among these qualities were joy and ecstasy. I had tasted the cosmic mystery and Oneness of existence through the use of psychedelics, but I didn't know how to bring that visionary imperative into the struggles and anxieties of everyday existence so as to transform the mundane into the holy. I realized that unlike Rabbi Israel Salanter or the Kotzker Rebbe, both of whom attacked the dark and resistant elements of human nature, the Baal Shem illumined the vast reservoir of human potential, a potential born of nurturing mystery, linking my small life to the great life of the universe.

I had been given just enough caring during my childhood to build a life. That love, together with the adversity I experienced during those years, had provoked me into a lifelong search for a deeper all-embracing love. I discovered the reality of universal Oneness and connectedness through my experiences with psychedelics. And I'd immersed myself in Rav Kook's poetic descriptions of this kind of ecstatic experience. But how might I nurture this love and integrate it into ordinary, everyday life? The PsychoGenesis Process enabled me learn how to face and deal with the impediments to love. I sensed that the Besht would not only be able to inspire me; he would also point me toward spiritual practices that would inculcate love in my soul.

RECONCILING WITH THE KOTZKER

I have embraced the path of the Baal Shem Tov for over forty years now, and yet the challenge of Kotzk still rings in my ears. It took a great deal of time, but I eventually came to a rapprochement with the Kotzker. The Besht helped in this endeavor. His watchword, "There is no place devoid of the Divine," taken from the Zohar, necessitated that I look more closely at the Kotzker to discover where God might be found in that master's earnest ongoing quest for truth.

I am subject to inertia. There were many times when I've become too comfortable and self-satisfied, when I've feared looking at blocks to growth, when I wanted to escape the outer challenges of the world and simply disappear into my spirituality. The Kotzker was able to break through all this reticence and awaken me to the inner or outer work that had to be undertaken.

Part of my aversion to the Kotzker had to do with his narrow, one-pointed obsessiveness. It cut too close to home; it was something I was trying to escape. But given his temperament I can understand his abhorrence of the ego and its self-justifying rationalizations. Much of the time, however, I'm inclined to a more lenient and compassionate attitude, knowing how easy it is for human beings to slip into self-deception, even when they might have the best of intentions. I now identify even more with the Kotzker's passion for truth, his quest to witness the world from a transcendent place, free of partisanship and prejudice of any kind. This was the boundlessness that the Besht was able to enter through his ecstatic, mystical experience.

The Kotzker's practice of compelling his disciples to struggle against their egos and continually extend themselves toward the truth is laudable, but I never felt his obsessive ferocity in this endeavor was warranted. I came to realize my aversion toward his path had to do, in large part, with my proclivity toward perfectionism and judgmentalism, habits I later came to understand were ways to justify and maintain my own lack of self-esteem. It was the Besht, with his high estimate of the value of every human being, who provided me with the incentive to change.

I have been involved in a discipline called spiritual direction for many years. This is an approach to counseling that helps "directees" discern God's presence in their lives. There are times when I have worked with directees who have perfectionistic temperaments. I have suggested they learn to accept imperfections in themselves and others, forgive themselves and others, and let go of extreme judgments. I remind them that the goal in life is to be human, not without fault. And I have offered practices that could help in this process of self-acceptance.

Menahem Mendel's voice continues to stir me out of excessive inwardness and spiritual self-concern. He rails about the dangers of a world gone mad. He carries the stern tones of the ancient Hebrew prophets crying out against injustice, mendacity, and moral callousness. It was, I now appreciate, this terrible suffering of conscience that motivated my mother to try to save European Jewry. And it is that voice that has, in large measure, been responsible for my political work on behalf of causes ranging from Soviet Jewry and nuclear disarmament to the struggle to end Israel's occupation of Palestinian lands and bringing about a just peace between the two peoples.

The Kotzker also forced me to examine my relationship with the Baal Shem Tov, which began naively. I discovered that I was using the Baal Shem's optimistic vision as a way to counter my melancholy. For many years the Besht's positive attitude was beneficial and healing, but eventually I saw that it had required me to defy and bracket my own pessimism. I came to understand that my outlook had to encompass the unredeemed and unredeemable chaos, absurdity, and horrors of human existence. A wholly optimistic, mystical vision of reality simply cannot adequately deal with the centuries of brutal antisemitism that culminated in the Holocaust, nor can it account for the omnipresence of human evil in the modern world: racism, genocide, the threat of nuclear and/or environmental devastation. I now believe that the Kotzker's heartbreaking view of the human tendency of manifesting senseless evil is absolutely necessary for an adequate grasp of the human predicament. It was this recognition that led to his passion for truth and practice of ongoing self-interrogation regarding his motives.

Studying the Baal Shem, I learned that he had a darker aspect to his vision, for he recognized that a single Lifeforce drives evil as well as goodness. And because of this the tzaddik has a responsibility to transform God's malevolence into goodness. So, integrating the teachings of the Besht and the Kotzker has been neither simple nor easy. The real problem is not the question of which teacher possessed the truth, but why I found it so necessary to embrace the one and reject the other. Together the two perspectives represent an entire range of spiritual and moral concern. There will be times when one rebbe's call summons my attention, and times when the other rebbe's voice must prevail. I have learned how to listen deeply to the promptings of my heart so I can more easily discern how to respond in a truthful way when I am confronted by difficult choices in life.

Nonetheless, for me, it is the voice of the Baal Shem Tov that must in the end prevail. The master's compassion undergirds and informs the Kotzker's demand for truth. "How can the harshness of existence be sweetened at the core?" the Baal Shem once asked his disciples. He then answered his own question: "By raising oneself toward the greatest desire of all: the longing for true goodness. And what is true goodness? It is perfect compassion."

THE BAAL SHEM TOV AND NEO-HASIDISM

Before my encounter with the Besht, I was drawn also to the religious philosophy of Martin Buber, arguably the most renowned Jewish thinker of the first half of the twentieth century. Buber's philosophy of dialogue was influential among Christians as well as Jews, and he was the major founder of the twentieth-century spiritual movement that today we call Neo-Hasidism. Buber was the first to recognize that the Baal Shem Tov and Hasidism contained truths desperately needed in the modern, secular world. And he saw Hasidim as the necessary catalyst for the renewal of the spirit in Judaism in our era.

Other important non-orthodox Jewish spiritual teachers felt similarly, including Hillel Zeitlin, Rabbi Zalman Schachter-Shalomi, Rabbi Shlomo Carlebach, and Rabbi Arthur Green. In an interview I once conducted with Reb Zalman, he told me, "If you were to remove every trace from my makeup, there would scarce be anything left of me!" Learning about the effect that the Baal Shem's vision had on all of these teachers led me to the realization that the founder of Hasidism was also at the root of the rebirth of Jewish spirituality in the twentieth century.

For me, most essential was the search for an identity. Who was I? What was my life's purpose? What part could my being Jewish play in all of this? And perhaps the most important question of all: On whose life could I model my own? How could I keep a vast sense of being One with the Infinite alive when the world demanded I behave in a way that would inevitably close it down? It was this that launched the quest that took me to Eastern spirituality and eventually to the Baal Shem Tov.

The Besht offered something that none of my previous Jewish mentors had given: a key that could open the realm of mystery and Oneness and a way to channel that richness into my life on this earth plane; and then to bring this to my work as a rabbi, helping to renew Judaism in our time.

CHAPTER FOUR

KABBALAH, VEDANTA, AND HASIDISM

*"Life's splendor forever lies in wait about each one of us in all
its fullness, but veiled from view, deep down, invisible, far off.
It is there, though, not hostile, not reluctant, not deaf. If you
summon it by the right word, by its right name, it will come."*
FRANZ KAFKA, FROM HIS DIARIES

In 1964, my year as a rabbinic student in Israel, I took a class in Zohar at Hebrew University. The Zohar is the masterwork of the Kabbalah, channeled and composed by the eminent Spanish mystic, Rabbi Moses de Leon (1240-1305) in the latter part of the thirteenth century. The class was taught by Dr. Rivka Schatz-Uffenheimer, a student of Gershom Scholem, the renowned scholar who had been the founder of the modern academic study of Jewish mysticism.

The Zohar is, in part, a kind of mystical novel. The central character in the work is Rabbi Shimon bar Yochai, a sage who lived during the second century in Palestine. All through the volumes that make up the Zohar, Shimon bar Yokhai is depicted as a denizen of both the visible and invisible worlds, a charismatic visionary, frequently receiving spiritual insights from the worlds beyond. He led his disciples into the deep mysteries of the words of Torah, and the world of nature, in order to unveil the vast mine of divine secrets hidden beneath the surface of all things. Through such daring inquiry, the Zohar sought to open the hearts and minds of students to celestial revelations that would allow them to penetrate secrets of the human soul and fathom the mind and psyche of the divine source of existence.

As the year in Israel went on, I became close with a fellow student named Michael. The two of us would regularly prepare for class by working our way through the assigned portion of the Aramaic text of the *Hak'damah La'Zohar,* the introduction to the Zohar. Early on we discovered that we were both photographers, and shared our work with one another. And when we studied Zohar, we often tried to visualize the symbols and metaphors in the sources. One day we were delving into the following passage:

> Rabbi Pinhas used to visit Rabbi Rehumai by the shore of Lake Ginnosar. Rabbi Rehumai was distinguished, advanced in years, and his eyes had transcended seeing the physical world. He said to Rabbi Pinhas, "Truly I have heard that our Companion, Rabbi Shimon bar Yochai, has a pearl, a precious stone. I gazed into the light of that pearl, which was issuing like the radiance of the sun from its sheath, illumining the entire world. That light extends from heaven to earth, and will illuminate the entire world until the Ancient of Days comes and sits fittingly upon the throne. That light is contained totally in your house, and from that light contained in your house there emanates a fine threadlike ray, radiating, illumining the entire world. Happy is your share! Go, my son, go out after that pearl illuminating the world, for the time is ripe."[8]

Michael and I felt a sense of wonder and exuberance as we attempted to puzzle out the text's profundities. What was the pearl that Rabbi Shimon bar Yochai possessed? What does the author mean when he states that this jewel illuminates the entire world? Which face of Divinity does the appellation "Ancient of Days" represent? What is the light that Rabbi Rehumai is referring to, and what does he mean when he tells Rabbi Pinhas that "that light is contained totally in your house"?

At one point in our preparation, Michael exclaimed, "Can you see this as an animated movie—like Disney's *Fantasia*? The two sages sitting on the edge of the lake—and as the blind sage speaks, the camera moves away from them and outward into space." He began to move his arms in the air, as if to mime the movement of the camera. "Now the two figures are becoming tinier and tinier, and slowly they disappear into a vast, luminous pearl shining down upon the globe of the earth in space, and the light enters all the crannies of the earth, and all the dark places become light—and then, superimposed on that scene, an immense mysterious figure, the Ancient of Days, enters and sits on a throne."

"Wow! What an idea," I exclaimed, "but how would you depict the Ancient of Days?"

"Ah, I don't know. Maybe just a robe, a shimmering, multi-colored robe. Or maybe the robe is glowing, glowing with gold and silver. No face, of course, no body, no body at all."

UNFOLDING THE COSMOS

Kabbalah is a visionary path and discipline that dominated Jewish spiritual life from the thirteenth through the seventeenth centuries. Kabbalists rank the Zohar as the central repository of Jewish mystical insight and one of the three fundamental scriptural sources of Judaism, together with the Bible and the Talmud. The three large Aramaic tomes that make up the Zohar were composed as a kind of commentary on the five books of the Torah; in actual fact, however, the Zohar is an independent composition that makes use of the contents of the Torah as the starting point for its own symbolic and mystical vision. Rabbi Moses de Leon, its brilliant author and compiler, employed many different literary genres in his writing: story, fantasy, myth, vision, and mystical reflection on the dynamic workings of the divine "mind."

At its essence, Zoharic Kabbalah is an esoteric teaching about the creation of the universe. It deals with questions such as, what is the spiritual origin of the physical world, and how is the physical linked to the metaphysical? The Bible begins with the words, "In the beginning God created the heavens and the earth" (Gen. 1:1), but the Zohar posits a very different kind of genesis: the universe was not created by a transcendent God; it was an emanation out of unfathomable mystery (*Ein Sof*). All the archetypal powers of Divinity, which formed the spiritual foundation for the physical universe, emanated out of the infinite enigma (*Ain Sof*) of which human beings can know nothing. The term "Ancient of Days," found in the quotation from the Zohar cited above, is another synonym for that mystery.

And where is God in all this? According to the Zohar, God (*Elohim*) too emanated out of the mystery, specifically out of the realm of cosmic wisdom that originated in the *Ain Sof!* In this way the Zohar emphasizes the notion that everything we can know about God as well as the physical world is an emanation out of the mystery. Kabbalists believed that what they called the Upper Worlds—or what we might call the higher spiritual dimensions—are ineffable. Nonetheless, they made extensive use of imagery in order to make those otherworldly realities more tangible. The kabbalists were profoundly fascinated by the God who emerged out of that greatest of mysteries. That God, they believed, possessed a kind of mind or psyche, and an inner life. They also supposed that they could infer the workings of God's psyche through the faculties of the human soul that we call intuition and imagination, i.e., through revelation, myth, symbol, fantasy, and dream.

One of the images they used to symbolize the divine psyche is known as the Tree of Life. This upside-down tree, rooted in heaven, was seen as having ten branches extending downward, known as the ten *sefirot*, the ten mystical dimensions of divine inwardness. In the process of their unfolding, the ten sefirot became the spiritual blueprint for the creation of the physical world. And through the human imagination, any verse in the Bible could be unlocked to reveal the hidden happenings within the divine psyche. These elucidations were usually remote from the original and literal meanings of the biblical verses they were based on.

Emphasis is placed on transcendence in the Zohar. Rabbi Moses de Leon's goal largely had to do with inspiring people to rise above the lowly physical plane and enter higher spiritual rungs of the Tree of Life. When early kabbalists entered states of expanded awareness, they believed they were experiencing a merging with the sefirot themselves. It was in and through such states of consciousness that they intuited the ineffable Oneness that lies behind and beyond the realm of multiplicity and division, the primal essence from which everything originally arose and continues to arise. If all of this seems overly complex, that is because the hierarchal world of the kabbalist's imagination is, indeed, extremely intricate and rich. Like modern-day physicists, Moses de Leon was attempting to describe the underlying realities of the universe, but he was exceedingly fascinated by the question of the spiritual origins of existence.

HEALING A BROKEN WORLD

I heard about Scholem's book, *Major Trends in Jewish Mysticism,* while in Israel, and purchased a copy when I returned to New York in 1965. This work is considered his most important attempt at elucidating the history of Jewish mysticism. I was intrigued by his descriptions of pursuits of the mystics throughout history. One of the chapters had to do with a later era in the development of Jewish mysticism, the so-called "new Kabbalah" of Rabbi Isaac Luria, also known as the Holy Ari (1534-1572). I was captivated by Scholem's dramatic description of Luria's spiritual worldview.

Born in Jerusalem, Luria lived for some time in Egypt, then moved to the little village of Safed in northern Palestine to join a community of kabbalists who lived, studied, and practiced an ascetic, mystical Judaism together. The world of the Zohar had been thematically anchored in the creation of the cosmos, but the Holy Ari's vision represented a revolutionary departure from de Leon's understanding of Kabbalah. Luria was absorbed by the question of brokenness and evil in the universe and human existence. Scholem believed that Luria was preoccupied with this question because he lived just after the trauma of the Inquisition and the expulsion of the Jews from Spain in 1492. Consequently, Scholem averred, Luria was drawn to the questions of how the cosmos could be redeemed from chaos and how human life could be liberated from wrongdoing and sin.

Before reading Scholem, I knew something about Lurianic Kabbalah because of my discussions with Arthur Green. But now, having spent a year studying the Zohar, I was taken with Luria's vision because it tackled the subject of evil in such profound fashion. I felt that if Luria's theology had addressed the adversity experienced by Jews following their expulsion from Spain, perhaps there was a way in which it could also speak to the suffering I was still experiencing in the wake of the Holocaust and my own growing up.

Luria wrote very little. Once asked by a disciple why he did not set out his ideas and teaching in book form, he is said to have replied: "It is impossible, because all things are interrelated. I can hardly open my mouth to speak without feeling as though the sea burst its dams and overflowed. How then shall I express what my soul has received, and how can I put it down in a book?"[19]

After the master's death, Luria's disciple, Rabbi Hayyim Vital, wrote four volumes that explained his teacher's system. To judge by Vital's writings, Luria's metaphysics was dramatic, subtle, and exceedingly complex. Why does the physical universe even exist? Why wasn't the Holy One content to remain the All? According to Luria, the Infinite desired the existence of something other than itself. But in its state of simple being-ness it could not manifest its hidden potentiality; only by becoming a differentiated universe could its perfection come into being. Such a process could not take place as long as the Holy One continued to fill the All. So the Infinite contracted itself (*tzimtzum*), receding deeply into the recesses of its own being, and in this way made room for a finite universe. The Infinite took on a new form, gradually becoming the personal God who could be known by human beings. Then, taught Luria, from out of God's eyes, ears, and nose wondrous lights beamed forth into the emp-tiness. God began to emanate out of Itself ten vast bowl-like vessels— Luria's main image of the ten sefirot—into the space that it had vacated, and began to fill these vessels with divine light.

Then suddenly an unexpected calamity occurred and the divine plan went completely awry. Too fragile to contain the light of the Infinite, the seven lower vessels fractured and burst (*shivi'rat ha'kelim*). Most of the light that these vessels had briefly contained then flowed back to the Infinite Source, but the remainder of the light fell into primordial space as tiny sparks (*ni'tzo'tzot*). These sparks clung to the shards (*kli'pot*) of the broken vessels and energized the fragments to which they were attached.[20] Animated by divine light, these shards, which filled existence, contained a ferocious power and brought into being evil and the demonic forces. This is the origin of the broken universe that humanity eventually came to inhabit. The cataclysm caused the Divine to be split into two parts, a hidden transcendent aspect, the blessed Holy One (*Kud'shah B'rikh Hu*) understood as masculine, and an immanent dimension, seen as feminine. It is the latter facet of God, known as the *Shekhinah*, that dwells in the physical world. And these two faces of Divinity, like pas-sionate lovers cut off from one another, long to be reunited.

This powerfully imagined description of the broken world inhabited by human beings posed the great questions that Luria attempted to answer: How might the Shekhinah, the divine bride, join her cosmic groom, the *Kud'shah B'rikh Hu*, once again? And how can this shattered cosmos be healed? Classical Judaism had taught that God would someday send the messiah to redeem the world, but the Ari had a very different sense of things.

Jews had been in exile at the mercy of the Gentile nations for so many centuries, and it had become obvious that God alone was unable to redeem the world. Not only that, but Luria understood that God himself must not be perfect; God, too, required redemption. It was because of this that God created humanity—or more specifically, the Jewish people—with the mission of repairing both the universe (*tikkun olam*) and reuniting the Shekhinah with her divine Husband (*tikkun Elohim*).

Human beings are composed of spirit and matter, light and darkness, sparks and shards, and God gave humans the freedom to decide which of these polarities they want to give their life energies to. The kabbalists saw themselves as defenders of the light, using magical practices that the Ari taught to repair and heal the broken world. By means of their special mystical contemplations and their sacred deeds—including absolute love for everyone and everything—Lurianic kabbalists were convinced that they could release sparks from the demonic husks that held them captive. In this way they believed that they could help restore the broken universe to wholeness and bring about the messianic era.

The universe that Vital describes is a marvelous, magical, and dangerous place. The kabbalists who followed his path believed that the attainment of holiness is difficult for human beings plagued by the wiles of the Evil Urge. They believed they could attain sanctity only through renouncing physical pleasures, mastering their passions, fasting, remaining awake throughout the night, continually atoning for sins, flagellating one another, tormenting themselves, and engaging in purifying ritual baths.

Scholem ends the chapter with an interpretive summation of Luria's path, focusing on how the Ari understood the exile of Jews from their homeland and the way they could bring about their own redemption. In all, the Lurianic mythos provided me with a new sense of the purpose of

Jewish existence—*tikkun olam*, the healing and restoration of the world to its original wholeness. For years, I championed the Ari's vision of healing the world and restoring it to its pristine unity. I came to feel that when I engaged in my religious obligations, or when I struggled against injustice, I was fulfilling God's vision and contributing to the perfecting of life on this planet.

BEGINNING A NEW LIFE

My encounters with kabbalistic metaphysics were fascinating, powerful, and energizing, but they were of no help just a few years later when I abandoned traditional Judaism altogether. Indeed, it seemed that the promise of world redemption in Luria's cosmic drama now seemed to be an inflated dream. His magic-based practices had not brought the Jewish people any closer to the messianic era. Indeed, in 1648, less than a century after Luria's death, there were major pogroms in Ukraine during which tens of thousands of Jews were brutally slaughtered. This was followed by the appearance of Shabbatai Tzvi, the Lurianic kabbalist who claimed to be the promised messiah and who was forced, on pain of death, to convert to Islam, deflating the hopes of the majority of Jews in the world who had put their faith in his promises. Then there were the 1881 pogroms in Odessa, and a hundred other localities in Russia and Ukraine, which spurred the beginnings of the Zionist movement. And then the Holocaust, during my own lifetime.

I had not given up on spirituality at this time. That happened when I was living in Boston. As detailed in the last chapter, I left aside my Judaism for a period of time. I needed a new path that would allow my sense of selfhood to grow. Deciding to explore the world's religions in greater depth, I purchased Joseph Campbell's four-volume history of world mythology and religion, *The Masks of God.* As I encountered the wonders and terrors of the religions that Campbell portrayed so well, I was especially taken with the author's portrayal of Taoism and Hinduism.

When I encountered the *Tao Te Ching,* the writings of the Chinese sage, Lao Tse, I was entranced by the book's sublime and lofty language, a form of sacred poetry that had the capacity to rouse the reader to actually experience the notions it was communicating. The word *Tao* (pronounced *Dao*) signifies the primordial essence or basic nature of the universe. It can also be thought of as the flow that provides the universe with balance, harmony, and order. Like water, the Tao is undifferentiated and endlessly self-replicating. But Tao also flows through the lives of people and has the power to transform human life. I found many different translations of the *Tao Te Ching* and compared them, trying to enter more deeply into the mysteries of that ancient wisdom. I learned that Taoists envision the human mind as an uncarved block before it enters the world of experience where it is sculpted into human form and shape. And even though the mind may be sullied through its experience with the world, the uncarved state of consciousness never completely disappears. Its oneness lies beyond dualistic distinctions such as right and wrong, good and bad, or beautiful and ugly. When one discovers the uncarved block, one finds alignment with the Tao.

I recall a lovely summer evening in the summer of 1970 at a campground in a state park on the California coast overlooking the Pacific Ocean. I was reading the *Tao Te Ching* in my little tent by lamplight, and in that serene environment the words took on a kind of numinous radiance. Then I heard music outside. I left the tent and wandered in direction of the sound. When I reached the campfire, there were twenty or thirty hippies sitting around, singing folk music, smoking marijuana, smiling and laughing. A few people were strumming guitars. I joined the group and we sang for hours into the night. It couldn't have been more blissful and harmonious. To me it was a living experience of the Tao.

Excited by what Joseph Campbell had to say about early Vedic religion, I then turned to the Upanishads, a collection of teachings composed by forest sages in India during the seven centuries before the Common Era. Two concepts that spoke most persuasively to me were *Brahman* and *Atman*. Brahman is the pervasive, genderless, infinite, eternal truth, and bliss that does not change, yet is the cause of all changes. Atman means the inner self, the soul, immortal spirit within individual human beings and all living beings, including animals and trees. Atman is their essential being, eternal and ageless. And in truth, the ancient sages proclaimed, Brahman and Atman are one. In one of these texts, a spiritual seeker named Svetaketu is told by his father that "An invisible but subtle essence is the Spirit of the whole universe. That is Reality. That is Truth. THOU ART THAT."

The Upanishads provided me with a direct kind of language for what I experienced through psychedelics: *my essence was one with the essence of the universe.* I encountered parallel ideas in Jewish mystical sources, but in the Vedantic sources they were stated much more clearly and simply than in the elaborate and highly symbolic kabbalistic texts I studied. Why couldn't Judaism offer such supreme truth in as simple and direct a way as this? Kabbalah seemed like a labyrinth of words, images, symbols, and myths that obscured rather than revealed truth. Normative Judaism was full of moral hedging. Yes, said the tradition, we all have something Divine within us, but be careful! Remember that Adam and Eve were created in the divine image, but they listened to the serpent and ate from that cursed tree and lost everything! You are no different; you are a fallen and sinful human being. So keep up your guard! Hold fast to the six hundred and thirteen commandments! One false step and you'll fall into the pit of sin!

BE HERE NOW

It was during this period that Ram Dass' *Be Here Now* appeared. The book was striking in appearance, printed on the kind of rough brown paper used for wrapping packages. The type was handset and the author's words were accompanied by whimsical illustrations. Ram Dass' message poured out in a playful, stream-of-consciousness fashion.

IF YOU ARE PURE SPIRIT

YOU ARE <u>NOT</u> MATTER . . . . . . YOU ARE THAT

ETERNAL SPIRIT

IF EACH OF US IS THAT VERY OLD BEING

AND NOT THIS YOUNG BODY

OR THIS BODY THAT IS GOING

THROUGH THIS LIFE . . .

<u>WHY</u> DON'T WE

REMEMBER?

WHY DON'T WE REMEMBER IT ALL??

WHY CAN'T WE READ

THE ENTIRE AKASHIC RECORD??

BECAUSE OF OUR ATTACHMENTS TO

THE PHYSICAL PLANE OF REALITY . . .
BECAUSE OF THE POWER OF OUR IDENTIFICATION
WITH OUR OWN BODY-SENSES
AND THOUGHTS.

The book certainly had its moments of humor, but Ram Dass' message was earnest. He called for a complete renunciation of attachment to desire and to ego:

DO YOU REALIZE WHEN YOU GO ON THAT JOURNEY
IN ORDER TO GET TO THE DESTINATION
YOU
CAN NEVER GET TO THE DESTINATION?
IN THE PROCESS
YOU
MUST DIE
MUST DIE
PRETTY FIERCE JOURNEY   PRETTY FIERCE REQUIREMENT
WE WANT VOLUNTEERS[21]

Words like these scared me. I didn't want to be a volunteer. I had a poor self-image and a weak ego. I knew that it would be years before I would be ready to renounce my ego—*if* that was to be my path. I had to first discover my potential, find a new identity. But I also knew that Hinduism was patient; the sages taught that an individual might have to go through many lifetimes before being ready to accede to a higher destiny. It was a matter of eventually attaining enlightenment; it had nothing to do with sin.

I needed to go beyond merely reading about Vedanta. I'd heard about the Ananda Ashrama in Cohasset, Massachusetts, near Cape Cod, from Rabbi Zalman Schachter. It was at that ashram that Reb Zalman first experienced LSD with Timothy Leary. This spiritual center was founded by Swami Paramananda in 1929. I drove down to Cohasset on several occasions, attending services, listening to lectures, and dialoguing with one of the teachers. On one occasion I even took my mother to the ashram for a visit.

I don't recall meditating at the ashram, but I was drawn to

contemplative practice, and it was during this time that I was initiated into Transcendental Meditation. TM, as it is called, is a form of practice from India, introduced into this country by Maharishi Mahesh Yogi. I began practicing daily, even though I found the practice somewhat boring. After three months, seeing no change in my myself, I gave it up.

Sometime after moving to the West Coast, I drove to New Mexico to spend a month at a spiritually-oriented commune called the Lama Foundation. At the time, Indian spirituality was pivotal to the folks living at Lama. Ram Dass had lived there and the community had published *Be Here Now.* I took part in community meditation, and got to know some of the adepts living on the commune.

When I returned to the Bay Area, I delved into the work of the Indian mystic Sri Aurobindo. He'd developed a method of spiritual practice called Integral Yoga. The central theme, drawn from Vedanta, was the evolution of human life into a life divine. He believed that spiritual realization would not only liberate human beings but would transform human nature, enabling a divine life on earth. This seemed promising. Nonetheless, I couldn't commit. Part of the problem had to do with the assertion made by Indian sages that the human self is an illusion, even though I knew from my experiences with psychedelics that this claim was in some sense true. But there was a second, deeper impediment to my adopting a Hindu path. Because of my upbringing and education, I was finding that I could not escape my Jewishness. It would take me years to figure out that I could only find healing for my broken Jewish soul through confronting and working through the Holocaust-related traumas I endured as a child, and gaining the knowledge and inner strength necessary to deal with the guilt I was experiencing for having abandoned Judaism.

I was conscious, then, of the lack of an imperative for social justice in these Eastern paths. There seemed to be no need for the transformation of society—as the Hebrew prophets had called for in ancient Israel—because evils that took place in the social, economic, and political realms were illusory. For millennia the caste system, so endemic to Indian society, had been shored up by religious authority. This aspect of Hinduism made me feel queasy—something I simply could not accept.

I have never lost interest in or respect for the visions and the practices of the Eastern mystics. Indeed, without having entered the precincts of Vedanta and Taoism, it is likely that I might never have looked for a Jewish counterpart to the teachings I discovered among the Asian mystics. It was partly because of my previous encounters with the spirituality of the East, along with my psychedelic experience, that primed me to discover the wealth offered by the Baal Shem Tov.

CHAPTER FIVE

THE BAAL SHEM'S TRUTH

As I mentioned in chapter 2, it was the vision of the great modern Orthodox mystic, Rav Abraham Isaac Kook, that first drew me back toward Judaism, even though I struggled with several of his key ideas and most especially his unyielding orthodoxy. Then, when I met the Baal Shem Tov in San Francisco, it was his teachings that took hold of me, providing me with a powerful incentive to return more fully to Judaism.

Some of the most important insights I had found in Hinduism leapt out as I read Heschel's *A Passion for Truth*, especially what the Besht had to say about the Divine within human beings. For example: "The soul is 'part of God from above,' but man thinks he is all from below, all made of dust. Every man must think of himself as a stairway set on the ground, its top reaching heaven. It is within his power to affect what should happen in the upper worlds." And: "Man has a soul which is itself a divine portion of Divinity and through it he can intuit something of the Divinity of God who is above."[22]

There is a Hasidic parable about the Baal Shem that encapsulates the essence of the Besht's revelatory gift to the Jewish people. Two nineteenth century rabbis were conversing about the founder of the Hasidic movement. One was Rabbi Aryeh Leib Heller (1745–1812), a brilliant non-Hasidic Talmudic scholar, and the other was Reb Tzvi Hirsch of Zhydatshov (1763-1831), founder of the Zhydatshov Hasidic dynasty.

> Reb Aryeh Leib asked Reb Tzvi Hirsch, "What is it that makes this age so different from times gone by? Since the Baal Shem has appeared, a tremendous number of scholars and followers have been drawn to his way of thinking. Isn't his viewpoint the same as that of Rabbi Isaac Luria, the Holy Ari? Yet the Ari's following was small. What has the Besht done to attract so many followers everywhere? What has he given us that is new?"

"Let me share a parable with you," replied Rebbe Tzvi.

"There was once a nation that had no ruler. Now the people of this land had heard that there was an extraordinary individual living in a distant land, who might make them a great ruler. This unusual person was said to be blessed with both physical beauty and nobility of character; there was none to compare with him in virtue.

"The people did not want to invite this individual to be their sovereign sight unseen, so they sent one of their number to that distant land to meet the candidate in person. In this way they would know whether the reports they had heard were true. Some time later the envoy returned full of enthusiasm, and yet he was able to convince only a small number of people of the candidate's worth.

"So a second emissary was sent. He returned even more enthusiastic than the first, and was able to convince a greater number of the people to accept the candidate as their ruler. Still, most of the people remained ambivalent, and the invitation was not offered.

"There was one man, however, who knew exactly what was needed. He undertook the long journey, and invited the candidate to return with him to his country. The nominee agreed to return with this man, and when all the citizens saw just how worthy he was, they set the crown upon his head in recognition of his greatness.

"This is the parable," said Rebbe Tzvi, "and now I will tell you its meaning. Rabbi Shimon bar Yochai, the hero of the Zohar, was the first envoy. He was able to reveal some of the secrets of God's great glory through the Zohar. But this was an esoteric work, accessible only to few. The Holy Ari, Rabbi Isaac Luria, was the second envoy. He was able to bring these teachings to a greater number of people, but he, too, spoke in terms of the celestial spheres and sublime matters, and most of the people could not appreciate his teachings.

"When the Baal Shem finally appeared, however, he was able to reveal the Divine in each tiny creation in this humble world. He taught us how to bind ourselves to God's holiness through all of our deeds and all of our thoughts—even through our ordinary conversations. In this way the Besht succeeded in bringing the Majesty of majesties before the very eyes of every human being."[23]

In a second version of this story, Reb Tzvi Hirsch answers his questioner this way: "Rabbi Shimon bar Yochai showed us that the world had a Creator, and R. Isaac Luria taught us how we could journey toward the Creator; but the Baal Shem Tov explained that we do not have to leave our place at all, for Divinity can be found exactly where we are."[24]

I lived with Reb Tzvi Hirsch's powerful parable for many months, trying to grasp its implications for my life. The more I entered into the parable's images and words, the more I came to appreciate its simplicity, its depth, and its way of describing the radical path of the Baal Shem Tov.

A RADICAL KABBALAH

The parable presents a picture of a people without a ruler. As I understand this, it means that the mystery of God ceased to be a living reality in the lives of the Jewish people. To make the spiritual realm a living reality once again, Rabbi Shimon bar Yokhai, and later the holy Ari, both attempted to move beyond the old paradigms of biblical and Rabbinic Judaism that had pictured the Divine in external, anthropomorphic terms, and to some extent they succeeded. Kabbalists discovered that beyond the personified deity there were many transpersonal dimensions or energies—the sefirot—and that beyond those energies there was sheer mystery, the Infinite (*Ein Sof*).

These approaches of classical Kabbalah, however, had been *symbolic* interpretations of reality. They lived in the realm of concepts and imagination, not the everyday world. Because of this they required the use of esoteric practices that would lift the kabbalists out of the physical into a celestial realm where they might experience the presence of the Divine. As such, traditional Kabbalah was accessible to only a handful of mystics.

Reb Tzvi Hirsch was claiming that the Baal Shem Tov enabled ordinary people to grasp, in ways they immediately understood, the sacred nature of the reality in which they were living. The alternative ending puts it directly: *"We do not have to leave our place at all, for Divinity can be found exactly where we are."* The Besht focused on the presence of the Presence, the immanent dimension of Divinity that one could sense in the here and now. In Heschel's words, the Besht was able "to reveal the Divine in each tiny creation in this humble world. He taught us how to bind ourselves to God's holiness through all of our deeds and all of our thought—even through our ordinary conversations."

To me, the teaching itself is paradoxical. The parabolic form makes use of the traditional anthropomorphic imagery of a monarch's relationship with his subjects. In actuality, though, the Zhydatshover is pointing toward a transpersonal understanding of reality, especially in the alternate version: *"The Besht explained that you and I do not have to leave our place at all, for divinity can be found exactly where we are."* The Holy Oneness is neither a king nor a father. Rather, the Divine is the ground of existence, the fiber of our being, the lifeforce flowing through everything. We live within its very presence.

As I studied the text in depth it struck me that what it was describing was in some ways similar to my first experience of LSD. In the grip of what was occurring I knew that I was part of the same world I encountered in my ordinary consciousness, but something much deeper had opened up. The earth was flowing with radiant colors and pulsing with life. Through the power of the psychedelic, the underlying energy giving everything its existence had become fully present, and despite the enormous differences between each and every thing in my field of vision, I had palpable recognition of the interlocking Oneness binding all together, as well as a profound sense of utter mystery pervading the whole. The Baal Shem Tov seemed to be promising me that it was possible to live my life with this kind of consciousness.

Also in the parable, the Zhydatshover makes the point that the people had the right to choose who would be their ruler. This claim seems radically modern and anti-authoritarian to me, for according to traditional Judaism, the covenant was imposed upon the Israelite people by an all-powerful God 3,000 years ago at Mt. Sinai, and was meant to last forever. Jews could not opt out of this eternal contract. According to one well-known midrash, God had lifted Mt. Sinai over the heads of the assembled Israelites and proclaimed that if the people refused to accept the Torah, he would drop the mountain on them![25]

Reb Tzvi Hirsch lived in the late eighteenth and early nineteenth centuries, and was undoubtedly aware of the democratic challenges to monarchal autocracy that sparked the American and French revolutions. Something a bit less radical had occurred much earlier in Poland, when, after 1572, kings were elected by the nobles. In his parable, R. Tzvi Hirsch seems to be saying that as in Poland, sovereignty was now invested in the "nobles"—that is, the Jewish people—and the *people* therefore have the power to choose to offer the crown to the One they wish to become their Ruler. Reb Tzvi Hirsch appears to be implying that the Baal Shem Tov knew that no Jew could be compelled to accept God's sovereignty on the basis of blind faith alone.

The Zhydatshover came from a pious Hasidic community made of Jews brought up with a love and reverence for the Torah and God. His disciples and colleagues were steeped in Jewish mystical lore. Like the Besht, he affirmed the teaching of the *Zohar Hadash,* "There is no place devoid of the Divine." Yet for those of us who live in a predominantly secular society, encountering the holy in the here and now is not so easy. How does one go about such a quest today?

In an interview he gave towards the end of his life, Abraham Joshua Heschel was asked, "You recently told an interviewer that 'what keeps me alive is my ability to be surprised.' What has surprised you lately?" In his answer, he cited the verse from the biblical book of Ecclesiastes, "There is nothing new under the sun," adding: "I disagree with that statement. I would say there is nothing stale under the sun except human beings, who become stale. I try not to be stale. And everything is new. No two moments are alike. And a person who thinks two moments are alike has never lived."

In *God in Search of Man,* Heschel offers a spiritual path inspired not only by his ability to be surprised, but by the vision of the Baal Shem Tov.

> The ultimate insight is the outcome of *moments* when we are stirred beyond words, of instants of wonder, awe, praise, fear, trembling and radical amazement; of awareness of grandeur, of perceptions we can grasp but are unable to convey, of discoveries of the unknown, of moments in which we abandon the pretense of being acquainted with the world, of *knowledge by inacquaintance.*[26]

And what does one find when one truly pays attention to such moments? Heschel cites one of the chief insights of the Baal Shem Tov: "The impenetrable fog in which the world is clad is God's disguise. To know God means to sense display in his disguise and to be aware of the disguise in His most magnificent display."[27]

WHAT DID THE ZHYDATSHOVER KNOW?

Since my encounter with the Zhydatshover's parable many years ago, I have studied a great number of the Baal Shem's teachings, and I've examined a good deal of the modern, scholarly literature about the master. Simply put, the message the parable contains is a vast oversimplification of the Baal Shem's spiritual thought. Nor were all the assumptions held by the Zhydatshover historically accurate.

Reb Tzvi Hirsch of Zhydatshov was a Hasidic rebbe born in 1763, three years after the Baal Shem's death; he therefore had no firsthand acquaintance with the founder of Hasidism. R. Tzvi Hirsch was strongly influenced by four different later Hasidic rebbes, all of whom had been disciples of Dov Baer, the Maggid of Medziritch, the most prominent disciple of the Baal Shem. The Zhydatshover probably received his initial knowledge of the founder of Hasidism from his own teachers, yet it doesn't seem clear that he studied the books of the Besht's direct disciples which contained the master's teachings. Still, he was aware of many of the tales about the Baal Shem's life and deeds.

The parable reveals, in a historical sense, that relatively soon following the Baal Shem's passing there were already those who had studied his teachings in depth, and who were adopting and simplifying the master's legend and wisdom for a broader audience. But the parable says more than this, too. The Zhydatshover is making an important statement regarding the Baal Shem's magnetism: It is through his charismatic presence that he was able to make the Divine Presence a reality.

Moshe Idel, a professor emeritus of Jewish thought at Hebrew University, believes that the Baal Shem's charisma had largely to do with the way he communicated with people, specifically, with the quality of his voice. In his teachings, the Besht makes the point that the Lifeforce, the *Hiyyut,* manifests in human beings as speech. It seems possible that he was able to mesmerize his students through the words he spoke and the way that he expressed them. It would not be long, however, until charisma would be replaced by the institution of the Hasidic dynasty, i.e., the eldest son of a given rebbe would become the head of his father's community, whether or not he manifested charisma.

THE POWER OF A PARABLE

This spiritual insight of the Baal Shem Tov has been called panentheism or acosmism. *Panentheism* means that universe is in God, but God is greater than the universe. *Acosmism* is a belief that there is no universe, and that everything is actually God. Reb Zalman Schachter-Shalomi wrote that this insight really means that *existence itself* is God. What would it be like to recognize that this world and everything in it, including oneself, is divine? To do so one would really have to learn to perceive and experience existence in a different way, as the locus of the sacred, as the ultimate miracle.

I interpret the Baal Shem's insight in the following way: If I can open my eyes to the depths of the realities of this world, I will discover that each moment is more than just that moment. And if I can open my heart to the people that I encounter in my daily activities, I will realize that each person I meet is more than just a person. Every human being, every creature, and every creation is a manifestation of the very essence of existence.

I look out of my window and see leaves of a tree being moved by the breeze. I cannot see the breeze itself. What then am I really seeing? Scientists from various disciplines would give different answers to a question like this. But the Baal Shem Tov said it simply: What you are witnessing is the *Hiyyut,* the Lifeforce giving existence its reality. It is in the leaves; it is in the breeze; it is in every phenomenon of existence. This notion is in some ways similar to that of the modern philosopher, Henri Bergson (1859-1941), who posited the existence of the *Élan vital,* a primary, non-mechanistic force that was part of the inner current of reality, bursting out from time to time in novel creations.

I certainly don't see the Hiyyut continually. Most often I find myself preoccupied by some concern or responsibility, and out of touch with what is happening before my eyes. But through experimentation over the decades, I have been able to find a way to sense the Presence in moments throughout the day, and this has subtly transformed my life in the world.

CHAPTER SIX

A LEGENDARY LIFE

"Out of the mists there appears to us the historic form of the founder of Hasidism; out of the mists of the wondrous tales with which popular legend had wreathed its favorite hero. A dense mask, spun by the fantasies of his contemporaries and his successors, conceals from our eyes the true picture of the Besht, until at times it seems to us as if this person had never existed but was entirely a figure of legend."

SIMON DUBNOW[28]

Tales about the Baal Shem Tov in Martin Buber's *Tales of the Hasidim* do not focus on the Besht's formal teachings; instead, they highlight the master's awesomeness, his ability to perform miracles, and his love. The spiritual lessons flow out of events that occur in the master's life when he is with people. One of my very favorite tales about the Baal Shem Tov in Buber's collection is a tale he titled "The Strength of Community." The following is my own translation from the Hebrew:

> The story was told: The holy work of Yom Kippur had been completed. One task yet remained: blessing the Holy One for the new moon of the month of Tishrei. The Baal Shem and his Hasidim left the synagogue and looked up into the heavens, but the night sky was cloudy and the moon could not be seen. This weighed heavily on the Baal Shem's spirit, for he felt that some enormous liberation was destined to be accomplished through the prayers he would offer during the new moon ceremony.
>
> The Besht returned home and entered his study. He sat down, closed his eyes, and concentrated all of his intentionality and power on the hidden light of the moon, trying to drive away the clouds that surrounded

it. Every so often he would send one of his disciples outside to see if the moon was yet visible, but each time he was told that the cloud cover had become even more thick and heavy. Finally, he gave up all hope.

Meanwhile the Hasidim—who knew nothing of their master's grief—had gathered in the front room of his house, and had begun to sing and dance, for the Day of Atonement was over, and all of their sins had been forgiven due to the intense priestly service of the Baal Shem. To them it was like a festival, a night of joy. As they danced, their rapture mounted higher and higher, and finally they invaded the Baal Shem's study. The master was sunk in gloom, but the Hasidim took no mind; overwhelmed by their own frenzy, they took him by the hands and drew him into the round.

Then, just at that moment, someone called outside. The night had suddenly grown light. The clouds were gone, and the radiant moon shone in the dark starry night.

The Besht is the rebbe. And as rebbe, he has a special responsibility that only he is able to accomplish, a redemptive responsibility he must bring about on behalf of his community and the world that has to be carried out right after the end of Yom Kippur. But now he's stymied, for his work depends upon the presence of the moon, which is a symbol of the Shekhinah, the indwelling presence of the Divine. Without her presence, this work could simply not be completed. He sinks into gloom. But he had taught his Hasidim how they were not to allow themselves to despair. They were to rejoice no matter what the circumstances. Yet, he himself is unable to do so! The Hasidim, however, have learned well from their master. Now it was *their* turn to "teach" what they had learned to their master. Their joyousness overwhelmed the Baal Shem and brought him joy. The disciples had so absorbed the Baal Shem's bliss that when their master was himself caught in grief, their fervor was able to draw him back into the joy that normally characterized his life. This in turn had a magical effect on the night sky. The clouds dissipated and the moon could be seen.

The story also implies that the action of the Hasidim magically brought about the uncovering of the moon. What are we to make of this element in the story—the belief that the joy of the disciples, which transformed the disposition of the Besht, also cleared the heavens of the clouds obscuring the moon?

I have taught this to people of all ages, from ten-year-olds to college students. Most of the adults were either puzzled or dismissive. The children understood it best. In the introduction to *Tales of the Hasidim*, Buber calls the stories that he gathered *legendary anecdotes*. "They go back to fervent human beings who set down their recollections of what they saw or thought they had seen, in their fervor." Nonetheless, Buber calls these anecdotes "reality—the reality of the experience of fervent souls."[29]

IN PRAISE OF THE BAAL SHEM TOV

One day I wandered into a bookshop on Telegraph Avenue and, looking at the titles on the Judaica shelf, found a new volume titled, *In Praise of the Baal Shem Tov: The Earliest Collection of Legends About the Founder of Hasidism.* The cover described the work as "a mixture of legend, parable, and history, these stories offer a fascinating introduction to the Baal Shem Tov, the kabbalistic wonder worker who founded Hasidism in the eighteenth century.... Originally published in Hebrew in 1814, this is the first complete translation into English and the first scholarly edition of the text in any language." The translators were Dan Ben-Amos, professor of folklore and folklife at the University of Pennsylvania, and Jerome R. Mintz, professor of anthropology at Indiana University.

I was expecting to find something like Buber's tales of the Baal Shem Tov, but I was completely disappointed. Although there were tales that highlighted the Baal Shem's spiritual and moral eminence, most of them emphasized his supernatural, curative powers and the miracles he supposedly performed. And the style in which they were recorded was frequently crude and awkward, at times even primitive. Some of the stories seemed to be important for an understanding of the Baal Shem's life and personality, like the anecdote I cited above, but others seemed trivial and beside the point. It took many readings of the book for me to learn how to appreciate what it represented.

The volume begins with the story of Israel Baal Shem Tov's father's life and deeds. This leads into the story of Israel's childhood and young adulthood, his first exposure to mystical teachings, marriages, and years of solitude, followed by his failed journey to the Holy Land. The chronological narrative, however, basically ends at that point; the remainder of the book is made up of a haphazard collection of testimonies from a large swath of people who claimed to have been in contact with the master at some point in his life, witnessing his miraculous healings, exorcisms, and other extraordinary feats. Many of the storytellers claim to remember their encounters with the Besht because they were amazed by what they perceived to be his superhuman abilities.

There are other testimonies that reveal a more human side of the master. Here, for instance, is a one of these testimonies:

> Once, people asked the Besht to preach to them after prayer. And he did so. While he preached he moved and trembled as if in prayer, and he inserted in his sermon, "God O God, it is known and revealed to you that I do not preach this sermon for my honor (but for the honor of my father's and my mother's families). I know many things and I can do many things, but there is not a person to whom I can reveal them."[30]

The anecdote reveals three things. First, that the anonymous individual who was present when the Baal Shem Tov gave this sermon could not help but notice that the way the Baal Shem preached was as passionate as an act of prayer. Second, that the Besht must have seen the impression he was making on those who were listening, since he was afraid God might judge him wrongly, thinking he was prideful. Third, that he was loathe to expose his knowledge and abilities to others, perhaps because doing so would seem again like an act of pride. This incident may have taken place before he had revealed himself publicly as a spiritual teacher.

In Praise of the Baal Shem Tov also presents descriptions of the Baal Shem's ecstatic prayer life and his uncanny trance ascent to the heavenly palace of the messiah to try to prevent a pogrom. Strangely enough, tales of his saintliness are mixed with others that depict him as being angry and prideful. Along with stories about the Besht, there are also tales involving his colleagues and his disciples.

Reading the translator's introduction, I learned that the volume's editor was Rabbi Dov Baer ben Samuel, the son-in-law of Rabbi Alexander the ritual slaughterer, who had been the Baal Shem's personal scribe for eight years. It is clear from the contents of the book that R. Dov Baer had no intention of composing a biography of his subject. In his introduction he writes, "The reader should realize that I wrote all this not as history nor as stories. In each tale I want the reader to perceive God's awesome deeds. He should infer the moral of each tale, so that he will be able to attach his heart to the fear of God, the beliefs of the sages, and the power of our holy Torah." In other words, the editor's purpose in compiling the work had to do with his desire to strengthen the reader's faith in God's supernatural powers by recounting the astounding exploits of the Baal Shem. Because the book's intent was to deepen the readers' fear and awe of God, the editor provides readers with an image of the Besht as an enigmatic wonder-worker and teacher, able to penetrate the humdrum veil of ordinary reality and reveal the miraculous and providential nature of existence. R. Dov Baer also desired to show his own generation how the founder of Hasidism had been able to bring hope and healing to those who were suffering. This is why so much of what would have been of interest to me was missing from the volume—the spiritual purpose of the Besht's life, the intentions behind his mysterious actions, and most important of all, the reality of his inner life.

This was unlike the image of the master Heschel had drawn in *A Passion for Truth*, and it was different from the stories in Buber's *Tales of the Hasidim*. I began to wonder whether Heschel and Buber had simply chosen to single out aspects of the Besht's life that they thought would appeal best to a modern sensibility. Despite my reservations, however, I was fascinated by all three sources, and felt more than ever before a desire to solve the conundrum of why their images of the Besht were so different.

SIMON DUBNOW: HISTORIAN OF HASIDISM

Then I learned that in the 1930s the great historian of Polish and Russian Jewish history, Simon Dubnow, had written the first history of Hasidism. I discovered a translation of his chapter on the Baal Shem Tov and eagerly read it. Dubnow begins with these words:

> The historical image of the progenitor of Hasidism is clouded by a fog of miracle stories with which the folk adorned its beloved hero. The veil woven by the imagination of his contemporaries and of later generations obscures the reality of the Besht's actual character to such an extent that it sometimes seems as if he was not a real person at all, but a myth, an imaginary name attached to the force that created a religious movement that shook the Jewish world. Those conversant with the literature of the time will not, of course, be so foolish as to doubt the existence of the Besht; after all, we have the testimony not only of his disciples and colleagues but also that of several contemporaries who opposed his teachings.... The silhouette of a person of real flesh and blood emerges even from the legendary biography of the Besht, if we know how to read it.[31]

Using the tools of modern historiography, Dubnow believed he would be able to distinguish history from legend. And with the exception of the supernatural elements in the tales, Dubnow basically trusted *In Praise of the Baal Shem Tov* as a historical source. He also added information from other sources he knew, and fashioned what he believed to be a chronological biography of the founder of Hasidism. Before laying out his account of the Besht's life, however, Dubnow undertook an analysis of the process through which he assumed *In Praise of the Baal Shem Tov* had come into being, comparing it with the way in which the first Christians had fashioned a biography of Jesus two generations after their master's death:

> Fifty-five years after the death of the Besht, a book appeared that purported to relate the events of his life—*Shivhei ha-Besht (In Praise of the Baal Shem Tov)*—comparable to the manner in which the first gospels of Jesus Christ appeared two generations after his death.

> The process of gestation for both mythic biographies
> was the same, despite the seventeen hundred years that
> separate them. Over the course of some decades, mira-
> cle stories began to spread among the folk about the son
> of Podolia, just as they had about the son of Galilee in
> his day.[32]

Dubnow explains that when the tales about Jesus and the Baal Shem Tov were first told, they were not far removed from historic reality, but as they were transmitted from one teller to the next, they became embellished and exaggerated. Afterward, the stories were collected and written down in differing versions, becoming "sacred scriptures." Finally, editors collated the different renditions and produced a published work.

I also learned that in the decades following Dubnow's pioneering work, historians were critical of both his assumptions and the methodology he employed to distinguish history from legend. Elie Wiesel, for example, criticized all the historians, strongly favoring a legendary approach to the Beshtian tales. Because of this, for many years I assumed the Besht's biography was probably only legend.

Then, in 2005, historian Immanuel Etkes' *The Besht: Magician, Mystic, and Leader* appeared in English translation. Etkes was able to show that most modern historians were in agreement with Dubnow, even though each scholar had developed his own particular method of analyzing the issue. As Etkes writes, "If we take a broader view of the positions of the scholars thus far surveyed, we find that the trend that emerges is one of increasing readiness to acknowledge the value of *Shivhei Habesht (In Praise of the Baal Shem Tov)* as a historical source."[33]

THE HISTORICAL BAAL SHEM TOV

Although there is a great deal of uncertainty, the synopsis of the Baal Shem Tov's life that I offer below constitutes my best guess regarding events and happenings that can be known about him. It is both speculative and approximate. I am certain, however, that there is a great deal that will forever remain unknown, especially about his early life, in large part because he chose to keep it secret. To fashion such a narrative, I made use of Dubnow's account together with what I gleaned from *In*

Praise of the Baal Shem Tov. I supplement those stories with letters written by the Besht, and with tales that appeared in later Hasidic legend that I believe to be historically accurate. I also add details discovered in scholarly books and articles. Dates I have assigned to the periods of the Besht's life are only approximate, and I received some help with the chronology from a doctoral dissertation by Hasidic scholar Yaffa Eliach.[34]

1. CHILDHOOD AND YOUTH (1698-1714)

The Baal Shem's father, a Polish Jew named Eliezer, lived during the latter half of the seventeenth century and the first years of the eighteenth century.[35] The tales recount that before his son's birth, Eliezer had been carried away by bandits to a foreign land and sold as a slave to a wealthy master whom he served for many years. Throughout his exile, however, Eliezer remained loyal to his religion and faithful to his wife back in Poland. After many years, he was finally able to escape and returned home to Okop in southeastern Poland, to be reunited with his wife.

We now have evidence that Eliezer and his wife originally hailed from Romania, and that most likely it was there that Israel was born.[36] If this is true, the family immigrated to the province of Podolia in Poland (now Ukraine) early in the child's life. We are told that both of Israel's parents were elderly at the time of his birth, and that his father died when the boy was young. Dubnow writes:

> Israel was orphaned in childhood. Eliezer, on his deathbed told his young son the conventional things: "My beloved son, remember this as long as you live—God is with you. You need not be afraid of anything." The boy took these words to heart and they strengthened his resolve as he embarked on the road of life. He would later come to think of his father's last words as a kind of prophecy and a confirmation of his own teaching that man is in a constant, solitary encounter with his Creator.[37]

Strangely enough, the tales reveal nothing about what happened to his mother; she simply disappears from the narrative. The community of Okop attempted to care for the orphan, but Israel was wild and willful, and would often absent himself from school, running into the woods to be alone.

As he grew up, Israel seemed to live an unremarkable life, at least to the villagers. Although he had been averse to formal study, during adolescent years he became an assistant teacher. He would conduct the children to school in the mornings and then accompany them home when school ended, all while singing cheerful prayers and songs. In this capacity he endeared himself to the children in his charge. On one occasion, we are told, he saved some boys from a wild animal that was about to attack them. Later, Israel became a watchman in the synagogue. During the day he would sleep, but at night, after the townspeople had gone to sleep, he would secretly study and pray in the synagogue.

In those years there was a spiritual master in Poland by the name of Rabbi Adam Baal Shem. This teacher had discovered a number of arcane Jewish manuscripts in a cave, and one night he dreamed that he was to give these documents to a young man named Israel, who lived at a distance in the small town of Okop. Rabbi Adam instructed his son that after he died, he was to travel to Okop and deliver the manuscripts to a young man by the name of Israel.

Rabbi Adam's son was able to locate Israel, and eventually gave him the manuscripts, asking if they could study these strange texts together. Israel agreed. The teachings were potentially dangerous, though, and it was clear to Israel that on no account could they fall asleep while studying them. But during a daring attempt to gain access to the mysterious secrets of the Torah, Rabbi Adam's son was unable to stay awake, and he died. Israel, on the other hand, possessed the spiritual stamina to withstand the risks of mystical revelation.

In Praise of the Baal Shem Tov portrays the Baal Shem as a kind of autodidact. He has only a single teacher, a spiritual guide who appeared to him in visions, whose name was Ahiyah of Shiloh. Ahiyah the Shilonite was a Levite prophet of Shiloh in the days of King Solomon, as mentioned in the first biblical book of Kings (1 Kings 11:29). In rabbinical tradition he is singled out as one of the seven long-lived *tzaddikim* whose successive lives extend over the whole history of humankind, each having transmitted the sacred lore from his predecessor to the one succeeding him, while shielding the generations of his time by means of his piety.

There are later Hasidic sources, however, that claim a succession of hidden tzaddikim spirited young Israel away from Okop and provided him with a strong traditional Jewish education. These traditions may reflect historical truth, for in the discourses recorded by the disciples, the master frequently references passages from the Bible, Talmud, and Kabbalah, showing a deep grasp of classical Jewish texts.

2. MARRIAGES (1714-1723)

The villagers became convinced that the orphaned youth had chosen a good path and they induced him to take a wife. Unfortunately, the woman, whose name went unrecorded, died only a year later. Israel then left the village of Okop and moved to a small settlement in East Galicia in the vicinity of the town of Brody where he became an elementary school teacher. He became known to the townspeople as a wise man, and was frequently called upon to be an arbitrator and mediator.

Once he was asked to arbitrate a legal case and his acumen made a strong impression on one of the litigants, the learned Rabbi Efrayim of Brody. Inspired by the holy spirit, Rabbi Efrayim offered the youthful mediator the hand of his daughter, a divorced woman, in marriage. Israel agreed on condition that the marriage contract reveal nothing at all about his personal or scholarly merits. *In Praise of the Baal Shem Tov* never mentions the name of the Baal Shem's mother or his wives. Other Hasidic sources, however, call his wife either Hannah or Rachel Leah.

Unfortunately, Rabbi Efrayim died on the road back to Brody. When his son, Rabbi Gershon of Kuty, discovered the marriage contract among his father's papers, he was astounded that his father had betrothed his sister to a man without a scholarly pedigree. "More shocking still," writes Dubnow,

> the prospective bridegroom soon appeared before the rabbi, dressed "as a coarse person" (in "a short jacket and a wide belt"), and spoke uncivilly to the rabbi as Jacob had spoken to Laban: "Let me have my wife!" The rabbi asked his sister if she would consent to marry this "boor," to which she replied that she was honor bound to respect her dead father's wishes. During the wedding ceremony, the bridegroom revealed his secret to his bride: that he

wished to remain incognito for the time being, so that
no one would think of him as a scholar and a kabbalist.[38]

Rabbi Gershon, however, was embarrassed to have such an uneducated
rustic for a brother-in-law and he made it clear that the couple needed
to live elsewhere.

3. THE YEARS OF SECLUSION (1723-1736)

Following their wedding, the couple traveled to a village in a valley
between the towns of Kuty and Kassowa. There Israel spent seven years
in the Carpathian Mountains living as a hermit in solitude and seclusion.
As a means of support for his wife and himself he dug clay from the earth,
and twice weekly Hannah brought a cart to collect the clay, which she
then sold in surrounding villages.

We have only later legends that attempt to answer the question of
what the Baal Shem did during his years in the mountains. Nonetheless,
Dubnow offers the following imaginative speculation:

> During his days of solitary meditation he would fast
> most of the time, taking only a bit of bread between fasts.
> The mystic's thoughts were lost in the upper spheres,
> while all around him loomed the majestic Carpathians,
> forested and blanketed with grass on the lower slopes
> and snow-capped up above. Here, amid the silence of
> nature, the recluse heard the voice of God. Here he
> felt His presence permeating the entire universe. This
> was the setting in which the basic idea underlying his
> later teachings germinated: "all the world is full of His
> Glory"—literally.[39]

During this period Israel became known as one who could perform
miraculous deeds, especially among the bandits who lived in the mountains. There were books published in Hebrew about methods of healing
which he may have studied, but it could have been that he learned about
healing modalities and herbal remedies from Gentile healers during
those years.

Dubnow calls Israel a kabbalist, and it must have been during this
time when Israel was also a student of Jewish mysticism. Later stories

have him apprenticing with a number of different Jewish mystics. He appears to have been under the sway of the teachings of the great mystic, Rabbi Isaac Luria, for like the followers of that school of Kabbalah, the Besht engaged in fasting and practiced austerities, including at times celibacy. But in his own teachings he cites many Jewish teachers whose books he must have studied.

During this period, Israel's spirit guide, Ahiyah of Shiloh, acted as his moral mentor and the revealer of spiritual wisdom to him. Ahiyah protected the young man from the demonic powers, and accompanied him on journeys to heaven, offering help when needed. Most importantly, Ahiyah enabled Israel to undergo a profound inner spiritual transformation. The future Baal Shem often lost himself in otherworldly experience, and found it difficult to relate to people. Ahiyah taught him to be present and how to connect with others, and how to stay in mystical alignment with the Divine while conversing with others.

After spending seven years alone in the mountains, later legends tell us that he resisted leaving his retreat, but Ahiyah convinced him to do so. The married couple decided to return to Kuty and Rabbi Gershon settled them near his house. Gershon took Israel as his personal servant, even though Gershon continued to remain hostile toward his uncouth and ignorant brother-in-law. From other sources we learn that during this period, Israel was peripherally involved with the small group of ascetic Hasidim in Kuty. These were scholarly kabbalists dedicated to the study and practice of the teachings of Rabbi Luria. The Baal Shem cultivated a relationship with the leader of this ascetic band, a certain Rabbi Moses.

In the mid 1730s, once again anxious to be rid of Israel, Rabbi Gershon leased an inn for the couple in a village near Kuty, which Hannah managed. Israel built a house of seclusion in the forest where he prayed and studied throughout the week, returning home only for the Sabbath, or when he was needed to attend to visitors staying at the inn. It was probably during this time that he and Hannah had two children, Hodel (or Udel) a girl, and Tzvi Hersh, a boy. Later legends suggest that the Baal Shem was closer to his daughter than he was to his son.

The inn did not bring in enough revenue to support the family and they moved to the Galician town of Tluste, where once more Israel became a teacher of children. It was apparently during this period when he achieved spiritual wholeness and perfection, so the moment had finally come for him to reveal his true identity to the Jewish world.

There are two quite different accounts of Israel's self-disclosure in *In Praise of the Baal Shem Tov.* The first version portrays him as a *Baal shem,* one who made use of holy names to work miracles, to heal the sick, and to give amulets the power to protect those who possessed them. The second report describes his vocation as that of a spiritual teacher who drew kabbalists to him by virtue of his charisma and profound teachings.

4. ITINERANT HEALER AND MYSTIC (1736-1740)

The Baal Shem Tov spent his next years wandering from village to village, acting as a miracle-worker and healer. He writes amulets, performs wonders, and heals individuals—Jews and Gentiles alike—through the use of herbs, incantations, and prayer. He exorcises demons and evil spirits and helps barren women conceive children. He has the ability to elevate fallen souls to heaven, and to ascend to heaven in order to annul evil decrees that have been promulgated against Jewish communities. He can foretell future events and communicate with Jewish figures from the past. He is able to discover when someone has committed adultery. He can travel long distances in the blink of an eye through supernatural means. And he is able to accurately predict the time of the deaths of many people.

There are numerous tales that speak of the Besht's superhuman powers and his heroic acts to help oppressed Jews. It is told that he could read the minds of craftsmen just by looking at the utensils they'd made; that he was able to cross rivers by the power of faith alone; that he had telescopic sight and was able to see tremendous distances and locate missing persons and lost possessions; that he was able to hear proclamations from heaven and witness all the realms of the cosmos with his supernatural sight.

He often comes over as charismatic and charming, and as knowledgeable and wise, possessing good judgment. He is concerned about people and seeks to ease the sorrow of those who are suffering. He champions the cause of widows and is willing to sacrifice himself for the welfare of others. He's also concerned about people's livelihoods. He does not believe in owning things and, after having paid off his debts, gives the remainder of his hard-earned money to the poor. Though impoverished himself, he asks wealthy people to support others in need, rather than give him monetary gifts, trusting that God will provide the support he and his family require.

Other sources testify that during this period he taught as well, offering short, pithy teachings delivered in homes, shops, and in the streets, but he did not generally preach in synagogues. He would speak to women as well as men, clothing his wisdom in stories and parables that could easily be grasped by the common people he addressed. He could be sincere and earnest, fierce, determined, and extremely intense and emotional. Yet, despite his usual earnest demeanor, on occasion he exhibited a rough but keen sense of humor, and he was sometimes given to drinking wine and smoking.

The Baal Shem believed that every member of his people was part of the Divine, and he felt called upon to love, serve, and champion them. He was bitter about the ways in which antisemitism affected his people. He used his magical skills to defend Jews, defeating both natural and supernatural enemies. But he was also indignant about the ways in which perfectionistic Jewish preachers regularly vilified common people. He exposed the ignorance of great rabbis and revealed the wisdom of the unlearned. He cherished devotion, truthfulness, lack of pretention, humility, honesty, piety, and dedication to one's work even if one's vocation seemed of small consequence. He could be harsh with wrongdoers, but there are also instances when he showed a deep concern for reprobates.

The tales also reveal the Besht's faults. He takes great pride in his abilities as a healer and wonderworker, and sometimes he has to struggle to curb his grandiosity. There are stories that reveal his anger, arrogance, and haughtiness. He could be blunt with people, sometimes insulting them, as well as vindictive and even physically abusive. While the storytellers reveal the Baal Shem's flaws, they do so without judging him, perhaps because he was held in such great reverence by those who had been touched by his gifts.

It was during this period that the Besht's daughter, Udel, gave birth to a son, Moshe Ephraim. According to one tradition, Moshe Ephraim lived with his grandparents until he was twelve years old, at which time the Baal Shem died.

5. THE TEACHER AND HEALER OF MEDZHIBOZH (1740-1760)

For many years, Israel longed to go to the Land of Israel. He often made plans to travel there, and once he actually set out on a journey to the Holy Land with his daughter Udel, but a series of obstacles kept him from attaining his goal. It was then that the Besht realized that such a journey had not been ordained from heaven.

Around 1740, the Baal Shem Tov settled in the town of Medzhibozh, near Brody in Podolia. There were a number of fraternities already in various locales in Poland, such as the group in Kuty he had been part of. These comradeships were made up of ascetic kabbalists of the Lurianic type. When the Baal Shem settled in Medzhibozh, many of these men gravitated to him, in large part because his charisma was so powerful, and despite the fact that they tended to be more scholarly than this newcomer. Dubnow writes, "Talmud scholars and kabbalists, rabbis and preachers, who could not find satisfaction in scholastic and ascetic religion and sought a new path, found their way to the Besht. Some came with the idea of testing him, and some came to bask in the glow of his religious passion."[40]

HE BEGINS TO TEACH

Only a few of the Baal Shem's actual teachings are recorded in *In Praise of the Baal Shem Tov,* but we possess a multitude of testimonies from disciples that portray him as a master teacher, even a source of divine revelation. We learn that he was able to hear Torah being taught in heaven that had originally been his own teaching. And that he often gave discourses at the third Sabbath meal just before nightfall. *In Praise of the Baal Shem Tov,* however, focuses on the founder of Hasidism as a charismatic presence. It does not deal at all with the Besht's overall spiritual vision of reality. Here is Dubnow's capsule version of the core message:

> Two ideas lie at the bottom of the "Doctrine of Piety," or
> the Hasidism of the Besht: The idea of Pantheism, of the
> Omnipresence of God, and the idea of the interaction of

the lower and upper worlds. The former may be approximately defined by the following utterances of the Besht: "It is necessary for man constantly to bear in mind that God is with him always and everywhere; that He is, so to speak, the finest kind of matter, which is poured out everywhere; that He is the master of all that happens in this Universe.... Let man realize that when he looks at things material he beholds in reality the Divine Countenance, which is present everywhere. Keeping this in mind, man will find it possible to serve the Lord at all times, even in trifles."

The second idea is borrowed from the Cabala, and signifies that there is a constant interaction between the world of the Divine and the human world, so that not only does the deity influence human actions, but the latter exert a similar influence on the will and the disposition of the Deity.[41]

Dubnow writes that other major elements of the Besht's doctrines and practices follow from these postulates: communing with God through fervent and ecstatic prayer, cultivating joy, and serving God in one's everyday affairs and through one's thoughts. The Baal Shem considered the study of Jewish ethics to be more important than engaging in Talmudic casuistry. "What is most important in religion," writes Dubnow, "is the frame of mind and not the external ceremonies: excessive minuteness of religious observance is harmful."[42]

The Besht's spiritual mastery was accepted by a number of prominent scholars, such as Rabbi Jacob Joseph of Polonoyye and Rabbi Dov Baer, the learned Maggid of Medziritch. Most of his teachings that we have are found in the four volumes that Rabbi Jacob Joseph wrote, and many of the Baal Shem's core spiritual ideas became the basis for Rabbi Dov Baer's own spiritual philosophy. By this time the master's brother-in-law, Rabbi Gershon of Kuty, had also become a devoted follower. Some of the Besht's disciples lived in distant areas and at times he would pay them personal visits.

In Praise of the Baal Shem Tov and the plethora of tales that followed in its wake underscore the Baal Shem's accomplishments as a master of mystical and magical prayer. Those who observed him worshiping in public describe his prayer life as extremely intense, indeed, so passionate that it could shake the cosmos. In the midst of his prayers his face could become enflamed like a torch, his body might quake, and his eyes would bulge from their sockets. He would make use of divine names in order to bring about the union of the masculine and feminine aspects of the Divine, so as to bring about the Oneness of God with all of reality. He would enter the *mikvah*, the ritual bath, close his eyes and describe the varied dimensions of existence he was witnessing. Throughout the day, whatever he was engaged in doing, he would continuously link his consciousness to the Divine Presence.

I have been particularly moved by stories that reveal ways he was able to penetrate the veil of ordinary reality with its endless suffering, revealing the wondrous and miraculous nature of existence. It was understood that by means of these same powers he was able to transform people's lives. Time and again we see him acting strangely and even bizarrely, performing mysterious symbolic actions that would in some way bring about positive transformations in the world.

His disciple, Rabbi Jacob Joseph of Polonoyye, preserved a remarkable letter from the Besht to his brother-in-law in the Holy Land, dated 1747. In the document, which never reached Rabbi Gershon, the Baal Shem describes a profound, life-altering experience he underwent. He writes that on Rosh Hashanah, the Jewish new year, he embarked on a heavenly ascent to the palace of the messiah seeking to annul a heavenly decree, a pogrom against a particular community of Jews. His attempt to stop the massacre failed, but in the course of his ascent he received a deeper understanding of his life mission. He was to teach his path and practices to others so that they would be able to do everything he was able to do, and in this way the world would become prepared for the messianic era.

HIS FINAL YEARS

Dubnow suggests that "In the last years of his life the Besht devoted more and more attention to public affairs. He was no longer oppressed by care for his daily bread, as the amounts sent to him by the many believers...

for amulets and other magic remedies or for special prayers and blessings represented a considerable income. Now he could in his turn distribute gifts generously to the poor. His special concern was the 'freeing of captives,' that is, paying debts owed by the small tenants on the estates of Polish landlords, who with their families were completely at the mercy of their masters and who in case of inability to pay rent had to suffer severe punishments."[43] But there was also the need to "free captives" for the support of the families of martyred men, murdered during pogroms because they had purportedly used the blood of Christian children killed to make matzot for Passover. (More on this in chapter 19.)

Legends state that the deceased false messiah, Shabbatai Tzvi (1626-76) once came to the Besht in a dream seeking redemption, but the Besht saw that it was too dangerous for him to attempt to redeem the man's soul. Another time, Shabbatai Tzvi tried to tempt the Baal Shem into declaring publicly that he was the messiah. The Besht told his disciples that Shabbatai Tzvi had actually had a holy spark within him, but that Satan caught him in his snare.

Similarly, a contemporary of the Baal Shem named Jacob Frank (1726-91) saw himself as the incarnation of Shabbatai Tzvi and claimed to be the messiah. Frank promised the Jews freedom from the yoke of the Law if they followed him. The Besht hoped he would be able to bring the Frankists back into the Jewish fold, but threatened with death by the Christian authorities, Frank converted to Catholicism; most of his followers accompanied him into the Church. It is reported that in 1759, a year before the Baal Shem's death, he participated together with traditional rabbis in public disputes with Jacob Frank.

However embroidered they may be, all these stories about the Besht reveal a man of great personal charm, remarkable magnetism, and ecstatic sensibility. He radiates power and authority. No one meets him without falling under the spell of his unique personality. Yet he is not pictured by his witnesses as a romantic dreamer or a flawless saint. He is a passionate and sometimes coarse man, extremely intelligent and knowledgeable, who feels called by a singular and joyous vision, and who works steadily to fulfill his destiny.

It is not clear when the Baal Shem's wife died, but there are tales that describe him as having experienced extreme grief and depression at her passing. There are also traditions indicating that toward the end of his life he became irritable and depressed, perhaps because of his wife's death and the heretical activities of the Frankists. Dubnow writes, "According to Chassidic tradition, 'it was decided in heaven that the master should depart this life shortly, due to his heavy exertions in the fight against the Shabbatian sect.' By this is meant, probably, that his impetuous praying... and his inconsolable grief over the mass conversions had consumed the last of his strength."[44] The master died on May 22, 1760, the second day of the holy day of Shavuot.

Two of the Baal Shem's disciples, Rabbi Jacob Joseph of Polonoyye, and Rabbi Dov Baer Friedmann, the Maggid of Medziritch, were especially important in transmitting his legacy. R. Jacob Joseph recorded many hundreds of the Besht's teachings and in his books redefined the very character of the *tzaddik,* the enlightened spiritual leader, based on Jacob Joseph's observations of the Baal Shem's life and activities. Dov Baer, on the other hand, was a charismatic teacher and a contemplative mystic, and it was he who inherited the mantle of leadership after his master's death. Dov Baer attracted many disciples, trained them to become spiritual leaders, and sent them out to various communities of Jews.

Before concluding my rendering of the Baal Shem's life, I want to reiterate my understanding of the possible historicity of my views. I would like to think that my reconstruction comes close to mirroring the master's life, but I cannot in all honesty make a claim for it being any more than an approximation.

CHAPTER SEVEN

THE QUEST OF A HERO

To comprehend the deeper meaning of the larger story found in *In Praise of the Baal Shem Tov*, I turned to another book that had meant a great deal to me earlier in life, mythographer Joseph Campbell's *The Hero With a Thousand Faces*. In this distinguished work the author elucidates the paradigmatic journey of the archetypal hero found in all world mythologies. He demonstrates that hero myths from around the world, many of which have survived for thousands of years, all share the identical narrative structure, which he calls the *monomyth*:

> A hero ventures forth from the world of common day into a region of supernatural wonder: fabulous forces are there encountered and a decisive victory is won: the hero comes back from this mysterious adventure with the power to bestow boons on his fellow man.[45]

Campbell states that every hero's journey is characterized by three steps or stages. The first of these he calls *Separation*. The hero begins life in the ordinary world, but then receives a call from beyond summoning them to depart from a commonplace existence and undertake a quest that will take place in an unknown world of strange powers and events. The person who accepts this call begins the second phase of the quest, *Initiation*. Now they must face tasks and trials, either alone or with assistance. In the most intense versions of the narrative, the hero must survive a severe challenge, often with help, and if they survive, they attain a great gift or blessing.

At this point a hero must decide whether or not to return to the ordinary world with this boon. The individual who chooses to go back to the world that they came from now undertakes the third phase of the journey, called *Return*. Heroes often face challenges on this return journey but if they succeed, the boon they bring may be used to improve the world. Campbell writes that "The hero, therefore, is the man or woman who has been able to battle past his personal and local historical limitations to the generally valid, normally human forms. Such a one's visions, ideas and inspirations come pristine from the primary springs of human life and thought."[46]

As I consider the first part of the Baal Shem's life, I find that the central themes reflect Campbell's archetypal phases of the hero's journey. Israel begins his quest in the ordinary world of Okop, the village in which he grew up. The death of his father, the disappearance of his mother, and his secretive behavior combine to set the scene for the genesis of his inner journey, that is, his *separation* from the ordinary life of the villagers.

The manuscript he receives from Rabbi Adam's son opens the way to his *initiation* as a hero. In Campbell's phrasing, destiny has summoned the hero and transferred his spiritual center of gravity to the unknown. Israel's tasks and trials include his death-defying quest with Rabbi Adam's son to gain access to the secrets of the Torah; the loss of his first wife after just a year of marriage; determination to marry his second wife, Hannah; devotion to the ascetic path; solitary years in the Carpathian Mountains; the struggle between desire to remain a hermit or return to the world; and acceptance of failure in his attempt to reach the land of Israel.

Like all spiritual heroes, the Besht needed to find supernatural help in order to continue on his journey. "Whether dream or myth," Campbell writes, "in these adventures there is an atmosphere of irresistible fascination about the figure that appears suddenly as a guide, marking a new period, a new stage, in the biography." And, "What such a figure represents is the benign, protecting power of destiny."[47] As we have seen, Israel's guide and helper through these tasks and trials was the biblical prophet Ahiyah the Shilonite, who protected him from the demonic, and accompanied him on heavenly journeys, offering help when needed. Ahiyah was also the Besht's moral guide, and a revealer of spiritual wisdom.

"The hero is the man of self-achieved submission," writes Campbell.[48] All the ordeals the Baal Shem underwent led him to displace his self-centered ego with submission to the divine. And like all heroes, the Besht discovers in the process that there is a benign power everywhere supporting him in his superhuman passage. By his thirty-sixth year he reaches spiritual maturity and wholeness. He has, as Campbell puts it, been able to reconcile his individual consciousness with the universal will, and has attained a realization of the relationship of the passing phenomena of time to the imperishable life. Then, he is primed to return to the ordinary world of his people, to act as a healer, spiritual teacher, and community leader. Here is Campbell once again: "The supreme hero...reopens the eye—so that through all the comings and goings, delights and agonies of the world panorama, the One Presence will be seen again."[49]

In the course of his teaching, the Baal Shem shared a number of parables with his disciples that made the point that he was the "son of the king." In other words, the Besht saw himself as a son of God. While this might sound like the Christian claim regarding the divinity of Jesus, in his book-length study, *Ben: Sonship and Jewish Mysticism,* Professor Moshe Idel has shown that the theme of divine sonship runs through the entire history of Jewish mysticism. Indeed, there were numerous Jewish mystical figures who experienced themselves as sons of God. With regard to the Baal Shem Tov, Idel writes, "[T]he Besht and his family cultivated the perception of a 'son of a king' as part of a vital parable of their self-understanding."[50]

Of course, the idea of divine sonship was not unique to Judaism. Campbell writes that this notion is actually a universal theme that runs throughout the myths of the hero:

> The godly powers sought and dangerously won are revealed to have been within the heart of the hero all the time. He is "the king's son" who has come to know who he is and therewith has entered into the exercise of his proper power—"god's son," who has learned to know how much that title means. From this point of view the hero is symbolical of that divine creative and redemptive image which is hidden within us all, only waiting to be known and rendered into life.[51]

Campbell's description of the archetypal pattern of the myths of the spiritual hero provided me with a universal way to grasp the deeper meaning of the Besht's life journey. This also became a way for me to link the Baal Shem's mission with those of the founders of many of the world's wisdom paths.

CONCEALED FROM THE EYES OF THE WORLD

There are a number of leitmotifs that run through the stories about the Baal Shem's life before he revealed himself publicly.

- The Besht had an unusual childhood and adolescence. He does not possess a scholarly pedigree, which makes the stories about his childhood and youth quite different from the usual claims made about distinguished medieval rabbis.
- He is depicted as having started out as a solitary seeker, connected only peripherally to the Jewish community. This, too, would have been unusual at that time.
- He seems to possess a definite self-understanding of his special destiny and life mission.
- He is fascinated by the supernatural and mystical and gives himself to experiences that are out of the ordinary.
- During the first thirty-six years of his life, he was concerned with concealing his true identity, but once he discloses himself to the Jewish community, gives himself wholly to the tasks he believes he has been called to carry out.

This last motif, the Besht's self-concealment, emerges again and again in the biography. Why all the secrecy? Why does young Israel go to such great lengths to hide his identity? Why does he shun a title of any kind, or a description of his virtues in the marriage contract? Why does he dress like a peasant and pretend that he has no knowledge of Torah? And why does he subject himself to the ridicule of his bride's brother?

Kabbalistic scholar Aryeh Wineman writes that in medieval Jewish folklore there are "many tales that point to the premise that it is of the nature of the highest level of holiness to be concealed from the eyes of the world. Such tales tell of the incognito master of mystical Torah who inevitably assumes some kind of mask that deceives the world concerning his real nature.... He might be bizarre in his appearance or mannerism or character, and even appear outwardly to follow a lifestyle remote from even the most basic of traditional Jewish values. Through such masks, the concealed mystic fully hides his knowledge of Kabbalah and his real level of spiritual power."[52]

In the Zohar, many of the great teachers of mystical teachings veil their true identities, and some—like the Besht—even appear in public disguised as Gentiles. Wineman writes that this notion "reflects the sense that all flows from what is intrinsically hidden, and is dependent upon what is unknown and unknowable. And Torah...emanates from the hidden region identified with the Concealed and Primordial Light."[53] So it would seem that one possible reason that the Besht went into hiding had to do with imitating the unknowability of the divine mystery, and in this way to coming closer to that mystery.

The notion of the hidden God is central to the Kabbalah. *Ein Sof,* the Infinite, is mysterious and ineffable—quite beyond the capacities of the human intellect to comprehend. For the Baal Shem Tov, however, it is not the hidden God but the *hiding* God that becomes significant. The Besht's mature teaching is that human beings have the capability to see through the physical world that veils the truth, connecting with the *Shekhinah,* the Presence that is always present.

The Besht's concealment also points to the fact that, unlike most Jews, he lived in two worlds. He was a healer and teacher in the Jewish community, but he spent a great deal of time in solitude, dwelling in the hidden worlds beyond. Rachel Elior writes, "Unquestionably, the Baal Shem Tov saw himself and was seen by others as one who had crossed the divide between the terrestrial and the celestial and had attained unmediated contact with those dwelling in the higher worlds."[54]

There is a second possible motive behind the Besht's concealment. As we learned above, during his years of seclusion he was an adherent of the Lurianic school of Kabbalah. The ascetic practices that were essential to his religious regimen at that time could have served as paths to atonement for sins he believed he committed. One such transgression, *ga'avah*—which can be translated as pride, grandiosity, or arrogance—required individuals to repent and give themselves to the cultivation of humility. The Besht's habit of concealment, then, may have been a strategy employed to compel himself to live in humility.

Due to all of these factors, and because the Baal Shem kept so much of his personal life private, the biography assembled in the previous chapter is missing many essential details. In addition, the story about Rabbi Adam's son and the secret manuscripts, which in *In Praises of the Baal*

Shem Tov acts as the phase in which the Besht is initiated into his role as a mystic is, in my opinion, a kind of replacement for the actual story of the master's initiation, which he kept to himself. In future chapters, I will offer my own theory regarding the Baal Shem's actual initiation.

INTROVERSION AND EXTRAVERSION

As I considered the theme of the Baal Shem's concealment, it occurred to me that Carl Jung might offer a lens through which certain features of the Besht's life might become more transparent. It was Jung who first distinguished between two fundamentally different types of individuals, which he termed *extroverts* and *introverts*. The extrovert is primarily other-oriented, while the introvert is self-oriented. Extroverts show a predominant interest in events, people, and things, and are both motivated and influenced by the world outside the self. They are sociable and confident in unfamiliar surroundings. By contrast, Jung writes, introverts are withdrawn from the world, and their energy is focused on subjective matters. "For him self-communings are a pleasure. His own world is a safe harbor, a carefully tended and walled-in garden, closed to the public and hidden from prying eyes. His own company is the best. He feels at home in his world, where the only changes are made by himself. His best work is done with his own resources, on his own initiative, and in his own way."[55] Introverts lack confidence in relation to people and things, and tend to be unsociable, preferring reflection to activity. Because they don't spend their energy trying to impress others, or dissipate it in social activities, they may often possess unusual knowledge. Many of the tales about the Baal Shem's life before his public self-disclosure reveal him as an introvert, at least during the first half of his life. He cherished solitude, had an intense inner life, and had few if any friends. At one point his inner spirit guide, Ahiyah of Shiloh, has to actually teach him how to relate to people.

Jung also distinguished between four functions that people use to orient themselves to the world: *sensation,* which is perception through the senses; *thinking,* which gives meaning and understanding; *feeling,* which has to do with how one values what he or she is perceiving; and *intuition,* which brings hunches or visions from the unconscious to consciousness. Jung believed that one of these four "modes of apprehension" dominates the perception of every individual. The stories about the Besht reveal that he was primarily an intuitive, as Jung described this type: "The peculiar nature of introverted intuition, when given the priority...produces a peculiar type of man, viz. the mystical dreamer and seer on the one hand, or the fantastical crank and artist on the other."[56]

Frieda Fordham goes on to explain this in greater detail: "This is the type that sees visions, has revelations of a religious or cosmic nature, prophetic dreams, or weird fantasies, all of which are as real to him as God or the Devil were to medieval man. Such people seem very peculiar to-day, almost mad, as in fact they are, unless they can find a way to relate their experiences with life. This means finding an adequate form of expression, something collectively sanctioned, not just a living out of fantasies. They can sometimes do this by finding, or even forming a group where their vision is of some value...except as mystics in religious communities there is little place for them in the world to-day. Usually they keep quiet about their experiences, or form esoteric sects or little groups concerned with 'other world experience.'"[57]

A rather perfect characterization of the Baal Shem Tov, I would say. And so much of the master's energy was taken up with forging a way to relate his inner experiences to the lives of the men who became his disciples. This gives us a clue as to why, during the second half of his life, the Besht appears to be much more of an extroverted teacher and community leader. How did this change come about?

Once again, Jung provides us with a deeper understanding of the Besht's personal evolution through his notion of "individuation." Jung used this term to describe the way an individual self develops out of an undifferentiated unconscious. The task of the first half of life is to build a conscious ego through deepening particular qualities and characteristics that are native to one's temperament and personality. But this creates a one-sided personality, leaving other potentials within the psyche undeveloped. It is during the second half of life, beginning around age thirty-five, that the healthy individual begins to engage with the undeveloped side of the self to integrate these newly revealed features into the personality, and move toward wholeness. What had been undeveloped in the Besht's life was extroversion. There are stories in Hasidic tradition that show him resisting such a change, which I think may have an actual basis in the master's life. If so, however, he eventually recognized that this kind of growth was necessary to fulfill his roles as healer, teacher, and defender of his people. His self-disclosure to the Jewish world marked his intention to move into his public role.

According to Jung, the development toward wholeness during the second half of life implies a movement away from preoccupation with the ego toward a concern with the greater Self, that is, the God-image within one's psyche. Jung also characterized the ultimate aim of individuation as realizing God within one's self and the world: "The whole man is an individual, but he is not individualistic, which means ego-centered, and is often used as an excuse to develop peculiarities at the expense of other people or to behave in an egotistical fashion. The individuated person, on the other hand, through his acceptance of the unconscious has, while remaining aware of his unique personality, realized his brotherhood with all living things, even with inorganic matter and the cosmos itself."[58]

It is clear that the Besht was deeply concerned with linking himself to God during the first half of his life, but his understanding of Divinity must have been restricted by his solitary existence. Furthermore, during that time he was also preoccupied with issues linked to his outsized ego. But when the Baal Shem transitioned to his role as a public spiritual leader, his spiritual awareness gradually widened. Following his revelation, the story of his life shows a major change in themes:

- A movement from private to public existence.
- A change from dealing with loss to becoming a force for healing in the world.
- A focus on love, compassion, and joy.

And, as I will show, an awakening from illusion to enlightenment.

MODELS FOR EXISTENCE WITHIN TIME

Some years ago, I encountered an interesting book by Leo D. Lefebure, a priest of the Archdiocese of Chicago and professor of theology, titled *The Buddha and the Christ: Explorations in Buddhist and Christian Dialogue*. It explores the two religious founders through the lives and views of their followers. Comparing the two, Lefebure writes: "[T]he lives of both Jesus

Christ and Shakymuni Buddha have served as hierophanies to their followers, manifestations of the sacred that overcome the alienation and fragmentation of temporal existence and offer an orientation for human life. These manifestations of the sacred overcome the terror of historical existence by providing models, paradigms for existence within time."[59]

Something similar occurred in Eastern Europe among eighteenth-century Jews, as Elie Wiesel has written, "The Baal Shem was a moment of rapture and exaltation in times of mute lamentation.... He had been the spark without which thousands of families would have succumbed to gloom and hopelessness—and the spark had fanned itself into a huge flame that tore into the darkness." The original tales, amplified by many hundreds of apocryphal stories, began to proliferate after the Besht's passing, offering a model of love and compassion, courage, hope, and joy to Jews living in the continuing exile. Once again, Elie Wiesel: "In the course of the next two centuries, his legend surfaced in many trials his followers endured: it helped people stay alive and sometimes to prepare for death. It appeared even in the kingdom of night. In the vision of a Jewish poet, the Baal Shem visits Jews massacred somewhere in the East. Their corpses fill the trenches to the very top. Suddenly their arms stretch up toward their illustrious visitor and a cry is heard: Welcome, Rebbe Israel Baal Shem Tov, thank you for your miracles, Rebbe Israel, son of Eliezer."[60]

Those Hasidim were my people. And even though I had grown up in America, far from the turmoil of antisemitism and the massacres of the Shoah, I hadn't fully escaped from their fate. Now, I too shared some of the hope that they had carried. No one who is sensitive to the ravages of adversity escapes suffering. We need models, paradigms for existence within time. For me, Israel Baal Shem Tov became such a model.

CHAPTER EIGHT

THE DISCIPLES' TESTIMONIES

I was embarrassed by the secret I held, but no one had to know, and for years I carried the shame within and did nothing to change the existing state of affairs. It was the early 1990s, and I had been immersed in my study of the Baal Shem Tov for more than fifteen years thus far. However, I had looked at only a small number of the original Hebrew teachings attributed to him. I was relying on the relatively few and scattered English translations of the Baal Shem's insights that existed at the time.

Why was I so lax? Hadn't I studied classical biblical and rabbinic texts in Hebrew and Aramaic for seven years at a prestigious seminary? And even though none of my classes had exposed me to Hasidic sources, they couldn't be that different from the kinds of texts I studied in such an intensive manner at JTS. Wouldn't it be possible to learn to decipher them with the skills that I already possessed?

The fact of the matter was that I had never fully mastered the sources in rabbinical school, and only got through the tough text-centered classes with a great deal of outside help. I was born with a learning disorder called dyslexia, and because of this had experienced great difficulty learning any subject matter that required holding sequences of previously learned information in memory while focusing attention on whatever it was that I was studying in the moment. I had always been poor at foreign languages as well as math, science, and history. During my years at JTS, learning to decode the various kinds of classical Hebrew encountered in my classes had been arduous, and the effort required to comprehend texts in Hebrew and Aramaic had been excruciating. The legal debates that characterized Talmudic argumentation—the principal subject matter of my classes—was exceedingly difficult to grasp. Had I not received help from fellow students during those years, I'm certain that I would never have qualified for rabbinic ordination. So it is not surprising that soon after ordination I gave up regular study of classical texts, and whatever language and text skills I'd acquired had certainly deteriorated since that time.

This was my quandary. I wanted to enter the world of the Baal Shem's wisdom but the language barrier seemed impossible to surmount. Nonetheless, I couldn't put the thought away that someday I might obtain the skills needed to decode the Baal Shem's teachings more deeply. I cannot remember why I didn't seek out a teacher at that time, who could have helped me become proficient in Hasidic Hebrew; probably, I was simply too embarrassed by my ignorance.

I do recall having come across a translation of a Beshtian teaching that eased my mind. It goes something like this: When you are reading from the scroll of the Torah and you experience the inner illumination that comes from the letters themselves, even if you don't grasp the meaning of the words, God will not be strict with you, providing that you read with great love and fervor. Think of a child whose father loves him greatly. Even if he stammers and doesn't speak properly, his father will be tremendously pleased because he dotes on his child. So when you read words from the Torah with a holy love, the Holy One will love you greatly and won't pay strict attention to whether or not you are saying them correctly.

Thinking about my dyslexia from this perspective, I realized I needed to be kinder to myself, and more self-accepting. After all, my learning disorder was not my fault. And no one was looking over my shoulder; I could go at my own pace. If I could be more patient with my linguistic limitations, I could begin to study the Baal Shem's words with the elementary knowledge and tools I already possessed, and gradually enter more deeply his world of values and ideas. And it was true. As the years went on, I found that I was becoming more proficient, able to penetrate the meaning of many if not all of the Besht's utterances.

ENLIGHTENING THE EYES OF ISRAEL

I remember asking a friend, Jeffrey Dekrow, then a graduate student specializing in the study of Hasidism, to suggest a volume of the Baal Shem's teachings that would be accessible to someone new to Hasidic texts. He recommended a volume called *Meir Einei Yisrael: Torat HaBaal Shem Tov,* which translates as Enlightening the Eyes of Israel: The Torah of the Baal

Shem Tov, edited by Yehoshuah Yosef Kornblit. Jeffrey told me that unlike
other books containing teachings of the Besht, this volume was organized
by subject matter, that is, each section contains teachings devoted to a
single theme about which the Besht had taught. When I looked through
my copy for the first time, I saw that it contained over 1,000 teachings of
the Baal Shem Tov, organized under 120 major subject headings.[61]

For the most part, the texts were not easy to comprehend. They
seemed to be written in a kind of shorthand, as if taken down by a ste-
nographer. Also, there were the inevitable Hebrew abbreviations of
technical terms that seasoned students would have recognized but were
unfamiliar to me. Despite these obstacles, though, I continued to pursue my goal, intent on engaging with what I believed to have been the
very words uttered by my teacher. Over the next few years, I would usually dedicate an hour a day to studying the teachings in this work. I used
Hebrew and Aramaic dictionaries, and other linguistic helps, and gradually found myself attaining enough fluency to comprehend most of the
Baal Shem's ideas. I was able to assemble and make sense out of texts
on major themes in the Baal Shem's teachings that interested me, such
as divine immanence and presence, love and compassion, awe and fear,
ecstasy and joy, and individual and collective liberation. Using this book
as a source, I eventually taught classes at weeklong Jewish Renewal gatherings and at the Academy for Jewish Religion in Los Angeles, as well as
in my own congregation.

In later years, I worked with two other collections of teachings. The
Reported Teachings of Israel (*Sefer Sh'mu'ot Yisrael*) is a five-volume collection of all the citations found in the works of the Baal Shem's chief literary disciple, Rabbi Jacob Joseph of Polonoyye. Its editor, Rabbi Ya'akov
Eliahu Daitch, excerpted these quotations from Jacob Joseph's works and
organized them according to the weekly Torah readings. Most valuable
to me were Daitch's extensive Hebrew commentaries, which explained
the meaning of puzzling teachings and traced their origins back to biblical, rabbinic, and kabbalistic roots. I gained a great deal of clarity from
his work, and it became evident to me that the Besht had been a deeply
erudite scholar as well as innovator.

Then I went on to the two-volume collection of all the Besht's
teachings called The Book of the Baal Shem Tov (*Sefer Baal Shem Tov*),

compiled by Shimon Menahem Mendel of Gowarczow early in the twentieth century. This comprehensive anthology also follows the weekly Torah portions. For each of the themes the Besht had taught to his disciples and colleagues, Shimon Menahem Mendel managed to collect the various parallel versions from a myriad of different Hasidic works. It was in this way that I was able to compare how different teachers heard and recorded the insights of the Besht. The editor also wrote a commentary on each passage based on the ideas of his own rebbe, Yehudah Yehiel Safrin of Komarno (1806–74), known as the Komarno Rebbe. Some of the texts in *Sefer Baal Shem Tov* were readily comprehensible to me; others completely eluded me. I was aided in my endeavor by Rabbi Ronnie Serr, an Israeli-born Orthodox rabbi and friend who teaches at the post-denominational Academy of Jewish Religion in Los Angeles, and who is himself a devotee of the Baal Shem Tov.

Then, in 2011, *Pillar of Prayer*, a bilingual volume of the Baal Shem's teachings on prayer appeared in print. Because the original texts were translated into English, it became rather easy for me to gain a deeper understanding of the master's complicated mystical practice of ecstatic and contemplative prayer. *Pillar of Prayer* was translated by Rabbi Menahem Kallus, who also provides footnotes in English illuminating the discourses. Kallus' knowledge of Tibetan Buddhism also adds a great deal to the meaning of the original texts. And I studied The Testament of the Rabbi Israel Baal Shem Tov (*Tz'va'at Ha'Ri'vash*), which I found to be important, accessible, and fascinating. Scholars, however, have surmised that, despite the title, the perspective in the volume reflects that of the Besht's disciple, R. Dov Baer of Medzeritch. Studying it, I found a number of teachings that appear to me to be authentically the Baal Shem's.

The modern Hebrew poet, Chaim Nachman Bialik once famously observed that reading a poem in translation was like kissing a woman through a veil. That's because a translation can only transmit a single denotative dimension of a text, whereas the text in the original language presents the student or reader with a multiplicity of connotative meanings that link it to the entire web of literature of which it is a part. I knew that the Besht had delivered his teachings in Yiddish, rather than Hebrew, and I was aware that the transcribed versions I was studying were concise renderings of what had originally been longer, oral teachings. But I also had a sense that these Hebrew versions of the master's teachings had actually been recorded by those who heard them from the mouth of the Baal Shem Tov, or by later writers who claimed to have heard them from reliable sources. Because of this, I felt I was entering the Baal Shem's universe of discourse, somehow at home in his presence. His world began to open to me in a new way. Instead of merely reading what modern thinkers and scholars had made of his legacy, I felt I was encountering his thoughts directly—or at least no worse than secondhand.

THE BAAL SHEM TOV IN HASIDIC MEMORY

I began my study of *Meir Einei Yisrael: Torat HaBaal Shem Tov* (Enlightening the Eyes of Israel) by reading through the first section, titled "At the King's Gate," a long introduction to the Hasidic image of the Baal Shem Tov. This is over 120 pages in length and contains an assortment of adulatory statements spoken or written by Hasidic teachers and leaders throughout the two and a half centuries of the existence of the Hasidic movement.

This is how "At the King's Gate" begins: "From the depths of my heart I bring forth praises and thanksgiving to the blessed Name for His great kindness, because He allowed me to collect roses from the Field of Holy Apples—the words of the Living God—that came from the mouth of our Master and the Light of Israel, the Radiance of the Seven Days of Creation, our Holy Rabbi, Israel Baal Shem Tov, may his merit protect us and the entire Jewish people."[62] I couldn't help but notice that the editor's flowery words of gratitude proclaimed his conviction that the teachings of the Baal Shem published in this book were actual revelations of God, thus making the founder of Hasidism not only king-like, but a veritable prophet.

I poured over this for three or four months, studying what the Hasidic writers said about the Besht's life, his personal qualities, core values he espoused, and spiritual foundations he provided for Hasidic thought. As I made my way through the testimonials, I was able to consider ways in which Hasidim viewed the founder of their movement. This is some of what I discovered.

After the death of the Baal Shem Tov, his major disciple, Dov Baer, the Maggid (Preacher) of Medziritch, became the leader of the emerging movement. "At the King's Gate" contains a number of stories about the

Maggid's relationship with his teacher, together with testimonials of the Maggid regarding the Baal Shem's prominence. For example, a certain disciple of the Maggid's reported that his teacher had told him the following tale having to do with what it was like to be in the presence of the Baal Shem Tov:

> Once on a holy day...I was asked to lead a blessing during the communal prayer service. It was either a blessing for rain or for dew—I don't quite recall. When I arrived at the synagogue, I found that the Baal Shem Tov was leading the service with great enthusiasm. I already knew from his greatest disciples that when the master prayed, he would utter a great cry and pray louder than anyone else. But I was actually quite sick at the time and I could not stand the noise of the Besht's praying, so I left the synagogue and went into a small room in the schoolhouse to worship by myself. When the Morning Service in the synagogue had been completed, my master entered the room where I was praying in order to put on his white robe before leading the Additional Service. I was amazed when I saw him, for he was filled to overflowing with the Divine Presence, and it was clear that he had transcended the physical world. Well, the Baal Shem put the robe on, but it was wrinkled around his shoulders. So I took hold of it in order to smooth it out. But when by accident I touched his body, I began to tremble. I grabbed a table, but the table began to shake as well. The Baal Shem returned to the synagogue, but I continued to tremble. And then I prayed to God that I be freed from this trembling because I could no longer bear it.[63]

This story comes from the earliest collection of tales about the Besht, *In Praise of the Baal Shem Tov,* published in 1814, seventy-four years after the Baal Shem's passing. It seems that the tale has historical roots.

And yet we have a Beshtian tradition from R. Israel Friedman of Ruzhin (1796-1850) that states that in Rabbi Dov Baer's eyes, the Besht's devotion to God and to his caring for people were far more important than the miracles he performed. For once when he was speaking to his own disciple, R. Shneur Zalman of Liadi, the Maggid told him: "Once when the Maggid was speaking to his disciple, Rabbi Shneur Zalman of Liadi, he said: 'When we were close to our holy teacher, miracles occurred beneath every bench, and the Holy Spirit overflowed from every pitcher, but we paid no mind to any of this. For what we sought and learned from the Baal Shem that was truly significant had to do with the ways of service.'"[64]

We see with what reverence Rabbi Dov Baer held the Baal Shem Tov. It was also reported that Dov Baer said that if his master had lived during the time of the Mishnah, he would have been considered a great rabbi by his colleagues. But if he had lived at an earlier time, during the era of the biblical prophets, what he had to teach would have been seen as fresh and new. And if he had lived even earlier, during the age of the patriarchs— Abraham, Isaac, and Jacob—the Baal Shem would have been seen as an exceptional human being. Another much later Hasidic teacher cited in "At the King's Gate" goes even farther, stating that if the Baal Shem had lived at the time of the patriarchs, he would have been counted as their full equal. Each assertion in the section seems more superlative than the one before it.

We also read that the tzaddikim, the righteous men of Karlin in Lithuania, proclaimed that "A soul like that of the Baal Shem Tov comes to this world only once in a thousand years." Another rebbe stated unequivocally that he was convinced the Baal Shem had been an angel of God. Another proclaimed that the Besht "was a flame of fire who descended from Heaven in human form." There were also Hasidim who considered the Baal Shem to have been divine![65] And here we have another tribute to the Besht by a later Hasidic teacher:

> The rabbi, our teacher, Rabbi Israel Baal Shem Tov—
> may his memory be for a blessing—was the father of the
> Hasidim. He is the head of those holy tzaddikim whose
> teachings and righteousness have continued to illumine
> the lives of Hasidim to this very day. All the tzaddikim
> since the Besht's time have only drawn from the well of
> his teaching. Even though his disciples have all forged

their own paths, nonetheless they all drink fully from his endless source alone. They are all his Hasidim and Hasidim of his Hasidim, and they enlighten the world, teaching people the ways of God: to cultivate the love and awe of the divine with a full heart and soul.[66]

Turning to the sizable sub-section of "At the King's Gate" having to do with the Besht's innovations, I found a number of statements that emphasized the master's unitary experience of the world. Here are the words of R. Kalonymus Kalman Shapiro of Piaseczno, the Rebbe of the Warsaw Ghetto: "The Baal Shem and his disciples taught that it is not enough to say that material forms cloak the Divine Lifeforce...for even the *physical* forms that we see with our eyes are sparks of divine light." And this testimony from another later source: "The spiritual philosophy of our teacher, the Baal Shem Tov, was a single teaching (*torah*) that can be expressed in two ways: 1.) The Divine is everything; 2.) Everything is Divine."[67]

We are told that the Baal Shem would often quote the medieval kabbalistic book, *Tikkunei Zohar:* "There is no place devoid of the Divine." And he was able to experience the presence of the Divine in every occurrence of his life. Such a view enabled him to recognize that he was only a tiny part of an awesome universe that is alive, conscious, and interconnected. And because God is present everywhere, every deed that he performed, whether religious or secular, became a way of serving God. According to these teachers, then, the Baal Shem's visionary worldview made it possible for the master to unite and integrate the various aspects of existence into a single fabric, linking everything to the divine.

One writer attested that the master had addressed the uncertainty many people felt regarding God's concern for people. The Besht's advice: Focus your awareness on the miracles that infuse your daily lives and you will have all the evidence you need to appreciate how you are being cared for by God. Following in this vein, Rebbe Nachman of Bratzlav, the Besht's great grandson, quoted the Besht's utterance regarding the need to wake up to the wonder of the universe. "Oi! The world is full of enormous lights and mysteries, but you put one small hand before your eyes and you see nothing!"[68]

As I read statement after statement about the Baal Shem's confident spiritual attitude toward life, I began to sense that the Hasidic writers must have felt the founder of their movement did not believe that the scriptures, beliefs, rituals, and institutions of the Jewish religion were the real essence of the Jewish path. At the heart of authentic religious living is the spiritual awareness of an ineffable living Presence continually enacting miracles that inform our daily lives. To these Hasidim, then, the task of the Jew has to do with learning to live in a way that would be commensurate with this reality. The traditions and practices were primarily meant to embody that kind of higher consciousness.

Several of the writers testified that the Baal Shem's vision brought about the eradication of the severe asceticism that had prevailed among pious Jews in early eighteenth-century Poland. In my own lifetime, the late Lubavitcher Rebbe, Menachem Mendel Schneerson, citing the Baal Shem's colleague, R. Pinhas of Koretz, told the story of a group of pious Jews that once appeared before the Besht with a question:

> "Rebbe, we are confused regarding how we are to serve God. Before you appeared, pious Jews fasted from one Shabbos to the next. But you have done away with the practice, teaching that those who impose hardships on their flesh are actually sinners, because they torment their souls. So please tell us what is the true service of God."
>
> The Baal Shem replied: "I have come into this world to point toward another way. Seek to cultivate three kinds of love: love for God, love for the Jewish people, and love of Torah. There is no need to mortify the flesh."[69]

Here was an anecdote that I really prized. Yet, I could not help but notice the authorities cited in "At the King's Gate" disagreed with one another with regard to the question of the Besht's most significant innovations. One teacher, for instance, stated that when the Torah was given at Mt. Sinai the Jews learned the importance of *sacred study*; and then centuries later, when the holy Temple was built by King Solomon in Jerusalem, Jews learned the significance of serving God through *sacrifice*. But the Baal Shem Tov, living almost two millennia after the destruction of the Temple, revealed a new core principle: the centrality of *human kindness*. The Lubavitcher Rebbe also wrote about the Baal Shem's embrace of joy, not only in carrying out the mitzvot, but in all of one's activities. He quotes the Besht as having said, "It is the aim and purpose of my pilgrimage on earth to demonstrate, through the way that I live my life, how one may serve God through happiness and rejoicing. When you are filled with joy, you are filled with love for people and all living things."[70]

A different modern teacher, Rabbi Aaron Roth (1894-1947) added that the Besht taught that years of abstinence and ascetic practice could not equal the power of joy in serving God, for such joy can connect the seeker to God with an immediacy unequaled by the path of self-restraint. Then there were those who pointed to the Besht's emphasis on worship as being his most essential innovation. The following citation comes from R. Kalonymus Kalman Halevi Epstein (1753-1823) of Krakow: "The most essential religious act is prayer. With the advent of the holy Baal Shem Tov, the sacred illumination that comes from the act of prayer gleamed and shone forth into the world for all those who wished to approach the worship of God, may the Name be blessed."[71]

Still others believed that the Baal Shem's primary innovation was the creation of a new approach to communal religious leadership. R. Shlomo Hakohen Rabinowicz (1801-66) of Radomsk wrote: "Through the work of the *tzaddik* all forms of spiritual abundance flow into the world. This was revealed to us by the Baal Shem Tov who shined his light over the earth."[72] And some teachers saw the Besht's role as an intermediary between heaven and earth, drawing down and channeling the flow of divine love and joy into the world, and spreading the celestial bounty to the Jewish people. Through the master's intervention, we are told, the common people were able to experience a taste of heaven.

It seemed to me that the differences in opinion regarding the innovations of the Besht meant that over time different views had developed among the Hasidim regarding the precise content of his legacy. Or perhaps each teacher wanted to identify the founder as the authority behind the particular Beshtian virtue he believed was primary. Nonetheless, as I explored these numerous opinions it became obvious that these teachers were simply speculating about the founder's larger vision, based on their knowledge of certain teachings with which they were familiar.

Reading all these accolades, I was struck by the boundless veneration that later Hasidim held for the Besht. Virtually all of the approbations come from later Hasidic sources. Do they reflect the actual character and deeds of the Baal Shem Tov or were they projections by later teachers onto the founder? It seemed that, for many, perhaps most, Israel Baal Shem Tov had been a new Abraham or Moses, a more than human hero who remade Judaism into a pristine spiritual path. The Baal Shem who appeared in "At the King's Gate" was in many ways similar to the master I first met in the writings of Heschel, Buber, and Wiesel, even though these modern writers never implied that the Besht had been divine.

UNCOVERING A VISION

One morning, I came across a remarkable and unique document titled, "Ten Statements That Lay Out the Foundations of the Baal Shem's Path."[73] The very existence of this source excited me, for it looked like it offered the view of a Hasidic writer who had studied a large number of the original teachings and had been able to synthesize a comprehensive picture of what he believed to be the master's visionary worldview.

Here, then, is an abbreviated version of the ten statements in the order laid out in the document:

1. The reality of the world is not separate from God. The essence of Divinity hides within each of the creations and in every event and thought, and because of this everything is Divine at its core.

2. The divine power that gives evil its "reality" has been severed from the wholeness of Divinity, yet that spiritual power does not disappear, because nothing can exist—not even something evil—without the vitalizing presence of God within it.

3. Human beings are able to experience both passion and desire, and even the temptations of sin, because they are the natural gifts of being alive. They are sent to us by God, and are meant to awaken our willpower and determination. Our responsibility is to guard ourselves from wrongdoing by channeling these energies into the service of the Divine. For we have the ability to

sanctify our passions and desires so they will become gateways that will open us to God.

4. Because God is present in everything, there is no absolute evil. The bad things we encounter and experience have, at their core, an absolute goodness, and it is this goodness that gives them their reality.

5. When one binds oneself to any of the dimensions of being, one is binding oneself to God, because all dimensions of being are divine.

6. Everything that exists comes from God.

7. We are called upon to awaken ourselves to the service of God, not through ascetic practices which require self-denial, but through the longing to bind ourselves to the goodness of the Source of life.

8. Every individual's life is a miraculous expression of the Divine, an actual Torah, a unique and complete revelation of Spirit. And yet one can only realize this when one lives one's life in a sacred way.

9. People should not offer prayers and concerns for their personal needs. Instead, all prayers should be offered on behalf of the Divine Lifeforce, the Shekhinah who dwells within them and inhabits all things.

10. Because a benign providence guides everything, there is a reason for and a positive meaning behind every event that occurs.

As I examined the document, each proposition made sense. I had encountered the ideas and principles articulated in this document elsewhere, in teachings that had come down in the name of the Baal Shem. Even so, the document as a whole seemed disjointed. I had a distinct sense that in a synthesis of this kind, the statements should relate to one another in a more logical and organic way so the text would offer its readers a coherent spiritual vision, laid out in a logical order. Yet I could not find a single underlying thread that might link the statements together.

Over the next few months, I returned to this statement—which I took to calling "The Ten Tenets"—over and over, attempting to find the invisible link that might bring unity to its principles. I wondered: Could the text have somehow been jumbled out of order during the years since its composition? No, I thought, that wasn't what happened, but maybe the writer had simply written these statements down as they occurred to him in no particular order. Even if this were true, there might be a way to grasp how they were related. Could I find a way to rearrange the ten principles into a coherent sequence? It was a bit like fitting the pieces of a jigsaw puzzle together. After a while, though, I began to see how the various statements were related, and to have an answer to the conundrum.

It took months of further delving into the document to uncover its invisible anatomy. My electronic file contains more than a dozen attempts at making consistent sense of the text. But one day I had a breakthrough. It occurred that if I could identify the underlying questions the author of the document was addressing, I might figure out the pattern that linked the ten statements together.

THE UNDERLYING QUESTIONS

Where do we come from? What is the nature of reality? What is the true essence of human existence? Why does evil exist? What happens to us when we die? What is the destiny of the human race? These are some of the questions that religious and philosophical thinkers address as they formulate their distinctive theologies or worldviews.

What I had to do was look at each of the Ten Tenets individually and try to figure out the question being addressed. When I completed my list, I compared the questions with one another. It then became clear that the author of the Ten Tenets was primarily concerned with a number of fundamental issues he believed were at the heart of the Baal Shem's speculations. I narrowed the larger questions underlying the document to three: (1) Where do we find God? (2) What is the relationship between the Divine essence and evil? (3) How can a human being manifest his or her own spiritual essence?

This led me to reorganize the Ten Tenets—again in abbreviated form. This allowed me to understand aspects of the document that I'd been unable to comprehend when I first examined it. And because of this, I have added a few notes in brackets that link the individual tenets in a coherent way.

QUESTION 1: WHERE DO WE FIND GOD?

1. Everything that exists comes from God, [the single mysterious Source of existence that lies beyond anything that we can ever know.]

2. [Nonetheless,] the reality of the world [we live in] is not separate from God, for the essence of Divinity hides within each of the creations, and in every event and thought. [And thus] everything is Divine at its core.

3. Because a benign providence guides everything, there is [an underlying order in the world] and there is a reason for and a positive meaning to every event that occurs.

QUESTION 2: WHAT IS THE RELATIONSHIP BETWEEN THE DIVINE ESSENCE AND EVIL?

4. Since God is present in everything there can be no absolute evil. The evil things that we encounter and experience have, at their deepest core, an absolute goodness; it is this that gives them their reality.

5. [Human beings do not experience evil as being an aspect of divine goodness because our awareness is limited. To us it seems that] the divine power that gives evil its "reality" has been severed from the wholeness of the Divine. But that spiritual power does not disappear, because nothing can exist—not even something evil—without the vitalizing presence of God within it.

6. [As human beings we have the ability to transform the evil of the world through our prayers.] But we should not offer prayers for our own [personal] needs and concerns [because those kinds of prayers center on the human ego, narrowing our awareness. The true reality is that it is the Shekhinah herself who is suffering, and the afflictions each of us individually experience are only a part of universal suffering. [Therefore,] all prayer should be offered on behalf of the Divine Lifeforce, [that is] the Shekhinah who dwells within us and inhabits all things.

QUESTION 3: HOW CAN A HUMAN BEING MANIFEST THEIR ESSENCE?

7. [Like all of the creations in the universe] each person's life is a miraculous expression of the Divine, an actual Torah, a unique

and complete revelation of Spirit. Yet one can realize this truth only when one lives one's life in a sacred way.

8. Human beings are able to experience both passion and desire, and even the temptations of sin, because these are the natural gifts of being alive. They are sent to us by God, and meant to awaken our willpower and determination. Our responsibility is to guard ourselves from wrongdoing by channeling these energies into the service of the Divine. For we have the ability to sanctify our passions and desires so they will become gateways that will open us to God.

9. [Because our passions are God's gift to us] we are called to awaken ourselves to the service of God, not through ascetic practices which require self-denial, but through the longing to bind ourselves to the goodness of the Source of life.

10. When one binds oneself to any of the dimensions of being, one is binding oneself to God, because all dimensions of being are Divine.

Once I felt I made sense of the tenets, I was curious about their historical origins. Following the text there is a parenthetical note that reads: "A hidden treasure found in the hands of the grandson of the Besht, may his merit protect us." The Baal Shem Tov had two grandsons, R. Moshe Hayyim Efrayim of Sudlikov, and R. Baruch of Medzhibozh. The statement does not indicate which of these grandsons owned this document, nor does it state who wrote it and how it had come into the hands of the Besht's grandson.

I photocopied the document and mailed it to my friend and teacher, Rabbi Arthur Green, asking him what he might know about it. In his return email he told me that there are other similar statements about the Baal Shem's worldview in Hasidic literature, but it was impossible to know anything about the text's origins. I have no proof, but I strongly suspect it was authored by an anonymous Hasid sometime in the nineteenth or early twentieth century.

It is now almost two decades since I first encountered the Ten Tenets, and I have become much more familiar with the Baal Shem's teachings than I was then. I no longer believe the document is as comprehensive as it first seemed. What it misses is the complexity of his teachings on a host of other issues, giving the impression that his vision was simpler than it actually was. And in some places, I believe it is actually inaccurate regarding the Baal Shem's views. For instance, the author was not fully aware of all of the Besht's teachings about evil, especially the ability and responsibility of the tzaddik in countering adversity and suffering. Despite these reservations, however, I believe the Ten Tenets do reflect many core aspects of the Besht's spiritual and visionary worldview that are preserved in Hasidic tradition. We have much to learn from them.

It is the first of the tenets that I believe embodies the central truth expounded by the Baal Shem. Here it is in full:

> The entire Torah and the entire universe contain nothing but the light of the Infinite that is hiding within them. When the Bible states that "There is nothing else!" (Deut. 4:39) or that "I fill the heavens and the earth," these statements are to be taken quite literally: the essence of Divinity is hidden and concentrated in every occurrence, and in each and every word and thought. And if you possess a spiritually discerning eye, you will behold each object that you come upon not merely in terms of the way it appears externally, but more in terms of its inner character, and the Lifeforce that saturates it. You will see only the Divine power pulsing within, enlivening it and giving it its very existence and its ability to subsist moment after moment through time. Moreover, if you listen with a discerning ear to the inner voice within any physically audible voice, you will hear only the Divine voice that enlivens and gives existence to the external voice that you are hearing at that very moment.

I believe this powerful declaration should precede the other nine statements, as if to say, *"Because of the Divine power pulsing through each creation and every process in the universe, the following statement is true..."* I further believe that it was this assumption which during the course of his life came to be the underlying foundational message of the Baal Shem's vision. But what the author of the Ten Tenets seems to have missed is the place of spiritual practice and visionary experience in his worldview. For the Baal Shem's teachings were not mere intellectual propositions; they expressed the way in which the master experienced reality in a heightened state of consciousness.

As central as the first tenet is to the Baal Shem's worldview, it is not unique in the annals of human spirituality. It characterizes the outlook of mystics and thinkers who have emphasized divine immanence, pantheism, and panentheism—the view that everything exists within God. Nor is it completely unique to Jewish thought as we will see in future chapters. For example, the affirmation expressed in this tenet reminds me of the final section of Allen Ginsberg's great poem, *Howl*. In the first part, the poet, like a biblical prophet, blasts away at Moloch, the false god of money and power, who dominates our culture and politics, destroying "the best minds of my generation." And then in "Footnote to Howl" Ginsberg declares the real truth of existence in lines that include: "Everything is holy! everybody's holy! Everywhere is holy!" Similarly, for the Baal Shem, one cannot behold the Divinity of existence with eyes caked over by absorption in the imperfections of outer existence.

MYSTICAL TEACHER

I found a number of descriptions of the Baal Shem as a teacher. One of the most prolific teachers on the Baal Shem in recent years, Yitzhak Buxbaum, cited a text that states there were times when the Besht's words were so passionate and evocative that they set the hearts of his disciples aflame with joy. At other times, his words were sweet as honey and his disciples experienced an ineffable sense of peace. We are also told that to the disciples who sat in his presence it was evident their master had been transported to another realm, intimately connected to God. Words that flowed from his mouth could not be his own, but must have come from the Shekhinah, the Presence of the Divine.[74] It is clear that for the Besht, studying and teaching Torah did not focus simply on an intellectual perception of meaning in a text. Rather, communion with the Torah was a kind of mystical revelation that linked a student to his teacher, and both of them to the Divine.[75]

The Komarno Rebbe, Isaac Judah Safrin (1806-74) imagined this charismatic aspect of the Baal Shem's classes, describing the experience of studying with him as a kind of revelation akin to the giving of the Torah to Moses on Mt. Sinai. "It is well known that when the Baal Shem Tov would study Torah with his holy students, a fire blazed about them and the heavenly angels gathered around them. The students experienced thunder and lightning, and the commandment, 'I am the EverPresent, your God,' could be heard emanating from the Blessed One."[76]

We also possess a number of stories that describe the Baal Shem's relationship with some of his closest students—like Jacob Joseph of Polonoyye and Dov Baer of Medziritch—in great detail. For the Besht, Jewish learning needed to be a totally-involving spiritual experience that would have a transformative impact on the student. Moshe Idel has noted that the Besht did not teach by commenting on traditional texts, as most other teachers did. He spoke directly to his students and his insights were delivered in an oracular manner, as if he himself were hearing them for the first time.[77] He was convinced that all creativity came directly from the divine mind. He once told his students, "When I link my thought to the blessed Creator, and I let my mouth utter whatever it utters, as I bind those words to their higher Root in the blessed Creator. Remember: Every word is rooted beyond, in the higher dimensions (*sefirot*)."[78]

There is a well-known story that describes the Besht's first encounter with the Maggid. The master asked Dov Baer to read and explain the meaning of a particular kabbalistic text. The Maggid gave a plain reading and explanation of the source. Then the Besht took the book from the Maggid's hands and read the words on the page aloud as a kind of sacred incantation, and suddenly the words of the text became a living reality. In the process the Maggid was radically transformed and, as a result, became the Besht's disciple.

We are told that the Maggid himself told a story about how the Besht's manner of teaching affected him:

> Once the Baal Shem Tov was speaking to his disciples, revealing to them secrets of the Torah that no mortal ears had ever heard, none of which could be found in the works of the kabbalists who preceded him.... The Maggid of Medzeritch said that on this occasion he heard teachings that perplexed him, and he found it

difficult to believe that a soul encased in a human body could have knowledge of such esoteric insights, notions which were probably beyond the grasp of the angels themselves. The Maggid was seized with the thought that the voice that was speaking must be the divine soul itself. Other disciples felt the same, and they drew near the Baal Shem and touched his hand to see if it was really made of flesh.[79]

THE PRIMORDIAL LIGHT

One homily in *In Praise of the Baal Shem Tov* reveals the Baal Shem's self-understanding as an enlightened teacher. But first, a little background will be necessary in order to grasp the Besht's insight.

The Bible famously begins with God's decree, "Let there be light!" (Genesis 1:1). From the context of the narrative it is clear that this luminosity could not have been the light of the sun, because the biblical account goes on to state that the sun was created on the *fourth* day. "Then God said: 'Let there be lights in the dome of the heavens to divide the day from the night'" (Genesis 1:14). So the light of the first day did not radiate from the sun. Could it be that the biblical writer imagined that the Creator required some light to see and illumine the pre-existing chaos and darkness so that he might reshape it into cosmos through his commands?

Whatever its original purpose, on the fourth day the sun and moon were created and the primordial light was no longer needed. What, then, happened to the original light? A well-known answer to that question is found in the Talmud:

> Rabbi Elazer said: That light which the blessed Holy One created on the first day was distinctive, for with it one could see from one end of the world to the other. But when the blessed Holy One looked into the future, he saw the generation of the Flood and the generation that would build the Tower of Babel. He knew that their works would be corrupt, and so he hid the light from them. (*Talmud Hagigah* 12a)

This midrash assumes that the primordial light provided Adam and Eve with a kind of cosmic consciousness so they, like God, were able to comprehend the intricate workings of the universe. Thus, it portrays the first human beings as enlightened beings. Yet such knowledge was dangerous and could become a curse as well as a blessing. The generation who lived at the time of the biblical flood and those who built the Tower of Babel made use of their cosmic omniscience to challenge God's authority, bringing collective evil into the world. Nonetheless, the primordial light was too precious to be destroyed, and so God concealed it: "He hid that light for the righteous (*tzaddikim*) in the future, as it is written: '*And God saw that it was good.*' There is no good but the righteous, as it is written: '*Say of the righteous person that he is good*' [Isaiah 3:10]. God rejoiced when he saw the light that he had hidden for the righteous, as it is written, '*The light of the righteous will rejoice*'" [Proverbs 13:9] (*Talmud Hagigah* 12a).

Because the light of cosmic consciousness was potentially dangerous, God concealed it and made it a reward for saintly people—tzaddikim—who would become enlightened and would know how to make use of such omniscience in spiritually and morally beneficial ways. Aware of this midrashic tradition, the Baal Shem Tov offered the following addition to the rabbinic vision, which is recorded in *In Praise of the Baal Shem Tov*:

> With the light of the six days of Creation, the first human
> beings could see from one end of the world to the other.
> Where did the blessed Holy One hide that light? In the
> Torah. And that which God revealed to the tzaddikim
> of that time—that the light was theirs to see by—was
> also meant for future tzaddikim. Any tzaddik who has
> the merit to uncover the light hidden in the Torah will
> be able to see from one end of the world to the other.[80]

The primordial light is hidden in the Torah, says the Besht, and therefore the true tzaddik has the ability to look beneath the surface of any and every biblical text, to perceive the primordial light through which both the universe and Torah came into being. And because the tzaddik is an enlightened human being, he is able to tap into the vast creative consciousness and wisdom of the Divine, using this power for the benefit of the world.

The Baal Shem Tov's interpretation of this Talmudic passage mirrors his own shamanic (more on that, below, in chapter 10) and mystical abilities, and his vocation both as healer and teacher. He was convinced that the inner light he experienced was one with the primordial light of creation. He believed he was able to illuminate the darkness of human existence, revealing and making tangible the underlying goodness of reality. And he revealed to his disciples how they could make use of the Torah to develop or deepen their own shamanic and mystical powers for the benefit of the people they were serving.

Those months of poring over "At the King's Gate" elevated my consciousness. The utterances of the Hasidic teachers praising the Besht seemed to make up an immense poem-like myth. I could see how the image of the founder of Hasidism had shaped a deep wellspring of faith that acted as a bulwark against the adversities of life that Hasidism met through the centuries. I have no doubt that some of the anecdotes actually happened. The story that the Maggid told his disciple, cited above, has a vital quality about it that makes it seem almost real—even though the memory of the event recounted might have been altered over time. Nevertheless, all through those months of study I was questioning the historic veracity of the pronouncements about the identity of the Besht.

I had read Dubnow's study of the Baal Shem Tov, as well as Raphael Patai's critical examination in *In Praise of the Baal Shem Tov*. I had a well-developed analytical approach to the study of history, beginning in college, when I minored in British history. Then at JTS I'd covered the entire field of Jewish history taught by a number of prominent historians including Gershom Cohen and Cohen's mentor, Salo Baron, who wrote the multi-volume *A Social and Religious History of the Jews*. My most important mentor in Jewish history, though, had been Professor Cohen himself. His academic research encompassed the many permutations of rabbinic culture, both classical and medieval. I admired his erudition, and it was in his classes on Talmud and Rabbinic Judaism that I gained a critical approach to historical methodology, becoming skilled at examining and interpreting historical documents. Because of all this, I had to ask the hard questions while reading "At the King's Gate," even though the answers might shatter the image of the Baal Shem Tov that meant so much to me. What kept me going was my conviction regarding the value of truth. Not the truth of the heart, but a larger more abstract truth guided by the intellect: the ability to ponder the events and personages of Jewish history in order to understand the past. I couldn't give up my heartfelt attachment to the Baal Shem, but for now, at least, I would have to live with a large measure of ambiguity.

SCHOLARLY SKEPTICISM

Simon Dubnow wrote his book on the history of Hasidism in the 1930s. It seemed to me that there must be more known about the Baal Shem Tov since that time. In my research I discovered that the earliest modern historians had been quite antagonistic toward the Besht and Hasidism itself. These scholars had all been influenced by the Haskalah, the nineteenth-century movement for Jewish enlightenment, which stressed the necessity of viewing Judaism as a preeminently rational religion. Heinrich Graetz, the first major Jewish historian in modern times, wrote that Hasidism taught "the grossest superstition to be the fundamental principle of Judaism." The image that Graetz drew of the Baal Shem Tov was likewise positively contemptuous.

Another respected scholar, Mayer Balaban (1877-1942), the founder of Polish Jewish historiography, later stated that there are no historical facts whatever against which to test the legends about the Baal Shem Tov, and thus he was dubious as to whether any authentic evidence related to the Besht would ever be unearthed. The Baal Shem, he wrote, "did not participate in the public life of the Jewish community, and did not come into contact with the leading personalities of his age. He did not compose books himself and did not write introductions to the books of others. Neither did he engage in business activities nor have any communication with the Polish noblemen. There is therefore nowhere to look for traces of his activities. All we have is a multitude of legends which often contradict each other."[81] Balaban, in fact, doubted whether the Baal Shem had ever lived. "A legend is a piece of folk poetry," he wrote, "and it should not be dissected. We must take the legend as it is or not use it at all."

Then, in 1985, Samuel Dresner, a devoted student of Abraham Joshua Heschel, published a volume of his teacher's writings, *The Circle of the Besht: Studies in Hasidism*. In the book's introduction Dresner writes that the single most important project which Heschel left unfinished at the time of his death was his book on the life and thought of the Baal Shem Tov. As readers may remember, in the introduction to this book I wrote about the fire that devoured the rare books collection of JTS including all of Heschel's precious work on the Baal Shem Tov.

Despite this loss, Heschel had previously published four essays describing the personalities of four of the men who had been part of the Besht's intimate circle. "In Heschel's adept hands," writes Dresner, "these men are revealed as formidable scholars and striking personalities who, no doubt, would have played a role in any period of Jewish history. In reading these essays, one beholds the image of historical figures and not simply legendary ghosts."[82] Studying these portraits it became clear that these men recognized the Besht as a distinctly remarkable teacher, but not necessarily the sole outstanding teacher of his generation, as later generations would come to portray him.

I now found myself wondering again about the other Baal Shem Tov, the legendary master who I found in "At the King's Gate," which pictures the Besht as a perfected saint, even a divine being. Was this purely apocryphal? Had all these stories been made up by the generations of Hasidim in centuries that followed the master's death? I don't think so. The view of the Baal Shem fostered in these legends, in my estimation, actually originated with the laudatory tales and statements in the oldest sources, and was elaborated and expanded by later generations of Hasidim who sought to exalt and idealize the founder of their movement.

The most comprehensive of all gatherings of tales about him in English came from my colleague, the aforementioned Maggid Yitzhak Buxbaum, may he rest in peace. Buxbaum spent twenty years collecting, organizing, and translating a vast number stories, and in 2005 published his magnum opus, *The Light and Fire of the Baal Shem Tov*. This is a magnificent treasury of stories. In his introduction, Buxbaum writes, "This book of stories about the holy Baal Shem Tov and his teachings is a book of remembrance written before the Holy One, blessed be He. It is written for all those who seek to love and fear God and desire His nearness. It is written for you."[83] My only difference with Buxbaum has to do with how to evaluate the stories from a historical perspective. Buxbaum believed that many or all of the tales could have actually occurred, and it doesn't seem that way to me.

All of these accolades demonstrate that the Baal Shem's contemporaries, as well as the Hasidim who followed in his wake, recognized that the founder of Hasidism was an extraordinary, multi-talented individual sent by God. That they made use of hyperbole in describing him, though, must be understood as coming from a penchant to idealize religious heroes. We see this tendency not only in Hasidism, but also in the Mahayana school of Buddhism, which envisions the Buddha as encompassing all of reality. It is present in Christianity as well in the doctrine of the Cosmic Christ who is identified with God.

In his perceptive book about King David, biblical scholar Walter Brueggemann writes, "David is one of those extraordinary historic figures who has a literary future. That is, his memory and presence keep generating more and more teachings and tales. One must, of course, recognize that others gave shape to these traditions, perhaps even fabricated them. But surely there can be no doubt that it was David's magnificent and mysterious person that generated them. None of the literary artifacts could quite comprehend him, let alone contain him."[84] Brueggemann is not referring to the great number of post-biblical legends about David, but to images of David found in the Bible itself, for even in ancient times the legends about Israel's second monarch had burgeoned. These narratives can be found in the books of first and second Samuel.

Something analogous to this occurred with the Baal Shem Tov: He also had a literary future. Because of their love for him, the tales that the Hasidim conveyed about his life and deeds kept proliferating after his passing. In fact, the only figure in the lengthy history of Judaism about whom there are more legendary tales is the Prophet Elijah. And, as in the case of David, it was the Baal Shem's magnificent and mysterious person that generated them.

I have come to feel that even if this large body of tales is primarily the creation of the Hasidic imagination, it should be read not only for an understanding of the needs of the Hasidim who generated it, but for the wealth of spiritual wisdom and truth it contains. This body of legends is similar to the way that modern novels about historical figures sometimes magnify the qualities of a historical figure, providing insight into their personalities and actions.

CHAPTER NINE

THE BAAL SHEM, JESUS, AND HISTORY

"What Heschel writes...about the Besht could, for some,
describe Jesus quite well. In both cases an individual arises
and in a very short time fundamentally alters everything.
He embodies a kind of spiritual 'event' that changes the very
nature of all that came before. And the 'personhood' of both
live on to this day—and this is what really matters."

SHAUL MAGID[85]

One afternoon, searching in the Judaica section of a used bookshop, I discovered Elie Wiesel's *Souls on Fire: Portraits and Legends of Hasidic Masters.* I was familiar with a number of his other books, including *Night,* the account of his horrific experience as an adolescent in the Auschwitz and Buchenwald death camps. I had read *Night* as a rabbinical student, and it was a gripping and unforgettable experience, calling to mind the buried memories of the Holocaust that had affected me so powerfully as a child. I'll never forget Wiesel describing a child being hung before all the prisoners in Auschwitz, slowly suffocating, too light to break his own neck: "Behind me, I heard [a] man asking: 'Where is God now?' And I heard a voice within me answer him.... 'He is hanging here on this gallows.'" And again: "Never shall I forget those moments which murdered my God and my soul and turned my dreams to dust."

I had assumed Wiesel's experiences in the death camps extinguished his religious faith. It was only years later, reading his memoir, *All Rivers Run to the Sea,* that I learned this was not the case. Like Job, Wiesel had his quarrels with God, and the novels reflect his anger and rage toward the inexplicable source who created a universe without justice. Despite the unrelieved and absolute evil he experienced during the Shoah, Wiesel states that he continued to believe in God and to affirm life. Those few tense hours I spent reading Wiesel's memoir contributed decisively to the eradication of my naive faith in the personal God of Jewish tradition, the God who would, at some mysterious future time, send his messiah to redeem his people.

Now, as I paged through *Souls on Fire,* it seemed Wiesel had taken a step beyond his preoccupation with the tragedy of the Holocaust. I purchased the book and took it home. In the first chapter, Wiesel recalls the special relationship he had with his grandfather, who introduced him to the Hasidic rebbes. "He made me enter the universe of the Baal Shem and his disciples, where facts became subservient to imagination and beauty." It was in that universe that "everything becomes possible by the mere presence of someone who knows how to listen, to love and give of himself."[86]

Wiesel states that the Besht provided the Jews of his era with a deep sense of meaning: "The Jew suddenly discovered within himself the desire and the strength to sing and celebrate life at a time when the sky was darkening with crimson clouds and the threat was becoming closer and more defined." And again, "The legend of the Baal Shem had fired Jewish imagination with such violence and in so many places, nobody could stop or even brake his momentum. He answered a need."

Wiesel shared a modern Hasidic legend in which the Baal Shem follows his disciples into the death camps, helping people stay alive and sometimes prepare for death. "What cannot help but astound us is that Hasidim remained Hasidim inside the ghetto walls, inside the death camps. In the shadow of the executioner, they celebrated life. Startled Germans whispered to each other of Jews dancing in the cattle cars rolling toward Birkenau." It seemed that the legends of the Hasidic masters Wiesel heard as a child planted a seed of spiritual truth in his soul, and in this way the legacy of his grandfather gave him the strength necessary to reject despair. "The Baal Shem's call was a call to subjectivity, to passionate involvement; the tales he told and those told about him appeal to the imagination rather than to reason. They try to prove that man is more than he appears to be and that he is capable of giving more than he appears to possess."

When I read Heschel's *A Passion for Truth,* I took it for granted that my teacher was writing about the actual Baal Shem Tov of history. But Wiesel makes it clear that the Besht of Hasidic memory was a figure of legend:

> Historically speaking, the character barely emerges,
> his outlines blurred by contradictions. Nothing can
> be said about him with certainty. Those who claim to
> have known him, to have come close to him or loved
> him, seem incapable of referring to him in terms other
> than poetic. He has made them dream so much that
> they describe him as in a dream. That is at least part
> of the reason why so many rationalists study him with
> thinly veiled hostility. By becoming a legend, his life has
> slipped from their grasp.

Wiesel emphasizes the enigmatic character of the founder of
Hasidism. There is nothing that we know about him that is not tinged
with mystery. Because the Baal Shem Tov was an oral teacher, we have
hardly anything that comes directly from his hand. His disciples ascribed
many insights to him, yet each saw him differently. As for the images of
the Besht found in the myriad tales told about him—they contradict one
another. The so-called "testimonies" abound with controversies, confusion of places and dates, and abundant paradoxes. All these contradictions have led some historians to doubt that he had been an actual
human being.

But the fact that the Besht was a legendary figure did not bother
Wiesel in the least. "There remains of him nothing but legend, a legend whose profound and lasting reverberations paradoxically gained in
strength with time." And none of Wiesel's disclosures about the legendary character of the Baal Shem concerned me then. I wasn't thinking in
historical terms.

THE BAAL SHEM AND JESUS

It turns out that Jewish scholars and writers have often compared the
founder of Hasidism with Jesus of Nazareth.

More than a century ago, the great rabbinic scholar Louis Ginzberg
(1873-1953) wrote, "It may be said of Hasidism...that, with the exception
of Jesus and the Judeo-Christians, there is no other Jewish sect in which
the founder is as important as his doctrines. [The] Besht himself is still
the real center of Hasidism." And Dubnow wrote: "Fifty-five years after the

death of the Besht, a book appeared that purported to relate the events of his life—*Shivhei ha-Besht* (Praises of the Baal Shem Tov)—comparable to the manner in which the first gospels of Jesus Christ appeared two generations after his death. The process of gestation for both mythic biographies was the same, despite the seventeen hundred years that separate them. Over the course of some decades, miracle stories began to spread among the folk about the son of Podolia, just as they had about the son of Galilee in his day."[87] And Gershom Scholem remarked, "The Besht was what modern scholars of religion call a charismatic leader... Rudolph Otto, in his study of Jesus, wrote that charismatic leaders had the gifts of being able to heal and to exorcize demons, together with the abilities of preaching, prophesying, and opening the eyes of people to the truths of the spirit, just as Jesus was able to do with his disciples."[88]

Rabbi Louis Newman (1893-1972), editor of *The Hasidic Anthology*, wrote that "Jesus developed his system upon the foundation of traditional Jewish teaching, and gave to it at the same time a personal direction and content; the Besht, also, accepted the fundamentals of the inheritance of Israel, but emphasized those features which appealed to his own individuality and temperament, thereby creating a new group in Jewry with its own creed and practices."[89]

Taking these statements together it seemed that if I examined the historical scholarship about Jesus I might find some indication about how to discern the original identity of the Baal Shem. I decided to get to know the methodological approaches that New Testament scholars used to portray the historical Jesus. Such knowledge might help me in my work. This knowledge also helped me in later years, as I pondered the numerous lacunae in historic data we have about the Baal Shem, and saw how New Testament scholars attempt to fill in the missing historical information about Jesus.

WHO WAS JESUS?

I was intrigued when the cover of *Time* magazine was "Who Was Jesus?" In the lead article journalist Richard Ostling wrote that modern scholars have offered a number of radically different portrayals of the founding master of Christianity: "How is Jesus to be understood? Did he stride out of the wilderness 2000 years ago to preach a gentle message of peace and brotherhood? Or did he perhaps advocate some form of revolution? Or did he instead look for heavenly intervention to establish the kingdom of God? What did it mean for Jesus to be tempted by sin? When did he realize that his mission would end with death upon a cross? Did he view himself as the promised Messiah? Did he understand himself to be both God and man, and what imponderable struggles of the soul would that have meant for him during his sojourn on earth?"[90] These questions were meant to point out the fundamental mystery of the identity of the founder of Christianity, an enigma that had, in modern times, provoked a surfeit of conjectures by biblical scholars.

Ostling sketched out several of those theories. There were those who pictured Jesus as an itinerant sage, like Gandhi or Socrates, a troublemaker and subversive. Many historians, on the other hand, saw him as an apocalyptic prophet who believed in the coming radical transformation of the world, and sought to get people to repent before the end times occurred. One particular scholar pictured Jesus as a Hellenistic Cynic, who advocated for virtue and self-control, and whose teachings were influenced by Roman and Hellenistic sources. But there were also Jewish scholars in Israel who portrayed Jesus as an inspired rabbi, a liberal humanist, connected to the rabbinic school of Hillel, who taught love, understanding, and identification with one's fellow human beings. At the same time, conservative Christians continued to champion the traditional Jesus, the Son of God who was the Christ, or Messiah. Ostling noted that each approach assumed that the recorded texts could be trusted completely, even though those texts contradicted one another. He also noted that there were scholars who simply didn't trust the historicity of the New Testament accounts at all.

In the fourth century, the Church Fathers canonized four gospels, four versions of Jesus' life and teachings—Mark, Matthew, Luke, and John—which they believed to be historically authentic. Yet now, Ostling wrote, we have knowledge of a copious array of ancient Christian gospels, perhaps as many as two hundred in all. These "heretical" documents were mostly suppressed by the Church, because they came from Christian splinter groups whose theologies and views of Jesus did not match those found in the four gospels.

I followed up the *Time* article by spending time in the Graduate

Theological Union library in Berkeley, paging through a number of books devoted to the question of Jesus' historic identity. Although I did not discover any clues I could use in my pursuit of the historic Baal Shem Tov, I did come to understand that New Testament scholars used various methods of inquiry in their analyses. The chief approach was called the historical critical method, examining the origins of biblical texts in relation to other contemporaneous documents, to discern the authorship, audience, and authenticity of those texts. The aim of this method was to get as close to the original text and its original meaning as possible.

Of course, this kind of methodology wasn't foolproof. Ostling pointed out that the historical critical method did not bring any unanimity to the study of the historical Jesus. On the contrary, scholars using this methodology had come up with a variety of Jesuses. A few years later, David B. Gowler's *What Are They Saying About the Historical Jesus?* summarized, analyzed, and critiqued the innumerable portraits of Jesus in a way that also made fascinating reading. He detailed the intricate and sometimes convoluted ways scholars have gone about fashioning their reconstructions, attempting to prove the accuracy of their theories. Gowler wrote: "The evidence is complicated, because the canonical gospels present somewhat divergent portraits of Jesus, and extracanonical sources present an even more complex situation. In addition, our presuppositions and biases—seen and unseen, admitted and denied—enter the mix. We always, inevitably and understandably, project a bit of ourselves and of our own epoch onto our conception of Jesus."[91] Gowler reviewed a rather large range of interpretations and reconstructions of Jesus. The first two chapters alone touched on twenty-three, and the final four chapters elaborated on four widely different others. An appendix at the end further highlighted twenty-nine more studies.

The debates between contemporary New Testament scholars include a number of questions: What sources should be used to reconstruct Jesus' life and teachings? How historically reliable are these sources? Which criteria or methodology should be used in interpreting the sources? Can scholars integrate various disciplines in their methodologies, and which of these are most appropriate and useful? What relevance does Jesus have for us today? Because of the dynamic nature of these debates, I view these many and various reconstructions of Jesus as at least partially if not completely speculative in nature, utilizing the scholars' intuitive and imaginative faculties. This is not necessarily a bad thing, but it signals the impossibility of attaining a definitive image of the historical Jesus.

One of the most prominent of these researchers, John Dominic Crossan, has published his own theory about Jesus' historic identity, portraying him as a healer and wise man who taught a message of inclusiveness, tolerance, and liberation. In Crossan's view, Jesus' strategy "was the combination of free healing and common eating...that negated the hierarchical and patronal normalcies of Jewish religion and Roman power.... He was neither broker nor mediator but...the announcer that neither should exist between humanity and divinity or humanity and itself."[92] Yet, Crossan admits, "our *best* theories and methods are just that: *our* (limited, dated, and doomed) theories and methods." He relativizes the process of attempting to locate Jesus, and speaks about "reconstructing the historic Jesus as best one can at any given time and place—with a clear method that is cogently communicated to encourage public discourse." He also states that every generation must reconstruct the historic Jesus as well as it can, knowing the impossibility of solving once and for all the enigma of his life.[93] I was impressed by Crossan's candor. I'm not sure that he would agree with this, but it seems to me his view provides a warrant for multiple speculative approaches to history, as long as a historian is open, honest, and truthful about what he is doing.

What, then, do I make of the search for the historical Besht in the light of all this? First, even though the problems in Baal Shem Tov scholarship are similar to those in the study of Jesus, they are not the same. Because the Besht lived in the eighteenth century, the historical issues are simply not as problematic as they are in Jesus scholarship. With all our questions about the historical Besht, we do have more information at our disposal for an accurate reconstruction of his life and thought.

I drew another lesson from Gospel scholarship, and from Crossan in particular. There was a time in my quest when I hoped to find *the* Baal Shem Tov of history. This was no longer the case. I came to believe that there may never be a single, historically definitive portrait of the Baal Shem's life, deeds, and thought. Yet, although I knew that my view of the Besht could certainly be challenged, I felt duty-bound to offer these honest probings to readers. This whole book, after all, is my personal quest to fill in the gaps of missing information and interpret our existing knowledge, amplifying our understanding of, and our appreciation for, the master's achievements. A Spanish Gospel scholar named Jose Antonio Pagola once wrote a book called *Jesus: An Historical Approximation.* This is what I have attempted—for the Besht.

WAS JESUS A HASID?

I did not get much further than this with my historical research before another possible avenue in my quest to discover the Baal Shem opened up. As I examined the various theories about Jesus, I found that a large number of researchers were focusing on Jesus' Jewishness, even though there was disagreement about what his relationship was to the forms that Judaism took in the first century. I was amazed to discover that there were scholars who thought that Jesus had been a *Hasid*.

In the course of Jewish history there have been a number of pietistic movements whose adherents were called Hasidim. The First Hasidim (*Hasidim Ha'ri'shon'im*) were members of a sect of Jews that may have originated during the second century before the Common Era. These saintly men were distinguished by their austerity in matters of religious observance, by their love of silence before prayer, and by their wonder-working abilities. They would guard themselves against the possibility of being the indirect cause of harm to fellow Jews through carelessness. They were later remembered for their uncompromising observance of the mitzvot, most especially Shabbat. The sect eventually faded or became part of the Pharisees, the forerunners of the Talmudic rabbis.

How was Jesus related to these early Hasidim? I first read about this possibility in *God and the Big Bang* by Daniel Matt, one of the world's preeminent scholars of Kabbalah. Based on his knowledge of Jewish piety, Matt wrote that throughout Jewish history there were certain features that always characterized this type of spirituality. A Hasid, he wrote is "someone passionately in love with God, drunken on the divine, unconventional and extreme in his devotion to God and to fellow human beings. The *hasid* is a nonconformist who demands much of himself and his followers. His intimacy with God, his confidence in the power of his words, and his unreserved personal authenticity conflicted with the conservative power structure." Matt sees Jesus as falling into this religious category. "Like later Hasidim, Jesus felt that it was not enough to follow the Torah: One must become Torah, living so intensely that one's everyday actions convey an awareness of God and evoke this awareness in others."[94] To me, this most certainly sounded like a description of the Baal Shem Tov!

The primary source Matt drew from included the work of the Jewish New Testament scholar, Geza Vermes. In *Jesus the Jew* and *The Religion of Jesus the Jew*, Vermes compares Jesus to two Hasidim referred to in rabbinic literature, Hanina ben Dosa and Honi the Circle Maker. According to legend, both men lived in the Galilee around the time of Jesus, and like the latter, they were charismatic miracle workers and healers in the mold of the early biblical prophets, Elijah and Elisha. In addition, Hanina was seen as a saint and sage for whom prayer was central. Vermes states that the life and teachings of Jesus testify to his having been a much more profound charismatic prophet than either Hanina ben Dosa or Honi the Circle Maker. Vermes writes that "the real Jesus of Nazareth remains Jesus the Galilean Hasid. Thanks to the sublimity, distinctiveness and originality of his ethical teaching, Jesus stood head and shoulders above the other religious teachers of his day. He was a faith-healer, a folk preacher and moral revivalist—a different kind of rabbi who represented a loving, forgiving, and yet demanding God. Jesus believed that he had been sent by God to give hope to downtrodden Jews and to heal those who were physically and spiritually ill."[95]

With this as a basis I began to compare Jesus and the Besht as Hasidic types. The traditions surrounding both leaders testify that they brought hope to their people and that each of them emphasized awe and reverence on the one hand, and love and compassion on the other. One of my favorite stories in the Gospels describes Jesus being approached by a scribe, a man who had knowledge of the Torah and who could draft legal documents. The scribes were associated with the Pharisees. The scribe asked Jesus,

> "Which is the first of all the commandments?" Jesus
> replied, "This is the first: Listen, Israel, the Lord our God
> is the one, only Lord, and you must love the Lord your
> God with all your heart, with all your soul, with all your

mind, and with all your strength. The second is this: You must love your neighbor as yourself. There is no commandment greater than these." The scribe said to him, "Well spoken, Master; what you have said is true...this is far more important than any burnt offering or sacrifice." Jesus, seeing how wisely he had spoken, said, "You are not far from the kingdom of God." (Mark 12:28-34, New Jerusalem Bible)

Similarly, according to a source cited by Rebbe Menachem Mendel Schneerson, the last Lubavitcher rebbe, the Besht interpreted the interrelated commandments of loving God and loving one's neighbor in the following way:

"You must love your neighbor as yourself." (Leviticus 19:18) This is a specific application of the commandment, "You must love the EverPresent your God with all your heart, with all your soul, and with all your strength." (Deuteronomy 6:5) When we love our fellow humans as ourselves we actually love the Holy One, for every person is part of God.[96]

Though both Jesus and the Besht emphasized the connection between the love of God and the love of people, they differed theologically regarding the nature of God. Like his predecessors in the Hebrew Bible, Jesus was theologically a dualist, seeing God (whom he often called "Abba," which means Father) as transcending creation, though at the same time deeply concerned about the world he had created. Because God and human beings lived in separate realms, Jesus spoke about the love of God and the love of human beings as separate commandments. The Baal Shem Tov, on the other hand, appears as a nondualist in many of his teachings. For him the separation between the Divine and the human is, in some real sense, an illusion. Thus, he taught that when a person loves their neighbor, they are at the same time loving God, since one's neighbor is part of the wholeness of reality that is divine. The Baal Shem doesn't claim that such love is the primary commandment, but he spoke about showing members of his community, through his actions, that service to God comes with joy and love.

Along with these similarities, there are a large number of other parallels between Jesus and the Besht. The Galileans whom Jesus addressed lived in a world filled with difficulty and harshness, and God seemed remote and exceedingly hard to fathom. With Jesus' help, however, these Jews were able to realize God's sovereignty in the present in their personal lives, and in this way their suffering was ameliorated. Jesus' own extraordinary "messianic" presence among the people he served was taken as a sign of the truth that he was proclaiming.

The Baal Shem, too, understood that for most people God seemed transcendent and out of touch with the suffering they were experiencing. But he emphasized God's actual presence in the here and now, i.e. the Shekhinah, immanent in all things and events. With the Baal Shem's support and with great personal spiritual effort seekers could learn to see through the evil and divisiveness of the present and live in the Presence, and in this way, their suffering could be sweetened. We are told that the Besht saw his own sacred work as preparation for the coming of the messiah, which would occur as human beings brought about the spiritual conditions necessary for that great event to occur.

Major theological differences separated Jesus and the Besht, but their similarities could not be denied. It would seem that these parallels resulted from the fact that both teachers shared a common Jewish heritage anchored in the Hebrew Bible. And if Vermes and Matt were correct, they both shared the heritage of being Hasidim. But there was another factor as well: Jesus and the Besht faced similar social and political issues: in both cases, the Jews whom they addressed lived in a world dominated by alien powers that had no respect for the Jewish people or their religious traditions.

Through my years of study, I kept a running list of other similarities I found:

- Both Jesus and the Baal Shem were folk healers and wonder-workers as well as spiritual teachers.
- Both were charismatics whose provocative teachings and

manner of delivery opened their followers' hearts to new ways of experiencing reality.

· They both made the sovereignty of the Spirit utterly immediate and palpable through the power of their own authority, convictions, and presence.

· Jesus and the Besht were highly intuitive and were certain that they had been sent by God to proclaim or reveal the existence of a higher spiritual order of reality that could be perceived neither by the senses nor by reason alone.

· Both teachers came to the realization that they were sons of God, that is, at one with the divine essence.

· Although they conceived of this spiritual order in radically different ways, each taught that God was sovereign over the cruel powers and principalities that dominated the visible world.

· Both reached out in compassion to marginalized members of society; nonetheless, they were suspicious of non-Jews and each directed their teachings to Jews alone.

· Both sought to renew Judaism, emphasizing the necessity of spiritual intentionality in all of one's deeds, while at the same time deemphasizing asceticism.

· Both were seen by followers as supernatural and divine redemptive figures who had come to prepare the way for the unfolding of the messianic era which would alter human consciousness and change the world.

These numerous parallels seemed positively eerie, as if comparable historical circumstances had given birth to two teachers who were also savior-figures, seeking to bring healing to the people of their time. In retrospect, however, I must admit that not all of these likenesses, enshrined in legend, may have characterized the actual historical personages of Jesus and the Besht. But an examination of their similarities helped me recognize the primary purposes of the Besht's ministry as it was perceived in Hasidic tradition.

CHRISTIAN INFLUENCE ON HASIDISM?

Throughout the long history of Judaism, the Jewish people resisted making any human being into a savior-like hero. There were precedents in history for the notion of the tzaddik as a saintly figure possessed with extraordinary abilities, but in general Jews were skeptical of the elevation of any human being to the rank of intermediary between God and people. The Talmudic rabbis, likely influenced by the Christian deification of Jesus, eliminated all references to Moses in the Passover Haggadah so that Moses would not be seen as the liberator of the Jewish people from Egypt. This changed with eighteenth-century Hasidism, for the Baal Shem Tov not only became a unique holy figure in the movement that he founded, but the model for a new kind of charismatic spiritual leader, the tzaddik or rebbe. How was it that such a radical break with tradition took place in eighteenth-century Poland?[97]

For her doctoral dissertation in the 1960s, Yaffa Eliach studied the Christian sects that existed in Poland when the Baal Shem Tov was alive. Eliach discovered numerous resemblances between Hasidic values, beliefs, practices, and styles of leadership with those of the Christian Raskolnik schismatics and dissenters who had broken with Russian Orthodoxy. One of these Raskol sects was called the Khlysty, and Eliach described a number of likenesses that characterized both the Khlysty sectarians and the early Hasidim. During their worship, members of the sect shouted foreign sounds, ran around, jumped up and down, and whirled around like Muslim dervishes or "holy rollers." In like manner, Eliach showed how the Hasidim engaged in ecstatic singing and dancing, and some of their dance forms resembled those of the Khlysty. During their worship, Hasidim would also engage in wild spontaneous movements.

To Eliach, the most striking and convincing parallel that characterized the two religious communities was the similarity of the Hasidic tzaddik to the leaders of the Khlysty, who were called "Christs." Just as the Besht and later rebbes were thought to have a special relationship with the Divine that made them godlike, so the Khlysty believed that their Christs reincarnated the very spirit of Jesus. The first collection of tales about the Besht, *In Praise of the Baal Shem Tov,* states that the Besht was psychic, able to predict the future, and that he could pick out sinners by observing their faces. These powers were also attributed to the Khlysty Christs. Eliach wrote, "It has been noted that the Besht resembled Jesus in a number of aspects. This is explainable by the close similarity between the Besht and the sect's local Christs, who resembled Jesus."[98] If Eliach was right, we may have a key to understanding why the Besht seems like Jesus in so many ways.

When Eliach published a small article containing her findings, her hypothesis was roundly attacked by Gershom Scholem, the founder of the academic study of Jewish mysticism. Scholem called her scholarship irresponsible speculation. Another contemporary historian, Moshe Rosman, was also critical and wrote that Eliach was able to point to parallels, but could not adduce "a single piece of evidence demonstrating that the Besht, or any Hasidic leader, was in contact in more than a superficial way with any Christian theologian."[99]

Speculation plays an important role in the study of history, pointing the way to future research by developing early ideas into hypotheses. Of course, speculation is not proof, and it seems to me that Eliach acted rashly in simply assuming her hypothesis was true. Nonetheless, her theory seems extremely suggestive, and I believe she was treated unfairly by the scholarly establishment. It is evident that if the Besht had been influenced by the Khlysty he would not have wanted this to be known for fear of being accused of heresy. Unfortunately, because of the criticism leveled against her work, Eliach never published her doctoral dissertation. I ordered it through interlibrary loan. It came on microfilm and I read it in the public library on a microfiche reader.

Eliach was neither the first nor the last to consider the possibility of Christian influence on Hasidism. In a chapter on Hasidism in his book, *The Jewish Mind,* anthropologist and historian Raphael Patai takes a strong position on this point. Besides citing Eliach, he calls attention to the work of Swedish scholar Torsten Ysander, who identified similarities between Hasidism and Russian Orthodoxy, as well as Russian dissenting sects.[100] Patai writes about a Ukrainian preacher, Gregory Skorovoda (1722-94), whose ideas were remarkably similar to kabbalistic and Hasidic notions, and compared Hasidic doctrines to those of Russian Orthodoxy, demonstrating similarities of the two faiths. The old Russian idea of God dwelling in the human soul and speaking through the human mouth was reaffirmed with new vigor. "The mystical Russian soul was filled with a desire for infinity and oneness with God. The mystics held that the purpose of human existence was to become part of the universal Divine and to become dissolved in it. They also maintained that love was the greatest value in life, love that filled the heart and embraced all—men, animals, birds, demons, and the totality of creation."[101]

Patai also compared Hasidic tzaddikim to the Russian Startsy (sing. Starets). These charismatic holy men, who were usually monks, commanded wide popular respect for their pastoral care and spiritual guidance in the eighteenth- and nineteenth-century Russian Orthodox Church. Just as Hasidim made pilgrimages to their tzaddikim, so Christian laypeople would make pilgrimages to the Startsy. Believers would become totally dependent on their Starets, abdicating their own will entirely. Patai also showed the similarities between the tzaddik and Catholic and Orthodox priests who were seen as mediators between God and the world.

Mainline Jewish scholars have by and large shied away from exploring the possibilities of these non-Jewish influences on the development of Hasidism. It's as if they want to preserve what they perceive to be the unique character of Jewish religiosity. Nonetheless, there are a handful of researchers who have engaged with the question of possible Christian influence on early Hasidism.[102] For instance, Moshe Idel, arguably the leading contemporary academic scholar of Jewish mysticism, commented on the possibility of Christian influence on early Hasidism, pointing out that the Carpathian Mountains—where the Besht purportedly lived for seven years—was home to Christian hermits and monks, and so he probably found himself in their company. Idel also compared the descriptions of Hasidic forms of meditation to Greek Orthodox models. Some of his observations echo those of Eliach and Patai. Idel notes that the Besht and other Hasidic rebbes understood themselves to be sons of God:

> It should be mentioned that the openness of Hasidism
> to other forms of behavior, *en vogue* in the Christian
> environment, like dancing, drinking, alcoholic drinks,
> special garments, or the importance of story-telling,
> reminiscent of what was found in the immediate vicin-
> ity of nascent Hasidism, are hardly explainable by Jewish
> antecedents. Therefore, it may well be that the adoption
> of a Christian understanding of [divine] sonship [by the

Baal Shem Tov and other Hasidic rebbes] is a small part
of a greater openness than witnessed earlier to non-Jewish religious practices and other phenomena.[103]

As I was working on this chapter, I recalled that many years ago Reb
Zalman Schachter-Shalomi had sent me a photocopy of a chapter from
a book that threw additional light on the Baal Shem's relationship with
Christians. I found the article in my files and re-read it, remembering
how it recounts a remarkable story about the Besht from his time in the
mountains. Stanislaw Vincenz, the article's author, was a well-known
Polish essayist who grew up in the Carpathians. He was intimately familiar with, and wrote about, the Hutsul Christians and the Jews who lived
there. Hutsuls and Jews, Vincenz writes, have lived side by side in harmony
for hundreds of years. They help and respect one another, work together,
and take part in each other's festivals. This fact is in itself remarkable,
since Jewish-Christian relations during that period were almost always
characterized by tension. Vincenz then describes a number of similarities shared by both peoples, noting that "the magical practices used in
urgent cases of need by the Christian Hutsuls and the Hasidic Jews were
fundamentally the same."

What struck me most, though, was Vincenz' comments about the
Baal Shem Tov. "Since childhood," he writes, "I too have heard many stories about the Baal Shem Tov, especially how he lived in Jasienov with
a Hutsul family named Fedieczkowi, who looked after him kindly and
nursed him when he was sick. The direct descendants of that family, who
still referred to that tradition, lived in the village of Krasnojila, not far
from Jasienov." So it is possible that the Besht witnessed Hutsul gatherings where the participants danced joyously all night long.[104]

Now, presuming that Ysander, Eliach, Patai, and Idel are correct,
we have one of the strangest ironies in all of Jewish history. Jesus was a
Jewish teacher who became the center of a new religion and was lost to
the Jewish people. For 1,700 years the two religious communities lived
side by side, each assuming that the doctrines of their respective religions represented the highest religious truth. Triumphalism and antisemitism were part of the Christian attitude toward the Jews through most of
those years, and in return Jews developed a great deal of hostility toward

Christians. Then, in the eighteenth century, a Jewish movement arose in Poland with a powerful Jesus-like figure at its head, who introduced innovative elements into Judaism that were quite similar to the beliefs and practices of his Christian neighbors.

For the longest time I carried with me a deep sense of ambivalence about this possibility. Despite my love for Hasidism, it felt as if there was something inherently inauthentic about a Jewish movement that may have adopted Christian forms of spiritual leadership. Intellectually, I believe that every religion is an expression of the underlying human quest for a relationship with that greater Reality out of which everything in the cosmos flows. Nonetheless, I carry an old tribal sensibility that longs for the unadulterated Judaism of the pre-modern world. Still, theories like Eliach's posit the possibility that even a parochial closed society like Eastern European Jewry might have been permeable to external religious influences.

I found it surprising, then, that Abraham Joshua Heschel, who grew up in the parochial Hasidic world of Warsaw, was not only able to entertain the historical possibility of Christian influence on Judaism, but even to celebrate it!

> The religions of the world are no more self-sufficient, no more independent, no more isolated than individuals or nations. Energies, experiences, and ideas that come to life outside the boundaries of a particular religion or all religions continue to challenge and to affect every religion.... *No religion is an island.* We are all involved with one another.... Views adopted in one community have an impact on other communities. For all the profound differences in perspectives and substance, Judaism is sooner or later affected by the intellectual, moral, and spiritual events within Christian society, and vice versa.[105]

Similarly, my friend and colleague, Rabbi David Zaslow, opens his book, *Jesus: First Century Rabbi,* with these words: "The time seems to have arrived when Christians and Jews are beginning to have a new understanding of each other. Old notions and prejudices are rapidly being discarded, making room for what the Holy One might have had us understand all along."[106]

EXPERIENCING JESUS' PRESENCE

My own strong interest in Jesus goes beyond the issue of how the study of his life and mission might illumine the life and legacy of the Besht. During the summer following my bar mitzvah, my parents sent me to the Eagle's Nest Boy's Ranch in the Texas hill country for a month, not knowing that the director and staff of the ranch were fervent evangelical Christians. I enjoyed the experience immensely, learning how to ride a horse, milk cows, make rope, and take care of a goat. We boys would swim in the Perdanales River and listen to stories of nineteenth-century life on the Morris Ranch when it had been the primary breeding ground for the nation's racehorses. On Sundays, I would remain alone at the ranch while everyone else went to church. During the final week of camp, however, we learned that we would be spending our last weekend together at a revival meeting in the hills. I had no idea what a revival meeting was, nor did I ask.

That Sunday morning the children's revival was held in the large tent following the adult meeting. Hymns were sung, and the preacher offered intense and heartfelt prayers to God. Then came the sermon. The preacher was serious and earnest. As I recall, he began by declaring how much God and Jesus loved us, proclaiming that God wanted us to dedicate ourselves fully and completely to Christ. He also warned us that if we refused to accept Jesus as our savior, God would be forced to punish us in hell, where we would burn forever. Then he called for each of us to come forward and give ourselves to Christ. I became panicky and frightened. What should I do? One by one the children walked down the center aisle to the front of the tent, most in tears. The preacher quietly blessed each boy or girl in turn, and then directed the children to leave through the rear tent flap. Something inside me deeply longed to join the other kids. It was partly because I didn't want to stand out, but it was more than that. What if the preacher was right, and I would burn in hell if I didn't give myself to Christ? And yet I knew that I was a Jew and that we Jews did not worship Jesus. If I left my seat and walked to the front of the tent to give myself to Jesus what would my parents say? How would my bar mitzvah teacher, Mr. Bendiner react? My heart was racing, I was sweating, and the moment seemed endless. By the end, I was the only child left seated in the large tent. I didn't leave my seat until after the preacher had exited.

I never told my parents or my bar mitzvah teacher what happened. Was I scared or ashamed—or both? I don't remember, but for decades, even during my years as a student in rabbinical school, I suffered an aching guilt at not being a Christian. That preacher had been so fully devoted to his religious beliefs, and maybe he had been right. Perhaps Christianity had superseded Judaism, and was the only true religion. Perhaps my being Jewish meant that I would have to suffer after death.

The issue surfaced again a few years later when I was giving a weekly course on the world's religions to a group of high school juniors. A few days before teaching the class on Christianity I began to panic. How could I teach such a class to Jewish students with all my unresolved conflicts? I called Reb Zalman on the phone to ask for his help, and without hesitation he suggested a detailed course of action.

On the following Sunday morning, I followed Reb Zalman's plan. I readied the youth room of the synagogue, pulling down the window shades and putting a recording of Gregorian chant on the turntable. Then I lit some candles and incense, placed a chair in the middle of the room, and turned off the overhead light. Upstairs in the usual classroom I greeted my students, took attendance, and then led them quietly down to the youth room. I sat on the chair and the students silently took seats on the large pillows surrounding me. After allowing the Gregorian chant to play for five or six minutes, I lowered the volume of the record player, opened my copy of the New Testament, and slowly read aloud selections from the Sermon on the Mount from the Gospel of Matthew (4:25 and 5:1-14), the longest teaching of Jesus in the Gospels:

> And large crowds followed Jesus from Galilee and the Decapolis and Jerusalem and Judea and beyond the Jordan River. And when he saw the crowds he went up onto a hill, and when he had sat down, his disciples gathered around him, and he began to teach them. And this is what he said: Blessed are those who are not bound to their desires, for theirs is the Kingdom of Heaven.

Blessed are the gentle, for they shall have the earth as inheritance. Blessed are those who mourn, for they shall be comforted. Blessed are those who hunger and thirst for justice for they shall have their fill. Blessed are the merciful, for they shall have mercy shown to them. Blessed are the pure in heart, for they already see God. Blessed are the peacemakers, for they shall be recognized as children of God. Blessed are those who are persecuted in the cause of righteousness, for theirs is the realm of God...

I read aloud for perhaps seven or eight minutes and then allowed for a period of silence. All of us, myself included, were awed by the spiritual power of Jesus' words. Later that day, I realized that my issues with Jesus and Christianity had simply vanished.

It took me many years to come to some kind of understanding of what happened to me that morning. In the Sermon on the Mount, Jesus was offering comfort and consolation to the poor and humble Jews living in the Galilee, assuring them that somehow God was present for them and would not let them be forgotten, despite the oppression they were suffering at the hands of Rome. Jesus' compassionate words had touched my soul as I read them to my students, and somehow for those few moments I had actually become Jesus. It was this experience that healed the wound that had been inflicted on the thirteen-year-old boy.

Over the years I have wondered whether my future interest in the Baal Shem Tov might have been kindled by my encounter with Jesus on that fateful Sunday morning with my students. It has certainly helped me to appreciate the attraction exerted by the figure of Jesus on so many Christians. Looking back at the terrifying event of my childhood, it seems to me now that in some odd and paradoxical way, the trauma I experienced had been, at the same time, an initiation into the world of earnest religiosity for me, a spirituality that was based on self-surrender to the Ultimate. Somehow, I must have unconsciously known that if I was not going to be a follower of Jesus, I would need to find a wise Jewish spiritual teacher, someone who would have the ability of showing me the way to God just as Jesus was able to lead Christians to God.

One of the Baal Shem's core teachings had to do with the notion of the hidden presence of the Divine in all our experiences, whether beneficial or damaging. When we are able to find God in our difficulties and adversity, we can begin to fashion meaning out of our suffering. In this way, our troubles can be transformed into something positive. This is how I have come to understand my traumatic encounter with Christian evangelism. Despite the scarring that the experience left on my soul, it did help propel me toward a sincere encounter with traditional Judaism and set me searching for a spiritual figure who might lead me to God. It would take decades, but eventually I found the Baal Shem Tov, a loving spiritual master who would teach me the power of a joy and a love that would make guilt and shame unnecessary.

CHAPTER TEN

THE QUEST FOR THE HISTORICAL BESHT

"The fact that there have been so many attempts to appropriate the Baal Shem Tov in the service of ideology and politics is testimony to the power of his image in Jewish collective memory. Perception of Israel Baal Shem Tov resonates through the ages and across the Jewish spectrum. The historian's Besht is but one component of the people's Besht—and not necessarily the most interesting one. The historian's Besht is essential, however, for understanding the history of Polish Jewry, Hasidism, and the process by which memory transmutes history to serve culture and society."

MOSHE ROSMAN[107]

In 1978, Moshe Rosman, an American-Israeli graduate student in Eastern European Jewish history, was working on his dissertation at Hebrew University. He'd journeyed to Poland to engage in research on the relationship between the Jews and the Polish nobles in the eighteenth century. The documents he needed were located in the Czartoryski Library in Krakow. He knew that the Czartoryski family had owned the town of Medzhiboz, where the Baal Shem Tov and his family had supposedly spent the last twenty years of his life, and he thought that perhaps he could examine town records. Perhaps there would be documents to verify the historical existence of the Baal Shem. "But I hesitated," he writes, for "researching the Besht was not my mission, and with limited research time available.... I dared not be distracted. Moreover, I feared what I might find—or not find. What if the Besht did not appear in the Miedzyboz records? Would that mean he was a mythological figure?"

For weeks, Rosman held his curiosity in check, but inquisitiveness finally got the better of him and he asked to see the Medzhibozh town tax records dating from the early 1740s. Thumbing through the documents, he was surprised. "Within minutes I found the Baal Shem Tov. He indeed appeared as 'Balszem' or 'Balszam,' even 'Balszam Doctor.' I was filled with excitement, as if my inner body would burst through my skin. I was also relieved." The records actually stated that the Jewish community owned the Baal Shem's home and paid the taxes on it. When Rosman returned to Israel, he shared his discovery with colleagues, but he wasn't really sure what to do with the information he'd uncovered. Eight years after making the discovery, he finally went public with his preliminary findings, and the news swiftly became a sensation in the Jewish scholarly world.[108]

MYTH VERSUS HISTORY

Rosman wrote: "The eighteenth-century Polish-Jewish mystic, Israel Baal Shem Tov—known as the Baal Shem Tov, or the Besht—is one of the key figures in Jewish history. As the progenitor of Hasidism and the perceived spokesman for the warm, humane side of Jewish religious observance, he profoundly influenced the shape of modern Judaism.... Much of what is believed about his life is based on stories...[which] serve more to mythologize than to describe the Besht." What did that last line mean— that the stories "serve more to mythologize than to describe the Besht"? Rosman stated that he was making use of a new approach in his study, and that he'd arrived at radically different answers to the basic historical questions regarding the identity of the reputed "founder of Hasidism." He discussed the social, religious, and economic conditions in the Polish-Lithuanian Commonwealth during the eighteenth century, and especially in Medzhibozh. Early historians of Hasidism had believed that at the time of the Besht, Poland was a country in decline. Not so, stated Rosman. The agrarian economy was booming as the international grain trade turned Poland into the breadbasket of Western Europe. The region of Podolia where the Besht lived was growing and was one of the most attractive places in Poland for Jews to live, and many Jews had moved there during the first half of the eighteenth century.

This new information, explained Rosman, changes our entire understanding of the origins of Hasidism. Previous historians had posited that Polish Jews lived a bleak, alienated, and dangerous existence, and those conditions were the fertile ground for the birth of Hasidism. Rosman disagreed. He acknowledged that there was violence against Jews, which produced insecurity in the Jewish consciousness, and yet, Jews and

Christians shared cultural similarities which eased the tensions between the two different religious communities. In fact, Jews actually cooperated with their Christian neighbors in defending themselves against common enemies. Rosman also showed that Medzhibozh was a prosperous town, providing a modicum of law, order, and economic prosperity necessary for the Baal Shem to function. The Besht filled a public role in Medzhibozh and maintained relations with Christians as well as Jews. All of this was completely new to me.

It was the second and larger part of the book that was especially distressing. Rosman stated that the reason why scholars have disagreed among themselves regarding the identity of the historic Baal Shem Tov has to do with the small number of eighteenth century sources available and the fact that these texts are extremely difficult to interpret. Because of the equivocal nature of the sources, Rosman said that many of the stories told about the Besht in *In Praise of the Baal Shem Tov* were simply not historically accurate. And because of this, he wrote that his reconstruction of the figure of the Baal Shem deemphasizes the stories. *In Praise of the Baal Shem Tov* is nothing more than hagiography, that is, a later idealization of the life and deeds of its subject, Rosman said. The tales in the book serve more to mythologize the Besht than describe the actual man.

As for the Baal Shem's teachings, they too were untrustworthy, for even though the disciples credit the Besht as their source, Rosman asserts that they most likely come from the disciples themselves. Because of this it's impossible to determine the Besht's religious philosophy. In fact, the historian admits that he finds it impossible to contribute anything at all to the intellectual biography of the Besht.

Not that all the records are equivocal. Rosman contends that his reconstruction of the Baal Shem's life and deeds is based neither on the tales about him nor the teachings ascribed to him, but on previously unexplored archival sources that haven't been mined for information. Looking at the historical evidence he trusts, Rosman believes the Besht was a conservative leader, not a radical innovator. He was known and respected by eminent reputable rabbis, and connected to the rabbinic and the Jewish political establishment. There is no evidence that he rebelled against the establishment or created new institutions; nor did he start a new religious or social movement. Rather, he was much more a representative and perpetuator of existing religious, social, political, and economic realities than he was an innovator.

Rosman contends that "most descriptions of the Baal Shem Tov over the past two hundred years or so tell relatively little about him but very much about the issues confronting Jewish culture in the Western world beginning at the end of the eighteenth century."[109] He notes that the Besht has been viewed by historians as both an enlightened teacher and as a benighted, superstitious conjurer. A Marxist historian saw him as the defender of the masses against the establishment. A Conservative rabbi believed he was a leader willing to compromise in order to win souls. And later Hasidim saw him as a precedent for the legitimacy, activities, and leadership style of the rebbes of their respective dynasties.

I was devasted by this. It went against virtually everything I had surmised in my attempt to interpret the Besht's contributions to the founding of Hasidism. If I was to assimilate Rosman's view, I could no longer trust the texts I was studying. The thought went through my mind that maybe I would have to give up my entire quest, or at least admit that what I had surmised was only imaginative speculation and nothing more.

So I went back and re-read the book's introduction. To his credit, Rosman admits that his own "presentation of the context and texts of the Besht's life contains within it my own notion of the Besht." He is also honest in his self-assessment of his contributions toward uncovering the historical Besht: "I do not deny that my construction of the Besht's life and activity, limited as it is, contains projections of my own preconceived notions and predilections, although, in the nature of things, I am blind to them." Nevertheless, he claims that he has "subjected the sources to more rigorous criticism than has been done previously."[110] For months I thought about Rosman's thesis, weighing the pros and cons. I felt that he was wide of the mark, but who was I to question a professor of Jewish history at Bar Ilan University in Ramat Gan, near Tel Aviv.

For years, before reading Rosman, I had been studying the teachings attributed to the Besht, and I was repeatedly meeting ideas, themes, and spiritual practices recorded by the disciples in the master's name. Could all of these disciples be lying—making up teachings and then presenting them in the name of their master? I sensed that all these citations must represent some kind of valid testimony regarding the Besht's actual views, even if this evidence did not meet Rosman's criteria for historic authenticity. I was also disturbed by Rosman's view that if a historian cannot speak with absolute certainty about the ideas held by a particular historical personage, he should say nothing at all. This seemed to represent a kind of methodological rigidity anchored in unwarranted skepticism. So although I admired Rosman's brilliance and historical rigor, I inevitably came to feel that his skeptical methodology left him tone-deaf to what the historic documents might reveal about the personality and vision of the Baal Shem Tov.

At that point I decided to contact my friend Rabbi Arthur Green to see what he thought. "It all depends on whether you agree with Rosman's assessment of the historical value of the sources," he told me on the telephone. "I don't agree with him and most of the scholars of the period don't agree with him either." I breathed a sigh of relief as I listened. Green had recently published a critique of Rosman's book, which he sent me. "We are told [by Rosman] that [the Baal Shem Tov] was not a revolutionary, but [that he] merely...made some moderate changes in existing forms...modified some conventions.... Why then is he so interesting? Why do devotees continue to flock to his name and historians struggle over his role? Is this all somehow a mistake? Merely a distortion created by the grand image given him in posthumous exaggeration of his role?"[111]

FOUNDER OF HASIDISM?

In 2005, nine years after Rosman's book was published, Professor Immanuel Etkes, his former teacher in Jewish history at the Hebrew University, published his own work on the Baal Shem Tov. In the introduction, Etkes addresses the differences between their viewpoints: "Although my research on the Besht commenced before Rosman's book was published, I freely admit that reading this book gave me an important incentive to complete my own study. While there was much that I learned from the chapters dealing with the background of the life of the Besht, I found myself in considerable disagreement with Rosman's conclusions about the credibility of the source materials.... As a result, my own reconstruction of the Besht...differs substantially from the one put forward by Rosman. One hopes that the appearance within so relatively short a time of two books offering different points of view on the Besht may only inspire and enrich discussions of this topic."[112]

Gershom Scholem had been one of the first modern scholars to research the Baal Shem Tov and prove that he had been an actual person. Etkes summarizes the voluminous amount of critical scholarship that has appeared since Scholem's study. Over the years, historians have challenged or disproved many of Scholem's assumptions. Nonetheless, like both Simon Dubnow and Gershom Scholem, they have paid a great deal of attention to the issue of the historical value of *In Praise of the Baal Shem Tov*. Etkes was able to show that most scholars now agree that the historian who seeks to rely on *In Praise of the Baal Shem Tov* for a reconstruction of the life and character of the Baal Shem Tov stands on firm ground.

One of the most important issues tackled by both Rosman and Etkes was the question of the origin of the Hasidic movement. It was here that Rosman had presented the most novel and extreme aspect of his portrait. Like historians before him, Rosman compares the Besht to Jesus:

> The Besht's relationship to Hasidism is analogous to Jesus' relationship to Christianity. Neither consciously founded a new religious movement. The ideals they exemplified in their teachings and by their behavior were adopted, developed, and made into institutions by later figures. Only when the differentiation of [the new] Hasidism from the [older forms of] Hasidism was in an advanced stage was the role of "founder" filled.[113]

Rosman asserts that the Baal Shem did not create a movement; instead, he modified existing conventions. He appears to have made some moderate changes in existing forms that were eventually transformed by others into the mature institutions of Hasidism. And early Hasidism, Rosman claims, was not a movement of social radicalism, but rather functioned in a way that would strengthen traditional social structures.

Etkes could not disagree more. He sees the Besht as a radical, whose personality and vision of divine immanence inspired the founding of

Hasidism: "Rosman argues...that the founders of Hasidism ascribed their teachings to the Besht and cited his authority for them. This formulation hints at manipulation. Why make such an implication rather than simply say that the Besht had a profound impact on his disciples, as indeed many teachers have done in the history of religion? Why deny the possibility that a personality of extraordinary spiritual vigor could bring about a revolution in the minds of associates, restructure their values, and inspire them to action? It is this that the founders of Hasidism claimed for the Besht. They repeatedly presented themselves as his disciples, cited him in their teachings, and maintained that they were developing ideas and practicing modes of worship they had learned from him. They regarded him as a model to emulate, a source of inspiration, and an authority. Does not this insistence of theirs imply a direct link between the Besht and the emergence of Hasidism?"[114]

Was the Baal Shem Tov, then, the real founder of the Hasidic movement? Etkes states that "the Besht was not a leader of a movement, nor did he even conceive of founding one.... Nevertheless...there are good grounds for regarding the Besht as having been decisive for the emergence of Hasidism as a movement, even if this outcome was not intended by him." As proof, Etkes quotes the Rebbe Meshulam Feibush Heller, who in 1777, just seventeen years after the Baal Shem's death, wrote, "The learned of the era, men of marvels possessed of the Holy Spirit, whom my eyes beheld and not a stranger's: like an angel of God is their fear and awe, and all had drunk at the same fountain, namely the divine R. Israel Baal Shem Tov of blessed and righteous memory."[115]

In 2013, Rosman's republished his book with a new introduction, in which he defends many of his assumptions, but is also willing to grant legitimacy to some of his critic's ideas. He specifically deals with Etkes' criticism, admitting that Etkes' "was the most systematic, detailed, and reasoned critique of my book." He also states that Etkes' work, along with that of some other serious commentators stimulated him to refine his views in different ways: "[T]he critics have convinced me about one thing. I should have tried harder to identify those of the Besht's ideas that influenced later Hasidism. There is some room, even within parameters, to say more on this subject than the modest assertions I made.... I should have analyzed notions such as divine immanence, the elevation of alien thoughts, the techniques of prayer *kavanah,* worship through corporeality, and the intensity of mystical experience as possibly belonging to the innovations, emphases, or attributes of the Besht himself."[116]

In fact, just a few years earlier, Roman Foxbrunner, a scholar of Hasidism engaged in research at Harvard University, took a very different approach in evaluating what is arguably the most reliable collection of the Baal Shem's teachings. Foxbrunner pointed to the 400-plus citations in the works of Rabbi Jacob Joseph of Polonoyye, the Baal Shem's foremost literary disciple, and states that in order to arrive at what the Besht actually taught, scholars would have to compare "many homilies and aphorisms on the same theme and by devoting particular attention to the contexts of the often cryptic aphorisms" can we hope to arrive at what the Besht meant to convey. However, Foxbrunner continues, he really trusts Rabbi Jacob Joseph since "he took pains to transmit the directly heard teachings as faithfully and with as little editorializing as possible. These works therefore comprise the largest and most reliable repository of the Besht's authentic teachings."[117] If we are ever to recover a fuller and more reliable understanding of the Baal Shem's vision, I believe Foxbrunner's suggested methodology will have to be implemented. *All* of the purported teachings of the Besht cited in Hasidic literature on each particular theme that he taught will have to be examined and analyzed in tandem.

WHAT WE KNOW FOR CERTAIN

When I completed Etkes' voluminous book I realized that despite his differences with Rosman, the two scholars actually agreed on most of the major points having to do with the Baal Shem's historical identity. Yet, because Etkes trusted the value of the sources more than Rosman, he was able to say a great deal more about the Besht. Both historians agree that the Besht served the Jewish community in four different ways: as a shamanic healer, a mystic, a teacher, and a community leader.

SHAMAN/MAGICIAN

Both Rosman and Etkes view the Baal Shem Tov as having been a shaman-like folk healer who believed he was able to cure patients using his magical spiritual powers and ecstatic prayer. Also like the shamans, the Besht ventured into the spiritual realm to defend both his community and the entire Jewish people. He struggled to channel divine abundance into the world, and attempted to provide protection against supernatural "accusers and detractors."

Etkes adds that Hasidic tradition makes it clear that in his community the Besht was thought to have remarkable spiritual powers of a prophetic nature, abilities like remote vision, prognostication, hearing decrees from on high, foretelling the future, locating missing persons, and finding stolen property. He was reputed to discover an individual's previous incarnations, and confront supernatural entities face-to-face, dealing with them on an authoritative basis. He was a successful healer who used ecstatic prayer as a healing technique. These practices were probably learned, writes Etkes, during the years that the Besht lived in the Carpathian Mountains and was exposed to the Gentile miracle workers practicing there.

The Besht held himself in high esteem as a Baal shem, and enjoyed reminding people of these powers. Nonetheless, despite such personal pride in his abilities, the Besht's caring for his people is fully evident in the stories that describe his shamanic work.

MYSTIC

Both Rosman and Etkes consider the Besht to have been one of the great mystics of his generation, a master of the unseen and unexplained. Etkes makes the point that the Besht's mystical experience—known as *devekut* in Hebrew—was at the core of his spiritual world. Etkes asserts that for the Besht, the purpose of prayer was the "delight" it produced, i.e., the mystical ecstasy, which the master compared to sexual intercourse. The master understood his experience as direct communion with the Godhead. During these encounters the Besht achieved a complete break with all that surrounded him. The external world ceased to exist. Consciousness of the "I" as a distinct entity was lost.

Etkes writes that the Besht was inspired by his mystical experiences to adopt the notion of divine immanence—that the Godhead saturates all worlds equally. The realization of God's continuous presence led him to abandon asceticism and self-mortification, and to deny the existence of evil as a separate demonic entity.

For the Baal Shem Tov, Etkes states, it was joy that would lift the soul to the divine realms. And it is through bodily pleasures that the soul is set free of its chains and allowed to rise to the heights of the Upper Worlds. The Besht taught that the way people conducted their earthly lives should be seen as divine worship. He urged his disciples to see each and every mundane act as an opportunity for practicing holiness.

TEACHER

Like Etkes, Rosman views the Baal Shem as having been a religious model and guide as well as a teacher of moral instruction, spiritual concentration, divine communion, and magical skills. He was also a wisdom teacher and served God not only through discourses with the members of his circle, but through telling stories and engaging in conversation with common people. He taught by example and through object lessons. And he believed his teachings held the kind of redemptive potential that those who practiced them might eventually bring about the messianic era.

Etkes maintains that the Besht did not teach his approach to achieving mystical union to the broad public. Rather, he revealed his discoveries only to his circle of disciples and colleagues. These men had all been members of the older ascetically-oriented Hasidic groups that existed before the Besht came onto the scene, and consequently his message was meant for the spiritual elite. It was out of this circle that seeds sown by the Besht would flower creating the mass movement of Hasidism.

To me it appears that the Baal Shem's focus on his role as spiritual teacher shows his concern for those in his circle, for he wished to enable his students to evolve spiritually. They, in turn, would be able to become greater spiritual leaders in their own communities. Two of these disciples, Jacob Joseph of Polonoyye and Dov Baer, the Maggid of Medziritich, laid the foundations for the Hasidic movement.

Rosman and Etkes passionately disagree with regard to the possibility of articulating the Besht's intellectual legacy. Rosman takes the position that the Besht's teachings were unwritten and inchoate, inspiring profound religious creativity by the Besht's disciples in their master's name. Etkes believes that it is indeed possible to reconstruct the Baal Shem's fundamental worldview, a groundbreaking spiritual philosophy that effected his disciples as well as all the Hasidic teachers who were to come in his wake.

COMMUNITY LEADER

Both scholars highlight the Baal Shem Tov's deep concern for the Jewish people. Rosman writes that the Besht was well known, and that he was a paternal figure to his family and everyone connected with him. He was involved with robbers, noblemen, priests, sinners, and even satanic accusers. Rosman maintains that as a community leader, the Besht felt he carried the burden of responsibility for the cosmic fate of his people, believing he had an important role in bringing redemption through his prayers, unification practices, and ability to return the holy sparks dispersed throughout the physical world back to their divine source. He made use of his shamanic abilities in attempts to counter antisemitic attacks and epidemics, and believed that he offered collective security for the Jewish people as a whole and not just for individuals.

Etkes' concurs that the Besht identified personally with the sufferings of his people. While he did not view himself as the leader of a new Hasidic movement, he did believe he bore responsibility for the welfare of all Jews. Etkes accepts as authentic the Besht's statements that he made ascents of soul into the upper worlds on behalf of the people during public prayer. The Baal Shem testified that during these ascents he confronted the demonic, and contested evil decrees imposed on the people, and that his work was aided by the messiah. He also believed he could assist the souls of sinners who were seeking salvation, and could guide lost prayers to their ultimate destination. But, Etkes states, he did not see himself as a messianic figure; his mission was oriented toward a world in which redemption has not yet occurred.

Etkes writes that the Baal Shem was a popular tzaddik who uncovered the exceptional spiritual qualities of common people. He had great empathy for people, tolerance and forgiveness for their failings, and sensitivity toward their sufferings. He also had forbearance toward people driven to sin by their personal misfortunes. And he appreciated simple Jews who worshipped their Creator with pure devotion.

THE LITTLE FLUTE

All of this leads me to ponder, how can a historian ascertain whether a particular story in *In Praise of the Baal Shem Tov* ever in fact occurred?

Etkes writes about one of my favorite tales in the book in order to show how a story's authenticity can be determined:

> There was a villager who year after year prayed in the Baal Shem's synagogue on the High Holy Days. Now this man had a son who was so simple-minded that he could not grasp the shapes of the Hebrew letters in the prayer book, and had no idea at all what the words meant. Because of his son's disability, the villager never brought him to Mezhibozh for the High Holy Days. But when the boy turned thirteen, his father had to take him with him for otherwise the boy might eat on the fast day.
>
> Now this boy had a little flute that he always played when he sat in the fields herding the sheep and calves. And when he and his father travelled to town for Yom Kippur services, he took the flute with him. Throughout the services the boy was quiet; it seemed as if he could not comprehend what was taking place. But during the day, just when the Additional Service began, he said to his father: "Daddy, I have my flute with me and I want to play it." The father was quite bothered and told the boy not to play the instrument.
>
> Hours later, when the Afternoon Service began, the boy once said to his father, "Daddy, please let me play my flute." The father became quite angry. "Where did you put it?" he asked. "It's in my pocket," answered the boy. Then the father put his hand over the boy's pocket so his son would not be able to take the flute out.
>
> The Closing Service began shortly before sunset, and the earnestness of the worshippers was apparent. The boy suddenly pushed his father's hand away from his pocket, pulled out the flute, and blew an earsplitting note. The entire congregation was terrified, but the Besht, unperturbed, continued to chant the liturgy, now more rapidly and effortlessly than usual.
>
> Later the Baal Shem said, "Through the sound of his

flute this boy was able to elevate all the prayers that were chanted in the synagogue today, and he made it easy for me. He did not know how to pray, but he heard our prayers throughout the day and our davening kindled a fire within him, and the flames of his longing burned higher and higher until his soul nearly expired. Because of the strength of his longing he blew on his flute with the entire strength of his soul, and that blast came from the core of his heart without any distraction, and was totally dedicated to the blessed One. And because the Almighty looks into the heart all the prayers that we uttered today were lifted up to God."[118]

Quite a tale, but, comments Etkes, "At first reading the story provokes disbelief for this story...has been graced by an editing with a discernably fictional component. The narrator develops and 'stretches' the plot so as to intensify the element of drama." However, the basic story is not necessarily a fiction, writes Etkes, for there is a possibility that it contains a nucleus of truth. "More than anything, what strikes me about the story as plausible and consistent with what we know about the Besht is its conclusion: that the pure intentions of this boy who did not know how to pray made a great impression in the Upper Worlds...there is a recognition here of the superiority of innocent prayer-intentions, even when these are unconnected with any formal knowledge."[119]

Does the story also embody another novel virtue that Hasidic tradition attributes to the Besht: the idealization of common Jews, even those who are ignorant of Jewish tradition? Etkes doesn't believe that this is an aim of the story, but I am not so sure. I believe that this virtue, which Hasidism traces back to the Besht, may also be one of the values being emphasized in the tale.

THE CROWN OF A GOOD NAME

One of the most intriguing aspects of Etkes' reconstruction appears in his chapter on the Baal Shem Tov as a mystic, where he shows how the master's mystical experience gave rise to key aspects of his religious thought—divine immanence, the nature and purpose of evil, worship through corporeality, the elevation of stray thoughts, and the dialectics of rises and falls in the worshipper's consciousness. And, he writes, these features of the Besht's understanding of the devotional life are crucial to an understanding of the foundations of Hasidism as a movement.

Historians have sought knowledge of the Baal Shem's life and accomplishments in the Jewish world of eighteenth-century Poland, and because of that they have focused on what could be learned from *In Praise of the Baal Shem Tov.* But, in fact, the Besht's inner life was equally and possibly even more important than his outer life, especially for those of us who see the master's spiritual experience and religious thought as essential for the renewal of Judaism in our own time. This information can only be fathomed through a sustained study of the entire oeuvre of his teachings, as Moshe Idel has emphasized. I have attempted such an endeavor in this book, but I know that I've only scratched the surface. Hopefully, future research will reveal a great deal more.

The Baal Shem Tov wrote very little. His ideas and practices have come down to us in fragments that were remembered and recorded by members of his circle. To make sense of the Besht's worldview one needs to view his utterances as pieces of a gigantic puzzle. Often the different passages seem like they don't fit together; with persistence and patience, however, the student can assemble a wholistic and visionary worldview that attempts to make sense of an often seemingly senseless existence. And the Besht continually reveals not only spiritual meaning, but makes palpable the mystery interpenetrating it all.

BETWEEN ECSTASY AND MAGIC

There are those who rank Moshe Idel as the true successor of Gershom Scholem. As a historian, he has endeavored to understand the ways Jewish mysticism evolved through time. He has also made use of the phenomenological method to illuminate how Jewish mystics understood and articulated their spiritual experience. *Hasidism: Between Ecstasy and Magic,* Idel's primary work on Hasidism, was published in English in 1995. Much of what he is concerned about in this rich and intricate book is relevant to our search for the historical Besht. He maintains that even though the Baal Shem cannot be considered the founder of Hasidism, as the most important forerunner of the movement he was likely the most influential figure in all of Jewish mysticism.

The Besht, Idel writes, was described repeatedly by his students as having enjoyed a variety of mystical experiences, and yet there was a single form of mysticism cultivated in the circle of his disciples—ecstasy. We have a letter composed by the Baal Shem in which he testifies that during his mystical flights, he would ascend to spiritual heights where he would unite with the Divine. But it's clear from his description of these experiences that he did not undertake such celestial journeys for his own benefit alone. Like other Jewish mystics before him, the Besht also engaged in magical practices during these experiences in order to channel *shefah*—divine energy—downward into the physical world for the benefit of his community and for the entire Jewish people. Idel calls the Baal Shem's experiential model "the Mystical-Magical Model," and it would become the prototype of the tzaddikim throughout the history of Hasidism.

What were the sources that the Baal Shem employed in developing this new model of the tzaddik? Idel shows that the Besht was intimately acquainted with the writings of two remarkable medieval Jewish mystics, R. Abraham Abulafia and R. Moses Cordovero. Abulafia was a twelfth century ecstatic kabbalist, and Cordovero was one of the leading kabbalists of the sixteenth century. The Besht drew from their visions and practices, developing his unique approach to both mystical experience and to elevating the Jewish community in Poland and the Jewish people as a whole.

In 2020, twenty-five years after the publication of *Hasidism: Between Ecstasy and Magic,* Idel published a second book devoted to the Baal Shem Tov. The primary aim of *Vocal Rites and Broken Theologies* has to do with describing and explaining the character of the ecstatic spiritual practices of the Besht and how they were put into practice. Together with this analysis, Idel offers important comments on the Baal Shem's body of teachings that illuminate the aim of this chapter, the quest for the historic Besht.

Like Immanuel Etkes, Arthur Green, and most of the other scholars of Hasidism, Idel accepts the authenticity of the citations of the master found in the disciples' books. He's even willing to recognize the validity of statements that don't seem characteristic of the Besht if he is able to find these same views attributed to the Baal Shem in other parallel sources. Idel recognizes that many of his teachings contradict one another, but he accounts for this by theorizing that during the thirty years of his teaching the Baal Shem evolved spiritually, and because of this he changed his mind on a number of ideas.

Throughout *Vocal Rites and Broken Theologies* Idel characterizes the Besht's thought as more conceptually complex than previous investigators have made it out to be. He takes other scholars to task for providing what he calls impressionistic, selective, and simplistic accounts of the master's message. In his view, the Besht did not have a single simple message, such as immanentism. He also makes it clear that the Besht had a great deal to say about a host of different themes, only a few of which have been addressed by scholars. Finally, Idel makes the point that the Baal Shem selectively drew many of his own ideas from a variety of different traditional sources. This is what he means by the term "broken theologies," i.e., the Besht's willingness to appropriate particular elements from different past systems of Jewish religious thought without needing to adopt the entire framework of any previous mystical thinker.

Idel believes that in order to understand the Baal Shem we need to understand that the teachings cited in the disciples' books come from three successive periods of his life, and that each of these phases was characterized by a distinct spiritual model. Even as he elucidates these models, however, he is willing to admit that what he is offering is impressionistic and tentative.

1. The first period of the Besht's life as a seeker was characterized by an inner struggle to reach a more sublime experience of the Divine. Presumably, it was during this early phase that he was still an adherent of the asceticism that characterized the Lurianic form of Kabbalah which so dominated the lives of Eastern European Jews in the early eighteenth century.

2. Idel identifies the second period of the Besht's life with what he calls "the Harmonic model." During this phase he was experimenting with an approach to the practice of ecstatic worship

that he adapted from the writings of R. Abraham Abulafia—the vocal use of the Hebrew letters and words found in the Torah and the traditional liturgy which he used as the means to elevate his soul toward the Divine. It was through this kind of experiential process that the Besht came to recognize that the letters and words of the ancient tradition actually contained divine power. And because of the rapturous effect of this practice, he came to believe that it had the magical power to bring about harmony in the external world. Thus, he felt he could draw down the divine power into his own life and channel it into the Jewish community that he was serving. This, Idel believes, was the beginning of the Besht's turn to immanentalism, but he did not yet believe that the Divine was immanent in the entire world—only in the Hebrew letters and words.

3. Idel calls the third period, which came toward the end of the Besht's life, "the Noetic" or "Acosmic" model." The noetic quality of a mystical experience refers to the sense of revelation. Acosmism denies the reality of the physical universe, and affirms that only the Divine is real. It was at this time, influenced by the writings of Moses Cordovero, that the master came to recognize and experience the Divinity of everything. This included the Baal Shem's recognition that God can be found in every form of movement, and even in alien thoughts, evil, and sin. And it was the Besht's recognition of divine immanence in everything that took him even deeper into the great mystery, as Idel writes: "The Besht, presumably one of the greatest of the known magicians in Jewish culture, describes, during what I conceive to be the last phase of his religious career as part of his noetic model, God as the great illusionist, by creating the world by means of an illusion."[120] Idel identifies this form of illusion with the Hindu notion of maya.

Why was it that the Baal Shem shifted from one type of model to another? Idel writes that these changes had to do with the relevance of each approach for an intensified experience of worship. He adds that even though the Besht espoused different models at different times of his life, the newer models never completely replaced what had come before. And Idel insists that if we wish to really understand the evolution of the Baal Shem we must not simplify his worldview by focusing exclusively on the third model, as virtually all other scholars of Hasidism have done.

I believe that Moshe Idel's rigorous thinking represents a major contribution to an understanding of the spiritual development of the Baal Shem Tov. As I read and re-read *Vocal Rites and Broken Theologies,* I found myself cheering, for over many years of studying the Besht's teachings I had come to similar conclusions. I hadn't considered the possibility that the Baal Shem's teachings might represent distinct periods of his spiritual development, but I was aware that the disciple's records attributed different views of the Besht, and had a sense that the master changed his mind on a variety of concerns. Idel gave me language and evidence to make more sense of this. On the other hand, I couldn't agree completely with everything he claimed. Idel minimizes the Besht's concern with kabbalistic concepts like the sefirot and the unification of the Shekhinah and the blessed Holy One, which I found to be central to the master's psychospiritual perspective.

CHAPTER ELEVEN

A REMARKABLE RESEMBLANCE

In both of Idel's books, he refers to the influence exerted on Hasidism by Muslim mysticism: He asserts that "Abulafia's Kabbalah interacted with Sufi mysticism," and that "Hasidism is a unique synthesis of primordial themes and concepts, traditions as old and primal as those of the paleolithic age and as late and refined as those of the Renaissance, and early modern religiosity."[121] I knew that Reb Zalman had been initiated into Sufism and had become ordained as spiritual leader in that tradition. So I decided I needed to learn about Sufism; perhaps such study would illuminate the path of the Baal Shem Tov.

SUFISM AND HASIDISM

One of the first books I read was Mary Blye Howe's memoir about her initiation into Sufism. She describes dancing with God under a huge canopy on a ranch in the Texas hill country. "It's nearing midnight and we've just finished a ritual called *zihr* (also known as *dhikr*)—an important Sufi ritual in which one *remembers* God through meditational chant and movement. In *zikr* we repeat certain Divine Names of God, representing attributes of God such as mercy and kindness, so that our hearts and lives may become more saturated with the characteristics of God.... My heart feels baptized in God's presence.... As I sit trying to talk myself out of participating, I suddenly find myself drawn into the vortex. With my right hand symbolically raised towards heaven and the palm of my left hand facing the earth—representing the intertwining of the two worlds—I begin to whirl."[122]

As I read Howe's description of dhikr, I recalled another memoir by Jiri Langer, a nineteen-year-old secular youth from Prague, who made a trek to the town of Belz in Ukraine, to experience Hasidic life first-hand. This is how he begins his description of the *davening* (worship) on Friday night as the Hasidim inaugurate the Sabbath: "Dusk is already well advanced when the rabbi enters the synagogue. The crowd quickly divides, to let him pass.... With long rapid strides he makes straight for the *bimah,* or reading desk, and the strange Chassidic service begins. *'O give thanks unto the Lord, for He is good; for His mercy endureth for ever.'* It is as though an electric shock has suddenly entered those present. The crowd which till now has been completely quiet, almost cowed, suddenly bursts forth in a wild shout. None stays in his place. The tall black figures run hither and thither round the synagogue, flashing past the lights of the Sabbath candles. Gesticulating wildly, and throwing their whole bodies about, they shout out the words of the Psalm. They knock into each other unconcernedly, for all their cares have been cast aside; everything has ceased to exist for them. They are seized by an indescribable ecstasy."[123]

This is what I also saw on a number of occasions during visits to various Hasidic enclaves in Brooklyn and in Jerusalem in the 1960s. The enthusiasm and ecstasy aroused by devotional singing and dancing in these two different religious communities seems to have called forth remarkably similar inner emotional and spiritual responses in their members. But was Moshe Idel correct? Did this resemblance actually stem from a historic contact or contacts?

In 2013 I was visiting a friend on the East Coast who was deeply interested in Hasidism. While we were conversing in his living room, I picked up a rather interesting looking book lying on his coffee table. It was titled *Shalom/Salaam: A Story of a Mystical Fraternity,* having to do with the historic connections between Islamic and Jewish mysticism. I wanted to ask my friend what he thought of the book, but because the intense conversation in the room was focused on other matters, I never inquired. Nonetheless, when I returned to California, I ordered a copy.

The book's author, Thomas Block, is not a scholar, but an artist and autodidact. *Shalom/Salaam* represents his view of the historic interactions between the two mystical traditions. Block breaks the contemporary myth that Jews and Muslims have always been enemies, revealing the ways Judaism affected the origins, teachings, and practices of Islam. Even more important to the author, however, are the ways Jews under Muslim rule during the earlier centuries of Islam were affected by the regenerative forces of their host religion. To make this point he cites the words of Abraham Halkin, a historian with whom I studied medieval Jewish history at Jewish Theological Seminary: "The vocabulary of

Islamic faith finds its way into Jewish books; the Koran becomes a proof text. The Arabs' practice of citing poetry in their works is taken over by the Jews. Jewish writings teem with sentences from the works of scientists, philosophers and theologians. Indeed, Arabic literature, native and imported, becomes the general background of all that the Jews write."[124]

Shalom/Salaam contains chapters devoted to the Jewish Sufis of medieval Egypt and the Sufi influence on Spanish Jews. But it is the chapters focused on Jewish mysticism that are relevant to the author's ideas regarding ways that Muslim mysticism would affect the Baal Shem Tov and Hasidism. Block cites Idel, who writes candidly about Sufi influence on Hasidism: "It is probable that the main, and perhaps single channel of information available to Jewish medieval authors was Muslim culture.... In general the magical and mystical models [of Hasidism] owe much to the vigorous Muslim culture that existed between the 10th and 14th centuries.... [T]hese models, significantly affected by Muslim culture, were transmitted to Jews in Europe through various channels and were formative in the emergence of Hasidism."[125]

Readers will recall that Moshe Idel ascertained that the twelfth century kabbalist, Abraham Abulafia, was a powerful influence on the Baal Shem's mystical practice. Block goes further than Idel, making the case that Abulafia was heavily influenced by Sufi spirituality. He cites Professor Harvey Hames: "It is worth considering a passage contained in the work of a disciple of Abulafia's which expressly mentions Sufi practices, the *dhikr*, or enunciation of the Divine names, which is a central part of Sufi discipline . . .[after a discussion of *dhikr*, the student] relates his own personal experience with his teacher, Abulafia, who teaches him to combine letters."[126]

Block writes that the practices and ideas that Abulafia published in his meditation handbooks affected many kabbalists in subsequent centuries, including Moses Cordovero, who we learned had a powerful influence on the Baal Shem. These notions included ideas drawn from Sufism such as the essence of God's power entering into the very soul of the kabbalist, and the channeling of that power from above into the world. Block makes the point that the idea of the Hasidic tzaddik's ability to draw down divine power into the physical world is similar to the Sufi notion, attributing such power to the Sufi sheikh.

In his chapter on Sufism and Hasidism, Block admits that "the Sufi and Islamic influence on 18th-century European Jewry is perhaps the most controversial aspect of this study—and one that has been overlooked by many 20th-century academicians."[127] He admits that there could not have been any direct Sufi influence on Hasidism because the Jewish movement took place in Eastern Europe. However, Block maintains that Sufi ideas and values came into Hasidism indirectly via the Kabbalah. These notions include the following:

THE PURPOSE OF CREATION

- According to both streams of thought, God created humans because he needed a creation other than himself who could perceive his existence. Therefore, human love of God represents an act of self-knowledge for God.

- In Kabbalah, creation is linked to the letters of the Hebrew language, which God used to speak the world into existence. Block quotes the Besht: "Even now the entire life of creation and all existence springs from the holy letters that are God's word standing always in heaven to give them life." He then states that this notion derives from the Islamic Science of the Letters (*Ilm al-Huruf*) which posited the same idea in relation to the Arabic language.

THE CENTRALITY OF ECSTATIC WORSHIP

- Citing Idel, Block writes that this Divine power is called *Ruhaniyut.* "It is important to point out the profound influence of the Islamic concept of *ruhaniyut* on Jewish mysticism.... Union with the Divine was portrayed as a spiritual force (Hebrew: *Ruhaniyt*) that descends upon the mystic during *devequt*. This way of understanding unitive experience is widespread in Jewish mysticism, though predominant in Hasidism."[128]

- Hasidism replaced sacred study with worship as the highest form of spiritual practice. Once again, he quotes Moshe Idel: "Abulafia's writings constituted the beginning of the process of absorption of the Sufi outlook within Kabblah.... The influence of the views sketched above may be traced through the writings of the Hasidic mystics."[129]

- In Hasidism the seeker attempts to empty himself of all impurities such as personal ego and desire, in preparation of receiving the divine flow of power. In Hasidic terminology this is called annihilation of the self (*bittul ha'yesh*), while in Sufism it is called *fana*. God "becomes the ear with which he sees, the hand with which he grasps, and the foot with which he walks."[130]

- Early Hasidic practice revealed that union with the Divine (*devekut*) obliterates the distance between God and human beings. This, writes Block, is also the main goal of Sufism.

- Any personal ego retained during worship comes between the seeker and union with the Divine. According to Sufism, the adept needs to cultivate equanimity, *Hishtawwut,* in Arabic. Block cites the Baal Shem Tov as having taught that equanimity (*hishtawwut,* in Hebrew) means that the seeker pays no attention whether people praise or despise him, and does not consider at all the affairs of the world.

- Both traditions emphasize the notion that earthly love and beauty can be the doorway to divine love.

SPIRITUAL LEADERSHIP

- Both streams of thought posit the notion of the perfect person. In Sufism, he is called the *sheikh;* in Hasidism the tzaddik. Both Sufism and Hasidism teach that the more that mystical awareness unfolds in the seeker, the more that God is reflected in the seeker's soul.

- The true spiritual leader (sheikh/tzaddik) is a mystic who loses himself in God and then returns to act as an emissary, teacher, intercessor, and spiritual director for his disciples. The spiritual leader also disseminates divine power through his acts in society.

- Both the sheikh and the tzaddik get their authority from their forerunners, and operate as the heads of a particular spiritual school. The organization of novices in both traditions forms around the spiritual leader whom they venerate. By the third generation after their founding, mystical lineages began to form in both traditions, sometimes following a hereditary line.

Block concludes his chapter on Hasidism with the words: "It is too far a stretch to assert that Hasidism is little more than re-worked Islamic mysticism, packaged in ancient Jewish lore and practiced by Jews from the 18th century through today. However, the influence of Sufism on the development of much post-10th century Jewish thought cannot be denied, and Islamic inspirations run deeply through Hasidic practice as well."[131] I was grateful for his prodigious effort in uncovering so many parallels between these two mystic streams.

Nonetheless, I was left with questions about these theories because Block provides no examples of actual contact between Islamic and Jewish mystics. I also wondered if the kabbalists had any influence on Muslim mysticism. Perhaps in his great excitement over Sufi influence on Jewish mysticism, Block distorted the historical picture. And since he didn't offer any conclusive proof for his theory, I would have been happier if he'd been more cautious with his claims. It also occurred to me that the similarities between the two traditions may have come about, in part, because of the zeitgeist of the times. And the remarkable similarities could have come from extensive contact, whether there was evidence for this or not. How was I to judge? I had no real background in this area of medieval history. I shelved *Shalom/Salaam* with my other Baal Shem related volumes, where it remained for many years.

Working on this chapter, however, re-awoke my curiosity about the relationship between Sufism and Hasidism, and I re-read Block's book. One of the authorities that Block cited was Paul Fenton, a professor of Jewish studies at the Sorbonne in Paris. I googled Fenton's name and saw that he's written a number of academic papers on subjects linking Kabbalah and Sufism. One is an article for the *Cambridge Companion to Medieval Jewish Philosophy.* Fenton writes that "in the broad lines of their respective historical evolutions, Jewish and Islamic esotericism betray a remarkable resemblance. Both went through formative periods characterized by ecstatic experiences and followed by periods of consolidation in which mystical tendencies were tempered by legalism and philosophy. Both underwent profound transformations and were entirely renewed in the late Middle Ages by novel cosmological and speculative systems, sometimes imbued with 'prophetic' aspirations, and both finally developed into institutionalized brotherhoods."[132]

Then Fenton comments, "Though the two tendencies appear to have developed quite independently, there have been significant points of intersection between them." He also states that "From a strictly chronological point of view, it was Judaism that initially influenced Sufism in its formative period in Baghdad. Surprisingly, while scholars have recognized the influence of Neoplatonism and Christian pietism on the evolution of Muslim asceticism at this time, they have failed to point out the profound mark imprinted on Sufism by the ambient Jewish milieu." And "it is interesting to speculate to what extent Sufi ideas percolated into Podolia and influenced the nascent Hasidic movement. The veneration of the zaddiq, visiting the tombs of saints, the importance of music and dance as forms of worship provide very striking and thought-provoking analogies to the Sufi model." And so while Fenton certainly believes in the existence of Sufi influence on Jewish mysticism, he is quite a bit more guarded in his assertions than Block.

I have no difficulty with Block suggesting his conjecture as a possibility. I engage in such speculation myself. But given the fact there are no actual records of Sufis and kabbalists meeting, it would have been better to offer his theory as a possibility, even a strong possibility, rather than writing about it as if it were an attested reality. Whether or not there was direct contact between Sufis and kabbalists, what stands out are the remarkable parallels between the two traditions, especially with Hasidism. I believe that many or even most of these features may have been introduced into Polish Jewish spirituality by the Baal Shem Tov himself, and we will be exploring this possibility in the remainder of the book.[133]

CONSTRUCTING HISTORY

Rachel Elior is professor of Jewish philosophy and Jewish mystical thought at Hebrew University in Jerusalem. Two of her many perceptive books were extremely valuable in my quest for the historic Baal Shem Tov—*The Mystical Origins of Hasidism,* and *Jewish Mysticism: The Infinite Expression of Freedom.* In the first of these, Elior offers her theories about the identity and contributions of Israel Baal Shem Tov to Jewish spirituality. The last chapter of *The Mystical Origins of Hasidism* is titled, "Scholarship on Hasidism: Changing Perspectives," and offers a broad sense of how scholars in the modern era have understood the world of the Baal Shem and the subsequent development of Hasidism. Elior writes that "since the 1970s the foundations of scholarship on Hasidism have been re-examined. New approaches have been formulated, and there has been critical evaluation of what had already been achieved.... In recent years, a new generation of scholars has contributed to a broader understanding and a more nuanced perception of Hasidic spirituality and Hasidic scholarship."[134]

Elior also made me aware of historian Haydn White's radical critique of all attempts at reconstructing history, which made perfect sense. White claimed that there is no way that historians can hope to present the facts as they really happened. Any written account of the past can only offer a selection of details drawn from the massive totality of spiritual, material, cultural, and social realities of particular times and places that the historian is attempting to understand. Because of this, White asserts, there is no such thing as history per se, there is only history as *story*, as *narrative*, constructed by the historian. And every historical narrative is the narrative of the particular historian who has constructed it.

What did White mean by the assertion that there is no history per se, but only historical narrative? While the narratives that historians construct do proceed from empirically validated facts or events, they necessarily require the scholar to employ imaginative steps in order to place those facts or events into a coherent narrative. White writes that instead of revealing the true essence of past reality, historical narrative imposes a mythic structure, devised by the historian, on the events it purports to describe. Comparable to good narratives, historical works carry the reader smoothly but directly to the conclusion that the author has in mind. Historical narratives explain why events happened, but are "overlaid by the assumptions held by the historian about the forces influencing the nature of causality." White's postmodernist concept of history as a literary genre calls into question the claims of truth and objectivity in all historical reconstruction.

In *The Mystical Origins of Hasidism*, Elior writes the following about Hayden White's thesis: "History is never divorced from story, and any story is only one voice among others vying to represent reality.... [T]he concept of 'history' that speaks in a single hegemonic voice has been replaced by the notion of rival voices recounting the past from a multi-tude of viewpoints, all of which carry merely relative weight."[135] White's thesis would explain the diverse opinions by the many Gospel scholars who have portrayed Jesus in many different ways—and also histori-ans like Rosman and Etkes regarding the Baal Shem. And it would also account for my own developing image of the master, and why it was so different from other historical approaches.

Deeply immersed in the world of the Baal Shem Tov, I naturally developed numerous intuitive suppositions about the master's life and thought for which there was no actual historical evidence. My knowl-edge of the lives of shamans, mystics, and the founders of religious move-ments from other religious traditions, however, offered me possible clues as I formulated my own speculations. When these conjectures first began to surface in my mind, I was somewhat uneasy about including them into my emerging image. Because of this I decided to study what natural and social scientists have stated about human intuition and imagination, and became convinced of the value of White's understanding of historic reconstruction.[136]

IMAGINATION VERSUS REASON

Academic approaches to a subject like the Baal Shem Tov often become all-consuming. My thoughts go back to Elie Wiesel's somewhat antag-onistic views about historical inquiry. One doesn't have to agree com-pletely in order to appreciate his perspective. Wiesel writes beautifully about what he learned from his grandfather: "My very first Hasidic tales I heard from him. He made me enter the universe of the Baal Shem and his disciples, where facts became subservient to imagination and beauty. What difference did it make that events and chronological dates no lon-ger matched? I surely didn't care. What mattered to me was not that two and two are four, but that God is one. Better still: that man and God are one. I can still hear my grandfather's voice: 'There will, of course, always be someone to tell you that a certain tale cannot, could not, be objec-tively true. That is of no importance; an objective Hasid is not a Hasid.'

"He was right. The Baal Shem's call was a call to subjectivity, to pas-sionate involvement; the tales he told and those told about him appeal to the imagination rather than reason. They try to prove that man is more than he appears to be and that he is capable of giving more than he appears to possess. To dissect them, therefore, is to diminish them. To judge them is to detach oneself and taint their candor—in so doing, one loses more than one could gain."[137]

I am grateful for the work of Rosman, Etkes, and Idel, who provided me with a great deal of information and understanding about the life and achievements of the founder of Hasidism. Still, there have been moments when I've wondered whether such academic inquiry is a kind of substitute, or otherwise stands in the way of a direct embrace of spiritual realities the Baal Shem Tov stood for. Elie Wiesel's experience and perspective are instructive. Still, there's no doubt in my mind that scholarly approaches to the Besht and Hasidism have succeeded in cutting through what so frequently appears to be legendary camouflage, uncovering significant truths that would otherwise remain hidden. And here, too, in these sober investigations, the Baal Shem's maxim, taken from the Zohar, must apply: "There is no place devoid of the Divine."

CHAPTER TWELVE

WHAT THE ARCHIVES REVEAL

For a few years in the late 1970s I lived in a communal house in Berkeley within walking distance of the University of California. Telegraph Avenue, the main thoroughfare, led to the entrance of the university, and it was usually packed with students on the go. Sidewalks were cluttered with longhaired vendors selling inexpensive jewelry, marijuana paraphernalia, tie-dyed tee shirts, multi-colored knitted berets, candles, and incense. Every once in a while, a group of Hari Krishnas, dressed in exotic clothing, would saunter down the street, chanting and drumming.

I frequented the bookshops on Telegraph Avenue—Shambala, Cody's, Moe's, Shakespeare, Logos—looking for anything relevant to my search. Salamo Birnbaum's little 1930s collection of texts, *The Life and Sayings of the Baal Shem Tov* was an absolute treasure. Louis Newman's *The Hasidic Anthology* arranged an array of teachings alphabetically, so I could find what the Besht had said on particular subjects and themes. Martin Buber's *The Legend of the Baal Shem Tov,* and his other books on Hasidism—*Tales of the Hasidim, The Origin and Meaning of Hasidim,* and *Hasidism and Modern Man* opened a world to me. I gradually built a small library of current and out-of-print volumes on early Hasidism and the Besht. I also had my eyes open for works having to do with spiritual experience, psychology of religion, and comparative mysticism—anything that might illumine my possible understanding of the Besht's life and journey.

My favorite bookshop was Shambala, which carried all the latest books from the world's wisdom traditions. The sixties had given birth to a tremendous interest in Eastern spirituality and mysticism, and Shambala carried translations of classical texts and contemporary interpretations of Asian wisdom. I also found volumes devoted to world spirituality and religious psychology. There were a few books on meditation; many more would be published in the next decades.

The Jewish section of Shambala was small, for at that time there were relatively few volumes dealing with Jewish spirituality. The spate of Jewish spiritual publishing would not begin in earnest until the 1990s. Once in a while, though, a new volume would appear on the shelf— books by Herbert Weiner, Lawrence Kushner, Zalman Schachter, or Aryeh Kaplan. After my tour of the bookshops, I would take a small table at the noisy Mediterraneum Coffee House, where Allen Ginsberg and the Beat writers had hung out. Sipping my latte, I would page through books I'd just purchased.

There were days when I would walk through Sather Gate, the entrance to the university, and spend hours in the dark stacks in the Doe Library or the Boalt Law School Library (which housed a terrific collection of Judaica), or walk over to the Graduate Theological Union library, just north of the university campus, which also had a good Judaica section. After completing my research, I'd visit the impressive bookshop located in the same building. It was there I discovered books about Christian mystics from different eras, as well as contemporary works on cultivating the spiritual life. If I became aware of an academic article or an out-of-print book, I'd order it through interlibrary loan at the Berkeley Public Library.

THE GLORIOUS PRESENCE

By the late seventies, I had embraced the Baal Shem Tov as my most important spiritual teacher, and felt I knew enough about him to compose a small book on his life and teachings. This simple seventy-five-page introduction to his life, personality, and worldview focused attention on insights that spoke to my heart and mind in a direct and deep way. *The Glorious Presence* was typed on my old Smith-Corona portable typewriter.

Perusing that manuscript some thirty-five years later, I find my early attempt at portraying the Besht and his spiritual message riddled with over-simplifications and errors. The writing also reveals that my knowledge of the history of the period was limited. Nonetheless, in my new-found enthusiasm I was attempting to express something genuinely important. As I re-read the manuscript, I find a statement regarding the Besht's relevancy for spiritual seekers today that still speaks in a powerful way. I wrote that members of my generation had grown up in a secular society and found its materialism and individualism deficient:

The transcendental dimension is missing from the promise of the American Dream. Because of this we have sought the Spirit through chemicals, meditation, yoga, therapy, Eastern religion. And some of us are searching for it in the Jewish tradition we never really knew when we were young. But the problem of integration is alive for us: How to be a human being and a Jew at the same time? We want to affirm our links with the Jewish people and its dreams—but we are wary of its parochialism and triumphalism, for we carry with us a universal vision of a world where all people are sisters and brothers, and truth can be found in all wisdom traditions.

We know that Judaism has much to teach us, but we refuse to submit to an authoritarian orthodoxy that would limit our growth as individuals and as human beings. We seek a kind of freedom that goes beyond the definitions of all previous religions and cultures, including Judaism. As we struggle to solve this dilemma, we draw forth some of the latent impulses of our tradition and create a Judaism for a new age.

To be Jews in our time is to have the courage to strike out on our own, to know that the Teacher manifests in each of us and, if we open ourselves, will inspire us to create a Judaism that embodies the broadest and highest levels of spiritual consciousness of which we are capable.

Traditional Judaism begins with Torah, Talmud, commentaries, and a religious lifestyle regulated by a medieval legal code. The new Judaism begins with you and me, with our personal experiences of the spirit, with what I call the Torah of the Heart. From the here and now it moves both forward and backward. Forward to the creation of a world in which Jews and all peoples can live and share and respect one another. Backward to those teachings that resonate with our own personal experiences of the spirit, insights that can help build toward the future we envision.

The teaching of the Baal Shem Tov, spoken and lived out over two hundred and fifty years ago is, to my mind, one of the best places to begin. There is an authenticity here. The words ring with a truth that speaks across time. The message is simple, direct, and personal. The Baal Shem does not ask us to surrender to tradition. He asks us to begin with ourselves, to discover our own potential. He shows us a path through which the symbols and sacred deeds of Jewish tradition can become vehicles for a rebirth into the awareness of the Glory that is always present.

I sent photocopies of *The Glorious Presence* to friends and several scholars of Jewish mysticism whom I knew. Some of the responses were enthusiastic, but most, especially those who knew a great deal about Hasidism, were lukewarm. And a few of the reactions were extremely critical. It was painful for me to admit, but it became clear that my thinking about the Besht was still unripe. I would have to learn a great deal more. Equally important would be the necessity to begin to integrate his teachings and practices into the way in which I live my life.

In my manuscript I had confidently written that the Baal Shem's "message is simple, direct, and personal." But one of the crucial discoveries I made during my long quest was that a large number of his teachings were neither simple, direct, nor personal. He was a complex man, and his ideas are not always readily accessible. He was a traditional, observant Jew who lived in a pre-modern world and his thought patterns— even where they break with previous tradition—were formulated in the language of that world. To comprehend his wisdom, the serious student must have a broad background in classical Judaism, especially in Jewish mysticism. To grasp the relevancy of many of the Besht's most profound insights for contemporary living also requires deep discernment and the ability to translate the ideas of an earlier age into contemporary language.

Furthermore, I learned that the Baal Shem Tov I'd discovered through Heschel might not be the actual Baal Shem of history. Soon after I began my exploration of the stories of his life, I discovered tales that portrayed him acting in repulsive ways. This raised doubts, and I began to wonder whether the Besht could really be my teacher. Yet, the stories also aroused great curiosity. I was going to have to plummet beneath the layers of the legends that both revealed and disguised the Besht.

MARTIN BUBER'S TALES OF THE HASIDIM

I found myself drawn again and again to Buber's collection of Baal Shem anecdotes, so much so that my old paperback copy of the book literally fell apart from use. In his biography of Buber, Maurice Friedman writes: "The most effective single portrait in *The Tales of the Hasidim* is the sixty-five pages devoted to the Baal-Shem. 'Worry and gloom are the roots of all the power of evil,' the Baal-Shem warned. 'Alas, the world is full of enormous lights and mysteries,' he exclaimed, 'and man shuts them from himself with one small hand!' Like Jesus, the Baal-Shem preferred sinners who were humble to scholars and the self-righteous who were proud. The 'service of men in the world to the very hour of their death,' said the Baal-Shem, 'is to struggle with the extraneous and time after time to uplift and fit it into the nature of the Divine Name.' What matters is not mystical exercises (*kavanot*) but the wholehearted turning to God (*kavana*). 'What are all special mystical intentions compared to one really heartfelt grief!'"[138]

Buber explains what it was that made the Baal Shem Tov such a powerful leader. People, he writes, tend to live as if the natural world and the world of the spirit exist entirely separate from one another, but the greatest teachers are those who are able to bring these two realms together, their lives testifying to the unity of existence. The Baal Shem was one such teacher, able to unify within himself the heavenly light of the spirit and the earthly fire of the natural world. Buber believed the Besht affected his students through his own presence, rather than through formal teaching. What was important was the way the master interacted with people, how he demonstrated the way to goodness, how he prayed, how he led people to a living connection with the Divine.

In the next few years, I searched local libraries for anything about the Baal Shem Tov or Hasidism. Before my brother Stuart took a trip to Israel, I asked him to inquire about the Hebrew version of Buber's *Tales*.

He found a copy in a bookstore in Jerusalem. When he returned, I began to read these texts using the English version as a kind of trot. I also discovered a small Hebrew book containing all the Besht's parables, which I photocopied and studied. These were more difficult for me to make out, but I stuck with it making use of a Hebrew-to-English dictionary, and to my delight was able to understand the meaning of most of the texts.

By the late seventies, I felt I had enough grounding that I could begin a second attempt at sharing my ardor for the Baal Shem Tov. I experimented by composing a commentary on an anecdote about the Besht in *Tales of the Hasidim.* Here is Buber's rendition of the story:

OBSTACLES TO BLESSING

> The Baal Shem once asked his disciple Rabbi Meir Margaliot: "Meirly, do you still remember that sabbath, when you were just beginning to study the Pentateuch? The big room in your father's house was full of guests. They had lifted you up on the table and you were reciting what you had learned? Rabbi Meir replied: "Certainly I remember. Suddenly my mother rushed up to me and snatched me down from the table in the middle of what I was saying. My father was annoyed, but she pointed to a man standing at the door. He was dressed in a short sheepskin, such as peasants wear, and he was looking straight at me. Then all understood that she feared the Evil Eye. She was still pointing at the door when the man disappeared."
>
> "It was I," said the Baal Shem. "In such hours a glance can flood the soul with great light. But the fear of men builds walls to keep the light away."[139]

I no longer possess the text of the essay I wrote, but the point I made had to do with the statement made by the Besht at the end of the tale: *"It was I," said the Baal Shem. In such hours a glance can flood the soul with great light. But the fear of men builds walls to keep the light away."* According to a number of legends, he was able to foresee the future, and he knew that this little boy would one day become a renowned tzaddik, which might be translated "an enlightened spiritual leader." Because he knew this, the Besht secretly came to the celebration to bless the child. As usual, he wore the clothing of a Polish peasant. When the boy's mother saw the stranger, she fearfully assumed he was a Gentile sorcerer and had entered their home to curse their son. Given the ever-present antisemitism in Poland, her impulsive action was reasonable, but it was also thoughtless, and it thwarted the Baal Shem's blessing.

In the ancient rabbinic source, "The Ethics of the Fathers," a rabbi by the name of Ben Zoma offers this advice: "Who is wise? One who learns from every person" (4:1). But this insight was not in Meir's mother's mind when she acted on impulse. The lesson of the Baal Shem's story, then, has to do with the necessity of cultivating a mindful openness to what one can learn from those who are remote from one's own experience of the world. Central to the Baal Shem's teaching was the Zohar's proclamation that "There is no place devoid of the divine." This means that God is present everywhere, even in that which is alien, and even in that which one might fear.

My commentary was only two or three pages long; nonetheless, given my earlier discouraging attempt at writing, I wasn't sure whether what I was formulating would convey to others the depth of the Besht's insight. That's when I turned to Richard Stone.

I met Richard in Berkeley when he registered for a class I was co-teaching with my friend, Barry Barkan, through the Lehrhaus Judaica adult education program. The focus of our course was how contemporary writers could work creatively with the symbols, myths, and legends of Jewish tradition. At the beginning of the initial session, Barry and I introduced ourselves and the subject matter, and then we asked each student to share something about why they had chosen this class. When Richard's turn came, he said that he'd grown up in New York City in an assimilated Jewish family and that he knew very little about Judaism. He picked the class because he was looking for ways to expand his poetic horizons and he thought there might be something he could learn from his ancestral traditions.

At the beginning of each session, I would teach something I thought might be spiritually and artistically provocative from Jewish tradition. Then Barry, a skilled and gifted creative writer, would take what I presented and turn it into a writing prompt. After twenty minutes of intense silence the group members would share aloud what they'd written. In class after class the pieces Richard wrote and shared were nothing less than remarkable.

I stayed in contact with Richard over the years, and eight years later it seemed obvious that he was the person who might best evaluate what I'd written. When I called him on the phone—he was living then in Fresno with his partner Avigdar—he protested that he knew nothing about the Baal Shem Tov, or Hasidism for that matter; nevertheless, he agreed. A week after receiving the manuscript he mailed it back with a few suggestions and a handwritten note at the top of the first page: "Maybe you can find something more valuable to do with your discretionary time." I was taken aback by his comment, but still wanted to learn what it was in my writing that he objected to.

In a follow-up phone call, Richard asked who I thought my potential audience would be for this kind of writing. "Spiritual seekers," I replied, "I want to share my love for the Baal Shem Tov with people who are looking for spiritual depth in Judaism."

"Well," he replied, "reading what you sent me, I had imagined that you were attempting to write for scholars. The style is dispassionate, even academic, and the tone is didactic and preachy. And I don't sense your personal presence on the page. If you really want to reach spiritual seekers, you will not only have to learn to write better. You will also need to put yourself and all of your feelings and senses into what you are writing."

I was disappointed by his criticism, but thanked Richard and hung up the phone. And as I thought about the matter over the next few days, I realized there was truth in what he had so honestly said, and I realized that I'd written my little commentary in the same dry, academic style I learned as a rabbinical student. My instructors at JTS had been primarily interested in the historical meaning of Jewish sources, not in their relevancy for modern living. The few essays that had been required of me were written in the academic style expected by my instructors. So even twenty years after ordination, I was still writing that way, attempting to make the case that my insights represented the authentic meaning of the Baal Shem's story.

I called Richard and told him this, asking if he would rewrite my piece so I could get a better idea of what he had in mind. He said he would, but then, after a moment's pause, he asked, "Burt, have you ever feared something that you later found contained a gift or a blessing that actually benefitted you?... I'm asking this because if you recall something like this you could add a paragraph or two to your piece that would make the Baal Shem's story personal for you."

"Let me think about that," I answered. I thanked Richard, said good-bye, and put the phone down.

Then I remembered an occurrence from my past that seemed relevant. I had grown up in a secular family, but during my sophomore year of college I made a leap of faith into traditional Judaism. By the time I entered rabbinical school a few years later I had become a rigidly observant Jew, carrying out the entire range of Jewish religious law in an obsessive manner. One day during my first year in rabbinical school, I was eating lunch in the cafeteria with an older, fellow student. He told me the story of a student who had dropped out of the seminary after a few years of study, completely turning his back on traditional Judaism. I was horrified. How could this have happened? Why had he become a heretic?

Interestingly, then, a decade and a half later, after years of psychoanalysis, psychiatry, and numerous experiences with psychedelics, I myself left the bounds of traditional Judaism. Despite the guilt I felt, my break with the past was truly liberating, indeed, a blessing. The decision came from deep within me. Had it been inspired by God? I wondered. If so, it was a far different sort of deity than the god of fear I had been subject to for all those years, a superego-god whose voice had been formed out of the angry demands of my punitive mother.

I wrote this incident up and mailed it to Richard. A week later I received his revision of my original piece, incorporating a reworking of the personal story I'd sent. I was astonished to see the way in which he refashioned my thoughts into an engaging, literate prose. The anecdote about my life gave the Baal Shem's tale a reality that it hadn't had by itself, and showed clearly how the Besht's story informed my personal story with a deeper spiritual resonance. I began my follow-up phone call to Richard with gratitude, thanking him for his revision, yet with a question: "Wouldn't such an approach to writing, which would include my personal responses to the Baal Shem's teachings, be seen by readers as self-centered—a way of putting myself in the limelight?"

"Tell me, Burt," he answered, "what is it you most admire about the Baal Shem Tov?"

"His love and compassion. The way he welcomed joy. His profound wisdom. His recognition that God is always present, and because of this his ability to find something precious in every moment. I feel like I've found a Jewish teacher whose vision speaks deeply to both my heart and my mind."

"Yes, good. And one of the best ways you can convey those truths to your potential readers is through sharing your experiences with readers along with your reflections on the Baal Shem's teachings. In this way you will be modeling a way to read the centuries-old texts. Your readers will then see you as a personal witness to the wisdom of the Besht. That's not self-serving at all. It's just the opposite." Richard then agreed to become my writing teacher as well as my editor, and he suggested I begin the manuscript with an autobiography that would provide readers with an understanding of how the Baal Shem Tov came into my life and how his presence had inspired and transformed my spiritual path.

Amazingly, for over thirty years, Richard worked hand-in-hand with me, patiently instructing me in the elements of good writing, helping me discern the direction of my work, and editing version after version of my manuscripts. This approach also affected the way I was preaching at my synagogue on Sabbaths and holy days. My sermons became much more personal and engaging. So if this book has any literary merit, it is because of his careful and patient mentorship.

ESSENTIAL QUESTIONS

Richard Stone's promptings compelled me to clarify what it was that I was searching for. Although I was tremendously interested in discovering the historical Besht, my primary purpose did not have to do with enhancing what we know historically. The question that gnawed at my soul was different from the factually-based questions pursued by historians: How might the life and teachings of the Baal Shem offer me a loving and joyous path to God anchored in my ancestral religion?

In the course of time, other questions about the Besht emerged as well, some of which overlapped with the academic research I was beginning to read: Who had this powerful teacher been historically? How did he come to such a radical vision of the world and of Judaism? What could he teach me about Judaism that would be spiritually and morally relevant to my life? How might his vision and wisdom help in the current renewal of Jewish spirituality? In what ways do his spiritual insights relate to those of Eastern spirituality? Are there spiritual practices I can learn from him that might aid me in transforming my life? Does the Besht's path offer healing modalities for the kind of traumas that I underwent growing up?

It is normative in the scholarly world to think and write about subjects from a dispassionate, objective perspective. I think it's possible that because I've been approaching the Besht as a latter-day disciple, there are aspects of his life and vision that I've been able to unearth that the historians have failed to notice because the questions they were seeking to answer were different from my own.

LITERARY RESOURCES

The process of getting to know the literature associated with the Besht took many decades. To say that I really mastered knowledge of this body of literature would be an overstatement. Yet as I embraced more and more of the tales and teachings, I felt I was coming to know the range of images held throughout the ages. The Hasidic literature which features the Besht has come down to us in a number of genres and literary forms.

ANECDOTES

An anecdote is a miniature story that reveals the master's wisdom and ingenuity in a quick burst of insight. For example, the following was reported by one of the Baal Shem's companions, the Rebbe Pinhas of Koretz:

> One day a man complained to the Baal Shem Tov about his son. "My son has left the Jewish path, and is becoming a heretic, God forbid! What shall I do, Rebbe?" he asked. "Do you love your son?" "Of course I do." "Then love him even more." The Besht later heard that the man's son had repented of his heresy.[140]

Reading this anecdote for the first time was surprising, for I had never seen anything quite like it in Jewish religious literature. The way in which the Besht highlights the value of love brought to mind Rabbi Akiva's statement in the Talmud that the entire Torah rested on the single commandment, "You shall love your neighbor as yourself." Also, the words of the renowned twentieth-century Orthodox mystic, Rav Abraham Isaac Kook: "Let love fill your heart and flow out to all." Yet this brief tale is more specific. It presents an actual situation in which a troubled father is guided to deepen his love for his wayward son by a teacher steeped in love.

The father's complaint has to do with the son's intent to convert to another faith. Readers may remember that something like this takes place in the Broadway musical, *Fiddler on the Roof,* where Tevya the milkman is horrified by his daughter Chava's decision to marry a Russian and to convert to Christianity. The prospect of losing a child to another religion would have been shocking to traditional Jewish parents in Eastern Europe during the eighteenth or nineteenth centuries, and they would have mourned their child as if he or she had died. The tale about the Baal Shem and the father who comes to him in such pain is truly astonishing, then, for the Besht expresses neither fear nor anxiety about the son's possible conversion. His entire concern is centered around *love.*

Notice that the Baal Shem reframes the anguish of his visitor as an opportunity to increase the love between a father and his son. This incident is an example of the Besht's conviction that "Suffering is the throne of goodness," (*"Ha'rah hu ki'sei el ha'vov."*) which might be paraphrased as, "Don't despair when something problematic happens, for the difficulty you are witnessing is, in reality, an opportunity for you to open your heart and to allow a deeper, more embracing love to shine through you."

STORIES

Hasidic tradition also gives us longer stories that build toward a climax, each of them demonstrating the master's acumen. Here, for instance, is one of a number of different reports about how Rabbi Jacob Joseph, the chief literary disciple of the Besht, became converted to the Hasidic path:

> Rabbi Jacob Joseph, the chief judge of the holy community of Sharogrod, heard that the Baal Shem Tov was coming to visit the neighboring community of Mohilev. Curious about the holy man regarding whom

he had heard so many rumors, Jacob Joseph traveled to Mohilev, arriving at the synagogue before the prayer service on Friday morning. When he first saw the Baal Shem, the master was smoking a Turkish pipe, which quite shocked Jacob Joseph.

"And later," he reports, "while I was praying, I wept profusely. It was unlike anything that had happened to me before, and I knew that this weeping had not come from me. And now I was completely captivated by the holy Baal Shem Tov. Soon after I met him, he set out on his journey to the Land of Israel and I became desolate until he came back to Poland. And then, when he did return, I began to travel to be with him for short periods of time. At one point the master told me that it was necessary to elevate me, and so I stayed with him for a number of weeks. Finally, I asked him when he would elevate me."[141]

This is where R. Jacob Joseph's report ends. What did the Baal Shem do to "elevate" his new disciple? We are not told. One modern commentator, Rabbi Samuel Dresner, writes that Rabbi Jacob Joseph "came, at last, to the Besht—that much we know—but precisely what transpired there, exactly how, the Besht 'elevated' his soul...despite the multiplicity of legends, remains a secret of God. And perhaps it can only be so. What took place between those two men must be the story of mind meeting mind, heart meeting heart, soul meeting soul, the joining of two flaming brands into one."[142]

Reflecting on this story, I realized there was something crucial missing. Perhaps in the process of oral transmission a storyteller had forgotten to include it. R. Jacob Joseph alludes to some miraculous deed that the Baal Shem did which drew him towards the master, and yet he doesn't reveal what the deed was. From what we know about the Besht as a clairvoyant, however, the original story must have shown him using psychic abilities to read what was going on in Jacob Joseph's mind. Then he used his paranormal powers to bring about a radical change in the rabbi's disposition toward the new Hasidic approach that he was advocating, a change in awareness. The poet Robert Bly writes that the main quality of consciousness is that it gives off energy. This energy then, in the form of longing and desire for what the Besht had to offer, could have passed from him to Jacob Joseph like an electric current, revealing the younger man's awareness of his purpose on earth.

How exactly did this occur? It is clear that at the time the incident supposedly took place, Jacob Joseph was in the same synagogue as the Besht, praying with the congregation. In a heightened state of worship, a curious Jacob Joseph could not have failed to witness the Baal Shem Tov's extraordinary davening. We have ample evidence that while the Besht was davening his consciousness would gradually ascend and open into a state of devekut—mystical union with the Divine. While this was happening, his body would at times shake violently, and he would double over, while loud and indistinguishable sounds bellowed from his mouth. We have testimonies from other disciples as well who, like Jacob Joseph, were deeply touched and transformed by witnessing their master at worship.

Tales like this form a vast genre of literature about the Besht. They cover a host of themes, including his birth and childhood; his life before he revealed himself as a healer and teacher; how he befriended simple folk; how he taught virtue; the ways he transformed wrongdoers; his visions and ascents to heaven; his supernatural powers; how he healed the sick; ways he defended his people against antisemitic acts; and his interactions with disciples. A great deal about the Hasidic traditions regarding the Baal Shem's character and presence can be inferred from such stories.

TEACHINGS

We turn now to another kind of testimony, the Baal Shem Tov's teachings. As an oral teacher, the Besht had no interest in recording his utterances, and the extensive body of sources that elaborate his vision of the Divine and his understanding of the path to spiritual enlightenment are found in the books of his direct disciples as well as in oral traditions that were later written down. Because virtually all the teachings are located in citations by others, we have no original source that provides us with anything like the master's overall vision and spiritual philosophy. Nor is it possible to date the teachings, or to discern much of a sense of the evolution of the Baal Shem's thought. Still, there is a great deal that can be learned about his views on a host of subjects through studying in tandem the citations gathered from the disciples' books. Two twentieth-century Hebrew compilations have made this possible: *Sefer Baal Shem Tov,* collected and edited by Rabbi Natan Nata Dunner and Rabbi Shim'on Menahen Mendel Wodnick; and *Meir Einei Yisrael,* edited by Yehoshuah Yosef Kornblit.

The anecdotes and stories, as discussed above, show us how the Hasidim believed that those in direct contact with the Besht were affected by his presence. The teachings, on the other hand, reveal aspects of the master's *inner* life—his thoughts and feelings, values and visions. These insights cover the following areas of his thought: the struggle for moral and spiritual wholeness; sacred practices and deeds; attaining mystical union; ethics and service; religious virtues; the nature of Divinity and the world; the psyche and soul; methods of healing; the sacred study of Torah; the meaning of Shabbat and the holy days; and preparing for religious leadership.

Those searching for a fully accurate systematic presentation of his teachings, or for a cogent theology, will be disappointed. His thought was always in motion, constantly changing and evolving. As Elie Wiesel writes regarding the Baal Shem's theories: "His disciples—the Maggid of Mezeritch, Shneur-Zalmen of Ladi, Nahman of Bratzlav—could formulate them later. For the moment, what mattered was to communicate experience rather than scholarship, intuition rather than logic."[43] This is why the Baal Shem's teachings come down to us as brief records of the master's utterances spoken to his disciples. These men translated what they heard in Yiddish into an idiomatic language that would have been familiar to students of traditional Jewish sources. As such they are characterized by a self-containment that often make them difficult for the newcomer to access, even in translation. In my survey of these teachings, I will begin with the shorter insights, which are more straightforward. And I accompany my translations of these teachings with examples of how I interpret them.

I learned to compare and sometimes juxtapose the texts I encountered. It was like assembling a jigsaw puzzle, but slowly the Besht's views on a subject would come together. Over time, it became clear that he'd been generally consistent. However, this was not always the case; sometimes he seemed to have taught views that contradicted statements made at other times. In these instances, I assumed that in the course of time he changed his mind—or possibly, that later teachers had attributed their own notions to him.

There were other difficulties, as well, for even when I was able to translate the texts, making sense of these compressed discourses demanded interpretation; and at times, this required intuitive or imaginative speculation on my part. I freely admit that I am not certain all of my attempts at understanding those problematic texts were accurate. As I studied the Besht, I attempted to corelate a teaching with what I knew about his life and deeds. When I succeeded in substantiating a connection, I would sometimes get more of a sense of the situation that might have given rise to notions found in the teachings. This mode of study provided clues that enabled me to formulate tentative theses about his spiritual biography as well as the larger message embedded in his vision. Following this, I would consult the writings of modern scholars who wrote about him, or about Hasidism, or Kabbalah. In some cases, I discovered that the master made use of a symbol or a motif that could be found in traditions other than Judaism. This was all tremendously helpful in grasping his wisdom from a more universal perspective.

APHORISMS

The Besht's teachings also sometimes take the form of brief aphorisms. Here, for instance, is a short and potent insight recorded by the Baal Shem's great grandson, Rebbe Nachman of Bratslav: "The world is filled with lights and mysteries, but you place your tiny hand before your eyes, and you see nothing!"

So much of the time we go about our lives buried in our day-to-day activities and fail to recognize the wondrous and awesome character of the world in which we live. But, declares the Baal Shem, the soul knows there is a great deal more to existence than what we experience through our senses. If we can learn to lower our hands and open the eyes of our souls, we too will be able to see that every moment is filled with a host of miracles. And if we truly experience the moment, what do we see?

The Baal Shem loved to cite the teaching from the Zohar, "There is no place devoid of the divine."[144] Wherever we look with the eyes of our souls we see the Shekhinah, the holy Presence. We are in truth living *within* the very presence of God—not just the physical universe, mind you, but God! Hasidic tradition records many of the master's profound teachings in this pithy form.

PARABLES

Through parables—simple stories to illustrate deeper spiritual truths—the master also communicated effectively. Here, for instance, is a potent parable of his that I've returned to again and again: "There was once a ruler of a great kingdom who sent his only son to a village far from the capital so that he would learn what life was like for the common people of the land. Living in this rural community the son became acquainted with the villagers, and gradually over time forgot his royal origins. When the king sent a messenger to bring his son back to the palace, the prince simply refused to believe what he was hearing. So the king sent a second envoy, but he received the same treatment. Finally, the king found a wise and clever messenger who disguised himself so he would look like one of the villagers. It was this third envoy who eventually convinced the son of his royal origins. This messenger brought the prince home to his father."[145]

The king in this parable is, of course, God. And the first two messengers? Perhaps Jewish spiritual teachers whose words were too complicated to reach the hearts of the common Jew. But the third messenger was the Baal Shem Tov himself. What gives this away is that we know the Besht dressed like a Gentile shepherd and often acted like a peasant, making himself more approachable to common Jews.

But who is the prince? Possibly the Jewish people, living in an exile so difficult that they have forgotten their divine lineage. Or maybe the prince represents every one of the Besht's disciples. They were all learned men, yet the Baal Shem presented himself without airs and in his presence they recognized a teacher who could take them to deeper places in their souls, where they would learn to recognize their true essence as images of God. I believe this parable has another function, as well, for through its storytelling the listener or reader is enticed to remember their own spiritual identity.

The Besht's use of parables also gives us a clue regarding his understanding of Divinity. In most of the Baal Shem's teachings he does not make use of anthropomorphic language, for he does not think of God in personal terms. Instead, he portrays the Divine using kabbalistic concepts, treated these ideas in a psychological fashion. In the parables, however, he often compares God to a human king, thereby explaining the actions of Divinity in human terms. Calling these descriptions of divine activity parables made it evident to his students that the Divine was in fact a reality that transcended the human.

MORE COMPLETE TEACHINGS

The Baal Shem also offered his wisdom through more extensive teachings, some of which included parables. These discourses were recorded by members of his circle, and provide a more comprehensive understanding of his larger concepts. They reveal him as a new kind of mystic whose understanding of Kabbalah emphasized experience over concepts and psychology over metaphysics. We learn what he experienced in his mystical experiences, and we get instructions on how to daven.

Frequently we witness the ways in which he interprets biblical and rabbinic texts in radical ways. His elucidations of traditional sources frequently depend on plays on words unintended by the authors of those texts, and by intentional misreadings of the plain meaning of the original sources. Here is an example of this: There is a tractate in the second-century collection of legal documents titled "The Chapters of the Fathers," (*Pirkei Avot*) which contains the wisdom teachings of the sages of the previous three centuries. One saying found in the collection comes from Rabbi Judah the Prince (170-220 CE), who edited the entire Mishnah. Here is the text:

> Keep your eye on three things, so you will not come into
> the clutches of sin. Know what is above you: An Eye that
> sees, an Ear that hears, and all of your deeds, written
> down in a book. (*Pirkei Avot* II:1)

Talmudic scholar Rabbi Jacob Neusner interpreted this teaching in the following way: "We are here on earth, with a God who cares what we say and do and who keeps track of it all. This is phrased in vivid images: an eye, an ear, a pen recording what the eye sees and the ear hears. The point, it is clear, is that there is a reward for doing one's religious duty and a penalty for not doing it or for committing a transgression."[146]

The Baal Shem Tov knew perfectly well what this text meant. What he does is excerpt a phrase from Rabbi Judah's teaching, reinterpreting it in a psychologically radical way. The phrase is "Know what is above you." The Hebrew for this literally reads, "Know what is above you from you." (*Dah mah l'ma'alah mim'khah.*) The Besht reads the text this way: "Know that what is above you comes from you," which means something like, "You can know what is happening in the transcendent heights beyond this world by looking into your own depths," or possibly, "That which you imagine in the heavens above actually has its origin in your own depths." This kind of free-ranging reinterpretation was fully accepted in his circle of disciples and companions. There was an assumption that because the Hebrew language is in some way God's own speech, the words and letters of every sacred text contain an infinite number of hidden meanings that interpreters in every age are able to discover using their intuitive abilities.

One of the myriad themes treated in the Baal Shem's teachings has to do with what it means to be a tzaddik, an enlightened spiritual master, a teacher concerned not only with his own spiritual progress, but also with bringing wisdom and blessing to the members of the community that he serves. These particular discourses define the qualities of the authentic tzaddik and provide instruction to disciples on how to attain the virtues necessary to become such a master. He often began with a verse from the Bible, or a passage from rabbinic or kabbalistic literature, and would interpret it radically. Here are just a few examples of this.

1.

We read in the book of Proverbs,
"The tzaddik knows the nature of his beast" (12:10)
This verse seems to refer to an animal owned by a tzaddik,
    but the Hebrew can be read in an entirely different way:
"A tzaddik is one who knows his own *animal nature,*
    and yet has the ability to bind his wild impulses to the Creator."

2.

> The tzaddik is a conduit drawing down the abundance of divine
>> energy from the cosmos.
> By means of his holy actions, he is able to channel blessings into the.
>> world
> And just as a conduit does not itself benefit from whatever passes
>> through it, so the true tzaddik does not want anything for
>> himself, and is concerned only for others.

3.

> When a sage reaches full spiritual realization,
>> his experience of being continually united with the Divine
>> is never disturbed by anything that happens in the world.
> Because of this, all the words that the tzaddik speaks with others
>> about matters of the world come out of this uninterrupted union.
> This, then, is the source of his immense wisdom.

4.

> Tzaddikim are able to elevate everything.
> They make it possible for their disciples to refine their character
>> traits and their ways of speaking with others.
> There are some tzaddikim who can elevate individuals through
>> their devotion to sacred study and prayer.
> But there are other tzaddikim who can actually elevate people
>> through ordinary conversation.
> For even though the mundane remarks of a tzaddik may on the
>> surface seem pointless, they always have a deeper purpose.[147]

How might one work with these kinds of teachings? I begin by asking what the various descriptions of the tzaddik tell us about the inner life of the Baal Shem Tov. In the parable about the messenger who brought the king's son back to his father, for instance, I imagine that the Besht saw himself as the enlightened envoy, sent by God in order to prepare a new kind of spiritual leader, one who would be able to awaken common people to spirit truth through his inspiring leadership. It seems then that the first of the four sources above describing characteristics of a tzaddik might reveal that the Besht recognized he exhibited wild impulses need-ing to be tamed, and that he learned to do this.

The second passage demonstrates how the Besht was convinced he had the ability to connect directly to God and to act as a conduit of divine blessing, which he was able to channel toward his people. The third source shows that the Baal Shem felt intimately connected to God at all times, and his consciousness had developed to the point where he was living on an equanimous plane that lay beyond the ordinary contortions of the ego. And the final passage reveals how he understood his extraor-dinary ability to affect the consciousness of those in his presence, even through what seemed to be ordinary conversations.[148]

A disciple would find these teachings demanding, but also empower-ing. They give the impression of an atmosphere in the Besht's classroom that was serious and deep. But through the years, I came to feel they failed to capture the electricity that must have filled the air when students sat in the presence of their master. Many of these stenographic teachings come to us only through the disciples' notes, written down long after the Besht's passing. It seems that while they preserved his ideas, they couldn't capture the heady atmosphere in which these ideas were shared. A state-ment by a later teacher, Rabbi Isaac Judah Safrin of Komarno (1806-74), attempts to capture that quality, imagining the experience of studying with the Besht as a kind of revelation akin to the giving of the Torah to Moses on Mt. Sinai: "It is well known that when the Baal Shem Tov would study Torah with his holy students, a fire blazed about them and the heavenly angels gathered around them. The students experienced thun-der and lightning, and the commandment, 'I am the EverPresent, your God,' could be heard emanating from the Blessed One."[149]

Readers may sense that this statement is hyperbolic, and this is likely so. Yet I can recall numerous visits to the Lubavitcher community in Crown Heights during the early sixties, when I stood amidst the crowd of Hasidim facing Rebbe Schneerson as he taught in his charismatic style and led the community in rapturous song. The hall pulsated with energy. Those were amazing experiences, never to be forgotten. Such memo-ries are what gave rise to my imaginative description of the Baal Shem's classroom.

Most of the Baal Shem Tov's teachings were meant for his direct disciples. We can get a sense of his mission as a teacher from this parable, "The Wise Courtier and the King's Son," that he shared with his students:

> There was once a prince whose father ruled a great nation. This king wanted his son to live for a time with common people so the young man would be able to learn how his future subjects thought and acted. In this way he reasoned that the prince would come to understand how to best govern his people in righteousness once he ascended the throne. And so the king exiled his son to a village far from the capital.
>
> The prince was not wise, however, and soon took on the ways of the common folk among whom he was living. As time went on the memories of his life in the palace seemed less and less real. He began questioning whether the splendid childhood he remembered had actually occurred. He finally decided that his "memories" were in truth only childish fantasies. As the months turned into years, his royal past dissolved like a dream in the morning.
>
> The king finally decided that the time had come to bring his son home, so he sent one of his highest officials to the village where his son was living with the message that the king, his father, wanted him to return to the palace. The nobleman was dressed in royal attire, but when he revealed his identity and mission to the king's son, the prince thought the man was completely mad and sent him away. The official returned to the palace with this news. The king then sent a second official with the same mission, but like the first noble, he too was rebuffed by the prince. When this official returned to the capital, he told the king that he believed that the prince was suffering from some kind of amnesia. *Hmm*, thought the king, *how might I wake my son to his true identity?*
>
> So he picked an astute and clever member of his court and told him the full story of what had happened.

"I know you will have the wisdom to bring my son home," he told the man. The courtier dressed himself in the clothes of a peasant, and when he reached the village, he befriended the prince, spent time with him, ate with him, and joked with him. In time the two became close and the prince came to love his companion and to trust him in all matters. When the courtier revealed his true identity to him, the prince believed him. Then the courtier brought the prince back to the palace and he was joyfully reunited with his father.[50]

At the root of the parable is a description of the spiritual quest and the role played by the teacher. The prince represents those who become lost in the values and norms of the material world, exiled from the spirit. Living in exile, the prince forgot his true identity, became alienated from his true home, and came to accept his present condition as normal. It took the loving ministrations of the wise courtier to awaken him to the reality of his spiritual essence and to lead him back to his true home.

The wise courtier is the Baal Shem himself. Like this noble, the Besht wore the clothes of a commoner, and didn't affect airs. He befriended his disciples, spent time with them, joked with them, revealed his love for them. Through the trust that developed, he was able to help each find a path to liberation. The parable seems dualistic, as if the king and prince were two different individuals, but in other teachings the Besht indicated that the king symbolizes the royal essence at the core of every person. In the language of Jungian psychology, the prince represents the personality, the small self, while the king symbolizes the greater Self, the psyche as a whole.

THE PRACTICE OF SACRED STUDY

The Baal Shem Tov made it clear to his disciples that their study of the Torah and the other sacred books had to be carried out with a spiritual sensibility. How does one engage in the process of study in a way that moves beyond the desire to gain knowledge? The Baal Shem's grandson, Chaim Ephraim of Sudilkov, reported the following:

When I was studying with my grandfather he quoted a teaching from the Talmud: "A student who goes over a subject one hundred times cannot be compared with a student who reviews a subject one hundred and one times." (Hagigah 9b) Then my grandfather asked me: "What's the real difference between these two different students? How could it be that adding a single repetition would distinguish an exemplary student from an ordinary student?"

And then, after a pause, he answered his own question: "Capitalize the word 'One,' and read the text this way: "A student who goes over a subject one hundred times cannot be compared with a student who reviews a subject one hundred times plus One."

What this means is that at the time when you are studying anything in our sacred tradition, you must let your mind be imbued with the awareness of the One![151]

Now, the original meaning of the Talmudic teaching has to do with going over a text again and again in order to fix it in memory, so that it will strongly influence the student's thought and action. But the Baal Shem's intentional and creative misreading transforms this literal meaning into a spiritual imperative. Authentic sacred study requires one to continually remember that he is living in the Presence.

There is another question to ask here. Philip Zaleski, the author of many books on spirituality and religion, has written that "among the lesser mysteries associated with great spiritual figures, there is this: that neither Jesus nor Buddha nor Muhammed nor Confucius nor Pythagoras nor Socrates wrote a book.... Great teachers, it seems, prefer oral instruction, with its intimate interaction between speaker and listener and its affinity for rhythm, rhyme, and parable."[152] Thus we see that the teachings of so many of the greatest sages in human history were preserved only because that teacher's disciples thought to do so.

We have a story about the Besht from R. Pinhas of Koretz, one of his companions, which seems to show that the master did not want his teachings recorded:

There was someone who was writing down what he heard from the Besht, and when the master found out about this he directed his disciple, Dov Baer of Medzeritch, to read what the man had written down. The Maggid saw that not one word that the master had spoken was in the student's notes. The Baal Shem then said that this man had not listened for the sake of heaven and therefore an evil force (*klipah*) had taken hold of him, and he had heard falsely.[153]

Why did all of the sages Zaleski mentions refrain from writing their insights down for future generations? Citing Saint Augustine, Zaleski writes that "what Jesus taught was too profound to be encapsulated in the written word, for in Jesus' lesson the surface veils as well as displays." Could it be that Augustine's words apply also to the Baal Shem? This story raises the question of how close those disciples who attempted to document their masters' words came to recording what actually came out of the mouths of their teachers. It also raises the question of whether a written record can ever really reproduce the transformative kind of experiences that disciples undergo when they are experiencing the radiance of their master.

PART TWO

PENETRATING A VISIONARY LIFE

CHAPTER THIRTEEN

THE STRUGGLES OF A FUTURE SAINT

*"Very often when we encounter hagiography, the description
of the lives of saints, the Rebbes of the past often seem like
plaster-cast statues or two-dimensional iconic representations.
That is not how we need to approach the Baal Shem Tov or
any other Rebbe today. Sociologists call these hagiographic
depictions of tradition[al] 'archetypal models'—models that so
perfectly embody our ideals that they are very difficult for us to
emulate, so perfect as to be above the human situation."*
ZALMAN SCHACHTER-SHALOMI
AND NETANEL MILES-YEPEZ[154]

As we have seen, it did not take long for the Baal Shem Tov to become a
superhuman savior-like hero to the masses of Eastern European Jewry.
Even more, for Hasidim entranced by the image of the Besht, it was
almost as if the founder of Hasidism had never really died. Elie Wiesel
writes that "More than any other Jewish historical figure, with the exception of the Prophet Elijah, the Besht was present in joy as well as despair;
every *shtibel* reflected his light, his warmth. Every Hasid had two Masters:
his own and the Baal Shem Tov—each drew strength from the other. The
first was needed to live, to second to believe. Whoever disclaimed kin-
ship with the Baal Shem found himself relegated outside of the Hasidic
community."[155]

What was it about him that made such a deep impression on so
many ordinary Jews? What did he evoke in the Jewish heart? Popular
storytellers passed down many hundreds of arresting tales, describing
him as the supreme exemplar of sainthood, and modern exponents of
Hasidism have followed in their wake. Martin Buber begins his groundbreaking collection of stories about the major early Hasidic masters
with this anecdote: "They say that once, when all souls were gathered in
Adam's soul, at the hour he stood by the Tree of Knowledge, the soul of

the Baal Shem Tov went away, and did not eat of the fruit of the tree."[156] The remark refers to the decisive moment in the Garden of Eden when Adam and Eve were seduced by the primordial serpent to eat from the fruit of the Tree of Knowledge. That fateful act brought about their fall from grace and expulsion from the garden. But just at that moment, the anecdote asserts, *"the soul of the Baal Shem Tov went away, and did not eat of the fruit of the tree."*

The teaching begins with the words, "They say that once, when all souls were gathered in Adam's soul." The remark assumes that every human soul that would ever live has its origin in the first human being ever created. And the story assumes that because Adam and Eve sinned against God, every future soul would somehow be tainted by their transgression—every soul, that is, except for the Baal Shem. For somehow his soul was able to foresee the calamity about to occur and bolted from the scene before the first human beings ate the fateful fruit. Because of this, the soul of the Besht was able to retain its primal innocence—its primal connection to God and to the natural world. Thus, his soul never experienced sin, guilt, shame, or suffering; he escaped the shackles of ordinary human destiny and was able to remain closer to the reality of the Divine than any human being who would ever live.

The storyteller obviously knew there was something marvelous and unique about the Baal Shem Tov. His anecdote symbolizes this quality as a kind of primal innocence. He could not have known how much adversity Israel Baal Shem Tov had undergone or the hurts he'd inflicted on other people. Nor could he have been aware of the inner struggle he had waged to purify and transform himself into the avatar that he became. This anecdote, like so many others, is part of the *hagiography* of the Baal Shem Tov.

A PERFECT MASTER?

Early in my investigation, I discovered an unorthodox and disturbing portrait of the founder of Hasidism by historian and folklorist, Raphael Patai. The stories in *In Praise of the Baal Shem Tov*, writes Patai, show him to have been a man of superior intelligence, a miracle worker, possessed of great piety, and a veritable saint. Yet interspersed among the legends are pieces of information incongruous with the general tone of admiration. These unflattering details, Patai states, reveal some unsettling aspects of the Besht's character: he was prone to violent temper tantrums, and he rudely accosted those who aroused his anger, calling them fools or idiots. "While temper is a matter of individual proclivity, the amount of control a person exercises over his temper is largely determined by the values inculcated into him by his environment. Jewish tradition has always favored mild, modest, peaceable, and temperate behavior. Temper tantrums and outbursts of anger were considered unbefitting a Jew. Numerous Talmudic sayings well known to all educated Jews decried temper and upheld meekness as the ideal behavior." Patai writes that the Baal Shem would angrily accost people, calling them fools, idiots, or worse. On one occasion, for instance, he shouted at a barren woman: "See to it that you give birth to a son! If not, I will break your bones with this stick!" Another time he beat a man who was feigning death.[157]

Where did this uncontrolled anger come from? "If the Besht did not follow these [traditional] directives," Patai writes, "it must have been due to the influence of the peasants with whom he associated and who were uncouth, unmannered, and would make no attempt to control their temper." Patai points to a number of other statements in *In Praise of the Baal Shem Tov* that he claims reflect the Besht's peasant-like character, including his physical closeness to his wife, preoccupation with sex, riotous joking, use of profane language, belief in evil spirits, fondness for horses, wine, and strong drink, and rustic clothing.

For many years, I took Patai at his word. It now seems to me that his view was greatly influenced by a belief that Hasidism was heavily influenced by Polish peasant culture. As I stated in Part One, it seems more likely that the Baal Shem's peasant persona was a ruse used to hide his true identity from the public. Still, for a long time I wondered what to make of the Besht's "un-Jewish" anger.

KINDNESS AND HAUGHTINESS

Along with numerous tales highlighting the Besht's kindness and generosity, there are a smaller number that expose his anger and rage. Here, for instance, is a lovely tale about the master as a compassionate healer:

Once, while the Besht was traveling, he came to a particular city on a Friday afternoon. When he arrived, he was instructed by a messenger to stay as a guest in a certain house for Shabbat. The Besht sent his scribe, Tzvi Hirsh, to the house to check with the householder about this, but when the householder's wife overheard the request, she became irritated. Interrupting the conversation between Tvi Hirsh and her husband she told the messenger that his master could not stay in their house because her son was deathly ill and she was in great sorrow. The householder was silent during this interchange. When Tzvi Hirsh left the house, however, the householder accompanied him so that he could mollify the Besht. When the Baal Shem heard the man's story, he promised him that if he allowed him to stay in his home the boy would live. The householder agreed.

When the Besht arrived at the house he ordered everyone to leave, including Tzvi Hirsh. The Baal Shem entered the sick boy's room and began to pray intensely. Late in the night Tzvi Hirsh returned to the house. He opened the bedroom door slowly and heard his master speaking intently to the child's soul: "I have sworn that the boy will live and I command you to reenter his body! I cannot swear a false oath, so you must reenter his body!" Tzvi Hirsh quietly closed the bedroom door.

Awhile later, Tzvi Hirsh entered the room and he found the Besht lying on the floor with his arms and legs stretched out as if he was being beaten with a whip.

Then the Baal Shem stood up and exclaimed, "Didn't I tell you to reenter the boy's body?" And seeing Tzvi Hirsh standing there, he shouted, "Hirsh, bring me wine for Kiddush (the blessing to sanctify the Sabbath)!" After reciting Kiddush in the bedroom, the two men left the room and ate dinner in another part of the house.

In the morning the Besht gave his scribe instructions

and medicinal herbs to administer to the child, and then he went to pray in the synagogue.

Throughout the morning the boy showed signs that he was on the way to recovery. When his mother saw what was happening, she began to sob.

"Why are you crying?" Tzvi Hirsh asked.

"How can I not cry when I cursed such a pious man?" she answered.

"Do not cry," he told her, "My rabbi is a good man and he will forgive you."

When the Besht returned from the synagogue the boy's mother was still crying. Seeing her sobbing the Baal Shem whispered to his scribe: "Tell her not to cry, Hirsch. She should prepare a good dinner. Tell her that I promise her that the boy will sit with us at the table for dinner."[158]

The most peculiar element in the story is the description of the Baal Shem lying on the floor with his arms and legs stretched out as if he was being beaten with a whip. Knowing that readers might be puzzled by this, the storyteller parenthetically states, "The reason for this was that the Besht had agreed to accept the punishment from Heaven of 'fiery lashes' because he had compelled Heaven to change the decree of death that had been decreed for the child." Throughout numerous stories of the Besht's feats we find his ability to miraculously alter the malicious decrees of divine providence when human beings are being affected badly. In this story, he was willing to suffer for his unrepentant defiance. This was a tale I loved because it demonstrated his courage and compassion.

But as I read more of *In Praise of the Baal Shem Tov*, I also encountered the stories Raphael Patai had pointed to, in which the Besht is blunt, loses his temper, insults people, and is physically abusive. And there was more in the book that disturbed me. Patai hadn't mentioned the many stories that reveal the Baal Shem's arrogance and grandiosity; I found tales that portrayed him as fully aware of his greatness and superiority, and vaunting that knowledge in public. Here, then, is a second story that reveals what I call the Besht's shadow side of anger and excessive pride:

When the Besht was staying in Istanbul on his way to the Holy Land he heard about a wealthy man whose only son had become blind. He went to the home of the boy's father and told the man that he was a healer and that he could cure his son's blindness using holy names. The wealthy man's wife, however, saw that this stranger was wearing unsightly clothes. She told her husband that she wanted nothing to do with this supposed healer, and she also spoke out against the Besht and against his use of holy names to heal. The Besht became angry because the woman disparaged his use of holy names. Nonetheless, he asked that the boy be brought before him. The woman suddenly became hopeful.

The child was brought to the Besht and the master whispered something in his ear. The boy was immediately able to see and the family was joyous. And then the Besht passed his hand over the boy's eyes and once again he became blind. The members of the family began to weep, and they bowed down before him, begging him to restore the boy's sight, even offering him a huge sum of money.

But the Besht turned to the man's wife and said to her, "You are a wicked woman. You mocked the holy names and thus you cannot benefit from such power. I did not come to your family in order to glorify myself—God forbid!—nor did I do it for the money, but simply to sanctify God's blessed name. I showed you the great power of the holiness of the divine Name, but you will not benefit from it." Then he left the house.[159]

The mother in this story is skeptical and hostile to the Baal Shem's methods of healing. In the earlier tale, the Besht is entirely forgiving of the child's mother, while in this one he is angry, cruel, and vengeful, taking out his hostility toward her by causing her child to return to blindness. Even though he states that he didn't act to glorify himself, I sense the Besht's wounded pride fueling his anger.

I bristled as I read this and other stories like it. How could a supposed holy man act this way? Why was he compassionate and forgiving in one instance and angry, vengeful, and arrogant in the other? And how was I to understand the Besht's haughtiness and grandiosity?

In 1979, I had the great fortune of spending an evening with Reuven Gold, a social worker and Hasidic storyteller from Chicago who was visiting a friend of mine in Berkeley. Reuven was bright, energetic, and highly intuitive. Most of our time together was given over to a discussion about the Baal Shem Tov. Reuven was unfamiliar with stories about the Baal Shem's negative character traits, but he wasn't entirely surprised by what I shared with him. He thought the stories might indeed be authentic, and that Raphael Patai's beliefs about the Besht coming from peasant origins might also be true. Then, Reuven paused, collecting his thoughts, before a stream of insights poured out of him as if he had been considering the issue for years.

"Here's what's coming to me," he said excitedly, "As an individual, the Baal Shem may have been crude and elitist toward the common people, those he served as a healer and miracle worker. But the disciples saw him completely differently because of the Baal Shem's incredible magnetism, and his power to affect and expand their minds." Reuven was speaking in a rapid, animated tone, gesticulating with his hands, as if he were telling a story. "So here's what I imagine: When the Besht gathered his disciples around him and began to expound his mystical teachings, the atmosphere must have been electric! The disciples were in a kind of trance-state. The Baal Shem was so on fire with his own potent giftedness that he must have been able to kindle the spiritual giftedness of his disciples. He had the ability of making disciples feel their own beings flowing together with the cosmos. And what the disciples offer us in their testimonies is the *inner spiritual reality* of their master as it manifested in the intimate circle of the Baal Shem."

Reuven paused for a moment and I asked him if he could slow down so I could get his words on paper. He nodded and waited while I wrote, and then took up again where he'd left off. "What was so unusual about the Besht was not that he was free of faults," Reuven continued, "but that he drew his disciples into a state of cosmic consciousness where the whole world seems glorious, where negativity is not opposed to positivity, but complementary to it. In such a state of expanded consciousness his followers paid no attention to his defects. In that sort of state, they would have seen human faults as transitory. The common folk who met the Besht as a healer or magician could only see him from the outside. They didn't know what was happening to him internally, spiritually. Like the disciples, they were also under a kind of hypnotic spell, because of the Besht's magnetism, his reputation, and miraculous power. But unlike the disciples, the common people were not that spiritually inclined. They stood in awe of him because he was the Baal Shem Tov. So we're dealing with two different kinds of awe here. One kind comes from an inner connection with the master that has a transformative effect on consciousness. This is what happened to the disciples. The other kind comes from witnessing things that happen that are psychic in nature—but this second kind of awe was not personally transformative, and the common people remained the same after their encounter with the Besht."

Reuven paused again until I stopped writing. "But here's where I think Patai was wrong. If the image of the Baal Shem in *In Praise of the Baal Shem Tov* represents the true and the only authentic image of him, he could not have become the founder of the Hasidic movement. He wouldn't have swept up so many people into a state of mystical wonder and unity. He would have remained a great healer and magician for his own generation alone." I was mesmerized by this intuitive grasp of the issue that had been plaguing me for months. The evening I spent with Reuven completely changed the way I understood the Baal Shem's alluring power and influence on the people of his time.

What Reuven called awe I would describe as charisma, arguably the most prominent feature of the master's personality. The sociologist Max Weber defined charisma as "a certain quality of an individual personality, by virtue of which he is set apart from ordinary men and treated as endowed with supernatural, superhuman, or at least specifically exceptional powers or qualities. These are such as are not accessible to the ordinary person, but are regarded as of divine origin or as exemplary, and on the basis of them the individual concerned is treated as a leader." Nonetheless, this didn't seem to me a complete solution to the problem. Were the disciples *always* in an altered state when they were in their master's presence? Could they have been entirely blind to the Besht's purely human faults? Or did they deliberately attempt to conceal his darker side in their citations of his teachings? And even if disciples were entranced by his charisma, was he himself oblivious of his failings? Was he then a charlatan—as the *Mitnagdim*, the Jewish opponents of Hasidism, later claimed?

THE BESHT'S TROUBLED CHILDHOOD

Some years after my encounter with Reuven Gold, I enrolled in an all-day seminar on Hasidism and psychology offered by my friend, Estelle Frankel, a psychologist and spiritual teacher intimately familiar with Kabbalah and Hasidism. It was Estelle who provided me with one of the key missing pieces of the puzzle.

At one point in the seminar, she talked about Israel Baal Shem Tov's childhood. As readers will recall, *In Praise of the Baal Shem Tov* states that Israel's parents were quite old when he was born, and we're told that his father died when the boy was young. In addition, his mother simply disappeared from the narrative without any explanation. The villagers saw him as a footloose child because he was an orphan. He grew up alone and quite secretive. Frankel spoke about Israel's loss of his parents as an experience of abandonment. She later detailed her observations in her profound and insightful book, *Sacred Therapy: Jewish Spiritual Teachings on Emotional Healing and Inner Wholeness*:

> Loss seems to have played a significant role in the lives of many Hasidic Masters.... Many were orphans or had lost a parent at a young age, including the famed Baal Shem Tov.... Like all children who suffer early losses, young Israel must have struggled to overcome feelings of abandonment and loneliness—perhaps even depression. As a child, he used to go out alone into the forest to commune with the divine. There, in his aloneness, he formed a deep bond of attachment with God called devekut—or union with the divine. Through devekut, the Baal Shem Tov was able to transcend his own wound of abandonment and to feel connected to all beings and all creation. In healing his own broken heart by cleaving

> to the ever-present love and unity of the divine, he
> blazed a spiritual pathway for others to follow.[160]

Just as we cannot know how historically authentic the various stories about the Besht's life found in *In Praise of the Baal Shem Tov* were, we cannot know with any certainty whether a modern psychological interpretation of these tales could be historically accurate. All the same, I was persuaded by Frankel's argument. The stories about Israel's childhood say nothing at all about the boy's personal distress at losing his parents. Perhaps the storyteller imagined that even as a child the Baal Shem's faith was so extraordinary that he experienced no grief at his loss.

I also realized that what Frankel said about childhood abandonment was true for me. My spiritual quest originated in the woundedness I experienced in my family of origin, and in my search for something transcendent that could provide a sense of meaning. Frankel also points out that other great spiritual teachers, such as the thirteenth-century Sufi poet, Rumi, experienced abandonment and found healing through mystical experience. After the death of Rumi's beloved and inspiring teacher-friend, Shams, Rumi went through a period of profound heartbreak and mourning: "In his grief, however, his heart didn't just break. It broke open, and thereafter his heart knew no boundaries. He began to find the presence of the Beloved One everywhere and in everything. Through the loss of his mortal beloved, then, Rumi's whole being opened up, and his heartbreak was transformed into the music and poetry of mystic love and longing."[161] Frankel implies that something like this had also happened to the Baal Shem. He, too, eventually discovered the presence of the Beloved One everywhere and in everything.

THE PATH OF "TURNING"

How did the Baal Shem's ongoing connection with God transform him? What was the healing process he went through? I could find nothing in *In Praise of the Baal Shem Tov* that might offer answers to these questions. One day, however, it occurred to me that a Jew living in eighteenth-century Poland had to have been aware of the importance and obligation of *teshuvah*, often translated as repentance, penitence, or "turning." Teshuvah is the process of evaluating one's life and deeds, working to transform one's life, making amends to people one has wronged, and seeking forgiveness from God. Because of the centrality of teshuvah in traditional Jewish life, the Besht must have been aware of his failings, and he would have made a great effort to transform his character.

I remembered a short tale in *In Praise of the Baal Shem Tov* that described a scene in which the master became furious with the guests at his table and his visitors hastily got up and left his home. Then his wife scolded him for having lost his temper. So the Besht leaned over the table and said, "I am ready to accept your rebuke." He sent a messenger to apologize to the guests.[162] This anecdote implies that the Besht was aware of his penchant for anger, and also that he was willing to apologize after wronging others. And so it appeared to me that the stories about the Besht's saintliness might be understood as evidence that he had undergone a prolonged struggle to transform his negative character traits. This would mean that the story about the Baal Shem and the family of the blind child was an early tale, while the story about the master and the child close to death happened later. I had very little textual evidence for my assumption, then, but through the years, as I studied many Hebrew texts containing tales about and teachings ascribed to the Besht, I was able to find abundant sources that made my theory plausible.

We are told in *In Praise of the Baal Shem Tov* that the Baal Shem spent seven years as a hermit in the Carpathian Mountains, and that he fasted and engaged in other ascetic practices. As readers will recall, the tales state that he did not reveal his identity and vocation as a healer and teacher to the Jewish world until he'd entered his thirty-sixth year. I wondered if he waited so long to disclose his gifts because he was working on refining those crude character traits, and didn't feel ready to become a leader and teacher.

Over the decades I discovered numerous teachings attributed to him that had to do with teshuvah.[163] The Hebrew word *ga'avah* can be translated as pride, vanity, egotism, self-inflation or grandiosity. In his ethical teachings, the Besht singles out ga'avah as being worse than sin. He states that ga'avah is a form of self-worship that cuts us off from God, equivalent to idolatry. The master also quoted a teaching from the Talmud that states that anger is a form of ga'avah. In another instance, he teaches that vulgarity and crudeness are worse than sin.[164] According to Jacob Joseph of Polonoyye, the Baal Shem's major literary disciple, his teacher once admitted that he had wronged God and had to undergo teshuvah. The Besht even told his disciple about the process that brought him to engage in teshuvah: listening deeply to the promptings of his conscience, understanding that the decree he heard was a revelation prompting him to transform his life and become good.[165]

In another utterance, the Besht cites Ecclesiastes, "There is no righteous man on earth who does only good and does not sin" (7:20), and then tells his disciple, "One cannot continually remain in a state of goodness in which one has no negative motivations or sins. This is impossible!"[166] I believe, then, that he had come to recognize that, even though he was a gifted healer and teacher, he was still human and had to deal with those human failings.

CULTIVATING HUMILITY

The Baal Shem Tov was fascinated by the figure of Moses. He often spoke about Moses' qualities and abilities. Here, for instance, is what he has to say about Moses' greatness: "The fully developed individual, the person who possesses a clear knowledgeable consciousness, is able to bring all the people of his generation together. And it does not matter what level they are on. He is able to raise them up, uniting them to their Root, and then uniting himself with them. Such a person is called *Moses*, for he contains within himself his entire generation. He is called *Consciousness*, and his generation is called *the Conscious Generation*."[167]

He is not merely speaking of the historical Moses. Reading such teachings, it became clear to me the Besht was portraying virtues that he thought were necessary for the spiritual leader of every generation. And because I was knowledgeable about so many of his other teachings, it became clear that he was, in fact, describing himself. Yet, the Baal Shem did not limit himself to speaking about Moses' merits. He also shared his perception of difficulties Moses had to undergo to become the greatest leader of the Jewish people. He once cited a rabbinic midrash that portrayed Moses as having started out as *kubiyustas,* which can mean either a kidnapper or a gambler. He interpreted this midrash as showing that as a young man Moses had little self-understanding, and that he had to grow spiritually in order to realize his potential to transform evil into good. He reached the point where he was able to bring unity into his own life and into the world by linking the lowest levels of reality with the highest.[168] The Baal Shem stated that "Our master, Moses, was born a complete scoundrel, and manifested every evil trait. But Moses reversed this, shattering every one of his evil traits. And he attempted to cultivate only good character traits."[169]

Rabbi Jacob Joseph also quoted the Besht as having cited the medieval philosopher, Sa'adia Gaon: "Human beings were created in order to shatter their natural tendencies toward evil."[170] From all of the references to pride and anger in Beshtian texts, and from teachings like those cited above, it is clear that the Baal Shem struggled with these dark forces within. He emphasized the atrociousness of anger and pride because of his knowledge of his own failings. I would imagine that he stressed their weightiness as a warning to disciples that they were not to imitate his negative traits; they were to emulate his ability to transform his shadow side. In fact, the disciples cite teachings in their master's name that assert the necessity of fighting against one's regressive traits.[171] At the same time, the Besht focused a great deal of attention on the need for the cultivation of *anavah,* humility.

One of the tales in *In Praise of the Baal Shem Tov* clearly demonstrates the Besht's struggle with pride:

> Once the Baal Shem travelled to the holy community Brody and stayed overnight in a place near Brody. During the night the Besht became so frightened that his knees were knocking against each other. The noise awoke Rabbi Tzvi, the Besht's scribe.
>
> The scribe asked the Baal Shem, "Why are you afraid?"
>
> The Besht answered, "My spiritual guide, Ahiyah, the prophet, came to me and asked, 'Who is more worthy—you or Abraham, our father, may he rest in peace?'
>
> "I then asked Ahiyah, 'And just why are you asking me this question?'
>
> "'Because you are going to the holy community of Brody,' he answered, 'and they will give you great honor.

And if—God forbid—you fail to resist their adulation, you will lose all of the merit that you have earned.'

"And that is when I became very frightened," the Besht told Rabbi Tzvi.

And the next day, just as Ahiyah had predicted, as the Besht and his scribe entered the community of Brody, the wealthy men welcomed him, and robed him in their finest clothes.

The Besht then turned his attention to the horses, stroking them with his hands in the manner of one who is familiar with animals.

And now you know the extent of the Besht's fear of sin.[172]

"And now you know the extent of the Besht's fear of sin." While the storyteller's final comment here appears to be true, it doesn't exhaust the full significance of the story. The tale is also meant to demonstrate the master's temptation by the sin of pride. In a footnote to this story, Dan Ben-Amos and Jerome R. Mintz explain why at that moment the Besht decided to stroke the horses: "The Besht feared the sin of pride. He played with the horses and thus behaved like a commoner or even a wagon driver, who had very low status in the community."[173] In other words, he was experiencing pride at being honored and was stroking the horse to displace vanity with humility. The Besht later taught that because human pride displaces the Divine, it is the worst form of idolatry.[174] When your attention is focused on your achievements, this leads to the false assumption that you have attained greatness through your own efforts. The person forgets that they exist only by dint of divine grace, and that all attainments come from God. The aim, then, should be a kind of equanimity (*hish'ta'vut*) with regard to the ego, together with humility (*ana'vut* or *shif'lut*) and the cultivation of a virtue of attachment (*devekut*) to the Divine.

The following text comes from a collection of rules of conduct from the school of the Maggid of Medziritch: "The Baal Shem Tov taught, 'When a person has no self-interest, and sees everything with equanimity, he is then worthy of experiencing all of the highest levels of Divinity.

And remember this: Humility is the highest rung of all.'"[175] When the self-centered ego is no longer standing in the way, the seeker becomes transparent to the higher energies, filled with compassion and love for all living things and ready and willing to sacrifice for the benefit of others. In the Besht's view, this is the very essence of saintliness, *hasidut*.

I found two quite different traditions regarding the Baal Shem's ability to overcome pride and cultivate humility. One stream in Hasidic literature claims that he struggled with arrogance and pride until he was finally able to restrain and transform it for good. This text comes from the school of the Maggid of Medziritch: "The Baal Shem Tov taught, 'Humility is loftier than all other spiritual attainments. For if you are able to cultivate equanimity, becoming completely unconcerned about yourself, you will then be able to reach the highest spiritual rung.'"[176] The other stream of tradition indicates that the Besht made peace with imperfection, knowing that pride was a trait he'd struggle with throughout his life: "Toward the end of his life, the Baal Shem's disciples came to him with a question. 'Master, which tzaddik should we bind ourselves to after your passing?' And the holy Baal Shem Tov—may his memory be for a blessing—replied, 'The man who gives you advice about how to rid yourselves of pride—don't take him as your rebbe. For there is no counsel at all about how to deal effectively with pride.'"[177]

Did the Besht change his mind about this? The second source states that the incident happened toward the end of his life. Perhaps he had second thoughts about the issue in light of his lifelong experience. But there was no doubt in the Baal Shem's mind about the absolute necessity of cultivating humility. He once told his disciples the following parable: "There once was a king who sought a magical elixir that would allow him to live forever. When he consulted with his advisors, he was told that he could attain his desire by learning to detach himself from pride, for pride brings with it death. The king attempted to follow his advisor's counsel, but the more he tried, the greater became his pride. *Look at me*, he told himself, *I'm such a great king and I'm so very humble!* When he finally realized his folly, the king consulted his spiritual teacher. 'You can't get rid of pride,' the teacher told him, 'nor should you attempt to do so. In fact, as king, you must possess a sense of self-importance so that you can conduct the affairs of the kingdom with the kind of authority that is necessary to get things done. So my best advice to you is to behave like a king in the world, and at the same time to cultivate humility in your heart. In this way you will merit eternal life.'"[178]

This parable reveals something about the Besht's internal process learning to manifest the kind of self-respect and self-esteem he needed to function as a healer and teacher, while at the same time working to restrain or break his pride and deepen his humility. In another teaching, he taught that self-worth is essential for the realization of one's mission on earth: "Too much humility causes a person to distance himself from serving the blessed One. You need to recognize that through your own practices of prayer and study you will gain the ability to channel the divine flow into all the worlds."[179] It is evident then that he was gradually transformed by his spiritual practices and especially by his mystical experiences. His conviction that the world is a manifestation of God's glory, and that there is no place devoid of the Divine, offered a path to mastering his pride, not through repression or suppression of his vital instincts, but through a process of learning to see through them to reveal the divine spark in each negative character trait. Digging deep into pride and anger, he learned to locate the life-flow that gave these traits their substance. And once he found that spark, he could begin to catalyze the change in his character and behavior that he wanted to see.

Such a personal journey of transformation is not uncommon. James F. Masterson (1926-2010) was an internationally recognized psychiatrist and psychoanalyst who helped inaugurate a new approach to the study and treatment of personality disorders. He wrote that early abandonment can lead to a number of different forms of psychological disorders—narcissism, borderline personality disorder, or obsessive-compulsive disorder. Masterson helped me see how the ga'avah that characterized so much of the Baal Shem's early life came out of the loss of his parents. Masterson states that this psychopathology leads to depression and the construction of a false sense of Self, characterized by narcissistic grandiosity, accompanied by feelings of anxiety, panic, and rage.[180] This theory seemed to agree with Estelle Frankel on abandonment.

So, when did the Besht undertake the process of teshuvah? There is no way to know with any assurance, but my best guess is that his recognition of this issue began early, before his second marriage. The Besht spent seven years as a hermit in the mountains. Perhaps it was during those years when he began to engage in teshuvah. Many of the stories that reported his having acted in deleterious ways, though, took place after his public revelation as a healer, so his engagement with teshuvah and his later transformation might not have happened until later in his life.

THE TESHUVAH PATH

With all this in mind, let us look at a few of the Baal Shem's actual teachings about the nature and practice of teshuvah, which appear in the citations recorded by his disciples. We begin with a very telling parable that he taught about four types of thieves and their different forms of relationship to the process of teshuvah:

> A king once appointed four officers to stand guard over his treasury. Since no one was appointed to watch over them, the officers began to conspire with one another. They agreed to divide the contents of the treasury into four equal portions and then each of them would take their share and flee the country on their own. The men succeeded in carrying out their plan. And what was the result?
>
> The first officer had no conscience at all and simply disappeared. He was never heard of again. Each of the other three, however, began to have second thoughts about their thievery.
>
> One of them recognized that he had done something completely wrong. He returned to the palace bringing back what he had stolen. When he told the king that he had returned because his conscience would not let him keep the treasure, the king was happy with him and honored him greatly.
>
> The second officer hadn't been quite sure what to do. He finally sought out a wise man and asked his counsel. The sage told him that he most certainly had to return what he had stolen. When the man arrived at the

palace and told the king what had occurred, the ruler said to him, "If you hadn't found that sage, you would not have returned the treasure." The king did not punish this officer but he was not at all as happy with him as he had been with the officer who had decided on his own to return the treasure.

The third officer found himself in a country where thievery was punished severely. This caused him to experience a great deal of fear lest he eventually be found and punished. Because of this he returned to the kingdom with the treasure he had taken. When he informed the king as to why he had come back, the king appointed him to a special position: For the rest of his life, he would be required to observe as people were punished for their transgressions. And the Baal Shem indicated to me that he himself was the third type.[181]

I find the candor here remarkable: *"And the Baal Shem indicated to me that he himself was the third type."* The Hebrew text actually says, "My teacher told this (to me) about himself." In other words, he admitted to Jacob Joseph that he'd been motivated to undergo teshuvah out of inner fear. But fear of what? It's not exactly clear, but it would seem that being "required to observe as people were punished for their transgressions" might mean he would have to live the rest of his life remembering what he'd done, and watching as other unrepentant people were also suffering from fear and guilt.

What did the Baal Shem steal from the King, that is, God? It seems that he regretted stealing God's glory for himself, that is, allowing pride in his own talents and abilities to displace the true origin of those gifts. The parable then offers us an explanation as to why the Besht was so insistent with his disciples that they learn to curb their pride and cultivate humility and equanimity.

There is also another Beshtian teaching that may provide us with a window into his understanding of how teshuvah could be initiated. The master begins this discourse by telling disciples how fundamentally there are just two kinds of wrongdoers. The first type is so oblivious of their condition that they imagine they are a complete tzaddik. Their conscience has become so dulled that they cannot even recognize they are engaging in evil. And, the text points out that for such a self-satisfied wrongdoer, there is no hope at all; he lacks not only the will to change, but the motivation as well. Then the teaching pictures the second kind of wrongdoer:

> This is an individual who actually knows who his divine Master is, but he's dead set on rebelling against him. His self-centered desire (*yetzer ha'rah*) seals his eyes from recognizing his own faults and, like the first type of wrongdoer, he thinks that he is a complete tzaddik. And even though this individual involves himself continually in sacred study, davens regularly, and abstains from sensual delights, all of his toil is really for nothing, for he is not bound in devotion to his Creator in complete faith.
>
> What is more, he doesn't know how to serve in a spiritual manner, or how to carry out a mitzvah for God. And yet, despite all of this, it is possible for this person to be elevated and healed, if he listens for the call to teshuvah. But then he must turn toward God wholeheartedly, and ask for direction so he can discover where the light of his liberation dwells.[182]

In formulating this description, the Baal Shem may have been characterizing his own path toward teshuvah. Although he may have harbored rebellion against God because of misfortunes of his life, he continued to observe the disciplines of his ancestral religion out of fear. Even though he carried out the mitzvot, everything he did was carried out because of habit or fear of the consequences of failing to observe the mitzvot. Nonetheless, at some point he came to recognize the error of his ways, as he tells Jacob Joseph, "And yet, despite all of this, it is possible for this person to be elevated and healed if he listens for the call to teshuvah, and then turns toward God wholeheartedly, asking God to show him where the light of his liberation dwells."

What was it that moved the Besht? I used the word "conscience" above, but the Besht didn't believe in a conscience in the modern naturalistic sense of the term, i.e., a sense or an awareness of the blameworthiness or moral goodness of one's conduct, intentions, or character, joined with a feeling of obligation to do right or be good. For a kabbalist like the Baal Shem Tov, the inner call had a sacred origin, the rung of consciousness called *Hokhmah*. Hokhmah is the highest of the ten *sefirot*, the levels or dimensions of existence that represent the kabbalistic model of the universe. The *sefirah* of Hokhmah is the all-embracing Oneness out of which the cosmos emanated. Because Hokhmah itself was born out of divine love, every form of goodness has its origins in its vast, enigmatic reality. And for the Baal Shem, who understood that these ten dimensions exist not only in the cosmos at large, but also in the human psyche, the call to teshuvah comes from the place of Hokhmah within.

Was there an actual "voice" that issued decrees from heaven? R. Jacob Joseph writes that he heard the following from his master concerning what the ancient rabbinic tradition called "the Divine decree from heaven": "The world of Hokhmah lies beyond anything we can know. It is a domain of silence—no sound, no words at all. Nevertheless, within our hearts that celestial Wisdom gives rise to thoughts of goodness. Because of this there is no wrongdoer who does not experience promptings of goodness that arise out of the power of the 'Divine decree' of goodness that emerges out of the realm of Hokhmah. However, when such benevolent thoughts enter the mind of a wrongdoer, they simply pass through and disappear. And because of this, he turns his heart toward things that have no real worth. In this way he forfeits his life, for he has been given a goodly treasure, and instead he has fled the majestic core of reality."[183] In another teaching, the Baal Shem emphasized the metaphorical nature of all religious language. He warned his students not to take the symbols used by the kabbalists literally, explaining that mystics make use of metaphors drawn from the material world to point toward truths that would otherwise be impossible to grasp.[184]

I came to realize that I had been so deeply shaken by the revelations of the Baal Shem's flaws because I'd internalized my mother's perfectionism, and her judgmental attitude toward me, my father, and brother. In my eyes, then, the Besht had to be a perfect saint who could model authentic piety. In fact, this was a pattern that repeated itself again and again in my search for the perfect male hero. Some of these men were living and others were found in the pages of books. Once I found a heroic figure whose life could serve as a model, I would exalt him in my mind's eye. Then, inevitably, at some point I'd discover what I considered a major imperfection in my hero's personality or in his thought. Disappointed, I'd discard him and once again resume my quest for the complete saint.

Now I began to notice the large number of stories and teachings in which the Baal Shem decries judgmentalism and instead displays compassion toward sinners. Finally, I came to understand that following the path of the Besht would require me to transform my judgmentalism into compassion. I had learned how to forgive my parents, so I could certainly do the same for the Baal Shem Tov who had, in a few short years, given me so much! After all, he had identified his own flaws and struggled mightily to turn his life around. And his loving presence had an amazing transformative influence on large numbers of people. Understanding that the master himself had been continually working on his self-transformation helped to make such a change of attitude on my part toward him possible.

SAINTLY IMPERFECTION

In his classic essay, "Saints and Saintliness," Rabbi Solomon Schechter wrote that "saintliness is the effect of a personal religious experience when man enters into close communion with the Divine."[85] The saint, then, does not focus their life on attaining perfection, but on deepening their relationship with God. Schechter points out that saints are intensely aware of their faults and are always attempting to purify their lives, ridding themselves of vices that stand in the way of connection with the Divine, expanding their practice of godly virtues. The emphasis is on striving for transformation, to become more and more worthy of being with God. The smugness of one's sense of perfection is perhaps the greatest hindrance in becoming transparent to the Divine. In a similar light, Martin Buber cites the following reflection of the Baal Shem:

> I let wrongdoers come close to me, if they are not proud.
> I keep the scholars and the sinless away from me if they

are proud. For the wrongdoer who knows that he is a wrongdoer, and therefore considers himself lowly— God is with him, for He "dwells with them in the midst of their uncleanliness" (Leviticus 16:16). But concerning him who prides himself on the fact that he is unburdened by wrongdoing, God says, as we know from the Talmud: "There is not enough room in the world for myself and him."[186]

Saints and spiritual teachers in every religious tradition exhibit a shadow side. They become saintly precisely because they recognize and struggle with their negative traits, working to transform them. Philosopher Ken Wilber has illuminated the problem of the relationship of spiritual teachers to their egos in a rather novel way. He writes that "most devotees want their spiritual sages to be devoid of all the messy, juicy, complex, pulsating, desiring, urging forces that drive most human beings.... All the things that frighten us, confound us." Yet, he writes, the great yogis, saints, and sages "were not feeble-mannered milquetoasts, but fierce movers and shakers.... Gautama Buddha shook India to its foundations. Rumi, Plotinus, Bodhidharma, Lady Tsogyal, Lao Tzu, Plato, the Baal Shem Tov—these men and women started revolutions in the gross realm that lasted hundreds, sometimes thousands, of years." These teachers did not avoid the human dimensions and the ego but engaged this facet of their selves with an intensity that was world-shaking. They were, says Wilber, big egos, and their egos existed within them along with their souls. But unlike most of the people in their societies, their egos were plugged into a deeper level of the psyche, which was in turn "plugged straight into God." These masters inhabited their egos fully and used their egos as necessary vehicles through which higher truths were communicated. The danger comes only when the ego is not plugged into God, for then it takes center stage and becomes self-serving.[187]

The image of the Baal Shem Tov as an imperfect human being who gives himself to the task of spiritual and moral growth is much richer and more realistic than the romantic view of the perfected master that characterized depictions of the Besht in later Hasidism. If my theory about his emotional issues and unruly behavior is true, his life is a powerful testimony to the ability of a devoted human being to free himself from the trauma of childhood abandonment and the self-centered traits that came about as a result of that trauma. He tried to stay aware of the possibility that he could always fall from his high rung because of pride or other forms of wrongdoing, and he attributed his ability to transform himself neither to his ego, nor his will, but to the Divine Soul, a gift of God.

SUFFERING AS A CATALYST FOR GOODNESS

Joseph Campbell states that tragedy means that "the world as we know it, as we have seen it, yields but one ending: death, disintegration, dismemberment, and the crucifixion of our heart with the passing of the forms that we have loved." And he writes that comedy is "the wild and careless, inexhaustible joy of life invincible." Then Campbell tells us that "It is the business of mythology proper...to reveal the specific dangers and techniques of the dark interior way from tragedy to comedy.... The passage of the mythological hero...is inward—into depths where obscure resistances are overcome, and long lost, forgotten powers are revivified, to be made available for the transfiguration of the world."[188]

In this way many of the great religious heroes of the world were able to transform their suffering into salvation. Gautama Buddha, surrounded by his family and his princely comfort is suddenly shaken by his exposure to dissolution and death, and flung onto a chartless path that finally takes him to enlightenment. Moses, another prince, discovers that his identity with the aristocracy of the Egyptian monarchy is an illusion. Fleeing from Egypt, Moses then becomes a nonentity—neither Israelite nor Egyptian. One day, shepherding his father-in-law's flock, he suddenly sees a bush on fire and is called by the Israelite God to return to Egypt to redeem his people. The traditional story in the book of Exodus pictures this as an external event, but from Campbell's point of view, the incident happened in Moses' "depths where obscure resistances are overcome, and long lost, forgotten powers are revivified, to be made available for the transfiguration of the world."

However difficult the emotional issues and attitudes that had been at the core of the Baal Shem's biographical legacy, he was, with divine aid, able to transform them. What is more, he came to see those undesirable traits as having played a positive role in furthering his spiritual formation. For having undergone such great suffering at a tender age eventually enabled him to empathize with the suffering of his fellow Jews and to develop the deep compassion even for wrongdoers that he became known for. As my good friend Barry Barkan put it to me one day, "The Baal Shem's own sense of abandonment allowed him to grasp the way in which his people felt abandoned by God." And the Besht himself said: "Evil is a catalyst for goodness," i.e., the suffering we experience has the power to serve as an incentive for growth.[189] I believe this was indeed the case for him. Once his vision had evolved into nondualism, he came to see that there was an organic wholeness to existence. He was able to understand that the universe had been fashioned in such a way that a true tzaddik could transform adversity and suffering into something good. He was able to do this because the cosmos was derived from divine compassion, and that compassion is found even at the depths of evil. In this way the true tzaddik is able to manifest the Divinity within himself for the benefit of his community, transforming divine harshness into compassion.

In a well-known parable, which we will be examining in the next chapter, the Baal Shem sees himself as a prince, the exiled son of the king of the universe, who is finally able to reconcile himself with his father. This is actually a universal theme, as Joseph Campbell writes: "For the son who has grown really to know the father…the world is no longer a vale of tears but a bliss-yielding, perpetual manifestation of the Presence."[190]

CHAPTER FOURTEEN

REALIZING ENLIGHTENMENT

*"[The] Baal Shem Tov taught adeptship as the purpose of
evolution and the goal of all aspiration...the attainment of a
supernal state of consciousness, wherein man ceases to be and
becomes God-Man. In the adept...is all life realized...in him has
Nature perfected itself, and consummated the fruition of the
ages.... He has, as the Hindus would say, attained
Moksham (liberation)."*
ISRAEL REGARDIE[191]

How did the Besht go about transforming his moral character? This is
only one of a number of questions that go unanswered. There are a number of others, as well: How did the Besht gain a classical rabbinic education? Where did he learn to be a healer and magician? How did he
attain enlightenment? What external influences might have affected the
Besht's formulation of the foundations of Hasidism? Here, I will attempt
to provide some answers.

THE BAAL SHEM'S EDUCATION

It is evident from the Besht's teachings that he possessed an extensive knowledge of Jewish literary sources, including the Bible, Talmud,
Midrash, Kabbalah, and Musar literature. And even though *In Praise
of the Baal Shem Tov* has nothing at all to say about this, later Hasidic
sources describe his relationships and mentorship with a series of saintly
teachers called *nis'ta'rim,* "hidden ones." These mentors, we are told, provided the young man not only with an extensive formal education, but
with a distinct sense of religious vocation. The tales also declare that
the Baal Shem apprenticed directly with the legendary biblical prophet,
Elijah. Were the writers who made those claims transmitting a tradition
that went back to the Baal Shem himself, or were they also wondering
about this question, and so invented an imaginary scenario to suit their

purposes? I once asked Reb Zalman Schachter-Shalomi if he thought these stories had any basis in history, and he affirmed his belief in their veracity.

Modern historians have not really dealt with the question of the Besht's education, limiting their inquiries to the information provided by *In Praise of the Baal Shem Tov*. By their silence they are asserting that these later legends are untrustworthy, and were probably fabricated by later Hasidim to account for the Besht's erudition. The scholars may be right about this, but every once in a while I encounter a tale or anecdote that supposedly took place during the master's hidden years that seems it might have its origin in the actual life of the Besht.

In Praise of the Baal Shem Tov presents an image of the young man as a solitary loner. Except for his relationship to the son of Rabbi Adam, and his brief marriage to an unnamed woman in Okop, he's pictured as having little contact with people until he moves to Brody. The impression is that all the Besht's inspiration and determination derived from his relationship with his inner spirit guide, Ahiyah of Shiloh. But is this really plausible? I cannot help but wonder whether he had living human models who exemplified the values he later espoused. And even if he lived a solitary life during those years, how could he have gained his fluency in Hebrew and Aramaic, and his in-depth knowledge of Jewish sources without a teacher?

EXTERNAL INFLUENCES ON THE BESHT

A number of scholars have suggested that the Baal Shem Tov may have been influenced by Christianity: beginning with Torsten Ysander, as well as Yaffa Eliach, Raphel Patai, and Moshe Idel. Furthermore, we have the memoir of the well-known Polish writer and essayist, Stanislaw Vincenz, who grew up in the Carpathians and heard stories about a Christian family that cared for the Besht when he was ill. Idel describes the young Baal Shem's background as "a rich amalgam of ethnic identities and religious convictions."

Many of the tales in *In Praise of the Baal Shem Tov* also depict the Besht as engaging in experiences that allowed him to interact with the world of the spirits, and directing his own spiritual energies toward the physical world for the purpose of healing and divination. Historian

Gershon David Hundert has written that eighteenth-century Jewish sha-mans in Poland drew on long traditions and bodies of knowledge stretch-ing back to the distant past. Even the use of the term *Baal shem,* which means one who uses the divine name for magical purposes, went back many centuries. Hundert also points out that the remedies and strategies for healing illness used by Jewish healers were often strikingly similar in form to those found among non-Jewish groups.[192]

Spirit guides are one of the universal features of shamanism and, as anthropologist Michael Harner writes, "To perform his work, the sha-man depends on special, personal power, which is usually supplied by his guardian and helping spirits. Each shaman generally has at least one guardian spirit in his service, whether or not he also possesses helping spirits.... Without a guardian spirit it is virtually impossible to be a sha-man, for the shaman must have this strong, basic power source in order to cope with and master the nonordinary or spiritual powers whose exis-tence and actions are normally hidden from humans."[193]

Now, according to *In Praise of the Baal Shem Tov* and many of the later legends, the Besht had a singular spiritual mentor or guardian spirit: the biblical prophet, Ahiyah of Shiloh. One of the many things that such a spirit guide does has to do with initiating the budding adept into his vocation. Yitzhak Buxbaum found and translated a Hasidic text that depicts Ahiyah of Shiloh opening the Besht's eyes to the existence of the all-pervading spirit of Divinity. The incident is set during the Besht's sev-en-year period as a hermit, preparing for the vocation he would be called to once he reached his thirty-sixth year. According to this legend, Ahiyah appears and directs him to immerse himself in the Prut River eighteen times, and to then retire to the cave in which he was living and stay there for three days and nights without eating. On the fourth day at dawn, Ahiyah reappears and leads the Besht outside the cave. Placing his hands on the young man's head, Ahiyah gives him this blessing: "May your eyes now be opened to see the Truth!" Then Ahiyah disappears again, and the Besht suddenly experiences the most intense yearning for God he has ever known. But just then the Baal Shem's eyes revealed a new light to him, more powerful than a thousand suns:

Everywhere he looked, he saw God's light shining out

through everything. The sky, the trees, the stones, the earth beneath his feet, the very air—were all Godliness, shimmering with divine vitality. Waves of joy thrilled his body. He saw God with his physical eyes. He saw Godliness first and everything else afterward, by the way. It was clear to him: God is everything and everything is God.... He knew and saw that God is more real than the world, for He is the essence of all that exists...

From that day on the Baal Shem Tov was established in God-awareness.... Even every movement of his, every feeling, every thought, was also from God. He saw God in all things and heard God in all sounds. He heard the divine voice in the rustling of tree leaves, in the flowing sounds of the river, in the singing and chirping of birds. When he listened to the inner sound that his ears heard, he heard the voice of God, which enlivened and brought into being the sound he was hearing. He felt at every moment that God was with him. His bliss was boundless.[194]

When I discovered this vision, I was overjoyed. At first, I believed the story was authentic, but later I wasn't sure. As we will see, the Baal Shem told his disciples that they should not attempt to engage in a form of teshuvah that would change them too rapidly, extinguishing their previous identities. And in his teachings the Besht admits that a permanent state of God-awareness (*gahd'lut*) is not something human beings are able to retain. Again and again he says that human consciousness is cyclic, and his disciples must be prepared for times when their awareness will be diminished (*kaht'nut*). Still, I think it possible that this source bears the kernel of an experience the Besht may have undergone.

Two scholars, Yaffa Eliach and Sharon Packer have gathered evidence that the Baal Shem Tov was exposed to psychedelic substances. I've come to believe that their claims could be true. Shamans in many, though not all, archaic cultures have employed psychedelics in efforts on behalf of their tribes. What could be true is that if the Besht underwent some or many extraordinary experiences through the unintentional or deliberate use of psychedelics, they may have inspired his quest for a transformational spiritual path. Nonetheless, I am not convinced that psychedelic experience by itself could adequately account for his radical transformation.

Roger Walsh, a professor of psychiatry, anthropology, and philosophy at the University of California at Irvine has argued that "these drugs seem better at inducing transient altered states rather than enduring transformed traits." He also states "that while it is clear that entheogens can produce religious experiences, it is less clear that they can induce religious lives." Walsh identifies two principles that have become clear to the researchers: first, that considerable enquiry shows how entheogens can occasion genuine mystical experiences and long-lasting benefits in a large percentage of suitably selected and prepared people. And second, that an enlightened life requires a long-term multifaceted discipline of psychological, spiritual, and physical practices.[195] From my personal experience with psychedelics, I agree.

A RADICAL FORM OF MYSTICAL WORSHIP

As we've seen, Moshe Idel has provided strong evidence that the Baal Shem was inspired by practices of the twelfth-century ecstatic kabbalist, R. Abraham Abulafia. It would seem like the Besht engaged in a long-term transformational psychospiritual practice that he derived from Abulafian sources. Abulafia was influenced by the writings of Moses Maimonides, but he was mystically-inclined and not satisfied by his study of philosophy, nor by any other branch of knowledge. At thirty-one he began to immerse himself in the study of the kabbalistic Book of Creation (*Sefer Yetzirah*) together with its numerous commentaries. This work described the creation of the world and human beings through the use of divine speech, made up of different combinations of the letters of the Hebrew alphabet. Out of this theory Abulafia developed a novel, ecstatic method of spiritual practice that made use of the Hebrew alphabet.

He wrote a number of meditation manuals, and maintained that through the spiritual techniques he was introducing, seekers would be able to expand their consciousness and be transfigured, becoming one with God, and part of the world of divine light. He also promised that the practices he was introducing would disclose prophetic visions through which all the mysteries of the universe would be revealed. Idel identifies Abulafia's experience as *unio mystica*, union with the Divine.

Just what were these techniques? Abulafia believed that all the letters of the Hebrew alphabet were part of God's great name, which is the underlying spiritual foundation of everything that exists. Through experimentation he discovered that passionately centering his attention and voice on those letters had the power to open him to expanded states of awareness. As he wrote, "every letter represents a whole world to the mystic who abandons himself to its contemplation." Through a variety of methods of repetitively combining the different letters of the alphabet with one another he was able to gradually expand his consciousness and attain intense experiences of bliss. In this way "the mystic consciousness perceives and becomes part of the world of divine life, whose radiance illuminates his thoughts and heals his heart."[196]

One of the methods Abulafia used in his practice was automatic writing. A disciple of his described what occurred to Abulafia the first time he combined the Hebrew letters through writing: "During the second week the power became so strong within me that I couldn't manage to write down all the combinations of letters which spontaneously spurted out of my pen.... When the evening came in which this power was conferred on me, and midnight had passed, I set out to take up the Great Name of God—Y-H-V-H—but in the form of the seventy-two names, and I permuted and combined those forms in writing. And when I had done this for some time, the letters took on the shapes of great mountains. I was then seized by strong trembling; I lost all of my strength, and my hair stood on end—it was as if I were no longer part of this world! Then something like speech came out of my lips, forcing them to move. And I said: 'This is indeed the very spirit of wisdom.'"[197] Idel describes Abulafia's approach as an "ongoing combinations of letters, their pronunciation according to a certain melodic code, movements of the head and hands, and some form of vocal melody and different rhythms of breathing, most probably influenced by the Yoga breathing technique."[198]

Idel shows how the Baal Shem adapted Abulafia's technique to the liturgical text of the *siddur*, the traditional prayer book, and in this way converting the Jewish liturgy into a spiritual procedure that would open to the kind of transformative experience we might call enlightenment.

In one of his instructions to his disciples, the Baal Shem taught: "When you offer your prayers, invest all of your energy in the words of the prayer book. Sound out letter after letter in an intensive manner, and you will eventually forget your physical existence. It will then seem to you that the letters that you are chanting are combining themselves and linking themselves one to the other without your aid, forming the actual words. This practice will give you immense pleasure."[199]

In a letter that the Baal Shem wrote to his father-in-law and disciple, R. Gershon of Kutov, the Besht explains in greater depth what is occurring during this practice: "In each letter of each word of the prayerbook there are three dimensions: worlds, souls, and Divinity. And when you daven in the way I have been teaching you, the worlds, souls, and Divinity in each of the letters ascend heavenward and become bound one to the other. And then they become united in true unification with the Divine itself. At every stage of this movement, allow your own soul to become united with them. Soon, all the worlds will become united as one, and they will ascend even further, and there will be immeasurable joy and pleasure. Think about how much joy a bride and groom experience when they unite physically in this diminished world. Well, the kind of joy that I am describing is so much greater!"[200]

In some of his reports about this practice, the Baal Shem testified that he was able to actually see a radiance within the words: "Focus your attention entirely on the words of prayer and Torah that you are chanting and you will eventually see lights within the words illuminating one another, as it is said, *'Light is sown for the tzaddik, and joy for the upright in heart'* (Ps. 97:11). Remember this: the letters of Torah are divine chambers into which God shines the emanation of sacred light, just as the Zohar teaches: *'The Holy One, the Torah, and the Jewish people are all One'"* (2:85b, 3:73a).[201] As important as this Abulafian technique was to the Baal Shem's mystical ascent, it soon became a foundational launch pad to even higher realms. As his awareness expanded into those supernal states of consciousness, he would eventually shed all signs of his physicality and ego, and enter into a profound state of awe. The Kabbalah declares that the physical world is merely the lowest of four different and distinct realms of being, all of which form a hierarchal unity. These cosmic realms are reflected and replicated within the human psyche, each realm taking the form of a widening state of consciousness. The Besht describes his approach to davening as a gradual ascent from the lower to the higher worlds.

The lowest level of all is the realm of ordinary human awareness of the world in all of its multiplicity (*Olam Ha'Ah'si'yah*). In the act of ecstatic davening, however, the Baal Shem's awareness would ascend upward (or inward) to the World of Formation (*Olam Ha'Yeh'tsi'rah*), where he felt fully embraced and loved by the Divine. And, still mounting, his soul would enter the World of Creation (*Olam Ha'B'ri'yah*), where his soul experienced the passionate and complete reunification with its source. The journey would culminate in the World of Emanation (*Olam Ha'Ah'tsi'lut*), an expansive state in which the ego together with all boundaries between things would dissolve into the supreme Oneness. When his ecstatic worship took him into this most spacious state of consciousness, he would discern that the three lower rings of awareness were only partially real. And he would know for certain that it was this ocean of Oneness that continually gives birth to the three lower worlds.

The supreme affirmation in the morning and evening liturgy is the *Sh'mah,* the declaration of Divine unity. For the Baal Shem, this was no mere verbal declaration. It was the opportunity to actually experience what the words express. Here is how one Beshtian text interprets the holy watchword of our faith:

> *"Hear O Israel: the EverPresent is our Power, the EverPresent alone."* When we say *"the EverPresent alone,"* we mean that nothing other than the Divine exists in the whole of the universe. Ponder this: Your separate self is absolutely nothing, for you are really only the soul within you, which is a portion of the Divine beyond. No, nothing at all exists in the universe except for the absolute Unity which is God.[202]

Rabbi Lawrence Kushner puts this mystical insight into contemporary terms: "Being at One with the Holy One of Being is not about becoming the same as God, but about forgetting the boundaries of self. You forget, at least for a moment, the mind game of where you end and creation begins. You understand that you are an expression of creation: It is in you and you are everywhere in it."[203]

Historian Immanuel Etkes describes the Besht's mystical ecstasy as an experience "in which his soul merged unimpeded with the divine spirit...that disclosed to him the truth about the presence of the divinity in all things." He adds that "ecstatic prayer is supposed to help the person praying achieve liberation from the characteristic consciousness of earthly life and to attain an unmediated proximity to the realm of the divine.... As the spiritual stimulation intensifies, the symptoms of ecstasy become involuntary and uncontrollable. The climax of the experience of ecstasy becomes the setting for awareness of direct contact with the Divinity. This is the experience of mystical ecstasy.... [I]t would seem that ecstatic prayer became a hallmark of the Besht at a relatively early stage of his career."[204]

Through my own experiences with psychedelics, I know that this kind of mystical experience leads the seeker to a state of a consciousness free of the ego. And when the ego dissolves, one becomes part of the unity of the whole. At the same time, the unity that one enters becomes a total embrace of compassion and love. Such an experience cannot last, but the Baal Shem would apparently enter that realm of absolute love day after day during his mystical ascents, and I'm convinced it was this discipline that inspired him to change his life so he could live in accord with his mystical vision.

He davened in public in his synagogue in Medzhibozh, and *In Praise of the Baal Shem Tov* contains a remarkable description of the master at prayer by a disciple, a certain Rabbi Abraham, who was the cantor in his master's synagogue:

> During the silent standing prayer (the *Amidah*), the Besht trembled greatly as he always did when he was in deep prayer. Everyone who looked at him while he was davening noticed this trembling. When Rabbi Abraham completed the public repetition of the silent, standing prayer and the time for the chanting of the Hallel psalms had come, the Besht was still standing in his regular place

of prayer. He did not go up to the holy ark to lead the communal davening as was his custom. And then, just at that moment, the Hasid, Rabbi Wolf Kitses, looked at the Baal Shem's face, and saw that it was burning like a torch. And his eyes were bulging and immobile, fixed straight ahead like someone who is dying—God forbid!

Rabbi Ze'ev motioned to Rabbi Abraham, and each man gave his hand to the Besht and led him up to the ark. The master went with them and stood before the holy ark. But he continued to tremble and the prayer leaders had to postpone the reading of the Torah until the Baal Shem finally stopped shaking.[205]

To judge by the description, the Besht was in a deep trance free of the encumbrance of his body. A similar instance is found in a text cited by Yitzhak Buxbaum. One of the high points in the morning liturgy is called the *Amidah* or *Sh'moneh Es'rei*. This is the silent standing prayer, and traditional Jews often cover themselves in their prayer shawls (*tallit*, pl., *tallitot*) to be in solitude with God: "Once, when the Baal Shem Tov was in Kolomaya, and praying the *Sh'moneh Es'rei* his face covered with his tallit, a little boy named Nachman, the son of Rabbi David of Kolomaya, snuck under his tallit (as children do) and looked at his holy face. He saw that each moment the Baal Shem Tov's color changed. One moment his face was entirely white, without a drop of blood, like a dead man; the next moment his face shone like the sun with a supernal light. From his fright and terror at seeing this, the boy became ill with a high fever, until they told the Baal Shem Tov, who healed him."[206]

Now the Baal Shem may have been completely silent, but from all appearances it seems that he was undergoing an emotionally intense form of ecstatic surrender. He testified that during these hours of worship he was entirely saturated by the Divine. In another striking teaching, the Besht tells his disciples how to prepare themselves before they begin to enter the intense realm of consciousness that will lead to union with the Divine: "Before you begin to daven, focus your entire intentionality on the reality that you might actually die because of the intensity of your davening. There are some worshippers whose concentration becomes so overwhelming that they breathe their last after having chanted no more than four or five words in the presence of the Divine. And when you become fully aware of this great risk, ask yourself: Why should I have any kind of ulterior motives in my davening? But know that you will remain alive and able to complete your prayers only because of the great mercy and strength that you receive from God while you are davening."[207]

PROPHET OF A NEW PARADIGM

We know that the Baal Shem's spiritual transformation took place over time and not in a single flash because he specifically states *teshuvah* shouldn't happen all at once, for a sudden conversion would crush the seeker's individuality. In his bilingual collection of the Baal Shem's prayer practices, *Pillar of Prayer*, Menachem Kallus translated a striking parable that compares the slow and careful progression of spiritual development to the making of wine. Here is Kallus' translation of the Baal Shem's teaching:

> Before one makes the decision to serve God with purity, one is like impure wine before straining, committing transgressions and *Mitzvot* randomly. Then one decides to serve God wholeheartedly, with purity, and separates oneself from his or her "sediments," that is, from the impurities within. And one proceeds along the proper path for some time. Then one undertakes a second examination, and again finds elements of self-service, though fewer and more subtle than before, and then separates oneself from these ulterior motives, proceeding for a while along a straighter path. Subsequently, one examines oneself yet again and still finds the service of God marred by self-interest, though of a more subtle nature, such as expecting reward in the coming world, etc. This is because the *Yetzer haRah'* [evil inclination] does not release a person so easily, and the more one escapes it the more diligently it pursues with ever more subtle ploys.[208]

In a footnote on a related passage, Kallus shows that the Besht charted seven stages of spiritual refinement, each one more subtle than the preceding stage.[209] It's clear that these discourses on individual spiritual evolution are autobiographical in character.

During the 1990s I was privileged to study a number of the Baal Shem's original teachings about sweetening suffering with a colleague, Rabbi Miles Krassen. A scholar of Kabbalah and Hasidism, Rabbi Miles is intimately familiar with Eastern mystical thought, and he has suggested the following reconstruction of the Baal Shem's path to mystical illumination: "Sometime in the 1730s, the Baal Shem Tov embarked on a multiyear spiritual retreat in the Carpathian Mountains, during which he perfected his spiritual powers and practice. Up until that time, evidently, while he was well-known as a powerful healer, he had attained neither the full realization and spiritual knowledge nor conviction that would characterize his later life and transform him into one of the most important spiritual teachers in Jewish history. In this sense, the Baal Shem Tov may be numbered among similarly realized masters, *siddhas,* and saints who after a lengthy period of secluded practice take their place in a spiritual pantheon consisting of some of the most highly spiritually evolved figures in the history of humanity.... The shamanic nature of this retreat is quite evident. The Baal Shem Tov had access to a method of entering not only altered states of consciousness but also hidden worlds. On these spiritual journeys he made contact with disincarnate spiritual guides who advised him, and he was able to gain knowledge of hidden matters regarding past, present, and future."[210]

This is a brilliant and accurate description of the Besht's evolutionary path. Krassen concludes: "It is precisely in this sense that we may see the Baal Shem Tov as a prophet of a new paradigm, the Messianic Age, characterized by a higher non-dual consciousness, rooted in direct recognition of a pervasive and unifying Divine Presence that is manifest everywhere and in everything." He saw the possibility that if his practices became widespread, they might have the effect of inaugurating a new and perfected era.

THE CASTLE OF ILLUSION

I have used the word "enlightenment" a number of times already. What do I mean by this term, which is usually employed in connection with Eastern forms of mystical experience, rather than Western spirituality?

In *How Enlightenment Changes Your Brain,* Andrew Newberg and Mark Robert Waldman write that the various Eastern paths define the word enlightenment differently. In Hinduism, seekers become one with the consciousness that is the essence out of which the universe emerged. Taoists, on the other hand, achieve enlightenment by being in harmony with the flow of life, that is, the principles of nature. In Chinese and Tibetan Buddhism, enlightenment is personal, brought about through a process of continual self-reflection, while in Japanese Zen Buddhism students only become enlightened when they realize the radical truth that everything is an illusion of the mind.

The concept of enlightenment is rarely found in Jewish, Christian, or Muslim sacred texts. Gnosticism was an exception, for the ancient Christian Gnostics were more interested in religious experience or mystical union than they were in conceptual knowledge of God. Gershom Scholem considered Gnosticism to be one of the two major roots of Kabbalah, the other being Neoplatonism. Newberg and Waldman write that in the centuries encompassing the time period of the Besht, practices that encouraged and referred to the possibility of mystical union with God were common in both Jewish Kabbalah and Islamic Sufism.[211] What then do we mean when we use the term in connection with the Baal Shem Tov? We are fortunate to have a remarkable parable of his that symbolically encodes his particular experience of enlightenment:

> There was once a very wise king who possessed great magical power. And with this skill he wove an illusory spell, enclosing himself in a great castle surrounded by walls, towers, gates, and moats. And then the king commanded that gold be placed before each of the gates. Finally, he invited all of his subjects to visit him in his castle.
>
> Hearing the summons, all of the people in the realm set out for their sovereign's castle. But when they arrived and saw the gold, they immediately filled their pockets with as much of the treasure that they could carry, and then returned to their homes.
>
> One seeker alone continued on his quest to reach the king himself—the king's own son. And finally, after

tremendous effort, the prince came into his father's very presence. At that moment there was no longer any separation between father and son. And just then, all the walls, towers, gates, and moats simply disappeared, for it had all been merely an optical illusion.[212]

Notice that the parable assumes the world is experienced differently by people who live in different states of awareness. The multitude of the king's subjects dwell in an instinct-driven dualistic state of consciousness, and are therefore dominated by their cravings. Because of this they easily give up the ideal they originally set out to fulfill. But the prince's awareness is dominated by a higher form of comprehension. He knows that there is more to existence than material reality. It is this certainty that brings him to the realization that all the delights of the world and all the barriers to enlightenment are, in truth, illusions.

Examining the parable closely, it seems the Besht's enlightenment is like the Zen perception that the physical appearance of the world is an illusion of the mind. Yet the Besht's experience was actually closer to Hinduism which, like Zen, would recognize the physical appearance of the world as an illusion of the mind, but would also affirm that seekers become one with the consciousness that's the essence out of which the universe emerged. In the parable the Baal Shem describes this merger in personal terms: "At that moment there was no longer any separation between father and son." In other, possibly later teachings, however, he used a transpersonal metaphor, saying that, ultimately, the whole of existence is *Ayin,* "No-thing," that is, no *particular* thing. In other words, a Oneness that embraces everything. Here is how the Besht put it: "Out of the strength that comes to you from the compassion of the Divine you will be able to enter the gate of No-thing, completely forgetting your own existence. The only aspects of yourself that will remain in place are your limitless thoughts, and your love, and all of your virtues. And these will be completely bound to your love for the One."[213]

William James said that this kind of unitary experience is common to all the world's mystics: "The overcoming of all the usual barriers between the individual and the Absolute is the great mystic achievement. In mystic states we both become One with the Absolute and we become aware of our Oneness. This is the everlasting and triumphant mystical tradition, hardly altered by clime or creed. In Hinduism, in Neoplatonism, in Sufism, in Christian mysticism, in Whitmanism, we find the same recurring note, so that there is about mystical utterances an eternal unanimity which ought to make a critic stop and think, and which brings it about that the mystical classics have, as has been said, neither birthday nor native land. Perpetually telling of the unity of man with God, their speech antedates languages, and they do not grow old." One would like to add Judaism to James' list, but in 1902 when he published *The Varieties of Religious Experience*, hardly anything about Jewish mysticism was known in the wider academic world.

METAPHORS FOR ENLIGHTENMENT

Ralph Metzner, a pioneer in the study of consciousness and transformative experience, discusses the metaphors used in spiritual literature to describe psychospiritual transformation. He explains that he came to realize "whereas there are literally hundreds of specific methods of bringing about psychospiritual transformation...only about a dozen or so key metaphors describing the process itself seem to occur over and over in the world's literature." One of these metaphors is "From Darkness to Light," i.e., the process of enlightenment. We find this in a number of the teachings and tales of the Besht. For example, *In Praise of the Baal Shem Tov* relates an amazing experience that a young disciple of the Besht's father-in-law underwent when he first encountered the Baal Shem. This unnamed student was staying as a guest at the inn of the Baal Shem and his wife. At midnight, he awoke abruptly and witnessed what he took to be a huge blaze burning on the oven. As he ran toward the conflagration, he was hurled backward and fainted. Israel and his wife revived the guest, and the Besht admonished him: "You should not have looked at what is not permitted to you." But the guest marveled at what he'd seen, for it hadn't been a physical fire, but a visage of the innkeeper himself, blazing like a fire.

Metzner writes that for mystics and visionaries of the Eastern and Western spiritual traditions, light is "an experience that is lived and felt in the mind, the heart, the body, and the inner recesses of the psyche. Enlightenment, then, is not merely a metaphor but rather an experience of one's own inner essence, the Self, as a Being of light."[214] We see this in the following teaching of the Besht: "Make your body into a dwelling place for the soul. And then make your soul (*nefesh*) a dwelling place for the spirit. And then turn your spirit (*ru'ah*) into a dwelling place for your higher soul. And finally your higher soul (*neshamah*) into a dwelling place for the light of the Shekhinah, which is above you. It will be as if the light is spreading all around you, and you are within the light, sitting and trembling in awe."[215] As Ralph Metzner writes, "Whatever the nature and origin of this 'light' may be, it is apparent that it can, on occasion, suffuse the body with such intensity that it becomes visible to others, even those who are not normally clairvoyant. The light may become visible in certain altered states: in psychedelic states, as well as after prolonged periods of meditation, many people, myself included, have seen patterns of light and flame around the heads and faces of individuals. Thus, it appears that either the sensitized vision of the perceiver or the intensity of the phenomenon in the subject can make the inner light outwardly visible."[216]

When I examined the twelve metaphors identified by Metzner, I recognized that in his teachings the Baal Shem employed not only the image of enlightenment, but five other, similar metaphors:

- *Uncovering the veils of illusion.* The Besht speaks of the universe as clothing of the Divinity. The adept is able uncover the outer physicality of the universe, and witness its underlying spirituality.
- *From captivity to liberation.* The Baal Shem employs the story of the Exodus as metaphor for individual spiritual liberation from the bondage of obsessive desire.
- *From fragmentation to wholeness.* The master engaged in *yihudim,* which were spiritual practices meant to reunite or reintegrate the fragmented character of consciousness and existence.
- *Reconciling with the inner enemy:* He came to the understanding that the yetzer ha'rah, self-centered desire, was in truth a face of the Divine itself, meant to provoke seekers into transforming its power into goodness.
- *Journey to the place of vision and power* and *Returning to the Source.* Our pilgrimage on earth has to do with finding our way

back to our ultimate Source, which is the place of vision and power.

ENLIGHTENMENT AND THE BRAIN

Earlier I cited Andrew Newberg's and Mark Robert Waldman's book, *How Enlightenment Changes Your Brain.* Newberg is a neurologist, and because of a pivotal spiritual experience while growing up, he became interested in scientific evidence for enlightenment. In the course of his research with more than 2,000 self-identified enlightened individuals, he discovered they had undergone profound, positive life changes as a result of their experiences. These included Brazilian psychic mediums, Sufi mystics, Buddhist meditators, Franciscan nuns, Pentecostals, and participants in secular spirituality rituals. By examining their brain scans, Newberg was able to identify the specific neurological mechanisms associated with the enlightenment experience.

Newberg and Waldman write that their analysis of the experience of enlightenment in subjects they investigated led them to conclude there are five basic elements that lead to the enlightenment experience, and that these are generally the same for everyone: (1) A sense of unity or connectedness. (2) An incredible intensity of experience. (3) A sense of clarity and new understanding in a fundamental way. (4) A sense of surrender or loss of voluntary control. (5) A sense that something— one's beliefs, one's life, one's purpose—has suddenly and permanently changed.[217] Nonetheless, they write, "the interpretation of these elements varies enormously from person to person. For example, one might feel unity with nature, or with universal consciousness, or with God." The book contains a number of examples of enlightenment experiences. One of these came from a sixty-five-year-old American Jewish woman: "It felt like an energetic merging and being One with the most powerful Creative Force/Being in and beyond all universes. In that moment, I was simultaneously the same individual consciousness of myself, but I was also part of 'God' (for lack of a better term, really). Infused with the power of Creation/Creativity, I was buoyed up with a joy so immense it infused my Beingness with an affinity for everything."[218]

The authors distinguish between enlightenment with a lower case "e," and Enlightenment with a capital "E." Experiences of enlightenment with a small "e" "shed light on our ignorance and bring ourselves out from the dark...often preparing us for the rarer big "E" experience where our entire worldview and values are radically transformed.... For some, the separation between God and oneself completely dissolves."[219] This research can help us understand the place of intense spiritual practice in the Baal Shem's life, for we have a tradition that states,

> The Baal Shem's soul once revealed to him that it did not open him to lofty insights because of his study of the Talmud, or because of his probing of traditional inter-pretations of Jewish law. Rather, his deep spiritual per-ceptions came to him because of his life of worship. The Baal Shem Tov davened with intense concentration, and it was because of this that he was able to attain such a high spiritual rung.[220]

Considering that as a traditional Jew the Baal Shem davened regularly three times a day, and that his disciples recorded a vast array of his instructional teachings about prayer, I think it probable that he underwent numerous experiences of enlightenment with a small "e" before his Enlightenment with a big "E" occurred. The authors state that this kind of experience radically transforms one's worldview and values. Does enlightenment then immediately turn an individual into a saint? Of course not. But being enlightened means becoming more sensitive to the existence of one's moral flaws, together with a new and deep-seated intentionality to transform attitudes and behaviors in order to live in alignment with the vision provided by enlightenment. This is fully in accord with what Judaism teaches about sainthood, as R. Solomon Schechter writes, "Consciousness of sin and the assurance of grace are the two great motive powers in the working of religion.... Under these two realities—the reality of sin and the reality of grace—the saint is constantly labouring."[221] And this, in my understanding, is what happened in the life of the Baal Shem.

He was an enlightened master, and while "enlightenment" is not really part of the lexicon of Judaism, the experience behind it became a normative aspect of what it meant to be a tzaddik, a Hasidic spiritual leader. The tzaddik was assumed to have attained the highest truth, and this awakening brought with it both spiritual and moral perfection. Menahem Nahum of Chernobyl, a disciple of both the Besht and the Maggid, puts it this way: "The fact is that *'the tzaddik is the foundation of the world.'* (Proverbs 10:25) He is both the foundation and also the channel through which divine abundance and life flow down into the world and into all of the world's creatures. He fashions the pathway through which this life flow will spread. Through his continual attachment to the Creator he becomes a dwelling place for the letter *Aleph,* the silent origin of existence, which lives within him, as it states in the book of Exodus, *'I shall dwell in their midst.'* (25:8) And thus he is in truth an actual part of God."[222]

DEVEKUT AND DAVENING PRACTICE

When I first encountered the Baal Shem Tov, I had left traditional Jewish prayer practices behind. In some bizarre way, marijuana had come to replace the missing religious modes of worship. And yes, I could get "high" with what we then called weed or grass, yet I soon came to recognize this was no substitute for a deeper connection with the cosmos and its spiritual source. Discovering the Baal Shem inspired me to begin a quest for a personal spiritual practice that could transform my consciousness in ways that he spoke about. Many insights I encountered in Beshtian texts offered clues regarding possibilities of establishing a transformative spiritual discipline. In my experiments, I would integrate the wisdom of the Besht with what I knew or was learning from other spiritual traditions.

When I began to study more, I discovered that he developed his own method of davening, drawing on the approach pioneered by Abraham Abulafia. We looked at some of this in Part One. I was powerfully drawn to the Besht's descriptions of this experience, but in my attempts to make use of his technique I found myself stymied. Even if I could find a way to project my consciousness into the letters and words of the liturgy, the method seemed cumbersome and over-complicated. Over time the Besht's method of worship fell out of use among the Hasidim, perhaps because it was so unwieldy.

Recently my wife discovered that an Orthodox rabbi, Abraham Leader, teaches Abulafia's ecstatic methods in Israel. Diane has studied with Rabbi Leader online and she testifies to the power and depth of the method. However, I have been using a different and I believe simpler set of practices now for almost twenty years, inspired by the Besht, which takes me where I want and need to go.

During the years I studied these teachings intensively, I looked for hints regarding spiritual practices that would allow me to open to grace and gratitude, to experience the luminous divinity of the world, and lose myself in the vastness of existence. At the same time, I was studying and experimenting with different forms of meditation. The forms that worked the best for me were somatically based. They utilized the ongoing cycle of breathing and/or continual repetition of a divine name to evoke an experience of divine presence.

The meditation masters of India have indicated that the key to understanding the power of repeating divine names is their vibration, which contemporary neurologists trace to the frequency of brain activity in the cerebral cortex. "The mantra forms a feedback loop as the brain produces the sound, listens to it, and then responds with a deeper level of attention," explains one of the most popular interpreters.[223] Meanwhile, modern investigators have discovered that traditional Asian forms of breathing practice calm and relax the body and mind by connecting different parts of the brain: the prefrontal cortex, limbic system (which includes the hippocampus and the amygdala), and brain stem. When the neurons from these four parts of the brain are stimulated together we feel good and it becomes easier to concentrate, to be kind, and make good decisions. About this process and experience, Rabbi Diane Elliot has written: "The movement of breath in and through the body reflects the cosmos's constant rhythm of expanding and condensing. The voice—amplifying, coloring, and riding on the breath—makes audible our participation in the vibratory patterns that are always shaping and reshaping all matter."

The Sanskrit word *yoga* refers to a group of physical, mental, and spiritual practices or disciplines. The actual word "yoga" means to join, to unite, or to attach the self to God. Central to Hindu contemplative practice is the journey into the depths of the Self, which can lead to what is permanent, reliable, and beyond which there is nothing else to be found or realized. Like yoga, the Hebrew word *devekut*—used by numerous kabbalists including the Baal Shem Tov—means joining, uniting, or attaching the Self to God. One can see the proximity of the Sanskrit and the Hebrew terms.

The approach that I use has a contemporary lineage—from 1968 to 1971, when I lived in Boston and was a member of the intentional neo-Hasidic community, Havurat Shalom. There, the davening was wonderful. I was regularly moved by it, for I had never experienced communal davening in a contemporary context as powerful as this. A quarter century later, living in California and having experimented with numerous forms of meditation and prayer from different spiritual traditions, I found myself returning to some of the sequence of core elements that we had incorporated in our davening at Havurat Shalom:

- The prolonged chanting of a *niggun,* a Hasidic devotional melody, often without words.
- Entering the silence and stillness of meditation following the niggun. I call my practice Yah Breathing Meditation.
- Contemplative davening using words drawn from the traditional liturgy, which I have named Unitive Love Practice.

In the remainder of this chapter, I will share my practice of the first two elements of the progression: niggun and meditation. Let me add that even though my practices don't duplicate those of the Besht, they were inspired by him, and I believe they allow me to experience core aspects of his vision as I understand it: awakening to the wonder of the here and now, recognizing that the present moment is the Presence of God, and realizing that I'm a small part of a mysterious universe that is Divine.

NIGGUN CHANTING

I was first exposed to the world of Hasidic niggun (melody) at the Lubavitcher community in 1961. Imagine hundreds of Hasidim standing on bleachers in a huge hall, loudly chanting the same joyous or devotional melody again and again. And the rebbe, Menachem Mendel Schneerson, at the front of the throng waving his arms, urging the entranced men to sing even louder and more passionately. And this goes on for perhaps a half hour without ceasing. Then the rebbe speaks for a while, and begins another niggun. It is as if the melodies transmute the rebbe's words into the transcendent language of music.

I cannot put the power of *niggunim* into words better than my good friend and teacher Rabbi Marcia Prager has already done: "A niggun is a sacred wordless melody, crafted to carry us to deep centers of awareness, opening new possibilities for self-reflection and spiritual deepening. Within a niggun, we can open our hearts to feel life most deeply. We travel again to the places in our souls that hurt, and the places that sing with joy. Sometimes, if we are willing, those can merge and a great unifying light envelops us. We feel an exaltation, and a nurturing love. We are lifted up, and along with us the melody floats higher and higher.... With eyes closed, a niggun can be traveled far and deep.... With eyes closed we are alone while not alone, in private space yet aware of and supported by the presence of those around us."

Robert Gass has written that most mystical sects seek to give devotees direct access to the Godhead and teach practices built on the uttering of certain sacred sounds.[224] Abraham Abulafia compared his ecstatic method of combining the Hebrew letters to music. The influence that Abulafia exerted on the Baal Shem's sound-based form of intoning the letters and words of the liturgy can explain, at least in part, the emergence and importance of sacred melody in early Hasidism. The Besht is reported to have taught that "through melody one can reach joy and devekut—deep connection—with the Infinite."[225] Velvel Pasternak began to record the niggunim of the various Hasidic communities in the sixties, and I purchased these long-playing records and listened to them again and again.

YAH BREATHING MEDITATION

We have learned about the Baal Shem's use of loud vocalizations of the letters and words of the traditional liturgy, a practice that thrust him into a state of exalted rapture. As Hasidism became less radical, this approach was replaced by niggun. But what about silence? The Besht's grandson, R. Hayim Ephraim of Sudlikov, writes the following:

> Be silent before you begin to daven until you are able to
> cut through the barriers that prevent you from binding
> yourself (*devekut*) to the Divine. Then you will be able
> to sweeten suffering at its very root. This is the secret of

prayer, as I was taught by my teacher, my grandfather, the Baal Shem Tov, who learned this from his teacher, Ahiyah of Shiloh.[226]

What is it that "sweetens suffering at its root"? As so many meditators have found, entering the depths of silence allows one to break through the noise and commotion of the world and to find one's spiritual center in the ensuing stillness. Here is what the Besht has to say about this: "At times it is possible to pray in great love and awe and ecstasy without any bodily movement at all. This can happen when one is bound in oneness with God, worshipping through the soul alone."[227] But what does one actually do during meditation? When I was first introduced to Reb Zalman in 1963, he gave me a copy of *The First Step,* a little treatise on personal spiritual development he'd written and hand-printed in 1959. That was the first time I read anything about a *Jewish* form of meditation. In his description of the practice, Zalman focused on an immediate *emotional* awareness of the presence of the Divine in the here and now in one's consciousness: "So you meditate on God filling the universe with life...you are now here, filled with life—with God.... When you finally face this tremendous fact, you feel something in your heart. But the feeling is not as important as whom you feel. When you have reached that point in your meditation, fasten on to it for a few moments. Nothing, neither your thought sequence nor your emotional response, is as important as He whom you are facing and who fills you with life. So hold onto this confrontation for a while. When you do this, you need not do anything else except face and behold him." At the time I didn't know that Zalman was adopting an approach to meditation that came out of the teachings of the Baal Shem. His contemplative visualization was a beginning for me, but however much I appreciated it, I found that it wasn't a form that would work for me in an ongoing way.

I was initiated into Transcendental Meditation in 1970, and by the time I discovered the Baal Shem I'd spent time at the Vedanta Center in Cohasset, Massachusetts; at Ananda Village in northern California, where Yogananda's teachings about self-realization were taught and practiced; and at the Lama Foundation in New Mexico, which at the time was oriented toward the teachings of Neem Karoli Baba under the tutelage of his disciple, Ram Dass. I also took a class in the variety of Buddhist forms of meditation in Berkeley.

I continued to wonder about *Jewish* meditation, and especially about what Reb Zalman had written in *The First Step*. Reading Yitzhak Buxbaum's *Jewish Spiritual Practices,* I found the following, which confirmed that the meditation suggested by Zalman originated with the Baal Shem Tov: "The Besht taught that you are to first establish strong *d've-kut* in small consciousness (*katnut*) in the Lower World by meditating on God's greatness, that His glory [the *Shekhinah*] fills the whole world and that you are in His presence; then you enter the state of expanded consciousness by ascending to the Upper Worlds. He taught that where a man thinks, there he is himself; and such a meditation is not just imagination, but reality."[228] It then occurred to me that perhaps I could fashion an ongoing Jewish form of meditation by combining Zalman's Baal Shem-based approach with the Eastern somatically-oriented forms of spiritual practice that I had witnessed and experimented with.

Conscious breathing would be pivotal. I remembered a classical midrash that I'd studied many years before: "Rabbi Levi taught in the name of Rabbi Hanina, 'Praise your Creator with every breath (*neshema*) that you breathe.' What is the biblical basis for this? The final verse in the Book of Psalms reads *'Kol ha'neshamah t'halel Yah, HalleluYah....* Let every living being praise Yah, HalleluYah.' Read this verse in the following way: 'Let every *breath* praise Yah, HalleluYah.'"[229] This midrash has as its unmentioned source the tale in the second chapter of Genesis about the creation of the first human being. "And Y-H-W-H Elohim formed the earthling from the dust of the earth. Then he blew into his nostrils the breath of life, and the earthling became a living being" (Genesis 2:7).

Yes—so why not use the divine name *Yah* as a kind of breath-mantra, vocalizing it with each outbreath, and in this way offer praise to Yah? Yah is a shortened form of the four-letter name of God, *Y-H-W-H*—considered by the rabbis to be the holiest name of God. In Rabbinic Judaism and in the Kabbalah, Y-H-W-H was understood to symbolize divine love. Combining Yah breath meditation with the intentionality that the Divine was present in this very awareness that I'm experiencing, became my form of contemplative practice, and as I sat in silence every day, I found that it could gradually open me to a sense that my existence, life, and consciousness are expressions of that Presence.

What is it like to practice this form of meditation? I have experienced transcendental periods of bliss, when everything simply radiates Divinity. I cannot distinguish myself from creation as a whole. I am enfolded by great love. At times there is an openness to my inner depths and to the vastness of the cosmos. A sense the ultimate mystery and unity. A loss of self-concern. An inexpressible joy. An unearthly freedom. But I must also acknowledge that most meditation periods are not this ecstatic. Still, I can often feel transported into a higher octave, as it were, becoming part of the song of creation. There are days when the practice just seems like a rote exercise. If this continues day after day, I stop the practice entirely for a few days, giving myself a rest.

The Baal Shem taught that joy and delight are essential to the spiritual life. Nonetheless, he was clear that attaining personal pleasure should not be the chief purpose of our practice. Desiring to "become high" merely reifies the ego, and authentic spiritual discipline is about de-centering the ego and making Spirit our center. There have been times when I have gone for days without engaging in my practices, and I can testify that I felt that my life was missing something precious—a sense of enlargement that transcends my ego.

CHAPTER FIFTEEN

TRANSFORMING THE SELF

One of the important Jewish literary developments of the high Middle Ages was the introduction of *musar*, an influential genre of religious literature which had the primary aim of guiding Jews in a quest to deepen personal morality. The word *musar* might be translated as "ethical discipline." These writings have names like *The Duties of the Heart, The Gates of Teshuvah, The Candelabra of Light,* and *Eight Chapters.* Originally, they were studied and their contents embraced and absorbed by individual Jews.

In the introduction to one such work composed in the thirteenth century, *The Book of the Pious,* its author Rabbi Judah HeHasid states that his purpose in composing it was that "all those who fear God, as well as those who wish to return (*teshuvah*) to their Creator with sincerity will now be able to see, know, and understand what they should do, and what they should avoid." HeHasid was the most prominent leader of the Ashkenazic Hasidim in Germany at the time, and the head of an earlier Hasidic movement in Germany.

THREE THEMES OF MUSAR

Here are three excerpts from this voluminous work, each having to do with the theme of teshuvah. The titles of the selections come from the translator, Abraham Yaakov Finkel.[230]

THE GREATNESS OF A BAAL TESHUVAH

Great is repentance, for it reaches up to the Throne of Glory, as it says, "Return, O Israel, to the Lord your God." (Hosea 14:2) Teshuvah is one of the things that was created before the world was created, and it is equal in importance to all the sacrifices. A *baal teshuva* (i.e., one who undertakes and masters the process of teshuvah) should not consider himself as being far removed from the rank of the righteous because of the transgressions he's committed and the mistakes he's made. Quite the contrary, he is loved and cherished by the Creator more than the tzaddikim, because he has tasted sin, yet subdued his evil tendency. Our Sages say, "Where the repentant sinners stand, the wholly righteous may not" (*Talmud Berakhot* 34b, *Talmud Sanhedrin* 99a).

DOING PENANCE

Consider a man who had sexual intercourse with a married woman who was not his wife, and the man wants to know what he should do in order to do teshuvah. In a case like this, we must determine whether or not he can do teshuvah at all, as set forth in *Talmud Chagiga* 9b. If his sin was in the category where teshuvah is effective, his teshuvah must entail a form of penance that's the equivalent of *karet* [divine punishment by premature death] or *malkot,* flogging. If his penance is to be done during the winter, he should chop a hole in the ice on the river and stay immersed in the water up to his nose for the length of time that he was with the woman. In the summer he should sit in a ditch that is crawling with ants and keep his mouth closed. He should prepare a container of water to bathe afterwards. In the spring or the fall, he should fast and break his fast in the evening on bread and water.

PERFECT REPENTANCE

What is perfect teshuvah? If a person has transgressed and has the opportunity to commit the same transgression again, but refrains from doing so because of teshuvah and not because of fear or weakness. For example, consider another case of a man who had illicit sexual relations with a woman. At a later time, he has a chance encounter with her and the opportunity to have relations with her again. He still loves her and still has his physical strength, but this time subdues his passion and does not transgress. This man is the paradigm of a baal teshuvah.

MUSAR AND THE BAAL SHEM

During the late Middle Ages there were itinerant preachers known as *mo'khi'khim* (chastisers) or *maggidim* (explicators of Torah and religious storytellers), who would travel from one community to the next preaching in synagogues, drawing their lessons from musar literature. Like the biblical prophets, they boldly addressed ethical and religious iniquities that they saw polluting the lives of Jews. Several of the Baal Shem's followers were moralistic preachers of this type.

By the time of the Baal Shem, musar books had become harsh, punitive, and ascetic, permeated with a belief in demons and evil spirits born of people's sins. And in their sermons the travelling preachers would scold people for not observing the Sabbath properly, for not studying Torah, and for committing numerous transgressions, including the enjoyment of sexual pleasure. Penalties that the *mo'khi'khim* would voice in their sermons ranged from burning in hell to every sort of physical and mental suffering, and falling victim to the millions of demons and evil spirits imagined to inhabit the world. As historian Bernard D. Weinryb (1900-82) put it: "They, as well as the spirits of the wicked, the ghosts, and Satan himself, are constantly waiting to attack people for the slightest transgression. To be more or less secure one must, in addition to using certain magical defenses, fulfill all the precepts and avoid all transgressions, one must study and pray most of the time, talk very little, and care little or nothing for secular matters; one should do penance and weep all the time, fast, roll in the snow, and mortify oneself."[231] The preachers emphasized the value of fear—of God, sin, and punishment. They urged Jews to forswear the vanities of this world and praised the value of asceticism, fasting, weeping, and self-flagellation.

Musar had a significant effect on the Baal Shem Tov and leaders of Hasidism. Mendel Piekarz (1922-2011), a prominent scholar who taught at Hebrew University, wrote that "close scrutiny of the *musar* books dating from the early days of Hasidic expansion will show that they are intimately related to the classical *musar* books.... The attentive reader of these books will find that sayings and maxims attributed by the early hasidic teachers, to the Baal Shem Tov or to other founding fathers of the hasidic movement—sayings which had been regarded by scholars as crucial to the understanding of the nature of Hasidism actually originated with authors who preceded or were contemporary with the beginning of hasidism but had no connection whatsoever with the new movement."[232] I think it highly likely that the Baal Shem began to engage in teshuvah while still young, and that he continued to do so throughout his life in tandem with ecstatic worship practices as he struggled to learn how to manage or alter irrational emotions that at times overwhelmed him. It seems probable that he studied both the classical musar books as well as those being composed during his lifetime. Somewhere along the way, however, he completely abandoned the guilt-inducing approaches advocated by those engaged in the study and preaching of musar.

Martin Buber provides us with a noteworthy source that attempts to indicate why the Baal Shem decided to embark on a very different approach. The tale takes place before the High Holy Days, which in Hebrew are called the *Yamim No'ra'im,* the Days of Fear or Awe. Traditional Jews believe that during these ten days, from Rosh Hashanah to Yom Kippur, God judges human beings for their actions, determining their individual destinies for the new year. Because of this, the entire Hebrew month of Elul, which comes just before the Days of Awe, together with the first ten days of the month of Tishrei, which begins the new year, were seen as a forty-day period of great trepidation, self-examination, and teshuvah:

> One year, just before Rosh Hashanah, the Baal Shem came to a small out of the way town. Because he was contemplating remaining in this town for the Days of Awe, he asked someone in the synagogue if he could meet the service leaders. He was told that the rabbi of the town himself led all the services. "How does he lead the services?" asked the Baal Shem, "What's it like when he davens?"
>
> "Well, you can tell his whole manner of davening from the way he chants the *vidui*, the confession of sin on Yom Kippur. He's not sad. He doesn't cry. He doesn't focus on how sinful our community has been during the past year. No, that's not his way. Instead he chants the confessions in the most joyful tones you can possibly imagine." "Hmmm..." mumbled the Baal Shem, "And where can I find your rabbi?"
>
> He was informed where the rabbi lived.
>
> The rabbi opened his front door and the Besht introduced himself, and then he recounted the story he had heard from the villager. The rabbi invited the young man into his home. When they were seated, Israel asked his question. "I've never heard of anyone chanting the Yom

Kippur confession in joyous tones. Your approach surprises me. What is your reason for this?"

Smiling, the rabbi said to him: "A king has many servants to do his bidding. But the lowest servant of all is he whose task it is to sweep out the dirt from the entrance to the palace. Is this servant sad because he has such a lowly job? Certainly not, for he knows that he is serving the king! And so he sings a joyful song while he works, knowing that cleaning out the entranceway will make the king happy.

"Well, on the Days of Awe I see myself as that servant. I too am sweeping out the dirt just to make the king of the universe happy. And this, in turn, makes me happy."

The Baal Shem thought about this for a moment and then he nodded. "And may my lot be with yours."[233]

Now, whether or not this story is historically true, at some point the Baal Shem Tov did undergo a major change of heart. And when he took on communal spiritual leadership, he reacted strongly to the dismal and rigid view of religiosity that the moralistic preachers were advocating. There are a number of tales about the Baal Shem's displeasure with the *mo'khi'khim* and *maggidim* of his time. We are told, for instance, that he once heard a preacher delivering a fire and brimstone sermon to a crowd of laymen, bringing the audience to tears. After the sermon, the Besht approached the preacher and reproached him: "What do you know about chastising? You have lived your life in a pure manner and you are unacquainted with sin. You are unaware of how common people live. How would you know what sins they commit?"[234]

In Praise of the Baal Shem Tov records his encounter with another preacher who had recently publicly chastised the people of a town he was visiting. With tears running down his face, the Besht told the man: "You say malicious things about the Jewish people and this is not right. I know a simple Jew in this town who goes to the market every weekday and works hard all day long. And then towards evening, when it is getting dark and the man is weary from all of his labor, he suddenly becomes anxious. '*Oy,* woe is me, I've missed the afternoon prayer service at the synagogue!' Dejected, he goes home and there he davens the afternoon prayers by himself, so tired that he is scarcely aware of the meaning of the words he is uttering. *And yet all the angels in heaven—the seraphim and the ofanim—are profoundly moved by his prayers!*"[235]

I find this anecdote incredibly affecting. "God desires the heart," we are told in the Talmud, so even though the poor man has offered an imperfect prayer due to his exhaustion from work, the angels are stirred by his unpretentious dedication and purity of heart. The Besht taught his circle of disciples and colleagues that when a tzaddik is called to the vocation of admonishing his people, he must do so in a spirit of love *or not at all.* In his study of the works of the Baal Shem's disciple, Rabbi Jacob Joseph of Polonoyye, Samuel Dresner comments: "Concern for the people and their plight flows over into love for them, a going out toward them, an embracing of them, a feeling of tender compassion and clement dismay for a dear one who has done wrong."[236] And Jacob Joseph writes that "There are two extremely different kinds of preachers, as in the parable I heard from my teacher, the Baal Shem Tov. A king once sent his son into exile, choosing two servants to accompany the prince. One of these servants later returned to the king and told him how disgusting his son was acting. The second servant came back with a similar report, but he spoke to the king about these matters with an anguished heart—for he felt distress because he knew the sorrow that the king was experiencing, and he also suffered anguish for the king's son, who had been exiled for so long that he had forgotten the royal customs. It was because of the words of this second servant that the king became filled with sympathy for his son."[237]

Rabbi Dresner comments, "The preacher should join himself to the people to whom he preaches. His ears should hear the words his mouth utters, and his soul should hearken to them. He should feel the failing of the people and his share in that failing, for he and they are one."[238] The Besht's approach to the right manner of admonishment flowed out of his emphasis on the value of love. He counseled people not to be hard on themselves, and he opposed fasting and self-inflicted pain. He advised his students to study musar every day, and told them that even if normally they didn't speak publicly to their communities about these matters, it was their responsibility to do so on Rosh Hashanah.

Yet he counselled them not to preach in a fiery or condemnatory way, which would only arouse divine judgment against the people. Preachers should rather speak out of love. Rabbi Jacob Joseph cites the words of the Besht: "Arouse the hearts of the people to return to their Father in heaven with words that will appease them, and directed to the heart of each individual, according to his or her spiritual level. This way of speaking will bring great benefit, for it will cause the blessing of divine bounty (*shefa*) to be drawn down on the community from beyond."[239]

THE GATE OF AWE

In the Baal Shem's day, the notion of the fear of Heaven (*yirat Sha'mayim*) was a primary impetus to keep Jews from breaking free of their observance of the mitzvot. In their sermons the chastisers would paint the kinds of punishments that awaited sinners in the next world who engaged in behavior unbefitting a Jew, or failed to observe the positive mitzvot. As the Besht developed spiritually and morally he must have come to see that such fear only exacerbated all the other worries and concerns that people were experiencing, and he would have none of it.

The Hebrew word *yirah* can be translated as either awe or fear, and the Besht distinguished between outer fear (*yirah hi'tzo'nit*) and inner awe (*yirah p'ni'mit*). His teachings about yirah emphasize the superiority of inner awe over outer fear. What is the difference between these two states of yirah? Outer fear arises out of a sense that something far greater than you is seeking to subjugate or to destroy you, and that you may not be able to withstand its power. Such fear is used as a tool to force people to behave properly. But, R. Jacob Joseph cites the Baal Shem Tov: "All of these are merely external fears. They are the same as the fears suffered by all living creatures: The mouse fears the cat; the cat fears the dog; the dog fears the wolf."[240]

Inner awe is different, for it has the power to expand one's awareness so that one can experience existence from a divine point of view. According to the Baal Shem's disciple, R. Menahem Nahum of Chernobyl, the master put it this way: "It is awe that the perceptive seeker experiences in the presence of the Divine, for God is the master and ruler, the very Root of all worlds. Just imagine: If the Lifeforce that energizes all worlds should disappear for even a single moment—God forbid!—then the whole universe would simply dissolve into nothing! So when you worship, stand in awe and trembling before the Holy One even to the point that your limbs shatter at the splendor of divine majesty overflowing all existence."[241]

We have a tradition from the nineteenth-century Rebbe Mordechai of Neskhizh that the Besht was once experiencing such a tremendous sense of awe that he exclaimed to his body, "I am astonished that you do not shatter to smithereens out of awe for your Creator!" This reminds me of Heschel's notion of "radical amazement": "Inquire of your soul what does it know, what does it take for granted. It will tell you only no-thing is taken for granted; each thing is a surprise; *being is unbelievable*. We are amazed at seeing anything at all, amazed not only at particular values and things but *at the unexpectedness of being as such*, at the fact that there is being at all."[242]

So the Baal Shem, unlike the musar preachers, didn't teach disciples to live in fear of God or punishment. What *did* he teach? A way to transform outer fear into inner awe. This is a practice in which he asks practitioners to link their fears to the Divine. Here is how one Beshtian source expresses this: "At the very moment that you are experiencing either love or fear, ask yourself, Where is this feeling coming from? Why it must be coming from God, for doesn't every feeling derive from Divinity? Even ferocious animals experience love and fear. And aren't these emotions part and parcel of what it means to be alive? Everything was broken when the cosmic vessels holding the divine light were shattered during the process of creation. But that divine light did not disappear, and it can be found in each and every fragment of physical existence. So why should I be afraid of this single spark of Divinity that comes to me in the guise of fear? Wouldn't it be better for me to bind this fear into the great awe of God alone? Now this principle is also true also when a feeling of love rises within you, or, for that matter, any feeling whatsoever. Look for the divine spark lying within it, and when you find it, lift it up to its Source. Isn't this why we have been gifted with divine souls—to uncover the divine sparks hiding in every aspect of our physical existence, and to then return them to their Source?"[243]

If one can accept outer fear and then convert it to inner awe in this way, said the Besht, it would also be possible to come to see inner awe as a form of love. Another source cites the Baal Shem as having taught: "The essence of your spiritual striving should be the cultivation of the awe of the Divine. And when you are actually able to experience such awe, the love of God will then be given to you as a great gift from Heaven."[244] In sum, what we see in the Baal Shem's musar teachings is an emphasis on inspiring people with a sense of the awesomeness of existence and the underlying love that gives birth to such awe, rather than admonitions that attempt to inculcate fear of punishment.

MOSES CORDOVERO AND THE BESHT

The fear-inducing form of musar that was regnant in Poland in the eighteenth century was characteristic of much of the musar literature. It also drew from the views of Rabbi Isaac Luria, whose form of Kabbalah was popular then. The Lurianic legacy emphasized the necessity of living an ascetic life, including the mortification of the body through self-chastisement and fasting. It would have been normal for the Baal Shem Tov to have practiced these kinds of austerities when he was young, and *In Praise of the Baal Shem Tov* reveals that this was indeed the case. It appears that the great change in his life came about, in large part, because of the intense effects his ecstatic worship practice had on his outlook. Those powerful experiences must have lifted his spirit, convincing him he could attain a deep and joyous connection with the Divine without need for an ascetic lifestyle. Rabbi Jacob Joseph of Polonoyye reports the following teaching of his master: "The flaws and sins that we commit do not reach the highest place within the Divine, for that realm is a completely pure, as it says in the book of Job: *'If you engage in evil, how will that affect Me?'* (Job 35:6). And this is why teshuvah is so effective, for our sins simply do not extend into that lofty domain. So even if you have transgressed sexually, in that highest realm within the Divine there is only love! Yes, what you did on the earthly plane generated something that was injurious. But if you sincerely sought pardon from those whom you wronged, and you received forgiveness, through your repentance everything becomes healed. And then my teacher added that there are wondrous depths to this teaching."[245]

The Besht was supported in his moral evolution by his discovery of and engagement with the teachings of Rabbi Moses Cordovero, the great kabbalist we met in Part One. As crucial as the Besht's ecstatic practice was in providing him with experiences that led to his enlightenment, he couldn't have made that vision real and tangible without having encountered Cordovero's teachings. And what about the traditional anthropomorphic notion of a humanlike God found throughout biblical and rabbinic literature? Cordovero had studied Maimonides and perhaps other medieval Jewish philosophers whose thought had been shaped, in part, by ancient Greek metaphysical ideas. And like those rational thinkers he warns his readers not to imagine God as an old man with white hair sitting on a throne of fire. "If you are enlightened," he writes, "you know that the Divine is devoid of corporeality. Then you wonder, 'Who really am I?' Astounded, you recognize how small you are, as tiny as a mustard seed enveloped by increasingly expanding dimensions of reality. Your awe is invigorating, and the love in your soul expands." It was this view—or rather *experience*—of the Divine that would have such a decisive influence on the Baal Shem's nondualistic thought two centuries later.

In *Vocal Rites and Broken Theologies,* Moshe Idel theorizes that at first the Baal Shem perceived the immanence of the Divine in the Hebrew letters alone, especially during his practice of ecstatic worship. Only later did he come to recognize the divinity immanent throughout the world. This makes sense to me. As the Besht's perception of Divine presence expanded, he drew on Cordovero's nondual language to express his experience of the divine fullness. Jacob Joseph quotes his master saying: "'The fullness of the whole earth is God's glory.' (Isaiah 6:3) Nothing great or small is separate from God for Divinity itself is the very Existence of all that exists."[246]

Idel also demonstrates how other major Hasidic concepts found in the Baal Shem's teachings trace back to Cordovero. Along with Abulafia, Cordovero was one of the first kabbalists to develop a psychological understanding of the soul, using the language of the sefirot, the archetypal emanations or dimensions that underlie the universe. And the Baal Shem's notion of the three-fold vocation of the tzaddik also owes a great deal to Cordovero: opening to the Divine; binding oneself to the Divine;

drawing down the divine flow of goodness into the world and channeling it to the members of the community. Yet, even though Cordovero's influence on the Besht was pivotal, Idel never equates the visions of the two mystics. He stresses that the Baal Shem's understanding of reality brought together elements from a number of diverse sources. And unlike Cordovero, the founder of Hasidism does not dwell on what we would call theology or religious philosophy. The Besht's emphasis was on enabling his students to experience and become one with the Divine in their devotional lives.[247]

THE PALM TREE OF DEBORAH

Cordovero was deeply attentive to the moral implications of his mystical vision, and he wrote a short but powerful musar treatise, called *The Palm Tree of Deborah (Tomer Devorah)*, which eventually became his most popular work. The kabbalist bases his approach on the spiritual notion of *imitatio Dei,* the idea that individuals should mold and refine their lives in such a way that they come to resemble the ten sefirot, the divine dimensions underlying all existence. "By performing deeds and acquiring spiritual qualities that are in harmony with each of them," writes the contemporary scholar Joseph Dan, "a person causes the divine flow of spiritual force from each divine power to vitalize his soul and create a link between himself and that particular *sefirah.* Thus, for instance, the performance of *teshuvah*—repentance—connects a person to the divine entity called by that name, which is the third *sefirah, binah,* which gives him the power to renew himself, to return spiritually to the infinite divine goodness and emerge from there purged of all sin and all the evil in him transformed into goodness."[248]

I first read *The Palm Tree of Deborah* in the early sixties, when the British scholar Rabbi Louis Jacobs first published an English translation of Cordovero's treatise. I was interested in Kabbalah, but knew very little about it. While working on this chapter, though, I re-read *The Palm Tree of Deborah* and was stunned at the way Cordovero's moral vision prefigured so much of what I've since found in the teachings and tales of the Baal Shem Tov.

According to the Kabbalah, *Ein Sof,* the Infinite is linked to this physical world through ten spiritual emanations that radiated forth at the beginning of time and space, each as an unfolding stage or dimension of the Divine. These dimensions of the Divine are the sefirot (singular, *sefirah*). The first sefirah is called *Keter,* "Crown." The sefirah of Keter is the locus of pure compassion. It is in this spirit that Cordovero begins *The Palm Tree of Deborah*: "It is fitting that we human beings model our lives on the image of our Creator, for when we do this, we find ourselves embraced by the mystery of the highest Form of all, and we ourselves become images and likenesses of the Divine.... The core of becoming a divine image and likeness has to do with one's actions in the world.... Therefore, it is right that the individual emulates Keter. The prophet Micah describes Keter as having thirteen virtues of compassion: (7:18-20): 'What divine being is like You, forgiving guilt, and passing over the wrongdoing of those who are Your heritage. You do not hold on to anger, for You seek love alone. You will renew Your compassion and overturn our offenses, casting our sins into the depths of the sea. Show Your faithfulness to the descendants of Jacob, and love the children of Abraham, as You promised our ancestors from the days of long ago.'"

Cordovero was constantly calling attention to the importance of developing and deepening one's love and compassion. At the same time, I could not help but observe the complete absence in his thought of fear as a motivation for change. Here, then, are just a small number of the moral teachings in *The Palm Tree of Deborah* that must have influenced the founder of Hasidism:

- Divine power and compassion are all-pervasive and infuse everything, and thus there is not a moment when one is not being nourished and sustained by God, even when sinning against God.
- We are commanded to love our neighbors as ourselves because we are part of one another.
- One should refrain from speaking in a derogatory way about any person.
- One should behave with a kindly spirit even toward those who transgress the Torah.
- God loves those who engage in teshuvah even more than those who never sinned at all.

- One shouldn't nurse hatred toward someone who hurt him. If that person has undergone teshuvah, one should show him both love and compassion.
- One should remember only the good that such a person has done, and put that person's past misdeeds out of mind.
- One should not behave cruelly toward wicked people. Rather, show them compassion, and love them.
- Even the things that happen in the world that come from the divine side of severity are, in reality, meant for the good.

What a highly developed and sensitive consciousness and conscience! In his introduction to his translation of Cordovero's book, Louis Jacobs writes that "The reader senses that he is being addressed in words which come from the heart of one of Jewry's saints who lived by his ideals." I could not agree more, and I imagine this is how the Baal Shem might have felt as he studied the book and took its contents to heart.

I imagine that Cordovero's treatise may have impacted the Besht in such a deep way because love and compassion had been so absent from his young life, and that while he was studying the older kabbalist's words, he came to recognize what was missing from his life. His own teachings made that kind of impression on me in large part because of the lack of love in my family of origin. And just as I used the teachings of the Baal Shem as a template for my own transformation, I believe that the Besht made Cordovero's moral vision into an objective for his own development.

A MORAL EXEMPLAR

The subjects of the Besht's moral and ethical directives include struggling with and transforming bad traits such as pride, hatred, and anger, and cultivating virtues such as love, compassion, humility, and equanimity. These teachings are not limited to inner teshuvah. They also have to do with how one should behave as an active member of the Jewish community. As a result of both his ecstatic practice and his study of Cordoverian musar, the Besht evolved both spiritually and morally. Historian Raphael Mahler writes glowingly about the moral image of the Baal Shem Tov in Hasidic literature: "Some of the legends praised Baal Shem Tov for his championship of the persecuted and the injured against their oppressors, for his advocacy of justice, his tribute to labourers living by the sweat of their brow and for his emphasis on the virtue of charity.... In practice, [the] Baal Shem Tov thought that the precept of charity was of greater importance than quoting from the Torah, and his friends testified that 'he never clung to any money; whenever he returned from a journey, he would pay his debts and on the same day disburse the remainder in alms.'"[249]

I find it fascinating that Mahler was a Marxist, and that he used a socialist lens in his analysis of Jewish history. Citing texts from Hasidic tradition, he writes that the Baal Shem would rebuke the lessors who deprived others of their incomes and increased the price of rentals, and he would defend the poor option-holding lessees against them. The Besht and his disciples would embark on the "redemption of captives"—rescuing Jewish lessees arrested by Gentile estate owners for failing to pay arrears on their rents—even though he himself was deeply in debt as a result of borrowing heavily from nobles to get these victims released. The Baal Shem was also scrupulous about honesty in business dealings with Gentiles. Nevertheless, he felt compassion for anyone who stole because of adversity.

The Torah forbids loaning money to fellow Jews in order to make a profit from the loan. We are told that through his psychic faculty the Baal Shem was able to recognize any money that had been acquired by usury in any form. On one occasion he threw away a ring he'd seen at a jeweler's because he sensed its defiled origin when he picked it up. There is also a touching story that describes a simple stocking-maker who worked for a jobber, performed his work diligently, recited all the Psalms that he remembered by heart while he worked, and prayed at the synagogue in a religious quorum. The Besht used to say of him: "He will be the foundation of the Jewish community until the Redeemer comes."

RABBINIC PSYCHOLOGY OF GOOD AND EVIL

It thus seems that the Besht reinterpreted the classical Jewish perspective on good and evil, applying a new understanding to the psychological struggle within human beings between self-centeredness and social responsibilities. One cannot study the Talmud or Midrash or the books of musar without encountering the notion of the yetzer ha'rah, "the evil inclination." Yetzer ha'rah might best be understood as a self-serving instinct that tempts us toward excessive self-gratification, and in this way causes us to rebel against God and against the moral underpinnings of society. Yetzer ha'rah is thus responsible for energizing the physical appetites, and stimulating personal ambition.

Talmudic sages taught that it is through promptings of this drive that the need for food becomes gluttony, the desire for procreation and physical pleasure becomes sexual license, and the necessity to earn a livelihood becomes boundless greed. Yet, however powerful its seductions, the sages insisted that this drive was resistible. Individuals always have the freedom to choose whether to go along with its provocations or to resist them. Despite its destructive power, there were rabbis who insisted that because it had been created by God, yetzer ha'rah had an essential generative purpose as well. Without its promptings, people would not procreate or do what was necessary to care for their family's needs. Furthermore, every person has the power to turn the destructive power of yetzer ha'rah to good purpose. And, the sages believed, humans were also endowed with a *yetzer ha'tov*, an altruistic instinct, that inspired them to engage in acts of goodness.

According to the Talmud, the primary weapons that one can use in the struggle against yetzer ha'rah are the study of Torah (i.e., the internalization of the moral and religious mitzvot of the Torah), the practice of the mitzvot, and accustoming oneself to carry out acts of loving kindness. The sages also maintained that through prayer God's grace is available in the struggle. To this classical psycho-biological understanding of the roots of human evil, the sixteenth-century kabbalists, under the influence of Rabbi Isaac Luria, added a cosmological explanation for its existence. At the beginning of time, when the seven lower vessels meant to hold the precious divine light shattered, the universe was filled with sparks (*ni'tzo'tzot*) of the original divine light, but these sparks were held captive by the fragments (*kli'pot*) of the broken vessels. The human race as a whole was contaminated by these fragments, and this innate brokenness continues to affect human behavior in deleterious ways. It is significant then that in kabbalistic thought it is God who is the ultimate source of human as well as cosmic evil. Human beings only receive blame for failing to stand up to these forces, because they were created to mend the brokenness and to return the sparks of light to their ultimate Origin.

The Besht's teachings mirror the emergence of a transformed view of yetzer ha'rah while at the same time revealing his own inner struggles. His focus had to do with the true character of yetzer ha'rah, and how this drive might be transmuted into something positive. We have learned that along with anger, the Besht's most problematic traits were grandiosity (*ga'avah*) and self-serving passion (the yetzer ha'rah). These characteristics are obviously related to one another, but they are not the same. The rabbis identified yetzer ha'rah with the serpent in the Garden of Eden. This is the drive within human beings that entices us to rebel against God. As Eve's reward for eating from the Tree of Knowing Good and Evil, the serpent promises her that the fruit of the tree will transform her and Adam into gods! This kind of self-centered inflation is ga'avah—the result of harkening to yetzer ha'rah.

Because of his developing nondualistic emphasis, the Baal Shem picked up on the rabbinic notion that yetzer ha'rah was actually divine at its core, for no power in the universe can exist without the activity of the Lifeforce that provides it with its reality. Desire and passion, then, are divine. Our passions only become malevolent when we fail to curb them, allowing them to become dominant. The Besht reasoned that since yetzer ha'rah was created by God, and is powered by divine energy, it cannot be completely evil. Radical instinctual desire has a spiritual purpose: to challenge the individual to stand against its unrelenting demands and fears and discern how to live a holy life in the face of its disconcerting presence.

The Baal Shem, on these points, seems to parallel Gautama Buddha's notion of the root cause of human suffering, called *tanha*. Huston Smith defines it this way: "*Tanha* is a specific kind of desire, the desire for private fulfillment. When we are selfless we are free, but that is precisely the difficulty—to maintain that state. *Tanha* is the force that ruptures it, pulling us back from the freedom of the all to seek fulfillment in our egos, which ooze like secret sores. *Tanha* consists of all those inclinations, which tend to continue or increase separateness, the separate existence of the subject of desire; in fact, all forms of selfishness, the essence of which is desire for self at the expense, if necessary, of all other forms of life."[250] Tanha is often simply translated as "craving." The Buddha taught a method to attain awakening from this condition. For the Baal Shem as well, yetzer ha'rah and ga'avah combine to immobilize both conscience and consciousness. And when individuals consider themselves to be the center of existence, there is no room for others, for the universe, or for God.

The Besht taught that even though yetzer ha'rah was created by God, no one should underestimate its power. He told his disciples to stay mindful of the attempts of yetzer ha'rah to undermine their integrity. These counsels have the ring of authenticity; he seems to be speaking from personal experience. Here are examples given by the Besht of the false claims of yetzer ha'rah. One way is through sublimation: "Let's say that the yetzer is attempting to trap you through arousing lustful thoughts in your imagination. If this happens say this to the yetzer: 'Okay, I'll do as you say; I'll let myself engage in lust—but it will be a lust for the study of Torah!'"[251]

The yetzer ha'rah may also attempt to provoke false guilt: "There may be times when it pretends to be your conscience, making you feel guilty for the slightest offence, or for doing something that was not really wrong at all. Why does the yetzer do this? To throw you into sadness, in order to goad you into withdrawing from serving your Creator. So if this occurs, stand up to the yetzer, and tell it in no uncertain terms: 'I see what you are trying to do, and I'm not buying it, for your words are only lies! Instead, I will serve God in joy, for this is the true path! How could I ever imagine myself ceasing from my service to God?'"[252]

Or the yetzer ha'rah may attempt to demean an individual by prying on a low sense of self-esteem, as in this quotation of the Besht recorded by R. Jacob Joseph:

> If the yetzer ha'rah attempts to humiliate you, you will need help to counter its false claims. Let's say that the yetzer says to you: "You are merely a stinking drop of protoplasm," soon to dissolve into nothing!
>
> "So how can you possibly imagine that you are worthy of entering the great circle of holiness and actually

becoming a Hasid, a pious person?" If the yetzer confronts you in this way, stand up to it and affirm your own greatness! Say this to the yetzer: "You are mistaken! My soul is part and parcel of the Divine beyond, and I am created in the very image of God. I am, indeed, worthy to enter the circle of holiness and become a Hasid!"[253]

I certainly recognize this last contention. In my younger days I regularly heard it speaking to me, even if it wasn't personified as a kind of psychic character. When I studied Freudian psychology, I learned that it represented a strong or dominant superego, a part of the self-image that had been instilled in my psyche by parents and teachers while growing up. According to psychoanalytical theory the superego represents the ethical component of the personality, providing the moral standards by which the ego operates. The superego's criticisms, prohibitions, and inhibitions form a person's conscience, and its positive aspirations and ideals represent one's idealized self-image, or "ego ideal." In my therapy work I learned that my domineering superego derived primarily from my mother's critical perfectionism—the heavy-handed constraints and obligations which she frequently voiced and which I had internalized. Once I left home and was on my own at college, I unconsciously transmuted my mother's criticism into the voice of the great male God of Jewish tradition. It was just this that drove me into psychoanalysis during my early years at JTS.

In the Baal Shem's teachings, however, he was not identifying this wily voice with God, but with yetzer ha'rah. How very radical! But if the Besht was speaking from personal experience, and if he really did lose his parents at a young age, where did such a punitive superego come from? Once again this argues for the young Israel having living mentors who cared for him, educated him Jewishly, and inculcated him with the imperatives of traditional musar. In advising his disciples and colleagues to be wary of a dominant superego, he was freeing them from a form of repressive conscience that has plagued Western religion for centuries. It was, I believe, his own musar work on himself, together with his mystical practices that freed him from the tyranny of an overactive superego. This achievement was not the least of the Besht's gifts to Judaism.

As he evolved spiritually and morally toward nondualism, he came to recognize that everything was divine, and like the rabbis in the Talmud he understood that the yetzer ha'rah was not unalterably evil. This Beshtian text reflects his later view that the yetzer can be transformed:

> In the story of the creation of the world, the Torah repeats itself again and again, saying, *"And God saw that it was good."* Where, then, did evil come from? The origin of evil is not evil; it is actually good, but it is a form of goodness that is less than absolute goodness. And thus, because evil contains the potential for goodness, it is possible to transform it into good. When you engage in wrongdoing, however, know that you are actually bringing evil into existence.[254]

Instead of *shattering* its power, the Besht began to speak about *restraining* and *transforming* the yetzer ha'rah: "We are taught in the Mishnah, *'Who is truly powerful? One who restrains his self-serving passions.'* Now notice that the verse says 'restrains,' (*kovesh*) not 'shatters' (*shover*). It doesn't take any real power to shatter your cravings. All you really need is a strong will, and you can rid yourself of the yetzer's power over you. But what does it mean to *restrain* your craving? Not merely holding it in check, but rather making use of its energies and its potential for good in the service of the holy." Compare this to the words of Cordovero in *The Palm Tree of Deborah:* "Indeed, the yetzer ha'rah should be bound and restrained, so it cannot be aroused to any physical activity—neither its desire for sex, nor for acquiring money, nor being provoked to anger, nor to attaining personal honor."

Suppose one has a strong craving for power. The natural tendency would be to attempt to control others for one's own benefit. But this drive can also be transformed into serving others, for instance, organizing a philanthropic organization that raises funds to help people in need. The Besht's approach is similar to that of depth psychologist Carl Jung, who held that the psychic energy of an individual—what he called the libido—is neutral in character, and can be transformed from lower urges into higher longings. Cordovero's *The Palm Tree of Deborah* contains a parallel teaching: "A person may purify the yetzer ha'rah and transform it into good, and then it will become rooted in the Holiness above. This is the level of teshuvah that one should practice, and every day one should reflect on it and engage in it in some way, so that all of one's days will be devoted to teshuvah."

In a commentary on a teaching in the Mishnah, the Baal Shem also speaks about learning from yetzer ha'rah how its power can be transformed into good: "Ben Zoma taught: 'Who is a truly wise person? One who learns from everyone' (*Pirkei Avot* 4:1). The Baal Shem Tov commented, 'Yes, you can learn from everyone, and also from everything. You can even learn from your own cravings. In this way you can transform your yetzer ha'rah into your yetzer ha'tov.'"[255]

How does one learn from one's cravings? We need to pay attention as they arise in consciousness, and not act on them in an impulsive way. Mindful knowledge of one's cravings eventuates in a greater ability to restrain and transform them:

> The EverPresent spoke to Moses: "Speak to the children of Israel. Tell them that they should take for Me an offering. Whatever moves their hearts—that should be what they offer Me." This means that if you desire to transform your bad traits, you must carefully examine your heart and see what it is that is driving your actions. What are your worldly desires and what are the bad traits that underlie them? From that knowledge you will know how to serve the Creator.[256]

The Besht believed that one of the most important virtues his disciples could learn from yetzer ha'rah was perseverance. Yetzer ha'rah will never give up trying to disconcert a human being, he taught, and from its obstinacy one can learn to be tenacious in one's ethical vigilance.

How did he use its energy? How did he transform his ga'avah? He dedicated his life to his people, becoming a teacher and healer. As we will see in the next section of this book, his healing was not limited to individuals, for he was also intent on healing the traumatic wounds that has been inflicted on his people in the seventeenth century, and which were continuing to fester during his lifetime. As Immanuel Etkes writes, the Besht possessed "an internal certainty that the exceptional powers and esoteric knowledge with which he was blessed were granted him so that he might use them for public benefit."[257]

INDIVIDUAL LIBERATION

I knew that both Hindu Vedanta and Buddhism promised liberation or enlightenment to individuals who followed the spiritual and moral paths of those traditions. Imagine then my surprise when I read Heschel's words, "The Baal Shem Tov even taught the spiritual redemption of the individual—a most daring idea, since Jewish thought had always seen redemption in terms of the people and the world as a whole."[258]

Some Beshtian sources state that the master never freed himself from the power of yetzer ha'rah, while others claim he was able to attain complete liberation from its power. Here again we may be dealing with sources that reflect different stages in his growth. Let us examine the more mature teachings. The Baal Shem spoke of two different forms of redemption or liberation: "There are two kinds of exile: First, there is the physical exile of the Jewish people among the nations of the world. Second, there is the spiritual exile of the individual soul, dominated by the yetzer ha'rah."[259]

This affirmation of human potential became central to his spiritual psychology. He came to believe that through teshuvah it would be possible for an individual to liberate completely from the enduring tension exerted by the urge to fulfill his self-serving passions. This would require the seeker to earnestly pray for its demise, while using all his energies to transform it. The Besht believed that as more and more Jews succeeded in transforming their lives in this way, they would make the liberation of the Jewish people and of humanity possible: "We read in the Psalms, *Draw near to my soul and redeem it*' (Psalm 69:19). This is a prayer for the liberation of the individual soul from its bondage to the yetzer ha'rah. And when each and every person is freed from craving in this way, the complete liberation of humanity will occur, and the messiah will appear. At that time everyone, young and old alike, will recognize the presence of the One, and every deed will be done for God's sake alone. May this happen soon, while we yet live. Amen!"[260]

In this vein the Baal Shem counsels to learn how to manage and direct such impulses when they first arise so that one can live a life of true self-mastery, untroubled by the yetzer ha'rah: "Be aware—for if you don't engage in this inner work of transformation, and merely attempt to drive your darker passions away, those cravings will surely return, and all of your days will be filled with struggle. And who knows if you will be able to continually battle against them. So use your intelligence, and from the very first accustom your yetzer ha'rah to serve your higher purposes, and then it will not bother you."[261] The way in which this insight is worded shows that he didn't feel unique, and taught his disciples how they, too, could achieve what he'd accomplished.

FINDING A WAY

Some years back I read Charlene Spretnak's notable book, *States of Grace,* an extended critique of the destructive forces that drive the modern world and how the ancient wisdom teachings, together with feminism, can bring healing to our fractured world. Spretnak observes ways in which life in the United States is becoming increasingly violent: rape, assault, child abuse, drug-related murders. "It is madness," she declares, "when a society panders to fragmentation, callousness, and cruelty that are the inevitable results of failing to comprehend—in an experiential as well as intellectual way—the truth of our existence: the profound communion of all life."[262] She writes about the need to move away from a society of consumption toward a culture of communion, from an emphasis on human mastery to an appreciation of mystery. Much of her book is devoted to a discussion of Buddhism, Native American spirituality, contemporary goddess spirituality, and the Abrahamic traditions—Judaism, Christianity, and Islam—and the critical insights that these wisdom traditions bring to contemporary social issues. "We *are here,*" she writes glowingly, "inextricably linked at the molecular level to every other manifestation of the great unfolding. We are descendants of the fireball. We are pilgrims on this Earth, glimpsing the oneness of the sacred whole, knowing Gaia, knowing grace."[263]

There's an array of social and political activities that we can and should participate in to engage in tikkun olam, but how do we process the tsunamis of grief that we experience as we read the daily headlines? Spretnak deals with the ways meditation can enable people to perceive the nature of mind, the nature of mental anguish, and a way out of these. She implies that Buddhist meditation can be an antidote to violence, teaching practitioners a way to deal with the various kinds of turmoil that rise in the mind. She writes that the happiest people she ever encountered were refugees from Tibet in Dalhousie who had lost everything to Mao Zedong's invading army in 1959. Spretnak was continually impressed by their cheerful expressions and almost wry sense of humor despite everything they suffered. She concludes with a powerful and poignant entreaty to her readers: "Will everyone then someday practice the meditation technique taught by the Buddha? Not likely. You may prefer a different way. But please, *find a way*. Find a way beyond the continuous chain reaction of craving, jealousy, ill will, indifference, fear, and anxiety that fills the mind. Find a way that dissolves the deeply ingrained patterns of negative, distrustful behavior caused by past cruelty and disappointment. Find a way that demonstrates to you that ill will and greed are damaging to your psyche. Find a way that grounds your deeds in wisdom, equanimity, compassion, and loving kindness. Find a way that reveals to you the joy of our profound unity, the subtle interrelatedness of you and every being, every manifestation of the unfolding universe. Find a way that will continually deepen your understanding of that knowledge. Then we could build community without hypocrisy. Then we would have a chance."[264]

I am grateful for what I've learned from my study of Buddhism over the years and especially from the practices of Insight (*Vipassana*) and Loving-kindness (*Metta*) meditation. They have added an important dimension to my spiritual practice. I think about the Metta Sutta scripture, and how close it comes to Moses Cordovero's teachings, and to those of the Baal Shem Tov:

> In safety and in bliss
> May all creatures be of blissful heart...
> Let no one work another one's undoing
> Or even slight him at all anywhere;
> And never let them wish each other ill...
> And let him too with love for all the world

Maintain unbounded consciousness in being
Above, below, and all round in between,
Untroubled, with no enemy or foe.
Through provocation or resentful thought.[265]

My knowledge of the Buddha's path has helped me understand the Baal Shem Tov's moral intent. It is clear that like the Buddha, the Baal Shem was seeking to end ill will and greed through the cultivation of wisdom, compassion, joy, and unity. Yet we must remember that for the Buddha the practice of meditation alone would not have been enough. The practice of meditation is imbedded in a spiritual and moral framework called the Eightfold Path—Right Views, Right Intent, Right Speech, Right Conduct, Right Livelihood, Right Effort, Right Mindfulness, and Right Concentration. If I understand it correctly, Buddhist meditation is connected with the last tenet of the Eightfold Path—Right Concentration—and is only a single component of the spiritual life. In *The World Could Be Otherwise,* my friend, the Zen priest Norman Fischer writes that the *paramitas,* or "six perfections"—generosity, ethical conduct, patience, joyful effort, meditation, and understanding—can help adepts reconfigure the world they live in. And then there are a host of Buddhist ideals and concepts about the nature of the human self that must also be accounted for by the seeker in the process of transformation.

In the very same way, the Baal Shem's core spiritual practice of devekut, union with the Divine, was embedded in the entire religious and moral discipline that make up halakhah, literally, "the Way" of living a traditional Jewish life. I do not subscribe to all of traditional Judaism's doctrines, nor do I necessarily follow the halakhah in my own religious practice, for even more important to me as a neo-Hasidic Jew is the cultivation and deepening of the inner voice coming from Mt. Sinai that the Baal Shem speaks about. This still, small voice within each of us is initially formed by social conventions and educated in the mores and wisdom of the society we live in and the religious ethos of our families of origin. As we mature, however, it begins to emerge within us as an independent voice with a wisdom all its own. If one learns to attend to its whispers, it will enable the seeker to discern the particular spiritual and moral directions that they are to take day after day. I am able to see the decisive role this inner voice has played in my own unfolding, and especially through my work with my spiritual director.

This is a path that requires both commitment and devotion—not only to the path, but more importantly to the source of the path, as we read in the Sh'mah affirmation: "Love the EverPresent with all of your heart, with all of your soul, and with all of your might." The Hebrew word translated as "might" is *meh'od,* means "very." Heschel suggests that a better way to render the word meh'od would be "veryness." Love God with the *veryness* of your existence. And the Baal Shem understands this as an unconditional imperative: "Love God with all of your heart, with all of your soul, and with all of your might despite all the harshness and suffering that God puts you through."

If I link these insights, I get something like this: Since each and every creation lives *within* God, learn to love everything in the world with the *veryness* of your being. And where there is suffering, work to bring about healing. This is the heart of the Judaism I practice.

CHAPTER SIXTEEN

STEEPED IN LOVE AND COMPASSION

"Regardless of the tradition, the effects of the spiritual journey on the person are the same. Contemplatives, mystics and sages, in whatever form of spirituality, undergo a radical refashioning of their being.... Their consciousness is greatly enhanced and deepened; they acquire a transcendental, subtle awareness. Their character becomes saintly; their will is fixed on love and compassion, mercy and kindness. They are exquisitely sensitive beings, gentle and patient."

BROTHER WAYNE TEASDALE[266]

The most absorbing history course I took as an undergraduate was taught by the eminent medievalist, Archibald Ross Lewis. Although sixty-five years have passed, I can still see Professor Lewis—tall, lanky, and bald—lecturing before some thirty students. Each week, he would examine the origins, development, and structure of a different medieval institution. We covered class divisions, social structures, the papacy, monarchy, knighthood, law, politics, and religion. By the end of the semester I had a comprehensive sense of Christian society in the Middle Ages.

During the week allocated to the mendicant religious orders, Lewis focused on the Franciscans and Dominicans, contrasting differences between the two societies of friars in a trenchant way. I've never forgotten the lecture he gave devoted to the life and deeds of St. Francis of Assisi. I had heard of St. Francis, but knew nothing about him.

Francis grew up in Italy during the age of chivalry. A wild young man, he idealized war and romance and became both a troubadour and knight. But after seeing the poverty and suffering that resulted from the tragedies of war, he gave away all his worldly possessions and became a friar (with vows like a monk, but not living in a cloister). The incident that catalyzed his transformation was, for me, especially poignant.

Francis had been repulsed by lepers and attempted to avoid them at all costs. One day, however, while returning from an errand his father sent him on, he heard the sound of a leper waving his rattle to ward people away. The stench of the leper nauseated him beyond measure. But at that moment something moved his heart and he dismounted from his horse. He hesitated briefly, but then ran up to the leper and pulled the man into his arms. In that moment Francis' fears simply dissolved. As he related the story of Francis' transformation, our professor began to weep. I was taken aback. I'd never witnessed a teacher so stirred by what he was teaching that he would cry before the class.

DISCOVERING A JEWISH SAINT

In chapter 1, I wrote about my first encounters with Jewish Orthodoxy. It was during my sophomore year that I began to teach children enrolled in the Hebrew school of the local Conservative synagogue in Austin. I also regularly attended Shabbat services at that synagogue, and it was there that I met Avraham Gottesman, an elderly Orthodox Jew who survived the Nazi death camps. On Friday evenings following services I would walk Mr. Gottesman home, and he would instruct me on the proper ways to lead a traditionally observant life. During the week following Dr. Lewis' lecture on the mendicant orders, I decided that the next time I accompanied my mentor to his home I would ask him about Jewish saints. I would not mention what prompted my question, however, because I knew that Mr. Gottesman hated Christianity, which he saw as the root of fascism and the Holocaust.

Gottesman told me that the idea of sainthood was not Jewish. Judaism, he said, has a superior concept—the tzaddik, the unique holy individual who dedicates his life to God and Torah, and is looked up to by the masses. He further suggested that I go to the university library and look for books about a particular modern tzaddik, Rabbi Israel Lipkin Salanter (1810-83). I eventually discovered the memoirs of Jacob Mark, an observant Jew who was also open to the wider European intellectual currents of the nineteenth century. Mark knew Salanter personally. "When I was young," he wrote, "I often met Rabbi Israel Salanter, and I heard his sermons and his private discourses and had the opportunity to observe him at close quarters. I once had the privilege of being examined by him on my knowledge of Talmud." Here, then, are two stories about Salanter that Mark wrote about.

> It was the evening of Yom Kippur, the holiest day of the year. On his way to the synagogue, Rabbi Salanter heard a child crying. He entered the house and saw an infant howling in its cradle, a bottle of milk just out of reach. The mother had prepared the bottle and gone off to the synagogue, expecting her six-year-old daughter to give the baby the bottle. The little girl, however, had fallen fast asleep and did not hear the baby crying. Rabbi Salanter fed the baby and put it to sleep. But just as he was ready to leave, the little girl woke up. She begged the rabbi not to leave because she was afraid to be alone; so he stayed until the mother returned. Then Rabbi Salanter left and walked to the synagogue.
>
> When he told the congregation what had occurred, people were disturbed and amazed. How could the rabbi miss Yom Kippur services because of a child's crying? Rabbi Salanter told them, "But don't you know that even if one is not sure whether one's act will save a life, a Jew is permitted to go without praying and even to break any of the laws of the Sabbath?"

And a second story: "It was the year 1848, and the cholera epidemic which had already killed thousands of people was still virulent. On the day before Yom Kippur, Rabbi Salanter had signs posted in all the synagogues of the city stating that because of the epidemic, services should be shortened. Furthermore, people were to stay outdoors as much as possible. Small portions of sponge cake would be available in the synagogue vestibules and those who felt weak were to eat. Following the morning services at the synagogue where he officiated, Rabbi Salanter mounted the pulpit and announced that anyone feeling weak would find food in the antechamber."[267]

I was a newly observant Jew who had fully taken on the stringent obligations of traditional religious observance. Reading these stories, I was both surprised and impressed to find a prominent Orthodox rabbi whose moral sensitivity was so great that he put the needs of people before the traditional laws. This enabled me to better understand what Gottesman had meant when he had identified Salanter as a tzaddik.

Rabbi Israel Salanter lived in Lithuania, the intellectual center of traditional Rabbinic Judaism. The great Talmudic luminaries in Lithuania despised Hasidism, seeing it as a heresy attempting to undermine traditional Judaism. Although Salanter was a leading Talmudist, he believed the study of the formation of Jewish law alone did not necessarily make one a spiritually deep and morally upright person. He was passionate about the necessity for the cultivation of the kind of rigorous spiritual and ethical behavior that was called for in the musar literature. In the past, pious Jews studied these books, and preachers taught the tenets found in them, but Israel Salanter decided to initiate a movement that would shape the lives of students in yeshivot, which would also act as an alternative to Hasidism.

Lucy S. Dawidowicz has written that Israel Salanter was one of the first East European rabbis to try to reconcile Orthodoxy with modernity, in large part because he wanted to try to stem the flight of young Jews from their ancestral religion. Salanter preached inwardness, self-awareness, ethical behavior, and personal morality through musar. He established study centers where both Talmud and musar were pursued, and he travelled from city to city to bring his message to the great urban centers.

Rabbi Salanter stressed the necessity of internal struggle. He taught that human beings are constantly being seduced by the evil inclination, and only through the most strenuous efforts could an individual beat down its dreadful power and gradually overcome the natural predisposition to sin. The greatest failing, he maintained, was living in a casual way, heedless of the dangers to one's soul. And despite his fear of being overpowered by yetzer ha'rah, he warned against fatalistic approaches to the matter of human sinfulness.

ENSCONCED IN MUSAR

Salanter's form of musar diverged in a number of ways from its medieval forebears. One of those differences had to do with its more modern psychological rather than theological orientation. Immanuel Etkes, who has written a superb volume about Salanter, writes that according to the rabbi, "The real problem with Musar is the gap between cognitive knowledge, on the one hand, and psychological motivation, on the other. In other words, the fact that a given individual knows God's commandments, acknowledges their validity, and wishes to fulfill them, is no guarantee that the individual will, in fact, behave according to them in practice. This is because the behavior patterns and reactions of a human being are not guided and directed by his rational consciousness but by powerful, irrational emotional drives."[268] Salanter believed that human beings have a natural desire for pleasure, and that this lust or appetite ceaselessly drives us toward self-fulfillment, often at the expense of responsibilities toward others.

The rabbi came to believe that there was only one tool capable of breaking the instinct's control over human action: fear of God. This meant, in large part, the fear of divine punishment, including the fires of hell that would consume an unrepentant sinner after death. In order to avoid such punishment individuals needed to deepen their fear of God while at the same time continually engaging in introspection and self-examination, discovering their weaknesses and faults. Salanter developed four rules for the practice of musar for the students in his yeshivah: (1) studying traditional musar teachings every day, (2) engaging in this study with emotional fervor so that the teachings become internalized, (3) reviewing the same ethical principles over and over until they become habitual, (4) and learning musar together with others, because in this way one can find the strength to overcome the yetzer ha'arah.

As I read and re-read Menahem Glenn's book, it seemed that Rabbi Salanter was describing me perfectly. I knew that I was lethargic, and I identified with the rabbi's doubts regarding the ability of most human beings to cope with yetzer ha'rah. It became clear that I had to learn how to suppress my evil impulses if I was ever able to perfect my life. I deeply wanted to serve God and it seemed that this was the authentic Jewish way of doing so. I couldn't believe in the literal reality of the torments of hell, but I did become God-fearing and thus stringent and rigid in my adherence to halakhah, and to the requirements of musar.

I hadn't yet studied Talmud, but Gottesman suggested a volume that covered all areas of personal religious observance—*The Abridged Shulchan Arukh,* by Solomon Ganzfried, a compendium of laws pertaining to correct religious conduct. The book was compiled in Europe in the nineteenth century, and written in a straightforward and exacting manner that matched Salanter's own sense of the gravity of Jewish law. What stands out in my memory was the puritanical approach to sex the author demanded of readers, and the way he depicted masturbation as an act that was virtually equivalent to murder.

Here I was living alone, fearful of intimacy, and never dating. And as I internalized the values and precepts put forward by Ganzfried and Salanter, I was also creating habits of constant judgement for any and every thought and act that violated the strict standards of Jewish law and morality. As the years went on, the guilt and shame I would experience when committing even small transgressions became enormous. Naturally, I felt that my excessive sexual urges had the power of destroying my yearning to become holy. And I saw my attractions toward men as well as women as major sins. It was in large part for this reason that I entered psychoanalysis during my early years as a seminary student.

Sharing my secrets with Dr. Gruenthal began a process of change, and by my third year in rabbinical school I began to repudiate the gloomy and repressive discipline of musar. It was only in later years when I learned that taking on musar, and indeed the entire regimen of Jewish religious practices, had served to replace my mother's severity and authority with the will of the demanding God of Jewish tradition. It was during those years when I was also learning about the human origins of the Torah and the Talmud, and this liberating knowledge finally enabled me to begin to distance myself from the yoke of divine authority that had buttressed my strict observance of the commandments and prohibitions. When I began to read about the Holocaust, my repressed anger toward God finally surfaced. It was becoming clear that the fear of God had never left me. And then my later experiences with LSD and other psychedelics revealed how a healthy religious outlook would have to be anchored in what Heschel called "radical amazement," rather than fear.

Many years later when I read psychologist William James' *The Varieties of Religious Experience,* I noted that religious people whose souls were sick maximize evil "based on the persuasion that the evil aspects of our life are of its very essence, and that the world's meaning most comes home to us when we lay them most to heart." I can't really identify this notion with Salanter's musar, but it does characterize how I internalized the precepts of musar. The truth of the matter, which I only discovered years later, was that I'd come to Jewish tradition and to Salanter's form of musar with a latent condition of what psychiatrists call Obsessive-Compulsive Disorder, brought about by the abandonment issues suffered during my childhood. My extreme adherence to Jewish law and to the beliefs and practices of musar had provided this disorder with a ready way to manifest itself. I realized that even though the psychotherapy I'd been undergoing was valuable, it was inadequate for healing the problem. If I was ever to become a free and responsible human being I would have to break completely with Judaism.

ISRAEL SALANTER AND ISRAEL BAAL SHEM TOV

It was a little more than a decade after abandoning Salanter that I encountered the Baal Shem Tov. Looking back at that period in my life, though, it seems a lot longer for I went through a great number of changes during that time. As I began work on this chapter, I noticed that I was still harboring residual anger toward Salanter's burdensome musar path. As I began my research into Salanter's life and thought, however, I began to feel a certain debt to him. For despite his extremism, it was he, more than anyone, who introduced me to the notion of Judaism as a continuous spiritual quest for self-transcendence. I still admire the man's moral idealism and the kindnesses he rendered so many people.

Like the Baal Shem, Salanter grew up in a traditional Jewish community that was bound to tradition and observance as obligatory requirements. That Salanter took this obligation in such an intense and serious way was part of his inheritance as an Orthodox Jew. He shared this legacy with the Baal Shem, and there are numerous similarities that characterize both teachers, even though the Besht was less exacting. To begin, the two men were both steeped in the ideas, values, and primary texts of classical Judaism—the Bible and Talmud. They were each committed to observe halakhah as codified in the Shulchan Aruch, the sixteenth-century code of Jewish law. Both were also grounded in medieval musar. They believed that without the wisdom provided by these inherited teachings, Jews would lose their authenticity and fall into a spiritual and moral morass. Moreover, like the Besht before him, Salanter possessed a psychological orientation toward the tradition, which included a positive evaluation of human emotion.

Nonetheless, setting their lives and teachings side by side, we can see enormous differences in their understandings of the constituents of an authentic Jewish religious life. Unlike most of the prominent Eastern European religious teachers in the eighteenth and nineteenth centuries, Salanter had no interest at all in Kabbalah or anything esoteric. His Judaism was based solely on the revelation at Mt. Sinai and its interpretation by the rabbis of the classical era. It was a religion grounded fully in the will of God. The Besht's Judaism, on the other hand, embraced the concepts, symbolism, lore, and mystical experiences of the Kabbalah. The underlying themes of the Zohar had to do not only with revelation and God's will, but with the creation and redemption of the world. The Baal Shem's Judaism was as much grounded in his kabbalistic understanding of the cosmos as it was on the Bible, Talmud, and Midrash.

Salanter imaged God as a king, a father, and a lord who was above and beyond the world, in whose image human beings were created. But the Baal Shem saw all of reality as existing within the Divine, and the Divine permeating the whole of existence. Like some of the kabbalists who preceded him, the Besht was psychologically oriented, and he believed the underlying forces of the universe were the same powers that drove human beings. This way of understanding the inner workings of the psyche prompted a great deal of speculation on his part regarding human behavior, and the ways that human character might be transformed through appropriate spiritual practices. The Baal Shem eventually came to see that everything comes from God, evil as well as good. This deepened his compassion for people, including evildoers, for he understood that human beings were not completely at fault for evils that existed in human society. This, in turn, motivated his certainty that the tzaddik needs to embody divine love and compassion in order to heal the brokenness of the people and the community that he serves.

The two men differed with regard to worship, as well. Although Salanter's approach to prayer was deep and sincere, it represented a less significant part of his religious life. Like other Lithuanian Jews, it was not prayer but the study of Talmud that drove him and his students. The dialectics of Talmud study focus on discerning how God would want Jews to deal with the many polarities of existence, and how to live an observant Jewish life. And for Salanter, this kind of sacred study was supplemented by the teachings of musar, meant to inspire the fear of God.

For the Baal Shem, it was not the will of God, but the experience of Divinity that was at the center of the spiritual life; and absorption into the oneness of the Godhead meant the transcendence of all the polarities of existence. Thus, for the Besht, the complete immersion in ecstatic worship became key to living a true life of devotion. Even though the study of the Talmud remained essential, it was no longer at the center. This led him to a more comprehensive understanding of serving the Divine: Everything one does, every situation in life offers the individual an equal opportunity for service.

While Israel Salanter intensified the fear of God, the Baal Shem Tov sought to transform such fear into awe. He taught his students the way to place the fears that normally arise in human life into a more spacious context, that is, a yielding into the mysterious reality that transcends the human ability to understand or alter. Even more, the Baal Shem was convinced that this kind of heightened awe could then be transmuted into love. This required that the individual learn how to fully surrender to aspects of his life that cannot be changed, only accepted in gratitude:

> When you experience divine love and kindness showering
> upon you through God's enormous mercy, you will come
> to realize that the purpose of all your external fears was
> only to awaken you to the inner awe of God. It is then that
> your fear of God will become transformed into the love of
> God, and you will be able to accept all of your outer fears
> in love. At this point you will recognize that there is noth-
> ing at all in the world that can make you afraid![269]

The Baal Shem taught that when we are faced with situations that cannot be changed, the best thing to do is fully accept what is occurring: "Accept everything that happens to you in this world with love. In this way you will be given both this world and the coming world.' On hearing this counsel, the man answered, 'May the Blessed One give me the strength to receive everything in love.' And the master replied, 'You have spoken the truth.'"[270]

CHAPTER SEVENTEEN

THE ESSENCE OF THE BAAL SHEM'S TRUTH

One day, several of Rabbi Israel Salanter's disciples saw him standing and speaking cheerfully and at great length with a man about worldly matters. They were perplexed because they knew their teacher was not accustomed to wasting time discussing frivolous things. After the conversation ended, one of the students asked their teacher why he'd behaved in such a lighthearted manner with the man. Rabbi Israel replied, "This man was feeling extremely bitter and depressed, and it was a great act of loving-kindness to cheer him up and make him forget his troubles and worries. Could I have done this by lecturing him about fear and about musar? Surely, I could only offer the man what he needed by conversing with him in a cheerful way about down-to-earth matters."[271] How very discerning and caring on Rabbi Salanter's part. Yet, from the bewilderment of the disciples, we can see that the encouragement of cheerfulness and joy was not a basic value in the Musar Movement.

There is a tale in the Talmud regarding two comedians who were granted their reward in the world to come because of their desire to cheer up depressed people. Rabbi Salanter doubtless knew this story, and it may have even been the source of his actions with the depressed man: "Rabbi Baroka was standing next to the prophet Elijah in a crowded marketplace. The throng of buyers and sellers were completely immersed in conducting their transactions, seemingly unaware of anything else. Then Rabbi Baroka asked Elijah, 'Is there anyone in this market who is actually worthy of entering the World to Come?' Elijah nodded in the affirmative, pointing out two brothers. When he saw the two men, Rabbi Baroka ran over to them and asked them what their business was. They replied, 'We are comedians. We make sad people laugh.'"[272] These two brothers were not at all concerned with the commercial activity that was consuming the sellers and buyers. Rather, they were dedicated to making sad people laugh, raising the consciousness of people lost in gloom. What a marvelous story!

Now we know that the Baal Shem Tov was familiar with this tale because he spoke about it with his disciples. He revealed that he had not really understood the deeper meaning of the tale, and that one night before sleep he prayed that an explanation of its significance be given him in a dream. This is what he then reported that he learned: The entire occupation of these two comedians was actually of a spiritual nature. They would meet each person who came their way and enter deeply into that individual's consciousness. Then they would link that person's awareness with the Divine. In this way the awareness of the person they had connected themselves with would expand, and he would realize that the world we live in is entirely divine. But when the brothers came across an individual who was in a state of pain and despondency, they were unable to enter that person's awareness and join his consciousness to the Divine. What did they do? They began with jokes, cheering the person with humor. Only then, once the person was feeling relief from his melancholy, would they enter his consciousness and link him with the blessed One.[273]

It seems that the Besht understood that his dream disclosed a practice that he should take up when out and about in the world—elevating the consciousness of everyone he met. Indeed, we have a number of Beshtian teachings that indicate one of the deployments of a tzaddik has to do with elevating the consciousness of the people one is with. His interpretation of the story about Elijah and Rabbi Baroka in the marketplace reveals one particular kind of practice that comes out of this understanding of the mission entrusted to him by God. In his mystical davening he felt privileged to unite with the underlying mystery and oneness of reality. As we saw earlier, this was a powerful and lifechanging experience, initiating him into enlightenment.

I imagine, though, that when the Baal Shem completed his practice, he could not avoid seeing how the celestial harmony he just experienced was now dissolved, replaced by the cacophony of ordinary existence. If I am correct, the Besht understood that it would be his duty to channel the mystery and unity he experienced during his altered state of awareness into the mundane, physical world. It seems that he realized it was in this way that he would be able to help bring about the recognition of the Divinity of the entirety of existence. Although this truth began in his consciousness, I think it placed a mandate on him to actualize it by how he lived. This would mean accentuating the virtues of joy, love, and compassion.

The Baal Shem's grandson, Hayyim Efrayim of Sudlikov, captured the Besht's understanding of this task in a teaching that he heard from his grandfather:

> In the Book of Psalms we read, *"And I will walk in the wide spaces for I have sought Your precepts."* (119:45) When King David spoke these words, he was enjoying his practice of spending time in marketplaces and other wide spaces devoted to fulfilling God's precepts. And what were these precepts?
>
> Throughout his life King David's only desire was to bring about unifications (*yihudim*) in the world. These unifications were meant to reunite the Shekhinah, the Divinity of the physical world, with the blessed Holy One, the Divinity of the transcendent realm.[274]

The Besht is projecting his own mystical practice onto King David, asserting that it is the duty of a true tzaddik to bring about a reunification of the dual faces of the Divine. This was a ritual act he would engage in wherever he was and whoever he was with. The kabbalists believed such a practice aided in the process of returning existence to the primordial unity that existed before the cosmic cataclysm occurred during Creation. It was this upheaval that had separated the Shekhinah from the blessed Holy One. The intentional act of the tzaddik contributes to healing that brokenness.

This reunification practice has the potential of empowering spiritual adepts in their relationships with the world. It does not necessarily require the kabbalistic intention that the Baal Shem employed. It does, however, necessitate the seeker bringing a spiritual mindset to all of the social connections and relationships they are involved in, with the intention of elevating those situations through empathic attention and deep listening. This may necessitate putting one's own preferences aside and adopting an attitude of equanimity. But it may also mean that the adept looks for ways to bring about greater trust and harmony among those who are engaged in dialogue. One of my close friends, Barry Barkan, is a master of this kind of uplifting spiritual practice. I am still trying to learn how to do this.

ONLY ONE LOVE

Contrasting the Baal Shem Tov with the Kotzker Rebbe, Abraham Joshua Heschel emphasized the Kotzker's having placed truth at the center of his spiritual quest while the Besht embraced the value of love and compassion: "The Baal Shem taught that love ranked higher than Truth. What really counted was a little compassion. There was only one kind of reality—love…. The test of love is how not how one relates to saints and scholars but to rascals. The Baal Shem was able to sense an admirable quality in every human being. In fact, he recommended a conciliatory attitude toward sinners and evildoers, true to his conviction that God loved all men."[275] And I must say that when I read the stories about the Baal Shem's love and caring, he seems in many ways closer to Francis of Assisi than he does to Rabbi Israel Salanter. There are many stories and anecdotes that were told about the Besht that reveal his love for people. For me the following tale is quintessential:

> A father once came to the Besht and told him that his son had broken away from Jewish tradition and was leaning toward converting to another faith tradition. "What should I do, Rebbe?" the man inquired. "Do you love your son?" asked the Besht. "Yes, I do," replied the man. "Then love him more," said the Besht.[276]

"Then love him more." I was simply amazed when I read this anecdote for the first time. This is not at all the way that Jewish parents in eighteenth-century Poland would have treated a wayward son. Abandoning the religion revealed by God and converting to another faith would have been seen as an act of arch heresy. And yet, in an alternate version of this

tale we are told that because the father followed the Baal Shem's advice, the son returned to his ancestral religion. For him, love was indeed a healing force.

Here is another remarkable statement of the master: "The Baal Shem Tov once told his disciple, the Rav of Kolomaye, 'I love the Jew whom you might consider the lowest of the low more than you love your only son.'"[277] What could have provoked this declaration to his disciple? My guess is that the Rav of Kolomaye had complained to the Baal Shem about how difficult it was to relate to common Jews who acted in crude ways. And I can almost see the Besht waving him away, as if to say: "You, sir, are the spiritual leader of Kolomaye, and no matter how coarse, how boorish, a human being in your community might be, he is an image of God and he deserves your love."

The Maggid of Medziritch once remarked, "I wish I could kiss a scroll of the Torah with the same love that the Baal Shem showed to a child who was beginning to read the Hebrew alphabet."[278] And we read how the master once told his disciples that the core principle of Hasidism was this: "One must love one's fellow human beings and never harm them, even if this entails harming oneself. Thus, love of the other takes precedence over love of oneself.... I have chosen to instill this virtue above all others into the hearts of my followers. And if you look deeply into their souls, you will detect at least a small part of this virtue in each of them."[279]

Rabbi Menachem Mendel of Chernobyl writes that his teacher taught that the Lifeforce (Hiyyut) that flows through all of creation takes a particular form in human beings: "The Baal Shem taught: The Lifeforce of every human being is love. One who is truly aware knows that the quality of love is among the most elevated of human virtues, illuminating our lives like a precious jewel."[280] Arthur Green has written, "Who more than the Baal Shem Tov stands to remind us that all love, even all of eros, is the fallen fruit of the great single love of God that animates the cosmos?... The point is that there is only one love, the love of God, and that all other loves or erotic attractions, including those forbidden by the Torah, are fallen expressions of that love, capable of uplifting or redemption. This is early Hasidism at its most radical."[281]

On another occasion, the Besht instructed his disciples:

As we know, the Torah teaches the basic principle *"As you love yourself, so love your fellow human being."* (Leviticus 19:18) But don't think that this mitzvah stands on its own, for it is a specific application of a greater, more inclusive mitzvah, *"And you shall love Y-H-V-H, the EverPresent, who is your Power, with all of your heart, with all of your soul, and with all of your strength."* (Deuteronomy 6:5) So you must stay aware of this truth: When we love our fellow humans as ourselves, we are actually loving the Holy One, for every person is part of God.[282]

On yet another occasion, the Besht framed this insight somewhat differently: "When you engage in an act of loving kindness, your intentionality and consciousness should be directed toward offering loving-kindness to the Shekhinah who dwells at the core of the person you are serving. Always remember: a human being is a portion of the Divine beyond."[283] The formulation of the mitzvah, *"As you love yourself, so love your fellow human being,"* takes it for granted that human beings love themselves, but we must admit that Jewish teachings have never really emphasized the love of self. Perhaps Jewish teachers have thought that the idea of self-love was dangerous, because it could lead to self-absorption.

Like the teachers before him, the Baal Shem Tov does not speak about self-love, yet he does take a strong position in terms of the necessity for individuals to recognize their Oneness with the Divine, the compassion latent in their souls, and their God-given abilities to mend and heal brokenness: "You may wonder, 'Who am I? What power do I have? How could anyone like me damage or mend anything in heaven or on the earth? How could any of my deeds affect God?' But it is because of your stubborn doubts that you give free rein to unholy habits of mind, imagining that you can live your life lost in false humility, saying to yourself: *'All will be well with me'* (Deut. 29:18). Don't be so modest! Know that through your deeds, you actually have the ability to bind yourself to God, as it is written, *'You shall be able to walk in God's very own paths.* (Deut. 28:9). When you act compassionately here on earth, you arouse divine compassion above, throughout all the divine realms."[284] In its own way, this teaching summons the individual to love their divine potential and to engage with people and situations in a way that can affect them for the good.

Professor Heszel Klepfisz, who was raised in Poland, calls the teaching about love and compassion "Hasidism's Teaching of the Heart": "Surely, the way was shown by Israel Baal Shem Tov.... But those who came after him also gave heart and soul to eliminate the individual's and community's sorrows. And even in a lifestyle where the cord of compassion for one's fellow man never ceased to vibrate, the Jewish spirit had to be stirred up by the waves of kindness and goodness which flowed with unrestrained vigor in Hasidism."[285]

We see this absolute commitment to compassion extended even into the abyss of the Holocaust. Writing in the Buddhist magazine *Shambhala Sun,* the poet, essayist, and naturalist Diane Ackerman tells the story of Rabbi Kalonymous Kalman Shapira of Piaseczno, Poland who made the decision to stay with his Hasidim in the Warsaw ghetto despite the danger to his own life, and then died with the ghetto's demolition: "During the war [Rabbi Shapira] suffered the same torment, fear, pain, and loss as other residents of the ghetto, and came to know the agony of howitzers bombarding friends and loved ones with shrapnel—in one week, he lost his mother, only son, daughter-in-law, and sister-in-law. His beloved wife of many years, whom he regarded as a soul mate...fell ill and died.... Nowhere in his writings does one read the factual reality of life for Jews in occupied Poland, nor even the words 'Nazi' or 'German.' Instead, his mission was compassion—'to project the supernatural powers of kindness into the realm of speech, so that they might take on concrete, specific form.'... The weak, sick, exhausted, hungry, tortured, and insane all came to Rabbi Shapira for spiritual nourishment, which he combined with leadership and soup kitchens."[286]

Many if not most of the Baal Shem's teachings on love and compassion refer specifically to the love of Jews and not human beings. Early on I was put off by what seemed to be a narrow and chauvinist attitude, but I came to understand that his focus on Jews makes sense historically. He lived among Jews, and he inherited the traditional Jewish notion of the chosenness. And the antisemitic pogroms that his people suffered could not have endeared him to Christianity. Nonetheless, as I pointed out in Part One, a number of scholars have suggested that the Besht may have had contact with Christians, which could account for similarities between Hasidic and Christian sects, including parallel spiritual practices.

I also note that in his famous letter to his brother-in-law describing his shamanic ascents in order to halt two antisemitic assaults, he doesn't blame those who were planning the attacks. For the Besht, everything that occurs in the world, both good and bad, comes about through heavenly decrees. And unlike the Musar preachers, he never assumes that antisemitic incidents might be punishments for sin. For the Baal Shem all evil comes from God's enigmatic harshness (*gevurah*), and wherever possible it was the duty of the tzaddik to inhabit divine love (*hesed*) and then to attempt to transform this irrational element within the Divine.

The kabbalistic tradition that the Baal Shem received definitely saw non-Jews as inferior to Jews. There are tales told about the ways in which he defeated Christian religious leaders who harbored malicious thoughts or plans against Jews. Some stories, however, seem to demonstrate his love for *all* people. He told his disciples that all human beings must be honored and respected because their souls are carved out of Divinity. Rabbi Mosheh Aaron (Miles) Krassen, a contemporary scholar of Hasidism, writes that "given the legendary and factual evidence regarding the Baal Shem Tov's relations with non-Jews as well as the radically non-dual inclination of his overall spiritual outlook, it seems to me more than reasonable to assume that his emphasis on love for others was more inclusive."[287]

Like Martin Buber, Hillel Zeitlin is considered a founder of contemporary Neo-Hasidism. Both men loved the Baal Shem Tov. But Zeitlin wrote that in the modern world the notion of love needs to be greatly expanded beyond the boundaries of the Jewish people. Zeitlin taught that the love of God needs to "shine forth and burn even more brightly" than in former times, Israel serving as a beacon to lead the entire world toward passionate engagement with a God present in all things and all moments, the great truth that he finds in Hasidism. "Love of Israel," a key teaching of the Besht and all later Hasidic tradition, will be expanded into "a great worldwide love of humanity." Love of Torah will no longer be limited to traditional rabbinic and Talmudic studies, but will be sought out in "all the finest works of art, in all worldly knowledge."[288]

COMPASSION IN THE CLASSROOM

I was so taken by the Baal Shem's teachings about love and compassion that in 2003 I offered to teach an intensive weeklong summer course on his approach to love and compassion to a class of rabbinical students at the Academy for Jewish Religion in Los Angeles. That summer I gave the course a second time at the Aleph Kallah, a weeklong gathering of Jewish Renewal folks sponsored by ALEPH: Alliance for Jewish Renewal, the organization whose founding was inspired by Reb Zalman Schachter-Shalomi. And during the following year I taught the class in my synagogue's adult education program.

In preparation for these classes I organized a collection of about one hundred Baal Shem stories and teachings along the following lines:

- Teachings in Praise of Love
- Love for God
- Human Problems in the Light of Love
- Loving Your Neighbor
- Loving Children
- Compassion for Women
- Love for Jews
- Compassion for Non-Jews
- Love for Sinners
- Compassion for Enemies
- Caring for the Poor
- Teachings on the Power of Compassion
- Radical Non-Judgmentalism
- Opening to Intimacy

One of my students at the Academy for Jewish Religion that summer was Diane Elliot. Diane and I had been dating for a few years, and it was during the weeklong class on the Besht that we became engaged. As I look back at that time it seems that the spirit of the Baal Shem's loving presence filling the classroom must have affected my spontaneous decision to ask Diane to marry me.

One of the questions I asked my students to consider and write about in their final class papers was how the Baal Shem's teachings might impact their future vocation as rabbis. Diane was moved by one of the stories I'd selected for inclusion in the section of the curriculum called "Love for Jews," which came from Martin Buber's *Tales of the Hasidim*: "The Baal Shem said: 'Imagine a man whose business hounds him through many streets and across the market-place the livelong day. He almost forgets that there is a Maker of the world. Only when the time for the Afternoon Prayer comes, does he remember: I must pray. And then, from the bottom of his heart, he heaves a sigh of regret that he has spent his day on vain and idle matters, and he runs into a by-street and stands there, and prays: God holds him dear, very dear and his prayer pierces the firmament.'"[289]

In her paper Diane wrote the following:

> The concern for the whole community, reflecting the Baal Shem's radical empathy with the pain of others along with joyfulness at their celebrations seems to me to be at the very root of caring community. To value all members of the group is perhaps the most difficult practice for those who aspire to be in spiritual community...
>
> Several years ago, I was invited to give a teaching for a Reform havurah.... It was on a Friday night, or perhaps a Sunday, that I arrived at someone's house and met a bunch of nicely dressed suburban couples. I struggled to converse with them, wondering what I was doing there, what I could possibly offer them that would knock a chink in their world. After dinner they sat down, and I tried to lead them in an exploration of how to "spiritualize" a few prayers, to bring their bodies and their voices into davening. One older man, a Holocaust survivor whom I had talked to before dinner, sat rocking and singing with a quietly blissful smile on his face. The rest of the group seemed somewhat embarrassed and inhibited. The only real energy surged when I demonstrated the Hebrew word *kavanah* (intentionality, focus) by miming a baseball pitch. I struggled during and after the presentation with self-judgment and with judging these people who were so unable to "respond" to my attempts

at initiating them into the realms of a renewed Jewish spirituality.

As I was working on this paper, I asked myself how the Baal Shem Tov might have acted in such a setting. The Baal Shem's teachings on love and compassion urge the practitioner to make an existential choice to work toward redemption. Deeply aware of the sufferings of the world and of our own shortcomings, we can nevertheless make and re-make the choice to open to each situation as it is, to engage in loving ways, rather than to hang back in disaffection. Focused lovingkindness meditation, when I can do it regularly, helps me to excavate and witness the obvious and subliminal disappointments and hurts that keep me caught in judgment. Then the natural goodness in myself and others breaks through like sun rays temporarily obscured by passing clouds. Here, then, is my story of the suburban havurah revisioned in the light of the Baal Shem's presence.

I arrive at the house for dinner. Instead of being worried about what I am to present, what "they" will think of "me," I look at each person's face with love and curiosity. I am genuinely interested in meeting them and in hearing their stories. I value the ways they are finding to practice Judaism and to serve God in their lives and reflect this worthiness back to them. Instead of approaching them with the assumption that they lack something, I simply share songs and stories that speak to them where they're at. Most of all I listen and help them to feel a bit more the God-presence that already imbues their lives.

The Besht's radical acceptance of people as they are, and the necessity to transmute judgment and fear of the other into love, form the springboard from which truly joyous service can be cultivated and spread. Diane said it very well. And since we met, our relationship has taught me how to love and forgive in an unconditional way. Our bond has also required me to learn to surpass my judgmentalism, selfishness, and inertia, and to give more of myself to the relationship. I am still learning these lessons.

LEARNING TO LOVE

Before concluding this chapter, I want to say something more about how the Baal Shem's teachings about love and compassion have impacted my personal life. In 1975, less than a year after having first read Heschel's tribute to the Besht, I moved from San Francisco to Berkeley to be part of the Aquarian Minyan, a New Age community inspired by Reb Zalman. The Minyan would become a laboratory in which I could begin to practice some of the Baal Shem's teachings.

Shabbat services in the homes of the members were unlike anything I had experienced before. Every Friday evening was different, and I never knew what to expect. At my first service, the singing and dancing were ecstatic, and the spirit of joy was entirely palpable. I sensed a spirit of love filling the room. People spontaneously shared the blessings they had received during the week that had passed, and they blessed one another for the coming week before joining in a vegetarian potluck. The only traditional liturgy that was chanted was the Sh'ma—the declaration of Divine Oneness—and I realized that many or most of the Minyan folks were probably not conversant with the siddur, the traditional Jewish prayer book.

These services uncovered a longing in me to return to Jewish modes of davening, but I knew that I could not use the traditional liturgy as it was. The ancient language was simply too ethnically focused, too centered on a heavenly father figure that I no longer believed in. Nevertheless, the ancient structure of the various services made a lot of sense to me. It was then that I began to alter the liturgy, taking prayers from the traditional liturgy and from the biblical Psalms and revising the language whenever I sensed that it was necessary to do so. I felt guilty for abandoning the ancient words of prayer hallowed by hundreds, even thousands of years of repetition, but I knew that this is what I had to do. The universalistic images that I used for the Divine were largely inspired by my psychedelic experiences, by Rav Abraham Isaac Kook, and by the American poet, Walt Whitman.

I found a poem by the Yiddish poet Yehoash (1872-1927) that spoke to my condition, and I would read or chant it before reciting the Sh'ma: "Happy is the one who says: Above all earthly might and fame I crave for love. Would that the words my heart and lips express were balm for wounds, to soothe and heal and bless. Oh, that my eyes would send forth a blaze of light, to be a beacon in another's night."[290]

Besides praying for help and support, how else could I cultivate love and compassion? For centuries Jewish tradition held the faith that the act of study, when undertaken with spiritual intentionality, had the power to inspire personal change. During the years that I immersed myself in the vision and teachings of Rav Kook, I found a Hebrew essay he wrote about universal love. It began with these words: "Love should fill one's heart for everything and everyone. The love for all creations in their entirety comes first. After this, love for all humanity. And then the love for the Jewish people, which includes the whole, since Israel is destined to bring creation to perfection. Each of these kinds of love becomes real through deeds, for to love God's creations means doing them some good, bringing them to higher elevations. Beyond all these circles of love is the love of God, which is fully realized love. It is not the essence of this love to bring about any change; but the heart fills with a love which is the highest experience of happiness."[291]

Rav Kook's Hebrew wasn't easy, and I spent almost ten years translating the essay. Yet I knew that I was not merely putting Kook's teachings into English; my study of the text was meant to alter my entire way of relating to people and to the world. This happened a second time a few years later when I encountered Heschel's portrait of the Baal Shem. I was deeply moved by Heschel's description of the Besht's loving character, and probed his words over and over, as if they were affirmations.

As important as such in-depth study about love was, however, it was not enough to really transform the damaging patterns that were lodged in my psyche since childhood. I wasn't skilled enough at that time to help create a climate of love and compassion in the Aquarian Minyan, and in fact there were numerous times when I acted out in deplorable ways. Yet I never gave up. I was determined to learn to love, whatever it would take. In 1978 I underwent a three-month psychospiritual process called "PsychoGenesis," based on the Hoffman Process, and in the years following gave myself to individual and group psychotherapy, working to extricate my soul from its bondage to the past. To be sure, the issues related to love and compassion were not the only issues I brought to therapy, but as I look back now, I believe they were the most critical. Perhaps the most crucial approach to inner healing I employed was a modality that has been called "inner-child work," enabling individuals to connect with younger damaged parts of themselves and work to heal those wounds. I also decided that I needed to live in a communal house with children, so I could gain some experience caring for youngsters.

All of this was important, and yet it was still insufficient. I needed some form of spiritual practice that would enable me to connect with the seed of love I'd lost growing up, and that I'd tasted during my psychedelic experiences. I remembered reading about a practice that the sixteenth-century kabbalist, Isaac Luria, had introduced into his morning davening. Before beginning formal worship, Luria would declare: "Behold, I am taking upon myself the positive mitzvah of loving my neighbor as myself." R. Shneur Zalman of Liadi, the founder of Chabad Hasidism, had engaged in this practice not only before davening, but after completing his davening as well, so he would have it in mind when he encountered the members of his community.

In the early 1990s I was studying to become a spiritual director at Mercy Center in Burlingham, California. One of the faculty members was Donald Bisson, a brother in the Catholic Marist religious order. I was deeply impressed by Don's knowledge and wisdom, and his psychological astuteness. Like me, he had been profoundly influenced by the work of Jung. I asked Don if he would become my spiritual director and supervisor while I was in the formation program. He agreed. I remember the day clearly. I was frustrated. I wanted so much to develop my capacity to love God and people and I didn't know how to go about it. I took the issue to spiritual direction, speaking at length about my problem. Don listened carefully as he always did, and when I finished he asked, "Do you love yourself?" I was taken aback. I finally answered, "Not really. I see self-love as a kind of narcissism."

"And do you sense that God loves you?" he asked.

I told him that the specter of the Holocaust stood in the way for me. "If God really loved people, then why did God allow so many millions of people to be tortured and massacred?" What I didn't say—but recognized later—was that I felt personally unworthy of God's love.

Don was not deterred by my theological argument. He emphasized that if I didn't allow for the possibility that God loved me, it would be difficult, perhaps impossible, to develop and deepen my love not only for God, but also for myself and for others. I left the session confused, but decided to read some books on God's love for humanity. At the time I was unaware of any Jewish books on this subject, so I turned to Christian writers. This was the beginning of an important journey for me.

Some years later I came upon a little book by Phillip Bennett called *Let Yourself Be Loved.* Bennett is an Episcopalian priest and a pastoral psychotherapist. His thesis is that the loving presence of God is always present unconditionally, ready to embrace and enfold us, despite all of our fears and all of our resistance. Bennett invites his readers to open themselves to this great love. The book was couched in Christian terminology, but as I page through my copy again today, I notice all the little notations I wrote in the margins, referencing Jewish wisdom sources that say similar things.

While reading *Let Yourself Be Loved*, I thought of the order of the Sh'ma and its blessings in the Jewish liturgy. Just before reciting the Sh'ma, there is a blessing that begins with the words, "With a deep love You have loved us, deep power that we are, embracing us with great compassion..." (*Ahavah rabbah ah'hav'ta'nu Yah Elo'hay'nu....*) Then the worshipper chants the Sh'ma itself: "O hear Israel: the EverPresent, our only Power, the EverPresent is one!" (*Shema Yisrael: Yah Elo'hay'nu, Yah ehad.*) This is followed by a declaration of our love for God: "Love the EverPresent, your own godliness, with all of your heart, with all of your soul, and with all of your passion." (*V'ahav'tah et Yah Elo'heh'kha b'khol l'va'vekha, u'v'khol nahf'sheh-khah, u'v'khol m'odekha.*)

"With a deep love You have loved us" is followed by the Sh'ma, declaring that God is one. Then, immediately come the words, "Love the EverPresent, your own godliness." The message is clear: We are able to love God because God already loves us and instills in us the ability to love.

One of the passages in Bennett's book deals with the question that Don Bisson had asked me. Do you sense that God loves you? "Ultimately, our attack upon ourselves is an attack upon God, a refusal to accept the self which God has made. There is a Hasidic saying that a host of angels goes in a vanguard before every human being crying out, 'Make way! Make way for the image of God!' When we attack ourselves, we are attacking the image of God within us, an image we are called to treasure and nourish in ourselves and others."[292] And at the conclusion of Bennett's book, he offers a meditation for opening one's heart to receive God's love. The practice then expands into a prayer for others, even people one has difficulty loving. Thinking about all of this so many years later, I realized that what Don Bisson had told me was eminently compatible with the teachings of the Baal Shem: There is a single love that penetrates the cosmos and binds everything together. The fact that I exist, that I have been given life, consciousness, creativity, and the ability to love is evidence that the universe has given me a gift. I have chosen to call this Something, God.

In the similar but better developed Buddhist practice called Metta, the practitioner begins by directing loving-kindness toward themselves, and then, in a widening circle, to others. Sylvia Boorstein, a Jewish/Buddhist meditation teacher, describes the long-term results: "*Metta* practice is transformative. The direct experience of the pleasure—indeed, the joy—of benevolence, over time, lessens the habitual self-centered, defensive actions of the mind and strengthens the habit of friendly acceptance. Responsive behavior—motivated by kindness—replaces reactive behavior. Benevolent, decisive, strong responses are possible. We become peaceful, passionate people."[293]

The Baal Shem Tov taught that because all of God's creations are divine, the love of God's creations *is* the love of God. Likewise, Sylvia Boorstein writes: "I don't think it's possible to love God with all your heart and not love everything else. Complete loving mandates and rejoices in complete acceptance. I learned that doing Buddhist *metta* (lovingkindness) meditation." Sylvia is also a traditional practicing Jew, and she associates Metta with the Sh'ma, the core affirmation of Judaism: The Sh'ma begins with the words, "Hear O Israel: the EverPresent is our Power, the EverPresent alone." Then the Sh'ma speaks of our relationship with the Divine: "And you shall love the EverPresent your Power with all of your heart, with all of your soul, and with all of your being." Sylvia writes that this is in fact the Metta practice of Judaism.[294] It seemed to me that I too could adapt metta to a Jewish context, associating it with the Sh'ma. I have been engaged with this practice for a quarter century now, and it has gradually transformed my life.

Soon after that I began to develop what I call the Unitive Love Practice. I have definitely noticed ways in which this gradually transformed my consciousness and behavior. Although I still get angry about social injustices, and I am still committed to engaging in tikkun olam, I find it difficult to hate the perpetrators.

Scientific studies bear out the effectiveness of meditation for the cultivation of compassion.[295] Have I become a more loving and compassionate person? I believe that I have, but I continue to learn and grow, especially in my relationship with my wife. I've discovered that the negative habits of a lifetime, especially when they are rooted in traumatic experiences, require a great deal of volition to transform. I have also learned that this is where inner struggle with regressive patterns needs to be balanced with a great deal of self-compassion.

CHAPTER EIGHTEEN

A JEWISH SHAMAN IN POLAND

"Shamans stand at the head of a long lineage of extraordinary individuals who have lived, excelled, or loved so well that ordinary mortals have regarded them with awe or jealousy or both. These are humankind's heroes, the healers, helpers, saints, or sages who exemplify our untapped potentials. Their lives have been immortalized in song, legend, and myth. Ordinary mortals have wondered and puzzled about them, venerated or even worshipped them, and often felt that they must be more than merely human, even when the heroes themselves made no such claims."

ROGER WALSH[296]

In chapter 14, we introduced the influence of shamanism on the Baal Shem. In this chapter, we are returning to this important theme.

Shloyme-Zanvi Rappaport (1863-1920), better known by his pen name, S. Ansky, was a Russian Jewish journalist, ethnographer, playwright, and socialist revolutionary who wrote in both Russian and Yiddish. In 1912, Ansky undertook a two-year ethnographic expedition to Podolia and Volhynia, the original centers of Hasidism, and among the treasures he brought back was a collection of 1,800 Yiddish folktales.

He was especially taken with the stories he heard about dybbuks. In Jewish folklore a dybbuk is a disembodied human spirit that, because of former sins, wanders restlessly until it finds a haven in the body of a living person. Following his expedition, Ansky wrote a play in Russian, later translated into Yiddish, called *The Dybbuk*. The drama tells the story of Khonen, a poor yeshiva student, and Leah, a rich man's daughter, who fall in love. Leah's father, however, scorns Khonen's proposal and arranges to have her married into a wealthy family. Undeterred, Khonen turns to kabbalistic magic, making use of esoteric invocations that he fervently believes will make it possible for him to marry Leah. But the practices are dangerous, and as he engages in them, Khonen tragically dies. Leah, meanwhile, is about to be married. But just before her wedding, Khonen's spirit enters Leah in the form of a dybbuk and refuses to leave.

The cause of the dybbuk's obstinacy is revealed before the Hasidic Rebbe of Miropol: before Khonen and Leah were born their fathers had sworn to one another that if one should have a son and the other a daughter, they would wed them to each other. Unfortunately, Khonen's father had died and Leah's father had completely forgotten his vow. So the rebbe discovers that the spirit of Khonen's father is demanding justice, and the father's spirit is summoned to a rabbinic court where he's told he must content itself with a compromise. The ghost of Khonen's father rejects the compromise. Lighting black candles and blowing a shofar, the rebbe excommunicates the dybbuk and drives it from Leah's body. Yet Khonen's spirit is relentless. Banished from his beloved's body, he returns and claims her soul. "It is only through your thoughts that I can remember who I am," Khonen's spirit declares to Leah. And the two lovers die united.

Despite its setting in Jewish mysticism and folklore, the play's theme of star-crossed lovers who could not be separated by death has a Shakespearean ring to it. Moreover, the central theme of romantic love was, for Jews, quite modern, for passionate love of this kind was not a value in traditional Jewish society. Yet so much of modern Yiddish culture represented a break with traditional values, and it seems that it was precisely Khonen's obsession with Leah that seems to have drawn so many to the play's performances, making *The Dybbuk* the most popular Yiddish play ever written. In 1928, the play was made into a stunning motion picture in Poland.

BAAL SHEM VERSUS DYBBUK

Now that we know what a dybbuk is, we can turn to one of the key stories about Israel ben Eliezer: the account of the revelation of his vocation as a Baal shem, a healer and a wonderworker in the Jewish world. As a young man, the Besht had been told by his spirit guide, Ahiyah the Shilonite, that he was not to disclose his professional identity to the Jewish public until he reached the age of thirty-six. The story takes place during his thirty-fifth year. It is told:

Israel and Hannah were living in a small village, earning their livelihood by keeping a tavern. After bringing a supply of brandy to Hannah, Israel would pack a few belongings, take a loaf of bread, and cross the Prut River, where he would seclude himself in a cave on a mountain for the rest of the week. At that time, he was still practicing austerities, and he ate only a single meal during the week. And then on Friday afternoons he would return home to be with Hannah for Shabbat.

Rabbi Gershon, Hannah's brother, had never reconciled himself with having Israel as his brother-in-law, and was still fretting over his sister's ignorant and ill-mannered husband. Whenever he was able to visit Hannah, Reb Gershon would try to persuade her to divorce her husband. But Hannah knew the secret of Israel's true identity, and she would always reject her brother's pleading.

After some time, Rabbi Gershon began to wonder what he might do to induce his brother-in-law to change his coarse ways and become a knowledgeable and pious Jew. He learned that there was a woman psychic living in a nearby village who was reputed to be able to reveal the virtues and vices of those who came before her. He thought, if I could just get Israel to meet this woman, she would reveal his flaws to him, and would reproach him, and then he will change his ways. Rabbi Gershon could not get himself to take Israel to meet the psychic, so he asked Rabbi Moshe of Brody to do this. Rabbi Moshe agreed. So he and Israel entered the woman's house along with others who wished to make use of her psychic powers. "Welcome," she greeted all of the guests, "welcome to all of you who are holy and pure." And then she spoke to each visitor in turn, greeting each man according to his particular merit. Israel was the last of the guests addressed.

"And welcome to you, Rabbi Israel ben Eliezer." But

then she paused, and suddenly her demeanor changed. She blurted out, "And do you suppose that I am afraid of you? No, I am not in the least afraid of you, for I know that there is nothing at all you can do to me. You have not yet reached the age of thirty-six, and so you may not use your knowledge of the holy names to exorcize me."

Shock and confusion filled the room. Was it possible? Had this woman been taken over by a dybbuk? The men yelled out insisting that the woman repeat what she had declared. But all through this encounter Israel merely stared at the woman, saying nothing. Finally, looking her in the eye, he exclaimed: "You, sir, are not at all who you appear to be. You are a dybbuk—and regrettably you've attached yourself to this woman. Now listen to me. If you don't keep quiet about my destiny, I will appoint a court of law to release me from my vow of secrecy, and then I will indeed exorcize you from this unfortunate woman!" Another shudder filled the room, for no one who knew Israel had ever seen him like this. It seemed as if he had quite suddenly become another person.

Among the guests there were a number of pious men knowledgeable in Jewish law. They briefly conferred with one another and then one of them turned to Israel and said, "Yes, three of us are willing to form a court of law right now, and we will release you from your vow. Then you will be able to exorcize the dybbuk from the woman, and she will be free." But Israel was already having second thoughts about what he had just said. "I'm not so sure," he told them, "for I can see that this spirit is extremely dangerous, and I don't know whether I'm capable of containing his demonic power once I free him from the woman." But the men could see that Israel was a master of divine powers and that he had the ability to penetrate the surface of a person and discover the truth that he was hiding. So they insisted that he use his power to exorcize the spirit.

Now during this entire interview, the "woman" stood there petrified. The dybbuk's secret was now out and she had a frightened expression on her face. "All right," the dybbuk implored, "I will be quiet. Just don't drive me out of her!" Seeing the terrified look on the woman's face, Israel changed his manner. "Just look at what you have done to this poor woman," he said in a sympathetic voice. "I advise you to leave her in peace and we will pray and study Torah on your behalf, so that you will find tranquility in the next world. Tell me your name so our efforts will succeed."

"I cannot tell you in front of all these men," answered the dybbuk, "Make everybody leave and I will reveal my name to you." The dead spirit did not want his children, who lived in the town, to find out that their father had become a dybbuk after his death because of his terrible sins. When all the visitors had left, the dybbuk told Israel who he had been when he had been alive. In fact, Israel did not have to break his vow, for the dybbuk left the body of the woman voluntarily.

This was how Israel ben Eliezer's identity as a Baal shem, a healer and wonderworker who made use of holy names, became known to the world. When Rabbi Gershon heard what happened from Rabbi Moshe, he was completely amazed and he changed his entire attitude toward his brother-in-law. In fact, he became the Baal Shem's first disciple. Not only that but the two men soon became intimate companions.[297]

SUPERNATURAL ABILITIES

A dybbuk. Clairvoyant mindreading. A psychic power struggle. Could such an incident have really occurred? Or if not, is there some kernel of truth in it? A bit of historical background will cast light on the story's origin and meaning.

The eighteenth century was an era filled with the miraculous and the demonic, the living and the dead. The boundary between the physical world and the world of the spirit was permeable, just as is the boundary between ordinary reality and dreams. The stories in *In Praise of the Baal Shem Tov* describe Israel as a Baal shem, a healer and wonderworker who was always on the lookout to save people, whether they were in danger because of life-threatening illness, pernicious enemies, or the demonic. He was also known to be able to help barren women bear children.

In Praise of the Baal Shem Tov describes the Baal Shem as a healer whose abilities surpassed those of physicians. He is portrayed as being aware of greater cosmic realities and how they related to human existence. We're told that he could predict the future because he understood the hidden spiritual patterns that shape events; in this way he was able to grasp the underlying meaning and destiny of human life. He knew what people were thinking. He could perceive a child's birth and send a gift of charity before the umbilical cord was cut. He was clairvoyant and could see at great distances. He was able to comprehend the reality beyond superficial occurrences so that he could perceive what was actually taking place on the spiritual plane. He is described as capable of traveling great distances in a flash. He was able to elevate the souls of the departed to heaven, and through the use of trance could ascend to and enter the celestial palaces in heaven. He communicated with spirits and even with the messiah. He revealed secret mysteries and engaged in sympathetic magic—a form of magic based on the assumption that a person or thing can be supernaturally affected through its name or an object representing it. He was also able to annul demonic decrees promulgated against the Jewish people. He used his magical skills to defend them, defeating both natural and supernatural enemies. He's portrayed as vigorous, assertive, and energetic, always on the offensive, and most often he accomplishes his goal. Quite a catalog of claims. Could they actually reflect historical truth about the founder of Hasidism?

WHAT'S A SHAMAN?

My friend Kenneth Cohen is the founder and executive director of the Qigong Research and Practice Center in Colorado. He is a world-renowned health educator and scholar of Chinese and Japanese culture and religion. Ken also trained with Native American and African shamans and authored an award-winning book in English on Native American healing. For many decades, he has taught Indigenous wisdom and healing techniques with the blessings and support of traditional elders of many Native American nations.

In 1978, Ken enrolled in the first course I taught about the life and teachings of the Baal Shem. Though Jewish by birth, Ken knew relatively little about Judaism, and he was captivated. We became friends at that time and have stayed close ever since. Twelve years later, I visited Ken and spent a few days with him at his mountain retreat near Boulder. Knowing his keen interest in healing and ancient magic, I asked what he thought about the claims made by Hasidic tradition regarding the Baal Shem Tov's supernatural abilities. "The Baal Shem fits the picture of a traditional shaman," he replied.

"I've heard the term *shaman* before," I said, "but I don't know what it means."

"Indigenous spiritual practitioners, often called shamans in Western literature, are the most ancient religious functionaries in recorded history," he explained. "The institution of the shaman goes back to the tribal cultures of the Paleolithic era. Shamanism is, in fact, the oldest religious phenomenon we know anything about."

I learned from Ken that shamans were often the spiritual advisors or leaders of ancient tribes, and that there are still shamans functioning in living tribal cultures today, though many prefer the term "traditional healer," or use words that describe the shaman and their activities from their own Indigenous languages. Ken also spoke about the psychic powers of the shaman. He told me that shamans are sensitive to levels and states of reality beyond the physical plane, and through the power of trance or other altered states of consciousness they're able to visit those planes and channel magical and healing powers. In these ways, they can effect changes in the physical world.

While Ken was talking about trance states, something suddenly clicked for me. "Do you know about the Baal Shem's ascent of the soul?" I asked.

"No," he said, "tell me about it."

AN ASCENT OF THE SOUL

At some point in his life, the Besht's brother-in-law Rabbi Gershon decided to immigrate to the Land of Israel. From that time on he and the Besht communicated by letter. For some unknown reason, one of these letters never left Europe and was instead preserved in Hasidic circles. The letter is known as the "holy epistle," and it's an extremely important document because it may be the only surviving piece of writing that the majority of scholars consider as having come from the Besht himself. The letter describes two different soul flights into the heavenly realms that the Baal Shem undertook, the first on Rosh Hashanah of 1746 and the second on Rosh Hashanah of 1749. The Besht writes Rabbi Gershon that he felt compelled to engage in these celestial journeys to save groups of Jews who might otherwise be massacred in pogroms. The holy epistle shows the Besht acting on behalf of these Jews, attempting to make use of magical means to halt the persecutions. He admits his attempt to stop the massacre failed, but that in the course of his ascent he received a deeper understanding of his life mission and the special mystical practices that he was to teach. "I saw wonderful visions," he writes his brother-in-law, "the like of which I had not seen since I attained mystical knowledge. It would be impossible to report to you what I witnessed and learned, even if we could speak face to face." During his vision, he writes, he encountered the souls of the living and the dead, as well as the souls of great rabbis, saintly figures of the past, and great heroes of the Bible.

At one point, the Besht came upon the wicked Samael, an important archangel in rabbinic lore who was seen as an accuser, seducer, and destroyer, and regarded as both good and evil. When he witnesses Samael destroying many souls, the Baal Shem becomes fearful and begs his spirit guide, Ahiyah of Shiloh, to accompany him as he continues his ascent. Finally, the Besht arrives at the palace of the messiah where he sees the great heroes of the tradition studying Torah and rejoicing. He comes before the messiah and asks him, "When will you come, master?" And the messiah replies, "This is how you will know that I am coming: your teaching will become well-known and revealed throughout the world, and the wellsprings of your wisdom will flow out to everyone. Others will then be able to employ the practices that I have taught you, and they too will be able to perform contemplative reunifications and ascents of the soul as you are able to do. Then all the shards that hold the sparks of light will be destroyed, and there will be a time of acceptance and redemption."[298]

The Baal Shem also writes that in his vision he was given three remedies and three holy names that he added to his healing and magic repertoire. And he learned a method of worship and study that would lead to blissful mystical union. He testifies that he was able to avert a demonic decree that would have laid waste to entire countries. Although he could not hold off the pogrom, he was able to lighten its impact so the massive death intended by the evil angel, Samael, would instead be transformed into pestilence and disease.

The Besht tells Rabbi Gershon that he was absolutely astounded by this vision. Nonetheless, his reaction to the messiah's sanguine answer to his question also reveals the Baal Shem's sadness and uncertainty about the fulfillment of the messiah's prediction: "I must say that I was bewildered by the messiah's response. I felt great anguish because of the length of time that would have to pass before the messiah would come, and I wondered when it would be possible for this to happen."

A SHAMAN'S VOCATION

When I finished describing the contents of the Besht's letter to Ken, he nodded his head. "Yes," he said, "it is clear that the Baal Shem Tov understood that this kind of shamanic activity was a major aspect of his mission as a spiritual leader of the Jewish people and of the world. What you have described clearly reveals the essential features of shamanism: the use of trance, the aid of an inner spirit guide, the ascent to heaven, the contact with a hidden reality, the interaction with spirits, the acquisition of knowledge, and the desire to serve the community." Ken suggested I do some reading about shamanism, and when I returned to Berkeley I purchased the first of a number of books he recommended, *The Way of the Shaman*, by anthropologist Michael Harner. Harner utilized the work of Mircea Eliade, historian of religion at the University of Chicago, to illuminate the vocation of the shaman:

> A shaman is a man or woman who enters an altered
> state of consciousness—at will—to contact and utilize

an ordinarily hidden reality in order to acquire knowledge, power, and to help other persons. The shaman has at least one, and usually more, "spirits" in his personal service.

As Mircea Eliade observes, the shaman is distinguished from other kinds of magicians and medicine men by his use of a state of consciousness which Eliade, following Western mystical tradition, calls "ecstasy." But the practice of ecstasy alone, he properly emphasizes, does not define the shaman, for the shaman has specific techniques of ecstasy. Thus Eliade says, "Hence any ecstatic cannot be considered a shaman; the shaman specializes in a trance during which his soul is believed to leave his body and ascend to the sky or descend to the underworld."

To this I would add that, in his trance, he commonly works to heal a patient by restoring beneficial or vital power, or by extracting harmful power. The journey to which Eliade refers is especially undertaken to restore power to a lost soul.[299]

Harner also observed that shamans don't rely on dogma or authority to provide them with evidence about the realm of the spirit. Rather, they seek to arrive at truth through personal experience and then derive conclusions from these experiences. Harner focuses on the individual as the locus of revelation. This insight immediately resonated with me, for even though he was a traditional practicing Jew, the Baal Shem Tov taught that spiritual seekers should not rely solely on the wisdom of the past. In one of his teachings, he stated that like the three original patriarchs—Abraham, Isaac, and Jacob—every individual must search for the unity of God and his own way of serving the Creator. It thus seems that the Besht's shamanic vocation may have affected the new emphasis he placed on individual spiritual intentionality and experience, and his teaching that each individual must find God on their own may have derived from his own shamanic practice.

The recognition of the Besht as a shaman also provides a deeper sense of his spiritual worldview. In a remarkable passage from his book, *The Elements of Shamanism,* Neville Drury writes that the shaman experiences "a feeling for the sheer alive-ness of the universe. Gone is any distinction between animate or inanimate. The whole universe is ablaze with energy—a vibration, a flowing and ebbing, a pulsing. All forms are perceived as interconnected, with a universal life-force underlying all. This in turn becomes a truly holistic vision because energy is matter, matter is spirit."[300] In my reading, I learned that the religious life of aboriginal tribes is centered around their shamans who, out of their knowledge of the cosmos and its forces, interpret the world for their people, teaching what life is about through stories and songs. These are all ways that Hasidic tradition characterized the life and work of the Baal Shem Tov, as well.

Ken Cohen had co-taught with Reb Zalman Schachter-Shalomi in what Zalman called his "mystery school." I wondered what Zalman might think about Ken's thesis, so when I next saw him in person, I asked. "Ken Cohen believes that the Baal Shem Tov was a shaman. Would you agree with him?"

"Something like that, yes," Zalman replied.

"And do you believe that the stories about the Besht's magical and healing activities were true? Could he actually do the things attributed to him in the legends?"

"Not only do I accept those reports as true," Zalman answered, "I believe these skills are foundational. We should be training sensitive people in the Jewish community to make use of those potent techniques."

CHARISMA

There is a second revelation story in *In Praise of the Baal Shem Tov* describing how Israel ben Eliezer disclosed his vocation in public. In this alternate tale, Israel reveals himself not as a shaman, but as a charismatic spiritual teacher:

> Israel and his wife managed an inn in a village near the town of Brody. On a Tuesday evening a student of his brother-in-law, Rabbi Gershon, happened to stop at the inn for dinner. Recognizing who he was, Israel received

the young man with great honor, even inviting him to stay for Shabbat. But the student was anxious to complete his journey and he declined the invitation.

After he left the inn, a wheel on the young man's coach broke and he had to return to the inn by foot. The Besht went with him and replaced the wheel. But just as the student resumed his journey, something else broke and once again he was forced to walk back to the inn, this time to spend the night. Strangely, every day of that week another accident would occur, preventing him from leaving. In the end he was forced to spend Shabbat with these peasants. Israel smiled. "Well, I knew that you would remain here for Shabbat, and so here you are!" he said in a cheerful voice. Although the evening meal was quite joyful, the guest could not remove the sadness from his heart. As the candles burned low, they all went to sleep.

Around midnight the guest suddenly awoke and saw what appeared to be an immense fire burning on the oven. Unnerved, he ran over to the oven. But no, it was not fire at all. But what was it? Some kind of strange and powerful light! Then, suddenly he was hurled backward and fainted. When Israel and his wife revived the student, the Besht admonished him: "You should not have looked at what is not permitted to you." But the guest marveled at what had occurred.

In the morning the Besht went to daven in his private prayer house. Afterwards he joyfully returned home with his head held high, singing as he walked back and forth in the house. And then in the course of the midday meal he asked his young guest to teach some Torah, but the student was confused and declined. And then the Besht spoke profound words of Torah. And in the late afternoon once again, he taught deep and novel words of Torah. Who is this man, the student wondered.

That evening, after Shabbat had ended, the Besht

instructed his guest to go to the Great Community of Hasidim in Brody, and also to the rabbi of the town and to say these words: "There is a great light living near your community, and it will be worthwhile for you to seek him out and bring him to Brody."

On hearing these words, the Hasidim began to walk toward the village where the Besht and his wife lived. At the same time the Baal Shem divined that the members of the community were coming to meet him. When they arrived, they all went to a place in the forest where the men constructed a makeshift throne out of tree branches. They placed Israel on the throne and accepted him as their rebbe. And then Israel spoke words of Torah to them.[301]

Like the first initiation story—the exorcism of the dybbuk—in this second revelation tale the Baal Shem performs actions and says things that are surprising and unexpected. The young student is completely disoriented, just as the Besht intended. What occurs, however, readies him for his task of teaching the Hasidim. All the while, the student is unaware that this mysterious innkeeper is manipulating reality in order to turn him into an envoy to the Hasidim of Brody. This second revelation story is in some ways even more bizarre than the first. Could such an event have actually happened?

We have learned in previous chapters how the Baal Shem Tov was a kabbalist, and in this tale we're told that his charismatic and mystical abilities led to his revelation as a spiritual teacher. Yet, *In Praises of the Baal Shem Tov* contains very few actual teachings of the Besht, for throughout the Besht is characterized as a folk healer and magician. If we want to study his teachings, we have to turn to the writings of the disciples where his insights are frequently cited. In these, I seldom found any references to the Besht as a healer and magician. This confused me to no end. It seemed as if the two genres of literature about the Baal Shem were picturing two very different men. I lived with this conundrum for years, wondering whether early Hasidism carried two completely different images of their founder.

Karl Erich Grozinger, a scholar of Jewish mysticism, offers a possible solution to the riddle. Grozinger writes that Hasidic literature reflects two quite different views about the Baal Shem's professional identity. And, he states, this is unusual in the genre of religious literature about spiritual heroes. "Only one revelation, reported in one revelation tale, may be allocated to each particular type of religious hero.... A new revelation-tale would be required only when a new type of hero, with a new role, has entered the arena." Because of this, Grozinger writes, "we have grounds to suspect that a new religious type is being promoted, and that the role of the hero is being defined in a new and different way.... [This] should raise our suspicion and point to the possibility that there may have been differences of opinion regarding the nature of the Besht's mission." Then he summarizes: "If we accept the premise of one revelation tale per hero, then we have to conclude that the narrator of this second revelation-tale in *Shivhei haBesht* (i.e., *In Praise of the Besht*) must have wished to define the Besht's mission quite differently from the first narrator. This suggests the presence of at least two conflicting views of the Besht's mission within the *Shivhei haBesht* itself, one defining him as a *Baal shem* and the other as a charismatic teacher of Torah. The first narrator sees the Besht as something like a latter-day physician, while the second regards him as the founder of a new religious community. My belief is that such a conflict of opinions did take place in reality. There were those in the first, second, and third generations of Hasidim, and even among the companions of the Besht himself, who preferred to see him primarily as a *Baal shem,* while others regarded him as a charismatic teacher."[302]

Grozinger's theory resonated with what I learned from my reading about the great differences between shamans and mystics. While both types of seeker pursue ecstasy, the forms of rapture they experience are different. Shamans employ magic in attempts to help their communities. They seek to navigate the spiritual worlds in an active way in order to bring healing and other benefits to their tribes. During their ecstatic ascents they may encounter evil spirits, who must be appeased or defeated, and they need to have strong egos in order to preserve their selfhood in the face of these dangers. The phenomenon of mysticism, on the other hand, evolved much later in the history of religion. The lone mystic seeks to break through the bonds of the physical world, surrendering his or her ego to an ecstatic union with the Divine. There is no magic in this, no attempt to alter reality for the benefit of the community.

At this point, Ken Cohen suggested I contact Dr. Ruth-Inge Heinze (1919-2007), a cultural anthropologist connected with the University of California at Berkeley who specialized in shamanic studies and altered states of consciousness. I knew that she was also familiar with mysticism, for years before I'd taken an experiential class in Buddhist meditation with her. I called her on the telephone. "Yes, it is possible that the Baal Shem Tov was a mystic as well as a shaman," she told me in her thick German accent. "There have been instances of this, but they are rare. A man who embodied both of these roles would be quite exceptional...he would have been a very great person."

And by this point, I was ready to turn to the work of Gershom Scholem: specifically, his essay entitled, "The Historical Image of the Baal Shem Tov."[303] My acquaintance with modern scholarly Hebrew was not extensive and it took me several months to work through the long essay. Most of the article is devoted to two questions: What are the reliable historical sources on which scholars can build a reconstruction of the Besht's life and thought? And what can we know about the Besht's historical identity?

First, the question of sources. Scholem writes that *In Praise of the Baal Shem Tov* certainly contains many legendary tales, but it is sometimes possible to distinguish the accurate stories from later legends. Scholem states that there are also four authentic letters written by the Besht. And in their own books, the master's disciples often cite numerous teachings of the Baal Shem. Finally, the Besht is mentioned by contemporaries in books and documents of the time. Some of these writers come from outside Hasidic circles.

Out of these materials Scholem constructs his own portrait of the historical Baal Shem. First, he states it is abundantly clear from *In Praise of the Baal Shem Tov* that he was a wonderworker and healer. He made amulets for people, and the numerous stories told about him attest to magical and telepathic powers. We also learn that he was able to understand the language of animals and birds, as well as the secret conversations of trees. From the time that he disclosed his vocation as a magician and healer to the Jewish community until his death, the Besht acted as a professional Baal shem. But, Scholem asserts, he had not only been a Baal shem, but also a spiritual teacher, even though he knew he was limited in his ability to communicate with people because of his continuous intimate connection with God. Scholem then reiterates what he had pointed out earlier in his chapter in *Major Trends in Jewish Mysticism,* that it is not possible to distinguish the Besht's professional work as a Baal shem from his vocation as a teacher of spiritual and ethical values.

The Besht was neither ignorant nor uneducated regarding Jewish tradition, Scholem writes, but neither was he a *talmid hakham,* a scholar with an encyclopedic knowledge of traditional sources. He was not an authority in Jewish law, yet he was certainly knowledgeable regarding Jewish mystical sources. When he taught, he used sharp epigrams to deliver his message. And when he quoted from traditional literature, he often altered the meaning of the original texts, giving them a novel, mystical depth. His message must have been profound because he drew great scholars into his circle. He believed that what he had to teach was crucial to the coming of the messiah, and that he himself had been sent by God to repair the world. He had confidence and pride both in his charismatic powers and his ability to bring the messiah. Scholem also wrote that the Besht's personality made a greater impression on people than his scholarship, arguing that the evidence pointed to him as having been a charismatic leader like Jesus. Both men possessed the gifts of healing and exorcism, and were preachers and prophets.

In Part One, we met Simon Dubnow, the first historian of the Hasidic movement. Writing before Scholem, Dubnow didn't use the terms "mystic" or "shaman," and his portrayal of the Besht leans more toward the founder of Hasidism as a healer and wonderworker. Nevertheless, Dubnow's profound description of the Besht's *inner* life encompasses both of these vocations: "Did the Besht himself believe that he was able to perform all the miracles and wonders that the people ascribed to him? Did he truly think of himself as a prophet and seer who could predict the future? To answer these questions we must try to penetrate to the very core of his personality. A man of this type, whose thoughts continually revolved around the divine, made no distinction between God and nature. He believed that the phenomenal world was connected with the transcendental worlds by an unbreakable bond, and he believed with all of his heart that these worlds constantly influenced one another. A man such as this could not distinguish between the 'natural' and the 'supernatural.' In his eyes everything was at one and the same time both natural and divine, physical and metaphysical, empirical fact and a wonder of God.... For him it was certain that in the ecstatic God-clinging worship of a *tzaddik,* a powerful spiritual leader, lay the power to bring about changes in the upper world."[304]

In 1996, Moshe Rosman's *Founder of Hasidism: A Quest for the Historical Baal Shem Tov* appeared in print, and to my knowledge this was the first time a prominent historian used the term "shaman" in reference to the Besht. "Baalei shem share many of the characteristics of what Mircea Eliade dubbed 'shaman,' an ancient type of holy man appearing in various forms in many of the world's religions up until modern times."[305] Since then, most scholars freely refer to the Besht as a shaman. He was in contact with a broad Jewish public who saw him as a wonder-worker and healer. His disciples knew their master was seen this way in the Jewish world at large. Some of them are even cited by name in *In Praise of the Baal Shem Tov.* But they also knew that he was more than a folk healer and magician, for they regularly saw him deep in mystical worship and listened as he spoke profound words of Torah. And what he was teaching them had little to do with shamanic healing and more to do with enabling them to transform themselves into tzaddikim.

IS THE MAGIC REAL?

Reb Zalman told me he believed the Baal Shem Tov had been a shaman, and that the psychic powers attributed to him in *In Praise of the Baal Shem Tov* were real. But what did I think? My memories took me back to the year 1970, when I had just made my break with Judaism, and besides reading about world mythology and the religions of the East, I was looking for some way to enter the world of the spirit. I found out about a psychic training process known as "Centering" which was based on techniques pioneered by the parapsychologist, Jose Silva. The "Silva Method" (also called "Silva Mind Control") promised to help participants change negative thought patterns and cultivate a positive mindset. I signed up for the weeklong training.

At the first gathering our instructor told us that the tools that we were going to be taught derived from the tradition of "white magic," and would enable us to awaken our natural healing capacities. The most important and remarkable skill that I learned was how to open my heart and mind to inner wisdom during times of difficulty, through accessing an inner voice of guidance called a "spirit guide." Just a few years later, I discovered that the Baal Shem Tov had had a spirit guide, and I was able to intuitively sense what that supernatural entity might have represented for him.

During the Silva Method workshop I also underwent a number of strange and astonishing experiences that were clairvoyant or psychic in nature. In one session we were learning how to employ our imaginations for healing purposes. My partner and I were sequestered in a private room together. We were each supposed to call to mind the name of an ill person. Then, taking turns, we were to give the name and location of the person to our partners. Our task would be to send healing energy to the person who needed it. My partner gave me the name and location of a friend of his who was sick. Using the techniques I was taught, I was able to accurately visualize his friend, and describe the illness this individual was suffering from. I was likewise able to picture his home. In my mind's eye I saw a bizarre green stained-glass window with the words "Screw you!" emblazoned in red at the center. This window was set next to a staircase that led to the second floor of the house. When I reported this scene to my partner, he told me that my descriptions were completely accurate, and that his friend actually had a stained-glass window designed and installed next to the staircase leading to the second floor of his home. The colors of the window and the inscription I saw on it were correct as well. I was flabbergasted by this. Since this exercise took place on the last day of class, I have no idea whether the healing tools I was given actually affected the health of the individual I was attempting to heal at a distance.

At the time, my maternal grandmother was in a hospital in San Antonio, and using his imaginative power my partner was able to provide an accurate image of her and also to identify the illness she was suffering from. His attempt at healing her was ineffective, however, and my grandmother died a few days later.

The second clairvoyant experience I underwent during that

workshop was also awesome and surprising. Following the conclusion of the Centering process, I was due to make an educational presentation in another city at a location I had never visited. Before the trip, I discovered that I'd lost the directions and there was no way I could contact anyone who might provide me with instructions on how to get there in my car. Yet despite this, my newly-acquired inner spirit guide accurately directed me to the site, taking me from Manhattan to a suburb in Boston! A few months later, I also had a psychic experience with the help of LSD. I was with a friend, and remember picking up a Bible, opening it at random, and reading a verse out loud. That biblical passage became a kind of key to penetrating my friend's psyche. I intuited facts about his life and about psychological issues he had with his father that I could not have known beforehand. He nodded and smiled, agreeing with everything that I said.

As I recalled all of these experiences, my questions regarding the paranormal experiences of the Baal Shem Tov began to resolve themselves, even though I wasn't certain that all of the extraordinary capabilities attributed to the Besht could have been true.

SCIENCE AND SHAMANISM

Most scientists would give no credence to the kinds of experiences I had during the Centering workshop, nor would they affirm the abilities of shamans to alter reality. The majority of books on shamanism don't even bother to ask whether shamanic magic is real. Experiences like this simply don't fit the regnant scientific paradigm. But Roger Walsh says something interesting: "There are many books on how to win friends and influence people, but surprisingly few on how to make enemies and alienate people. Here is a suggestion to fill the gap. Walk into a group of scientists and announce that you believe in parapsychology. Three things will quickly become clear. First, most scientists, like most of the public, hold very strong opinions on the topic. Second, despite these strong opinions, they know very little about the relevant research. Third, parapsychology is, to put it mildly, a very controversial and highly charged topic." Walsh concludes this subject with these cautious words:

> Having surveyed ethnographic, clinical, and laboratory
> research, what can we conclude about the possibility that

shamans employ psi (psychic phenomena) in their diag-
nostic and healing work? Certainly there are remarkable
anecdotal reports of psi in shamans and other native
healers. In addition, the conditions used in tribal magic
rituals often correspond to those reported to facilitate
psi, and many laboratory studies and meta-analyses
seem supportive of psi. However, as yet we have no good
experimental studies of shamans. Therefore, for those
whose minds remain open, the question of whether psi
plays a role in shamanism also remains open.[306]

During a later trip to Boulder, I once again met up with Ken Cohen. I
asked whether he thought shamanic powers could be empirically tested.
He smiled and went to his filing cabinet, removing a typewritten letter
from the Menninger Clinic, placing it in my hand. The letter stated that
he and eight other healers had been part of a rigorous scientific study of
exceptional healers that was part of the Clinic's Copper Wall Experiment.
The nine healers had each been tested separately over a nine-week
period. The letter attested to Ken's abilities and stated that all nine subjects of the experiment had successfully generated unusual electric phenomena, measured through bio-electric fields and brainwaves. In an
interview about the experiment, Dr. Elmer Green, director of the project,
said he believed the experiment proved that psychic healing at a distance
was a scientific fact. Curious readers who would like to learn more about
these matters might begin with Dean Radin's *The Conscious Universe: The
Scientific Truth of Psychic Phenomena*.

Radin is one of the most respected students of parapsychology. At
the time of this writing, he was the chief scientist at the Institute for
Noetic Sciences, and had held appointments at Princeton University, the
University of Edinburgh, and several Silicon Valley think tanks. He also
produced cutting-edge research for the U.S. government. The book provides statistical evidence for the veracity of thousands of experiments in
telepathy (mind to mind perception), psychokinesis (mind-matter interaction), clairvoyance (perception at a distance), precognition (perception through time) and other psychic phenomena. Radin made use of
quantum physics as well as the teachings of mystics, to demonstrate how

psychic phenomena has been tacitly acknowledged and exploited by the U.S. government and by corporations. He also carefully outlines the critical weaknesses in the arguments of those who attempt to debunk the findings of parapsychology. While the idea of psychic phenomena is ancient, Radin writes, its scientific truth has only been demonstrated in the last hundred years. Psychic phenomena, he writes, have "been shown to exist in thousands of experiments. There are disagreements over how to interpret the evidence, but the fact is that virtually all scientists who have studied the evidence, including hard-nosed skeptics, now agree that there is something interesting going on that merits serious scientific attention."[307]

Before the experiences I underwent in the Centering process, I too was skeptical of the claims of parapsychology. I assumed this attitude because of the scientific prejudice in our culture that opposes views that don't conform to the rational outlook of the current scientific consensus. And despite experiences that I personally underwent, and notwithstanding evidence I uncovered regarding the efficacy of shamanism, there are still times when my rationality tells me that it was all some kind of illusion. But I cannot deny what I know. I believe that we human beings have undeveloped psychic abilities that could, if developed, open us to a greater appreciation of the mysteries of the human mind and the universe.

The premodern society in which the Besht lived was in many ways radically different from the world that came into existence following the European Enlightenment. It seems to me that perhaps the dominant emphasis we place on rationality and science has cut us off from being able to perceive realties that pre-modern peoples were and are still able to recognize.

HISTORIANS AND THE BAAL SHEM'S MAGIC

Historians of Hasidism have disagreed regarding the truth of the stories about the Baal Shem's magical abilities and the miracles attributed to him. Simon Dubnow was a rationalist, and for him *In Praise of the Baal Shem Tov* was "a legendary biography." Dubnow's attempt to reconstruct the life of the Besht tended to omit references to the miracles, even though he fully recognized the fact that the belief in the possibility of magic was an integral part of the Baal Shem's worldview.

Beginning with Gershom Scholem, however, there was a willingness to accept the Baal Shem as a miracle worker who used magic for healing purposes. Scholem even suggested that the history of religion would benefit from an investigation into the realm of parapsychology. Most recently, Immanuel Etkes has stated: "Should we lend credence to claims that the Besht healed the sick and exorcized dybbuks and cleared demons out of houses? Yet the Besht was after all a *baal shem;* if he had not acted like other *baalei shem* he would not have been able to meet the demands of his professional calling. And what about his performances in the Upper Worlds and the powers of seeing from afar? Is the critical scholar to believe in all of these too? Well, why not? There is no doubt that Besht himself believed he had such powers.... Given that this is the case, the miraculous element in the tales of *Shivhei Habesht* are not only to be considered a reality the veracity of which the historian is permitted to acknowledge, but one that he is in fact required to recognize."[308]

Where would the Baal Shem have learned the worldview and techniques of shamanism? Historian Gershon Hundert writes that "magic and magicians had never been absent from Jewish society, and the eighteenth-century figures drew on long traditions and bodies of esoteric knowledge stretching back to the distant past.... In central and eastern Europe in earlier periods, most often particular rabbis were known to possess shaman-like skills. The use of the term *Baal shem* extended back many centuries."[309] Hundert states that the number of Baal shems began to increase at the end of the seventeenth century, and proliferated in the eighteenth. In fact, during the Besht's lifetime, the vocation of Baal shem became a fully legitimate profession, honored by all sectors of Jewish society.

The Baal Shem's description of his soul ascent actually has its origin in the Talmudic period. The Merkavah mystics would make soul ascents in order to attain a lofty vision of the throne of God on high. This kind of experience drew from the biblical vision of the prophet Ezekiel, who saw "the likeness" of the appearance of a man enthroned on "the likeness" of a celestial throne (Ezekiel 1:26). Nonetheless, Idel remarks that the Besht's soul ascent is different from the Merkavah accounts. The Besht states that he actually left his body, which is rare in Jewish mystical experience. But such practices were known among Gentiles on the Moldavian side of the Carpathian Mountains. As Idel writes, "Thus, less than a century before the revelation of the Besht, in the immediate vicinity of the place where the founder of Hasidism spent his time in solitude, ecstatic practices similar to his ascent to heaven were known and performed by Gentiles. These practices have nothing to do with Jewish sources but stem from Eurasian religious heritage."[310]

If Idel's hypothesis is correct, the Besht's knowledge of such practices among Gentiles might point to his having personal contact or perhaps apprenticing with shamans during that time. There are also shamans in the Carpathians called *molfars,* who were members of the Indigenous Hutsul culture with whom he could have mentored. This would account for his knowledge of spiritual and healing techniques. The implications of Idel's findings are of great consequence, for they show that unlike most of his Jewish contemporaries, the Baal Shem Tov might have been in direct contact with Gentile spiritual practitioners, and that he was willing to experiment with non-Jewish approaches to healing as well as shamanic spiritual practice.

In a fascinating scholarly study of medical practices in Poland and Eastern Europe, Yohanan Petrovsky-Shtern states that the Baalei shem were not influenced by the healing procedures of Polish healers and doctors. Rather, both Jews and Gentiles shared the same natural medical techniques. This foundational approach to healing had been pioneered by Paracelsus (i.e., Phillip von Hohenheim, 1493-1541) whose alternative medical theories were in many ways reminiscent of Kabbalah. Petrovsky-Shtern writes that "Paracelsus emerges as a common source of both Polish and Jewish healers: *Baalei shem,* barbers, paramedics, and medical doctors. Catholic, Russian Orthodox, and Jews drew heavily from handwritten, printed, and oral sources."[311]

SPIRITUAL ACTIVISM VERSUS MYSTICAL SURRENDER

I was intrigued and even titillated by the Centering process, and those experiences that I described earlier. They opened an alternate world of possibilities that I'd known nothing about, and for years I made use of several of the techniques I learned. In the end, however, the most important and lasting skill I acquired was a way to access spiritual guidance from within. This ability was absolutely essential to me because for so long I had been other-directed, depending on the authority of Jewish tradition to direct my life.

I came to see that neither the goals nor the methodologies of "white magic" were what I was seeking. I would describe it to friends as a kind of *spiritualism* rather than *spirituality*. In truth, I was not interested in learning how to control reality; rather, I wanted to learn how to become one with ultimate reality. Today I might call what I learned "spiritual activism," as opposed to "mystical surrender," and I would give it much more of a rightful place in the authentic life of a spiritual community.

At the time, my studies of Eastern religion, particularly the Upanishads, the Tao Te Ching, and Zen still felt like my best hope in discovering a path that would enable me to bind myself to the Ineffable, to release myself from the straitjacket of the rigid Judaism I'd been burdened with, and to free my soul from the entanglements and anxieties of ordinary existence. It was to this end that I was also initiated into the Maharishi Mahesh Yogi's form of Transcendental Meditation, hoping to learn a way to experience the divine presence. I spent the requisite time every day silently chanting my mantra, but I never encountered anything of a transcendental character in the meditation, on top of which I found the practice to be quite boring.

In the end, after all of these experiences, I realized that they did not really speak to my spiritual needs. What I ardently desired was a teacher who could offer a Jewish path to spiritual transformation that included guidance in practices that could enable me to live daily life in connection with the Spirit. This is what I found in the Besht, who was a miracle worker, a healer, and much more.

CHAPTER NINETEEN

ABYSS OF DESPAIR

I have had issues with sleep for decades. When I entered my seventies, I began to develop a new and more helpful nighttime pattern. I wake up at three or four in the morning and move to my study where I most often read a book that is related to whatever I am writing about. It is a quiet time, and I find that I can concentrate without any interruptions. Then I return to bed after forty-five minutes or an hour.

One of the books I had planned to read for this chapter was Rabbi Nathan Hanover's *Abyss of Despair*. Hanover lived through the devastating pogroms in Poland that began in 1648. It is a small chronicle, only a hundred pages in the English translation, and I knew that I could make my way through it in just a few nights. But week after week I avoided taking it from the shelf, choosing other reading instead. Finally, I knew that I had to overcome my resistance.

At first, I pondered the dirge-like words of the narrative. The first four chapters describe the atrocious deeds of the leaders of the massacres: Nalevaiko, Pawliuk, and Bogdan Chmielnicki. Subsequent chapters focus on cities and provinces in which Jews were butchered: Nemirow, Tulczyn, Polannoe, Ostrog, Zaslaw, Konstantynow, Lithuania, Bar, Lwow, Narol, Zamosc, Ostrog. At one point, Hanover writes, "What can we say, what can we speak, or how can we justify ourselves? Shall we say we have not sinned? Behold, our iniquities testify against us. For we have sinned, and the Lord found out the iniquity of his servants. Would the Holy One, blessed be He, dispense judgement without justice?"

Searching the history, I discovered one account claiming that 300 communities had been destroyed and 100,000 people killed. According to another report, 744 communities were wiped out and 650,000 people died. Contemporary historian Shaul Stampfer, however, estimates that 13,000 Jews died in the Chmielnicki uprising and more perished in the subsequent Swedish and Muscovite invasions.[312]

THE HOLOCAUST OF 1648

What was it that brought about the pogroms of 1648 a half century before the Baal Shem's birth? Feudalism was the dominant social and economic system in medieval Europe, and during the seventeenth century it continued to prevail in what was then known as the Commonwealth of Poland and Lithuania. The landlords of the great estates held territory from the Crown in exchange for military service. The vassals were tenants of these nobles, while peasant serfs were obliged to live on their lord's land and give him homage, labor, and a share of the agricultural produce in exchange for military protection.

The Commonwealth of Poland and Lithuania was ruled by a Catholic monarch, and the aristocratic landlords of the great estates who were in league with the king were also Catholics. The nobles loathed the lowly peasants who lived on their lands, not only because of class differences, but because the peasants were adherents of the Greek Orthodox faith. Landlords behaved in appalling ways toward "their" peasants. On the other hand, they had a somewhat greater regard for Jews who lived in their territories, even though they treated "their" Jews in a paternalistic and patronizing way. Why were the Jews regarded differently? There were very few vocations that Jews by law were permitted to pursue, and one of these was working as overseers. The nobles would use Jews to squeeze money from the peasants, and because of their own powerlessness the Jews went along with this vile arrangement. In exchange for their service, landlords provided Jews with a sense of physical security they would otherwise not have. The peasants, of course, were completely unaware of the predicament in which this arrangement had placed their Jewish neighbors. And, of course, the Jews were anyway guilty of deicide, according to common Christian teaching at that time. Without any thought, then, the peasants associated the Jews with their hated landlords.

By the mid-seventeenth century, the rift between nobles and peasants became extremely tense, and in 1648 one of the peasant leaders, a Ukrainian named Bogdan Chmielnicki, launched a revolt against both the king of Poland-Lithuania and the nobility. The Cossacks, a group of predominantly East Slavic-speaking Greek Orthodox Christians, made common cause with Chmielnicki's hordes, and the combined forces attacked nobles and Jews without discrimination. In 1654, the fate of the Jews in southeastern Poland was duplicated in northern Poland due to the invasions of the Russians and the Swedes. This was this situation that Nathan Hanover was describing in *The Abyss of Despair*, my dismal night-time reading. Hanover recounts in detail atrocity after atrocity:

> Some were skinned alive and their flesh was thrown to the dogs; some had their hands and limbs chopped off, and their bodies thrown on the highway only to be trampled by wagons and crushed by horses.... The enemy slaughtered infants in the laps of their mothers. They were sliced into pieces like fish. They slashed the bellies of pregnant women, removed their infants and tossed them in their faces. Some women had their bellies torn open and live cats placed in them.[313]

The wars, invasions, and epidemics brought death, devastation, and exile. The regions of Podolia, Volhynia, and Ukraine in southeast Poland were the hardest hit. The Jewish governing body of Poland-Lithuania, called the Council of Four Lands, was unable to meet the vast challenges faced by the Jewish people. A massive number of Jews immigrated to the west. And the longing for messianic redemption became palpable. At the same time, pious Jews who believed that the sins of the people had brought on the pogroms, turned toward penitence and asceticism.

In 1658, King John Casimir began to bring peace to Poland. He made efforts to compensate his Jewish subjects for their suffering, and assisted them in recovering from their afflictions, but for the Jewish masses throughout Poland life remained harsh. A renewed Cossack insurgency began in the 1680s, continuing until about 1715. The Northern War against Sweden and the strife within Poland that accompanied it lasted from 1700-21, and this discord was accompanied by enormous destruction, epidemics, and famine. The Baal Shem Tov was born in 1698 or 1700, just at the beginning of that gloomy period.

All this may seem like past history in the light of the horrors thrust upon Jews during the Holocaust, but William Helmreich, who wrote the introduction to the translation of Hanover's history, links the two tragic events in a remarkable way. He writes that "it is important to recognize that this last tragedy dwarfs all previous holocausts only in magnitude but not in kind, and that the brutality of Chmielnicki made that of the Nazis much easier. It is no accident that Eastern Europe was the location for most of the major concentration camps. The Ukrainians in particular tended to cooperate with the Nazis in their efforts to exterminate the Jews."[314]

THE PROMISES OF A FALSE MESSIAH

The historic tragedy did not end with the slaughter. An ancient Jewish tradition had foretold that the coming of the messiah would be preceded by war and pestilence, and many kabbalists predicted the messiah would begin his reign in 1648. Groups of Christian millenarians also believed 1648 was the year of the second coming of Christ, and this was also the year that brought peace to Central Europe and freedom to England. Also in 1648, a twenty-two-year-old Sephardic rabbi named Shabbatai Tzvi, who lived in the neighboring country of Turkey, claimed he heard a voice proclaiming he was to become the promised messiah. Tzvi later married a woman from Poland named Sarah, an orphan of the 1648 massacres, whose dead father had revealed to her she was destined to become the bride of the messiah. Tzvi vowed to avenge the sufferings of Polish Jewry, and many of these downtrodden Jews who had suffered such despair believed in Tzvi's promise. Most of the rabbis in the Jewish world repudiated Shabbatai Tzvi as a false messiah; nonetheless, the excitement mounted and Tzvi drew the frenzied allegiance of huge numbers of Jews—from England to Persia, from Germany to Morocco, from Poland to Yemen. Such was the extreme longing for redemption and healing.

The messianic movement actually began in 1665. It is not known precisely how large a following Tzvi had in Poland-Lithuania, but there was a penitential fever as many Jews readied themselves to leave Europe and return to the land of Israel. In 1666, some Polish Jews, expecting their immediate deliverance by the messiah, rose up against Christians in Pinsk, Vilna, and Lublin. About a year later, Shabbatai Tzvi was arrested by Turkish authorities and charged as a rebel of the Ottoman Empire. He was offered the choice of conversion to Islam or execution. He chose conversion. The effect of this decision on Jews in Poland-Lithuania who pinned their hopes on him was devastating. Still, there were those who regarded him still as the messiah, believing that there was a secret reason he had converted which had to do with the destined unfolding of the messianic plan; so they too converted to Islam.

It was this sense of being sinners that caused pious Jews to turn inward toward penitence and asceticism. And along with messianic yearning there was a new turn toward mysticism, especially the Kabbalah of Isaac Luria, which had made its way to Poland from the land of Israel. Luria's cosmological myth of a shattered universe requiring tikkun olam, healing and repair, fit the needs of a broken people. The number of individual mystics along with numerous groups of ascetic kabbalists multiplied.

JEWISH SUFFERING AND NEW BIRTH

It was natural for modern historians to link the historic calamities of the seventeenth century to the birth of Hasidism, seeing the new religious movement as a response to collective tragedy. Simon Dubnow argued that the aftermath of the massacres and the failure of the Shabbatean messianic movement left the Jewish people depressed and impoverished. The inability of the rabbis to provide leadership that was needed during this time of instability led to a perception among the masses that religion had failed them. It was this, Dubnow asserted, that brought about a spiritual vacuum which Hasidism came to fill in the 1740s with its emphasis on hopefulness and joy.

The Hasidic literature I have studied over the years never refers to the carnages of 1648 or the debacle of Shabbatai Tzvi. Because of this, contemporary historians downplay Dubnow's insight into the connection between tragic events of the seventeenth century and the birth of Hasidism, attributing the rise of Hasidism to other nonhistorical factors. But I had to wonder: could the heartbreaking events of the previous century have been forgotten? Was it possible that the recent tragic past really played no role in the Baal Shem Tov's sense of his responsibility to his people? My wife, Rabbi Diane Elliot, holds a different view. As a rabbi, she was familiar with the historical conditions in Poland during the seventeenth and eighteenth centuries. She is also a somatic therapist, trained in an approach to healing known as Body-Mind Centering. Over the years, Diane has worked with numerous victims of trauma. She has co-taught courses with me focusing on the teachings of the Baal Shem in which she often unpacks the Besht's teachings in an embodied way, sharing powerful somatic exercises with our students. Here is what she wrote regarding the connection between the trauma of 1648 and the debacle of Shabbatai Tzvi: "Contemporary somatic psychology and family systems theory have shown that, without intervention, traumatic suffering is held in the body and the collective unconscious, and is handed down from generation to generation. How poignantly we have seen the ways in which children of Holocaust survivors vicariously inherited the traumas of their parents. I believe that there had never been a healing following the trauma of 1648 and the Shabbatai Tzvi debacle, and Polish Jews were living, however unconsciously, with terrifying memories of the past, anger, and grief locked away inside. Fears of a resumption of antisemitism lay, ever-present, just beneath the surface. People continued to pray for the messiah, but perhaps with jaded hopes."

Jewish apprehension and anxiety could explain, at least in part, the popularity of religious asceticism in Poland at the time of the Besht. But Diane suggests that the ingrained habit of fearing the worst may have translated into feelings of sinfulness, the belief that punishment was deserved, and the obsessive need to atone for imagined wrongdoing.

HISTORICAL DEVELOPMENT

In 2014, I attended an academic conference on Hasidism at the Graduate Theological Union in Berkeley sponsored by the Center for Judaic Studies. One of the presenters, historian David Biale, spoke about the origins and history of Hasidism, recapitulating the current scholarly opinion on the subject. During the question and answer period, I spoke about Diane's background and shared her observation that traumatic suffering is held in the body and the collective unconscious and is handed down from generation to generation unless there is some kind of intervention. "The trouble with that," answered Dr. Biale, "is that there are no texts from the period, no evidence at all that can be brought as verification for such a theory."

Just a few years earlier, I'd attended a lecture on the history of Jewish mysticism given in San Francisco by Rachel Elior, professor of Jewish thought and mysticism at Hebrew University. In the course of her remarks, Elior shared her perception that every Jewish mystical movement in history has been a response to Jewish persecution and suffering, an attempt to employ the imagination to realize infinite freedom in a world that denied outer freedom. During the question and answer period following her lecture, I asked Dr. Elior if she agreed with contemporary Jewish historians regarding the lack of connection between the tragic events of mid-seventeenth century Poland and the founding of Hasidism. Elior was adamant. She argued that the contemporary historians are wrong, and that the pogroms of 1648 and the Shabbatean response were a primary historic cause for the rise of Hasidism. She affirmed the views of earlier Jewish historians such as Dubnow, pointing to the fact that during the Besht's lifetime there were over thirty blood libels in Poland. I later read her book, *The Mystical Origins of Hasidism,* and found her views to be a bit more circumspect. She wrote that "there is little doubt that the earlier social and religious crises had left their mark on Jewish society, and that hasidism may have been a response to this. However, these background crises are not sufficient to explain its distinctive characteristics.... Hasidism originated in a mystical awakening that altered conceptions of the relationship between man and God."[315] Apparently, Elior changed her mind about this historical issue, and came to the realization that the rise of Hasidism had indeed been profoundly affected by the social and political crises of the previous century.

It would seem, however, that with the sole exception of Elior (whose academic field is not Jewish history), the common assumption among contemporary Jewish historians is that the tragic events of the seventeenth century had no effect on the origins of Hasidism. Nevertheless, I felt that I had to engage my own research to determine if there was evidence to support her thesis. As I reflected on the numerous teachings of the Baal Shem Tov, I recalled text after text that spoke about adversity and that for him the alleviation of suffering was a major theme. However, he never mentions the cause or causes of suffering. Was he thinking only about the dismal events currently affecting his people in Poland? Knowing the sad history of the period, it seemed that the adversity he was referring to could not have been merely due to natural causes like illness and plagues. I also considered the possibility that his references to suffering might have included the continuing effects on his people of the atrocious events of the previous century.

Given that the Baal Shem Tov believed in the divine control of history (*hash'ga'hah pra'tit*), he must have thought that the Chmielnicki massacres and the messianic pretentions of Shabbatai Tzvi had originated as divine decrees, stemming from the cruel side of God (*Gevurah*). What I imagine him thinking was that these disastrous events occurred because there were no tzaddikim who knew how to transform those decrees. This was all the more reason for him to engage in teaching his disciples the shamanic methods he was employing to halt pogroms in his own day. It seems that this also might have been one of the reasons the Besht abandoned R. Isaac Luria's contemplative methods for bringing about tikkun olam. The fact is that those practices were not working, as evidenced by the major tragedies of the time. In fact, the phrase "tikkun olam" is hardly ever found in the Baal Shem's teachings. The evidence is slight, but perhaps one of his motivations when he began forming a cadre of students was to prepare community leaders who could use shamanic methods to counter antisemitic attacks on Jewish communities.

I discovered a single tale that recounts an encounter between the Baal Shem and Shabbatai Tzvi. According to this legend, the false messiah came to the Besht seeking redemption for his soul, and the Besht actually attempted this work of healing. But as the master was engaged in attempting to redeem Tzvi's soul, the latter tried to entrap the Besht; the Baal Shem hurled him to the lowest pit in hell. He later told his disciples that Shabbatai Tzvi had had a spark of holiness within him, but Satan trapped him in his snare. He also said that Tzvi fell due to his pride and anger, two of the issues that he himself had faced.[316]

Did the Besht's recognition that Tzvi had a spark of holiness within amount to more than a recognition that everything in the world is sourced in God, including evil? One modern scholar of Jewish mysticism, Professor Isaiah Tishby of Hebrew University, actually posited a direct connection between Shabbateanism and the origins of Hasidism. And another prominent scholar of Hasidism, Yehuda Liebes, has pointed to numerous possible connections between Shabbatean and Hasidic teachings.[317]

But were the contemporary historians correct? Was there no evidence, but only Diane's theory about historic trauma, that would back up her thesis? I think of one of the great spiritual heroes of the Holocaust,

Rabbi Kalonymus Kalman Shapira, known as the Piezetsner Rebbe. The rebbe and his community lived in Warsaw, and when the Nazis walled in the Jewish population of the city, creating the infamous ghetto, he chose to remain with his followers despite the fact that he could have escaped. Rabbi Shapira felt that it was his duty to stay with his community and give its members succor. We know from his surviving writings that he continued to affirm the teachings of the Baal Shem Tov—that the world with all of its defects, is divine. The Piezetsner Rebbe perished when the Nazis obliterated the Ghetto. *The Holy Fire* was one of the remarkable volumes that the rebbe composed during the siege, and in his book about *The Holy Fire*, contemporary scholar R. Nehemia Polen points out that nowhere in the volume do the words Germany or Nazi appear. No public figures of the day or place names are mentioned. There is nothing at all about events taking place in the ghetto, no mention of communal policies or any critique of leadership. And there is very little about the impact of the external events on the rebbe personally. Nonetheless, Polen shows that the theme of each of the rebbe's discourses reflects the external circumstances in which the teachings were composed, even though there are no actual details of the actual events. And, Polen writes, the social atmosphere of the ghetto and the psychological and religious problems that arose there are fully reflected in the book.

Why did the rebbe compose his book in this manner? Polen writes that "hasidic literature is, on an overt level, quite indifferent to history.... One would be hard-pressed to find even one instance of an early hasidic theoretical text that as much as mentions a contemporaneous event or circumstance.... It is remarkable that one can read many pages in *Esh Kodesh* (*The Holy Fire*) without gaining any idea of when and where they were written.... Primacy is given to Torah, not the shifting events of the outside world. The external realities provided the context for the discourses, but the internal dynamic was rooted in the author's own creative engagement with Torah."[318] This literary tradition goes back to the Baal Shem and his disciples. When the Besht speaks about suffering, he might be referring to current adversities affecting Jewish life, or he might be remembering the persistent effects of ravages that took place a half century before his birth. Or the collective awareness of what happened might have been so pervasive that the Baal Shem had no need to refer explicitly to that sad history. Perhaps he felt that speaking about those heartbreaking events would in some way tarnish the holiness of his teachings. Or that even mentioning those events might have a depressing effect on his students. I also think it's possible that Chmielnicki's very name had become anathema to eighteenth century Polish Jews.

As further evidence that the Jews of the Baal Shem's era were still aware of the horrendous events of the seventeeth century, we have the fact that *Abyss of Despair* was being published during the Besht's lifetime. In fact, Hanover's book was so popular that in some communities it was customary to read it like a sacred scripture during the "Three Weeks," the period leading to the Fast of Tisha B'Av, which commemorates the siege of Jerusalem and the destruction of the Temple by the Babylonians. It seems clear that the Baal Shem was aware of the tragedies. How could he not have been?

CONDITIONS OF JEWISH LIFE IN POLAND

A comparison of Jewish life in Poland before and after the Chmielnicki massacres strongly points toward the continuing impact of the tragedies of the seventeenth century into the eighteenth century. Let me explain. Historian Anthony Polonsky has written that the Jewish community in Poland-Lithuania grew rapidly in the century before the 1648 massacres, and became one of the main religious centers of the Jewish world. The rabbinate became professionalized and gained power. Along with power, its members enjoyed increased prestige. Polish Jewry produced a whole pantheon of sages and scholars. A large number of Jewish books were published and widely distributed. The final section of *Abyss of Despair* bears this out. Rabbi Hanover prefaces his description by remarking that Jewish life in Poland was "founded on principles of righteousness and justice." He states that in all of the diaspora communities of the Jewish people, "there was nowhere so much learning as in the Kingdom of Poland.... There was scarcely a house...where its members did not occupy themselves with the Torah."

Hanover then describes the numerous Talmudic academies and their faculties and curricula. He points out that the heads of the academies were respected and honored, and he elaborates on the ways in which study and prayer took precedence over concerns about business matters. He also describes how members of the community cared for one another, and how Polish Jews would help their co-religionists who lived elsewhere in the world. Altogether, the picture we get is of an integrated and peaceful life. It seems that even if Hanover's portrait might in some ways be an idealization, there must have been more than a measure of truth in it, as well.

Polonsky writes that after 1648 the relative security of the community was severely shaken. Jewish religious life began to recover from the traumas, but it never regained its former eminence, and the fabric of Torah learning was permanently diminished. It became normal for unqualified men to buy rabbinic positions of power.

Did Jewish life ever fully recover? In his portrayal of Jewish society in Poland during his time, Rabbi Jacob Joseph of Polonoyye, the Baal Shem's chief literary disciple, reveals an enormous amount of social dysfunction. Samuel Dresner writes that R. Jacob Joseph viewed the Jewish world of his time with the disparaging eyes of a biblical prophet. Jacob Joseph was sensitive to the disrespect that Jews had for one another, and the hollow ways they practiced their religion. Dresner describes thoughts he imagines going through Jacob Joseph's mind that prompted the rabbi's condemnation of Jewish life in Poland. The Baal Shem's disciple "was well aware of the physical suffering of his people. Each day he walked amidst hatred from noble, king and priest, as well as from peasant and tradesman, a hatred which crushed and tormented the innocent. He saw how lack of work and empty larders caused aching hearts and empty stomachs. He suffered for the physical suffering of the people, knew their hunger, poverty and pain—not only through the sympathy of his soul, but also because of the wretched life he himself endured. But he suffered infinitely more for their spiritual privation."[319]

And just what was their spiritual privation? Jacob Joseph writes that the core of the problem of Jewish life in Poland was a lack of love and compassion, the very virtues that had been so emphasized by his teacher, the Baal Shem Tov.

> The suffering caused by divine harshness (*gevurah*) may be sweetened in two ways that are really one: First, by not judging people in the world in an unfavorable way.

And second, by opening one's heart to compassion and looking for what is good in everyone.[320]

Dresner weaves together a series of stark pronouncements taken from various teachings in Jacob Joseph's works describing the society of his time:

> [F]or the cause of our misery in this bitter exile is that there is no brotherliness or unity.... This exile continues because of the needless hatred which exists.... No one inquires into the welfare of his neighbor, but one hates the other.... Hatred brings about division between men "below," causing division "above".... Therefore the commandment which encompasses the whole Torah is, "Thou shalt love they neighbor as thyself. I am the Lord"; that is, one should take pity on the glory of the Lord, encouraging brotherliness and love between a man and his neighbors, so that hatred and division on earth should not cause, God forbid, separation of the letters of His name in heaven.[321]

R. Jacob Joseph writes that the malignancy of hatred affected not only relations between people, but also the relationship between people and God. He points to the emptiness of prayer and the rote practice of religious observance among the people, stating that Jews had forgotten that study, prayer, Shabbat, and the festivals were meant to draw them closer to God. Instead, Jews observed these mitzvot in a habitual and routine fashion. In fact, many people were more enthusiastic in their pursuit of material cravings than they were about their religious duties. And among the ruling class there was a lack of respect for scholars, even a refusal to support scholars' livelihoods.

And yet if common Jews had gone astray, the rabbi writes, it was not really their fault. Jacob Joseph blames most of the problems on the spiritual leaders of the community: the rabbis, scholars, cantors, and teachers. Motivated by self-interest and pride, they were concerned for their welfare alone; for the common people these so-called leaders had only contempt. And as he often does, Jacob Joseph cites the Baal Shem in this connection:

> I heard a parable in the name of my teacher (may his memory live on in the future world). There once was a very tall man who was exposed to the heat of the sun all day, until he had become completely sunburned by its rays. A wise man saw what had happened—that he had no water for his parched tongue. So the sage approached the tall man, sat down, took out his container of water and drank from it, so that the tall man would see what he was doing. Then he offered the man some water, but the tall man refused to bend down to drink because this would show that he was in need of another's help. The wise man understood this, but he could find no other way of getting some water to the tall man other than by throwing it upward into his face. But concerned only with his pride and what others might think of him, the thirsty man tightened his lips so that not even the slightest bit of the sage's water should reach his mouth...and so he died.[322]

R. Jacob Joseph states that this pride was manifested in jealousy and rivalry among the rabbis. They were unconcerned with hearing the teachings of others and only sought to assert their own points of view. Such competitiveness gave rise to petty quarrels and diverted energy away from aiding the plight of the people. Moreover, the rabbis mocked the truly pious people, the tzaddikim. It was no wonder then that the common people had so little respect for rabbis, or why the wealthy failed to provide them with adequate financial support.

He also charges the rabbis with competing against one another for their own financial security, and coddling the rich for material advantages. And because they compromised their calling in this way, unduly concerned with maintaining their own positions, they were unable to criticize the wealthy. There are rabbis who are fully observant and studious, Jacob Joseph acknowledges, but they feel little obligation to look after the needs of the people. Instead, they focus on seeking their own perfection. These rabbis formed a world apart, immersing themselves in the intricacies of the Talmud and Kabbalah, while looking down on common people whom they perceived as being simple and crude. Then there were the fiery preachers who would travel from town to town preaching in synagogues, portraying the religious life as continuous warfare against the hostile Gentile environment without, the instincts within, and demons everywhere. They represented the religious life as demanding intense asceticism, zealous fulfillment of the mitzvot, and constant, anxious vigilance.

What brought about these deplorable conditions? There were indeed terrible things happening in Poland during the lifetime of the Besht, as we've seen. It was a period of almost complete chaos in Poland and Lithuania. The Northern War waged by Poland against Sweden and the internecine strife within Poland that accompanied it brought about destruction, epidemics, and famine. Jewish communities suffered along with the rest of the country, and for much of the eighteenth century the population was subject to constant attacks from foreign armies, and outbreaks of civil unrest were numerous.

Along with all this chaos, the Catholic Church in Poland had reinstated its medieval antisemitic constraints. These included the coerced conversion of Jews to Catholicism, the abduction of Jewish children in order to baptize and raise them as Christians, false accusations against Jews in economic, social, and religious areas. There were also the numerous blood libels—claims that Jews murdered Christian children to use their blood in their Passover rituals. So even if the events of the previous century had been forgotten, the current events would have created a climate of fear among Jews. The terrors experienced by eighteenth century Jews could have kept the fear of mass pogroms alive.

We also know that during the time of the Baal Shem Tov there were communities of Sabbatian Jews active in Poland. It would seem that in his travels the Baal Shem avoided visiting those communities. Along with this, a second false messiah by the name of Jacob Frank appeared. Frank claimed to be a reincarnation of Shabbatai Tzvi and promoted a messianic cult in the same geographical area. Like the Shabbateans, the Frankists opposed the observance of Jewish law which they found both authoritarian and arduous. The entire Frankist community eventually wound up converting to Catholicism.

In 1754, in the town of Lanskorn in Poldolia, a group of Frankists was caught in the act of performing crude sexual rites. The Jews of Lanskorn began to persecute the heretics, and in their distress the Frankists turned for support to Bishop Dembowski of Kamenetz. Dembowski saw this as an opportunity to prove the superiority of Christianity over Judaism, and he ordered the Jews of Lanskorn to engage in a debate with representatives of the Frankists over the contents of the Talmud. Of course it wasn't much of a debate, for the bishop himself was the sole judge and he knew the outcome before the confrontation. After the "debate," the bishop rendered the verdict that the Talmud contained material incendiary and offensive on matters sacred to Christianity and that all copies were therefore to be burned. The decision was enforced in the town square of Kamenetz in October 1757, and the rabbis of the communities in the Lvov region were made to witness the public book burning. These events left a deep impression on the Jews of Poland.

Soon thereafter, Dembowski was appointed bishop of Lvov, and there was a genuine possibility that he would order all copies of the Talmud in the region under his jurisdiction to be burned. Some Jews were so fearful of this that they sent all the volumes they possessed across the Turkish border. One of the tales in *In Praise of the Baal Shem Tov* refers directly to this event:

> It was the day before Yom Kippur, the Day of Atonement, and the Baal Shem Tov was despondent, for he had experienced a premonition that Gentiles were about to destroy the Talmud. Toward nightfall, the Jews of Medzhibozh came to his home so that he might bless them as he did every year before Yom Kippur. The master began to bless a few of these individuals, but because of his despair he didn't have the heart to continue.
>
> The congregation gathered in the synagogue for Kol Nidrei but then, just before the evening service was to begin, the Besht stood up and cried out to his community, begging them to look into their hearts and engage

in deep repentance. Then he approached the Holy Ark and fell down before it, crying, "Oi! Oi! They are scheming to take the Talmud from our hands. How will we survive among the nations for even half a day without our holy teachings?" And then he screamed out against the rabbis who were distorting the teachings of the Talmud with their self-serving casuistry.

The Besht's words evoked a deep sense of anguish and sorrow in the hearts of the assembled worshippers, and there was silence for several minutes. Then the designated men took all the scrolls of the Torah out of the ark and carried them around the synagogue. Then they gathered around the cantor; the congregation arose and the cantor solemnly chanted the Kol Nidrei three times in a plaintive voice. But this was not an ordinary Yom Kippur; the Baal Shem, visibly distressed, stood up again and cried out that the danger was growing even worse.

All through the night and the following day the Besht agonized over his dark premonition. As the long day began to wane and the congregation approached Neilah, the final service of the day, he once again pleaded with the congregation to dig deeper into their souls, and give themselves with greater vigor to the inner work of repentance. Then he wept aloud, leaned his head backwards, sighed and cried out. When he began to pray the Amidah, the entire community joined him. The silence was heavy. Then he chanted the Amidah aloud. When he reached the words in the prayerbook, "Open the gates of heaven to us," he began to gesture violently, bending backward until his head nearly reached his knees. His eyes bulged and his voice sounded like a bull being slaughtered. This continued for some two hours.

When the master emerged from his trance, his face calm and his demeanor serene, he straightened his body and quickly concluded the service. After the final blowing of the shofar, which ended Yom Kippur, the entire community came up to greet him and to find out what had taken place during the final prayer service. The Besht's face was beaming as he told them what had occurred.

"I was able to pass from one celestial world to another unhindered, and I came to a certain palace, and there I discovered fifty years of prayers that had not been able to rise to their destination because they had been uttered without any real intentionality. But because all of us prayed with such depth of soul both last night and today every one of the prayers ascended, and each prayer glowed as a bright dawn. So then I asked the prayers, 'Why did you not ascend until just now?' And they answered me, 'We were waiting for your Eminence to guide us to our destination.' And then I said to them, 'Come with me.' And so we moved through each of the gates toward higher and higher worlds, but the lock on the last gate was huge and it was bolted in such a way that I was unable to open it. Even my teacher, Ahiyah of Shiloh, who I summoned for help, could not open it. But Ahiyah did lead me to the palace of the messiah, and the messiah gave me powerful spells to use as keys to unlock the gate. I then returned to the gate and unlocked the bolt. When we entered, all the prayers of fifty years ascended together all at once. There was great rejoicing throughout heaven. Satan could do nothing and the decree to destroy the Talmud was cancelled."

In this account we again meet the Baal Shem Tov in his role as shaman, but here his ascent to heaven is carried out on behalf of the entire Jewish people. But notice: the entire story revolves around the Baal Shem's miraculous intervention. There is not a word about Jacob Frank and his followers, or any of the events that precipitated the attempted book burning.

All of the political and military occurrences that took place during the Besht's lifetime must have severely impacted the Jewish communities in Poland and Lithuania. But could these events alone have brought about the shattering of Jewish social life that R. Jacob Joseph painted in such dark colors? I don't think so, for however harsh life was, it was nothing like the damage wrought by the bloodbaths of the previous century and the fiasco of Shabbatai Tzvi. I see nothing in the historic chronicle that would indicate that the troubles affecting the Jewish community in the early part of the eighteenth century produced the societal dysfunction Jacob Joseph described. On the contrary, it appears that the situation described by Anthony Polonsky following the massacres continued into the new century. It also seems that the Baal Shem's powerful shamanic journeys on behalf of his people against antisemitic attacks may have been inspired by his knowledge that there were no such attempts at bringing about heavenly intervention before or during the carnage in 1648. If this is true, his conception of the Hasidic tzaddik as an intercessor may have been influenced by what occurred during the previous century.

A NEW TYPE OF SPIRITUAL LEADER

Underlying Rabbi Jacob Joseph's laser-like critique of the Jewish society of his time was his certainty that the Baal Shem Tov could provide exactly the kind of model of spiritual leadership that Jews in Poland needed. Because Jacob Joseph saw the problems of the Jewish community as a crisis in spiritual leadership, what was needed was a new kind of spiritual leader, as Samuel Dresner explains, "one whose humility would permit the word of God to penetrate his mind and heart, giving him unshakeable faith and the willingness to sacrifice, one who was strong in belief and compassion at once and could perform the double miracle of going out to the people while at the same time remaining bound up with God. Through such a man all else would be affected. Around the zaddik a new community of souls could gather; both synagogue and school could be transformed; teacher and cantor rededicated; rich and poor brought to repentance."[323]

Jacob Joseph was thinking of his teacher when he described this kind of leader. He declared that the tzaddik stands between heaven and earth. He is the means by which heaven reaches the people, and also the means through which the people reach heaven. He is a channel, receiving divine *shefa,* the spiritual outpouring which endlessly and lovingly flows from heaven, and transmits it to his people. Jacob Joseph cites the Besht: "I heard from my teacher (may his memory live on in the future world) an explanation of the following passage. *'A heavenly voice declared: All the world exists for the sake (bish'veel) of Hanina, my son, and Hanina, my son, is sustained by the fruit of the carob tree from the eve of one Sabbath to the eve of the next Sabbath.'* (Talmud Ta'anit, ch. 3) The word *bish'veel* implies that he made a channel (*sh'veel*) to bring to all the world the heavenly outpouring, and therefore it says, all the world is sustained through the channel of Hanina, my son. But it seems to me that not only did Hanina *make* a channel, but that *he himself became a channel* through which the outpouring passes."[324]

The people rise upward toward heaven through *devekut,* clinging to God. And, writes Jacob Joseph, this is at the heart of all the mitzvot. Through the tzaddik simple people who have to spend most of their time earning a livelihood can come close to God. The tzaddik recognizes that in every soul, no matter how dark the pit into which it may have fallen, there are sparks of holiness seeking to be redeemed. The tzaddik does not wait for these individuals to come to him; he goes out and down to their level, trying to find some way to reach them so that he may return them to God.[325]

How were Jacob Joseph's books received in Poland? There was anger among the Jewish opponents of the new movement, and his books were burned in public. But he had touched a nerve and many found inspiration studying his words. As Heschel wrote in the preface to Dresner's book, "The surprise, the joy, the refreshment which the publication of his books brought to the Jewish world are quite understandable to those who are acquainted with the spiritual atmosphere of the eighteenth century.... These books offered a fresh vision of what is at stake in Jewish faith and existence, and a singular sensitivity for the divine.... God's presence is felt on each page."[326]

CHAPTER TWENTY

HASIDISM AS HEALING COMMUNITY

Rabbi Tirzah Firestone's book, *Wounds into Wisdom*, explains a great deal the impact of trauma in the Jewish world, including the traumas that gave rise to Hasidism. Even more importantly, her work provides insight into the ways Hasidism brought about collective healing for the Jews of eighteenth-century Poland.

Wounds into Wisdom: Healing Intergenerational Jewish Trauma represents the fruit of research on the impact of collective trauma on Jewish lives, and on the ways Jews deal with that trauma in the contemporary world. Rabbi Tirzah draws on the fields of neuroscience, psychology, Jewish literature, and mythopoesis, and she employs interviews, case studies, and her own autobiographical narratives to demonstrate how trauma residue passes from generation to generation and how it can be transformed. "In the aftermath of traumatic events," she writes, "it is extremely common for strong mental images to be harbored in our minds, playing and replaying themselves. I propose that these unintegrated memory fragments can be transmitted, or 'deposited' within young porous minds by their parents and caregivers. This is largely an unconscious process."

She cites the work of Dr. Vamik Volkan, a psychoanalyst who spent his professional life studying the effects of war, terror, and displacement on the psychology of populations around the world. Volkan's experiences in war-ravaged areas taught him that "even persons who have no actual war experiences are influenced to one degree or another by mental images of wars or warlike conditions, due to identifications, transgenerational transmissions, and psychological links to their parents' or ancestors' history." Rabbi Firestone elaborates on this process: "Clinical studies give us evidence that stress and struggle can imprint itself not only on us, but upon future generations. The science of epigenetics shows that a person can carry evidence of their parent's, grandparent's, and even great-grandparent's social history. If, for example, a person's grandparents lived through starvation, deportation, or ethnic persecution, their descendants may show propensities to similar stress responses, both physical and psychological. Sometimes the similarities between generations are uncanny."[327]

Think back to what Rabbi Jacob Joseph reported about the deleterious religious and moral conditions of Jewish society in the eighteenth century, and to what Rabbi Nathan Hanover reported about the splendor and order of Jewish life in Poland prior to the pogrom of 1648. The second part of Firestone's book is devoted to the healing of intergenerational trauma. She cites a number of principles based on her work with her own Jewish patients and on interviews conducted with traumatized individuals in the U.S. and Israel. As I studied these healing modalities, I was struck by how similar they were to the spiritual innovations introduced by the Baal Shem Tov and his followers. Apparently, the modes of healing that Firestone identified have maintained some sort of continuity through time. Let us examine each one in light of our knowledge of the innovations of Hasidism.

DISIDENTIFYING FROM THE TRAUMA

Traumatized Jews have tended to see themselves as victims, and this negative self-image has perpetuated their distress. Rabbi Firestone writes about the necessity for trauma survivors to disidentify from their victimhood: "[T]here can be no discussion about disidentifying from Jewish victimhood without first acknowledging that Jews have, in fact, been the victims of persecution for thousands of years."[328] Firestone does not refer to psychedelics, but today there are numerous psychotherapists and practitioners pioneering the use of these drugs in the healing of Post-Traumatic Stress Disorder, and this is offering new hope for the healing of trauma. These substances bring about a state of disidentification from trauma for those with PTSD, while providing them with a sense of connection to the totality of existence. This experience allows them to see their traumatic issues in a new, more transcendental light. As we have seen, the Baal Shem Tov and his disciples may have been exposed to psychedelic substances. And even if they were not, it seems certain that the Besht was able to bring about such disidentification from suffering through practices he employed in his mystical prayer life. In his teaching, he employed kabbalistic imagery to depict what it meant to enter such a state of consciousness. He spoke about becoming *Ayin,* "No-thing." That is, he lost his identity as a separate human being and became one with everything. And it is clear from the citations in their books that he taught this approach to davening to his students. I am convinced that this kind of practice liberated the Baal Shem and his disciples from their earthly identifications, including those tied to suffering and victimization.

A VISION OF MEANING AND HOPE

Rabbi Firestone cites Robert Jay Lifton's observation that all survivors of trauma undergo a struggle to give "form or meaning to an otherwise incomprehensible experience, and above all, to their survival," adding: "There is evidence, Lifton says, that the offspring of survivors must undergo a similar struggle. But because they are working with events that are physically removed from their lived experience, it is often like groping in the dark for clues. In my own practice, I have heard second- and third-generation survivors report feeling crazy, abnormal, and even mentally ill due to the trauma symptoms they internalized growing up with traumatized parents."[329]

The Baal Shem's views about the nature of Divinity, derived from his mystical experiences, provided ultimate meaning for him and his disciples. He apparently entertained different views about the origin of evil at different times during his life, all of them found in the Kabbalah. But it seems that once he experienced nondualism, he understood that both good and evil stem from the Holy One. He taught his disciples to recognize that everything they encountered or experienced was divine, and that no matter how dark or dismal the world might seem, there was no way to fall out of God. He also taught that divine evil could be transformed into good. Most importantly, the tzaddik acts as a catalyst for such transformation. It was in this way that the Besht inspired hope and optimism that became hallmarks of the new Hasidism. He refined kabbalistic spiritual practices and devised novel practices to bring the healing presence of God into everyday life.

THE IMPORTANCE OF BEING WITNESSED

Firestone writes that for survivors of the Holocaust "there was an unprecedented loss of the divine witness. That is, the seeing, loving, divine protector who had watched from on high, whose presence had forever given meaning to Jewish history, had ostensibly vanished." She writes that to ameliorate the persistent suffering "we need to find a person whom we can trust, a person who has the ability to receive our words with an open mind and no agenda of their own. With such a witness, we can create a safe place where the unspeakable can finally be spoken."[330] From the abundance of stories describing the Besht's life, I imagine him as a person who could hear and witness the tales of woe people shared and then offer them his love and compassion. Furthermore, I believe part of the reason the Besht was so idealized by the Hasidim had to do with the way he was able to channel the flow of spiritual energy and goodness (*shefah*) from the higher world into their lives. In this way he acted as an intermediary, reconnecting his people to God. The Baal Shem Tov then served as the prototype for the Hasidic rebbe who was seen as being a channel of the Divine throughout the centuries of Hasidic life.

BREAKING THE PATTERN

Firestone identifies repetition as a hallmark of trauma. What she's refer-ring to is "the paradoxical but well-documented tendency of survivors to find or recreate situations reminiscent of their original trauma.... Whether survivors recreate their trauma situation to gain comfort, mas-tery, or resolution, this pattern remains unconscious and so yields little but further pain."[331] Many Jews of the Baal Shem's time practiced severe forms of asceticism, including fasting for long periods of time, which were sourced in the Kabbalah of Rabbi Isaac Luria. These stark practices took root because so many Jews were feeling guilt, sadness, and unwor-thiness as a result of the teachings of traditional musar. We have indica-tions that, as a young man, the Besht undertook such practices. But after his enlightenment he came to recognize this asceticism only reinforced depressive emotions. It is well-documented that he eventually sought to end ascetic practice entirely and instead to cultivate joy and pleasure as ways to experience God's immediate presence.

We also witness the Besht's formidable critique of the itinerant musar preachers who continually reproached Jews for their sins. He refused to blame Jews for the continued existence of the exile; instead, he made it clear that God was the ultimate cause of everything, including suffering, and that it was the responsibility of the tzaddik to transform God's harshness into love.

RECLAIMING EMBODIED LIFE

The asceticism that Jews practiced was, at least in part, a response to the pain that had been inflicted on the Jewish body. As Firestone puts it, "Trauma disconnects us from our bodies. Once we have turned to face our situation, we must learn to reinhabit our physical selves."[332] The Besht taught an embodied form of spirituality, summoning his disciples to reclaim their own physicality as God's handiwork. Along with joy, pleasure—including sexual pleasure—became a matchless way of experiencing God's presence. He formulated a new vision of Jewish spirituality geared toward individual transformation and enlightenment, allowing his disciples to concentrate on their healing. He showed them how to enter the depths of their souls to discover and actuate the potential for growth hidden within. This inner work also prepared them for roles as rebbes, giving them tools they needed to aid their own followers in healing. Hasidism thus began the reclamation of the Jewish body. And not only sexuality, but also embodied celebration through dance.

ENDING COLLECTIVE TRAUMA

Rabbi Firestone writes that "If individual trauma is a blow to the psyche that breaks through defenses with such suddenness and force that one cannot react to it effectively, then collective trauma is a blow to the living organism that is community. Over time, a trauma-informed worldview may become embedded in the identity of the culture."[333] This is a rather exact picture of the Jewish society in the time of the Baal Shem Tov, as Rabbi Jacob Joseph portrayed it. The result was a self-perpetuating dysfunctional community. This brought about resentments and divisions in the community that could not be overcome, for, as Firestone states, "when we distance ourselves from those who are unlike us, when we make them into the faceless objects of our distrust and fear, we are only one step away from denying their humanity. And so the cycle of violence and trauma is set in motion once again."[334] The master exhibited great compassion toward common folk, and the work he engaged in was meant to prepare leaders who would be able to nurture their spiritual communities in healing ways. He spoke about the need to reestablish empathy, love, and compassion among Jews, regardless of the differences of class and knowledge that separated them.

Was the Baal Shem consciously aware of the tragedies of his time? There is no textual evidence for this, but I cannot imagine that he was ignorant of history. His parapsychological capacities also would have provided him with an awareness of that bitter past. And the healing modalities he introduced may have been intended to heal the traumas his people had undergone. Even if some or all of these spiritual interventions came about through the creativity of his disciples and their disciples, the need by people for these innovative values and practices could well explain the tremendous success of Hasidism in the decades following the founder's passing.

Given the divisiveness in our world today, including within the Jewish community, it is clear that collective trauma is still a major issue that needs to be faced and dealt with. Spiritual teacher Thomas Hübl has written, "The underlying consequence of trauma—whether in individuals, families, communities, or societies—is that it damages our innate human capacity to form and sustain healthy relationships. We say trauma breaks relation. By supporting one another through times of difficulty, we can prevent traumatization."[335] Hübl has developed a mutual practice of group coherence, shared presenting, and collective healing. He has found a home for his work in Israel, and has led large-scale healing events there, bringing together hundreds of Israelis and Germans to address the collective wounds of the Holocaust.

Reading Firestone's book made me aware that many of my life choices have been responses to childhood trauma that I experienced. My early and persistent sense of being a victim came about due to my having conflated the asthma that almost killed me with the words my mother used over and over again at the dinner table: "You have to eat—the children in Europe are starving." I would feel enormous guilt if I did not eat everything on my plate. I soon learned that the children she was referring to were Jewish.

In college, I was drawn to an extreme form of traditional Judaism by a Holocaust survivor whose unvoiced message was that only the observance and faith of traditional Judaism would allow one to survive the kind of unspeakable trauma he'd undergone. Then came my later agnostic revolt in rabbinical school, fueled by rage toward an untrustworthy God who had abandoned his people. In the long run there was the anxiety, depression, and despair that at times almost overwhelmed me, and the pessimism that lurked just beneath the surface of my everyday life.

Abraham Joshua Heschel and Zalman Schachter-Shalomi, both my teachers, had been able to retain their religious faith despite having gone through the Holocaust. I came to understand that like Hasidism itself, the neo-Hasidic form of Jewish renewal in our time was a healing response to that tragedy. Most importantly, just as the Baal Shem Tov had been a kind of savior figure for Jews in the eighteenth century, so he had been able to resurrect my life as a Jew. The story I tell in this book has to do with the form of Jewish renewal initiated in eighteenth-century Poland, but it is my belief that the Baal Shem was not only addressing the issue of trauma in his time. The Jewish people, in Israel and the diaspora, are suffering from the collective trauma brought about by modernity and by the Holocaust. My hope is that the path of the Baal Shem can further the necessary healing of our people.

WHAT ABOUT GOD AND EVIL?

The Baal Shem Tov's vision of a nondual God resolved for me the major theological conundrum: How could a good God allow the Holocaust to happen? In the last four books of the Torah—Exodus, Leviticus, Numbers, and Deuteronomy—God comes over as a transcendent potentate, often concerned and compassionate, but at other times imperious, violent, and vengeful. The biblical God is never merely a force for goodness alone. For years I struggled mightily with this image of an impetuous God, eventually rejecting it completely. At a certain point in life, I came to sense that some kind of "divine order" that laid beneath our messy lives no longer made sense. The strands of goodness and evil are interlaced in inexplicable ways, and human existence is often confused and irrational. I had to admit that the impetuous way in which the God of Torah was imaged actually does reflect the eerie reality of our existence.

The many explanations for the existence of evil often take God off the hook by placing blame on human beings. But look at our world: it is filled with violence and suffering, and not only among human beings.

As Darwin came to recognize, cruelty is built into the very fabric. People may have free will, as the Torah claims, but it has become clear that not all people possess an equal amount of choice. Humans are constrained by their social conditioning which tends to limit their freedom. And like the animals from which our species descended, we have a proclivity for violence that can often override any "choice" we may have. What we have learned about trauma only deepens the issue, for individuals whose lives have been severely affected in this way have an even more limited ability to make free choices, and often act out in irrational ways.

While there is a magnificent coherence in the cosmos, that harmony is laced with violence. And everything in the universe is intertwined and enmeshed with everything else in such a way that distinguishing good from evil often becomes impossible. Here on earth all life feeds on life, and violence is a normative aspect of human life. Because of this I cannot affirm his belief that at its root everything we perceive as evil is really good. Were there any Jewish teachings that spoke to this reality directly? I recall coming upon a verse in Isaiah in which the prophet declared in God's name, *"I form the light and create darkness; I make harmony and create chaos; I, the EverPresent, do all these things"* (45:7). Then, when I studied Job, I saw that its anonymous author actually refutes the view found in many narratives in the Torah regarding the human origin of evil. The author of Job makes it clear from the outset that his human protagonist is not being made to suffer because of some sin he committed.

Years later, I discovered that the Baal Shem had come to espouse a view of good and evil that paralleled the book of Job. The Besht came to understand that the world was constructed in such a way that evil and suffering both came from divine decrees over which human beings have no control. We are thrown into a world that at times makes no sense in human terms. Nonetheless, this doesn't mean we have to remain pawns in hands of some inevitable fate. For God makes it possible for certain human beings to become tzaddikim, spiritual heroes who are able to transform evil into good, bringing hope to tragic times. In becoming godlike, that is, embodying and manifesting the Divinity that is our true nature, it is possible to transform the world. This notion still lives. There are religious heroes who act to rebalance the world in a positive direction. I immediately think of Mohandas Gandhi, Nelson Mandela, Bishop

Desmond Tutu, Martin Buber, Abraham Joshua Heschel, and Martin
Luther King, Jr.

THE BAAL SHEM AND THE MESSIAH

Many stories about the Baal Shem Tov picture him as the primary spiritual defender of the Jewish people. Apparently, he believed it was his duty
to save Jews who were at risk of losing their lives in pogroms. Earlier in
this book we encountered a letter, the "holy epistle," that the Besht wrote
to his father-in-law, Rabbi Gershon, describing his ascent to heaven and
his encounter with the messiah. In this letter the Besht writes:

> I asked the messiah, "When are you coming, master?"
>
> He answered me: "This is how you will know I am
> coming: Your teaching will become well-known and
> revealed throughout the world, and your wellsprings
> will flow out to everyone.
>
> Others will then be able to carry out the practices
> that I have taught you, and they too will be able to per-
> form contemplative unifications and ascents of the soul
> as you are able to do.
>
> Then all the shards that hold the sparks of light will
> be destroyed, and there will be a time of acceptance and
> redemption."
>
> I was bewildered at his response, and I experienced
> great anguish because of the great length of time it
> would take until he came.
>
> I wondered when it would be possible for this to
> occur.[336]

The Besht's encounter with the messiah shows how much he longed for
the healing and redemption of his people. The messiah tells him that the
mystical practices he has been taught are the key to such redemption,
and that when these practices become widespread, the masses committed to them would create the necessary spiritual climate for the messiah's
coming. Rather than finding hope in this, however, the Besht experiences
anguish because the messiah's words seem so unrealistic.

There have been historians who believe Hasidism was founded as a messianic movement, but most scholars disagree.[337] The tradition itself does not claim the Baal Shem as the messiah. The deeds he accomplished in his lifetime did not fulfill the expectations and promises associated with the messianic role. And it would have been dangerous, in the wake of the Shabbatean catastrophe, for the Baal Shem to make such a claim. However, in the text above the messiah does tell the Besht: "This is how you will know that I am coming..." Instead, the messiah says, "you will know," which implies that the Baal Shem himself will witness the onset of the time of redemption. He, however, is more realistic than the messiah and he finds it difficult to believe the words he's hearing. During this soul ascent the messiah appears to him in the traditional similitude of an external savior, but the Besht seems to have reflected on his experience and then interpreted it in a new way:

> Every Jew needs to cultivate the part of the messiah contained within his own soul until the entire messianic prototype has been completed (*tikkun*) and prepared. Only then will the total universal unification of all reality be accomplished for all eternity. May this happen soon, while we still live.[338]

In this teaching the Baal Shem sees himself as a teacher sent by God to instruct disciples and perhaps others regarding how they might discover the spark of messianic consciousness in themselves, so that collectively people might bring about a new world. Although enlightenment was the initial goal in the training of a tzaddik, this was only a prerequisite to the fundamental goal of the tzaddik becoming an agent for community healing. What the Besht learned from the messiah must have affected his view of himself as a precursor of a messianic era.

THE TRANSFORMATION OF SUFFERING

We see this core function of the tzaddik functioning in the Baal Shem's radical interpretation of the story of the Binding of Isaac, known as the Akedah, in Genesis chapter 22:

> *And then, sometime after these events had occurred,* ***Elohim*** *put Abraham to the test. He spoke to him:*

"*Abraham!*" "*I am here,*" *replied Abraham.* "*Now take your favorite son, the son who you love, Isaac, and go forth to the land of Moriah, and offer him up there as a burnt offering upon one of the mountains that I will tell you of.*" *And Abraham arose early in the morning and saddled his donkey, and he took his two serving lads with him, and Isaac his son. And he split the wood for the burnt offering, and he readied himself and journeyed to the place that* **Elohim** *had told him about.*

On the third day Abraham lifted up his eyes and saw the place from afar. Then he said to the lads, "*Stay here with the donkey, and I and the lad will go yonder, and we will worship and then return to you.*" *Abraham took the wood for the burnt offering and he placed it in Isaac's hands, and he took the firestone and the knife, and the two of them walked together.*

Isaac said to Abraham his father, "*Father!*" *He replied,* "*I am here, my son.*" *And Isaac said,* "*Here is the firestone and the knife, but where is the lamb for the burnt offering?*" *Abraham answered,* "**Elohim** *will see to it that we have a lamb for the burnt offering, my son.*" *And the two of them walked on together.*

They came to the place that **Elohim** *had told him about, and Abraham built the alter and arranged the wood, and he bound Isaac his son, and placed him on the alter on top of the wood. And then Abraham stretched out his hand and took the knife to slaughter his son.*

But just then a messenger of **Y-H-V-H** *cried out from heaven:* "*Abraham! Abraham!*" *And he replied,* "*I am here.*" "*Do not stretch out your hand against the lad, and do nothing to harm him, for now I know for sure that you fear* **Elohim,** *for you have not withheld your favorite son from Me.*"

Then Abraham lifted up his eyes and saw a ram behind him, caught in a thicket by its horns. Abraham took the ram and offered it up as a burnt offering in place of his

son. And Abraham called the name of that place "Y-H-V-H
Sees," as the saying goes, "On that mountain Y-H-V-H was
actually seen."

The story concludes with the messenger of Y-H-V-H rewarding Abraham for his deed by giving him a blessing—that his progeny would multiply like the stars in the heavens and like grains of sand on the seashore. He also promises that Abraham will triumph over his enemies and that all nations of the earth will enjoy blessings that his progeny will bring to pass.

My imaginative understanding of the Baal Shem's interpretation of the Akedah comes from a few fragments that remain of what must have been a full Beshtian discourse. I was so taken by these fragments, that I attempted to reimagine the complete narrative. The Besht's interpretation turns around the Torah's use of two different names for the Divine in the Akedah, *Elohim* and *Y-H-V-H.* The first of these, *Elohim,* is regularly translated into English as "God," whereas *Y-H-V-H,* usually rendered as "the Lord," may actually mean something like "the Source of Being" or "the EverPresent." In Kabbalah, these two names took on very different meanings, in fact, opposing moral qualities. *Elohim* came to refer to God's rigor and harshness (the sefirah of *Din* or *Gevurah*), while *Y-H-V-H* was understood as the boundless love and grace of the Divine (the sefirah of *hesed*). The Baal Shem was struck by the fact that the narrative uses the name *Elohim* at the beginning of the story, and *Y-H-V-H* at its end.

The Besht's version of the tale begins with *Elohim*—divine rigor and harshness (*Gevurah*)—coming to Abraham, commanding him to sacrifice his son as a test of his faith. If my understanding of the story is correct, the Baal Shem interprets this occurrence as a blow to Abraham's faith in the God who promised his progeny would fill the earth like the stars fill the heavens and sand fills the seashore. The patriarch fell into a depression in which his consciousness contracted, as the Besht comments:

> When a person is undergoing a trial, he enters a state
> of diminished consciousness. We know this because the
> Torah says: *"Now after these events **Elohim** put Abraham*
> *through a test . . ."*[339]

This state of constricted consciousness diminished the patriarch's capacity for mustering his discernment and will, and he simply capitulated to *Elohim's* ruthless command. The Baal Shem's comment implies that if Abraham had been in a more expansive state of awareness, he would have perceived the Divine as the loving *Y-H-V-H,* who would never have put Abraham through such a cruel test.

"*Now after these events Elohim put Abraham through a test.*" The Hebrew verb that the text uses for "test" is *NiSaH.* But the Besht picked up on another meaning of the Hebrew verb root, *N-S-H*— "to lift up." Thus, he reads the verse in the following way: "Now after these events, *Elohim was lifted up by Abraham.*" How remarkable! The Baal Shem believed that as a representative of God's unconditional love (*hesed*), Abraham's task is to elevate and transform God's harshness and rigor (*gevurah*) through his own essence of love and kindness. The tale concludes with **malakh Y-H-V-H,** a messenger of *Y-H-V-H's* love, telling Abraham *not* to sacrifice Isaac.

As I understand the Baal Shem's radical interpretation of the story, then, Abraham soon recovered from his initial shock and, during the three-day journey to Mount Moriah, the patriarch used his own kabbalistic/shamanic powers to transform *Elohim* into *Y-H-V-H.* By the time Abraham lifted the knife, the elevation that he had catalyzed has been accomplished. He has succeeded in changing the face of *Elohim* to *Y-H-V-H.* The Besht's interpretation highlights an essential aspect of the vocation of the tzaddik: the enlightened one who has the responsibility of transforming suffering into blessing—even if that suffering had been decreed by Heaven.[340]

How did he do it? How did the Besht manage to change *Elohim* into *Y-H-W-H*? It is possible because these two names and the qualities they represent are in actuality two different faces of a single underlying divine force. Even more, evil can be transformed into goodness because both good and evil are part of a single continuum.

The Akedah was the portion of scripture that I read from the scroll of the Torah on the day of my bar mitzvah in 1949. It laid the groundwork for the kind of religious Jew I wanted to become during my adolescence, fully dedicated to God, whatever the consequences. But this sensibility didn't last. I eventually understood that giving myself uncritically to a mythic authority figure was a denial of my own experience and moral judgment. During my student days, I learned that human beings actually wrote the text of the Bible. When I thought about the many narratives in the Torah that reveal God as a magnified man who could act in despicable ways, the Akedah stopped making any sense at all. Yes, there was an interpretation of the story that claimed its real meaning was demonstrated by the ending of story: God does not want human sacrifice. But such a moralistic interpretation seemed to me to be a misreading of the plain meaning of the narrative.

I was both amazed and thrilled when I came across the Baal Shem's interpretation. As a loving and compassionate human being and teacher, he appears to have felt that the original story was morally questionable. After all, Abraham was the father of the Jewish people, a man who supposedly exemplified the most basic ideals of Judaism. In the Kabbalah, Abraham is seen as the primary human representative and channel of God's boundless grace and love. Would such a noble individual agree to sacrifice his beloved child to an arbitrary and willful deity? Of course, the Baal Shem accepted the divine origin of the Torah, and he would never have criticized anything in the scriptures openly, but he also believed in the possibility and duty of reinterpreting ancient texts in humane ways. And through his reading of the Akedah, he turned the story on its head.

I've tried to do this in my life, in various ways, including those detailed in this personal quest with the Besht. I believe that we each carry a rebbe-tzaddik within us. This power is identical with what the Baal Shem identified as the messianic capacity within every individual. It is our responsibility to learn to cultivate and activate this potential in order to bring our bit of healing and renewal to the Jewish people and the world.

CHAPTER TWENTY-ONE

ON SUFFERING AND JOY—
THE BUDDHA AND THE BESHT

*"Every great and deep difficulty bears in itself its own solution.
It forces us to change our thinking in order to find it."*
NIELS BOHR

*"The most authentic thing about us is our capacity to create,
to overcome, to endure, to transform, to love and to be greater
than our suffering."*
BEN OKRI

The question that began to trouble me so deeply during my third or fourth year of seminary was greater than personal affliction. It was concerned with mass suffering, especially the kind foisted on my people and other victims during World War II. Many years later, while studying Buddhism, I discovered that Gautama Buddha had not been interested in this question. Unlike the prophets of the Bible, he did not inveigh against those who caused suffering to others. Nor was he drawn to investigating the metaphysical reasons for the existence of evil, for he was unconcerned with God or gods. His sole interest had to do with illuminating the cause of human suffering, and providing individual seekers with a method for ending it.

According to legend, Siddhartha Gautama was born to a royal family in India during the sixth century before the common era. The young man's father was intent on hiding every manifestation of human misery from his son's awareness, yet Gautama was irresistibly drawn to witness the sorrows of the world and he discovered disease, decrepitude, and death. "Life is subject to aging and death," he declared, "but where is the realm of life in which there is neither aging nor death?"

Was it possible to put an end to suffering? Gautama knew that he could not find an answer to this question if he remained a prince living an opulent aristocratic life, and so one night he left the palace, abandoning his wife and child, never to see them again. There followed six years of wandering and experimenting with the different paths of Hinduism—raja yoga, asceticism, and mystic concentration—but none of these brought him the answers or resolution he was seeking. Finally, we are told, he sat down beneath a peepal tree and made a vow that that he would not move until he found an answer to his quest.

It was a most challenging resolution, filled with temptations that would have dissuaded someone with a weaker will. But after forty-nine days of meditation, something happened that radically altered his identity and destiny. His experience of nirvana opened him to an intuitive vision of the true nature of reality. The boundary between his finite self and the boundless infinite was extinguished. His personal desires dissolved and everything that had restricted his previous life died. Nirvana offered the Buddha the joyous rapture of complete Oneness with reality together with compassion for all of the creatures in the universe.

Following enlightenment, the Buddha gave his first sermon to five monks in the Deer Park in Varanasi. He asked the key question: If nirvana is the true nature of reality, why is it that most people don't experience this? What is it that stands in the way? The answer he gave is known as the first Noble Truth: suffering, *dukkha*. It is our suffering that prevents us from experiencing nirvana. Huston Smith offers a more exacting translation of the term *dukkha:* "Life (in the condition it has gotten itself into) is dislocated. Something has gone wrong. It is out of joint."[341] What is it that's out of joint? Why do people suffer? The second Noble Truth teaches that human suffering arises out of the craving for individual fulfillment, *tanha*. Selfish desire cuts individuals off from the totality of existence.

The third Noble Truth asserts that it is possible to put an end to suffering and to attain enlightenment. But to do so, the seeker must give up selfish craving.

The fourth Noble Truth lays out the path to enlightenment: The practice of eight virtues, the Eightfold Path, would bring freedom from one's suffering: Right Views, Right Intent, Right Speech, Right Conduct, Right Livelihood, Right Effort, Right Mindfulness and Right Concentration (or Meditation).

The Buddha's story deeply stirred me. There was such nobility in his search. I was also taken by his quiet and attentive presence and the equanimity he attained following his awakening. Mostly, though, I was impressed by the way he gave himself totally to his quest, his unremitting drive to find the truth no matter what it would exact of him.

Nonetheless, I didn't concur with all of the Buddha's assumptions about existence or about ending human suffering. It was a time in my life when I was looking for a personal identity that went beyond my allegiance to Judaism and the Jewish people. I was seeking my own independent path to truth. I did feel my life was out of joint, but I didn't believe the notion of *dukkha* was consistent with all of my experience. Life could be joyous as well as sorrowful, and the goal posited by the Buddha to end suffering, the overcoming of *tanha*—the greed, grasping, and the egoistic drive for a separate existence—seemed extreme to me. The most important thing I learned from him at that time was the possibility of personal psychospiritual transformation, and the intentionality and resolve required to bring such change about. This idea wasn't entirely new to me. I simply didn't know how.

My contrary feelings about the Buddha's path were confirmed by Herman Hesse's marvelous novel, *Siddhartha.* The book's protagonist, whose name was also Siddhartha, was a spiritual seeker who spent many years seeking the truth. In the course of the story, he actually meets the Buddha. He tells the master that he recognizes the truth of his path, but will not follow him because, as an individual, he needs to do what the Buddha himself did—seek the truth independently. Siddhartha undergoes many hardships along the way, but each encounter teaches him something absolutely essential for his life. Then, finally, he's taught by a ferryman whose name is Vasudeva, to truly see his entire existence in the river that they are crossing. The Buddha had taught, "Be a light unto yourself; do not give yourselves to any external refuge. Hold fast to the Truth. Do not look for a refuge in anyone besides yourselves." Hesse's spiritual hero honored the Buddha by not following him in person, but by following his example.

THE BUDDHA AND THE BESHT MEET

During the nineties, I co-taught a class in my congregation on Buddhism and Judaism. My partner in this endeavor was the extraordinary Sylvia

Boorstein. Sylvia was an early student of Reb Zalman, but for her there had been something missing in Judaism. Before her encounter with Buddhism, she felt that she "was stuck forever with my worrying, fearful, often sorrowful mind—the victim of whatever events my life had in store for me." She writes that when she heard the Four Noble Truths for the first time, she "shook and quaked" at the news that a liberated mind, a mind at ease in wisdom and filled with compassion, was a possibility. "Long before I had any confidence that I would be able to see clearly, it was thrilling just to know that it was possible for human beings—like the Buddha, who was a human being—to become, through practice, free of suffering." Sylvia summarized the Buddha's teaching in these words: "When we see clearly, we behave impeccably."[342]

In the class we co-taught, Sylvia introduced the Vipassana and Metta forms of Buddhist meditation. Vipassana (also called Insight Meditation) centers on transformation through self-observation. Metta is a method for developing compassion. It was then when I decided to experiment with Buddhist meditation myself. Vipassana gradually taught me how to become aware of the passing phenomena of existence without having to identify with them, and Metta helped me deepen my compassion and love.

As I was writing this chapter, I immersed myself again in the Buddha's teachings. I found his insights to be direct, methodical, demanding, angular. And then, every so often, the words seemed to glow—perhaps an echo of the master's experience of enlightenment. For example:

> However young,
> The seeker who sets out upon the way
> Shines bright over the world.
> But day and night
> The person who is awake
> Shines in the radiance of the spirit.
> Meditate.
> Live purely.
> Be quiet.
> Do your work, with mastery.
> Like the moon,

Come out from behind the clouds!

Shine.[343]

And this teaching on developing loving-kindness: "Put away all hindrances, let your mind full of love pervade one quarter of the world, and so too the second quarter, and so the third, and so the fourth. And thus the whole wide world, above, below, around and everywhere, altogether continue to pervade with love-filled thought, abounding, sublime, beyond measure, free from hatred and ill-will."[344]

My thoughts went back to that time in 1974 when I was immersed in Abraham Joshua Heschel's newly-published portrait of the Baal Shem Tov. There was a moment when it occurred to me that for a Jew living in eighteenth-century Poland to have attained such a high level of inner realization and saintly behavior, he must have undergone some kind of awakening or transformation like that of the Buddha.

THE BESHT AND SUFFERING

When I first looked into *In Praise of the Baal Shem Tov*, I was drawn to the tale told about the birth of the Besht. I discussed this in Part One, but I need to return to it here because it is crucial for an accurate understanding of the Baal Shem's concern with suffering: "Rabbi Eliezer, the future father of Israel Baal Shem Tov, had been exiled from his homeland for many years. Toward the end of that period in his life the prophet Elijah revealed himself and gifted him with a promise: 'Because of the merit of your behavior, a son will be born to you who will bring light to the Jewish people.' With God's help Eliezer arrived home and found his wife still alive. Israel was born to them in their old age, for they were each close to a hundred years old. The boy was weaned, and then the time came for Eliezer to leave this world. He took his son into his arms and said to him, 'I see that I will not enjoy the pleasure of raising you. You will instead light my yahrzeit candle, commemorating my passing each year. My beloved son, I ask you to remember this all your days: God is with you. Do not fear anything.' Now even though Israel was only a little child, because of the intensity and sincerity of their relationship his father's words were fixed in his heart."

A child born of two people, each close to a hundred years old. The boy's father dies, while the mother's disappearance goes completely unmentioned. It is a rather laconic legend; so much seems to be missing. Nonetheless, the central occurrence, that the boy grew up as an orphan, seems to have historical roots. The strangest feature of the tale is that Israel shows no grief at the loss of his parents. Why is this? I believe that another anecdote may reveal a clue toward the answers: "After his father had died, the child grew up, and because the people of the town revered the memory of his father, they tried to take care of him, sending him to study with a teacher. He did very well in his studies, but every few days he would run away from school. The townspeople would find him sitting by himself in the forest and they would bring him back to the town. But this happened again and again and the townspeople finally gave up in despair. They attributed his behavior to his being an orphan and a footloose child."

Could his running away to the forest have had something to do with the loss of his parents? It would have been the norm in virtually any Jewish community for some family to adopt him, but according to this account that didn't happen. Was the boy just too wild, perhaps too angry at the loss of his parents for any family to take him in? The villagers apparently thought so, for they attributed his behavior to his being an orphan and a footloose child.

In Part One, I cited the views of Estelle Frankel, a psychotherapist and scholar of Kabbalah, yet they are so pertinent to this issue that I need to return to her reflections a second time: "While all transitions provide an access point to the sacred realm, the experience of losing a loved one can be a particularly powerful trigger for spiritual wakening. When someone we love disappears, we immediately develop a relationship with the invisible realm. And as we continue to feel connected to someone who is not in the finite world, our connection to the infinite, the God realm, is potentially activated.... For this reason, loss was frequently the gateway to spiritual awakening for the ancient mystics.... Loss seems to have played a significant role in the lives of many great Hasidic masters as well. Many were orphans or had lost a parent at a young age, including the famed Baal Shem Tov, whose mother died in childbirth and whose father passed away when he was five. Like all children who suffer early losses, young Israel must have struggled to overcome feelings of abandonment and loneliness—perhaps even depression."[345]

Now, *In Praise of the Baal Shem Tov* does not mention that the Baal Shem's mother died in childbirth; it's an anecdote that Estelle Frankel must have found in a later Hasidic collection about the master's life. Interestingly, as my wife Diane recently reminded me, according to legend the Buddha's mother died seven days after her son's birth. The Buddha's concern with suffering may have been initiated by this very early traumatic experience. In both Judaism and Buddhism, we are dealing with legendary material, but given what Frankel has to say about the effect that the death of a mother can have on a child's future life, one must take seriously the psychological truth revealed in both stories. And the coincidence of both the Buddha and the Besht having lost their mothers to childbirth is remarkable.

THE ORIGINS OF SUFFERING

The Baal Shem often turned his attention to the problem of suffering and its amelioration. This must have been a quandary for him on a personal level, and his experiences of adversity sensitized him to the issue. His personal wounds may have been the reason why he eventually chose to become a public healer.

He doesn't see suffering as a punishment for sin. Rather, he adopted R. Isaac Luria's view that suffering is a metaphysical flaw that came about during the creation of the world. Before fashioning the universe, God was all in all, but in order to make a place for the universe God had to first withdraw (*tzimtzum*) into Godself. This is where the problem of human affliction had its ultimate origin. As the Baal Shem taught: "In the beginning, God was everywhere, divinity was all in all. But in order to create the universe, God had to withdraw from the whole, limiting the domain of the divine. This contraction occurred throughout the universe, for the Infinite contracted itself so that existence might receive its light. Separation and suffering—without these there would be no universe."

"Separation and suffering—without these there would be no universe." Adversity, then, is part of the very fabric of existence, not to be ended until the era of the messiah. But in Luria's cosmology there was a second tragic act that occurred during the process of creation that made matters even

worse. An unexpected cosmic shattering (*sh'virat ha'kelim*) took place bringing about chaos on a universal level. It was this brokenness that separated the Shekhinah from the blessed Holy One. And yet the Baal Shem Tov was in agreement with Luria that human beings have a potential to heal this cosmic brokenness and to alter the face of existence, for they understand how to bring about cosmic unifications that can restore the wholeness of existence. R. Jacob Joseph writes, "I heard from my teacher, the Baal Shem Tov, that all the tribulations that affect this world come about when the Shekhinah is not united with her Lover. But when such a unification takes place, suffering is sweetened and is transformed into compassion."[346] Notice that suffering is *sweetened,* not ended. The real miracle is that suffering can be transmuted into compassion.

The Zohar is endlessly fascinated by the complex ways in which the universe came into being. Moses de Leon and the kabbalists believed that God's motivation in creating the universe was unbounded compassion and love. Thus, despite the flaws brought about by the divine contraction and the breaking of the vessels, there yet remained, the Besht believed, a consummate beauty and a harmonious balance in the cosmos: "The hiddenness of Divinity is in truth a blessing, for reality is twinned: A creation may exist only by virtue of its opposite. Without evil, there would be no good. Without sadness, no joy. Without God's hiding, there could be no revealing, no creating." Also: *"For I said: A world of love shall be built'* (Psalm 89:3). Why did the Source of love withdraw from creation, allowing harshness and division to dominate the world? Every being lacks something that another can provide. Through giving, we may build a world of love."[347]

The Baal Shem did not criticize Luria's cosmology, but he disagreed with his predecessor in at least one fundamental way. As a student of the writings of Moses Cordovero, he adopted that kabbalist's nondualism, and from a nondual perspective how could it be possible for the universe to exist without the presence of the Divine permeating every moment and every bit of space? After all, divine sparks continue to shine despite their being captives of the husks of brokenness, which obscure their presence. Thus, for the Besht the divine contraction did not bring about the actual absence of God from the universe; it precipitated the *illusion* of God's absence.

Suffering was, in a way, sweetened. According to the first creation story in Genesis, it was the intent of the Creator at the beginning of time to fashion a world of goodness. This is why the story keeps repeating the assertion that what God was fashioning was good. And after the creation of the first human being on the sixth of the primordial days the biblical text reads, *"And Elohim saw everything which he had made, and behold it was all very good"* (Genesis 1:31). For the Baal Shem, that original goodness and love never really disappeared. Neither the divine contraction nor the breaking of the vessels, which together made evil and suffering possible, could obliterate God's original intent. Nor could the sinful acts of human beings destroy what God had brought into being out of pure boundless love. And because of this, evil can never fully prevail. Yet the master goes even further, for if God created everything, God's goodness can be found in everything, *even in evil.*

> This is the counsel that the disciples of the Besht received from their holy teacher: Look deeply at all the things that happen to you, and at all of the occurences that trouble you, and find the source of goodness in them. Search carefully for the root of goodness that is glowing within them. For when you find the divine core that is present, that evil can become a foot stool for goodness. Yes, in this way evil can be transformed into good.[348]

There is a line in Psalm 34 that the Baal Shem often quoted, always reinterpreting its meaning: *"'Turn from evil and do good.'* (Psalm 34:14) Understand the line this way: In order to turn away from evil, do what is good. Which means: Transform evil into good!"[349] He actually developed a three-stage process that he and his disciples would use to sweeten suffering—not to end it, but to take the sting out of it. Rabbi Jacob Joseph writes, "When you know that the Master of the world dwells in everything that is moving in the world, then you will be able to endure whatever happens to you. I know this personally to be true, and I also heard it from my teacher, the Baal Shem Tov: When you are aware that the fullness of the earth is God's glory, and that every motion of your body and each thought in your mind arises from the presence of the Divine, then this very knowing and awareness will rid you of suffering. And this is true even though in many instances the opposite of what you prayed for will occur. But to achieve such an understanding you will need to engage in Yielding, Discernment, and Sweetening."[350]

Yielding, Discernment, and Sweetening. This is the process of ameliorating suffering that the Besht refers to at numerous places in his discourses. Here is how I have come to understand his approach:

1. **Yielding** (*Hach'na'ah*): This means surrendering to and fully accepting the difficult situation that one finds oneself in because it is God who brought it about.
2. **Discernment** (*Hav'da'lah*): Looking deeply into the difficult situation to see where divine goodness is present in it, for when seekers find the divine spark in their suffering they will be able to find meaning and even joy, regardless of the adversity they're experiencing.
3. **Sweetening** (*Ham'ta'kah*): Focusing one's entire attention to the light of the divine spark that one has discovered, and disregarding the pain.

R. Jacob Joseph reported that Rabbi Nachman of Kosov, an important member of the Baal Shem's circle, interpreted this process as a method to discern how to curb one's judgmentalism and arouse one's compassion toward all the people in the world.

Let me share a single example of this process that came out of my personal experience. During the first year of the Covid pandemic in 2020, I found myself focusing all my attention on work and not thinking about what was happening in the world. In retrospect I think that I was unconsciously attempting to put the pandemic out of my awareness because I imagined that staying aware of it might paralyze my mind. But then, as the High Holy Days neared, I began to think about *teshuvah,* turning my awareness to the holy. I saw that my failure to look at what was happening was a form of escapism, and I began to ponder the immense amount of suffering and death that this plague was bringing to people. Yet, in my eighties, and with my own medical problems, I felt helpless to do anything that might actually be beneficial to those who had contracted the disease.

My congregation has a custom of offering workshops on Yom Kippur afternoon to members and others who attend our services. That year, of course, all of these sessions were to be given online over Zoom. I decided to offer a workshop titled "Spiritual Living in a Time of Adversity." To prepare for the offering I sat down with pen and paper and began to look at the current situation from the Baal Shem Tov's point of view. How might I find a way through the difficulties presented by the pandemic? I went through the three steps of the Baal Shem's process. This is on the order of what I wrote and later shared with those who attended the workshop:

1. **Yielding.** Let me admit the truth: Before all this adversity struck my life it was more or less easy for me to bury my head in the sand with regard to the pandemic. Sure, life was rough at times. I am getting old. I have many medical issues. But I don't really have to leave my house for anything. Our food and other necessities are being delivered to our door. I have felt that Diane and I had what we needed to get along in the world. And yes, I've been reading the headlines every day and I see how many people are dying from Covid. I also know the ways that African-Americans are being trampled on in this society; and how President Trump is doing dreadful things to immigrants; and of course there are human-made disasters happening due to climate change. Nonetheless, so far Diane and I have not been touched.

   As I think about all of this, I have to acknowledge that I have been swept up in the maelstrom, and am really in the same boat as everyone else. I'm breathing this rotten air from the West Coast wildfires. My suitcase is packed and sitting near the front door in case we are told to evacuate. And at my age I am highly vulnerable to the virus. Really, this is how it is, perhaps how it's always been for most people in the world: sickness, poverty, conflict, war, natural disasters, death. Ultimately, we're simply not in control of our lives.

2. **Discernment.** How do I make sense of all this? Where is there meaning in all of this chaos? The pandemic is forcing me to further admit my ultimate powerlessness. I live in an imperfect world, and I can't escape my mortality. I may avoid the ravages of the pandemic, but sooner or later I will suffer, and I will die.

God, the Shekhinah, the Lifeforce, the Universe, Existence—whatever name I give it, I'm a part of it for as long as I'm alive. Everything is interconnected; everything is one. And every living organism suffers and dies. But who am I anyway? Covid could get me at any time. That should make it clear to me that this little ego I cherish is not the be all and end all of life. If I can get out of my self-centeredness, if I can accept the limits placed on me by nature or God, and if I'm willing to let go of my attachment to my individual identity, I will suffer a great deal less.

All this is to say that I need to surrender to what is happening in the here and now. I don't mean to give in to it. But I have to become more aware and serious about my spiritual practices which enable me to see that everything is God, to take greater care of my body, and to accept whatever final destiny awaits me now in these last years of my life. And, retired or not, I have to teach the Baal Shem's truths to people in my congregation.

3. **Sweetening.** Daily spiritual practices—what more can I do? I need to look for opportunities to experience some joy every day, and I should focus attention on gratitude for this small life that I've been lent for these few years that I'm alive. After all, what is really important is that the existence of this universe will continue long after I'm gone. And how do I do this? (a) Through the practices that I'm already engaged in—chanting, meditation, affirmations, prayer. (b) Continuing to study the Jewish and universal teachings of the great sages who struggled with issues of suffering and adversity. For me this primarily means studying or writing about the Baal Shem Tov's teachings every day. (c) Cultivating greater perseverance so I don't give in to despondency. (d) Deepening my relationships with family, friends, community—even if this can now happen only over Zoom. (d) Regard my bodily needs as a manifestation of God, and do what it takes to care for my body. (e) Taking my attention off myself, with all of my qvetches, and instead find ways to stand up for people of color, for the poor—whether my efforts succeed or fail. For if I don't stand up against iniquity, I am no longer fully human. And I need to pursue my plan of finding a

way that activists in my congregation can ally ourselves directly with a Palestinian village and in this way contribute to rectifying what my fellow Jews in Israel did to that people. Such an allyship would sweeten the bitterness of the conflict and provide those involved in it with a sense of hope.

FEAR OF DEATH

Those reflections came out of a period of intense inner struggle I went through, beginning in the years before the pandemic. The process started during my eightieth year as I remembered my mother dying on the operating table at age eighty. After many years of relatively good health, my own body began its inexorable decline.

There were months when I was consumed in fear. How will I die? When will I die? And what will become of this person who I now am? Will my "I" continue in some other form? Or will it simply dissolve into the enigma out of which it arose? Of course, there could be no conclusive answers to any of these questions. I knew that when my time would come, I would have to simply let go and enter the unknown. I told myself that perhaps I could look at death as a blessing, saving me from the rank indignities of an increasingly decrepit body. During that time, I used a method of discernment that allowed me to tap into my inner guidance.

At one point I received this directive from what I sometimes call the still, small voice within: "Embrace life fully; embrace death fully." Yes, that seemed completely right; but was I up to the challenge? As I reflected on this question, my thoughts went back to a teaching of the Baal Shem that I had first encountered years earlier, a process for the transformation of fear. I found what I'd written in my computer files and examined it to see if his outlook could aid me in my present plight. Indeed, it offered me a perspective that I found exceedingly valuable.[351]

The Baal Shem spoke about two types of *yirah,* a word that is most often translated as "fear," and sometimes as "awe." He calls the first kind of *yirah* "outer fear," (*yirah hitzonit*). This is the existential fear or terror experienced by all living beings when they undergo extreme pain or face annihilation. How is one to deal with such raw fear? He suggests enlarging one's outlook, beginning to transform one's outer fears into what the Baal Shem calls "inner awe" (*yirah p'ninit*). The master suggests that you step outside of your body and consciousness and attempt to see the issue from a more universal and transcendent perspective. When I am able to do this, I become aware that my small self is only a particular cell in the body of this vast amazing universe. The cycle of my own birth, life, and death is a single instance of a great archetypal phenomenon, for every creation in the cosmos is bound to go through such a process. If I can learn to surrender to the whole of Existence, and accept this process, then I become amazed at the awesomeness of Existence and astonished to be a privileged part of both its joys and even of its suffering for the span of my life.

In my experience the transformation of external fear into inner awe comes about through meditation practice, which enables me to temporarily detach from identification with my body and individualized consciousness, freeing me to recognize that I am one with the fullness of existence itself. At this transpersonal stage, I realize that I don't "own" my fears. They are part of a universal process which the Besht identified as the exile and suffering of the Shekhinah herself.

The final challenge, the Besht tells us, is moving from awe (*yirah*) to love (*ahavah*): "The essence of your spiritual striving is the cultivation of the inner awe of God. Then the love of God will be given to you as a great gift from Heaven."[352] Such love requires that you surrender to the Divine and fully accept the inevitable. In such a state of acceptance you embrace the coming of death as part of existence. It was this call that I heard from my inner guidance: "Embrace life fully; embrace death fully."

This love is the single love that binds all things together. It is love for an existence filled with pain as well as joy. It is a love that tenderly embraces our smaller fearful selves. A love that assures us, "It will be okay; death is no enemy." It would seem that the Baal Shem himself had to face this darkness one last time before his death. Elie Wiesel recounts a series of tales in which the master's spiritual strength was tested to its limits: "Toward the end of his life...he displayed increasing signs of irritation and depression, expressing himself in ways 'defying the laws of language.' He who had worked so hard to make himself understood, no longer succeeded. Faces, words and incidents were forgotten; he was losing touch with his surroundings. He could be seen knocking his head against a tree or following what seemed to be a strange choreography with his body. He

expressed regret at having used his powers; he was no longer himself....
He had lived too fast and had made too many promises that God did not
keep. At the age of sixty he became ill; his insides were tearing him apart.
It was Passover. Deviating from habit he celebrated the Holy Day far from
other people, plunged into silent and uninterrupted meditation."[353]

If these anecdotes about the last phase of the Besht's life are true, it
seems that somehow he was able to transform his confusion and uncertainty into an all-embracing love. In the same passage, this is how Wiesel
describes the master's preparation for death: "Seven weeks later, during
Shavuot, feeling the end approaching, he gave his intimates detailed
instructions for his burial. He requested them to sing at his bedside and
invited a *minyan* for the last service. 'I have two hours to chat with God,'
he said. Seeing tears on the faces of his faithful, he added: 'Why do you
cry? I am leaving by one door only to enter by another.'"

I recently listened to a fascinating interview with the Zen teacher,
Jun Po Denis Kelly Roshi, who was suffering from neuropathy, cancer,
and Parkinson's Disease. During the conversation, Jun Po called attention to a number of points that I also had found in the thought of the Baal
Shem Tov. He spoke of radical self-acceptance. He stated that witnessing
one's dying in an expanded state of consciousness is amazing. And he
said that out of this "your heart breaks open into unconditional love."[354]
This insight dovetails with a view of suffering that psychologist Viktor
Frankl came to while he was incarcerated in Auschwitz: "Everything can
be taken from a man but one thing: the last of human freedoms—to
choose one's attitude in any given set of circumstances, to choose one's
own way." I also know that there is a part of me that will welcome death.
As a respite from this life of incessant motion, from this mind that is continually occupied with its plans and fantasies, from a world pervaded by
so much tumult and sorrow. Death, then, is the true complement of life.

Does this wider awareness take away the existential fear of dying?
Not completely. There are moments when I can still feel lost in dread,
and these can be quite terrifying. I wake up in the middle of the night
unable to fall back to sleep because of an intestinal ailment. I desperately
want the problem to go away, but it doesn't. There is nothing I can do. I
know that I must yield to this discomfort, sense that it is also God's presence, accept its heavy burden. Can I do this now, once again? I must. But I

also have to embrace my resistance, for it too is human, and divine. Thus, it seems that if everything is divine, not only death but the resistance to entering death's gates must be Divine. I'm not alone in this. Most living organisms struggle against death. At those times I feel my fear as deeply as I can and then take a step back and view the whole panorama with my eyes focused on eternity.

R. Jacob Joseph reported that he heard from the Baal Shem that a man once came to him complaining of suffering.

> "Accept whatever happens to you in this world with love," counselled the Baal Shem Tov, "and you will have life both here and in the world to come." "That's not really in my power," the man replied, "for it is God who gives a person the ability to accept everything that happens to him in love." "Yes, that is certainly true, and I pray that you will be able to do this," replied the Besht.[355]

What does it mean to accept suffering in love? My understanding of this is that there are two ways to react to suffering. We can whine over it, or we can fully accept it. Whining can lead to bitterness and dejection, while acceptance can steer us toward gratitude. How so? Acceptance comes from recognizing the gifts we have been given throughout our lives from family, friends, and the world around us, and especially the gift of life itself that comes from the source of all life. The Besht knew how difficult and counterintuitive his advice was, and that those who were suffering could only do this with help from beyond. I find comfort in this, for I cannot say that I myself can choose to accept suffering in love. And it's certainly unwise to squelch our human feelings in the face of adversity; I believe that there is Divinity present in our painful emotions. I must live with paradox, with both of these perspectives simultaneously, both grieving my suffering and learning to accept it.

The Besht's teachings about fear have become a great boon to me. I cannot alter the process of aging. I cannot rid myself of my medical issues. I cannot avoid death. Yet I still have the ability to choose my attitude toward the fears that sometimes ambush me. I don't have to be a victim.

THE FIVE CERTAINTIES

Like the prophet Second Isaiah, the Baal Shem asserted that God was the ultimate source of suffering. After all, had not God himself declared: *"I am Y-H-V-H, the EverPresent, and there is none else, forming light and creating darkness, making harmony* (shalom) *and creating chaos* (rah). *I do all of these"* (45:6-7)? Y-H-V-H is the coming together of all opposites, including good and evil, suffering and healing. As the Besht taught, "Because the Shekhinah encompasses all the worlds, everything that has been created, whether good or evil, is part of a single reality. The Shekhinah is the true Unity."[356] The Talmud asserts that the world was created through the Hebrew letter *hey,* which means five (*Menahot* 29b). But the Baal Shem noticed that the text didn't identify what those five things were. In his interpretation, he outlines what seem to be five certainties which he believed were woven into the very fabric of existence:

- *Tza'ar,* Suffering;
- *Kabbalat tza'ar,* Acceptance of suffering;
- *Tefillah,* Prayer;
- *Ye'shuah,* Liberation;
- *Ho'da'yah,* Thanksgiving.[357]

The entire teaching from which this comes is extensive, but strangely the Baal Shem says virtually nothing about the actual meaning of these five certainties, nor the reason he listed them in this order. Perhaps he shared these details with his disciples and they were so obvious to those that heard them that they felt they didn't have to record them. At any rate, all we have is what he taught about how each of the certainties is linked to particular sefirot on the Tree of Life.

What could the underlying meaning of this teaching be? This is my educated guess. The five certainties appear to be arranged in a particular progression, delineating an ascending spiritual process that an individual can go through to ameliorate suffering. Studying the full text, it seems that the Besht was suggesting a step-by-step process for the transformation of suffering. One must:

- Yield to and accept the adversity being experienced in a state of awe.

- Engage in a form of prayer that establishes connections through compassionately uniting all extremes into a unity, and in this way elevate your consciousness beyond the anguish into a more spacious realm.
- In that expanded state, experience the liberation that sweetens suffering.
- And this finally leads to an acknowledgment of thankfulness for the goodness of life, despite all of the difficulties one encounters.

Returning to one's ordinary life the seeker brings a wider perspective on the suffering they have been experiencing. This points toward the stages of a process that the Besht believed an individual had to undergo in order to attain enlightenment, which means becoming fully aware of the Divine permeating everything: "God's reign embraces *everything*. Yes, the Divine is present even where potent evil exists, and even where the demonic seems to rule, as it is written, "You enliven *all* things." For what appears to be evil is merely a shell. Crack the shell open and you find the spark of light within. If you grasp this truth, you will no longer fear suffering, for you will know that the light of goodness dwells at its core."[358]

The Baal Shem promised his disciples and colleagues that engaging in such a process would give them the insight and courage to carry on despite their suffering: "When you know that the Master of the world dwells within every movement that occurs in the world, you can endure all things."[359] In like manner, the Christian theologian Dorothee Soelle writes that God can be found in the darkness, and even though suffering cannot be totally overcome, it can be moved through.

I believe that the Besht's teaching about the five certainties alludes to an encounter he underwent that may have been something like the kind of awakening the Buddha experienced under the peepal tree. For the Baal Shem the experience of cosmic No-thing-ness obliterated good and evil as opposites in a final realization of the nature of reality as total goodness. The Buddha attained nirvana through intense prolonged meditation. The Baal Shem reached *Ayin,* the state of No-thing-ness, through his ecstatic devotion. This process began with the vocal sounding the Hebrew letters and words of the liturgy with immense surrender and intensity. The Baal Shem put it this way: "Entreat the letters of prayer by uniting with the divine light at their core. Then pray from that place so that you will be able to sound them with a true intentionality for their own sake. In this way the suffering will be sweetened at its very roots."[360]

ALLEVIATING SUFFERING IN THE MOMENT

Also from the Baal Shem's teachings, I have developed a way of dealing with the inevitable forms of adversity that occur in daily life. It might be mild irritability or physical pain, or it could be anxiety or melancholy, inner conflict or doubts, or worry about a difficult decision that has to be made. Or a feeling of being overwhelmed by work, or by life itself. Whatever it is that might bring on the difficulty, I have neither the time, energy, or patience at the moment to attempt to sweeten the suffering by going through the Besht's entire three-stage discernment process. The master himself was aware of this predicament: "At the moment you find yourself experiencing suffering remember and affirm that whatever is happening to you is being energized by the Lifeforce of the EverPresent, and that this Lifeforce is entirely good." He further taught: "Know and hold to the faith that the blessed Presence fills the whole earth with divine splendor, and is found in each and every movement and thought. If you can remember this truth, then *'all the workers of evil will be scattered'* as the psalmist has written, and you will no longer be overcome by fear. This is the true meaning of the words, *'Know the God of your ancestors'*" (1 Chronicles 28:9).[361]

I have found that remembering and affirming is not enough. I have to yield and surrender to what is happening out of love for the life I have been granted. I do this by simply breathing in and then breathing out the divine name, "Yah." And with each exhalation, letting myself go a little more into God, recognizing that everything is part of the Oneness, and sensing my gratitude for the life I've been given. If I can, I close my eyes while engaging in this practice. In addition, I affirm my ability to withstand whatever is happening, and not to fall back into feeling like I'm a victim. This is the method, and I have found that it works a lot of the time, but remembering to do it has not always been easy, and mustering the energy it requires to make the practice work can be a real challenge. The actual pain may not go away, but the suffering is usually ameliorated.

Rabbi Shefa Gold calls this process, "Enlarging the Context," which she sees as "opening to the Soul-perspective, knowing and experiencing the physical universe as a thin sliver of the larger Reality, and resting into what I call the widest embrace. When I enlarge the context, I face all the same challenges of the world, but I am not overwhelmed by them, because they exist in a vast framework. The moment I lose my reactivity and sense of overwhelm, a new calm, clarity emerges. When I lean into and feel held by the wide embrace, I relax all of my egoic struggles and I am suddenly connected to the flow of immeasurable resources of love and wisdom."[362]

When I connect my awareness with the Divine, I am expanding my consciousness, giving the pain a larger frame, linking it to the natural processes of the unfolding of life, while at the same time adopting a posture of acceptance of whatever is happening to me. I come to see myself as a tiny part of the vast universe, and my ego-consciousness with its suffering most often opens into that larger awareness. This is yet another practice with an analogue in Buddhism, as the Dalai Lama explains: "For every event in life, there are many different angles. When you look at the same event from a wider perspective, your sense of worry and anxiety reduces, and you have greater joy."[363]

WHEN SUFFERING CAN'T BE SWEETENED

Like the author of the Genesis creation story, the ancient Greek philosopher, Heraclitus, affirmed the fundamental goodness of existence. "To humans," he wrote, "some things are good and some are bad. But to God all things are good and beautiful and just." Perhaps it was the Baal Shem's conviction of the truth of this notion that provided him with the power to convey a new kind of hope to his disciples, who in turn brought it to their communities. This legacy of faith was manifest even during the Holocaust. Elie Wiesel writes that "What cannot help but astound us is that Hasidim remained Hasidim inside the ghetto walls, inside the death camps. In the shadow of the executioner, they celebrated life." On the train taking Wiesel to a concentration camp, he witnessed Hasidim dancing in the boxcars as they were ushering in the holy day of Simchat Torah.[364] Still, I find it difficult if not impossible to believe that goodness really lives at the heart of existence and can be found in every form of suffering. There are just too many people who go to their deaths in agony, their only redemption being death itself. Nor do I believe that all suffering can be sweetened. I could name instance after instance of events in human history when people were swallowed by despair or massacred without pity. What stands out sharply in my memory at this moment are the showers in the Nazi concentration camps that poured death on hundreds of unknowing victims at a time. Fully half of the six million Jewish victims of the Shoah were Polish Jews; a large number were Hasidim and their rebbes. An entire civilization obliterated in a few short years. And now the world is facing a form of universal annihilation—the possibilities of global climate catastrophe and nuclear war.

The Baal Shem believed it was the duty of a tzaddik to embody goodness in the face of evil. When antisemites stalked the Jewish community, he didn't ruminate on how the destructive effects of their attacks could be sweetened; he gathered his strength and drew on all his shamanic powers in an attempt to halt its dark advance. Sometimes he succeeded; at other times he admitted that he failed. I also recall Wiesel's description of the Besht, approaching death: "He could be seen knocking his head against a tree or following what seemed to be a strange choreography with his body. He expressed regret at having used his powers; he was no longer himself." Even the most spiritually astute human beings must sometimes face situations over which they have no control. At times like these, they can only recognize the fact that human beings are ultimately powerless in the face of mystery.

It is because of this that I have had to reinterpret the Baal Shem's approach to dealing with adversity in a radical way, redefining it as a process akin to what contemporary psychologists call "cognitive reframing" or "positive reappraisal." For me, the Besht's second step, discernment, is not necessarily about finding the goodness hidden within one's adversity, as much as it is a way to make use of our own innate meaning-making powers to actually transform negative situations into something positive. And where do our meaning-making powers come from if not our souls, which are sparks of Divinity?

The example I gave earlier in connection with the Covid pandemic is a case in point. I believe that it is possible to reframe many, but not all of the challenging events of our lives in ways that can transmute absurdity into meaning. I know, though, that there is a dimension of reality in which goodness is revealed to be absolutely true and fully present. I often enter its presence during my morning spiritual practice as I ascend onto a more expansive rung of consciousness. Once there, all the issues and obstacles that I usually have to cope with simply dissolve, and everything becomes One. I am learning to carry the energy of those experiences with me as I start my day.

The Baal Shem, like the kabbalists before him, recognized the limitations of the human mind. He taught that we have the ability to touch into *Ayin,* the No-thingness that is Everything, evil as well as goodness and everything in between. But beyond that we are left with *Ein Sof,* the absence of anything that we might recognize as having existence, the mystery of mysteries that has no end out of which everything was created. All we can do in the end is to surrender to that great enigma.

LIVING IN JOY

Polish Jews in the eighteenth century had to deal not only with the natural infirmities of life, but also with plagues. And not only did they encounter antisemitism on a regular basis, they were steeped in the traumas of the immediate as well as the longtime past. Inspired by his ecstatic devotion, the Baal Shem Tov was able to begin to shape a very different form of Jewish living. If God is fully present in every moment, and if pain and sorrow could be spiritually transformed into joy, then it became possible to experience daily living in an extraordinary way, filled with wonderment and exaltation. As Heschel put it: "The Baal Shem proclaimed joy to be the very heart of religious living, the essence of faith, greater than all other religious virtues. He and his disciples banished melancholy from the soul 'and uncovered the ineffable delight of being a Jew.' God is not only the creator of earth and heaven. He is also the One 'who created delight and joy.'"[365]

For the Baal Shem, joy (*simhah*) was not the mere enjoyment of life on the physical plane, nor was it "getting high," for such states only make the ego-self feel good for a limited time. Sacred joy asks the seeker to open his or her heart to the vast realm of the spirit. The problems and irritations of physical existence melt in the recognition of the overpowering truth of the marvelous nature of existence.

There is a tale in *In Praise of the Baal Shem Tov* that reveals not only his joy, but his sense of humor:

> Once on Simchat Torah the Besht's disciples were at his home, and they were extremely happy—dancing and drinking a great deal of wine from his cellar. The Besht's wife saw that the Hasidim were consuming all of the wine they had in storage, and she worried that there wouldn't be any left for Kiddush or Havdalah—the ceremonies that inaugurate and end the Sabbath.
>
> The Besht had already retired to his study when his wife rushed in and told him what was happening. "Tell them to stop drinking, Israel, please..." she pleaded.
>
> The Besht laughed. "You're right. Go tell them that I said they should stop and go home."
>
> When she returned to the main room, the Hasidim were dancing in a circle, and she was amazed to see a fire blazing around them like a canopy. She took all the empty pitchers, went down to the cellar, and brought up all the wine that was there.
>
> A while later the Besht still heard singing and dancing and he asked his wife, "Well, did you tell them to leave?" She replied, "You should have told them yourself."[366]

Such ecstasy and joyousness were at the heart of the celebration of the Sabbath and many of the Jewish holy days, but this ideal of exaltation was also meant to affect the ways in which the early Hasidim lived during the ordinary days of the week. For even though the Baal Shem urged people to carry out the mitzvot—the divine directives of the Torah—with joy, such exuberance should characterize everything we do—eating, drinking, lovemaking, engaging in business, because this is the best possible way of serving God.

The traditions regarding his capacity for sacred joy are legion. There were many Hasidic masters who believed that his teachings on joy were among the most precious gifts. Reb Arele Roth, for instance, the twentieth-century rebbe of the Shomrei Emunim Hasidic community of B'nai Brak, wrote that the Baal Shem Tov revealed the primacy of joy. Before the Baal Shem's time, Reb Arele taught, an individual who wished to serve God in joy would experience guilt and sadness because Satan would make him feel that his desire for joy was a great transgression. But the Besht revealed that the desire for joy was not sinful. On the contrary, it is through joy that one can truly turn to God. Hasidic tradition asserts that the Baal Shem introduced sacred song and dance as communal forms of joyous spiritual practice. He and his followers borrowed secular songs from the Polish peasants and they may have borrowed Polish modes of dancing as well. Such song and dance drew people to the spirit, but they could also be expressions of the soul intoxicated with holiness.

There are even teachings ascribed to the Besht which state without qualification that people must live in a state of joy at all times. Some of these assertions make it seem as if sadness and melancholy are actually sins: "It is essential to always be happy. Such happiness is part of the experience of devekut with the Divine. Without joy it is impossible to be continually attached to God."[367]

In another teaching, the Baal Shem speaks about the connection between joy, love, and pleasure:

> It is the purpose and the true meaning of my pilgrimage
> on earth to show my comrades by my own example how
> one may serve God through pleasure and rejoicing. And
> one who is filled with joy is also filled with love for peo-
> ple and for all fellow creatures.[368]

Jungian psychologist Verena Kast surrounds such teachings by writing movingly on the subject of joy and its relationship to love: "Joy moves us upward and outward, toward ecstasy, toward others. It opens us, leads us to give things away, bonds us with others, suspends gravity, inspires us to sing and make friends.... Joy and love can, of course, complement and intensify each other.... When joy is present, affiliation takes the place of backbiting, and paranoia disappears.... Joy is inclined toward transcendence, transcendence of present relationships and of the world's resistance. Every movement connected with joy, even a quiet joy, is an elevating movement, relieving us of our normal weightiness, causing us to rise up and see matters from another perspective."[369] Discovering and pursuing this link—between joy, love, and compassion in daily life—is at the heart of what it means to be a student of the Baal Shem.

PART THREE

EXCAVATING THE BAAL SHEM'S
LEGACY

CHAPTER TWENTY-TWO

MARTIN BUBER'S DISCOVERY

Martin Buber was a Renaissance man: philosopher, scholar, theologian, cultural anthropologist, Bible translator, and social critic. If the Baal Shem Tov and Hasidism are at all known in the Western world, it is because of Buber's groundbreaking work through his translations and lectures. What was it that brought this Austrian, who identified as a Polish Jew, and had once imagined that he had abandoned Judaism, into the heart of a spiritual movement scorned by modern, Western Jews?

As a small child, Buber's father or grandfather would sometimes take the boy to a small Hasidic synagogue for worship on the Sabbath, and it was there that he had his first encounter with a rebbe. He later wrote what he remembered from those experiences: "The palace of the *rebbe*, in its showy splendor, repelled me. The prayer house of the Hasidim with its enraptured worshippers seemed strange to me. But when I saw the *rebbe* striding through the rows of the waiting, I felt, 'leader,' and when I saw the Hasidim dance with the Torah, I felt 'community.' At that time there rose in me a presentiment of the fact that common reverence and common joy of soul are the foundations of genuine human community."[370]

During his late adolescence, while attending university in Germany, Buber suffered a major spiritual crisis. He found himself restless and confused. He didn't feel rooted in Judaism, humanity, or the Divine. His disorientation was so serious that it led him to contemplate suicide. Instead, he turned to modern thinkers like Immanuel Kant and Friedrich Nietzsche, who inspired him to take up the study of philosophy. It was only later that he became involved in Zionism, then Hasidism, both of which—especially Hasidism—brought him back to a profound connection with his Jewish heritage.

Buber credits a small Hebrew book of teachings, *The Testament of Rabbi Baal Shem Tov,* for setting him on a path toward spiritual meaning. One day, while studying the book, a particular passage leapt out at him:

Embrace the quality of fervor. Rise from sleep with fervor, and you will become a radically different person, capable of giving birth just as God gave birth to worlds. Perform each act with fervor, and each of your deeds will become a path to serving the One.[371]

Buber wrote that reading this passage instantaneously opened him to the realization that through his *own devotion* and his *own deeds* he would be able to unite the divided powers of his soul and create something new that never existed before. By taking personal responsibility for his life, he writes, he would be able to embody the creative power of the Divine. He experienced the Baal Shem's teaching as a joyous summons. The experience also opened him to the Hasidic soul, that which was "primally Jewish," and which was at the same time "a primal human reality, the content of human religiousness."[372]

As crucial as that encounter was, even more essential was the spiritual breakthrough that began for Buber before World War I and lasted over eight years (1912-19). He characterized this inner revolution as a great experience of faith. Maurice Friedman, in his biography of Buber, writes that what happened to Buber was "something that transcended all experience and seized him whole, transporting him in *all* his being, his capacity for thought and reason included. The very validity of this religious totality is witnessed by the fact that nothing separate was given to Buber, that he received no message that he might transmit.... As he was to say in *I and Thou,* what he received was not a specific 'content' but a Presence, a Presence as power.... The only description that Buber could give of these experiences of being that converged into a single great experience of faith was just a pointing to this ineffable wholeness that transported him in such a way that, all the doors springing open, the storm blew through all the chambers of his being."[373] This was one of the crucial breakthroughs that became the foundation for Buber's lectures on "Religion as Presence," given in 1922. In those discourses Buber redefined religion in a radical way. In the first lecture he stated that religion is not the remembrance of something sacred from the past, nor is it the hope for a perfected future. Rather, it is the "lived presence" of the Divine in the here and now, as a presence that can never become past.

He came to realize that the reality of God cannot be found in the recorded events of the past, or in some imagined and hoped-for future. Nor can genuine religion be reduced to a set of doctrines, or to the contents of traditional texts or inherited rituals or ethical teachings. Authentic religiosity—what we today would call spirituality—centers around God, and God has a real presence that transcends human consciousness/experience when one is aware of and present to the preciousness and sacredness of each moment. Buber added that this understanding of the truth of the religious life means that all people at all times can share in the truths of authentic religiosity, whether they are adherents of a particular religion or not. Buber credited this understanding of Divine Presence, in part, to the lives and wisdom of two Jewish teachers, the Baal Shem Tov and Jesus of Nazareth.

He may have accentuated the importance of the present moment because of the increased pace of events and myriad concerns that increasingly occupied people in the twentieth century. Lost in the swirl of occurrences, the uniqueness of the particular moment had vanished. What would happen if an individual could just let the calendar and clock go and be fully present? Through such peaceful centering one might truly experience the sacred.

Earlier in his life, in the 1890s, Buber became interested in Eastern religion, and had been especially drawn to Taoism and Zen. The Taoist notion *wu wei,* which he greatly admired, refers to the cultivation of a state of being in which human actions exist effortlessly in alignment with the ebb and flow of elemental cycles of the natural world. *Wu wei* is characterized by ease and awareness; without even trying the individual is able to respond perfectly to whatever situations arise. I assume that Buber's high regard for *wu wei* contributed to his notion of religion as presence.

I and Thou, his landmark work of religious philosophy, was composed soon after he delivered his lectures on "Religion as Presence." In that book Buber grounded his experience of the immediate presence of "the Eternal Thou" in what he called the "I-Thou" (or "I-You") encounter. When two individuals meet, engaging one another in an openhearted and mutual way, something inexpressible arises between them. Two poles of being become linked into a single present, a single presence.

(In German, the word *geganwart* can be translated either as "present" or "presence.") It is in and through this present moment that the Divine becomes present as the "Eternal Thou." Between his lectures on "Religion as Presence" and the writing of *I and Thou* Buber came to realize that the perception of Presence is not merely something that can happen to an individual. The Presence, he attested, is something objective and eternal that appears *between* an I and a Thou.

THE BAAL SHEM TOV AS A LIVING TORAH

Buber later brought this understanding to his portrayal of the Baal Shem. In *The Origin and Meaning of Hasidism* he wrote that the Besht evoked the sense of Presence in his students, affecting them through his own presence and presentness, rather than through formal teaching. Most important was the way in which the Baal Shem interacted with people, how he demonstrated the way to goodness, how he prayed, and how he led people to a living connection with the Divine. Buber wrote that "the Baal-Shem belongs to those central figures of the history of religion whose effect on others has arisen through the fact that they lived in a certain way. These men did not proceed from a teaching, but moved to a teaching, in such a way that their life worked as a teaching, as a teaching not yet grasped in words."[374] It was in this way that the Baal Shem Tov became, as it were, a living Torah, for the disciples experienced him not merely as a teacher but as a living and embodied *teaching*. He modeled what it was to be a tzaddik, "the man who leads the community in place of God, the man who mediates between God and the community."[375]

Buber explained that the Baal Shem did not teach about the higher planes of reality and how to transcend this lowly world. Rather, he offered people help in making their daily or everyday lives holy. Connected to the reality of existence in its fullness, the Besht was able to inspire others to live in the fullness of existence. One of my very favorite passages of Buber's—a teaching that I have returned to again and again—describes how the path forged by the Baal Shem Tov made everyday existence holy through the spiritual practice of intentionality:

> One may and should live genuinely with all, but one
> should live with it in intentional holiness; one should

make holy all that one does in one's natural life. No renunciation is commanded. One eats in intentional holiness, one savors the taste of food in intentional holiness, and the table becomes an altar. One works in intentional holiness and lifts the sparks that are hidden in all tools. One walks over the fields in intentional holiness, and the silent songs of all creatures, those they speak to God, enter into the song of one's own soul. One drinks to one's companions in intentional holiness, each to the other, and it is as if one studied together with them in the Torah. One dances in intentional holiness, and a splendor radiates over the community. A husband is united with his wife in intentional holiness, and the Shekhina rests over them.[376]

Still, although I admire the way Buber understood this teaching, it will be clear that he was incorrect regarding the master's relationship with transcendence and the higher planes of reality. As we have already seen, the Besht practiced a form of mystical ascent that took him beyond the confines of the existential world to an ecstatic state of awareness in which his ego dissolved into the totality of being.

BUBER AND JESUS

For Buber, Jesus' presence and teaching paralleled that of the Baal Shem. Throughout his adult life Buber was profoundly interested in Jesus, seeing him as a kind of precursor of the Baal Shem. Both teachers, Buber declared, sought to renew Judaism with a focus on moral deeds against the rigidity of the law and the emphasis on correct ritual performance. And like the Besht, Jesus found eternity not in a spirit that transcended this world, but in concrete moments: "For the actuality of the faith of Biblical and post-Biblical Judaism and also for the Jesus of the Sermon on the Mount, fulfillment of the Torah means to extend the hearing of the Word to the whole dimension of human existence."[377] I have long been moved by Buber's confession of his personal relationship with Jesus: "From my youth onwards I have found in Jesus my great brother.... My own fraternally open relationship with him has grown ever stronger and clearer, and today I see him more strongly and clearly than ever before. I am ever more certain that a great place belongs to him in Israel's history of faith and that this place cannot be described by any of the usual categories."[378]

In an illuminating article, Shaul Magid, a contemporary scholar of Hasidism, writes that "Buber fashioned Jesus as the quintessential 'religious anarchist' and as a precursor to the Baal Shem Tov, whom he regarded as the great rebel of Jewish modernity who pushed aside the normative conventions of Judaism to make way for its spiritual renewal."[379] As moved as I have been by Buber's insight into Jesus and the Besht as conduits of Divine Presence, however, I'm unconvinced that either of these teachers sought to decenter the principles or practices of the Judaism they inherited. What they were seeking, in my view, was the radical renewal of their religion through the heightening of personal devotion and intentionality. Nor do I believe that the Baal Shem would have limited the presence of Divinity to what is occurring now, for in his understanding the Shekhinah embraced *everything* that can be perceived by human beings. This would have included past and future events as well as what was occurring in the moment. Whatever is happening now is uniquely alive and real in the awareness of the one experiencing it, yet this moment is always born out of what came before, and pregnant with the moment that is emerging.

I first became aware of the issue of being awake to the present moment through teachings of Ram Dass. His *Be Here Now* became a sensation in the counter-culture in the 1970s. Ram Dass got the idea for the title of the book in India from Bhagwan Dass, who was taking him to meet the man who would become his guru, Neem Karoli Baba. "I would say to Bhagavan Dass something like, 'How long do you think we are going to be on the road?' and he would say 'Don't worry about the future, just live now.' So we would be silent for a while, sleeping on our wooden beds and I would say, 'Gee, this sure is strange in relation to the past. You know when I used to...' and then he would say, 'Just be here now.'"

Buber's life story is packed with the testimonies of people who acknowledged the sense of presence that Buber emanated. My own bar mitzvah teacher, Milton Bendiner, was one of them. Milton—who later became a lifelong mentor and friend—once told me that the most memorable experience of his life was the hour he spent with Buber in Jerusalem. Like Buber, Milton exuded a forceful presence, influencing the formation and futures of countless students, many of whom became rabbis. His influence was not limited to Temple Beth El in San Antonio, where he served as educational director, for he also taught existential philosophy in universities and Christian seminaries. For me, his presence was the primary gateway to a life that valued the intellect but was centered on the importance of the spirit.

TEACHERS OF PRESENCE

In his celebrated book, *The Quest for the Historical Jesus,* Albert Schweitzer (1875-1965) argued that Jesus believed he was the messiah, and he expected that God would intervene in history and bring about the apocalypse. This supernatural act would end not only the domineering rule of Rome, but the entire dreadful world of history as human beings had known it. In its place God would inaugurate the eternal kingdom of God. It was in preparation for the final day of reckoning that Jesus believed would soon come that he sought to get his people to repent. Of course, the expected end didn't occur, and Jesus himself bore the suffering that was destined to sweep over the Jewish people and the world. Schweitzer's reading of the message of the Gospels has been accepted by a large number of historians. Yet since his time there have been many also who have disagreed, believing that Jesus taught something quite the opposite of apocalypse—that God's kingdom was already mysteriously present and available to those who are willing to enter it. When Jesus spoke about the kingdom, these scholars assert, he was not referring to a political insurgency but to a revolution in *consciousness.* Jesus believed that through his own deeds and words he was ushering in the kingdom, making it possible to experience God's presence inwardly despite the constrictions of the outer world.[380]

I am not qualified to take a position on this issue, but I resonate with this second understanding of God's kingdom. It seems that these contemporary scholars have come close to Buber's perception of the spiritual gifts that Jesus—and later the Baal Shem Tov—brought to the

Jewish people. In *The Gospel According to Jesus,* Stephen Mitchell restates in his own way and with great clarity the fundamental reality that Buber had earlier recognized:

> Like all the great spiritual Masters, Jesus taught one thing only: presence. Ultimate reality, the luminous, compassionate intelligence of the universe, is not some-where else, in some heaven light-years away. It didn't manifest itself any more fully to Abraham or Moses than to us, nor will it be any more present to some Messiah at the end of time. It is always right here, right now. That is what the Bible means when it says that God's true name is *I am*.... Jesus speaks in harmony with the supreme teachings of all the great religions: the Upanishads, the Tao Te Ching, the Buddhist sutras, the Zen and Sufi and Hasidic masters. I don't mean that all these teachings say exactly the same thing. There are many different resonances, emphases, skillful means. But when words arise from the deepest kind of spiritual experience, from a heart pure of doctrines and beliefs, they transcend reli-gious boundaries, and can speak to all people, male and female, bond and free, Greek and Jew.[381]

Mitchell's words about Jesus mirror those of Arthur Green, writing about the founder of Hasidism: "The Baal Shem Tov offered a clear per-ception of the divine presence in the most immediate here-and-now. He claimed that experience of this palpable presence was available not only to him, but to anyone who learned to open his inner eye. He read an array of texts, Biblical, rabbinic, and kabbalistic—indeed we may say he read all of Judaism—as an invitation to such experience. He sought to wave away any obstacles, including demands of learning, ascetic prac-tice, and especially guilt or brooding over sins, that would keep one from this transforming religious moment."[382] If we assume that the views of these two scholars are historically accurate, then both the Baal Shem and Jesus made the teaching of Divine Presence a reality through their char-ismatic presences, and even after their deaths the memories of their lives and deeds remained vivid, making it possible for devoted followers to re-experience the presence of the Divine in the here and now.

Like Jesus, the Baal Shem Tov remained alive in the hearts and souls of his followers. "More than any other Jewish historical figure," declares Elie Wiesel, "with the exception of the Prophet Elijah, the Besht was present in joy as well as in despair; every *stibel* (Hasidic synagogue) reflected his light, his warmth. Every Hasid had two Masters: his own and the Baal Shem—each drew his strength from the other. The first was needed to live, the second to believe."[383]

PRESENT TO HIS DISCIPLES

To ground the notion that the Baal Shem Tov lived his life in relation to his disciples, I would like to share a tale about the first meeting between the master and the man who would become his chief disciple, Rabbi Dov Baer, the Great Maggid of Medziritich. I first read the story of their encounter in Buber's *Tales of the Hasidim*. Here is my own rendition of that fateful meeting:

> Rabbi Dov Baer was an astute and perceptive scholar, equally at home in the intricacies of the Talmud and the depths of the Kabbalah. He had heard a good deal about the Baal Shem Tov, and he finally decided to go to see him in person to determine for himself whether the man's wisdom really justified his reputation.
>
> When he arrived at the Baal Shem's home, Dov Baer stood before the master and greeted him. Then he immediately stated his business. "I have heard a great deal about you, sir. Can you share some of your wisdom with me?"
>
> The Baal Shem sat in silence considering Dov Baer's question. Then, in a quiet voice, he said, "Once my coachman was driving me through a wilderness. The journey took many days, and we ran out of food. I was feeling quite bad for my coachman. But just at that moment a peasant happened to come along and he sold us some

bread." There was a moment of silence, and then the Baal Shem simply said goodnight to his guest.

Dov Baer left the master's house completely bewildered. Such a simple and meaningless story! Nonetheless, he decided to give it another try, and the following evening he returned to the Besht's home. The master welcomed him, and once again the visitor asked to hear some of his wisdom. Once again, the Besht sat in silence. And then he told another story. "It once happened that I was travelling on the road for number of days and I had no hay for my horses. But a farmer came along and fed the animals." And then the Baal Shem said goodnight to the visitor.

Dov Baer was now thoroughly baffled. He concluded that there was nothing to this man, and he determined to go back to his home immediately. Returning to the inn where he had been staying, he ordered his servant to prepare the coach and horses for their journey. "I see that the sky is now cloudy," he told the man, "but as soon as the moon appears we will leave." Around midnight the sky became clear and the Maggid entered the coach. But just as they were about to depart, a messenger came from the Baal Shem Tov. "Rabbi Dov Baer," he announced, "my master, Rabbi Israel Baal Shem Tov, asks that you to come to his house without delay." The Maggid went at once.

The Baal Shem took him to his study.

"How well do you know Kabbalah?" the Besht asked the preacher.

"I am well versed in the mystical teachings," answered the Maggid.

The Baal Shem picked up a book of Lurianic teachings, The Tree of Life, and placed it in front of the Maggid. "Now open it to any page and read aloud." Dov Baer did as he was told. The section had to do with the nature of angels.

"Now take some time and consider what you read." Several minutes passed in silence. "Can you tell me what the passage means?" asked the Besht. The Maggid explained the meaning of the text in detail.

"You have no true knowledge of Kabbalah!" said the Besht sharply, "Stand up!" The Maggid arose. The Baal Shem took the book and stood before the Maggid and with great fervor intoned the passage in a piercing voice as a kind of incantation. Suddenly the entire room went up in flame, and through the blaze the Maggid heard the rush of angels. And then he lost consciousness.

Sometime later he awoke and again found himself facing the Baal Shem Tov. "You explained the meaning of the text correctly, but you have no true knowledge, because in what you know there is no soul." And then in silence he accompanied the Maggid to the door.

Rabbi Dov Baer returned to the inn, and bade his servant to go home. He stayed in Medziritch with the Baal Shem Tov.[384]

What happens in this tale? We know that Dov Baer was a scholar with a broad knowledge of Jewish tradition. But like so many of the rabbis during that period, he was filled with pride regarding his intellectual attainments. He comes to the Besht out of a sense of curiosity mixed with skepticism. As the Baal Shem listens to Dov Baer's question, he recognizes the man's arrogance, but also senses his latent spiritual potential. He knows there is no way he will be able to break through his future disciple's haughtiness with words alone.

The two simple stories he relates on successive nights point to what seem like trivial events. In both instances the Baal Shem tells the Maggid that he was aided by someone who just happened to pass by at the right time. These are coded messages meant for the Maggid: If you could just let go of your skepticism and open your heart in faith and simplicity you would see that there is help available that could quench your unconscious hunger for a fuller and deeper spiritual life. But why the code? Why not tell this to Dov Baer straight out? At that moment the Maggid was being defensive. Had the Besht said this to him directly, the younger man might have merely denied what he was being told and dismissed the Baal Shem as an ignorant critic who had insulted him. In the context of the larger narrative, however, the obscurity of these koan-like anecdotes served to gradually break down Dov Baer's resistance, preparing him to open to something deeper than mere verbal wisdom.

During the confrontation in the study, the master is able to reveal to Dov Baer the experiential reality of a mystical teaching, the actual presence of the Divine encoded in the words on the book's page. As scholar Moshe Idel has commented, "The text is not ancient history, not a metaphor or symbol for something else, but the appropriate performance; the text, when performed enthusiastically, includes the experience itself."[385] The experience of what? Of a mysterious reality locked in words on a page. If one has the psychic ability to perceive the genuine truth that lies encrypted in a mystical text, one can experience that reality. In this way the Maggid finally realizes that Israel Baal Shem Tov has the power to take him beyond his intellect, to experience the reality of the sacred. This is an awakening, a transformative moment, and the first step toward enlightenment.

Rabbi Miles Krassen has commented incisively about the role of the Besht highlighted in this story. "This encounter points to another of the Baal Shem Tov's important charismatic gifts: *the power to awaken in others the capacity for direct mystical experience....* We may consider this another example of Rabbi Israel's function as Teacher, an initiatory power that thoroughly transformed the Maggid's spiritual life and made him the Baal Shem Tov's disciple for life."[386]

The Baal Shem comes over as being severe, even judgmental. Perhaps this is why Buber placed the following touching anecdote right after the story of the first meeting of the Besht and the Maggid in his *Tales of the Hasidim*: "Once, at parting, the Baal Shem blessed his disciple. Then he bowed his own head to receive the blessing from him. Rabbi Baer drew back, but the Baal Shem took [the Maggid's] hand and laid it on his head."[387] Buber was the first to compare Hasidism with other forms of world spirituality, especially Eastern religion, and he noted that in both Zen and Hasidism the relation between teacher and disciple is central. The harsh demeanor of the Besht reminds me of stories I've read about exchanges between Zen masters and their disciples, which on the surface often seem blunt and nonsensical. Here is one such tale:

> A young man comes to a Zen teacher for spiritual direction. The teacher shuts the door in his face. The stranger knocks on the door again. "What do you want?" the master asks through the closed door. "I am able to look at the ground of my existence and I desire to receive instruction," replies the aspirant. The teacher opens the door, gazes at the man, and once again shuts the door in his face. The youth goes away, but then returns again, and the same scene is repeated. The man returns a third time and when the master opens the door just a crack, the man forces his way inside. The teacher grabs the man by his chest, and cries, "Speak!" When the young man hesitates, the teacher screams at him "You blockhead!" and throws him out. But just as the master is forcefully shutting the door, the man's foot gets caught in the door's hinge and his foot breaks. Screaming in pain the young man experiences inner illumination.

Shocking. Even cruel. But this is the way that the master breaks through the disciple's arrogance.

In the Rinzai school of Zen, a teacher gives a disciple a *koan*—a paradoxical statement, story, or question meant to confuse the aspirant's mind, forcing them to sharpen their intuitive ability. The disciple attempts to solve the puzzle, meeting with their master regularly to report on progress. According to the ninth-century *Rules of Hyakujo,* these meetings afford "the opportunity for the teacher to make close personal examination of the student, to arouse him from his immaturity, to beat down his false conceptions and to rid him of his prejudices, just as the smelter removes the lead and quicksilver from the gold in the smelting pot, and as the jade-cutter, in polishing the jade, discards every possible flaw."[388] The story of the Maggid's meeting with the Besht serves this kind of function. Like the Zen master, the Baal Shem gives his full and caring attention to Dov Baer, concerned for his soul and spiritual growth.

How did the Maggid respond to what he received? Over the years he fashioned his own spiritual vision based on that of his teacher, adding elements and terminology from the Kabbalah, and taught this to his own disciples. But, as Arthur Green has written, "The maggid was much more a contemplative than an ecstatic, plumbing the depths of mystical ideas, rather than seeing visions, hearing voices, or engaging in shamanic rites [like the Baal Shem Tov]. This is not to say that his mysticism lacked an experiential dimension, but it lacked the dramatic manifestations of the Besht's *ekstasis*."[389] The Maggid's disciples then took what they received from their master to communities in Poland and Russia, and in this way created the Hasidic movement.

CHAPTER TWENTY-THREE

TO LIVE IN THE PRESENCE

"Together we shall explore the question of the extent to which
there is religion as presence. That is, religion not as remem-
brance and hope but as lived presence...we must ask to what
extent religion is absolute presence, absolute present that can
never become past and must therefore become present and be
present in every time and for every time."

MARTIN BUBER[390]

The Baal Shem was convinced that the experience of the Presence could
be cultivated through spiritual discipline: *devekut*, "communion with
God." Gershom Scholem writes that through this practice the seeker
becomes continually aware of the omnipresence and immanence of
God and becomes "united" with God in the sense that "the core of his
own being is bound up with the core of all being."[391] Scholem launched a
wide-ranging investigation into kabbalistic and Hasidic literature regarding the origins and history of the notion of devekut, devoting much of
his investigation to the centrality of devekut for the Baal Shem. Scholem
writes that the Besht taught that through devekut the perfected Hasid
is able to transform ordinary existence into "one single sphere of holy
action." Many kabbalists had seen this practice as the pinnacle of mystical attainment, but Scholem averred that for the Besht it became the *first*
step, a way to live in perfect faith:

> As a classical illustration of the meaning of *devekut*...we
> have the daring reinterpretation of Psalm 81:10, "There
> shall be no strange God in thee." These words, said
> the Baal Shem, can be taken according to the Hebrew
> sequence of words to mean "God shall not be a stranger
> to thee." And when is God no longer a stranger to man?
> When man constantly fulfills the admonition of the

psalmist, "I set the Lord always before me." It is communion with God through *devekut* that makes God an intimate friend of man, instead of a forbidding stranger.[392]

Reading Scholem's essay, I wondered how I might learn to practice devekut. I recall asking Reb Zalman Schachter-Shalomi about this
once, and was taken aback when he recommended a little book called
The Practice of the Presence, written by a seventeenth-century Carmelite
monk named Brother Lawrence of the Resurrection (1614-91). I was surprised to discover that Christians also engaged in this practice.

Brother Lawrence was a humble cook living in a monastery who
experienced life to its fullest by learning to commune with God everyday—and every hour of the day—even during his ordinary work. In
short, he learned the art of living in the presence of God throughout the
day. This discipline produced such a change in the monk that those who
encountered him saw him as a saintly person. People would come to visit
him and try to learn how they too could learn to practice the presence of
God. "Think often of God," he wrote, "by day, by night, in your business,
and even in your diversions. He is always near you and with you; do not
leave him alone." But the quotation from Brother Lawrence's book that
made the greatest impression on me was: "The time of business does not
differ with me from the time of prayer; and in the noise and clatter of my
kitchen, while several people are at the same time calling for different
things, I possess God in as great tranquility as if I were on my knees."
Brother Lawrence didn't actually tell people how to engage in practicing the Presence. I think, like the Baal Shem, people watched him for his
example of how to do this.

The Baal Shem also instructed disciples in the practice of devekut:
"Contemplate the many and varied creations of our world with the depth
of true vision. Look beneath their outward appearance, for in truth the
essence flowing through everything is the Lifeforce, the Divine Power,
animating, energizing, and sustaining all existence." He offered other
instructions too. Engage yourself fully with whatever you are doing,
remembering in the moment that everything you are encountering is a
manifestation of the Divine. On one occasion he taught: "When you are
engaged in any activity, bring your most spacious state of consciousness

into relation with whatever you are doing, binding such awareness with each of your actions. This is called the unification of the blessed Holy One and the Shekhinah."[393] Another time, he put it differently: "Bind yourself (*davuk*) to God to such an extent that when you look at any object in the world what you primarily see is the Divinity shining through that creation. Here's the truth: We cannot move our bodies even slightly without the aid of the divine flow that is making that movement possible."[394] Hasidic tradition calls this path, *Avodah Buh'gahsh'mi'yut,* which literally translates as "serving [God] through physicality." Sometimes we think of the material world as a barrier to the spirit. It doesn't have to be that way, taught the Besht, for God made the corporeal world and God dwells in materiality. Immanuel Etkes writes that this understanding "demonstrates the possibility of granting a state of sanctity to the most mundane action possible.... This is an activism that seeks to elevate the material state in which man lingers and to have it be bound to the Upper Worlds."[395]

The Baal Shem's practice of devekut, both in his ecstatic davening and during the activities he engaged in each day, must have contributed to the sense of Presence radiating from him. There is a well-known passage in the Talmud which states that God declares "the entire world is nourished for the sake of my son, the Hasid, Hanina ben Dosa" (*Talmud Berakhot* 17b). The Besht looks beyond the literal meaning of this, noting that the Hebrew word *bish'vil,* translated "for the sake of," may also be rendered "through the conduit of" or "through the path of." And he translates the Talmudic statement: "The entire world is nourished *through the conduit of,* through the path of his son, the Hasid, Hanina ben Dosa."

For the Besht, then, the essence of the true Hasid or tzaddik is that he is a conduit, a path through which the abundance of Divine Presence is channeled into the world.[396] Moshe Idel writes that what may be essential to the very nature of the tzaddik is not only his ability to achieve an expanded state of consciousness, in which his ego becomes dissolved in the Divine, but a capacity to perform miracles and channel the abundance of divine blessing (*shefah*) toward the community he serves, and in this way lift the community toward its Divine Source.[397] I witnessed this firsthand in visits to the Lubavitcher community in the early sixties. Rebbe Menachem Mendel Schneerson was extremely impressive, and the effect of his presence on the lives of his Hasidim was palpable. I was so drawn to what I found in that community that I came close to leaving the Jewish Theological Seminary and entering the Habad yeshivah. Had I done so I most probably would have become a very different kind of person and rabbi than I became.

I came to call this practice Living in the Presence, which implies that the Presence is always present, whether we're aware of it or not. I've made it a habit to punctuate my activities throughout the day by breathing out "Yaaaah..," letting go of whatever is on my mind and coming into the Presence in the present moment, recognizing that everything is part of the Oneness. If I am able, I close my eyes while engaged in this practice. In this altered state I may recognize the preciousness of this moment, or I sense the wonder or awe of existence. Or I may just surrender to the underlying Oneness of it all, or that I am a particular embodiment of the universe. I may simultaneously sense a combination of any or all of those experiences. If I am in some kind of pain, I recognize that this too is part of the Divinity of existence.

BUBER'S TRANSFORMATION

Because Buber placed so much emphasis on the spiritual reality of what was occurring in the moment, his representation of the Baal Shem Tov was built around select stories in the Hasidic canon describing incidents in the master's life. Buber was far less interested in the Besht's conceptual teachings. He was convinced that it was the tales, anecdotes, and sayings that conveyed how the disciples were shaped in relationship to their master. Buber never claimed that these tales were historically true. In the introduction to *Tales of the Hasidim: The Early Masters,* he writes, "The purpose of this book is to introduce the reader to a world of legendary reality. I must call it legendary, for the accounts which have been handed down to us, and which I have here tried to put in fitting form, are not authentic in the sense that a chronicle is authentic. They go back to fervent human beings who set down their recollections of what they saw or thought they had seen, in their fervor, and this means that they included many things which took place, but were apparent only to the gaze of fervor, and others which cannot have happened and could not happen in the way they are told, but which the elated soul perceived as reality and, therefore, related as such. That is why I call it reality: the reality of the experience of fervent souls, a reality born in all innocence, unalloyed by invention and whimsy."[398]

Early in his career, Buber took a deep interest in mystical experience. Soon after Buber published his first two books about Hasidism—one on Rebbe Nachman of Bratslav and the other on the Baal Shem Tov—he published *Ecstatic Confessions*, with gathered testimonies by mystics from all over the world who experienced euphoric states Buber described as "the most inward of all experiences...God's highest gift." In those years, Buber was involved in rapturous spiritual practices that elevated his consciousness. Strangely enough, *Ecstatic Confessions* has only a few texts drawn from Hasidism.

During World War I, in his late thirties, Buber underwent an experience that changed the direction of his life. He described the circumstances that it brought to his student, Aubrey Hodes. A young man had come to see Buber for counseling, but Buber didn't truly listen because he'd just been engaged in his practice of mystical ecstasy and was inattentive to his visitor's unspoken questions. Buber later discovered that soon after that meeting the man took his own life. Buber took this as a judgment not only on the mistaken character of his mystical practice, but on the erroneousness of his nondualistic view of reality. In *Between Man and Man*, Buber wrote about the incident and concluded with a reflection:

> Since then, I have given up the "religious" which is nothing but the exception, extraction, exaltation, ecstasy; or it has given me up. I possess nothing but the everyday out of which I am never taken.... I know no fulness but each mortal hour's fulness of claim and responsibility. Though far from being equal to it, yet I know that in the claim I am claimed and may respond in responsibility, and know who speaks and demands a response.[399]

This conversion was a crucial event in Buber's life that led to the formulation of the dialogical philosophy found in *I and Thou*. His friend Nahum Glatzer later characterized Buber's newfound relational spirituality as "co-existentialism." In later writings, such as "The Question to the Single

One" (1936, in *Between Man and Man*) and "What is Common to All" (1958, in *The Knowledge of Man*), Buber argues that special states of unity are experiences of self-unity, not identification with God, and that many forms of mysticism express a flight from the task of dealing with the realities of concrete situations, and substitute a private sphere of illusion for the actual world shared by human beings. Drawing on Hasidic thought, Buber argues that the world is not an obstacle on the way to God, but the way itself.

I have pondered Buber's story about his transformation again and again over the years. I certainly find it touching—but also problematic. In the later nineteenth-century school of Hasidism known as Habad (or Lubavitch), true ecstasy means that the Divinity in one's soul comes into contact with the divine light that is usually screened from view in ordinary awareness. Rabbi Dov Baer of Lubavitch, the son of Shneur Zalman of Liadi, the founder of Habad, wrote a *Tract on Ecstasy* in which he states that in the highest form of ecstasy the worshipper experiences a form of self-transcendence that contains little or no self-awareness. But is such rapture morally irresponsible? There is a story about this same Rabbi Dov Baer in Habad tradition that illuminates this question:

> Rabbi Dov Baer of Lubavitch and his wife lived with Dov Baer's parents. One day while his wife had gone on an errand Dov Baer was studying by himself next to the cradle in which his infant daughter was lying. The child happened to fall out of the cradle onto the floor and lay there crying. Because of his deep concentration, however, Dov Baer heard nothing. His father, R. Shneur Zalman, was studying in an attic room and heard the baby's cries. He came down, picked the child up, soothed her, and put her back in her cradle.
>
> Then he turned toward his son: "It's amazing to me that your mind is so constricted that you couldn't even hear the baby crying. When you are involved with something there is no room in your mind for anything else."
>
> Dov Baer was taken aback by these words, and then his father continued. "I am not like this. When I

am involved in deep contemplation, I can still hear the
noise of a fly crawling up the window pane."[400]

Such a mature ability requires real presence of mind during meditation or contemplation. Even though the adept is rapt in ecstasy, he
remains aware and mindful of everything taking place. This kind of consciousness is inclusive of all reality within the immediate environment
of the meditator. With this story in mind, I suggest that perhaps at the
time Buber met with the young man, a transformation was already taking
place in his consciousness that would require him to give up his self-indulgent form of mysticism in order to undertake a more responsible existential attitude toward the world.

The reorientation toward existence that Buber underwent also initiated a changed view of the Baal Shem Tov. In his early book, *The Legend
of the Baal-Shem*, Buber had written glowingly that *hit'la'ha'vut* (ecstasy)
"is an ascent to the infinite from rung to rung."[401] But in *The Origin and
Meaning of Hasidism*, published in the late fifties, where he offers his fullest portrait of the Baal Shem, Buber omitted mentioning anything having to do with the master's mystical transcendence of the physical world.
While one can understand Buber's motivations in this matter—whether
conscious or unconscious—his portrait fails to account for an extremely
important aspect of the Besht's mystical life. Likewise, Buber's aversion
to Kabbalah seems to have closed him off to two other vital aspects of the
Baal Shem's worldview: his use of kabbalistic concepts in fashioning his
psychospiritual understanding of human nature, and the panentheism
(everything is in God), acosmism (there is no physical world), and nondualism evident in many of the Besht's teachings.

GERSHOM SCHOLEM'S ASSAULT

As a young man, Gershom Scholem had seen himself as a kind of disciple of Buber's, but in 1961, *Commentary* magazine published an article by Scholem severely criticizing the older scholar's methodology.
Scholem attacked Buber's use of the legendary stories that were popular
among the Hasidim to characterize Hasidism. Instead, Scholem identified authentic Hasidism with the theoretical thought of the great rebbes
found in the books composed by those masters. This body of teachings

included sermons, commentaries on biblical texts, tracts on prayer, and other aspects of the devotional life. Scholem was also critical of Buber's view that Hasidism stood in opposition to Kabbalah. Buber was averse to Kabbalah because he thought it denigrated physical reality, instead focusing on an esoteric and unworldly "gnostic" form of religion. He wrote that Hasidism, in contrast, asserted the primacy of embodied existence. But in his critique, Scholem made the case that the Hasidic masters were not primarily interested in physical existence. He argued that they perceived the essence of reality as something beyond the physical world. Scholem also contended that Hasidism did not at all oppose kabbalistic esoterism. Instead, the Baal Shem and other masters interpreted kabbalistic concepts in a psychospiritual way, as dynamic realities of the human soul. Indeed, as we will see in the next chapter, Scholem was correct. Scholem also attacked Buber's entire approach to Hasidism as lacking the necessary objectivity and rigor required of a scholar.

Buber was hurt by Scholem's allegations, and two years later, in an article in the same periodical, he responded. Buber did not challenge the historical method championed by Scholem, but laid out two ways through which a great tradition of religious faith might be "rescued from the rubble of time and brought back into the light." The first, he wrote, is by means of historical scholarship that seeks to be as comprehensive and exact as possible. Its primary aim is to advance the state of knowledge about the body of religious faith in question—though it may also contribute to the instruction of future generations in the faith. Such a task of historical reconstruction and clarification requires the objectivity and detachment that make the scholar what he is. But, Buber maintained, there is also a second way to interpret a movement such as Hasidism: "[R]ecapture a sense of the power that once gave it the capacity to take hold of and vitalize the life of diverse classes of people. Such an approach derives from the desire to convey to our own time the force of a former life of faith and to help our age renew its ruptured bond with the Absolute.... To affect such a renewal one must convey the reality of the way of life that was once informed by these teachings, the life of faith that was lived by exemplary individuals and by the communities they founded and led.... [T]he work of transmitting the old faith to one's contemporaries does not require a complete presentation of all these connections, but rather a selection of those manifestations in which its vital and vitalizing element was embodied."

This dispute set off a heated debate that lasted for many years. Those were the days before personal computers and search engines, and I can remember ordering periodical after periodical from my local library's interlibrary loan program, and photocopying everything that arrived. For years I pondered, which of these two scholars is correct? I finally came to understand that while Buber was not a historian, that didn't mean he wasn't a scholar. His approach to Hasidism was primarily phenomenological, that is, an examination of the experience of Hasidic spirituality. This was why he chose to focus on the tales rather than the theoretical works of the various rebbes. Nevertheless, Buber's desire did have to do with the renewal of Hasidism for people living in the twentieth century, and thus Scholem was correct in criticizing Buber's distorted understanding of the movement's historical aims. At the same time, Scholem's rendering of Hasidism was distorted since it didn't take into account ways the movement's relational character was understood by the masses of Hasidim. Even after all these years, I react negatively to the disrespectful verbal harshness expressed by Scholem, and also to the refusal by Buber to admit that from an historical perspective Scholem's criticism might have merit.

I came to recognize that Buber's way of reinterpreting Hasidism was, in its own way, similar to what the masters themselves had done with the teachings of their forbears, for each rebbe adopted, interpreted, and renewed what he received from the Baal Shem Tov and the rebbes who came in his wake. In his turn, then, Buber fashioned an existential interpretation of that tradition. It would have been more honest if Buber had admitted from the first that the approach he adopted had grown out of his own philosophical concerns. Buber may not have taken the sermons, biblical commentaries, and the works that dealt with prayer and the devotional life as seriously as he did the stories and anecdotes.

Readers will recognize that in this book I have drawn from the approaches of both Scholem and Buber. Like Scholem, I have attempted to portray the Baal Shem Tov in his historic context, not wishing to distort either his identity or his worldview merely to make him more attractive or accessible to contemporary people. Nonetheless, I most certainly connect with Buber's overall aim—to highlight those aspects of the Besht's legacy that seem to nourish seekers in our time. And because my primary wish has been to speak to others through my writing, I have, like Buber, been selective regarding the particular aspects of the Baal Shem's legacy that I present.

I recall a class that I took with Reb Zalman Schachter-Shalomi in which he made the point that both Buber and Scholem had been short-sighted in their ways of understanding Hasidism. To really understand the Baal Shem Tov or any Hasidic rebbe, Reb Zalman told us, one needs to know four things about each rebbe: the tales that were told about him by his disciples; the teachings recorded in his books; the way that he davened; and the niggunim that he composed. It was the latter two aspects of the various rebbes' paths that both Buber and Scholem neglected. Zalman even made a fascinating video in which he enacted the various forms of davening that he imagined some of the greatest rebbes had practiced, based on what they had written about prayer.

AN ONGOING INSPIRATION

Martin Buber has been an important influence on my life and spiritual journey ever since I came across *I and Thou* as a rabbinic student. The book spoke deeply to me, teaching me to value my relationships as potential or actual epiphanies of the Divine. Years later, when I forsook traditional Judaism and moved to California, Buber remained one of my links to my heritage, for the guidance I found in his writings enabled me to adopt an existential approach to living guided in every situation by the spirit, rather than by a book of laws. Much later, when I came to spiritual direction, and studied to become a spiritual director at a Catholic institution in the early nineties, I very much wanted to bring this discipline into a Jewish context. It was Buber's understanding of human relationships that provided me with a framework to do so.

In the seventies, when I was trying to make sense of the Israeli-Palestinian divide, I also found guidance in Buber's writings. His Zionism was strongly affected by the love and compassion that he had discovered in Hasidism. He came to believe that the Jewish community in Israel could only thrive if they broadened the Zionist dream to include Jews and Arabs living together in mutual respect, and he worked tirelessly to persuade the Zionist movement to assent to an inclusive vision. In later years I came to know Buber's great-granddaughter, Tirzah Agassi (1950-2008), an Israeli-born psychologist who worked as a peace activist before moving to the U.S. Tirzah worked diligently to get Paul Mendes-Flohr's book, *A Land of Two Peoples: Martin Buber on Jews and Arabs* republished. She contracted cancer and in her final months came to live in the communal home I shared with Abigail Grafton and Shoshanah Dembitz in Berkeley.

Buber's political thought has been crucial to my way of thinking and acting in the world. His critique of capitalism and emphasis on communitarian socialism have been essential to my view that synagogues must become authentic communities of radical resistance, standing above all for social justice, compassion, and love.

During my junior year in Israel, I was privileged to study with Ernst Simon, an educator, religious philosopher, and writer who was one of Buber's close friends. I was looking forward to the meeting with Buber that Dr. Simon had been arranging for our class. But this was not to be, for at age eighty-seven, Buber broke his hip, became bedridden, and died before the gathering was to take place. I planned to attend his funeral, but just as I was getting ready to leave the dormitory, I was told by a friend that I had the date wrong; the interment had taken place the day before. I was disappointed. Why hadn't I been more mindful? I later learned that Ernst Simon was one of the speakers at the funeral. He described Buber's activism in attempting to reframe the Zionist dream so that it would envision a land of two peoples living in harmony. "He was alone when he fought," Simon said, "and the support he was given was small—even smaller in times of peace than in times of crisis.... During his last years he did indeed begin to find people like this among the young generation— Jews and Arabs alike."[402]

CHAPTER TWENTY-FOUR

JUNG, THE BESHT, AND THE SACRED PSYCHE

"The longing for growth is not wrong. The nub of the problem now is how to flip over, as in jujitsu, the magnificent growth-energy of modern civilization into a nonacquisitive search for deeper knowledge of self and nature."
GARY SNYDER[403]

My fascination with psychology began in my twenties, during three years of psychoanalysis I underwent while studying to become a rabbi. I would meet with psychoanalyst Max Gruenthal three times a week in his small office in Manhattan. He would encourage me to speak about everything troubling me without holding back, and ask me about my childhood and my growing up. Dr. Gruenthal was kind and accepting and above all, a good listener. I found the process to be a tremendous relief, especially at the beginning of our work together, for I had never before shared my inner life with another human being. What came out were vivid memories of the past as well as fantasies, many of them erotic, that continued to provoke a huge amount of fear, guilt, and shame. Gruenthal never took a moral stance with me, nor did he ask me to consider changing who I was.

What occurred during those sessions did not cure my neuroses, but the process of speaking about my psychic knots with someone who did not judge, allowed me to begin to develop a sense of myself as an individual worthy of human concern, whatever faults I might have. I also learned the enormous value of pursuing self-knowledge and self-understanding. Almost sixty years later I remain grateful for Dr. Gruenthal's gifts.

My first exposure to psychological ideas came in a class in pastoral psychiatry a few years later. During the year-long course of studies my classmates and I were instructed by three different psychoanalysts, all schooled in Freudian theory. I found those theories interesting, but they

didn't seem germane to my religious or personal concerns. I also wondered whether this kind of theoretical knowledge was really a necessary
component of my future work as a rabbi.

Then I read a book on my own that detailed Freud's theories, but the
materialistic premises of his worldview contradicted my own views in
denying the reality of anything metaphysical. I discovered that Freud had
written a book on religion, *The Future of an Illusion,* and was interested
enough to spend time reading it carefully. I was struck by his labeling
religion "a collective obsessive-compulsive neurosis." I'd never heard this
term before, and what I learned from the book enabled me to recognize
for the first time the major neurotic syndrome that had been plaguing
me. Still, Freud seemed to have a narrow view of religion, or at least
Judaism; it was simplistic and reductionistic.

A few years after that, during my first encounter with psychedelics,
it came as a kind of revelation that even though Freud's theory of human
nature had probably expressed something valid about the biological and
psychological underpinnings of our species, it had completely missed
the essence of human potential and possibility. I wondered what might
have happened to Sigmund Freud's worldview if the founder of psychoanalysis had been exposed to LSD.

DISCOVERING JUNG

William James' *The Varieties of Religious Experience* opened my eyes to
the psychology of religion from one of the great pioneers of the field.
There were many different valid states of consciousness, as James was
able to demonstrate, yet I needed to know more. When I discussed this
with my brother, Stuart, a clinical social worker, he suggested I might want
to explore the thought of depth psychologist, Carl Jung. This turned out
to be the perfect suggestion, initiating my long and fruitful relationship
with Jung's work. My study of Jungian psychology was of immense value
when it came to interpreting the life and teachings of the Baal Shem Tov.

Jung had worked with Freud for several years, but they split over
their very different views of the psyche. Unlike Freud, Jung was drawn
to religion and spirituality, and he developed an understanding of the
human mind that illumined the relationship between the psyche and the
spirit. *Psyche* is a Greek word meaning soul, and Jung often wrote about

the psyche in soulful terms. He stated that the psyche is "natively religious," and that the "religious impulse rests on an instinctive basis and is therefore a specifically human function."[404] He understood myths, symbols, dreams, and fantasies to be projections of the unconscious mind onto the external world, and was convinced that when these creations of the psyche are interpreted psychologically, they can provide in-depth knowledge of the human unconscious.

It was Gershom Scholem who recognized that one of the chief characteristics of Hasidism, demarcating it from classical Kabbalah, was its turn toward psychology. Commenting on the Habad school, Scholem wrote: "[T]he distinctive feature of the new school is to be found in the fact that the secrets of the divine realm are presented in the guise of mystical psychology. It is by descending into the depth of his own self that man wanders through all the dimensions of the world; in his own self he lifts the barriers which separate one sphere from the other; in his own self, finally, he transcends the limits of natural existence and at the end of his way, without, as it were, a single step beyond himself, he discovers that God is 'all in all' and 'there is nothing but Him.'"[405] In this way, Scholem explains, the entire range of kabbalistic concepts, which had been focused on theosophy (a metaphysical understanding of the universe at large) had been transformed into psychology. "What has really become important," Scholem states, "is the direction, the mysticism of the personal life. Hasidism is practical mysticism at its highest. Almost all the Kabbalistic ideas are now placed in relation to values peculiar to the individual life."

I could see that this psychological perspective did not begin with Habad, but with the founder of Hasidism. And as I studied text after text, I found that Jung's perspective allowed me to penetrate the psychological dimensions of the Besht's thinking. Along with this, I found many teachings strongly resonating with Jungian ideas. Still, Jung and the Besht used different vocabularies. Jung adopted terminology from existing schools of psychology, using words such as complex, libido, neurosis, psychosis, the unconscious, and defining these terms in his fashion. He also came up with or adopted new vocabulary for different aspects of the psyche and for the processes that take place within it: archetypes, persona, shadow, anima, animus, Self, introversion, extraversion, etc. The Baal Shem Tov, on the other hand, employed the existing language of the Kabbalah to identify the forces at work in the psyche, as well as making use of potent images found in the Torah such as creation, enslavement, exile, redemption, and the messiah. We will be investigating this terminology in the course of the chapter.

In 2000, psychologist Sanford L. Drob published *Kabbalistic Metaphors: Jewish Mystical Themes in Ancient and Modern Thought*, and Freud and Jung were among the modern writers whose links to Kabbalah he surveyed. What Drob had to say about Jung and Kabbalah expanded my thinking about the relationship between the Baal Shem and Jung's notions of the psyche. Ten years later, Drob came out with *Kabbalistic Visions: C. G. Jung and Jewish Mysticism,* the first full-length study of Jung and Jewish mysticism in any language, and the first book to present a comprehensive Jungian/archetypal interpretation of kabbalistic symbolism. Reading Drob was a confirmation of what I had been pursuing; somehow Jung had become aware of the psychological dimensions of Hasidism. On his eightieth birthday Jung told an interviewer, "The Hasidic Rabbi Baer from Mesiritz, whom they called the Great Maggid...anticipated my entire psychology in the eighteenth century."[406] Drob explains Jung's remarkable profession in the following way: "The Maggid had held that the Godhead has a hidden life within the mind of man and that while the Godhead himself is the foundation and source of thought, actual thinking can only occur within the framework of the human mind, a notion that clearly anticipates Jung's own psychologization of the objects of religious discourse."[407]

But recognizing that the sefirot had a life within the human mind did not begin with the Besht or Hasidism. We find a parallel to this way of thinking in the teachings of a number of the kabbalists who, having experienced the numinous directly, recognized that the symbols and myths they employed to describe it were human in origin. The following remarkable teaching has come down in the Maggid's name, but Moshe Idel believes it was based on the teachings of the Besht:

> Once the Maggid admonished a certain man, because he
> had been teaching Kabbalah in public. The man seemed
> puzzled: "Then why is it, master, that that you yourself
> teach Kabbalah in public?"

The Maggid answered, "I teach the world to understand that all the matters about which R. Isaac Luria,
Holy Ari taught exist in this world and within human
beings; but I do not pretend to comprehend the depths
of the spiritual matters revealed by the Holy Ari. In this
way I am able to transform matter into spirit. But you
teach that everything revealed by the Ari literally exists
in the mysterious realms beyond, and when you teach
in this manner you turn spirit into matter. But you must
know this: There is nothing we can say at all about what
exists beyond."[408]

*"I teach the world to understand that all the matters about which R.
Isaac Luria, the Holy Ari taught exist in this world and in human beings."*
In other words, the Maggid confines his discourse to insights about the
physical world in which we live, and the inner world of the human psyche. *"In this way I am able to transform matter into spirit."* That is, the
Maggid is able to reveal the ways in which what seems to be matter is
actually spirit in disguise. *"But in truth we can say nothing at all about
what is beyond."* Here, he warns the man not to take symbolic representations of the Divine as being in any way literally true.

To summarize: If we imagine that we can know anything about the
cosmic sefirot underlying and structuring the universe, we are fooling
ourselves. For even though the ten sefirot within human beings develop
out of and resonate with the ten cosmic sefirot, our mental faculties are
incapable of grasping those lofty dimensions of being. We can only dimly
know what that enigmatic reality might be like by looking at events
occurring in the physical world, and by peering deeply into our psyches
and examining the patterns of our mind and forms that they take as we
go about our daily tasks. Nonetheless, we are able to know a great deal
about this world because the capabilities of our sacred psyches are enormous and unique.

COLLECTIVE UNCONSCIOUS AND HIDDEN TORAH

Jung wrote about two different levels of the unconscious, which he called
the personal and the collective: "A more or less superficial layer of the

unconscious is undoubtedly personal. I call it the 'personal unconscious,' but this personal layer rests upon a deeper layer, which does not derive from personal experience and is not a personal acquisition but is inborn. This deeper layer I call the 'collective unconscious.' I have chosen the term 'collective' because this part of the unconscious is not individual but universal; in contrast to the personal psyche, it has contents and modes of behavior that are more or less the same everywhere and in all individuals."[409] He elaborates on this definition, stating that although consciousness is capable of indefinite expansion, it always finds its limit when up against the unknown. The collective unconscious is made up of universal contents that are omnipresent, unchanging, and everywhere. In the end, consciousness opens up and becomes one with the world itself. In the psychotherapeutic processes that Jung developed, especially in his work with dreams, fantasies, and the exercise of the imagination, certain contents of the collective unconscious can be made conscious, which assists patients in their healing process.

To someone like the Baal Shem, who was educated in the Kabbalah and studied it from a decidedly psychospiritual perspective, the notion of the collective unconscious would not have been foreign. For as he told his disciples, as the mystic ascends the Tree of Life, he begins to enter expanded levels of awareness that become less and less comprehensible. An adept can apprehend that he's approaching some kind of vast and spacious reality, but as he soars upward his mind is unable to fathom where he is or where he's going. This, for the Baal Shem, was the sefirah of Hokhmah, Divine Wisdom. The kabbalistic adept can know nothing about this domain, which is the realm of the Hidden Torah.

This notion of Hidden Torah parallels Jung's idea of collective unconscious. According to the ancient rabbis, the Torah existed before creation. It was the primordial wisdom that God drew from in order to fashion the world. As Scholem writes, for the kabbalists, "Everything that we perceive in the fixed forms of the Torah, written in ink on parchment, consists, in the last analysis, of interpretations or definitions of what is hidden.... It is embodied in a sphere that is accessible to prophets alone."[410] And despite this, when wise students study the written Torah—the portion of the Torah that has been revealed to us—and they use their imagination and creativity to plumb its depths, they are able to extract and reveal some of its secrets to help restore the souls of people today. This, the Besht teaches, is what Moses was able to accomplish on the mountain. Thus, he sees the written Torah as a remedy for the restoration of the soul, healing those engaged in its study and practice:

> The Baal Shem taught: The Torah is eternal, just as the Divinity which was its origin is eternal. All the verses in the Torah are eternal within the mind. And the meaning of those verses can always be found in every moment of one's study through one's wisdom and intelligence. Through mystical unifications one can learn the secrets of each of its verses, and in this way the Torah can become a guide to the service of the Holy One.[411]

THE ARCHETYPES

Central to Jung's psychology was his notion of archetypes of the collective unconscious. Jung posited that alongside our physical instincts, which we share with animals, the unconscious contains innate and inherited psychological dispositions that react, behave, and interact with the world in certain predictable ways. These universal patterns and forces he called the *archetypes*. They are native to the human psyche, and shape all of human experience. Jung came to understand dreams, fantasies, symbols, and myths as embodied expressions of the archetypes.

These can never be apprehended directly. They appear, though, as motifs in myths, dreams, fairy tales, and literature, such as the creation of the world, the hero's journey, or the birth of the divine child. They also appear as personalities like the Great Mother, the Wise Old Man, or the Trickster. And they manifest as events in our lives such as birth, death, separation from parents, initiation, marriage, and the union of opposites. Archetypes also show themselves in the psychological structures that define every human being's existence. For Jung there were five such structural archetypes. The *persona* is the interface between the individual and society: the way a person presents themself and is seen by the human world. The *shadow* contains all the rejected and unaccepted parts of the personality that are repressed. The *anima* is the archetypal image of the eternal feminine carried by men, while the *animus* is the archetypal image of the eternal masculine carried by women. Finally, there is the *Self,* the totality of who an individual is in relationship to the world at large. Jung's writings made it clear that even though the archetypes of the collective unconscious are universal, forming the psychospiritual foundations for all of the world's religions and fields of art, those dispositions manifest themselves in extremely divergent ways in different historical and cultural settings. This explains differences in the various beliefs and practices of the religious traditions of the world as well as the dissimilarities in artistic forms all over the world.

The Baal Shem developed a notion somewhat akin to Jung's view of the archetypes. He seems to have believed there were particular innate structures or aspects of the human psyche shaping all human experience. He saw the sefirot as representations of the divine energies and states of consciousness within human beings: "There are ten sefirot at the core of every human being, for each of us is an image of Divinity itself. This is to say that every individual is a microcosm, just as Rabbi Abraham ben David taught: 'Whatever exists in the celestial worlds beyond also exists in the realm of time, and within the human soul.'"[412] And: "The sefirot within a human being enclothe one another, just as the sefirot in the universe at large enclothe one another. Thus, all of the enveloping forces within us are interconnected."[413]

For the Besht, then, everything that human beings engage in manifests one or more of the ten sefirot. It was his way of affirming that the Divine is always present within us, manifesting through the sefirot that constitute the underlying structure of the soul. He also taught that the key events of Jewish sacred history were not only part of collective memory and future hopes, but prototypical or archetypal representations of eternal verities, somehow etched into the soul of each and every Jew.[414] This novel approach becomes clear in a teaching of his offered on a verse in the book of Numbers having to do with the forty years of wandering in the wilderness: *"These are the journeys of the Children of Israel who went forth from the land of Mitzrayim according to their hosts, under the guidance of Moses and Aaron"* (33:1).[415] He commented, "Moses wrote about these different journeys in the Torah because of their surpassing importance. And they not only have to do with the travels of our forbears through the wilderness, but also with the journeys of individual human beings in every era. They form the underpinnings of our lives from the very moment that we emerge from the womb until we pass from this earth and arrive in the supreme land of eternal life. Moses made sure to include in the Torah each and every one of these wanderings of the ancient Israelites through the wilderness, so that every person in the future would be able to learn the particular path that God ordained for her or him.... It is in this way that individuals can discover in the Torah a wellspring, a source of wisdom, which can guide them in how best to serve the Blessed One throughout their lives, each individual according to his or her own spiritual level."[416]

ARCHETYPE OF EXODUS

The notion of human life as journey of discovery is a universal, archetypal motif found in myths all over the world. Perhaps the major motif in Judaism is the Exodus from *Mitzrayim*, which exemplifies the universal experience of escape from danger, in this case, the escape of an entire people from slavery. This sacred event is celebrated every spring during the holy season of Passover. What makes the Baal Shem's understanding of the Passover narrative unique is the way in which he applies it to the life of the individual.

The Haggadah, the traditional liturgical script for the Passover seder, contains a statement that became the cornerstone of the Besht's perspective on the Exodus: *"In every generation each individual must see himself as though he personally came forth from Mitzrayim."* The Baal Shem read this powerful affirmation in a hyper-literal way: "Every human being is a microcosm. Within each of us lie the secrets of the bondage to Mitzrayim, the Passover, the Exodus, and the journey to Mt. Sinai. If you attain wholeness, you carry within yourself Moses and Aaron—and also Mitzrayim." And: "As for the exile and the liberation from Mitzrayim, these events happened to our ancient forbears, but they also occur in each of our lives as well, as the psalmist says, '*Liberation is close to my heart*'" (Psalm 69).[417] In other words, in the unfolding of our lives we recapitulate the collective motifs of Jewish sacred history. Each of us undergoes bondage, redemption, and personal revelation on our path to wholeness. And because of this, as we read the story of the formation and liberation of the Israelite people in the Torah, we can apply its lessons to our own personal lives.

For the Besht, every individual carries within their depths all the major protagonists of the Exodus—Moses, Aaron, Mitzrayim, and the Pharaoh. Each of us must choose whether to identify with the narrow repressiveness of Mitzrayim and the Pharaoh, or with the liberatory aspects of Moses and Aaron, which can free us from Mitzrayim. When individuals identify with Mitzrayim, they are dominated by their inner Pharaoh, the yetzer ha'rah, the psychological predisposition to make the fulfillment of egocentric desires the center of their lives. If, however, they choose to undertake the inward path of Moses and Aaron, they will move toward freeing themselves from bondage to their inner and outer Pharaohs.

According to the Besht, we have the capability of attaining redemption from the yetzer ha'rah here and now, even before the collective redemption of the messianic era. But to become free and whole, we must come to understand what it is that's actually enslaving us. For the desire of the Pharoah within is to enslave us to self-serving cravings, blocking out the real truth of existence:

> What was the true meaning of the bondage to Mitzrayim? It was just this—that the consciousness of the Jewish people lay in exile. The children of Israel had lost the truth that all existence flows from the light of *Ein Sof,* the Infinite.[418]

> The exile in Mitzrayim occurred because the people had lost their ability to perceive that the world has a single Creator; and that the universe is filled with divine splendor; and that each and every day the Creator is continually renewing creation.[419]

Contrary to the narrative of the Exodus in the Torah, the Baal Shem taught that it was not an external, outer Pharaoh who brought about the enslavement of the Hebrews. Rather, the people brought this bondage on themselves. Living in Mitzrayim, subject to the yetzer ha'rah, they lost connection to the larger spiritual truth of existence and gave themselves to a false and narrow view of reality limited to the physical world in which they lived. This weakened them and made them vulnerable to the whims of Pharaoh. Had they remained conscious of the reality and centrality of the Divine they would never have allowed themselves to become enslaved:

> People could not even recognize what it was that they lacked, and this brought about the exile, just as the Holy Ari taught: "Consciousness of the Divine departed in Mitzrayim." Then the people came under the dominion of Pharaoh, the stiff back of the neck, the place of forgetfulness. Pharaoh said: *"I do not know God,"* for he represented the opposite of spiritual consciousness.[420]

> To the wicked it seems as if the world has no plan. And this perception seems true, because the appalling schemes of wrongdoers always seem to triumph. But this cynical attitude comes about only because of a lack of deeper understanding of existence.[421]

The Baal Shem's view of the Exodus story, then, is a description of how we lose knowledge of our true essence, paired with a vision of how we can again regain a living connection with the Divine to liberate us from the dimness of sheer instinctual existence. I imagine he assumed that before our enslavement—in other words, before we enter this world—our souls dwell in a state of enlightenment, of absolute freedom, unfettered by self-centeredness. In such a state we are able to continually experience the radiance of being. But when we are born into the physical world we fall from grace. It is the Pharaoh—our own self-centered desire for power, fame, unfettered sex, and worldly possessions—that incarcerates us in the prison-house of mundane consciousness. This is what the Baal Shem calls *ga'avah* in many of his teachings, as we saw in Part One. And to get what we physically crave, we agree, perhaps unconsciously, to close down our awareness, hiding from the awesome and marvelous character of life and the vast spiritual potential that lies at our core. We ignore and devalue all that goes on outside the realm of personal will and understanding—all the other ways of seeing and knowing existence.

It is possible, he asserts, to live in freedom from slavery, i.e., from worldly adversity by practicing non-attachment to that suffering, while opting to link one's consciousness with the splendor and spaciousness of Divinity. It is the true and full experience of divine majesty and dominion that frees one's consciousness from the domination of the Pharaohs of the earth. In other words, an experience of identity with the whole of existence and the great mystery at its core which displaces the narrowing egoic form that one's Mitzrayim takes. Estelle Frankel articulates how the Exodus then became a paradigm for personal change and transformation in Hasidic literature:

> The exile of the Israelites in Mitzrayim represents a condition of self-alienation, of not being in one's true place. In exile we become disconnected from our own true nature and inner being; our outer lives slide out of sync with our inner essence. When we are not grounded in our essential being, we don't have access to the vital energies we need in order to be creative, and we are unable to realize our true potential. Deliverance from exile, or redemption, on the other hand, implies a return to one's true self, to one's inner heart of hearts. When we come home to ourselves we find that our innermost essence may be expressed in our outermost lives.[422]

Along with narratives linked to the Exodus found in the Torah, Jewish sacred history also highlights the future. The notion of a messianic redemption to liberate the Jewish people and the world began to take shape in the Bible, and then was developed in greater detail in Rabbinic Judaism. As we saw in our earlier discussion of individual liberation from the yetzer ha'rah, the Baal Shem applied the same individualizing approach to the messianic theme as he had to the Exodus. In order for a new order to come about and radically transform the world, every person would have to embody the hope for such liberation: "The liberation of humanity as a whole will come about only when each and every person has undergone such a liberation."[423]

He also taught: "At that time the experience of divine splendor will become universal. Everyone will sense and see that the whole world is filled with God's radiance…. All people will know that every event is an expression of God's simple will enacted through the divine plan down to the minute particulars. Yes, everyone will clearly see that the Master of the world abides in every motion, for the power of the One who acts shines within the enactment. Just as the shell of the tortoise grows out of and is one with the tortoise itself, so the world grows out of and is one with the Divine."[424] Thus, the entire sacred history of the Jewish people exists archetypally within the sacred psyche of the individual Jew, and can be recapitulated in the particular life of every conscious and conscientious individual.

Now even though the Besht employs imagery drawn from Jewish sacred history to create his vision for individuation, these movements of the psyche can also be understood to represent universal *human* psychological patterns, like Jung's archetypes. Perhaps this is why the story of the enslavement and the liberation and the hope for a messianic future have been adopted and adapted by so many suffering peoples and religious traditions all over the world as a way to speak about this universal desire.

CHAPTER TWENTY-FIVE

THE CASTLE WITHIN

"Who looks outside dreams; who looks inside awakes."
C. G. JUNG[425]

Anthropologist David Maybury-Lewis has perceptively written that "Modern society is intensely secular; even those who regret this admit it. The irony is that after excluding the mystical tradition from our cultural mainstream and claiming to find it irrelevant to our concerns, so many of us feel empty without it."[426] Carl Jung found this kind of emptiness dominating the lives of many of his patients, particularly those who were older. "Among all my patients in the second half of life—that is to say, over thirty-five—there has not been one whose problem in the last resort was not that of finding a religious outlook on life" wrote Jung. "It is safe to say that every one of them fell ill because he had lost what the living religions of every age have given their followers, and none of them has been really healed who did not regain his religious outlook."[427]

Jung stated that once his patients healed from the neurotic aspects of their personalities with which they struggled, he was able to help them forge links between the conscious and unconscious aspects of their psyches, to move away from the ego as the center of their lives and toward what he called "the Self," the center of the psyche, and the origin of all the archetypes. It is the Self that organizes and guides the unfolding of the various stages of psychic development, gradually bringing the individual toward integration and wholeness. Jung's view of human development, then, was rooted in a teleological view of the Self; he was convinced that the human psyche had particular goals to fulfill during its span of existence. "Unless it is blocked by special circumstances," comments Jungian psychologist Jolande Jacobi, "it will spontaneously produce everything that is needed for the fulfillment of individual development."[428]

He termed the movement toward wholeness that's directed by the Self, *individuation.* In his formulation of this process, he was influenced by Eastern notions of paths that led to enlightenment. Even the word he employed to designate the archetype of wholeness, "Self," drew from one of the synonyms for the Atman in Vedanta. And yet, Jung's understanding of the Self differed from Indian thought in a number of crucial ways. A great deal of Hindu thought regards the world as *maya,* illusion, but Jung was a European, and his Western psychological approach to individuation embraced the reality of all aspects of the psyche and of individual development, from childhood to old age. And unlike so much of eastern thought, Jung did not attack the worth of the human ego, which he believed was absolutely essential in the process of human development.

Jungian individuation provided me with a model for my own psychological and spiritual development. His optimistic reports about the ways his patients eventually found wholeness provided faith that it might indeed be possible for me to end the severe internal conflicts I lived with, and to finally become whole. He affirmed my hope that what I'd momentarily tasted through psychedelics might be realized in the rest of my life. When I entered the world of the Baal Shem Tov, Jung's understanding of the individuation process enabled me to grasp the master's struggles and successes on his path to personal redemption. Later, it also helped me identify the Besht's aims in the formation of his disciples into tzaddikim. From such a perspective a large part of the spiritual purpose of our pilgrimage on earth has to do with ending the blockages that prevent us from connecting with our divine souls, as we gradually refine our lives and become spiritually whole, loving, and compassionate beings.

BECOMING ONE WITH THE DIVINE

We have briefly examined Jung's notion of individuation, the process of moving through the different stages of one's life toward integration and becoming whole, knowing oneself to be part of the greater totality of the cosmos. In a comparable progression of psychospiritual development, the Baal Shem describes the individual seeker's pilgrimage to reach God. He portrayed this process in one of his best-known and brilliant parables, a teaching we encountered earlier in Part One. Here we will examine it from a slightly different angle:

"There once was a monarch who possessed great magical power. And with this skill he wove a spell, enclosing himself in a great illusory castle, surrounded by an illusory wall, tower, gate, and moat. And around this wall the king created nine more illusory walls, each of them with towers, gates and moats. And then the king commanded that gold be placed before each of the myriad of gates. Finally, he invited all of his subjects to visit him in his castle.

"But if this monarch really wanted his subjects to visit him, why then did he encircle his castle with so many walls, towers, gates and moats? It was because he wanted to know how deep was the love of his subjects for him, how fervent their desire to see their ruler, how strong their perseverance, and how much effort they would expend to reach his presence.

"Hearing the summons, all of the king's subjects set out for their sovereign's castle. Soon, a large throng had gathered before the first wall of the castle. They found the treasures at the gate of the first wall, and many of them collected all the gold and silver that they could fit into their pockets, and then turned around and made their way back to their homes. Yet there were some who remembered that they had been summoned to actually meet the king, and they sought and found a way to cross the moat, entering the first gate.

"But then these subjects encountered a second wall, tower, gate, and moat. And lying at its gate they saw even more precious treasures than there had been at the first gate. Some of them took the gold and silver and returned to their homes while others stayed the course. Those who continued on the journey met gate after gate and at each gate the heaps of gold became larger, and the temptation all the greater. More and more of the king's subjects were overcome by their material desires, taking the gold and returning home.

"Finally, only one seeker continued on his quest to reach the king himself—the king's own son. After tremendous effort, he came into his father's presence in the castle. Then suddenly all the walls, towers, gates, and moats simply disappeared and there was no longer any separation between father and son."

When the Baal Shem Tov had completed narrating this parable, he explained its meaning: God hides behind many barriers, and is veiled in many garments. But what is true is that the fullness of the whole earth is God's glory. Every thought, every movement comes from God. Everything is made of God's own essence. Those who truly understand this know that the walls, towers, gates, gold, and castle are only God in hiding, for there is no place devoid of the divine.[429]

How might Jung have understood this parable? Notice that the journey the king's son undertakes is from distance and separation towards an intimate connection with his father. In his theory of individuation, Jung affirmed that in the latter part of life, this process involves moving away from the narrow ego toward the more expansive Self. The discovery of God within the Self, or the full experience of the archetype of the Self. Sometimes Jung identified the Self as the *imago Dei,* the image of God within every human being. Realizing one's identification with the Self is thus the actualization of one's true self as an image of the Divine.

This motif is central to several of the Baal Shem's parables—the prince who has been banished from the royal palace and needs to be reunited with his royal father. Often the king's son is pictured by the Besht as unconscious of this necessity; at other times, as in the parable we are exploring, the son is fully aware of his need. Erich Neumann interpreted this as representing the alienated ego assimilated into the surrounding culture, oblivious to its connection with the numinous source of being. "The Copernican revolution in the development of Judaism, which begins with Hasidism," Neumann wrote, "displaces the ego from its position at the center of the world. The cosmic universe that emerges consists of the unconscious, organized in hierarchal levels, with the sun of the Self at its center, around which circles the earth of the ego-complex."[430] I believe that Neumann as well as Jung would have understood the castle parable to be a symbolic representation of the archetypal passage from experiencing the ego as the center of personality to making the Self the ultimate destination. The king is a representation of the archetype of the Self, the unconscious potential for wholeness and integration at the depths of the psyche.

Yet because the archetype of the Self is the unknowable, transcendent center of the personality, linked to the cosmos, Jung's notion is a close parallel to the kabbalistic understanding of the *neshamah*. In the Zohar, neshamah is the highest level of the soul, the divine core of every human being. According to Jung, it is the numinal attraction to the Self that entices some human beings to embrace a journey that will take them toward consciousness, wholeness, and unity. Most people, like the king's subjects in the parable, might imagine such fulfillment, but they never reach the destination. Caught up in ego attachments and appetites, they remain largely unconscious, identifying with inauthentic goals such as wealth, power, prestige, or surface beauty. Jung would say that in giving up their relationship with the Self these subjects have opened themselves to a loss of psychic balance and have become merely "fragmentary personalities," incapable of reaching their full potential.

Jung writes: "The decisive question for man is: Are you related to something infinite or not?"[431] The king's son knows, from the very beginning, that he has a unique relationship with the king and it is this that provides him with the motivation he needs to remain on the path. As Jung writes, "What is it, in the end, that induces a man to go his own way and to rise out of unconscious identity with the mass as out of a swathing mist?... It is what is commonly called *vocation;* an irrational factor that destines a man to emancipate himself from the herd and from its well-worn paths.... Vocation acts like a law of God from which there is no escape.... Anyone with a vocation hears the voice of the inner man: he is *called.*"[432] This eventually will take the seeker to God, as Jolande Jacobi comments, "For Jung, then, the experience of God in the form of an encounter or *unio mystica* is the only possible and authentic way to a genuine belief in God."[433] When the king's son finally reaches the castle and enters into his father's presence, the illusion of separateness dissolves as he becomes one with him.

In his study of sonship in Jewish mysticism, Moshe Idel has shown that the Besht saw himself as a son of God, and thus, the king's son in the parable can be seen in the first instance as the Baal Shem Tov himself. But Rabbi Jacob Joseph also wrote that his master would share this particular parable with his congregation before the blowing of the Shofar on Rosh Hashanah. From this we deduce that the Besht was promising members of his circle that if they realized they too were sons of God, and were willing to persist in the challenging journey, they would be able to discover their oneness with God.[434]

The language of parables is always anthropomorphic. But in other, possibly later, teachings the Baal Shem expresses this same experience of mystical union in a non-anthropomorphic way. Recall his play on words: the "I" (*ANiY*) becomes "No-thing" (*AYiN*); it is as if to say that one's very substance is transformed into the totality of being. Here, then, is the Besht's non-anthropocentric description of mystical union:

> Out of the strength that comes to you from divine compassion you will be able to enter the gate of No-Thing, completely forgetting your own existence. The only aspects of yourself that will remain in place are your limitless thoughts, and your love, and all of your virtues. And all of these will be completely bound to your love for the One.[435]

Does the parable, then, represent the process of individuation? Jung lived in the modern era, a time when the bonds between the individual and community had dissolved for many, and individualism had become the norm. The Baal Shem, on the other hand, still lived in a world that centered around the community and saw its members and leaders as part of the communal organism. And even though the Besht speaks about seven stages of the development of the soul, I have not found any elucidation of those stages. The master's burning desire, rather, had to do with dissolving the ego and getting to God.

The Hebrew word *shefah* means copiousness or abundance. In Hasidic terminology it refers to the abundance of divine energy that the mystic receives during the experience of devekut, the overflowing inspiration or influx that he channels to members of his community, renewing them spiritually. In his book exploring the Baal Shem's ecstatic approach to worship, Moshe Idel translates shefah as "supernal power," and explains the aims of the master's mystical worship: "The Besht is interested not only in the experience of adhering to God, but also in the reception of supernal power [i.e., shefah] that is imagined to be accumulated during the experience of recitation [of the letters and words of prayer] and *devequt,* and in its ensuing magical effects."[436] And in *Hasidism: Between Ecstasy and Magic*, Idel shows how the Baal Shem's practice of channeling shefah became part of his legacy to future tzaddikim: "What may be central for the nature of the Hasidic righteous man is, therefore, not only his [own] 'annihilation,' [i.e.,] the expansion of his consciousness, but his capacity to bring down and distribute divine power, or influx, to the community he serves as spiritual mentor." And again, "The Zaddik imitates the revealing divinity by becoming instrumental in the transmission of divine influx from the Sefirotic realm to the mundane one."[437] From this we can see that the Baal Shem's ultimate concern did not have to do with his own individuation, but with becoming a conduit through which he could channel shefah that he experienced during his mystical flights for the benefit of the Jewish people.

This has been a concern of great mystics around the world throughout the ages, as Erich Neumann writes: "The duty of self-sacrifice, which has the force of law in all high mysticism, demands precisely that the mystic teach, write, establish schools. In other words, this mysticism sees itself as a road to the redemption of men. Wherever this is the case, we have to do with the mysticism of the hero, who aspires to give the world a new face by his creative rebirth."[438]

FINDING MY WAY TO THE SELF

Like so many others, my journey has had ups and downs. I've stumbled along, succeeding and failing, in my efforts to evolve. And I've spent a great deal of time reflecting on the Baal Shem's parable as an expression of my journey. I've written about the barriers that held me back—psychological issues, my learning disorder—and there have been other obstacles too. Traditional Judaism, my entrance point to the quest, provided a religious foundation, but early on I naively took on its author-itarian dimension and its identification of text study as the highest ideal. In time, observing the mitzvot became rote and stale, a way to fulfill my religious obligations, lacking any transcendental meaning. One reason I allowed this to happen had to do with my overpowering inertia, my tendency to go to sleep. Often I would get trapped in secondary concerns and small comforts, losing my sense of vocation and self-worth. I was derailed by the moats of the castle, the apparent obstacles, and by the seeming treasures at the gates: my physical appetites, pride and sense of superiority in having found the truth, obsessions with photography and classical music, tendency to take on the personae and agendas of other people as if they were my own, and even my self-conscious devotion to my own growth!

Eventually I would find my way back to my spiritual aspiration. Reb Zalman used to speak about what he called "the heliotropism of the soul." Like a plant seeking the sun, I sought healing for my psychological issues through psychotherapy and spiritual direction. And my neshamah, my divine soul—which Jung called the Self—sought to steer me toward my true home in the depths of both my psyche and the world. This still, small voice could not be stifled. Eventually it led me toward my greatest pas-sion, deepening my love for God and for all of God's creations.

Despite the moats and the temptations of lesser treasures, I've pur-sued the path that the Baal Shem Tov laid out, aspiring to decenter the ego and to make the Self the true center of my life. This has opened me to greater love and compassion for other people, and for those who are suf-fering. I'm certainly not living in the Presence every moment, but when I engage in my spiritual practices, I can discern that I'm getting closer. When I falter, I seek guidance from within and find what I need to hear.

NOTHING WITHIN YOU BUT GOD

The Baal Shem asserted that the human psyche or soul is "a portion of Divinity beyond." Here is how he puts it: "You long for the Divine to descend upon you and enter your life? Then the most important thing for you to know and grasp is that there is nothing within you but God!"[439] This is the core of his psychological orientation. Idel believes that it was only late in life that he came to recognize God as the totality of every-thing. That's when the following insight must have come to him: "The lifegiving soul within a human being is one aspect of the lifegiving soul within all living and created being. And this great soul is itself the blessed Holy One."[440]

Does this claim mean that God encompasses evil as well as good? Jung certainly thought so. He was critical of traditional Christianity for its insistence that God was only good and then assigning the realm of evil to Satan or Lucifer. And Jung pointed to many places in the Hebrew Bible where God is depicted as having an evil as well as a good side, espe-cially the book of Job. Neumann was in complete agreement with Jung on this point. "It is only when man learns to experience himself as the creature of a Creator who made light and darkness, good and evil, that he becomes aware of his own Self as a paradoxical totality in which oppo-sites are linked together.... Only then will the unity of creation and of human existence escape destruction."[441]

As we've seen, the Baal Shem also emphasized the notion that every-thing, including evil, stems from God. I cannot put it better than the great neo-Hasidic teacher, Hillel Zeitlin:

> In seeking to present the essential teachings of Hasidism in consistent fashion, we have only the statement by the Besht and that which necessarily proceeds from it. On this basis we say that Hasidism recognizes no duality in creation, just as it knows none in the Creator. Hasidism sees only a single unified divine force, giving life in an absolutely equal way to all that is, both good and evil. Divinity, descending from "the Hidden of all Hiddens," is a force that proceeds from rung to rung, becoming ever coarser and more sensate. Only as it reaches the very end is it so hidden that it can barely be detected. When we contemplate those lower rungs, where no divine clarity can be perceived, we call them evil. The person who is attached only to them (their outer, not their inner qualities) we call an evildoer or a sinner. But when that

very person abandons those lowly rungs and reaches higher, or when he begins to see divinity within those lowly rungs themselves, he is engaged in redeeming and uplifting evil. To say it differently: he is raising up God's own Self, hidden within the coarseness of material existence, restoring it to its Source.[442]

The Besht was not the first kabbalist to recognize the existence of the sefirot within human beings, but his insights regarding the dynamics of the psyche show that he was keen on depicting the inner processes in a detailed way, using the language of the Kabbalah. In this sense, he is one of the precursors of modern psychology. In my studies of the Baal Shem's psychology, I've identified six ways that I believe he grasped the psychological character of the human soul:

- He sought to demonstrate ways that sacred narratives in the Torah could provide a kind of map for psychospiritual development.
- He wished to show how the great human virtues of love, awe, and compassion were anchored in the human soul through the sefirot.
- His psychological acumen shows through his use of the terminology of sefirot to describe ascent and expansiveness of the soul that occurs during ecstatic worship.
- He set out to understand ways in which individual consciousness expands and contracts, changing moods of the individual.
- He was concerned with linking and integrating the psychospiritual aspects of the psyche into a whole in such a way that the higher, more expansive levels would interpenetrate the lower levels to elevate the consciousness and conscience.
- He wished to explain how it was possible for tzaddikim to attain special psychic powers that would allow them to work for healing in the community.

My sense, then, is that the Besht's psychospiritual insights were meant to describe the inwardness of the soul as the tzaddikim went about their task of spiritualizing and elevating the lives of their own followers in the external world.

ERICH NEUMANN'S ROLE

It was Erich Neumann who persuaded Jung to study Kabbalah and Hasidism during the last decade of his life. Neumann left Germany and immigrated to Palestine to escape Nazism, where he composed an important book on Hasidism. *The Roots of Jewish Consciousness: Hasidism* wasn't published during its author's lifetime, and only saw the light in an English translation in 2019. Unable to read the original texts in Hebrew, Neumann depended on both Buber's interpretations and translations of Hasidic stories for his interpretation of Hasidism, along with what he had read by Scholem and other scholars.

Neumann makes the case that the new thing Hasidism brought to Judaism was an ethos of receptivity to the soul's ever-present guidance. He also focuses much of his attention on showing how the rebbes were engaged in the process of individuation. Reuven Kruger writes that Neumann's purpose in writing *The Roots of Jewish Consciousness* was his recognition that modern Judaism was in a spiritual crisis and the only way for it to be reborn was through the teachings of Hasidism. For Neumann this meant a "passionate call for constant inner renewal and self-contemplation."[443]

It seems fitting to end this chapter with two passages from Neumann's writings. The first comes from his essay, "Mystical Man," and has to do with the accomplishments of mature mystics from all of the world's mystical traditions, who have renewed their lives through undergoing individuation in a conscious way: "Only in the integrated man, who is attached to a center which is his own creative center and which he experiences as the creative center of the world, can the circle close; that circle is peace. For this illumined man the world is transparent and one.... In him lives the creative word and also silence. He lives in multiplicity and unity."[444]

And then, in his book on Hasidism, Neumann cited one of the Baal Shem Tov's ways of couching the same insight: "The human being has the duty to remember at all times that he is the son of the king of all kings, therefore he must not fall [in isolation] [with himself]." That is to say, no one is ever really isolated, for Divinity is always present within. And Neumann comments, "To achieve this level of undetermined freedom, unchained and unbound by all the world's conditions and determinations, counts as the fulfillment of the individual at the messianic level."[445]

CHAPTER TWENTY-SIX

THE IMMANENCE OF GOD AND CONTEMPORARY COSMOLOGY

"Religious experience is largely the experience of immanence,
of the divine as dressed in the garments of this world. We
discover the godly in the natural, through our own sense of awe
and wonder. It is this experience of immanence that leads us to
intuitive intimations that there is something 'beyond' as well."

ARTHUR GREEN[446]

"No Jew before had said, 'All is God.' He said it in Hebrew, '*Hakol Elohim*,' which means really practically, 'All is God.'" Those were the first words out of the mouth of Dr. Rachel Elior during a radio discussion panel about the Baal Shem Tov aired in 2010. Elior is a professor of Jewish mysticism and philosophy at the Hebrew University in Jerusalem. Her book, *The Mystical Origins of Hasidism* is a landmark in Baal Shem Tov scholarship. Later in the program, Elior admitted to being more at home with mathematics than with mysticism. But again and again, she returns to the same theme—Jewish mysticism reveals the deepening of inner freedom as a response to outer oppression. The Jewish mystics, Elior explains, "paved the way to new avenues in the history of freedom, where human beings succeeded in changing the course of history against all odds and managed to transform historic exile into different forms of human liberation." And one of the most important of those mystics was the Baal Shem Tov, for in his mystical ascents "he was capable of transcending the limits of time and place," and through his teaching and his example he "inspired his followers with a profound sense of freedom, imagination, and creativity."[447]

Much of *The Mystical Origins of Hasidism* is devoted to the Baal Shem, and more than any other modern scholar I've encountered, Elior's interest in him has to do with his mystical thought. "Too little attention has been given to the distinctiveness of the Baal Shem Tov's teachings and their tremendous impact on the development of Hasidism in its various forms in subsequent generations." What was it that was most novel and revolutionary about the Baal Shem's thought? Elior writes: "The Baal Shem Tov...focused his new order on the all-embracing divine reality that animates the universe and illuminates it with the light of *hesed* (mercy) and greatness, binding together the totality of revealed elements in a hidden unity. For him the visible world was inseparable from the divine spirit that animates it, and accordingly he required his followers to seek at all times the divine infinity lying beyond the limits of corporeality."[448]

ENDING SEPARATENESS

Elior cites the following teaching of the Baal Shem to substantiate her view of his worldview: "Whatever you are thinking about, that's where you will find God, for God's splendor fills all the earth, and there's no place devoid of the Divine. And wherever you happen to be, that's exactly where you will be able to bind yourself to the Creator."[449] She offers a novel perspective on this feature of the Besht's thought. But to comprehend her view, we first need to understand an important feature of traditional Judaism: the notion of *separation*—a deeply-rooted religious value that goes back to the earliest strata of biblical thought.

Jewish law meticulously distinguishes between the polarities of sacred and secular, virtue and sin, kosher and non-kosher, purity and uncleanness, Israel and the nations, men and women. And there is a definite sense of the superiority of the first term of each of these polarities. David Gelernter, a modern Orthodox Jew, writes that the multitude of laws that constitute the *halakhah*—Jewish law—cohere in an organic way, and that the unifying idea behind the entire system of Jewish law is *separation*.[450]

When three stars appear in the sky on Saturday night, religious Jews engage in a lovely and affecting ritual called Havdalah, during which participants bid farewell to the restfulness and joyousness of the Sabbath. The word *havdalah* means distinction or separation, separating the Sabbath from the coming week. A special braided candle with multiple wicks is lit and a blessing separating the new week from the departing Sabbath is chanted over a cup of wine. During the ceremony it is customary for those attending to gaze at their fingernails reflecting the light of the havdalah candle. This flame also symbolizes the light of the disappearing Sabbath, offering participants a symbolic bit of that light to carry them through the rigors of the coming week. A decorative box containing sweet-smelling plant spices, such as cinnamon or nutmeg, is handed around so that everyone can smell the scent of Shabbat and carry its fragrance into the week. Finally, the leader chants the havdalah blessing: "Blessed are You, our EverPresent God, Sovereign of the universe, separating the sacred from the ordinary, light from darkness, Israel from the nations, the seventh day from the six days of labor. Blessed are You, EverPresent, separating the sacred from the ordinary."

"To live by halakha," writes Gelernter, "means to use ritual acts of separation to create sanctity, and thereby make life into one continuous act of sanctification. Sanctity requires separation: between man and the beast inside; between our high aspirations and our animal nature."[451] And he explains that the value of separation also means traditional Jews insist that the natural world and people must be separate, and Jewish people must physically withdraw from others. Likewise, for many religious Jews, modern as well as traditional, it is a foundational theological tenet that God, humanity, and the world are ontologically separate. The gap between God and humanity is vast, even though for traditional Jews it can be bridged through prayer, study of Torah, and holy deeds.

But Rachel Elior writes that the Baal Shem attempted to put an end to this ancient view of separation, for central to his thought was his tendency "to blur the borders between the divine and the human, between the fantastic and the real.... The basis of his innovative authority was the intensity with which his consciousness breached the bounds of imagination and reality, sanity and madness, self and other, human and divine. The revolution that the Baal Shem Tov engendered is anchored in the blurring of distinctions upon which tradition is based."[452] This is where Elior finds what she believes is most innovative in the Besht's worldview. The Kabbalistic Tree of Life and the sefirot are arranged in a hierarchal descending order. Thus, the sefirot at the very top of the tree are closer to the underlying essence of reality than the sefirot lower down. But what if God is everywhere and everything? "Attention has long since been drawn to the centrality of the idea of immanence in Hasidism," Elior states, "yet evidently it has yet to be realized that the presumption of immanence... entirely uproots the point of the Kabbalist hierarchy."[453]

Because the Besht "blurred" the distinctions which form the basis of Jewish religion, it became difficult if not impossible to distinguish matter from spirit. Elior makes the point that he did not feel hemmed in by the multitude of polarities and categories that characterized traditional Judaism, and this allowed him to open his heart and soul to a profound sense of inner freedom, imagination, and creativity. At the same time, it is important to note that in practice the Besht did not abandon the norms of Jewish communal life, nor did he attempt to reform Jewish law.

TWELVE MYSTICAL CONCEPTS

What else was new in the teachings of the Besht? In an academic article issued in English after the publication of *The Mystical Origins of Hasidism,* Elior discusses twelve mystical concepts he formulated. These, she writes, were intended to be understood, practiced, and shared equally by all male members of the community and through all modes of worship by virtue of the radical claim that God, who fills the universe with glory, is present in human thought and human speech. Thus, "God wants to be served in all modes.... God can be served in everything."

We have met a number of these concepts and values already in this book, but I'd like to summarize Elior's views here, since she makes the point that they have a special meaning in the life and work of the founder of Hasidism.

1.   *Devekut,* which is unity with the Holy One, or attachment or adhesion to God, is a principle demanding total devotion to God to the extent of renouncing the realities of the material world and transcending one's own self in order to enter the domain of Nothingness and achieve true unification with the divine through higher levels of spiritual apprehension.

2.   *Thought.* By virtue of its divine source, human thought is able to overcome the limits of physical perception, recognizing the essential infinite Nothingness of being.

3.   *Letters.* The Baal Shem Tov maintained that the infinity of language in general and every letter of the holy tongue in particular are the most obvious location of the Divine Presence.

4.   *Bitul hayesh,* the negation or nullification of being, is the effort

to transcend physical reality in order to uncover the divine element that animates it.

5. *Nefesh elohit*, the divine soul or the eye of the intellect. The divine soul that every Jew possesses in potential strives to elevate everything to the spiritual level, to strip away materiality in order to reveal the divine element underlying the concrete manifestation.

6. *Hafshatat hagashmiyut*, the divestment of materiality or the stripping away of corporeality. A process that expresses the desire of the divine soul to transcend corporeality by means of prayer and contemplation and uncover the divine element that animates it.

7. *Hishtav'ut*, equanimity or indifference. Equanimity is an ascetic state in which all values and concepts relating to concrete existence are to be regarded as meaningless.

8. *Hitbonenut*, contemplation. Meditation on the Divine Presence that underlies physical manifestations in order to see in everything its supreme root and source.

9. *Avodah begashmiyut*, worship through corporeality. This concept refers to the name for the quest for the divine essence in the multi-faceted nature of material reality or the expansion of religious worship to all areas of human life by according religious significance to all ordinary activities.

10. *Olam hadibur medaber b'adam*, the Shekhinah, the Divine Presence, is also called the world of holy speech that can speak through the mouths of human beings. The Besht stated in an unprecedented way that every human being can become a vessel for the divine voice.

11. *Kavanot*, expressions of mystical intent, and *Yihudim*, unifications, are mystical meditations aimed at restoring the ultimate unity of the divine realm that was shattered in the process of creation in a cosmic catastrophe known as the "Breaking of the Vessels" or *Shevirat ha'kelim*.

12. *Gadlut*, greatness of spirit, is the sense of broadmindedness and expansive vistas generated by distancing oneself from worldly concerns and coming closer to God and to the sense

of redemption; *Katnut,* on the other hand, is pettiness or small-mindedness generated by submission to the constraints of reality which is perceived as exile.[454]

I find Elior's description of the Baal Shem's consciousness and thought dizzying. His was a unique consciousness, she writes, more expansive and wide-ranging than that of his contemporaries, able to embrace the panorama of human and divine existence. From a psychological perspective, one could say that the normal bounds that keep most people locked in their ego consciousness were missing from the Besht. I was thrilled by Elior's crystal-clear clarity and precision. She goes into greater depth than any of the current scholars in her portrayal of the master's worldview. And yet as I reflected on her assessment in the light of my own knowledge of his teachings, it seemed to me that perhaps she took her insight a bit too far.

First, I'm not convinced that the Baal Shem did away with all hierarchy. Even though he experienced the presence of Divinity in everything, he continued to distinguish between the differing levels of holiness as defined by Jewish tradition. He frequently made use of traditional vertical imagery, speaking of higher and lower dimensions of reality. He also distinguished between inner and outer, emphasizing the superiority of inwardness. The Besht also honored the distinctions between Shabbat, holy days, and weekdays. Though he extended honor toward common people, even those who were unlearned, he definitely exalted the tzaddik as an extraordinary human being because of attainments that led him into an enlightened relationship with God. He also distinguished between Jew and Gentile, often portraying the former in a more positive light. The Baal Shem did not seek to eliminate hierarchy which, as Huston Smith has shown, was part and parcel of virtually every religious worldview before the advent of modernity.[455] What the Baal Shem was certain of was that every rung of reality, whether high or low, was imbued with Divinity. And since "there is no place devoid of the Divine," the tzaddik was bound to pay equal attention to each and every occurrence, and to every human being and creature in his orbit, acknowledging everything and everyone as a manifestation of the sacred.

It also seems that Elior's terminology, "blurring the boundaries," is not quite right. Perhaps from a rational discursive perspective anchored in ordinary dualistic consciousness "blurring" might be the correct term, but I can personally testify that in the throes of mystical experience there are no boundaries to blur. In the kind of unitary state of consciousness that I have experienced both through psychedelics and mystical worship things simply flow into one another because all things are fully interconnected and one at their core.

What was the origin of what Elior calls the Besht's "blurring" of the distinctions between things? Undoubtedly this feature of his thought derived from the tremendous experience of Oneness that he experienced during his mystical experiences. This was an embracing unity that dissolved the myriad details of the world, returning his consciousness to *Ayin,* the No-thing-ness out of which it originally arose. The Maggid of Medziritch describes that experience this way: "You must forget yourself in prayer. Think of yourself as nothing and pray only for the sake of God. In such prayer you may come to transcend time, entering the highest realms of the World of Thought. There all things are as one; distinctions between 'life' and 'death,' 'land' and 'sea,' have lost their meaning. But none of this can happen as long as you remain attached to the reality of the material world. Here you are bound to the distinctions between good and evil that emerge only in the lower realms of God. How can one who remains attached to his own self go beyond time to the world where all is one?"[456] Also, Jacob Joseph of Polonoyye cites a teaching in the Baal Shem's name that states how in the highest dimensions (i.e., the sefirot of Binah, Hokhma, and Keter) in the Tree of Life, the Divine is absolutely one; and in the lower dimensions, opposites of all kinds prevail and Divinity is thus perceived as being manifold. This multiplicity includes what is permitted and what is forbidden, impure and pure, etc. And the Besht does not seek to denigrate the lower forms of divine reality.[457]

I am grateful to Elior for locating the twelve mystical concepts of the Besht. However, I find myself disagreeing with her judgement that he placed so much emphasis on transcendence. I don't read the texts that way. When the master states "there is no place devoid of the Divine," I believe he meant just that—that every manifestation of the finite is occupied by the Infinite. Elior's depiction of the Baal Shem's attitude toward the mundane world belongs more to his disciple, Rabbi Dov Baer, the Maggid of Medziritch who, as Elior states, "spiritualized" Beshtian views. I do believe, however, that his experience of *Ayin,* No-thingness, brought him to a recognition that the creations of the physical world are all ephemeral, and therefore have only a relative reality.

THE BESHT'S THOUGHT AS PHILOSOPHY

Ontology is part of a branch of philosophy known as metaphysics, and those dedicated to its study deal with concepts that directly relate to being, in particular becoming, existence, reality, as well as basic categories of being and their interrelations. As I studied her formulation of the Baal Shem's thought, it seemed that Rachel Elior was primarily interested in his ontology. Her presentation of his vision is a translation of the mythic kabbalistic language used by the Besht into a philosophical interpretation of the meaning of that vision. Although she doesn't state this outright, it is clear that Elior believes the Besht's mystical thought doesn't lend itself to a linear and logical presentation, and thus she summarizes his views as a series of interrelated conceptual strands. Some ideas may seem to contradict others, but that is because of the paradoxical character inherent in mystical thought.

- *Divinity is the all-embracing unity of existence.* The visible world appears to be an amalgam of independent particulars, but this perception is false. A profound unity animates the universe and illuminates it with the light of mercy and greatness, binding together the totality of revealed elements in a hidden unity.
- *Divine vitality is present in every being and is the basis of each being's existence.* God is the essence that animates all physical forms. And because God is equally present everywhere and in all things, there is actually no gap between God and humanity.
- *Reality may be perceived from a human perspective or a divine perspective.* When we look at the world from the human perspective, we see only physical reality, yet this is merely a barrier created by the human imagination. But when we perceive the world from a divine perspective—that is, in a state of mystical illumination— the physical world turns out to be an illusion without substance. All is divinity. But to reach such a level of awareness requires

cultivating a sense of detachment from the manifest world and concentrating thought on the truth of reality from the divine vantage point.[458]

· *Being implies the simultaneous existence of the physical and the spiritual in dialectical relationship.* The world is filled with polarities, things that seem to be in opposition to one another; but these polarities don't have independent existences, for everything is interrelated. Thus, physicality always implies spirituality. And finite being means that there is also an infinite nothingness. Revelation implies concealment. Divine perfection lies in the unification of these opposites, and human perfection lies in the recognition of this unity of opposites and the internalization of this recognition in the service of God. But just as the divine spirit emanates and withdraws, expands and contracts, ebbs and flows, so the human spirit experiences an alternation of spirituality and physicality, expansiveness and contraction.

· *Every physical phenomenon has at its root a divine element, a hidden truth that lies beyond manifest reality.* No aspect of reality should be taken at face value, because every manifestation conceals a divine essence. To put it another way, everything in the physical world is a manifestation of the hidden divine.

· *The transition from the mundane to the divine is achieved through the power of human thought.* Because human thought is divine in origin, it seeks to return to its source; human thought is able to transcend the senses and physical world, reaching beyond the finite and entering the infinite. This is how the mystic becomes one with God.[459]

· *In the beginning, God spoke the world into existence, and thus the world consists of the divine speech of God.* Just as the infinite light of the vitality of the universe fills everything, so it fills the letters of the Hebrew tongue, the language used by God to create. Thus, God can be found in the very words that we pray, study, and speak. The Torah is written in Hebrew, the sacred language, and because of this its study can link us to the Divine. Language is also the vehicle of the act of prayer that transports a worshipper back to God because God can be found in the words of prayer.

All human beings use language, and so every individual comprehends this world and has access to the higher worlds as far as their thoughts permit. Through speech a person becomes a partner in the divine process of creation.

- *Everyone, at all times and in all places, can contemplate the hidden divine root of manifest physical being and come closer to the divine essence.* Human beings must strive to recognize God's presence in every thought and action. We have a responsibility to seek God in the material world, even in ordinary activities that are not usually thought of as religious. In this way we become attached to God at all times and in all ways. And we also unite the Shekhinah with the Blessed Holy One, that is, the indwelling divine presence with the transcendent holiness. God is present in the world through the holy sparks of divine light that fill all creations. Through our good and holy acts, we elevate those sparks back to their source.

- *Finally, according to some Hasidic traditions, the Besht's teachings were meant to be egalitarian.* His social ethos was directed to broad public dissemination rather than to a scholarly elite. He taught that every individual should be aware of the divine presence at all times, striving to see things from the expansiveness of the divine perspective, and listening for the divine voice ever renewed in the human mind. Those who are unable or unwilling to attain this level may rely on the zaddik to act on their behalf.

I am not certain that Elior is correct on this last point. It would seem that the Baal Shem's teachings were directed toward his disciples and colleagues, and not to all the members of the Jewish community.

NONDUAL REALITY

What strikes me most profoundly about the Baal Shem's vision as seen in Elior's philosophical interpretation is its universality. It seems that by focusing on the Besht's ontology she lifts him out of his eighteenth-century Jewish setting and reveals his discoveries as a gift for those seeking a worldview centered on the sacred character of the earth, humanity, and the cosmos, coupled with a profound sense of the Oneness and mystery of existence. What message could be more relevant for an age in which human beings have lost their sense of the sacred and have no compunction about degrading and destroying the planet of which we are part?

Her interpretation of the Besht's wide-ranging perception of reality also recalls the descriptions of existence that I found in the writings of some of the world's greatest mystics. Her formulation reminded me of Lao Tzu's Tao Te Ching, the classic teaching of philosophical Taoism, one of my favorite spiritual texts. It states, "Every being in the universe is an expression of the Tao.... The Tao gives birth to all beings, nourishes them, maintains them, cares for them, comforts them, protects, them, takes them back to itself."[460] It also reminds me of the wisdom of the Upanishads. In the religious vocabulary of those ancient sages the word "Self" is a primary term for the Divinity that is immanent in all reality. One finds there: "Self is everywhere, shining forth from all beings, vaster than the vast, subtler than the most subtle, unreachable, yet nearer than breath, than heartbeat." Etc.[461]

In the Baal Shem's vision, as in these eastern sources, there's a recognition of a nondual reality at the center of existence and at the core of the human self, and that reality represents the underlying truth of the universe. For all three of these sources, reality is nondualistic—a recognition that underlying the multiplicity and diversity of experience there is a single, infinite, and indivisible reality whose nature is pure consciousness, from which all objects and selves derive their apparently independent existence.

I don't believe that the kind of philosophical rendering of the Baal Shem's vision Elior offers can replace the master's original mythic framework and the symbols and metaphors he used. Joseph Campbell asserted that myths offer a greater truth than anything in the realm of logic. They are filled with riches because they have multiple layers of meaning. And they are clues to the spiritual potentialities of the human life. "Every myth," Campbell stated, "is psychologically symbolic. Its narratives and images are to be read, therefore, not literally, but as metaphors." I ultimately find Elior's approach to be analogous to summarizing a poem in prose. While the conceptual meaning of the language employed by the poet may become clearer, there is a loss of the imaginative awareness and emotional power that poetic language or mythic imagery can, at its best, evoke. There is something about a sacred image that has the evocative power to take one to a deeper place in the heart than a philosophical concept.

CHAPTER TWENTY-SEVEN

KABBALAH, VEDANTA, AND GOD

I have shared my fascination with the Upanishads, the teachings of the ancient forest sages of India. I have been most taken by the truth revealed by those teachers that the Atman, the spiritual core in human beings is one with Brahman, the Divinity of the universe. And when I discovered the Baal Shem Tov, I was amazed to find that the mystical anthropology of Vedanta paralleled his understanding of the relationship of the human soul to God.

The Besht's views about God come directly from the Kabbalah, even though he modified them, focusing more on the human psyche than on the universe. In the course of my studies, I came upon a small book by James N. Judd that compares ancient Hindu thought with the teachings of the Kabbalah. In *Two Ways of Light: Kabbalah and Vedanta,* Judd writes that the two paths seem different from one another, but this is only true on the surface. When seen through a spiritual lens they provide the same basic message, and, in fact, augment one another, shedding a brighter light on various spiritual issues:

> There is one truth behind this universe. The various religions have different names for it—God, Jehovah, Brahman—but they are all talking about the same Being. God is God, regardless of what men say about Him. It is the same God who is sought and worshipped in all the religions of the world. Man's attempt to establish contact with this one Being is the core of all religions.[462]

Judd lays bare both the differences and the similarities of the two paths. I was particularly interested when the author compared passages from the Isa Upanishad with statements found in kabbalistic writings. Here's a translation of the eighth verse of the Isa Upanishad followed by a parallel text from the Kabbalah:

He, the self-existent One is everywhere, without a (subtle) body, without muscles (a physical body), and without the taint of sin; radiant, whole, and seeing all, knowing all, and encompassing all. He has duly assigned their respective duties to the eternal Prajapatis (cosmic powers).

Furthermore, the Most Holy Ancient One is symbolized and concealed under the conception of the Unity, for He Himself is One, and all things are One. And thus all the other lights are sanctified, are restricted, and are bound together in the Unity or Monad and are One.[463]

In his commentary on the two passages, Judd writes that everything in our human world is encompassed by the divine Self. Therefore, all human beliefs, even those that deny the existence of God, are actually views of the same reality. Furthermore, arguments about which views are most accurate are unimportant and "push us farther away from the One Cause that is the unifying reality behind all these discords and conflicts. Our energies should be expended in searching deeper within to find the self-existing One."[464] It has become clear to me that the Hindu and the Jewish mystical visions both understand the spiritual journey as a movement from ego-centeredness to God-centeredness, and both profess that what comes with enlightenment is the recognition that the core of the human self (*atman/neshamah*) is the divine Self (*Brahman/Y-H-V-H*).

Let us now take a closer look at another text, the Brihad Aranyska Upanishad, the oldest and largest of the collection, where we will find more similarities between the two traditions. In it, we discover:

- Brahman is the single underlying reality beneath the multiplicity of existence. This reality is ineffable and is impossible to grasp or to define in human language, but it is both the cause of existence and its absolute ground.
- Despite its multiplicity the world is nevertheless one. This unity includes the no-thingness beyond the world that is eternal and unchanging.
- The Divine is simultaneously immanent and transcendent,

and because of this all things are interconnected. Thus, human beings are linked to everything else.

· Because Brahman is everywhere, it is everything that we experience through our senses.

· The immortal, unchanging self (atman) within our depths is different from the external ego self (*ahamkara*) which is separate, transitory, bound to the body, and subject to suffering and death.

· When the seeker is transformed from the ego-self (*ahamkara*) to the immortal, unchanging self (atman), the atman becomes the knower of all knowledge.

These parallel views make clear, at least in part, why I was so drawn to the Baal Shem Tov's vision of existence. It seems that with the help of the Kabbalah, he was able to reach an understanding of the nature of the world and the identity of the human being quite similar to the vision described in this Upanishad. I cannot prove this because nowhere in the immense collection of teachings recorded by the master's disciples do we find a text that organizes them into a step-by-step progression that would demonstrate affinity with the Upanishads. But as far as I can tell, every one of the steps in the Brihad Aranyska has its analogy in the Baal Shem's thought.

SANKARA VS. RAMANUJA

In later Indian tradition, there are two major interpretations of the Vedanta teachings in the Upanishads. Sankara, a sage who lived in the eighth century C.E., taught that Brahman is absolute reality. It is true, Sankara maintains, that existence as we ordinarily perceive it in all of its multiplicity holds a certain reality for most people. And Sankara even recognizes that this conventional reality is Brahman, but he maintains that physical forms represent a lower form of Brahman. But when the seeker overcomes his ignorance, he will come to recognize that this limited perception is in truth illusion (*maya*). Sankara's school is known as Nondualism.

Then there was Ramanuja, an eleventh-century sage whose school is called Qualified Nondualism. Ramanuja taught that the physical world and individual souls are the actual forms through which God manifests himself. As Joseph P. Schultz writes, for Ramanuja, "God or Brahman is both transcendent and immanent, transcendent as pure being and intelligence, immanent in that he holds within Him as His body the individual souls and the world of matter.... Brahman has transformed Himself into the world, and the many souls that are particular states of Him are at the same time one with Him and yet have a real existence as His parts or states."[465]

The Baal Shem Tov's outlook is closer to that of Ramanuja than to Sankara, while the stance of the Maggid of Medziritch comes closer to Sankara. A careful reading of Elior's depiction of the Baal Shem's ontology reveals that she included the contradictory views that characterized the approaches of both Sankara and Ramanuja in her paradoxical understanding of his ontology. I believe there may be a way to reconcile the presence of both viewpoints.

As previously pointed out, in his instructions to his disciples the Baal Shem often refers to two major states of awareness, *gahd'lut,* expanded consciousness, and *kaht'nut,* contracted consciousness. He explained that the life of the mystic brings with it a periodic shuttling of awareness back and forth between the two states, and he taught his disciples to embrace this alternating rhythm of awareness as the will of God. As Rabbi Jacob Joseph writes in the name of his teacher:

> There are two primary states of consciousness, *gahd'lut* and *kaht'nut.* When you are in a state of *gahd'lut,* you are able to pray in deep awe and love, knowing that you are speaking with the great Sovereign, and that you are intimately bound to God's blessed presence. Certainly there is no greater delight than such an experience, and yet it is not possible to remain continually in such a state. When you are in the state of *kaht'nut,* you will have to undergo a great struggle in order to once again get close to the blessed One. But nevertheless, you will receive great rewards for your efforts.[466]

Also: "What is contracted awareness like? Your service to God derives from neither awe nor love. Instead, you do what you know you must do without experiencing any pleasure."[467] But even though there is greater reality to the experience of expanded awareness, there are reasons why God allows the seeker to lapse into contracted awareness: "I heard this from my master: If it happens that you are drawn away from the study of Torah, or from the act of prayer, understand that this, too, comes from God's hand. You are being pushed away in order that your longing for closeness to God will become stronger"; "When you find yourself in a contracted state, remember where you are, for through such awareness you will be able to sweeten adversity at its root."[468]

In other teachings, the Besht explained that the soul always longs for God but the body has desires for food and sex and other physical needs, and these, too, come from God and must be fulfilled. The great task of separating the holy sparks from the husks that hold them captive can only be accomplished in kaht'nut. The Besht counselled disciples to engage in devekut even when they found themselves in a contracted state, because God can be found in all of experience, whether spacious or limited in character. The enlightened tzaddik, however, has greater access to the state of gahd'lut, and it becomes his responsibility to channel the abundance (shefah) he receives while in that state to the denizens of the world, and in this way elevate earthly existence toward the sacred.

The state of oneness with the Divine is experienced in gahd'lut, and thus it seems to me, gahd'lut may be closer to nondual awareness, while the designation kaht'nut may point to a more dualistic apprehension of existence. If I am correct about this, the Besht was making room for both nondual and dualistic awareness at different moments in the seeker's life. For him it was important to continually link dualistic with nondual consciousness, reunifying the fragmentariness that results from losing contact with the greater whole. This was the ultimate purpose of his practice of *yihudim* (unification or integration).

GOD'S PRESENCE AND IMMANENCE IN EARLY HASIDISM

In what was possibly the first essay on Hasidism in the English language, Solomon Schechter wrote: "The keystone of all Baalshem's teachings is the Omnipresence, or more strictly the Immanence, of God.... The idea of the constant living presence of God in all existence permeates the whole of Baalshem's scheme; it is insisted upon in every relation; from it is deduced every important proposition and every rule of conduct of his school."[469] In this chapter and the last we have explored the Baal Shem's views about divine immanence in great detail and now we need to look at the ways in which the master's notions about divine presence informed the experiences and tenets of Hasidism in the early days of the movement.

In *The Mystical Origins of Hasidism,* Rachel Elior admits that she has integrated the views of the Baal Shem Tov with those of his disciple, Dov Baer, the Maggid of Medzeritch, whose views she finds "more spiritual" than the Besht's. Arthur Green also assumes that Hasidism was built on foundations established by both the Besht and the Maggid.

How do the two founders of Hasidism differ from one another? Green writes that the Baal Shem was a shaman as well as a mystic, and he was ecstatic and experiential, while the Maggid was more scholastic and contemplative. "This is not to say that his mysticism lacked an experiential dimension," writes Green, "but it lacked the dramatic manifestations of the Besht's *ekstasis.* While one disciple claimed that the Besht taught the Maggid his supernatural ways, the two seem quite different in their mystical practice, and there is no evidence that Dov Baer passed these teachings of the Besht on to the next generation."[470] Green goes on to identify eight tenets he believes lay at the heart of the nascent Hasidic movement. I have simplified his more detailed account of these values, in what you see below. The theme of God's presence and immanence is integral to each point:

1. The purpose of life is the joyous service of God. Our task as Jews is to accomplish that through constant good works and joyous praise.

2. God needs to be served in every way. All of life, including the mitzvot and the fulfillment of our physical needs, is to become an avenue of devotion.

3. The essence of religious life lies in inwardness and spiritual intensity. The great battle to be fought is that against routinized religious behavior, the opposite of spiritual enthusiasm. Outer deeds are the means to bring divine light into the soul.

4. All of existence originates in the mind of God, where Being is a simple, undifferentiated whole. Because God is beyond time,

that reality has never changed. In ultimate reality, our existence as separate individuals is mostly an illusion.

5. God's presence underlies, fills, and includes all existence. Sparks of divine light are therefore to be found everywhere. The Jew's task is to seek out and discover those sparks in order to raise them up and bring joy to Shekhinah, re-establishing the divine unity that embraces all of being in Oneness.

6. Prayer is the most essential act of devotional experience, more important than sacred study. All of life—including but not limited to Torah study and mitzvot—should be seen as an extension of the prayer experience.

7. Our human task is uplifting and transforming our physical and emotional selves to become more perfect vehicles for God's service. We need to realize that the only true love is the love of God and the only worthy fear is awe at standing in God's presence.

8. The person who lives in accord with these teachings may become a tzaddik, a channel for bringing that flow of blessing not only to himself, but to those around him and ultimately the world.[471]

Green writes that points one, three, six, and seven are especially prominent in the Maggid's discourses. I'm not expert in the teachings of the Maggid, but my studies of the Baal Shem have revealed that all these points have their origin in his vision, with the exception of number four. In the sources I've encountered, the Besht does not focus on the unchanging transcendental nature of the Divine, nor does he view human experience as illusory. A better way of characterizing his view of ordinary human perception would be that it is *partial*, and yet, even with its limitations, "there is no place devoid of the Divine."

THE WORLD AS LOVER

Does the concept of immanence have a place today in a secular world bound to the certainties of science and technology? Not really, for the notion of immanence implies that something beyond human comprehension is manifesting in and through the physical world. Mainstream science, on the other hand, has nothing to say about the possibility of a transcendent reality, even though there are scientists who affirm something enigmatic beyond or deep within the material world. But by its own definitions the discipline of science can only deal with that which can be measured.

For all intents and purposes, then, most scientists conceive of the universe as a material entity, even though quantum physicists claim that at root matter itself is an illusion! It seems to me that a moral problem arises from this reductionistic view, for it can easily abet the belief that the natural world has no inherent sanctity and therefore can be used by humans for their own benefit. And coupled with an economic system like consumer-oriented capitalism, as in the West, this so-called "objective" attitude toward the world has led humanity toward a lack of respect for and responsibility toward the world of nature. The environmental catastrophe we are facing is a direct outcome of this proprietary posture of science and technology toward the world.

This utilitarian way of looking at the natural world displaced the more holistic views of mythmakers and poets going back to the beginnings of humanity. Many of those visionaries testified to the existence of something wondrous, awesome, and inconceivable that informed the cosmos, a mysterious presence that lay beyond the confines of the physical world. These wisdom teachers made use of numerous kinds of imagery and language to describe that reality, but however they described it they knew in their hearts that it was sacred and that it required respect and responsibility. While the undeniable advances of science and technology have eclipsed the concerns of the soul for many today, there are still those who can see through the illusions of materialism. They know the preciousness of existence, whether there is something that transcends the physical world or not.

Joanna Macy, an activist and scholar of Buddhism and general systems theory, coined the phrase "the world as lover," i.e., the world beheld as a most intimate and gratifying power. In Hinduism, she writes, Krishna evokes in his devotees the desire for the bliss of union with the Divine. "As you sing your yearning for the sparkle of his eyes, the touch of his lips, the blue shade of his skin...the whole world takes on his beauty and the sweetness of his flesh. You feel yourself embraced in the primal erotic play of life."[472] And, Macy writes, this kind of affirmation is not limited to Hinduism. "Ancient Goddess religions, now being explored (at last!) carry it too, as do strains of Sufism and the Kabbalah, and Christianity has its tradition of bridal mysticism." And, I would add, Hasidism. Once again, I imagine the Baal Shem Tov making love to the Shekhinah in his davening; but also embracing in love all those particular creations—human or non-human—whom he encounters as he moves through his ordinary yet extraordinary life.

THE DISAPPEARANCE OF GOD

Although mainstream science still affirms and works within a materialistic framework, there is a shift going on. A growing number of scientists are acknowledging the limitations of the old paradigm and looking for ways to integrate the spirit into their worldviews. One of the first of these was Albert Einstein. "The most beautiful experience we can have is the mysterious," he famously wrote. Physicist Alan Lightman explains: "What did Einstein mean by 'the mysterious'? I don't think he meant that science is full of unpredictable or unknowable or supernatural forces. I believe that he meant a sense of awe, a sense that there are things larger than us, that we don't have all the answers at this moment. A sense that we stand right at the edge between known and unknown and gaze into that cavern and be exhilarated rather than frightened."[473]

In 1995 I attended an evening book reading at Cody's Books, which was at the time the largest bookstore in Berkeley. The theme of the evening was Kabbalah and modern physics and cosmology, and two authors shared the podium, Daniel Matt and Richard Elliot Friedman. At the time Matt was a professor of Jewish spirituality at the Graduate Theological Union in Berkeley. He was also a longtime friend, and I'd read his *God & the Big Bang* when it was first published a few years before. I loved what Matt did in the book. Drawing from modern cosmology and ancient Kabbalah, he showed how science and religion could together enrich our awareness and help us recover a sense of wonder. Science and spirituality, he wrote, are distinct but complementary. "Science enables us to probe infinitesimal particles of matter and unimaginable depths of outer space, understanding each in light of the other. Spirituality guides us through inner space, challenging us to retrace our path to oneness and to live in the light of what we discover."

Richard Friedman was one of the preeminent biblical scholars and had written many popular books in that field. His new work was really a change of pace for him. *The Disappearance of God: A Divine Mystery,* (later retitled, *The Hidden Face of* God) deals with a remarkable historical phenomenon, the gradual eclipse of God as a tangible presence in Western civilization. Friedman shows that while God is a fully present character in the early narratives of the Hebrew scriptures, he gradually disappears from view in the later books of the Bible, leaving human beings to fend for themselves. And Friedman emphasizes that from that point on the experience of God's presence is replaced by faith and belief and an adherence to sacred scripture in western religion.

This insight was quite striking to me. It was like seeing the seeds of secularism beginning to emerge in the biblical period itself. Friedman then jumps to the modern era. In the nineteenth century, Dostoyevsky and Nietzsche both recognized that religion had been displaced by secularity, and they proclaimed that God was dead or irrelevant for most people. What, then, might revive God as a living reality? Friedman asks. He turns toward parallels between Big Bang cosmology and Kabbalah, looking for a way that contemporary people might connect with the awesome mysteries of existence that are being explored by scientists today. Toward the end, he offers a prediction of what he imagines a reunion with God might be like for humanity: "What we encounter may or may not fulfill what we have historically sought or needed from a God. It may or may not be what anybody means by God now. It may not be a personal God. In the light of discoveries concerning the origin of the cosmos that we have made already, we can anticipate that, whatever we find, it will be everywhere, function everywhere, it will be in us, and we will be in it, as conceived in Big Bang and in Kabbalah; it will be in stars and in stones and in light and in flesh; it will determine everything, and explain everything, it will relate to our consciousness in some way; and it will impart awe. And this approaches what we, in Western civilization, call God. It may turn out to be something closer to the concepts of Eastern religions, which are not centered in a deity the way Western religions are. Or it may be a deeper force, in which both Western and Eastern religions respond in their respective ways."[474]

"It will be in us, and we will be in it . . ." This would be one way of translating and updating the Baal Shem Tov's vision of reality for today. More recently, Stuart Kauffman, a theoretical biologist who taught at the

University of Chicago, reached a similar conclusion. He is critical of the reigning scientific paradigm that reduces everything in the universe to the sub-atomic particles that make up existence, and believes that the qualities of Divinity we hold sacred—creativity, meaning, and purposeful action—are in fact properties of the universe itself that can be investigated scientifically. Kauffman argues for the continued use of the word God. He writes that "no other human symbol carries millennia of awe and reverence," and then continues:

> The God we discuss, then, might be God as the unfolding of nature itself.... Thus we may wish to broaden our sense of God from the creativity in nature to all of nature.... Then all the unfolding of nature is God, a fully natural God. And such a natural God is not far from an old idea of God *in* nature, an immanent God, found in the unfolding of nature.[475]

Pondering Friedman's and Kauffman's words I thought of the text I first encountered so many years before: "The basic approach of our teacher, the Baal Shem Tov, was a simple teaching that can be expressed in two different ways: 1. Divinity is all; and 2. Everything is divine."[476] If it is a single truth, why express it in two different ways? The first statement answers the question, "Who or what is God?" And the second, "What, really, is this world in which we live?" But for a mystic like the Baal Shem, such a brief theological summation would hardly be enough, for what these words attempt to express in such a pithy way was to him the very essence, the living core of his consciousness and existence.

I really like what Kauffman has to say about God. I, too, believe that no other human symbol carries such awe and reverence. And for me the word "God" has to do with recognizing the sacredness of all existence. In this time of the degradation of the natural world, of the mad and foolish misuse of its resources, of the possible end of life as we know it on this planet, it becomes a primary religious obligation to stand for the sacred in all of its forms and to say no to those who care only for their own profits. But I'm not unalterably wedded to the word "God." I understand those who would never use a name for the great mystery that is so freighted with centuries of negative overlay. But for me, as for Richard Friedman, the primary question is not what to name the ultimate, but rather the cultivation of the qualities of amazement, reverence, appreciation, gratitude, and love elicited by paying attention to the unbelievably marvelous nature of existence.

EMBODYING THE COSMOS

Earlier I cited the mathematical cosmologist Brian Thomas Swimme, a gifted writer who has written books for laypeople laying out the story of the unfolding universe in lyrical and accessible language. His book, *The Universe Is a Green Dragon,* is a *tour de force.* Recognizing the beauty, wonder, and sacred character of it all, Swimme develops a new vocabulary of immanence, describing the cosmos as a mysterious, enchanting, and almost living reality. When Swimme writes about the universe and its genesis one gets the sense of his utter respect for the greatest reality that human beings can know. *The Universe Is a Green Dragon* is fashioned like a Platonic dialogue, a youth in dialogue with an elder named Thomas. The book opens with the youth asking Thomas, "Why do you say the universe is a green dragon?" And Thomas answers, "for several reasons. I call the universe a green dragon to remind us that we will never be able to capture the universe with language."

> YOUTH: How can you be certain of that?
>
> THOMAS: Because the universe is a singularity! To speak, you need to compare things. Thus we say that the house is white, not brown. Or that the man is hostile, not kind. Or that it happened in the nineteenth century, not before. But there is only *one* universe. We cannot compare the universe with anything. We cannot *say* the universe.
>
> I call the universe a green dragon because I want to avoid lulling you into thinking we can have the universe in our grasp, like a stray dog shut up in its kennel. I want to remind us of this proper relationship as we approach the Whole of Things.[477]

And here Swimme gives himself away. The universe is *the Whole of Things*; in other words, what nondual spirituality has often identified as

"God." Swimme grew up in the Catholic faith, but it's obvious that he's no longer comfortable using theological language. And yet his cosmological framework is most certainly spiritual.

Later in the book, Swimme speaks of gravity as "cosmic allurement," the love inherent in the universe that draws all things together. It is as if the universe is being stimulated to progress from within: "The universe can no longer be regarded as a result of chance collisions of materials, nor as a deterministic mechanism. The universe considered as a whole is more like a developing being.... We need to understand the human within the intrinsic dynamics of the Earth. Alienated from the cosmos, imprisoned in our narrow frames of reference, we do not know what we are about as a species. We will discover our larger role only by reinventing the human as a dimension of the emergent universe."[478] At another point in the dialogue the youth asks where it all came from, and Thomas replies that it emerged from "the same place out of which the primeval fireball comes: an empty realm, a mysterious order of reality, a no-thing-ness that is simultaneously the ultimate source of *all* things."[479]

In a later book, *The Hidden Heart of the Cosmos,* Swimme writes that when Albert Einstein was asked about how he made his discoveries, he replied that he didn't simply study data and then look for equations that would fit the data. He admitted that he relied primarily on imagination. "I want to know how the Old One thinks. The rest is details." The Old One? But we know that Einstein did not believe in an anthropomorphic God, so what did he mean by this term? Was he aware that according to the Kabbalah "the Old One," *Atika Kadishah,* is a designation of *Ein Sof,* the endless, limitless, undifferentiated reality, the absolute Oneness underlying and interpenetrating all being?

Quantum physicists today tell us that there is a nonvisible reality, sometimes referred to as "quantum potential" or "universal wave functions" that can never be seen because it is neither a material thing nor an energy constellation. Swimme calls it "all-nourishing abyss," an unseen ocean of potentiality, an infinity of pure generative power. And he imagines what it was like for Einstein during the great moment when the scientist was in the midst of his most important discoveries, "*Einstein was not contemplating something apart from himself.* He was absorbed in the experience of the feelings in his body, his viscera, his bowels, that were caused by the causes permeating the universe. That Great Power that had, there, at the birthplace of the universe, gushed forth in all the energies and galaxies was now bringing forth its own self-portrait in the symbols of Einstein's field equations."[480]

I'm certain that the Baal Shem Tov touched into this immensity as well. He knew that human psychology and consciousness somehow reflect and embody the universe. And it is because of this mirroring that we are able to resonate with the universe. Swimme's comprehension of the Whole of Things is then remarkably similar to the Baal Shem's vision of relationship between the blessed Holy One and the Shekhinah. But who or what would the Holy One be? It is what physicists call "quantum potential." Swimme actually uses the same name for it as the Baal Shem Tov: *Ayin,* the No-thing-ness that is everything. I feel swept up in the immensity of it all, a momentary embodiment of the majesty, the fullness, and the emptiness of the nourishing abyss.

CHAPTER TWENTY-EIGHT

COSMIC CONSCIOUSNESS

I was standing in a vast cathedral, staring at the altar. At the center, where the cross would usually be, hung a colossal question mark. And in the chancel of the cathedral priests were moving about in front of the question mark, each wearing identical ritual vestments with a question mark emblazoned on their chests. The sonorous hymns they were chanting in unison lauded the Great Unknown Mystery. I whispered to myself, "I've finally found it! The Secret of all secrets, the Great Mystery!" Then I heard a laugh, a thunderous chortle that filled the cathedral. And then the building collapsed and there was nothing but hilarity. Suddenly the entire image disappeared.

That was a vision that broke into my awareness during one of my psychedelic experiences in the sixties. I later recognized where the notion it represented had originated, at least in my consciousness—a startling passage in the Zohar describing the creation, but not of the world. Rather, the creation of God! The book of Genesis opens with the words, *"In the beginning, Elohim created the heavens and the earth . . ."* (Genesis 1:1) But in biblical Hebrew verbs usually come toward or at the beginning of sentences. Thus, the Hebrew actually reads: *"In the beginning created Elohim."* This grammatical construction allowed the author of the Zohar to reimagine the origin of the universe in a radical manner. *"In the beginning/_____/ created /Elohim . . ."* *Elohim* has become the object rather than the subject. But if *Elohim* is the object that was created, who or what is the subject? The Zohar doesn't say, for the actual subject, the origin of the cosmos, is completely impossible to name. Thus, we might read the Zohar's construction of the first three words in the Torah: *"In the beginning (Something Unknown) created Elohim."* This is the Mystery beyond all mysteries.

It was this Mystery that created Elohim. What then is the meaning of Elohim? In the Bible it's a generic name for Divinity. But even though the biblical writers read it as a singular noun, it can be understood to have a plural ending, and could be translated "gods." It was as if the ancient Israelite God was absorbing all the pagan gods into a singular unity. But the Zohar reads this differently. It treats Elohim as a plural noun referring to the sefirot, the ten underlying archetypal dimensions of existence which emanated out of the great Mystery.

What is the Zohar really telling us? Try as you may, use all of your cognitive faculties, but you will inevitably fail to fathom where the universe came from. Human beings have come up with a vast array of answers to the foundational questions about reality, but the very existence of such a plethora of myths and philosophical positions is testimony to our basic ignorance of trans-physical reality and the genesis of being.

Scientific investigators may have revealed a fabulous amount of information about the physical origins and the constitution of the universe, and about the laws undergirding the natural world. Yet, in the end, with all their sophisticated ways of understanding, scientists meet only incomprehensible Mystery. Most of these explorers are interested only in what can be made comprehensible, yet it was Albert Einstein who famously stated, "The most beautiful experience we can have is the mysterious. It is the fundamental emotion which stands at the cradle of true art and true science."

The more we learn about the world in which we live, the greater we're stunned by our ignorance. There have been so many failed attempts throughout history to disrobe the inexplicable that we must conclude, our minds are unequipped for the task. We are left with the presence of the knowable, and the mystery of what is beyond. Yet there are scientists— predominantly those engaged in physics and cosmology—who fully recognize that something metaphysical exists—even if they do not use that term. Brian Swimme has shown that physicists are convinced there is a nonvisible reality "which can never be seen, because it is neither a material thing nor an energy constellation. In addition, the nonvisible world's nature differs so radically from the material world it cannot even be *pictured*. It is both nonvisible and *nonvisualizable*. Even so, it is profoundly real and profoundly powerful."[481] Physicists express its existence through numbers, and have various names for it such as "universal wave function," but Swimme prefers the term "all-nourishing abyss": "The universe emerges out of all-nourishing abyss not only fifteen billion years ago but in every moment. Each instant protons and antiprotons are flashing out of, and are suddenly absorbed back into, all-nourishing abyss. All-nourishing abyss then is not a thing, not a collection of things, nor even, strictly speaking, a physical place, but rather a power that gives birth and that absorbs existence at a thing's annihilation."[482] This is nearly identical to what kabbalists like the Baal Shem Tov called the *Or Ein Sof*. Referring to that reality, he taught that "The highest knowing is the realization of not knowing," for the world is a manifestation of an Enigma untouched by human thought.

According to Jewish mystics, what emerges from the Light Without End is the loftiest and most expansive sefirah known as *Hokhmah* (Wisdom), also known as "What?" This is possibly the deepest realization that a person can attain. I call it mystical agnosticism, for the mystic knows there is something there, but is also aware that the human mind is unable to penetrate its enigmatic reality. It is the first flash of intellect, the creative spark, writes Arthur Green. Then, out of Hokhmah comes *Binah* (Contemplation), also known as "Who?" Binah, Green writes, is "the depth of thought that absorbs the spark, shaping it and refining it into itself. And either of these two points would be inconceivable without the other. The light seen back and forth in those countless mirrored surfaces is all one light, but infinitely transformed and magnified in the reflective process." I learned from Arthur so long ago, and experienced firsthand through paychedelics, how those sefirot are states of expanded consciousness that the minds of the true mystics among the kabbalists were able to enter.

WALT WHITMAN'S VISION

As an undergraduate majoring in English literature, Walt Whitman was my favorite poet. His verse enthralled me—the breadth of the language, music, and cadences. And his optimistic vision of American democracy was bracing. Whitman's way of directly reaching his readers' hearts through words was almost uncanny. There were times when I felt he was speaking to me personally. His certainty about his own significance as an individual affected me deeply and I longed for the kind of self-acceptance he proclaimed. He began his acclaimed poem, *Song of Myself,* with these words,

> I celebrate myself, and sing myself,

And what I assume you shall assume,
For every atom belonging to me as good belongs to you.

A bit later, he amplifies his self-appreciation:

I know I am august,
I do not trouble my spirit to vindicate itself or be
    understood,
I see that the elementary laws never apologize,
(I reckon I behave no prouder than the level I plant my
    house by, after all.)

I exist as I am, that is enough,
If no other in the world be aware I sit content,
And if each and all be aware I sit content.

One world is aware and by far the largest to me, and that
    is myself,
And whether I come to my own to-day or in ten thou-
    sand or ten million years,
I can cheerfully take it now, or with equal cheerfulness
    I can wait.

And if such self-evaluation seems immodest, it is not at the expense of anyone else. In this sacred world the judging mind has dissolved, and the soul sings what it knows of itself, of the earth, of every living thing. This self-love leads Whitman to the love of others:

Whoever degrades another degrades me,
And whatever is done or said returns at last to me.

The poet's praise for democracy and for the equality of all people was also thrilling. He constantly expressed his love of and sympathy for people of all ranks of society. And he never doted on God, but once in a while linked his own experience to the Divine, inviting readers to join him in embracing both the natural world and humanity from an expansive stand-point where there was "extasy everywhere touching and thrilling me":

Swiftly arose and spread around me the peace and
    knowledge that pass all the argument of the earth,

And I know that the hand of God is the promise of my
    own,
And I know that the spirit of God is the brother of my
    own,
And that all the men ever born are also my brothers, and
    the women my sisters and lovers,
And that a kelson of the creation is love,
 And limitless are leaves stiff or drooping in the fields,
And brown ants in the little wells beneath them,
And mossy scabs of the worm fence, heap'd stones, elder,
    mullein and poke-weed.

So much of traditional religion throughout the millennia has served repression in the name of authority. But in Whitman we sense the opposite—the freeing of the emotions and imagination from traditional constraints, and the propulsion of the self into delirious heights, dissolving matter into spirit.

In the first chapter of this book, I wrote about my college years. Living on my own, away from my parents for the first time. I stood in stark opposition to my family's materialism, but I didn't really know who I was or what I believed in. Yet there had been one man who acted as a spiritual parent to me throughout my adolescence, my mentor Milton Bendiner, and he was a committed, traditional Jew. In college, an Orthodox Holocaust survivor, Avraham Gottesman, took me under his wing. Then came my absorption in the musar of Rabbi Israel Salanter, cementing my connection with Jewish tradition. So even though I admired Whitman's sense of self-importance and self-confidence, this was not at all the way I experienced my own life, nor did it seem to be a trait valued by the Jewish sources I was studying.

The religious life I led during the fifteen years I identified as an observant Jew was in large part rooted in fear and anxiety, lest I transgress any of the ritual or moral mitzvot. Unknown to me then, I suffered from a mild form of obsessive-compulsive disorder, and because of this the complex structure of Jewish observance ruled my life. At times I would rebel, but that only made me feel guilty. It would take years of psychotherapy, mystical experience, a complete break from my Jewish past, and finally the discovery of the Baal Shem Tov for me to recognize and seek to cultivate many of the qualities I'd first met in Whitman—self-worth, love, empathy, compassion, joy, ecstasy, and the presence of divinity in all of existence.

Richard Bucke was a close disciple of Whitman's. His book, *Cosmic Consciousness: A Study in the Evolution of the Human Mind,* proved to be a major discovery, one that would open my awareness to the underlying unity of all human instances of mystical awareness. Bucke was a British-born Canadian psychiatrist. Inspired by Whitman's spiritual depth, he decided to investigate the reports of people from different cultural and religious backgrounds throughout history who experienced what Bucke called cosmic consciousness. The author's claim is that he was unveiling the deepest potential of the human spirit.

Bucke's personal story is itself interesting and significant. In 1872, while visiting London, he underwent a personal spiritual awakening, an experience he described in the third person: "[Bucke] and two friends had spent the evening reading Wordsworth, Shelly, Keats, Browning, and especially Whitman. They parted at midnight, and he had a long drive in a hansom. His mind, deeply under the influence of the ideas, images and emotions called up by the reading and talk of the evening, was calm and peaceful. He was in a state of quiet, almost passive, enjoyment. All at once, without warning of any kind, he found himself wrapped around, as it were, by a flame-colored cloud. For an instant he thought of fire—some sudden conflagration in the great city. The next [instant] he knew that the light was within himself. Directly after [that] there came upon him a sense of exultation, of immense joyousness, accompanied or immediately followed by an intellectual illumination quite impossible to describe. Into his brain streamed one momentary lightening-flash of Brahmic Splendor which ever since lightened his life. Upon his heart fell one drop of Brahmic Bliss, leaving thenceforward for always an aftertaste of Heaven."[483]

Bucke describes the various types of animal and human awareness, and he asserts that *Cosmic Consciousness* represents the pinnacle of all states of awareness. And just what is cosmic consciousness?

> ... a consciousness of the cosmos, that is, of the life and
> order of the universe.... Along with the consciousness of
> the cosmos there occurs an intellectual enlightenment

or illumination which alone would place the individual on a new plane of existence—would make him almost a member of a new species. To this is added a state of moral exaltation, an indescribable feeling of elevation, elation, and joyousness, and a quickening of the moral sense, which is fully as striking and more important both to the individual and the race than is the enhanced intellectual power. With these come, what may be called a sense of immortality, a consciousness of eternal life, not a conviction that he shall have this, but the consciousness that he has it already.[484]

He profiles fourteen cases that he believed fulfilled these criteria. These included the Buddha, Jesus, Paul, Plotinus, Mohammed, William Blake, and of course, Walt Whitman. Following this Bucke chronicles thirty-six instances of "lesser, imperfect and doubtful" instances of such awareness, which include Moses, Isaiah, Socrates, Spinoza, and Ramakrishna Paramahansa. Bucke came to believe that cosmic consciousness will appear more and more often until it becomes a regular attribute of adult humanity.

His book has been compared to William James' *The Varieties of Religious Experience,* which appeared a year after Bucke's. According to scholar Michael Robertson, "Both Bucke and James argue that all religions, no matter how seemingly different, have a common core; both believe that it is possible to identify this core by stripping away institutional accretions of dogma and ritual and focusing on individual experience; and both identify mystical illumination as the foundation of all religious experience."[485] The two books have become part of the foundation of transpersonal psychology.

AN IRREPRESSIBLE JOYOUSNESS

Whitman's visionary illumination transformed his life. At one point, Bucke reports it this way: "In such hours, in the midst of the significant wonders of heaven and earth...creeds, conventions, fall away and become of no account before this simple idea. Under the luminousness of real vision, it alone takes possession, takes value."[486] In Whitman's poem,

"Prayer of Columbus," Bucke finds evidence of Whitman's recognition of the poet's own debt to God.

> With ray of light, steady, ineffable, vouchsafed of Thee,
> Light rare untellable, lighting the very light,
> Beyond all signs, descriptions, languages ...

Summarizing Whitman's experience, Bucke writes that the poet encountered a subjective spiritual light, moral elevation, intellectual illumination, an absolute conviction of eternal life, and the absence of both a sense of sin and the fear of death.

Cosmic consciousness exists. Abraham Maslow, writing from a psychological perspective in 1970, called such states of intense awakeness "peak experiences." Bucke goes on to create portraits of the Buddha and Jesus as two further examples of this. If Jesus experienced cosmic consciousness, what did he call it? Bucke tells us that he used the old Jewish messianic notion of "the kingdom of God" in a new and novel way, and he provides an exhaustive anthology of Gospel citations about the kingdom to back up his claim. The most telling, perhaps, is one of the last that he offers, from the Gospel of Luke chapter 17: "And being asked by the Pharisees when the kingdom of God cometh he answered them and said: The kingdom of God cometh not with observation; neither shall they say, Lo, here! Or there, for lo, the kingdom of God is within you." Bucke ends the chapter with these words: "Looked at from the present point of view, the objects of the teachings of Jesus, as of Gautama, were two: (*a*) To tell men what he had learned upon entering into Cosmic Consciousness, which things he saw it was the very greatest importance that they should know; and (*b*) to lead men up into or at least towards Cosmic Consciousness, or, in his words, into the kingdom of God." I find it interesting to recall that academic members of the contemporary Jesus Seminar have portrayed Jesus' notion of the kingdom of God in the same way as Bucke did at the turn of the last century.

PLOTINUS AND NEOPLATONISM

A third century religious philosopher, Plotinus (205-70 CE), was another of the fourteen adepts whom Bucke identified with experiences of cosmic consciousness. Plotinus was the founder of an influential school of philosophy in Rome that in modern times has been called Neoplatonism. His thought derived from an 800-year-old tradition of Greek philosophy dating back to Plato, but because of his spiritual proclivity, Plotinus interpreted the work of his predecessors in a distinctly mystical fashion. Bucke quotes from a letter that Plotinus wrote to his disciple, Flaccus: "You can only apprehend the Infinite by a faculty superior to reason, by entering into a state in which you are your finite self no longer—in which the divine essence is communicated to you. This is ecstasy. It is liberation of your mind from its finite consciousness. Like only can apprehend like. When you cease to be finite, you become one with the Infinite. In the relation of your soul to its simplest self, its divine essence, you realize this union—this identity."[487]

Later in the same passage, Plotinus reveals to Flaccus that he's undergone such experiences three times in life. He was to experience four more such encounters with the spirit before his death. Plotinus described these overpowering occurrences as experiences of love—love of the Good. "It is an invasion of the soul by a presence which leaves no room for anything but itself."[488] He understood that his experience was not an ascent out of himself toward some transcendent place beyond physical reality. Rather, it was a descent into his own deepest self, the center of his soul. What he discovered at his own depths was the ineffable One that paradoxically "is Everything and Nothing; it can be none of the existing things, and yet it is all."[489]

Neoplatonism became an important current in Jewish, Christian, and Islamic mystical thought during the Middle Ages. Gershom Scholem identified this philosophical school as an important influence on the formation of Kabbalah, particularly Plotinus' notion of the stages of emanation leading from the ineffable One to the material plurality of the universe, which may have been the origin of the kabbalistic sefirot. And as early as 1903, Martin Buber recognized the Baal Shem's debt to Plotinus calling Hasidism "a warm-blooded renewal of neo-Platonism."[490] I can't imagine the Baal Shem ever heard of Plotinus, but I can say with confidence that he was one of the master's chief spiritual ancestors. And I believe the Besht would resonate with Plotinus' statement that the completely illuminated human being is one who can "see all things, not in process of becoming, but in Being, and see themselves in the other.

Each being contains in itself the whole intelligible world. Therefore All is everywhere. Each is there All, and All is each. Man as he now is has ceased to be the All. But when he ceases to be an individual, he raises himself again and penetrates the whole world."[491]

The Baal Shem integrated his own mystical experience, resembling Plotinus, into the very heart of an innovative Judaism that drew most of its inspiration from biblical, rabbinic, and kabbalistic traditions, taking this vision in directions that the earlier sage would not have imagined. Yet as similar as they are, the visions of the two mystics, separated in time by sixteen centuries, also have their dissimilarities, for the religious and cultural contexts of the Baal Shem and Plotinus were considerably different. Did the Baal Shem recover these Neoplatonic insights from his knowledge of Kabbalah, or did he crystalize his own vision through contemplating his mystical experience in a way similar to that which Plotinus had done? We cannot know for sure, but intuition tells me it might have been a combination of both factors.

CHAPTER TWENTY-NINE

THE HIDDEN LIGHT

---

*"Now when a tzaddik studies Torah for it own sake, and looks
into its depths with the eye of his intelligence, that hidden light
shines upon him and opens a path so that he will truly see from
one end of the cosmos to the other. He becomes like the first
human being before the exile from the garden, able to see the
innermost truth of everything."*
ISRAEL BAAL SHEM TOV[492]

The Baal Shem Tov was enthralled by a large vision of the cosmos that
brought him to a new plane of consciousness. His teachings and many
of the tales demonstrate a state of moral exaltation and an indescribable
feeling of elevation, elation, and joyousness. He realized the oneness of
the universe, and envisioned the presence of the Creator in and through
the universe. He was able to reach a state of awareness free of the shadows of sinfulness, evil, disaster, and death. We have also seen that he
came to understand love as the rule and basis of all.

Ahiyah of Shiloh opened the Besht's eyes to the existence of the
all-pervading spirit of divinity. The incident took place during the Besht's
seven-year period as a hermit in the mountains. According to the legend,
Ahiyah appeared to him and directed him to immerse himself in the Prut
River eighteen times, and then retire to the cave where he was living,
remaining there for three days and nights without eating. On the fourth
day at dawn, Ahiyah reappeared and led the Besht outside. Placing his
hands on the young man's head, Ahiyah gave him this blessing: "May your
eyes now be opened to see the Truth!" Then Ahiyah disappeared, and the
Besht suddenly experienced the most intense yearning for God he'd ever
known. Just then the Baal Shem's eyes revealed a new light to him, more
powerful than a thousand suns:

Everywhere he looked, he saw God's light shining out

through everything. The sky, the trees, the stones, the earth beneath his feet, the very air—were all Godliness, shimmering with divine vitality. Waves of joy thrilled his body. He saw God with his physical eyes. He saw Godliness first and everything else afterward, by the way. It was clear to him: God is everything and everything is God.... He knew and saw that God is more real than the world, for He is the essence of all that exists...

From that day on the Baal Shem Tov was established in God-awareness.... Even every movement of his, every feeling, every thought, was also from God. He saw God in all things and heard God in all sounds. He heard the divine voice in the rustling of tree leaves, in the flowing sounds of the river, in the singing and chirping of birds. When he listened to the inner sound that his ears heard, he heard the voice of God, which enlivened and brought into being the sound he was hearing. He felt at every moment that God was with him. His bliss was boundless.[493]

When I discovered this vision, I was overjoyed. I believed the story was authentic, but later I wasn't so certain. It appears in a later text, and it makes it seem as if the Baal Shem's enlightenment and transformation happened in an unforeseen and abrupt way. You may recall that the Besht told disciples they shouldn't attempt to engage in a form of teshuvah that would change them too rapidly, extinguishing their previous identities. Also, he states that a permanent state of God-awareness (*gahd'lut*) is not something human beings are able to retain. And he cautions students that human consciousness is cyclic, and they must be prepared for times when their awareness will be diminished (*kaht'nut*). Nonetheless, this source probably reflects the kernel of an experience the Besht underwent.

PRIMORDIAL LIGHT

We've already encountered the Besht's experiences of cosmic consciousness, and I attempted to show what his mystical experience might have been like—merging the Shekhinah and his further ascent into the cosmic No-thing. We also pointed toward the Baal Shem's cosmic consciousness in his teaching about the tzaddik's ability to open toward, and make use of the primordial light of creation. I'd now like to reexamine that particular report from a somewhat different angle. There are a number of descriptions of the incident in the literature, and the following version comes from R. Zev Wolf of Zhitomir (d. 1798) a disciple of the Maggid of Medziritch:

> Once the Baal Shem's disciples asked their master a question about an event that was taking place in another part of the world. The master picked up his copy of the Book of the Zohar that was lying on the table before him. He opened the volume at random and looked into it, and gave them a full explanation of the occurrence that they had asked him about. Sometime later the information that he revealed to them turned out to be true.
>
> The Besht was able to do this because he made use of the Zohar, employing it in a psychic manner. In this way the Besht was able to discern the truth from afar. One time the disciples asked their master how he was able to accomplish this, and in response he gave them this teaching:
>
> "The primordial light that the blessed Holy One created on the first day shone from one end of the universe to the other; and the first human being was able to see the entire cosmos because of that potent light which shone on the earth and everything that lives on the earth. But when the blessed Holy One saw that the world was not worthy to use that light, God hid it for the tzaddikim in the future.
>
> "But where then is the place that holds that dazzling light—where is it hidden? God hid the light in the Torah, for the Torah is the treasure of the blessed Holy One's goodness.
>
> "Now when a tzaddik studies Torah for it own sake,

and looks into its depths with the eye of his intelligence, that hidden light shines upon him and opens a path so that he will truly see from one end of the cosmos to the other. He becomes like the first human being before the exile from the garden, able to see the innermost truth of everything.

"Truly, we don't know that we have these abilities. We simply don't understand just how far we are able to see. This is why we pray and ask for direction from the blessed Holy One: 'Open our blind eyes and enlighten us in Your Torah so that we are able to see the hidden Torah that shone during the seven primordial days of creation.'"[494]

There is nothing in this book about the Besht's views on the subject of life after physical death, and I haven't found teachings of his that elaborate on this theme, so perhaps the subject was not of great importance to him. But here is an anecdote found in Buber's *Tales of the Hasidim* in which the master makes it clear that attaining entrance into the world to come was not a concern that occupied much of his attention: "Once the spirit of the Baal Shem was so oppressed that it seemed to him he would have no part in the coming world. Then he said to himself: 'If I love God, what need have I of the coming world!'"[495]

Faith in the existence of an afterlife had been a conviction of belief for many Jews since the rabbinic period, and there's no reason to suspect that the Baal Shem did not affirm this notion. In some of his teachings, he does refer to the kabbalistic notion of reincarnation.

BECOMING LIKE MOSES

The Baal Shem placed an expanded sense of consciousness at the center of his understanding of the qualities that characterize an authentic tzaddik. And he characterized Moses, the greatest of the prophets, as the very embodiment of consciousness, a man whose soul contained both the root of every Jewish soul, and the full value of every individual:

The fully developed individual, one who possesses a clear knowledgeable consciousness, is able to link all the levels of his generation, and raise them up, linking them to their Root, and uniting himself with them. Such a person is called *Moses*. He contains within himself his entire generation. He is called *Consciousness,* and his generation is called *the Conscious Generation.*[496]

Notice that in the second of these sources, the Besht characterizes the greatest leaders throughout Jewish history as having been able to attain the consciousness of Moses. The text is clearly self-referential; it is clear that the Baal Shem thought of himself as having the ability to embrace the entire Jewish people in his consciousness and conscience.

Another Hasidic teacher, Rabbi Uri Fievel, cited the following interesting teaching:

"And the EverPresent spoke to Moses face to face." (Exodus 33:11) In the Book of Proverbs it is written, *"Just as the image of one's face in water reflects one's own face, so the heart of one person reflects the heart of the other."* I heard the following insight given in the name of the Baal Shem Tov, whose soul lives in the hidden places on high: When an individual stands near a body of water, his reflection will spread wide over the water. But when he bends down, moving closer to the water, his reflection becomes smaller. And as he moves even closer toward the water, the image he sees will come to match the exact size of his face. And if he then dips his face into the water itself, the reflection will then merge with his face. So too it is with regard to the heart of one person in relation to another. If you think of yourself as unduly important, your companion will do the same in relation to you, and you will never be able to attain true intimacy. But if you are humble with your friend, he will be humble towards you. Then you will consider yourselves to be equals, and you will be able to become intimate with one another. This, then, is the meaning of the verse, *"And the EverPresent spoke to Moses face to face, as one person speaks with another."*

Moses humbled himself before the blessed Creator, and then the Creator—so-to-speak—humbled himself in relation to Moses as well. It was in this way that the "face" of God became like a reflection of the face of Moses. And at that moment they were able to communicate face to face. This was a rung of awareness that no one but Moses has ever been able to attain, because Moses was the human manifestation of pure consciousness.[497]

"And the EverPresent spoke to Moses face to face, as one person speaks with another." Such a profound level of closeness to the Divine Wholeness may have been unique to Moses, but to the Baal Shem Tov it was clear that a true tzaddik would also be able to attain a connection similar to the union that Moses merited. Furthermore, he affirmed that every Jew had within them some of that potential, for he taught: "Every human being is a microcosm embodying Moses and Aaron, as well as the Egyptians."[498]

SPIRITUAL AWARENESS IN ORDINARY LIFE

One major characteristic of the Baal Shem's sense of cosmic consciousness was how it brought out the profound spiritual dimensions of everyday living. This is why he placed so much attention on the manifestations of the sefirot, not only within the psyche, but within everyday human experience. Rabbi Jacob Joseph reported: *"Know the Divine in all of your ways'* (Proverbs 3:5-6). Whatever you are engaged in doing be aware that you are living in wonder. This is just as I heard from my teacher, the Baal Shem Tov when he taught me how to bring my consciousness into every physical act."[499] Jacob Joseph also remembered the following medieval tradition together with the Baal Shem's commentary on the source:

> *"And Enoch walked with the Divine"* (Genesis 5:22). Our sages have stated, "Enoch was a cobbler, and while he was sewing the pieces of leather together to fashion a sandle, he would focus all of his attention on the cosmic meaning of the act. And with each and every stitch he would unite the blessed Holy One and His Shekhinah."
>
> The following explanation of that tradition was transmitted in the name of the Baal Shem Tov.... "The

realm of the mind is infinite and unbounded, while the realm of deeds is narrow and limited. But when you are engaged in carrying out a deed, and you integrate the consciousness of the Infinite into that action, the two realms become one. This is what we mean then when we speak of the Unification of the blessed Holy One and the Shekhinah."[500]

Not that the practitioner is actually drawing the spaciousness of Infinity into the act, for the *Ein Sof* is eternally present in everything, including every deed. It's just that carrying out any deed in an ordinary state of mind usually reduces it to a commonplace action. What the Besht's practice calls for is a willed enactment in which the individual seeks to access the vastly expanded consciousness hidden in their depths, and brings that awareness forward into each activity. In this way, the practitioner awakens to the infinite dimension hidden in finite action. Such an expansive way of living allows one to witness the wondrous character of existence from moment to moment.

I earlier gave a number of examples of the Besht's teachings that illustrated his practice of integrating an expanded state of awareness into consciousness while engaging in actions of various kinds. What I called there the practice of the presence is the same as what I here call microcosmic consciousness: "When you are engaged in any activity, bring your most spacious state of consciousness into relation with whatever you are doing, binding the two spheres together. This is called the unification of the blessed Holy One and the Shekhinah."[501] This discipline effected the Besht's vision.

The following anecdote, translated by Yitzhak Buxbaum, may not be historical, yet there are so many different tales about the Besht's ability to envision reality in an expansive way that I believe this could have happened:

> The Baal Shem Tov was once at a village inn in Podolia with a number of his disciples, when they became aware that the Jewish innkeeper was exploiting a pair of orphans by using them as servants without paying them properly. The Besht's disciples began to angrily rebuke

the innkeeper for his wrongdoing, but the Besht said to them, "I received a tradition from my father, of blessed memory, that the thief needs more compassion than the person he's stolen from! The person whose possessions were stolen will get over his loss, but how will the thief get over his wickedness? There are many accusers in the heavenly court against someone who's guilty of sin. There's no need for us on earth to add fuel to the fire." After this, the Besht took care of the orphans' needs and also brought the innkeeper and his wife to repentance.[502]

This tale raises a host of questions. How did it come about that the disciples discovered the situation that the orphans were subject to? What was the immediate response of the innkeeper to the charges leveled at him? Was the innkeeper present when the exchange happened between the disciples and the Besht, or did it happen later in private? How did the disciples react to their reprimand? How did the Besht bring the innkeeper and his wife to repentance? Yet, one also notices that none of these questions seem important to the storyteller. All that concerns him is the Baal Shem's reactions to the disciples' behavior and the adverse effect that this concern had on the innkeeper and his wife. And the Besht's response to the situation was one of compassion, rather than the kind of judgment the disciples had vented.

Yes, the exploitation of the twins needed to be halted, and exposing and condemning the innkeeper's actions would certainly do this, but what about the innkeeper? Would belittling him, especially in public, actually change him? Perhaps he would become defensive, and then what? A legal case? All of this would only produce further animosity. Wouldn't it be better to treat the innkeeper in a humane way that encourages him to undergo a moral transformation? The Baal Shem's actions come from a discerning heart and a sense of consciousness that sets the entire incident into a loftier spiritual context.

But let's look a bit deeper at the meaning. If one was unfamiliar with the Baal Shem's teachings, recognizing the Infinite in the finite, one might conclude that his response to the actions of his disciples was spontaneous, since he was naturally a loving and compassionate human being. There are a tremendous number of teaching stories like this in Hasidic literature, yet they are usually repeated without reference to the kind of spiritual discipline that had been necessary for him to cultivate his empathic response. Remember, however, how the Besht had to struggle with his anger and grandiosity to become the enlightened individual he became. And remember his practice of Cordoverian musar, and the kind of mystical davening he engaged in which opened him to cosmic consciousness. What the story is really conveying, then, is not only the Baal Shem's immense kindness, but also the way his inner work transformed him into the tzaddik he became.

The story of the Besht at the village inn in Podolia reminds me of something I recently read about the Vietnamese Zen Buddhist teacher, Thich Nhat Hanh: "Twenty years ago, the Rodney King riots had just exploded in Los Angeles, and the image of a fallen man being beaten by police replayed itself over and over on television sets everywhere. That same week, I went to a talk at the Berkeley Community Theatre featuring Thich Nhat Hanh. The auditorium filled with thousands of people as this small man in robes, little known to me at the time, took the stage. He immediately started talking about the news—the beating, the riots, the events in Los Angeles that were triggering anger around the world. He spoke about his sadness for the beaten man. And then he spoke about his even greater sadness for the men doing the beating—the rage they must have had inside and the deep suffering that would cause them to act out in this way. You could hear a pin drop as the audience took in his words, his understanding, and his compassion for every person in this struggle."[503] As in the case of the Baal Shem Tov, to really appreciate Thich Nhat Hahn's response, one must understand the central place occupied by the various practices fostered by Zen which enabled him to become mindful, to develop insight, and to bring peace and happiness to himself and to others.

MICROCOSMIC CONSCIOUSNESS

There is more than one kind of cosmic consciousness in Jewish mystical sources. To judge from what Gershom Scholem wrote about Isaac Luria, whose form of Kabbalah was prevalent in Eastern Europe before the coming of the Baal Shem, the Ari was largely concerned with what I would call the macrocosmic cosmic process of the universe: divine activities that brought forth the creation, the shattering of the divine design, magical actions of the kabbalists that he believed could bring tikkun olam, and the reparation and healing of the world's brokenness. Most of the Ari's concerns lay in what today we might call cosmogeny, cosmology, and metaphysics.

The Baal Shem was familiar with Luria's mystical ruminations, which I'm sure he accepted as authentic. But for the most part, the Besht's concerns were not speculative in this way. His macrocosmic concerns had to do with the practice of a form of mystical ascent that would allow him to merge with the Shekhinah, and then to dissolve into the cosmic No-thing. As Moshe Idel has stressed, the tremendous overflow of spiritual energy (shefah) that he brought back with him from these mystical flights became the primary font and source for his work in the world in a very different form of awareness. This is what I call *microcosmic* consciousness.

The Baal Shem's interests lay more with the inner and outer worlds of his disciples and the members of his community, and with the well-being of the Jewish people. He seldom spoke about tikkun olam—a central concept of Luria's—for he saw his primary task as bringing healing to individuals, to protecting endangered Jewish communities in Poland, and enabling his disciples to become enlightened and saintly teachers and leaders who would carry on the healing work that he pioneered. And, as we have seen, when the master pondered the Tree of Life his attention was focused on the dynamics of the sefirot *within* the lives and psyches of actual human beings, not in the cosmos at large. Unlike current forms of psychology, the Besht grasped the dynamics of the human mind in a way that maintained its connection with the sefirot underlying the universe. I call this approach "cosmo-psychology."

There's a Hasidic legend that suggests that in the afterlife the Baal Shem Tov met Isaac Luria and asked him why he had put all his energy into such a cerebral understanding of the cosmos, and had devoted so little of his concern to worship, which was the true essence of the religious life. The Ari told him that had he lived longer—he died at age thirty-eight—he would have done just that!

CHAPTER THIRTY

RELIGION AND THE QUEST
FOR MEANING

*"Now when a tzaddik studies Torah for it own sake, and looks
into its depths with the eye of his intelligence, that hidden light
shines upon him and opens a path so that he will truly see from
one end of the cosmos to the other. He becomes like the first
human being before the exile from the garden, able to see the
innermost truth of everything."*

ISRAEL BAAL SHEM TOV[504]

When I moved to Cambridge, Massachusetts in 1968, I became the principal of a large Conservative afternoon synagogue school in one of Boston's suburbs, where one of my responsibilities was to teach a course in comparative religion to twenty high school juniors. This was going to be a real challenge because the only religions other than Judaism that I knew anything about were Christianity and Islam—and my knowledge of Islam was limited to what I'd learned informally from a Muslim roommate in college. The synagogue's rabbi gave me a copy of the textbook for the class, Huston Smith's *The Religions of Man*.

I found the book exciting, and it opened new vistas at a time when I was having doubts about Judaism and Jewishness. Because of Smith's emphasis on experience, I decided I would teach the course in a way that would also accentuate experience in the classroom. Each Sunday morning, we would examine a different religion and I would attempt to present the essence and concerns of that faith tradition in a way that would enable students to sense what that path might feel like from the inside. Thus, as I developed the plans for each lesson, I tried to sense what it would be like to be a devotee of the particular religion we were encountering.

I was especially drawn to Smith's description of Zen. My students had been preparing diligently before each class, so I took it for granted that they had read the chapter, and I started the lesson by asking for a concise definition of Zen. Hands flew up. I called on each student in turn, but whatever they said, I shook my head no. They were baffled and there was complete silence. After a pause, I announced that I brought along a recording by a prominent Zen master who would provide the answer. I turned on my portable tape cassette recorder, but no sounds emerged. The tape was completely blank. A minute later, I turned off the recorder and sat in silence. The students looked even more bewildered. Then a hand shot up in the back of the classroom. "You can't put it into words!" the boy shouted, "You just can't put it into words!" Smiles and giggling filled the room.

I too smiled, and then read a paragraph from Smith's book: "A master, Gutei, whenever he was asked the meaning of Zen, lifted his index finger. That was all. Another kicked a ball. Still another slapped the inquirer." And then Smith comments, "Words...can deceive, or at least mislead, fabricating a virtual reality that fronts for the one that actually exists... [and] as mystics emphasize, our highest experiences elude words almost entirely."[505]

I was living in Somerville at the time, which borders Cambridge where Huston Smith was teaching at the Massachusetts Institute of Technology. He was a respected academic, and in the decades following the publication of *The Religions of Man,* perhaps the most well-known scholar of religion in the world. At last count *The Religions of Man* (later revised and retitled *The World's Religions*) sold over three million copies.

Born in China where his parents were serving as Methodist missionaries, Smith remained a Christian throughout his life. But he was also a universalist. He begins the introduction to the book with an incident that had just occurred. He'd returned from church where together with members of his congregation, he'd participated in the celebration of the Holy Eucharist. But in church his mind had wandered to the wider company of God-seekers. He remembered Yemenite Jews that he'd seen six months earlier in Jerusalem, sitting shoeless and cross-legged on the floor of their synagogue, "wrapped in the prayer shawls their ancestors wore in the desert. They are there today, at least a quorum of ten, morning and evening, swaying backwards and forwards like camel riders as they recite their Torah." Then he described other forms of worship simultaneously taking place around the world by Muslims, Hindus, Buddhists, and Zen monks. "What a strange fellowship this is," he writes, "God-seekers in every land, lifting their voices in the most disparate ways imaginable to the God of all life. How does it sound from above? Like bedlam, or do the strains blend in strange ethereal harmony? Does one faith carry the lead, or do the parts share in counterpoint and antiphony where not in full-throated chorus? We cannot know. All we can do is try to listen carefully and with full attention to each voice in turn as it addresses the divine."[506]

In the bibliography at the end of the chapter, Smith cited Abraham Joshua Heschel's books as works readers might go to if they wished to learn more about Judaism. And as I read the passage cited above now again after these many years, I notice how closely Smith's words echo those of Heschel in *A Passion for Truth:* "The Baal Shem exhorted us to prize highly everything that exists. How else can we come close to the Creator, if not through the things He has made? It is hardly possible to revere Him and at the same time despise His creation.... Man must cherish the world, said the Baal Shem. To deprecate, to deride it was presumption. Creation, all of creation, was pervaded with dignity and purpose and embodied God's meaning."[507]

But notice that unlike Smith's description, the Baal Shem does not use the language of the sanctification of life. The Besht was far more interested in experiencing God's presence in and through the things of the world than merely hallowing life. In the following teaching he offers a contemplative spiritual practice that centers on mindfully exploring the details of our ordinary existence, looking for signs of the spirit.

> What is the way of true seeing? Let's say that you attracted to a lovely woman. Do you dwell on her beauty—do you fantasize about her? Well, if this is happening, you need to turn your attention instead to this question: *What is the true source of this woman's beauty?* And then ponder this: If she were no longer alive, would she possess such an attractive face?
>
> From where, then, does her radiant beauty arise? It can only be the power of Divinity unfolding within her. And isn't it really this spiritual quality that is drawing

you to her earthly beauty? And then ask yourself: Why should I let myself be attracted to a mere fragment of the sublime when I can bind myself to the Whole, the root of all being?

Here, then, my students, is what I am asking of you: Look at every creation in this way, for the underlying cause of its existence. There is divine life even in those things that seem, on the surface, to be inanimate. The shape and stability of a stone point toward something transcending its materiality. And when you see something beautiful—for instance, an artistically-fashioned goblet—ask yourself: What is the true source of this object's grace and elegance? By itself the material of which it is made is quite worthless, for its true life comes from its form and delicacy, and these are of inspired origins. Also, when you are eating, be aware that the flavor of your food arises from its vital energy, and that this tastiness derives from a hidden essence. So wherever you look, making use the power of awareness, you will see the Lifeforce undergirding existence. Such seeing serves the Infinite, the blessed *Ein Sof,* for through this kind of mindful seeing, you will be actually drawing divine energy into that object, and bringing to it God's blessing.[508]

Although the Baal Shem Tov doesn't use the vocabulary associated with holiness, the practice itself would definitely alter a disciple's seeing in a way that eventually everything he witnessed would be perceived as sacred. I've found this to be quite difficult, but if and when I stay attentive, I find this way of seeing to be effective, enabling me to recognize that "the fullness of the earth is God's glory."

JUDAISM AND MEANING

We turn back now to the beginning of Huston Smith's chapter on Judaism. He begins his inquiry with a question: How could a tiny people like the Jews have survived the travails they underwent while at the same time making a profound and lasting moral and religious impact on the world? And then he writes: "[W]hat lifted the Jews from obscurity to permanent religious greatness was their passion for meaning."[509] Indeed. But doesn't every religion do the same? Aren't all philosophies and paths to wisdom concerned with finding and providing their followers with some kind of meaning? What is it then that makes Judaism different?

From its very beginning, writes Smith, Judaism's prophets, historians, and teachers were concerned with discovering meaning in the world in which they lived. What concerned the God of the Jews was not some mythic dimension somewhere above and beyond everyday human experience, but the here and now of this world. Then Smith spells out ways that Jews discovered meaning in eight areas of life: God, creation, human existence, history, morality, justice, suffering, and messianism. I'd like to look at Smith's first category of meaning—God.

He writes, "[F]rom beginning to end the Jewish quest for meaning was rooted in their understanding of God." How did the Jews perceive God? We do not create ourselves, Smith states, we issue from an Other, and this Other is neither prosaic, chaotic, amoral, or hostile. Above all, this Other is meaningful. In the ancient Middle East, it was taken for granted that there was a multitude of gods and that they were often in conflict with one another. The Jews, however, saw through the turmoil of the world, and what they found was a single and singular divine power who was ultimately in control. Of course this view of existence is not universally acknowledged as true. Smith underscores the idea that such an attitude toward the world affected the way Jews dealt with the challenges and defeats they suffered in the course of their 3,000-year history: "However desperate their lot, however deep the valley of the shadow of death they found themselves in, they never despaired of life itself. Meaning was always waiting to be won; the opportunity to respond creatively was never absent. For the world had been fashioned by the God who not only meted out the heavens with a span, but whose goodness endured forever."[510]

Perhaps Smith's use of the category of meaning applies to the teachings of the Baal Shem Tov. A good part of what the founder of Hasidism brought to his people in Poland was a restatement of the classical Jewish affirmation of meaning despite suffering. *"And Elohim saw all that he had created was good."* (Genesis 1:31) And, to the Besht, what God had declared as good at the beginning of time would be good in perpetuity:

> The Baal Shem Tov taught, it was not only the heavens and the earth and all their array that were fashioned during the six days of creation. At that time the Creator of the world also made every kind of remedy and cure that would ever be needed to heal any and every kind of wound that would ever occur. And God also created consolations for every form of suffering, whether individual or communal. These remedies will continue to be effective through all generations.[511]

One principal way that he spoke about meaning was through the traditional concept of God's providential caring (*hash'ga'hah p'ra'tit*): "The holy Baal Shem Tov once said to his students: Imagine that a farmer is driving his wagon along the road, and the wagon is loaded with straw, and then a tiny piece of straw falls from the wagon. Now the exact place on the ground where that piece of straw will land has been decided by a heavenly decree!"[512]

HESCHEL AND ULTIMATE MEANING

I mentioned that the bibliography of the original edition of *The Religions of Man* praised the writings of Abraham Joshua Heschel. Now Heschel's thought focuses a great deal on the question of meaning, and books like *Man Is Not Alone* and *God in Search of Man* were an inspiration for Smith. "On the certainty of ultimate meaning we stake our very lives," Heschel writes, "In every judgement we make, in every act we perform, we assume that the world is meaningful. Life would come to naught if we acted as if there were no ultimate meaning."[513]

Heschel writes about the meaning of our earthly existence in a way similar to Smith's understanding: "All things carry a surplus of meaning over being—they mean more than what they are in themselves. Even finite facts stand for infinite meaning."[514] But not just the meaningfulness of the events and things of the world, for Heschel, like the Besht, went beyond Smith's understanding of the significance of meaning for the religious life. He writes that "religion...comes to light in moments in which one's soul is shaken with unmitigated concern about the meaning of all meaning, about one's ultimate commitment which is part of his very existence; in moments, in which all foregone conclusions are suspended; in which the soul is starved for an inkling of eternal reality; in moments of discerning the indestructible sudden within the perishably constant."[515]

I have often wondered at the steadfastness of Heschel's faith in light of his experience of the Holocaust. Heschel lost his mother, his three sisters, and many of his relatives during World War II. And he suffered the loss of his home and his civilization. It was a miracle that Heschel was able to get out of Europe just before the Nazis entered Warsaw. How was he able to maintain his faith in ultimate meaning, having gone through such suffering and travail?

Heschel's family came from Medzhibozh where the Baal Shem Tov spent the last twenty years of his life. But Heschel's ancestor, Rabbi Abraham Joshua Heschel of Apt (1748-1825) had also headed the Hasidic community in Medzhibozh from 1814 until his death in 1825. The Apter Rebbe, as he was called, was so loved and revered that he was buried next to the tomb of the Besht. And most of the wondrous deeds that Heschel heard from his father as a child had something to do with Medzhibozh, his own ancestral home.

Heschel's father, Rabbi Moshe Mordecai, was a Hasidic rebbe in Warsaw, and countless numbers of people came to him with their petitions for support because he was known for his compassion, especially for the poor, and for the power of his prayers. But Rabbi Moshe Mordecai was a highly sensitive man and he lived in a state of anxiety for those whom he attempted to aid.

Moshe Idel has closely examined Heschel's relationship with the Besht, pointing out that Heschel did not hesitate comparing the Besht with Moses. Did Heschel then conceive of himself as the spiritual inheritor of the Besht? Idel wonders. "In fact the ideal religion as Heschel proposed it featured the centrality of prayer, decribed sometimes as an emanation of man to God, a view that echoes the axiology of the Besht." Furthermore, Heschel saw the Besht as the equal of Moses. In Heschel's words, Moses revealed the necessity of observance, but the Besht contributed both the notion of and the practice of exaltation. "The Besht taught that Jewish life is an occasion for exaltation. Observance of the Law is the basis, but exaltation through observance is the goal."[516]

Heschel refuses to indict God for the evil in the world. It is not God who is a problem, he maintained, but human beings. Our physical and mental reality is beyond dispute, but our meaning, our spiritual relevance, is a question that cries for an answer. This is the mainstream view of Judaism going back to the Bible: human beings are responsible for the evils in the world. And if my conjecture is correct, Heschel's faith during and after the Holocaust was buttressed by his faith in the Baal Shem Tov. But there was another factor to Heschel's view, as well: the power of worship to lift the spirit and deepen faith, something that was also part of the Baal Shem's teachings. Heschel writes that worship is an answer, "For worship is an act of man's relating himself to ultimate meaning."[517] What was the kind of worship that Heschel engaged in?

It was the evening of Simhat Torah, the holy day of rejoicing with the Torah, and I was celebrating together with my fellow students and faculty members in the seminary synagogue. As the special ritual began, worshippers took all the scrolls of the Torah from the ark at the front of the synagogue and carried them around the auditorium in seven joyful processionals, accompanied by ritual chant. Between each of these *hakafot* (processionals) the entire congregation would sing and dance ecstatically with the Torah. I watched Abraham Heschel holding a Torah in his arms. He was not dancing, but swaying with it as if he were cradling a baby. His eyes were closed, his face on fire, and it seemed at that moment that he was truly free in God. In one of his books, Heschel wrote that "inner freedom is spiritual ecstasy, the state of being beyond all interests and selfishness. Inner freedom is a miracle of the soul."[518]

I cannot prove this, but I believe that Heschel understood that even when there is a seeming lack of meaning in our earthly existence, there is meaning in transcendence, where a davener comes into a mystical oneness with the Divine. This is in consonance with the teachings of the Baal Shem Tov. I believe that the path of the Besht provided my teacher with a sense of exaltation and ultimate meaning even when virtually everything he had valued from his life in Europe had been shattered.

It was only in his last book, *A Passion for Truth,* that Heschel began to admit the ways in which the Holocaust challenged his faith, especially through his sympathetic portrayal of the Kotzker Rebbe: "To live both in awe and consternation, in fervor and horror, with my conscience on mercy and my eyes on Auschwitz, wavering between exaltation and dismay? I had no choice: My heart was in Medzibozh, my mind in Kotzk."[519]

There have also been times in my life when existence appeared to be absurd, times when I would have agreed with John-Paul Sartre when he stated in *Being and Nothingness*, "Man can will nothing unless he has first understood that he must count on no one but himself; that he is alone, abandoned on earth in the midst of his infinite responsibilities, without help, with no other aim than the one he sets himself, with no other destiny than the one he forges for himself on this earth." But my apprenticeship with the Baal Shem Tov through the writings and the life of Heschel opened the way to a perception of existence that recognized every creature, all of creation, filled by the universal powers that make life possible. And it deepened my devotional life. I've come to believe that human beings must either *find* transcendent meaning or *make* existential meaning out of absurdity. And from a non-dualistic standpoint, finding meaning or making meaning amount to the same thing, for if human beings are part of the cosmos—single cells within the living organism that is God—when we are engaged in making meaning, we manifest and enact the divine potential within us. But while we as individuals contribute to the creation of meaning for ourselves, it is a mere trick of the ego to imagine that the attainment of meaning is the result of our powers alone.

On the other hand, the Holocaust and other such horrors tragically demonstrate that our ability to advance meaning is tentative and impermanent, for human beings are also able to regress and bring about "devolution," obliterating human meaning, turning existence into absurdity, and returning the Divine to what it was before it gave birth to humanity, as if the experiment that we represent had never been.

FORGOTTEN TRUTH

One afternoon, I happened to meet Abraham Heschel in the seminary mail room. "Dr. Heschel," I said, "I just finished reading *God in Search of Man*." "And how did you find it?" he asked. I didn't know what to say and I blathered something fatuous. "And did you read *Man Is Not Alone?*" he asked. I shook my head no. "Well, you should have read *Man Is Not Alone* before reading *God in Search of Man.*"

God in Search of Man is a philosophy of Judaism; *Man Is Not Alone* is a philosophy of religion. In that book my teacher attempted to find the common ground in all religion, or at least in all Western religion. What he was telling me was that I needed to ground myself in the universal foundations of all religion if I was to truly understand Judaism. *Man Is Not Alone* asserts that the religious quest begins with radical amazement at one's existence, at the existence of others, at the very existence of the world. The mystery of being that we sense leads us to the desire to stand in the presence of ultimate reality.

Huston Smith also moved in the direction of universalism. Although *The World's Religions* was by far his most popular book, in later years he became more deeply concerned with the question of what it was that linked the various religions with one another. His thinking on this theme is found in at least three of his later books: *Forgotten Truth: The Common Vision of the World's Religions; Beyond the Postmodern Mind;* and *Is There a Universal Grammar of Religion?* After having taught for many years at MIT, he became critical of the ways modern science reduces the world to physical categories. He began *Forgotten Truth* by demonstrating how science obscured and eliminated the primordial wisdom underlying all religions, reducing reality to a single material plane. The results of this, he declared, have been appalling, for the world's religions recognize that reality is multi-tiered, and that there are many levels or planes to existence, not merely the material or physical, which is only the outermost level. He went on to show how every traditional religion without exception points to the existence of four levels of reality, each more ethereal and more complete than the one below it. Then he devoted a chapter to demonstrating how these four planes of being also manifest as correlative levels within the human self. That is, the world's religions all take for granted that human beings are microcosms of the cosmos and replicate within themselves the four levels of reality that characterize the universe itself.

Finally, in the appendix to *Forgotten Truth*, Smith cites the work of Stanislav Grof, a Czech psychiatrist who researched what psychedelics reveal about the human psyche more systematically than had any other scientist. Smith understands Grof's findings regarding human nature to be completely in accord with the religious concept of the human self that was and is held in traditional societies. Smith provides a graphic chart to show how each religion describes the four levels of reality. With regard to Judaism, he indicates that the four "worlds" of the Kabbalah (Action, Formation, Creation, and Emanation) are virtually identical with the four levels of reality found in all the other religious systems. And he shows that those four worlds are linked to the four levels of human selfhood as defined by the Kabbalah—the body and the three levels of soul/spiritual life, physical vitality (*nefesh*), spirit (*ru'ah*), and soul (*neshamah*).

During his ninth decade, Smith gave a public lecture that distilled his understanding of the universal truths shared by the world religions. His starting point was linguist Noam Chomsky's notion of the existence of a universal grammar which is innate in the human brain, and which structures every particular human language. Smith argued that if such an inherent capacity of the mind exists for language, it must exist for religion as well. As he put it, "we are hard-wired in our minds for the divine."[520] The book that contains this lecture, *Is There a Universal Grammar of Religion?* was edited by Smith's colleague and friend, Henry Rosemont, Jr., a scholar of Chinese religion. The book crystallizes fourteen points Smith believed are essential to and characterize every religion. He doesn't speak about meaning in the lecture, but studying his views it seemed to me that he could have just as well titled it, "Religion and the Quest for Meaning," for these fourteen points also highlight how the founders and teachers in all of the traditional cultures recognized their most significant values.

I also saw commonalities between what Smith claimed to be the glue underlying and uniting all religion, and what was true for the Baal Shem Tov and Judaism. So I reframed the Baal Shem's religious worldview using Smith's categories. Following each of Smith's points I have set in italics the way I imagine the Besht might have expressed this statement.

1. Reality is infinite. *The entire universe manifested out of Ein Sof, the infinite mystery.*
2. The Infinite includes the finite. *Everything in the finite physical universe is encompassed within Ein Sof, the Infinite.*

3. The contents of finitude are hierarchically ordered. *Divinity descends the Tree of Life through each of the Four Worlds depicted by the Kabbalah. The descent occurs in ten stages from the sefirah of Divine Wisdom (Hokhmah), which is closest to Ein Sof, to the Shekhinah, which is the most distant.*

4. Causation happens from the top down. *The higher sefirot are closer to Ein Sof, and thus more spiritually potent than the lower sefirot; and the entire Tree of Life is made possible by the mystery of Ein Sof.*

5. The One becomes the many, and the parts of the many are virtues that contain the perfection of the One. *The first three sefirot are the highest manifestation of Ein Sof. The absolute unity and perfection of Divine Wisdom (Hokhmah) is followed by the perfection of the next two sefirot, Understanding (Binah) and Consciousness (Da'at). Although differentiation is prefigured in this trinity, it doesn't actually occur until the appearance of the seven lower sefirot: Love, Rigor, Balance, Victory, Yielding, Foundation, and Shekhinah. Nonetheless, the seven lower sefirot each contain some of the perfection of the higher sefirot.*

6. As the virtues ascend the causal ladder, their distinctions fade and they begin to converge until the finite differences, which stand for separation, completely disappear in the divine simplicity. *This is exactly true in the realm of the sefirot. And the kabbalists call the sefirot Virtues (Middot). And such a convergence can actually be experienced in the process of ascent during ecstatic worship.*

7. Absolute perfection reigns at the top of the hierarchy, so even though the world may be in the worst shape imaginable, all is well in the eye of the cyclone. The physical world is transitory and will come to an end at some point in time—not wiped out, but redeemed. *Despite the challenging conditions under which the Jewish people live, there will be a time when divine perfection will reign, brought on by a large preponderance of tzaddikim. Their leadership, potent spiritual practices, and compassionate acts will bring about the healing and liberation necessary for the emergence of the messianic era.*

8. As above, so below, that is, everything that exists in the external

world also exists within human beings. *The four worlds and the ten sefirot that form the reality of the external world also exist within the human being as four different levels of the human soul or spirit.*

9. Human beings cannot fully know the Infinite. What we do know about the Infinite comes from revelations by the Infinite itself. *The foundation of the Jewish path to the Divine comes from the revelation of the Torah to Moses and the Israelite people which took place at Mt. Sinai after the Israelites escaped from Egypt. This is a Torah meant for living on the finite physical plane. But as a kabbalist, the Baal Shem understood that long before Moses there was an infinite Primordial Torah (Torah Kedumah) meant for the messianic era and rooted in the compassion that brought forth existence.*

10. Revelations have to be interpreted; the Bible and the sacred texts of the world must be interpreted to understand their intended meaning. *The five books that make up the Torah were revealed through Moses and are called the Written Torah. But the Written Torah can only be understood through the lens of the Oral Torah— the interpretations of the rabbis found in the Talmud and Midrash, and also revealed by later sages like the Baal Shem Tov, using intuitive powers that derive from the Primordial Torah.*

11. All of these factors were once taken for granted, but this changed in modern times with the success of science on the one hand, and the rise of fundamentalism on the other. *With the rise of Enlightenment rationalism in western Europe, which was taking place during the lifetime of the Baal Shem Tov, traditional religious understanding of the world came under attack. This effected Jews as well as Christians. Modern Jews have accepted the methodology of science as true, and many who are secular have come to see rationality and science as better guides to truth than traditional wisdom. Orthodox Jews, on the other hand, fearing the inroads of modern secularism, became increasingly bound to a literal understanding of what they saw as the exclusive truths of Jewish tradition.*

12. There are two ways of knowing: the rational and the intuitive. *The Talmudic sages made use of both approaches in methods they*

developed to interpret the mitzvot of the Torah. At the same time, the Aggadic interpreters of the non-legal parts of the Bible used intuition in their approach to those texts, and the medieval kabbalists followed in their wake. The Baal Shem favored the intuitive approach.

13. There are those who seek to understand the Infinite in humanlike terms, and others who envision the Infinite in more abstract terms. Both approaches are legitimate. *The Baal Shem uses anthropomorphic imagery when he speaks of God in his parables. He also uses such imagery in his discourses on cosmic unification (i.e., his kabbalistic understanding of the relationship between the Shekhinah and the blessed Holy One). But in his descriptions of the ways the sefirot interact within the human psyche, the Besht employed the abstract symbolic language of the kabbalists, referring to the sefirot as dynamic aspects of the Divinity within human beings.*

14. What we know is ringed about with darkness; we are born in mystery, we live in mystery, and we die in mystery. *The Baal Shem taught that even though the language he used to describe the workings of the Divine pointed toward the truth, the highest form of knowing is not knowing.*

And I would add a fifteenth principle, which I believe Huston Smith might agree with: Despite the absurdity of existence that often perplexes people, every religion provides a way for its adherents to discern the spiritual meaning of existence. Certainly, the Baal Shem Tov did this for his people after the calamities of the seventeenth century. I see the larger aim of his mission not only as collective healing, but as restoration of spiritual meaning to his people.

A UNIVERSAL TRADITIONALIST

Huston Smith might be called a universal traditionalist. He believed that the fourteen metaphysical points he identified were not only true of the underlying structure of the human psyche, but also with regard to the ontological reality of the world, completely independent of human perception. This was a radical claim to make, and it flies in the face of all modern philosophy, psychology, and science.

I am not so sure. My Western education has conditioned me to see the metaphysical views of Judaism and the religions of the world as human projections onto the mysteries of the cosmos. For me, the kabbalistic notions of the Four Worlds and the ten sefirot of the Tree of Life represent the different states of awareness that the mystic experiences, and not necessarily actual levels of reality in the external world. At the same time, pondering how thinkers like Smith and Heschel can take the kind of stances they do, makes me wonder. Heschel was able to show the common experience underlying every faith tradition, and Smith identified the common ontological features held by *all* the world's religions. Is it then possible that the traditional religionists had it right after all? Is the human mind really constituted in a way that it is able to grasp some of those ultimate mysteries?

I find that I have no answers. Often, when I encounter problems that I cannot solve, I open my journal and address my quandary to my inner spiritual guidance. A few days later I will open my journal again and simply let my hand write what it is directed to write by the spirit. So I wrote down my question: Are the four levels that Huston Smith talks about aspects of the universe at large? And the next day I had my answer: What you are seeking to understand is not something you could ever fathom with your mind. As for your soul—that is a different matter. But even though your soul realizes that something more exists, there is nothing of those deeper enigmas that you can know, much less affirm.

HUSTON SMITH IN SYNAGOGUE

The holy day of Shavuot celebrates the ancient barley harvest, but it later came to commemorate the giving of the Ten Commandments and the Torah at Mt. Sinai. The medieval kabbalists introduced a custom called *Tikkun Leil Shavuot,* which involves remaining awake the entire night of Shavuot and studying Torah communally in the synagogue. As the light of the new day dawns, members of the community daven the morning worship service and then chant the narrative of the revelation at Sinai out of the scroll of the Torah. The custom continues to this day.

During the nineties, I would usually attend a Tikkun Leil Shavuot celebration in Berkeley where I lived. One year, however, I heard that a Conservative synagogue in a neighboring town had invited Huston Smith to teach at their Tikkun celebration. This would be something I could not miss. The evening was a delight, for Professor Smith spoke both about Judaism, and about his personal relationship with our religion in warm and heartfelt words. I can't recall everything that he said, but I remember him sharing with the congregation the story of his eldest daughter, Karen, who converted to Judaism and married a traditionally observant Jewish man. Karen had contracted an incurable form of cancer and had recently died, but, Smith emphasized, he was so glad that his daughter's Jewish faith had given her the courage and consolation she needed to accept her death. He then introduced his son-in-law, who spoke briefly, and finally his grandson, who had just become bar mitzvah. The boy surprised us by chanting his *haftarah* for us—the portion from the biblical prophets that he had recently chanted at his ceremony.

Afterward, Smith told us that even though he himself was a Christian, throughout his life he had incorporated spiritual practices into his daily and weekly regimen from religions other than Christianity. These practices included Indian yoga, Zen meditation, and Sufi chanting—and that he had learned about Shabbat observance from his daughter and son-in-law, and was now practicing this as well. In a later interview, he revealed that in his last sustained conversation with Karen she'd spoken about angels. "I sensed at once," Smith said, "that she was thinking of the kabbalistic view in which every mitzvah, every good deed that people perform creates an angel. Those angels don't vanish with the acts that brought them into being. They live on as permanent additions to the universe, affecting the balance between the forces of good and evil."[521]

A similar openness was present in my teacher, Abraham Joshua Heschel. Reared in a home and culture that most likely exalted Judaism as the only true religion, his pursuit of the truth led him beyond the parochialism of his past, inspiring me to do the same.

CHAPTER THIRTY-ONE

THE DOMAIN OF PERENNIAL WISDOM

As a young man in the 1940s, Huston Smith was strongly influenced by the writings and presence of the British-American spiritual teacher Gerald Heard (1889-1971). An initiate of Indian Vedanta, Heard believed that human beings could effectively work to develop their consciousness through meditation and other spiritual practices. He was trained as a historian at Cambridge University and later served as science commentator on the BBC. Immigrating to the U.S., he founded and directed Trabuco College in California, which advanced comparative religious studies. His approach to philosophy influenced many. Heard was also one of the spiritual forerunners of the New Age spirituality that emerged in the counterculture during the 1960s.

I was surprised to learn that Heard had been a powerful influence on my teacher, Zalman Schachter-Shalomi. "There are some pivotal encounters in our lives," Reb Zalman writes, "and for me one of these was meeting Gerald Heard. It isn't easy to estimate the impact of his person and thought when it has become so pervasive in the system files of my thought processor."[522]

Heard once sent Huston Smith to meet Aldous Huxley (1894-1963), another of his proteges, a British-American intellectual, philosopher, novelist, poet, and screenwriter. Smith trekked out to the wilds of the Mojave Desert where Aldous and his wife Maria were retreating from the hustle and bustle of Hollywood. That encounter was pivotal for Smith's development, and Huxley became both a mentor and friend. Years later, when Smith was teaching at MIT, he brought Huxley to lecture at that institution. Huxley's lectures were wildly popular among the students.

Many consider Huxley to have been one of the greatest intellectuals of the twentieth century. He is probably best known for his early novel, *Brave New World,* a frightening dystopian exploration of modern culture which, in retrospect, shows itself prescient. Over the years, I had attempted to read several of his novels, but his fiction style did not appeal to me. But Huxley also wrote non-fiction, and books that did excite me included *The Doors of Perception*, a memoir that elaborates Huxley's experience using mescaline. He recalls the insights he experienced, both aesthetic and spiritual, having ingested the drug, and reflects on the philosophical and psychological implications. This experience, which Huxley underwent in 1953, gave him experiential proof regarding the origin of timeless truths that he'd only minutely detailed in his earlier work, *The Perennial Philosophy*, published in 1944.

EYELESS IN GAZA

Early in life, Huxley identified as an atheist and a sexual libertine. But his mind was mercurial, and he was too consumed by the issues posed by twentieth-century life to remain as cynical as he had been when writing the early dystopian novels. He eventually turned to existential questions: How should human beings live? Can nothing halt the chaos of our existence? Is there a way to stop technology from destroying civilization? And his friendship and mentorship with Gerald Heard led him toward a spiritual resolution to these questions.

This influence can first be seen in Huxley's 1936 novel, *Eyeless in Gaza*. Through the book's protagonist, Anthony Beavis, the author begins to fashion a mystical vision that he would elaborate in later works. It is here where Huxley first promotes the spiritual goal of union with God. Evil is that which separates people from one another; good is what unites people. And love, compassion, and understanding are manifestations of unity. Anthony Beavis' notebook contains a statement of Huxley's own mysticism: "Empirical facts: One. We are all capable of love for other human beings. Two. We impose limitations on that love. Three. We can transcend all these limitations—*if we choose to*. (It is a matter of observation that anyone who so desires can overcome personal dislike, class feeling, national hatred, colour prejudice. Not easy; but it can be done, if we have the will and know how to carry out our good intentions.) Four. Love expressing itself in good treatment breeds love. Hate expressing itself in bad treatment breeds hate. In light of these facts, it's obvious what inter-personal, inter-class and inter-national policies should be. But, again, knowledge cuts little ice. We all know; we almost all fail to do. It is a question, as usual, of the best methods of implementing intentions."[523]

A PHILOSOPHICAL DISCOVERY

The Perennial Philosophy, composed eight years after *Eyeless in Gaza,* was a landmark statement of Huxley's commitment to the mystical path, and a discovery of what perhaps lies behind all philosophical quests. Unlike *The Doors of Perception,* which is both personal and urbane, *The Perennial Philosophy* is more detached, serious, and challenging. It is a work of advocacy describing the outcome of visionary experience, that is, what such experience must lead to in terms of a universal path of life that can steer someone through the dark thicket of worldly existence.

If Richard Bucke's *Cosmic Consciousness* was mostly concerned with the visionary origins of mystical truth, *The Perennial Philosophy* focuses on ways mystics through the ages transmuted those visions into spiritual insights to illumine the way to truthful living, conjoined with a broad survey of moral and spiritual paths and practices that mystics have followed to live the truths they discovered. Huxley explains that the Perennial Philosophy is an approach to truth affirming an underlying and universal wisdom that appears across cultures and ages in different guises. The Perennial Philosophy is a metaphysic, a psychology, and an ethic that is "primarily concerned with the one, divine Reality substantial to the manifold world of things and lives and minds." This philosophical tradition was first committed to writing some twenty-five centuries ago. "Rudiments of the Perennial Philosophy may be found among the traditionary lore of primitive peoples in every region of the world, and in its fully developed forms it has a place in every one of the higher religions." He also notes that it can be seen in Vedanta, Hebrew prophecy, the Tao Te Ching, the Platonic dialogues, the Gospel according to John, Mahayana Buddhism, the philosophy of Plotinus, among the Persian Sufis, and Christian mystics.

Originating in ancient India, Perennial Philosophy appears in different guises in all the Eastern spiritual traditions, but it also forms the basic core of Western mysticism and esoterism. In antiquity it appeared in Hermeticism, Gnosticism, and Neoplatonism, and during the Middle Ages and Renaissance its basic tenets could be found in Kabbalah, Christian mysticism and philosophy, Rosicrucianism, and Freemasonry. During the nineteenth century Perennialism reappeared in movements such as Theosophy and New Thinking, and in the twentieth century it was allied with the New Age Movement. Carl Jung's understanding of human individuation is also a psychospiritual rendering of the Perennial Philosophy.

The Perennial Philosophy focuses on the common features of the great wisdom traditions of humanity, assembling parallel quotations from the world's scriptures, organizing them under headings such as "The Nature of the Ground of Reality," "God in the World," and "Self-Knowledge." Among the moral qualities Huxley treats are charity, right livelihood, and right action; among the spiritual qualities are non-attachment, spiritual exercises, and ritual. He informs readers about his approach: "In studying the Perennial Philosophy we can begin either at the bottom, with practice and morality; or at the top, with a consideration of metaphysical truths; or, finally, in the middle, at the focal point where mind and matter, action and thought have their meeting place in human psychology."[524] He shows the differences that distinguish each approach. Practical teachers like the Buddha begin at the bottom because they want to turn their followers into highly moral individuals. Philosophers and theologians start at the top because of their inclination to think and speculate. However, Huxley writes that "the middle gate gives entrance to the exponents of what has been called 'spiritual religion'—the devout contemplatives of India, the Sufis of Islam, the Catholic mystics of the later Middle Ages." Although Huxley doesn't discuss Judaism, I can add here that it was primarily the biblical prophets, the Talmudic masters, and the musar-oriented moralists in our tradition who emphasized ethical living. And it was the medieval philosophers and kabbalists who were largely drawn to metaphysical truth.

Huxley decided to gear his book to the middle way, that is human psychology. This is also the Baal Shem Tov's approach, beginning with the kind of psychospiritual self-understanding that brings the adept to an understanding of the Divinity of the soul: "You long for the Divine to descend upon you and enter your life? Then the most important thing for you to know and grasp is that there is nothing within you but God."[525]

As I paged through *The Perennial Philosophy* for the first time, I could not help but notice that it contained only a few citations from Jewish sources. Sometime later I discovered that Gottfried Wilhelm Leibniz

(1646-1716), the German mathematician and philosopher Huxley credits with the discovery of the existence of Perennial Philosophy, had been familiar with the Kabbalah, and this knowledge may have influenced his understanding. But why are Jewish sources missing from Huxley's book? It's not only Judaism that is missing from *The Perennial Philosophy*; I also found few references to Islam or Sufism. In fact, most of the teachings found in the volume come from either Vedanta, Buddhism, or Christianity. A smaller number of quotations represent Chinese wisdom. Was it Huxley's ignorance of Kabbalah, Hasidism, Sufism, Taoism, and Confucianism that led to these omissions? Or did he have some kind of antipathy to their teachings? Or was it the paucity of translations of perennial wisdom texts from those traditions in the early 1940s when Huxley was writing? Whatever the case, the fact that he was able to extrapolate universal spiritual and moral principles from the evidence of Indian and Christian mystics, principles that I intend to show apply equally and fully to the vision of the Baal Shem Tov, is further testimony to the universal validity of Perennialism.

THE PROBLEM OF THE EGO

Huxley was deeply troubled by the morally ruptured character of the world, and he attributed this brokenness to the human ego and its blinding desires, which have usurped the all-embracing truth that's experienced by those fortunate souls who experience spiritual enlightenment. It is this that is leading the human race toward the precipice. This recognition is nothing new, but the core of the tragedy, Huxley claimed, is that even when people recognize the problem of the ego, they so often fail to assent to the solution offered by the sages of the Perennial Philosophy.

I resonate with what Huxley was saying. He included the biblical prophets in his characterization of Perennialism, and that would likely extend to the later Talmudic rabbis since so much of their understanding of what constitutes a good society derived from the prophets. Huxley also included the Kabbalah, which would embrace the Baal Shem Tov. But what spoke most deeply to me was his critical analysis of modern society and its discontents from the point of view of perennial wisdom. This opened my eyes in a new way to the fact that Judaism and the

Gentile faiths are all part of a single spiritual family whose truths have been eclipsed by a mad world of individual and collective egotism.

THE PERENNIAL TRUTHS

Huxley wrote that "the mystical or esoteric components of religious traditions—as opposed to exoteric ritual, doctrine, ethics, and the like—call forth strikingly similar descriptions of reality, across cultures and regardless of era."[526] He believed that every version of the Perennial Philosophy was characterized by four fundamental truths:

> First: the phenomenal world of matter and of individualized consciousness—the world of things and animals and men and even gods—is the manifestation of a Divine Ground within which all partial realities have their being, and apart from which they would be nonexistent.
>
> Second: human beings are capable not merely of knowing *about* the Divine Ground by inference; they can also realize its existence by direct intuition, superior to discursive reasoning. This immediate knowledge unites the knower with that which is known.
>
> Third: man possesses a double nature, a phenomenal ego and an eternal Self, which is the inner man, the spirit, the spark of divinity within the soul. It is possible for a man, if he so desires, to identify himself with the spirit and therefore with the Divine Ground, which is the same or like nature with the spirit.
>
> Fourth: man's life on earth has only one end and purpose: to identify himself with his eternal Self and so come to unitive knowledge of the Divine Ground.[527]

Examining these four truths, we can see that they answer four central spiritual questions: What is the origin and nature of the universe? How can an individual intuit the existence of the Divine? How may an individual experience their identity with the Divine? What is the purpose of human life?

Huxley's book remains an amazing achievement, a work of genius that brings together and synthesizes some of the world's deepest wisdom regarding living an authentic spiritual and moral life. At the same time, it is a prodigious challenge to the materialistic and individualistic values that contemporary society takes for granted. He came to believe that if the Perennial Philosophy was widespread enough, it could actually change the direction of human existence on this planet, and his questions are still with us.

In a recent interview, *New York Times* columnist David Brooks was asked why Americans today are so sad and mean. "The statistics are horrific: rising suicide rates, rising depression," Brooks says, "The number of people in the lowest happiness category has gone up by 50 percent. It's a societal breakdown. When people feel invisible and unseen, they regard that as an injustice. They get angry and lash out and become mean." Then Brooks points to the fact that people are less likely to go to church or synagogue or mosques, or to join the Elks Club or Kiwanis Club. And he adds that people are not good at socializing: "There were all sorts of morally formative institutions that were very popular in American life, ranging from the Boy Scouts to the schools to the McGuffey readers. Then sometime after World War II, people decided human beings don't need to be trained anymore in the basic skills of how to be a good person: how to listen well, how to ask for forgiveness, how to end a conversation gracefully."[528]

I resonate with the critique, but it seems that it doesn't even go far enough, and that the heart of the matter is a toxic individualism—egotism—characterizing much of modern culture. In their in-depth sociological analysis of the ills plaguing the United States, *Habits of the Heart,* sociologist Robert Bellah and his fellow authors wrote that "American culture tradition defines...the purpose of human life in ways that leave the individual suspended in glorious, but terrifying, isolation."[529] They showed the ways in which community has gradually eroded, and the cult of individual self-interest has become the norm. Again and again, they made the point that a meaningful life can only be lived in a community sustained by tradition and by service to others.

KEN WILBER AND THE PERENNIAL PHILOSOPHY

For many years I attempted to formulate the underlying principles of the Baal Shem Tov's path using the principles of the Perennial Philosophy.

But as I studied more and more of his teachings, I found that many of his statements contradicted one another. What I didn't realize at first was that his teachings reflected a continuously evolving sense of truth. Where did the Besht wind up? Did he finally reach a comprehensive view of reality? My encounter with *The Perennial Philosophy* convinced me that he did, because I discovered that what seemed to be among the Besht's most advanced teachings matched the principles that Huxley identified.

At the same time, it seemed that something essential in the Baal Shem's teaching was missing from Huxley, for Huxley's formulation seemed to take as its premise the notion that the quest for salvation is a preoccupation of the individual in isolation from community, perhaps even in opposition to it. Notice how he framed his fourth truth: "Man's life on earth has only one end and purpose: to identify himself with his eternal Self and so come to unitive knowledge of the Divine Ground." This may be the case in some cultures, but it is not true for Judaism, nor most or many of the other perennial paths. What helped me deal with the inadequacy of Huxley's formulation was an alternative description of the Perennial Philosophy by contemporary spiritual philosopher, Ken Wilber, who added the principle that the individual's liberation leads him to acts of mercy and compassion on behalf of all sentient beings.

In *Grace and Grit,* Wilber explains his understanding of perennial wisdom in a dialogue with his wife, Treya Killum Wilber. He tells Treya that "the perennial philosophy is the worldview that has been embraced by the vast majority of the world's greatest spiritual teachers, philosophers, thinkers, and even scientists. It's called 'perennial' or 'universal' because it shows up in virtually all cultures across the globe and across the ages." Then Wilber explains that the human mind, like the body, harbors deep mental structures that are essentially similar across cultures. The mind has the capacity to form images, symbols, concepts, and rules. All of these vary from culture to culture, and on the surface they may not look alike, but the underlying mental structures are the same wherever they appear. Just as the human body grows hair, the human mind grows ideas, and the human spirit grows intuitions of the divine. It is those intuitions and insights that form the foundation of the world's wisdom traditions. "When you can find a truth that the Hindus and Christians and Buddhists and Taoists and Sufis *all agree on,* then you have probably found something that is profoundly important, something that tells you about universal truths and ultimate meanings, something that touches the very core of the human condition." Treya then asks Wilber how he views the modern argument that human knowledge is molded by specific forms of language and culture. And because these vary so much there is no way that any universal truths about the human condition can be posited. Wilber agrees that this is valid, but says it is not the entire truth, for numerous similarities appear in different cultural contexts, such as linguistic structures and mating customs.[530]

Central to the Perennial Philosophy, asserts Wilber, is the notion of a hierarchy of levels, and the possibility that spiritual seekers can ascend that hierarchy. Like Huston Smith, Wilber states that all wisdom traditions subscribe to the notion that reality manifests in a variety of dimensions, and each dimension is higher and more inclusive than the preceding dimension, and closer to the Spirit or Godhead. Then he speaks of the paradox of such a hierarchy, for "Spirit is the summit of being, the highest rung on the ladder of evolution. But it is also true that Spirit is the wood out which the entire ladder and all its rungs are made." He writes that the central claim of the Perennial Philosophy is that "men and women can grow and develop (or evolve) all the way up the hierarchy to Spirit itself, therein to realize a 'supreme identity' with Godhead—the *ens perfectissimum* toward which all growth and evolution yearns."[531]

THE BAAL SHEM AND PERENNIAL PHILOSOPHY

Instead of the four fundamental principles spelled out by Huxley, Wilber counts seven, and I believe these tenets do roughly represent the most important elements found in the Baal Shem's thought at its most advanced stage: "One, Spirit exists. Two, Spirit is found within. Three, most of us don't realize this Spirit within, because we are living in a world of sin, separation, and duality—that is, we are living in a fallen or illusory state. Four, there is a way out of this fallen state of sin and illusion, there is a Path to our liberation. Five, if we follow this Path to its conclusion, the result is a Rebirth or Enlightenment, a direct experience of Spirit within, a Supreme Liberation which—six—marks the end of sin and suffering, and which—seven—issues in social action of mercy and compassion on behalf of all sentient beings."[532]

Let me lay out what I consider to be the Baal Shem's view of these seven principles. I have changed the order in order to show how each emerged from his life experience:

1. *We are living in a world of sin, separation, and duality—that is, we are living in a fallen or illusory state.* Israel Baal Shem Tov underwent tremendous struggles as a young man, including a deep sense of alienation from people, from the world, and from God. At some point in his life, however, he came to recognize that without having been aware of his condition, he had indeed been living in a state of sin, separation, and duality, and he began to struggle in order to find a way out of this condition. Eventually, he came to sense that the brokenness he had experienced was not the fault of human beings. It is part of the flawed condition of the physical universe, which came about during the process of creation when the cosmic shattering—*sh'vi'rat ha'kelim*—occurred. Because of this cataclysm human beings were cut off from the harmony and unity originally intended by the Divine.

2. *There is a way out of this fallen state of sin and illusion, there is a Path to our liberation.* Although it may have been his contact with psychedelics that first opened the Besht to transcendence, it was the teachings of the Kabbalah, and especially those of Cordovero and Abulafia, by which he came to understand there was a way out of the darkness. The Baal Shem taught that through devotional practice, individual seekers can experience the true nature of existence. But it is also clear that the path includes teshuvah, a purification process that transmutes one's negative traits in such a way that the energy that has been tied up in craving is then transformed into positive energy.

3. *Spirit exists.* Through devotional practice one can experience the true nature of existence: that we are all part of *Ayin,* the vast wholeness of being. He both affirmed and experienced the central spiritual teaching of Judaism: "Hear O Israel: the EverPresent is our Power, the EverPresent is the Oneness of existence."

4. *If we follow this Path to its conclusion, the result is a Rebirth or Enlightenment, a direct experience of Spirit within, a Supreme*

Liberation. The Besht pursued the path that he had discovered to its conclusion, and found that it led to his own wholeness.

5. *Spirit is found within.* The Besht's devotional practice led him to the realization that the Spirit existed not only in the infinities beyond the world, but also hidden within himself and within every human being and creature. Using the kabbalistic map of the sefirot he was able to illuminate the ways in which the Spirit operated in the human psyche.

6. *This marks the end of sin and suffering*—and of the illusion of a world in perpetual exile.

7. *And this path of liberation leads in social action of mercy and compassion on behalf of all sentient beings.* The Baal Shem's personal process of enlightenment drove him to a realization that his life's task would be finding compassionate ways to heal and transform his people. He became a shamanic healer and spiritual teacher whose vision offered hope and renewal to many. His disciples continued to develop his legacy and created the Hasidic movement.

So here we have it. This is what I understand to have been the foundational curriculum of the Baal Shem Tov. In identifying the perennial framework of the Besht's wisdom, I believe that these teachings remain relevant despite the centuries that separate us from their initial expression.

DEEP ECUMENISM

Earlier I considered what might be called the universal mystical path to Oneness, and the Baal Shem Tov's place on that path. And yet one could search the entire body of traditions connected with him and conclude that none of his experiences or ideals were specifically shared by seekers and teachers of other faiths. This doesn't mean he was ignorant of other religious paths. If the suggestions offered by Yaffa Eliach, Moshe Idel, and others are accurate, the Besht may very well have had knowledge of beliefs and practices of other faiths, and may have even borrowed from them. But for Hasidism and pre-modern Ashkenazic Jewry as a whole, those other religions were both false and off-limits. Even if there were

Hasidim who knew something about the Baal Shem's links with members of other religious communities, such information would have been suppressed, both among the Hasidim and in the records of the literature associated with the movement's founder.

Such narrow parochialism would likely have characterized most of the pre-modern religionists and mystics in the Western world who lived and practiced exclusively in their own religious communities. This kind of insularity, combined with the tribal character of pre-modern religious institutions, was in large part responsible for the triumphalist views that adherents of these religions held. It was this kind of chauvinism that fostered Christian and, to a far lesser extent, Muslim antisemitism. At the same time most Jews, partly in retaliation, held to a version of Jewish chosenness that blocked their ability to appreciate whatever might be positive or true in either Christianity or Islam.

This kind of exclusivist fundamentalism was one reason why secularists dismissed religion. Today it has become essential for those of us involved with traditional religion to emphasize the ideals and values that unite us and to see one another as part of a single human family. And this is at the heart of the truths proclaimed by most of the mystical and esoteric teachers of the world: *there is only One.*

This is not a new insight. Long before the modern era the sages of India recognized that "Truth is one; the wise call it by many names." The modern Hindu mystic Ramakrishna expressed this in the following way: "Many are the names of God and there are infinite forms through which He may be approached. In whatever name and form you worship Him through that you will realize Him." In his book on the influence of Indian religion in the U.S., Philip Goldberg writes, "Vedanta's ecumenical spirituality has never been more necessary. In an ever-shrinking world, authentic pluralism—by which I mean genuine respect for religious differences within a framework of underlying unity—is obviously a needed counterweight to the deadly forces of tribalism, ethnocentrism, and fundamentalism."[533] We find this same attitude among some medieval Muslims, particularly Sufis. The renowned twelfth-century teacher Muhyiddin ibn Arabi wrote, "Do not praise your own faith so exclusively that you disbelieve all the rest; if you do this you will miss much good. Nay, you will fail to realize the real truth of the matter." This sensibility has begun to flourish in the West, especially through interfaith dialogues. Catholic monk, Brother Wayne Teasdale (1945-2004), gave this broad ideal a name: "Interspirituality, and the intermystical life it entails, recognizes the larger community of humankind in the mystical quest. It realizes that we all have a much greater heritage than simply our own tradition. It acknowledges the validity of all genuinely spiritual experience. Interspirituality honors the totality of human spiritual insight, whether or not it is God-centered. To leave out any spiritual experience is to impoverish humanity. Everything must be included, that is, everything that is authentic and genuine, that springs from contact with the divine, however we know or conceive of this."[534]

My teacher Reb Zalman not only studied the world's religions, but participated in the practices of many of them. He was even ordained as a Sufi sheikh by Pir Moineddin Jablonski. He was also the first major Jewish spiritual teacher to take a principled stand against what he called religious triumphalism. He wrote that "Most Jews in Orthodox communities...still hold on to a triumphalist vision of Judaism. Their thinking goes like this: 'When the end of days will come, the Messiah will show that they were in the wrong and we were free of error all along; we alone were right, and the others were wrong.' This is the Jewish version, but it sounds the same in the Vatican, in Mecca and Medina, and in hard-line communities everywhere."[535]

Reb Zalman asked a very simple but telling question: If God really had nothing to do with the founders of Christianity or Islam, where was God at the time that these teachers were on this earth revealing their teachings? And he went even further, stating the necessity for the existence of each and every religion, and declaring that Judaism was a world religion with a particular task meant to be of service to the human community. This goes hand in hand with God's command to Abraham: "I will bless you, and you shall be a blessing...and all peoples on earth will be blessed through you" (Genesis 12:2-3). In Zalman's words:

> When we look at our planet itself as an organism, we realize that every expression of diversity on this planet is part and parcel of Earth. At the highest level we are all one. But nowhere in nature do we find pure

universalism: the universe always expresses itself in the
particular. The nations and faiths of the world are the
organs of this planet. And we as the Children of Israel
have functions to carry out in this world for the benefit
of the organism as a whole.[536]

He believed that Jews have a covenantal vocation to contribute to the
breaking down of barriers that separate and alienate human civiliza-
tions: "If we extend our imagination beyond a meeting of two religions
to a place where all the religions of the world find ways of connecting
deeply with one another, each time that happened, we would come a
little closer to the sense that the kingdom is coming." Zalman called this
universal vision "Deep Ecumenism." He stated that what makes contemporary Jewish Renewal—a form of neo-Hasidism—different from
traditional Hasidism "is that it is post-triumphalist. It is ecumenical, recognizing that there are other people who are *'ovdey hashem* (servants of
God), from whom we can learn, and with whom we can have a *shituf
p'ulah* (action that is shared), and who also love God.[537]

It is in this way that my own neo-Hasidic journey brought me to the
form of Judaism framed by the Baal Shem Tov, and yet I remain extremely
appreciative of my encounters with Vedanta, Taoism, Buddhism, as well
as Christianity and Islam. I believe that one of the greatest insights of the
interspiritual approach is how it points toward transcending religious
triumphalism, recognizing that beneath all the culturally and historical-
ly-conditioned paths of spiritual awakening there's a common human
passion for a truth that lies beyond the material world. It seems to me
that the Baal Shem's watchword, "There is no place devoid of the Divine,"
might be a starting place for nurturing this kind of reverence for other
spiritual paths for those of us who identify with the Jewish faith.

Reb Zalman loved to foster and participate in gatherings that brought
spiritual teachers from manifold backgrounds together to share their
views about religious truth with one another and with laypeople. Just
recently I watched a video of one such panel that occurred in Ashland,
Oregon in 2006, hosted by Rabbi David Zaslow of Havurah Shir Hadash,
a Jewish Renewal synagogue. The panel featured teachers from many
perspectives, including Tibetan Buddhism, Hinduism, Christianity, and

Native American traditions. More than half the presenters were women, and what they had to share was often forceful and persuasive. My hearing aids were not functioning well—I was due for a new pair—so when I first watched the video I missed many of the doctrinal points as well as the positive comments of the speakers. But in a way this enabled me to appreciate the body language of the participants even more. From their smiles and attentiveness, I could see how deeply interested they were in learning about traditions other than their own. The respect, joy, and laughter were continuous throughout the three-hour presentation. It felt like these teachers, whose beliefs and practices had been separated by historic circumstances, were part of a large family coming together to a longed-for reunion. I sensed that those who sat in the audience were deeply moved, even ecstatic. The gathering was an immersive spiritual experience, one that I believe could only happen in our era.

CHAPTER THIRTY-TWO

CLEANSING THE DOORS OF PERCEPTION

---

*The Baal Shem Tov would serve God's creatures by day, but
during the hours of darkness his soul would free itself and fly
towards the Infinite. And each night his soul would soar higher
and farther toward the Oneness. But there came a night when
a wall of earth rose up before his soul, a wall with an enormous shadowy face, the face of the human life that he had left
behind. And then he heard a great voice coming from beyond
the wall. "Soul, you have reached the boundary. You cannot
pass without sacrificing yourself, for beyond this point Oneness
begins. Break your bond with the earth and I will open to you—
or turn back. But know that once you have entered my realm
you will not be able to return. Now you must choose." And just
as the soul was about to break its bond with the earth, the voice
of a woman, seeing the pale face of her husband lying next to
her, screamed: "Israel!" And her cry flew upward into the heavens. And the soul turned and returned to the earth. This was
the last journey of the master to heaven.[538]*

Now whether this legend, recorded by Martin Buber, was rooted in an
actual occurrence or not, we have no reason to suspect that the Baal
Shem ever halted the ecstatic practices that elevated him into *Ayin*.

I have recounted the legend here because of its resemblance to an
experience that occurred in my life during one of my psychedelic journeys. My companion gave me the sugar cube containing LSD a short
time before we got into his car, and just a few minutes later we were driving on the Massachusetts freeway that would take us to the ocean. As
the medicine began to take effect, the highway altered its appearance,
and became a map of the sefirot. We were travelling on the Tree of Life.
Every sign, every turnoff was pointing to another cosmic destination.
This way was *Hesed* (Love); that way was *Gevurah* (Severity). And there

was *Binah* (Understanding). But I realized that I was not going to any of those places; I was leaving my ego behind and ascending toward some unknown destination.

We pulled into a parking lot at a state beach, got out of the car, and began making our way toward the ocean. It was a cold gray weekday, and the beach was deserted. We came to a restroom, and my friend asked me to wait a few minutes outside. "Please don't leave," he told me earnestly, and I nodded my head in agreement.

I stood there alone, gazing out at the continual rise and fall of the gray-blue waves. And I began to feel the call of the ocean; I was being summoned. I slowly began to walk and within a minute's time entered the water. I was coming home, and I longed for the embrace of the sea. By the time my companion caught up with me the water was up to my chest. He gently turned me around and we walked back toward the shore.

Out of the plethora of disparate astonishing moments that rush by during a psychedelic encounter, certain occurrences can leave indelible imprints on the soul, becoming touchstones for future journeying. This was one of the instances that eventually persuaded me that using psychedelics was too dangerous to continue. Nonetheless, over the years what occurred on that day profoundly affected the future of my life, for that experience drove home what I knew from previous psychedelic experiences—that deep within me there was a longing for a greater reality beyond my ego with its endless cravings and complaints. What remains essential from that experience is the necessity of surrendering to the call of transcendence, which is the key to an authentic spiritual quest.

PEAK-EXPERIENCES

Abraham Maslow was one of the pioneers of a new approach to psychology that focused on a positive approach to understanding human potential, rather than psychopathology. He was interested in what he called self-actualized people, those who were able to fulfill their human potential. He put it this way: "According to the new third psychology... the far goal of education—as of psychotherapy, of family life, of work, of society, of life itself—is to aid the person to grow to fullest humanness, to the greatest fulfillment and actualization of his highest potentials, to his greatest possible stature. In a word, it should help him to become the best he is capable of becoming, to become *actually* what he deeply is potentially."[539] Maslow was fascinated by enlightened individuals who exemplified wholeness, intensity, virtue, achievement, and delight. He wondered what an entire society led by such people might achieve. His lifework had to do with describing them, explaining their excellence, and spreading the word that this richness was in fact an inborn human possession.[540]

The core issue Maslow addressed was how psychology might enable people to self-actualize. He uses the term "peak-experience" to describe certain transpersonal and ecstatic states of consciousness, particularly states characterized by euphoria, harmonization, and interconnectedness. He interviewed a large number of students at Brandeis University, where he taught, and discovered that most people underwent such experiences. Participants described these moments as possessing an ineffably mystical or spiritual quality or essence. Maslow states that peak-experiences are feelings of intense happiness and well-being that come on suddenly, often accompanied by the awareness of an "ultimate truth" and the unity of all things. It is an experience that fills the individual with wonder and awe; they feel at one with the world. He found that peak-experiences usually come on rapidly and may be inspired by deep meditation, intense feelings of love, exposure to great art or music, or the overwhelming beauty of nature.

Peak-experiences tend to be uplifting and ego-transcending; release creative energies; affirm the meaning and value of existence; give the individual a sense of purpose; provide a feeling of integration; and inspire the individual to become more loving and accepting. Such experiences can leave a permanent mark on the lives of individuals. They can be therapeutic in that they tend to increase one's free will, self-determination, creativity, and empathy. When peak-experiences are especially powerful, the sense of self dissolves into an awareness of a greater unity.

Most important for me was Maslow's discussion of what he called the "Being values" or "B-values." These ideals represent a particular type of cognitive knowledge that he thought one could gain through peak-experiences. He identified seventeen of these values: truth, goodness, beauty, wholeness, dichotomy-transcendence, aliveness, uniqueness, perfection, the sense of inevitability, completion, justice, order, simplicity, richness, effortlessness, playfulness, and self-sufficiency.[541] "What is important for us in this context," Maslow states, "is that this list of the described characteristics of the world as it is perceived in our most perspicuous moments is about the same as what people through the ages have called eternal verities, or the spiritual values, or the highest values, or the religious values." And indeed, I had experienced all of these during my psychedelic ventures. Maslow writes that the Being values "may well turn out to be defining characteristics of humanness in its essence…. The statement, 'The fully human person in certain moments perceives the unity of the cosmos, fuses with it, and rests in it, completely satisfied for the moment in his yearning for oneness,' is very likely synonymous, at a 'higher level of magnification,' with the statement, 'This is a fully human person.'"[542]

Maslow theorizes that "the peak-experience may be the model of the religious revelation or the religious illumination or conversion which has played so great a role in the history of religions. Because peak-experiences are in the natural world and because we can research them, and because our knowledge of such experiences is growing and may be confidently expected to grow in the future, we may now fairly hope to understand more about the big revelations, conversions, and illuminations upon which the high religions were founded."[543]

The Baal Shem Tov must have undergone the kind of peak-experiences that Maslow described. Even more important, the Besht adopted those B-values as his own and integrated them into the new form of Judaism that he taught his disciples. While he may not have thought that ordinary people were able to become illumined individuals, he believed that those under his tutelage could attain a high level of development and become true tzaddikim. He knew this possibility through his own struggles and breakthroughs, and also from his ecstatic worship practice.

Although Maslow appreciated traditional religion, and declared that religious experience in its pure form represents the ultimate human rapture, he came to believe that peak-experiences were natural human phenomena, endemic to the psyche. This indicated to him that there was a common essence underlying all human religion; yet it also meant that the search for spirituality was not confined to mystics or to even religion, but it was a universal human quest, such that even agnostics and atheists could have spiritual experiences.

Re-reading his work recently, I was sympathetic with Maslow's views about the universality of the spiritual quest, yet I found myself disagreeing with his scientific naturalism. There are just too many strange, inexplicable happenings in the world that most scientists tend to deny because they do not fit into the regnant rational paradigm. Maslow considered himself a scientist and it appears that he was attempting to refute the exclusivist claims of different religions, thus reducing them to mere peak-experiences. Yet there is a qualitative difference between the kind of peak-experiences that ordinary individuals undergo and the extraordinary revelations reported by the founders of the great religions. I'm not really comfortable with the term "supernatural," but neither am I willing to relegate all phenomena to purely naturalistic causes. I find myself far more receptive to a remarkable passage Maslow wrote toward the end of his volume which seems to contradict his naturalism: "We must remember, after all, that all these happenings are in truth mysteries. Even though they happen a million times, they are still mysteries. If we lose our sense of the mysterious, or the numinous, if we lose our sense of awe, of humility, of being struck dumb, if we lose our sense of good fortune, then we have lost a very real and basic human capacity and are diminished thereby."[544]

Reading Reb Zalman's memoir, *My Life in Jewish Renewal,* I discovered that he was deeply interested in Maslow's research. He writes that he met Maslow on an airplane in 1962, flying back to Winnipeg from Brooklyn, where he had celebrated Simhat Torah with the Lubavitcher Rebbe. The loudspeaker called out, "Could Dr. Abraham Maslow identify himself to the flight attendant?" To Zalman's surprise the passenger next to him raised his hand. Although Zalman was dressed in Hasidic garb, he identified himself as a professor at the University of Manitoba, and the two began to talk. They spoke for several hours about self-actualization and peak-experiences. Zalman had recently taken LSD with Timothy Leary and he was eager to hear Maslow's view of psychedelics. To his surprise Maslow was harshly negative. As Zalman remembers it, Maslow said: "I've discussed this with Tim Leary...he knows my viewpoint. I don't think you can have a genuine peak experience by such easy, chemical means. Life isn't like that. Real growth is hard work. As I tell my students, to achieve anything worthwhile in life, you have to sweat for it. Taking

LSD to have a mystical experience or a peak experience is like taking a cable car to Mont Blanc instead of climbing it. At best, you get the illusion of growth and enlightenment."[545]

But it would seem that Maslow's views changed during the next few years, for in *Religions, Values, and Peak-Experiences* he writes: "In the last few years it has become quite clear that certain drugs called 'psychedelic,' especially LSD and psilocybin, give us some possibility of control in this realm of peak-experiences. It looks as if these drugs often produce peak-experiences in the right people under the right circumstances, so perhaps we needn't wait for them to occur by good fortune. Perhaps we can actually produce a private personal peak-experience under observation and whenever we wish under religious or non-religious circumstances. We may then be able to study in its moment of birth the experience of illumination or revelation."[546] What Maslow didn't recognize is that psychedelic experience is not just another form of peak-experience. Unlike most peak-experiences, which are short-lived, psychedelics can provide a prolonged intense immersion in ecstatic consciousness and they also have the capability of initiating deep changes in one's personality and thinking.

Reb Zalman recalls that he and Maslow later spent time together at Brandeis University. "We talked genially about our mutual interest in Martin Buber's writings and the Hasidic concept of the *tzaddik* as one who self-actualizes and leads others in the midst of the world and not apart from it."[547]

WHY DO PSYCHEDELICS MATTER?

Huston Smith took the title for his book, *Cleansing the Doors of Perception,* from William Blake: "If the doors of perception were cleansed every thing would appear to man as it is, Infinite. For man has closed himself up, till he sees all things thro' narrow chinks of his cavern." And his mentor and friend, Aldous Huxley, had titled his book about his psilocybin experience, *The Doors of Perception.* But Smith didn't like the word psychedelics because of the way it had become tainted by its association with the culture of the sixties. He preferred the term "entheogens," which means something like substances that release the Divinity within the Self.

Smith reveals that he met Timothy Leary in 1961. Leary, together with

Richard Alpert—later known as Ram Dass—did a great deal to introduce the U.S. to psychedelics. And Leary accompanied Smith during his first encounter with psychedelics. Smith later wrote that he experienced a world that was "strange, weird, uncanny, significant, and terrifying beyond belief." A subsequent experience with mescaline provided him with the only powerful experience he ever had of God's personal nature. In a chapter of Smith's book to do with origins of religion, I was startled by his statement, "More interesting than the fact that consciousness-changing devices have been linked with religion is the possibility that they may have actually initiated many of the religious perspectives which, taking root in history, continued after their entheogenic origins were forgotten." That's an eye-opening theory. He mentions a number of scholars and writers who have made the same claim, including Henri Bergson, Robert Graves, Alan Watts, and Mary Barnard. Barnard hypothesized that psychedelic experience "might have had an almost explosive effect on the largely dormant minds of men, causing them to think of things they had never thought of before. This, if you like, is direct revelation."[548]

A number of scholars and archeologists have also applied the theory of psychedelic origins to particular religious experiences recorded in the Hebrew Bible. Dan Merkur conjectures that the manna, "bread from heaven," which the Israelites ate in the wilderness during their forty-year trek to Canaan, was psychoactive in nature. Merkur writes that when Moses fed manna to the Israelites, he told them that after eating the miraculous bread they would see the glory of God. And indeed they did: "They looked toward the wilderness, and behold, the glory of Yahveh appeared in a cloud." Merkur identified the manna as bread containing ergot—a psychoactive fungus containing the same chemicals from which LSD is made.[549] Benny Shanon, a professor of psychology at Hebrew University, has also speculated that ancient Israelite religion was associated with the use of psychedelics. His ideas are based on the fact that in arid areas of the Sinai Peninsula and southern Israel there are two plants containing the same psychoactive molecules found in the plants from which the powerful Amazonian hallucinogenic brew ayahuasca is prepared. These plants are species of the Acacia tree and the bush *Peganum harmala*.[550] And Rick Strassman, a clinical associate professor of psychiatry at the University of New Mexico School of Medicine, has theorized that dimethyltryptamine

(DMT), a natural psychedelic chemical found in the human body, has the ability to open the mind to the spirit world. Strassman applies his theory to the visions of the biblical prophets, concluding that what he calls "the prophetic state of consciousness" may share biological and metaphysical mechanisms with the DMT experience.[551]

Even more compelling than these conjectures is the actual evidence of cannabis discovered at an ancient Israelite shrine by three Israeli archeologists, Eran Arie, Baruch Rosen, and Dvory Namdar. Natalie Lyla Ginsberg of Multidisciplinary Association of Psychedelic Studies comments on this find: "We also recently discovered cannabis at Tel Arad, which was such exciting evidence that our ancestors used cannabis ritualistically as far back as the eighth century BC—currently the oldest discovery of ritual cannabis use in the world! Though some people may still debate whether the *kaneh-bosm* described in the Torah is actually cannabis—with detractors saying it refers to a different 'fragrant cane'—I think it's pretty clear that *kaneh-bosm* means cannabis.... And thanks to the Tel Arad discovery, there's no debating that there was an ancient Jewish altar, in a shrine inscribed with the word YHVH, containing cannabis."[552]

WHAT ABOUT THE BAAL SHEM?

As I have mentioned, I've come to believe it's likely the Baal Shem Tov experienced psychedelics. I base this opinion on the work of two scholars, whose hypotheses I now want to explain in depth, together with my own further research and reflections—because if either or both of their findings are true, this might alter our understanding of the origins of the Baal Shem's vision as well as the roots of Hasidism.

In 1998, Dr. Sharon Packer, a psychiatrist, psychopharmacologist, and historian of medicine who teaches at the Icahn School of Medicine at Mount Sinai, published a scholarly article about fungal epidemics in medieval Europe and the possible relationship of those outbreaks to the origins of certain medieval Jewish mystical movements. Packer writes that the most important grain eaten by poor people in Europe during the Middle Ages was rye, and this grain would regularly attract the psychoactive claviceps fungus known as ergot. When an ergot epidemic occurred, whole communities could be struck by strokes, seizures, and psychosis. But, Packer reveals, ergot is the same fungus from which penicillin and other neuroactive medicinals are made—and it is also the source of LSD-25!

She points out that three major mystical movements of Judaism appeared at the same times and places as these ergot epidemics: Ashkenazic Hasidism in the twelfth and thirteenth centuries in Germany, the messianic heresy of Shabbatai Tzvi in Turkey during the mid-seventeenth century, and eighteenth-century Hasidism in Podolia and Volhynia in Poland. Regarding the latter movement, she states that "ergotism was so consistently present that it was said to be *endemic,* as well as epidemic. The year 1722 brought a severe outbreak."[553]

If ergotism was a source of inspiration for the Baal Shem, Hasidic literature would never have preserved any stories about this, because the use of substances that could alter consciousness among the Hasidim was limited to alcohol. Any other substance would have been censured, and would have discredited the user. Let us suppose, though, that the Besht was exposed to ergot. In the year 1722, when the epidemic broke out, he would have been in his early or late twenties. This would most likely coincide with the seven-year period that *In Praise of the Baal Shem Tov* states he spent as a hermit in the mountains. During that time he ate nothing but the bread he baked. I would assume that on her weekly trips to collect the clay her husband had gathered, the Besht's wife would bring him the flour that he baked with, and it could have been contaminated by ergot. Dr. Packer also writes that personal letters plus the first collection of stories about the Besht, *In Praise of the Baal Shem Tov,* tell us that the pipe-smoking Baal Shem Tov experienced visions in which he saw rainbows, felt his "soul ascend, and burst into paroxysms of joy—all experiences that sound strikingly LSD-like. At times he would tremble and stare straight ahead during prayer, as though in the midst of an epileptoform event.... It is still uncertain what he smoked in his ever-present pipe, but even nicotine could intensify the effects of ergot."[554]

Long before Packer wrote her article on this subject, Yaffa Eliach, a young scholar of Hasidism, had written a doctoral dissertation at the City University of New York on the influence of Christian dissenting sects on the Baal Shem. Toward the end of a scholarly article summarizing her thesis, Eliach wrote about the Besht's use of a long-stemmed pipe: "When smoking the pipe (*lulke*) the Besht experienced joy, was stimulated to prayer, and above all saw visions.... It seems that the Besht had developed an addiction to his pipe and on occasions when he could not smoke, as during holidays, he suffered visible physical changes: his eyes bulged and he maintained a fixed expression, his face was aflame, and his body shook violently. At times he began to cry, and he once doubled over. Others who came near the Besht while he was smoking had strange experiences. The Mochiah of Polenoa once came upon the Besht while the latter was smoking and the Mochiah began to cry uncontrollably." In a footnote, Eliach notes that while there are a number of stories in the literature about the Besht's smoking, in only one is the substance he smoked identified as tobacco (*tutun*); in other stories "the substance smoked is not identified and the pipe is referred to as a *lulke* (Persian for 'pipe'), having a long *zibuk* (Turkish for 'shank'). While smoking the *lulke,* the Besht remained in a stationary position lying or sitting in his room or carriage."[555]

Was it actually tobacco that the Baal Shem was smoking? Possibly. In *Honoring the Medicine,* my friend and colleague Kenneth Cohen devotes a chapter to the use of tobacco in Native American religion and culture. Cohen states that tobacco had many uses in Native American cultures, one of which was intentionally altering consciousness. He cites an authority, Dr. Robert E. Svoboda, who describes the effects of tobacco on human consciousness: "Tobacco can make task performance easier by enhancing alertness and concentration, improving memory (especially long-term memory), reducing anxiety, increasing pain tolerance and reducing hunger." Cohen adds that all of these effects depend "on how much tobacco is consumed. A few puffs stimulate the nervous system; a five or ten-minute period of smoking calms it and may produce feelings of euphoria. Excessive smoking is toxic."

Cohen also notes that when used in moderation, Native tobacco does not have the toxic characteristics of the modern varieties, which are filled with chemical additives. And he states, "My hypothesis is that among healthy participants in Native American ceremony, tobacco filters a potentially confusing array of realities and perceptions. It allows a person to focus deliberately on any reality or aspect of reality, whether conventional or alternate. Tobacco invokes spiritual forces and strengthens the faculty to perceive them."[556] According to Cohen, Native Americans employed a very strong tobacco for sacramental purposes, but that by the eighteenth century the tobacco exported to Europe was usually a cultivated variety whose physiological effects would have been weaker than that used by Native peoples. Nonetheless, even cultivated tobacco can have mind-altering properties when combined with traditional drumming or chanting. "If the Baal Shem smoked tobacco along with chanting Hasidic *niggunim*," he explained to me, "this could have deepened his mystical trance states."

We have no conclusive evidence that the Besht engaged in drumming or chanting niggunim. Readers will recall, however, that he employed the kind of chanting of the letters and words of the traditional liturgy similar to the ecstatic chanting used by the medieval kabbalist Abraham Abulafia. This alone could have expanded his consciousness. What if the chanting was preceded by the Besht's use of his pipe?

In an interesting article on the use of tobacco by Hasidim, Louis Jacobs writes that Shimon Z'ev of Meyenchov in his book *Doresh Tov* reported that "When the Baal Shem Tov wished to proceed to the upper worlds he would inhale tobacco and at each puff he would proceed from world to world."[557] Nonetheless, it is certainly possible that the Besht was smoking something other than tobacco, at least some of the time. Eliach cites a story from *In Praise of the Baal Shem Tov* about the particular value that the Baal Shem and others placed on his pipe, which appears to have been a Turkish pipe, or *nargile*:

> Once the rabbi was travelling and smoking his pipe. Now the shank of the pipe was so long that it extended outside of the carriage, and as they were riding, an officer, accompanied by two horse cavalry soldiers, approached them. They took the pipe from the Besht and continued on their way, as did the rabbi. After an hour the rabbi stopped the coach and told his servant: "Take a horse and catch up to the soldiers, and get the pipe back from them; and so he did. When the servant found the soldiers they were sitting on their horses fast asleep! So he took the pipe and went on his way.

Now, tobacco is not a soporific, while psychedelics can induce sleep. For despite the ecstatic effect that comes with psychedelics, the moment can be short-lived. Following the desired effects comes the crash that results from chemical imbalances in the body. Aside from mood and physical changes, energy is depleted, and either drowsiness or insomnia often follows. It appears that the soldiers in the story above collapsed and fell asleep. How did the Besht know that his servant would find the soldiers and be able to retrieve the pipe? It may have been that he knew the effects of the psychedelic, and guessed that the soldiers themselves would not have known what it was they were smoking and simply crashed in their saddles.

One final witness: Solomon Maimon (1753-1800) was one of the founders of the Jewish *Haskalah* movement of rational enlightenment, and he also became one of the most important philosophers in eighteenth-century Germany. Maimon was born to a traditional Jewish family in Lithuania and schooled in both the Talmud and Kabbalah. And so around 1770, before migrating to Germany, Maimon made a pilgrimage to the court of the Maggid of Medziritch. His memoir is the only document we have in any European language describing early Hasidism.

The philosopher's skeptical characterization of the court of the Maggid is filled with his attempt to show the irrational character of early Hasidism. At one point he writes that "Some simple men of this sect, who sauntered about idly the whole day, pipe in mouth, when asked what they were thinking about all the time, replied, 'We are thinking about God.'" Maimon proceeds to criticize what he sees to be self-delusion. Yet his testimony points to the likelihood that the Baal Shem's practice of smoking had spread among the Maggid's disciples and that they, too, were smoking in order to expand their consciousness.[558]

PSYCHEDELICS IN THE JEWISH WORLD TODAY

The evidence we considered in the first half of this chapter strongly suggests that the Baal Shem's vision and spiritual practices were affected by psychedelics. This will be of interest to Jewish spiritual explorers searching for the experiential roots of Jewish mysticism. The fact of the matter is that psychedelics were instrumental in catalyzing the widespread counterculture in the sixties, and the Jewish counterculture that began then as well. This was when the Havurot and Minyanim movements, the Jewish Renewal movement, and many of the advances in communal worship and individual spiritual practice that have been affecting liberal forms of Judaism ever since, began.

I can testify from my own experience that the nascent Jewish counterculture—the Havurah movement, Shlomo Carlebach's House of Love and Prayer, and Jewish Renewal—were deeply affected by a spiritual sensibility that stemmed from the use of LSD and other psychedelics. My own quest for a Judaism anchored in the kinds of ideals and values that Maslow identified as endemic to peak-experiences was influenced by that exposure. The two most visible Jewish religious leaders who advocated for the use of psychedelics as spiritual tools were Rabbi Zalman Schachter-Shalomi and Rabbi Arthur Green, both rooted in Hasidism.

* * *

I interviewed Reb Zalman once about the influence of the Baal Shem on his life and he said, "If you were to remove every trace of the Baal Shem from my makeup, there would scarce be anything left of me!" He once wrote that the Baal Shem's greatest miracle was "to take a person who had despaired of being able to attain anything spiritual or divine in the world, infuse him with the spirit, show him that the possibility was still there, and what is more important, to show him how he can do it."[559] And this is precisely what Reb Zalman himself was able to do with large numbers of young Jews. A great deal of his motivation for undertaking this, and for renewing Jewish spirituality, came from his experiences with psychedelics.

Before his encounter with the medicine, Zalman had imagined that a psychedelic experience might resemble the well-known firsthand report by the Baal Shem Tov of his heavenly ascent. At the end of an account of his first experience with psychedelics, Zalman asks, "So was it a genuine aliyat ha'neshamah (ascent of the soul)?" He writes that he isn't sure. Unlike the Baal Shem's heavenly ascent to the palace of the messiah, Zalman's journey didn't have a destination. He didn't go anywhere. But, he wonders, perhaps he ventured to a place beyond all destinations.

Although his experience with LSD was unlike the Baal Shem's ascent of soul, it made him curious about Hasidic spiritual experience. "I started to reread some Hasidic material in order to see whether any parallels with LSD experiences stood out; I found there were many things I had read and had passed over before now took on a new, psychedelic dimension. I realized that even the Hasidic mystics couldn't always slip in and out of the expanded state of mind at will. It happened."[560]

Zalman tells his readers that over the course of numerous psychedelic experiences he was able to learn a great deal about himself and as a result he was no longer satisfied with unconscious self-deception. He also admits that he has more questions and fewer answers, and is able to see views other than his own with greater clarity. "I am sure," he addresses the reader, "that when you have it all figured out, you yourself will provide the next question that starts another round of games. While we exist, what else are we going to do? We exist forever in the now." Zalman also wrote, "The psychedelic experience can be not only a challenge but also a support of my faith. After seeing what really happens at the point where all is One and where God immanent surprises God transcendent and They merge in cosmic laughter, I can also see Judaism in a new and amazing light."[561] Only a few years later he began to bring the treasures of Kabbalah and Hasidism to a generation of younger Jews, founding the trans-denominational Jewish Renewal movement which, through its organizational arm, ALEPH: Alliance for Jewish Renewal, has been reinvigorating Jewish life.

* * *

Which brings me back to my old friend, Rabbi Arthur Green. "[Psychedelics] opened my mind to understand that there were infinite other levels of reality beyond ordinary consciousness, and that the states these Hasidic texts were talking about, *gadlut ha-mochin* ['greatness of mind'] and so on, were forms of expanded consciousness. I immediately translated what happened on acid to what I had studied," explained Arthur in an interview about twenty years ago.[562]

He was born in 1941 and grew up in an atheistic home in New Jersey. Discovering Judaism through his grandparents, he went through an intense observant period between ages eleven and eighteen. But soon after matriculating at Brandeis University he left religion behind. His re-entry into Judaism came a few years later through his discovery of Jewish mysticism. He later attended Jewish Theological Seminary, where we met.

Green became one of the world's premier scholars of Jewish mysticism as well as a neo-Hasidic pioneer. He developed what I and many others consider to be the most cogent spiritually-oriented contemporary Jewish theology. He is author, editor, or translator of many books and even more scholarly articles. He's taught at a number of academic institutions, and for many years was president of the Reconstructionist Rabbinical College in Philadelphia. Among his other accomplishments include founding the independent neo-Hasidic rabbinical school, Hebrew College of greater Boston.

Green took LSD for the first time in 1965, and it affected him in life-changing ways. He wondered how he could share with others the mystical awareness that he'd experienced. At the time it was dangerous for a rabbi to associate himself with LSD, and he wrote an article, "Psychedelics and Kabbalah," under a pseudonym. In it, he mapped out the stages someone undergoes during a psychedelic journey. These include: "When coming to speak of the deeply religious quality of the experience many of us have had through the use of psychedelic drugs, I balk before conventional religious language. Members of the religious establishment have been too quick to say that any experience brought on by a drug is necessarily cheap. I rather tend to fear the opposite: to speak of psychedelic/mystic experience in terms familiar to religionists might indeed cheapen that experience."[563]

Green describes the way in which psychedelics change one's perspective. The "I" stands aside, he writes, and the seeker begins to see reality from God's point of view, along with the realization that only this divine way of grasping reality can be real. Then he points to parallels between such an encounter and the teachings of Kabbalah and Hasidism. Ascending into "God's point of view" is also an ascension into utter freedom from all of the ego-based problems that had seemed so important before. He identifies this with what Jewish mystics call "stripping all the physical." In such an expanded state, everything is flowing, becoming, moving, and constantly changing. "If there is a 'God' we have discovered through psychedelics," he writes, "He is the One within the many; the changeless constant in a world of change." And this, too, is a basic motif of Kabbalah: the divine Self is both *Ein Sof,* possessing no attributes or personality, and it is also the *sefirot,* the varied forms of divine life, the ever-changing face of divine personality. "When we further compare both the psychedelic reports and the kabbalistic doctrine with the myths of oneness and change in Hindu mysticism, we can only conclude that psychedelic experiments have indeed led us to one of the major mystic insights common to East and West."[564]

Green goes on to speak about what the psychedelic experience has to tell us about renewing traditional symbols and rituals, especially rituals that have to do with sacred time. "As with the Hasidic Sabbath, time in psychedelic consciousness takes on a cosmic co-ordinate. The moment exists, but eternity is mysteriously contained within it." Then he turns to what he calls the deepest, simplest, and most radical insight of psychedelic/mystic consciousness: "We refer of course to the realization that all reality is one with the Divine. *Tat tvam asi,* in Hinduism: 'Thou art God...' This insight has been so terribly frightening to the Jewish consciousness, so bizzare in terms of the Biblical background of all Jewish faith, that even the mystics who knew it well generally fled from fully spelling it out." Of course, Hindu mystics said this unabashedly: Atman and Brahman are one. But, Green asserts, in the West we have built a colossal civilization on the premise of the reality of the individual ego. Nevertheless, the Kabbalah is not as reticent as other primary Jewish sources on this score, and "despite all the fears and reservations, the feeling of the true oneness of God and man is encountered with surprising frequency in the literature of the Kabbalah. The *Shechinah,* the last of the ten *Sefirot* within God, also contains all the lower worlds within itself. As God achieves His own inner unity, all the worlds, experimentally implying the mystic's own soul as well, enter into the cosmic One. The human soul, according to mystic doctrine, is in some particular way 'a part of God above.' In the oft-repeated parable of early Hasidic literature, the true son of the King, when entering his father's palace, discovers that the very palace itself, insofar as its chambers separated him from his father, is mere illusion."[565]

We recognize that the parable to which Green refers was told by the Baal Shem Tov to his congregation before the blowing of the shofar on Rosh Hashanah as a way to waken them to the work of the Days of Awe: returning to the palace of the One who is our spiritual parent, linking our lives with that truth, and knowing that the illusions of earthly life don't have to smother our souls. How interesting that both Reb Zalman and Art Green came to the same conclusion, that the kabbalistic texts did not merely represent arcane doctrines conjured up by esoteric minds, but were rather attempts at devising a religious language for actual mystical experiences! I also remember Art telling me that Heschel understood the language of the Kabbalah in this same way.

As I've explained, Green left his mark on me. Although there is much in this book that he would probably take exception to, the psychedelic experiences that I underwent with him changed my life and set the direction and tone for the passionate relationship I would later experience with the Baal Shem. And a class that Green gave focusing on the Baal Shem's mystical practices at Havurat Shalom was my first exposure to teachings of the Besht.

* * *

After the federal government made LSD use illegal in 1968, most people in the U.S. came to view psychedelics from a place of fear. Other than the threat of stiff penalties for possessing or distributing psychedelics, perhaps the bigger risk in using them has been the question of potential harm the drugs might cause. In many cases people who took them had bad "trips" or scary flashbacks. But over the last several decades attitudes toward psychedelics and related drugs have begun to change, and the federal government has given permission to a number of academic institutions to experiment with these substances.

How to Change Your Mind is Michael Pollan's recent book about research into psychedelics. He details the history, science, and effects of these potent drugs and details how psychedelic substances temporarily obliterate the ego and engender a deep connectedness with the universe. Pollan writes that his personal experience with the drugs softened his materialistic views and opened him to the possibilities of higher consciousness. He describes his own underground first experience: "I had always assumed access to a spiritual dimension hinged on one's acceptance of the supernatural—of God, of a Beyond—but now I'm not so sure.... Maybe to be in a garden and feel awe, or wonder, in the presence of an astonishing mystery, is nothing more than a recovery of a misplaced perspective, perhaps a child's-eye view; maybe we regain it by means of a neurochemical change that disables the filters (of convention, of ego) that prevent us in ordinary hours from seeing what is, like those lovely leaves staring us in the face."[566]

He writes that he became interested in psychedelics while working on an unrelated piece of journalism for *The New Yorker.* That article examined the use of psilocybin in the treatment of patients with terminal illnesses. The results were startling. For many, psilocybin made death seem less horrible. As the drug expanded their notions of connection, there were patients who lost their fear of death completely. In this vein, *How to Change Your Mind* contains a series of chapters devoted to the ways psychedelics can help people end addictions, deal with trauma, anxiety, and depression, as well as prepare for death. In one interview Pollan was asked how scientists explain the ways that psychedelics effect the human brain. "The feeling among the scientists is that these chemicals allow us to essentially reboot the brain. If the brain is stuck in these narrow grooves of thought—whether it's an obsession or a fear or the story you tell yourself—all those deep grooves that lock us into patterns of both thought and behavior are dissolved and temporarily suspended in a way that allows us to break those patterns."[567]

An online discussion took place in 2021 between Pollan, who is Jewish, and Dani Passow, an Orthodox rabbi who works with religious students at Harvard Hillel. Passow had taken part in a psilocybin experience at New York University as part of a group study of rabbis. Asked by Pollan whether the experience had been specifically Jewish or more universal, Passow shared some of his traditional background and explained how his religious orientation helped frame and anchor what he experienced from the drug. And though he was cautious, Passow suggested there might be a place for psychedelics in the Jewish religious world.

Pollan is a professor of journalism at the University of California in Berkeley. He and a number of researchers from different disciplines at the university recently initiated a new program, the UC Berkeley Center for the Science of Psychedelics. The curriculum for the Center was developed in partnership with the University of California in San Francisco, and Berkeley's Graduate Theological Union, and combines spiritual wisdom with the latest cognitive neuroscience.

* * *

The first Jewish Psychedelic Summit was held online in May 2021. The gathering brought together sixty speakers—twelve of them rabbis—taking part in panels and sessions with topics such as "Did Psychedelics Play a Role in Ancient Jewish Practice?"; "What Draws so Many Jews to India?"; and "Jewish Trauma and Psychedelic Therapy: What Is Culturally Informed Care?" The Summit was a collaborative effort of three people: Zac Kamanetz, founder of Shefa: Jewish Psychedelic Support; Natalie Lyla Ginsberg, director of policy and advocacy at the preeminent Multidisciplinary Association for Psychedelic Studies; and Madison Margolin, editor of the psychedelics magazine *DoubleBlind*. I found the presentations to be stimulating and forward-looking.

The idea for the Summit came from Kamanetz, a rabbi, community educator, and artist based in Berkeley. Kamanetz had been part of a group of clergy who volunteered to take psychedelics in a clinical setting at Johns Hopkins University, and was transformed by the experience. He went on to found Shefa, a Jewish organization that advocates for individuals and communities to heal individual and inherited trauma, has inspired a Jewish religious and creative renaissance in the twenty-first century, and integrated safe and legal psychedelic experiences supported by the Jewish spiritual tradition. Kamanetz described his first experience at Johns Hopkins in these words, "I had the image of a very large tree, where I saw these two branches of red and blue coming out from the trunk, the energy moving back and forth, from side to side, and I was able to immediately understand that this was about the integration between *chesed* and *din*— generosity/compassion and boundaries/power." His second and final experience at Johns Hopkins was completely unlike his first: "It was dark, there was no frame of reference inside, I felt like I was stuck in a hole with no light, I was incredibly bored and disappointed." But he later came to understand this was totally normal. "Yes, there is the bliss and color and light, but then there's a higher reality that falls away of experiencing the void. In kabbalistic language, there is a point at which there is no imagery, no words, nothing that can be experienced," he said. "We call that the *Ein Sof*, that which is without end."

During another interview, Kamanetz stated that those experiences were among the most powerful of his life and convinced him of the need for the use of psychedelics to awaken authentic spiritual awareness in the Jewish community. "Judaism as a vehicle for occasioning mystical experience seems to be a reality for very few American Jews.... The idea that there is a non-ordinary state that you can learn from, heal from, experience the unity of all creation and maybe the divine—doesn't seem to be on the forefront of current Jewish imagination."

He believes that psychedelics can bring about healing from trauma and other debilities that exist in the Jewish community. The drugs are increasingly being used in clinical settings to heal intense psychological trauma. And the Jews, Kamenetz believes, could use some of that: "How can we understand years of exile, diaspora, antisemitism? How can we heal multi-generational traumas? Maybe through these substances, we can heal our people." The rabbi's plan is to become a professional psychedelic therapist. There is now a training program of this kind in the Bay Area, and his intention is to become the first rabbi certified as a psychedelic-assisted therapist. He would also like to establish a place where Jews will be able to experience psychedelics in a Jewish context.[568] I see both of Kamanetz' aims—awakening spiritual awareness and the healing of trauma—as central themes of the Baal Shem Tov's understanding of how to best serve his people and renew Jewish life.

In a highly interesting interview, Madison Margolin, one of the co-facilitators of the Summit, interviewed the third co-facilitator, Natalie Ginsberg, on a host of issues related to the use of psychedelics by Jews today. Margolin writes that Ginsberg is unabashed in her Jewish identity and her commitment to social justice, and that she's inspired by the potential of psychedelics to help reveal and heal intergenerational trauma, and build empathy and community. Ginsberg codeveloped a study interviewing Palestinians and Israelis who've sat in ayahuasca circles together. Her work with the Multidisciplinary Association for Psychedelic Studies has propelled today's "psychedelic renaissance" in science and mainstream cultural acceptance, proposing psychedelics as a method of healing, consciousness shifting, and radical systemic change on a global scale.

One of the topics the two women discussed was how the current renaissance in psychedelic studies and use is affecting young Jews.

Ginsberg tells Margolin, "On the one hand, we're seeing many people who maybe don't feel so connected to their Jewish heritage, but who *are* finding spirituality in the path of psychedelics. Sometimes that path ends up awakening their interest in Judaism or their own heritage. We hear many anecdotes of people's psychedelic trips taking unexpected 'Jewish' turns—whether people recount seeing scenes from the Torah, or from the Holocaust, or of their ancestors. And on the other hand, we're seeing a lot of religious Jewish folks who are using plant medicines and diving deeply into Jewish mysticism and observance, or still others who are departing from a strict religious life and seeking a Judaism that feels less rigid and dogmatic, and more personal and spiritual."

"Among all of those groups, people are growing more open to the idea that their Jewish practice doesn't have to be totally separate from their spiritual psychedelic practice. So that's really exciting.... On a larger scale, I think we're seeing a conversation emerge, and a willingness to excavate our ancestral practices. It's no coincidence that people are reaching for ancestral rituals at a time when so many of us are searching for a greater sense of spirituality. But traditional religion hasn't always served that purpose for people in modern times. I think this concept of Jewish psychedelic spirituality is allowing people to forge bridges, and inspiring people to reexamine elements of Judaism they might not have noticed before."[569]

Having been part of the first wave of psychedelic experience, I'm gratified to see the ways this new research and usage is motivating and engaging people today in their spiritual search.

SOME QUESTIONS

If the mystics are correct, and the true essence of a human being is their unity with Oneness, why then are we destined to live out our lives in separate bodies? For this separateness means we are inevitably moved by self-serving desires to both protect and magnify the egoic self with which we identify.

Even more fundamentally: If the essence of reality is Oneness, why is the world constituted in such a way that this deepest of truths is hidden and multiplicity dominates, often leading to opposition and conflict—and on this earth where living forms have arisen, to what Darwin called "the struggle for existence"? It is as if God or nature put limits around what human beings can know, and then, as an afterthought, threw some medicinal plants into the mix that had the power to dissolve those limits—but just for a few hours. And what do those substances reveal? Images that live for a moment and then dissolve, immediately replaced by other images.

So, I wonder: Is it possible that any of those multiple facets can disclose eternal truths? Or are they mere allusions to a greater truth that we cannot grasp? I don't have an answer to any of these questions, but I know that the medicine does have the power to take someone all the way to that place beyond all images, beyond all knowing—to *Ayin,* No-thing. And once one has been there, there is no denying the existence of a supreme reality beyond all knowing.

CHAPTER THIRTY-THREE

RENEWING THE AMERICAN SYNAGOGUE

In 1974, living in San Francisco and still ambivalent about Judaism and my Jewish identity, I heard that Reb Zalman was offering a week-long seminar on the Zohar at the Hillel House in Berkeley. I decided to attend. When Zalman saw me enter the hall he came up and hugged me as a friend, inviting me to go for a walk during the lunch break so we could catch up on our lives.

As we strolled around the campus of the University of California, I revealed to him that I was going through a major crisis. I wasn't certain I could trust God—not after the Holocaust and my personal difficulties growing up in its gloom. I wasn't sure I could even continue being a Jew, because my Jewish identity had been so deeply bound up with my sense of personal victimization. I was exhausted as well by the authoritarian character of the tradition as I knew it, by the heaviness of the approach to observance of the rituals, and by the narrowness and parochialism of Jewish religion. I also told Zalman that I'd recently read Heschel's portrait of the Baal Shem Tov in *A Passion for Truth*, and that I'd been extraordinarily moved by this account.

"The Holocaust has really changed everything," he told me. "No honest Jew today can open to God or develop a sense of faith until he first faces the darkness of the Holocaust and struggles through its challenges. As for the authoritarianism of the tradition and Jewish parochialism—this must all change. We're living in a new era, one that calls for an entirely new approach to our tradition, an approach that comes out of love and offers people spiritual sustenance. The Baal Shem Tov knew something about this, Burt. I really admire the path you are on and I'm confident that you'll come out of this stronger and more whole."

It was a pivotal moment for me. Zalman's concern was comforting and empowering. That same year, he came to Berkeley and spent five nights a week for four weeks providing the attendees in his seminar with tools they would need to form their own community of prayer. Members of the group wanted to continue Zalman's work by observing Shabbat and Jewish holy days together, and they began to meet in one another's homes on Friday evenings. I signed the mailing list for Zalman's seminars and so I received a notice in the mail regarding the formation of the Aquarian Minyan of Berkeley, the name they eventually chose for themselves.

The word "Aquarius" is an astrological term referring to a new age in world history, a time of peace, love, and compassion. Many young people in the sixties and seventies believed that this new age was about to be ushered in. Late one Friday afternoon in January 1975, I drove from San Francisco to Berkeley to attend one of their Shabbos evening gatherings. The attendees seemed sweet-natured and welcoming, and the service was loving and open-hearted. I recognized some of the folks I had met at Shlomo Carlebach's House of Love and Prayer in San Francisco and at Zalman's seminar on the Zohar. During the service the singing and dancing were ecstatic, and the spirit of joy was palpable. People shared the blessings they received during the week that had passed, and blessed one another for the coming week. The only traditional liturgy that was chanted was the Sh'ma, and I realized that many or most of the Minyan folks were not conversant with the siddur, the traditional Jewish prayerbook. But I was convinced and moved to Berkeley to become a member.

I soon discovered that some of these young seekers were students or professors at the University of California; a few were dropouts from the Orthodox world; others were hippies with hardly any knowledge of Judaism. Others had experienced the mystery and unity of existence through the use of psychedelic drugs or eastern religious practices, and they wanted a way to link these visions with Judaism. For many months I told no one that I was a rabbi. I simply wanted to experience what seemed to be a healthy, non-judgmental form of Jewish community, and see what it felt like to be openly Jewish once again. Within six months I became one of the Minyan's spiritual leaders.

RESTORING THE CONNECTION

I was immediately drawn to Barry Barkan, one of the Minyan's founders. This exuberant man seemed to embody many of the qualities of the Baal Shem Tov that I'd read about. He was one of the most high-spirited and loving human beings I ever met. Openhearted, warm, and kind, he could also be forceful and articulate. He seemed to find something unique and precious in everyone. And you never knew what to expect from him—he could be deeply inspiring, or wildly humorous, or completely outrageous.

Barry's social and political views were shaped by the spirit of the time, and even earlier he had been an investigative journalist for an African American newspaper in the South. Unlike so many of the leftists I met, he didn't dote on what was wrong with American society. Instead, he came to see the problems and issues facing the U.S. and the planet as God-sent challenges. He fully believed that it was possible for human beings to solve and heal the problems we faced through the visionary power of our souls.

I recall many conversations with Barry. I would often try to convince him that his optimism about the future was naïve and exaggerated; he would counter my pessimism and cynicism, challenging me to deepen my faith. I recognized that Barry shared the Baal Shem's vision of human possibility. Although I never fully acquiesced to his incredible optimism, through his influence I eventually began to focus more on human poten- tial than on human failure. Describing what it was that brought him to Jewish spirituality, Barry wrote:

> My life in Jewish Renewal began even before I imagined the existence of such a movement. While on an identity quest in New York's Central Park in the late sixties, I met new friends who connected me with the living power of the ancient tradition. I read one line by Reb Martin Buber, "For me Hasidism was the restoration of the con- nection..." and I intuited that for me, too, the spiritual lineage of the Baal Shem Tov provided the connective tissue to a spirituality that I had not yet experienced. But where to find its living expression? It wasn't there for me in the Hasidic enclaves I visited in New York and Boston.[570]

Drawn by the personal example and the teachings of two char- ismatic neo-Hasidic Jewish teachers, Shlomo Carlebach and Zalman Schachter, Barry had joined with Judith Wallach and Minucha Gleich to found the Aquarian Minyan. The term "Jewish Renewal" had not yet come to identify this new Judaism, and Barry's name for it was "Native American Hasidism": "Many of the people in the [Aquarian] Minyan and its many sister communities that have sprung up around the world do see ourselves as a uniquely American incarnation of an ancient Jewish shamanic tribal tradition which previously had its last major flowering in Eastern Europe in the late eighteenth century." Through his contact with Reb Zalman, Barry came up with the notion of what he called "the rebbe within," an idea that was somewhat at odds with Zalman's more traditional understanding of what it meant to be a rebbe. As Barry wrote, "Shaped and formed by the egalitarian notions of the sixties, many in our movement have advanced the notion that the shamanic quality of the Rebbe figure resides not in one person or in a dynasty, but in the community and its members who take this form of service seriously... as we sing, dance, and tell stories, as we bring the presence of the Holy One, blessed be the Name, into the realms of our personal, communal and work lives."[571]

When I first came upon the Baal Shem Tov in Heschel's writings, I was intent on continuing to pursue my spiritual journey just as I'd done since leaving the East Coast. This expanded for me in large part because of the decision to join the Minyan in Berkeley, and my ensuing friendship with Barry. I lived with a lot of self-doubt, then, and Barry's modeling of "the rebbe within" made the Aquarian Minyan a place where I could begin to transform that negative pattern. Barry's presence in my life was a continual reminder that my spiritual quest was viable. His prompting strengthened my sense of self, empowering me to realize the potential I had not known I possessed. The Minyan was a place where I could use my skills and Jewish knowledge, and experiment with leadership. I made blunder after embarrassing blunder, and yet people seemed to forgive me.

Our closeness also proved to be an incentive for turning in earnest to the study of the Baal Shem's life and teachings and finding ways to incorporate these into my life. As I engaged, I did so with Barry's image in my mind, and this helped the texts come alive. It was during that time that I wrote a small book about the Baal Shem Tov, which I shared with members of the Minyan. I later discovered that many of the assumptions I held at that time about the Besht were questionable, if not mistaken.

SPIRITUALITY IN THE LIBERAL SYNAGOGUE

In 1977 I received an unexpected phone call from a rabbi in the Bay Area. He was about to take a sabbatical leave for nine months. Would I be open to take his place while he was abroad? I wasn't sure. I told him I would need a few days to think about his proposition. The truth was that I really disliked institutional synagogues; I was rather disposed to havurot and minyanim, the smaller kinds of face-to-face community that I believed needed to replace synagogues. Nonetheless, over the next week I debated with myself over the offer. As I thought about it, I realized that synagogues were not just going to disappear. I also knew that Reb Zalman had worked with several Reform rabbis, mentoring them in fashioning new experiential modes of davening that opened the hearts and minds of congregants to a greater spiritual reality. Perhaps I could use my temporary position as an opportunity to experiment with some of the new kinds of creative davening that we'd been experimenting with in the Aquarian Minyan.

Soon after my responsibilities at the temple began, I met with the cantor and suggested we work together to bring more warmth, joy, spirituality, and openness to services. Cantor Richard was excited by the prospect. Friday evening dinner is one of the highlights of Shabbat observance. In traditional homes the family and guests gather around the table, which is covered in a white tablecloth and laid out with the best china and silverware to honor the holy day. Candles are lit, blessings are said over wine and bread, delicacies are served, festive songs are sung, and conversation is lively. At the Minyan, we blended these home rituals with elements of the evening synagogue service, making our weekly celebrations intimate family-like events. Why not try something like this at the Reform temple as well?

The cantor and I wasted no time. The following Friday evening, we gathered congregants together in the social hall adjacent to the sanctuary. We invited everyone to make a circle around a large round table covered with a white tablecloth. Tall silver candlesticks stood in the center of the table, along with a silver goblet filled with wine and many loaves of challah, the special Sabbath bread. We paused for a minute of silence and then a woman congregant lit the candles and chanted the blessing. After that I invited everyone to place their arms around one another's shoulders to welcome the Shabbat angels through song. The cantor strummed on his guitar and led the singing of the traditional hymn, "Shalom Aleichem," welcoming the angels of peace. I then offered a contemplative meditation on the power of the Shabbat rituals to affect the soul. We blessed and drank the wine and then held up the challahs. I asked everyone to touch either the bread or someone who was touching the bread. People smiled at one another and I felt a sense of communal warmth and connection as we blessed and broke the bread and fed one another challah.

Then the large automated partition that divided the social hall from the sanctuary opened dramatically as the organist began to play "L'kha Dodi," the hymn that welcomed Shabbat, and the entire assemblage paraded into the sanctuary. When people found their seats, Cantor Richard began to wander through the sanctuary strumming his guitar and leading a spirited Hasidic niggun to prepare congregants for the evening service that would follow. People naturally began to clap to the joyous melody. I felt a collective sense of joy well up in the congregation as we began the evening service.

Much of the traditional language of the siddur did not evoke the kind of spiritual inspiration that I felt was necessary in our era. A few years earlier, I'd begun to compose new liturgy for Aquarian Minyan services, feminist-oriented renditions of the traditional prayers that also balanced Jewishness with a more universalistic embrace of humanity and the cosmos. Influenced by the teachings of the Baal Shem and Rav Kook, I'd replaced the traditional transcendent masculine imagery for God with an invocation of a loving and awesome Presence flowing through all reality. For example, instead of the traditional words, "Blessed are You, O Lord our God, Ruler of the universe," my version of the blessing (*b'rakhah*) began with the words, "Blessed is this moment within the Whole of Existence and the Mystery at its depths." The Hebrew transliterates as *Barukh atah, ha'havayah kulah, v'sod om'kah*; The word *atah* means "you," when it is spelled with the letter *aleph,* but when spelled with an *ayin,* it means "now." And because of my universalism, I had replaced the traditional language of Jewish chosenness with more comprehensive images that embraced all of humanity as well as the Jewish people.

I also preached on a number of issues that were taboo in most liberal synagogues at the time, such as the need to do away with nuclear weapons, and the rights of LGBT individuals and couples. I always encouraged the congregants to discuss these matters publicly after my sermons. There was, however, one issue that I never brought up: Israel's treatment of Palestinians. I knew that if I spoke about this all hell would break loose!

Before the rabbi left for his sabbatical, he told me that his temple had become too large, and that I might consider starting another synagogue in the area. Even though I had come to care for the temple's congregants, it became clear that my own spiritual and political sensibilities were too radical for this geographical area. I also knew that if I took a position at any liberal synagogue, I would have to hide my views on Israel and Palestine. If I was going to start a synagogue, then, it would have to be in Berkeley, which was still bathed in sixties activism.

RETHINKING JEWISH EDUCATION

For many years I'd worked as an attendant for disabled people in Berkeley. It was a valuable experience and I made friends in that community and came to understand the personal and political issues that people with physical disabilities experienced. Following my stint at the Reform temple, I returned to that work again. But I had also just gotten married, and my wife had a fourteen-year-old daughter. This was the Bay Area, an expensive place to live. I was, after all, a rabbi and perhaps there was a way that I could serve unaffiliated Jews in Berkeley. So I started "Kehilla: The Bay Area Synagogue Without Walls," conducting weddings and funerals for families of unaffiliated Jews. Then parents approached me requesting that I prepare their children for their bar or bat mitzvah.

I'd been a Jewish educator on the East Coast, but had also come to detest the ways in which bar/bat mitzvah students were prepared for what was supposed to be a rite of passage into Jewish adulthood. Classes were often extremely large, the kids were rowdy, and there was often no real personal connection between teachers and students. Ceremonies became enactments of prescribed rituals, and students were essentially judged on how well they performed. The culmination was an ostentatious party. I recall a joke that was passed around during those years: *The bar was more important than the mitzvah!* It was no wonder that for so many young people, bar and bat mitzvah represented a rite of passage *out of* Judaism!

Could bar and bat mitzvah preparation be something different? How might the experience become a genuine rite of passage, the beginning of a journey toward adulthood? And how might the Baal Shem Tov advise me to work with youngsters? The answer was in plain sight: The Baal Shem disciple, the Maggid of Medziritch once remarked, "I wish I could kiss a scroll of the Torah with the same love that the Baal Shem showed to a child who was beginning to read the Hebrew alphabet."[572] I had to apply the Baal Shem's values in my relationships with each student, treating them with love and care, and respecting their developing intelligence. Working with one, two, or three young people at a time in an openhearted personal way made the program work. And it wasn't long before I had the idea of starting an elementary Hebrew school for younger kids. I was joined in this endeavor by a superb Jewish educator, Deborah Enelow. We kept the class size to five so we could work with each young person alone in the course of a weekly two-hour session. In this way we were able to get to know every child in the school. What came next was the starting of our own synagogue, because the families of these kids were asking for something more.

A PROPHETIC VERSUS MYSTICAL SYNAGOGUE

The fundamental issue I had to solve for myself before starting a synagogue had to do with the kind of synagogue it would be. I loved the Baal Shem Tov's vision of a community in which love, compassion, and joy would be paramount, yet this didn't seem to connect with the biblical prophet Amos' radical vision of the centrality of justice.

It was around that time when I discovered a form of counseling practiced in the Christian world that was called "spiritual direction." A spiritual director meets with a directee and together they work to discern where the Divine is present in the directee's experience, and how the directee is being called to serve the spirit. I made an appointment with the man who would become my first spiritual director, Pastor Ted

Pecot, a Methodist minister. To my surprise, Ted told me that he'd been deeply influenced by Martin Buber, and said he felt there was no one in the Christian tradition who embodied the kind of joy that he found in the Baal Shem Tov. Without any prompting, he assured me that he would never attempt to convert me to Christianity. I knew from the start that I was working with the appropriate counselor. Ted later told me that he had written a paper about the Baal Shem as an undergraduate.

Sitting with Pastor Ted for hours on end, I was able to speak freely about all my personal and professional issues. Over the months I shared with Ted my desire to initiate a synagogue and my hesitancies and fears about committing myself to such a task. He encouraged me to put my dream into action. When I spoke about the Baal Shem/Amos polarity, he suggested that I reflect on the mission of this new congregation in a more inclusive way, making room for both spiritual seekers and political activists, and also for those who might seek to integrate both perspectives into their lives. With Ted's guidance, I began to integrate the visions of Amos and the Besht. I came to understand the ways that spirituality and community could provide a firm and lasting foundation for political action and change. I saw that I could work to provide my future congregants with the strength and courage to act in the world out of love, compassion and a sense of justice, and not merely out of righteous indignation.

As I pondered how to strike the Amos/Baal Shem balance, I remembered Rabbi Everett Gendler (1928-2022). Everett had been one of my most important mentors in rabbinical school. He'd successfully led congregations by combining spirituality with politics. I wondered why I hadn't thought of his example earlier instead of agonizing in an either/or way over the question. Rabbi Gendler was a leading civil rights advocate, environmentalist, pacifist, pioneer of modern Jewish spirituality, and advocate of Jewish universalism. As a friend of Martin Luther King, Jr., he was one of the first rabbis to join the Civil Rights movement. Meanwhile, he endeavored to sway fellow Conservative rabbis to get involved. Even on that most hot of hot button issues—he favored a Jewish community in Palestine, opposed nationalism, and stood for a community of Jews and Arabs living together in peace. In his book *Judaism for Universalists,* Everett recalled that early in his career he was referred to as "a radical universalist with a rabbinic degree." If this taunt had come at a later time, he wrote, he would have replied, "Of course I'm a universalist! How could I dare to be a rabbi without being concerned for all human beings? Abram's original command from God, as he was sent on his journey and assured that 'I shall make of thee a great nation,' was 'Be thou a blessing... in thee shall all the families of the earth be blessed.' Not to be a universalist, not to be concerned that through the quality of Jewish life all human families would be blessed, would represent a betrayal of the original purpose of God's call to Abram to become Abraham, the father of all three monotheistic traditions, Judaism, Christianity and Islam."

Early in my student years at the seminary, Everett had gently pushed me to examine my rather rigid, guilt-inducing traditionalism. He introduced me to the importance of silence during worship which I later learned was called "meditation." And his love of the natural world taught me the necessity for embodied worship as a way to open to the world's blessings. Most important of all, through his courageous example, he taught me to stand up for what I believed in, even when this flew in the face of what most Jewish leaders tolerated.

Kehilla Community-Synagogue held its first High Holy Days in a church in Kensington in 1983. There was a signup sheet for attendees who might be interested in a new congregation in Berkeley that would combine spirituality and politics. There were over twenty names on the list.

INSPIRED BY THE BAAL SHEM TOV

At about that same time, Arthur Waskow published his seminal book, *These Holy Sparks: The Rebirth of the Jewish People*, which began by tracing the history of contemporary Jewish Renewal: "In the late sixties out of their sense of alienation from America, these American Jews began to cluster together...in a dozen out-of-the-way houses and unused rooms scattered across the continent. In each place, to begin with, there were only twenty or thirty of these people; later, the number of groups began to multiply while the groups themselves stayed small and intimate. The number is still growing.... What is more, the sense of bafflement, of alienation from an America turned inside out did not end when the Vietnam War and the Black uprisings ended: so new waves of 'new Jews' have kept emerging."[573] But the largest part of *These Holy Sparks* was an exploration of the emerging directions that Jewish Renewal was taking, and what this could mean for the individual, the family, synagogue, world-wide Jewish community, and ultimately for humanity itself. Like Everett Gendler, Waskow inspired my vision and gave me the courage to pursue it. I began to compose a vision statement for a new synagogue which I titled "Re-Visioning the American Synagogue."

This vision-mission statement argued that the majority of American Jewish religious institutions were failing to come to grips with the challenges facing American Jews and Judaism. What was needed was a new form of American Judaism, one that would nurture our Jewish lives in profound ways, integrating wisdom from the past with the best and most wholesome values and ideals of contemporary living. It would aspire to a vision of the future based on our knowledge of the potential of the human spirit. Kehilla Community-Synagogue would embody a form of Jewish renewal that would bring together in an integral fashion the personal and communal, the mystical and intellectual, the moral and political. It would seek to create a religious perspective that would be at once imaginative and passionate, as well as clear-sighted and rational.

Today most liberal congregations have become fully open to feminism, and there are a host of women rabbis, but this wasn't the case when I was getting started. And at that time LGBT-identified individuals and families were still seen by many rabbis and their congregations and by all of the Jewish denominations as being deviants. Nor were most synagogues truly welcoming of inter-married couples. But the Baal Shem Tov had been non-judgmental, loving, and compassionate even toward transgressors in his eighteenth-century community. What would such compassion look like in a twentieth-century synagogue? The community that I would initiate would necessarily be fully inclusive, welcoming individuals and families as members regardless of the exclusivist norms of Jewish tradition.

Many of the small Jewish countercultural communities in the seventies and eighties were centered around charismatic spiritual leaders, but I knew that this could not be my path. I was not opposed to that kind of leadership, yet I did not possess a charismatic gift. I was convinced that the heart of the community-synagogue would be a set of ideals, a compelling vision that would fuse together a particular notion of community, a spiritual understanding of Judaism, and a progressive mission of engagement in tikkun olam. So again inspired by the Baal Shem Tov, the founding statement I composed in 1984 declared that "the divine lives in the depths of every individual, just as the divine lives at the core of every creation and in every process in the universe.... At its best, religious tradition can teach us how to listen to our own depths, and how to incorporate the teachings of the spirit into our daily lives." We would also be attuned to the demanding call for justice and compassion expressed so ardently by the ancient Hebrew prophets. The statement called for a community that would emphasize "the necessity for a strong political thrust in active opposition to human suffering, together with the quest for international peace." I was haunted by the Holocaust, but made a conscious decision not to emphasize that tragedy, or for that matter, the entire lachrymose aspect of Jewish life in the diaspora. Here too, I felt that I was following in the footsteps of the Baal Shem, who accentuated joy and love.

When I completed the first draft of the statement, I showed it to Barry Barkan, as well as to a number of other individuals whose counsel I admired. I incorporated their valuable suggestions into the final version. Then I sent copies to the people who had signed the list at High Holy Services six months previously, and I invited interested people to an organizing meeting, where we formed a steering committee and began to plan religious services. Kehilla Community-Synagogue had begun.

THE SYNAGOGUE AS CARING COMMUNITY

In 1988, four years later, I was invited by Rabbi Arthur Green, then president of the Reconstructionist Rabbinical College, to speak at a conference on "Imagining the Jewish Future." I accepted the invitation and began to think about what was necessary for a fully flourishing and efficacious Jewish life in the U.S. My thoughts ran back to my experiences at Havurat Shalom and the Aquarian Minyan, as well as the many other communes and experiments in communal life that I had sampled. What many of us had sensed in the sixties was how individualism had gradually destroyed community in American life. I found it strange that even though I had called Kehilla a "community-synagogue" in my founding statement, I hadn't thought about this question. Perhaps I naively thought that this issue was a given and would not need to be addressed in Berkeley.

My mind went back to an article I'd written in the early seventies for

The First Jewish Catalog titled, "Blueprint for a Havurah." I began with these words:

> Many of us are lonely and hunger for meaning beyond
> our limited selves. We seek fellowship and joy with oth-
> ers, the excitement of encounter with the Transcendent,
> and the discovery of our roots in the past. One answer
> to our quest seems to be emerging from the youth cul-
> ture—the creation of a new form of extended family:
> communes, co-ops, and, in the Jewish counterculture,
> the havurah. A havurah is a core community of indi-
> viduals who care for one another personally, and strive
> to attain a shared human and Jewish consciousness
> through shared activities and experiences. In this way
> a community structure is gradually built, and the havu-
> rah becomes a meaningful center in the lives of its
> haverim.[574]

I realized that what I'd written would have to become more central to the vision of Kehilla. What was needed was a genuine community in which people could share important aspects of their lives with one another, including moral and spiritual passions. And to be present and supportive for one another, especially during times of joy and sorrow. It would have to exemplify the best values of *shtetl* life in Eastern Europe, especially those emphasized by the Baal Shem Tov: love, caring, joy, and an atmosphere free of judgmentalism. With these thoughts in mind, I composed an address for the conference on "Imagining the Jewish Future," which I called "The Synagogue and Caring Community."

I told the audience that our congregations are primarily goal-oriented organizations, rather than communities. Basic to the synagogue is a shared desire for the survival of Judaism and Jewishness. The congregation provides a locus for communal worship and celebration, and it offers educational programs to pass down our heritage to young and old. Through the work of committees, individuals in the congregation work together on common projects which benefit the synagogue as a whole. Sometimes these various activities engender friendships among individuals and families. But friendship, intimacy, and caring are not usually high on the list of synagogue priorities. What seems to be missing is a larger sense of connectedness among members, a recognition that we are all part of a larger organism.

Martin Buber wrote that every genuine community has a center and its members have a common relation to that center overriding all other relations. For Buber, this emphasis would imply that such communities nurture the prospect for genuine I-Thou encounters and relationships in which people would exhibit openness, trust, and mutuality. And it is this kind of relationship that would make God, the Eternal Thou, truly present as the center of communal life.

INSPIRED BY THE BAAL SHEM

When I returned to Berkeley I began to wonder whether I could really ask such a commitment of our members. I decided to offer an adult class called "Creating a Caring Community." Eleven women signed up, but no men. It was a great class, but at our last meeting I asked whether the participants were willing to help engage our congregants in deepening authentic community. No, they all said; they were simply too busy, and they each had ties with many other organizations. And they felt that this kind of intensive community would be too demanding on their lives.

A few years later, the congregation hired Rabbi Zari Weiss, who also loved the idea of caring community. Rabbi Zari thought of new ways to implement the vision. Gradually, over many years, larger numbers of people saw how this form of intensive community could benefit their lives. It was around that time that I made the decision to set aside time to engage in research about the Baal Shem Tov, and begin to write about him in a regular and consistent way. I decided to step back from my role as the main rabbi. David Cooper was appointed to lead Kehilla. He was the ideal choice, for David's acumen and energy had been at the core of Kehilla's growth and staying power for years already. He had organized a cadre of spiritual leaders to serve the congregation. Rabbi David served the congregation as its community rabbi for fifteen years. Since then, under the leadership of Rabbi Dev Noily and Cantor Shulamit Wise Fairman, Kehilla has become a 550-family congregation with a sizeable religious school. Over the years many havurot developed, and a large core of our members have formed communal bonds and personal friendships.

Almost from the beginning there have been many spiritual leaders, musical prayer leaders, educators, teachers, and committee chairs in the congregation. Activists in the congregation have tackled social and political issues, such as sanctuary for refugees of El Salvador and Guatemala, Jewish-Black relations, homelessness, and the Israel-Palestinian conflict. Committees are devoted to: eliminating racism, Middle East justice and peace, economic justice, environmentalism, opposition to the death penalty, and immigration.

Kehilla is also engaged in interfaith spiritual peace-building with a progressive Protestant church and an Islamic cultural center. There is a committee that responds to incidents of domestic abuse within the community. The congregation has a chesed committee that aids members who are ill, or recovering from surgery, or mourning the death of a loved one. And there is a *hevra kadisha*, which prepares the bodies of those who have died for burial.

One of the Baal Shem's core spiritual practices had to do with bringing a compassionate consciousness to all of one's daily activities. He taught that this compassion transcends all polarities and divisions because it's rooted in the light of oneness out of which the universe was fashioned. I've come to feel that, through such spiritual practice, it may be possible to bring compassionate awareness to all our struggles for justice, peace, and sustainability. We have the ability to cultivate a compassion that allows us to struggle with forces of oppression, and with those individuals and organizations that represent such oppression, without investing our energy into reactionary hatred.

Inspired by the Baal Shem, I gradually learned how to love the people I was serving. Apparently, at some deep level, becoming a congregational rabbi was what I had to do in order to repair certain defects in my character. I deliberately framed my work as a part-time vocation, which I thought would leave time to pursue my study and inner spiritual work. This wasn't always easy, however, for as the congregation grew the professional demands required more and more of my time and energy. Early on I enjoyed teaching and inspiring people and I could be a sincere and enthusiastic service leader, but I could also be impatient as I struggled to carry out the detailed tasks of the rabbinate, especially those of an administrative character. Over the years, though, I did come to master some of those skills, or to collaborate with other leaders who could carry them out in a more skillful manner than I was able to do.

I did not feel I had to be a kind of CEO, especially since I had no understanding about community organizing and little experience leading a congregation. The vision statement invited members of the community to take part in leadership. This proved to be an essential building block. As the years went on, I was called on more and more to deal with my congregants' personal issues and by the professional tasks necessary to maintaining and developing the synagogue. I attended numerous meetings, some of which went far into the night. The duties before me each day were numerous, and I often had difficulty prioritizing values and tasks. I had difficulty tending to my inner life, and I was not studying except to prepare for teaching. I gradually felt myself becoming hollow. It became much more difficult to pursue my research and writing about the Baal Shem Tov.

In the summer of 1997, I underwent emergency heart bypass surgery. My cardiologist told me I would need to spend a good deal of time recovering at home and warned me I had to ease up on my workload. During those months I had a great deal of time on my hands and began to examine how I was living. I didn't like a lot of what I was seeing. I read books about how to slow down and simplify. I signed up for a seminar with the Franklin Covey Organization to learn how to prioritize my time and organize my work life. I spoke in depth with my spiritual director. I also began to connect more regularly with my inner spiritual guidance.

I had another motivation to change, as well. I came to the realization that much of my overwork as a rabbi had been tied in with fulfilling particular ego needs such as feeling successful and receiving praise for my efforts, both of which had been substitutes for a lack of self-esteem. My spiritual director suggested I examine my motives, and I came to understand how I needed to learn to serve people and the world from a more soulful and pure-hearted place. Studying the Baal Shem's teachings about humility, love, and compassion, and engaging in my form of Unitive Love Practice, then had a powerful effect on my attitude. I had to dedicate time to the kind of spiritual growth that would allow me to move from an ego-centered life to a God-centered life, and during the next several years I began to repattern my work.

My colleague Rabbi Shefa Gold has described her vision of what it means to be a rabbi in a way that speaks for my aspirations as well: "The intention I have is to make my life into a spiritual practice that will help to heal my own traumas and wounds, show me a path of exploration, discovery and adventure, and connect me with God, the Great Mystery, so that I can become self-realized. I want to take risks and learn from my mistakes. I know myself as an artist of the Holy. As an artist I need to play and be creative. My love of God moves me to expression and service. I want to always leave behind what I think I know, in order to step into the unknown, the Mystery. And I want to enjoy each moment and bring joy to whatever I do. My practice is about becoming radiant, which means I need to clear the veils that conceal the God-light that wants to shine through. I dedicate myself to this work, daily.... It's clear to me that when I am loyal to my own evolving dynamic practice, then my students will benefit. *My leadership becomes the overflow of my practice.* And I want to become trustworthy, because when someone trusts me, they can receive that overflow.

"My idea of leadership is staying true to my own soul's purpose and inspiration. I never know whether others will understand or come with me. I just want to stay in my integrity and follow that spirit of guidance that will show me the very next step. It may seem like a risky way to live—every day letting go of my attachment to security, affection and control in order to embrace this moment and unlock its potential. Every day I need to connect myself to Source and fill up. My faith is that the world will receive my overflow."

I wish that I had had such wise advice before I started Kehilla, although I'm not sure that I would have known how to follow it at that time. The historical traumas that we Jews carry is a primary reason for a problem that begs for a spiritual perspective, and once again I cite Rabbi Shefa Gold:

> It is time to put **Love at the Center**.... It is time for us to "live" it, to place Love at the center of our religious/ spiritual practice and let the force of that love radiate out to penetrate every other aspect of our lives.... This love is a force that connects the finite with the infinite,

the known with the unknown mystery that lures us beyond our small lives. This love reveals the beauty that is everywhere hidden in Nature, in relationships and in the depths of our hearts.[575]

I believe that Rabbi Shefa's vision represents the very essence of the Baal Shem Tov's path of spiritual leadership for our time.

JEWS AND SPIRITUAL PROGRESSIVISM

While I identify myself as a progressive, I have difficulty with the stridency and self-righteousness that I sometimes encounter in progressive and liberal circles. Although I fully understand and appreciate the anger that comes out of sympathy with the suffering of those who are oppressed, the demonization of the oppressor can lead to hardhearted or ruthless behavior. When we hate, we lose a measure of our humanity. This attitude is a far cry from the kind of nonviolent love that Mohandas Gandhi or Dr. King or Martin Buber practiced toward their adversaries. King put it this way: "Darkness cannot drive out darkness: only light can do that. Hate cannot drive out hate: only love can do that." And the Baal Shem Tov taught that when one person reproves another for having acted badly, such reproval must be carried out from a place of love—or not at all!

The Besht's loving proclamation that "there is no place devoid of the Divine" must now be boldly carried into the social, economic, political, and environmental realms of our world. There is so much suffering to be sweetened, so many myriads of sparks to be liberated, and all of human civilization to be elevated. Engaging in this work is at the core of what it means to be a spiritual person and an authentic Jew in this era. The Baal Shem Tov expressed this notion using the traditional Jewish symbol of the messiah in a way that was radical for its time. He taught that the soul of every Jew contains a part of the messiah, and because of this "Each of us is bound to heal (*l'taken*) and prepare...the particular portion of the messiah that is linked to his or her soul...until the entire messianic infrastructure is healed and prepared. Then the universal and eternal unification will be completed. May this happen soon while we yet live!"[576] This makes it clear that we're not to wait and hope for a miraculous figure to descend from heaven and bail humanity out of our catastrophic predicament. We have the potential and responsibility to work to transform the brokenness that we have been assigned to repair or heal. Would that our love for Jews and for all people and for the earth could be experienced as the love for God!

I have known Michael Lerner, the co-founder of *Tikkun* magazine and founder of the Network of Spiritual Progressives, since the early sixties. Michael was befriended by Abraham Joshua Heschel as a teenager, and studied privately with Heschel as a student at Jewish Theological Seminary. After having been ordained by Reb Zalman in 1995, Rabbi Michael started his own Jewish Renewal synagogue in the Bay Area. Always a leader in the progressive movement, Lerner advocated for a very different sort social concern and activism. He writes:

> Liberal and progressive movements need to move beyond a focus on economic entitlements and political rights to embrace a new discourse of love, kindness, generosity, and awe.... I am calling for both our American and global societies to embrace a new bottom line, so that every economic, political, societal, and cultural institution is considered efficient, rational, and/or productive—not according to the old bottom line of how much these institutions maximize money, power, or ego but rather how much they maximize love and generosity, kindness and forgiveness, ethical and environmentally sustainable behavior, social and economic justice.[577]

Echoing Heschel's own concerns, Lerner calls people "embodiments of the sacred," and encourages people to respond to nature "not solely as a resource for human needs but rather through awe, wonder, and radical amazement at the beauty and grandeur of this universe." He not only addresses Jews or Jewish institutions. What this brings up for me is the necessity for synagogues to deal not only with expressly Jewish issues; we need to see an authentic Jewish communal life with a responsibility as citizens of the U.S. and the world, and our contribution to the restoration of community in this country. Our concern for the earth and its inhabitants should lead to environmental and social justice. Humanity faces the possibility of global environmental collapse. Do we see physical reality as divine? Do we really love the earth? What about the tremendous amount of violence plaguing our planet? Our economic system is rife with social inequities and represents a great danger to the sustainability of our planet. Racism is an ongoing wound.

What can synagogues contribute to changing the status quo? When Rabbi David led Kehilla, he saw the congregation as analogous to the radical religious communities of Latin America that are based on liberation theology, applying Christian theology to the issues of poverty, social justice, and human rights. In those communities, local churches act as centers for both religious life and efforts to resist oppression. The comparison is apt. What if American synagogues were reconceived as revolutionary centers of social transformation? They would provide solidarity, shared dedication, education, and celebration. And they would also represent the kinds of progressive Jewish values that truly enable their members to resist the excesses of the materialistic and individualistic society that seem so prevalent. Guided by love, compassion, and justice congregants would not only support one another during difficult times. They would also gather together for protest, and work to build communities of resistance against oppressive social, political and environmental policies. Such community-synagogues, guided by ideals drawn from both Hasidism and the biblical prophets, could contribute to the kind of a radical awakening that must happen if we are to create a new and sustainable way of living on the planet.

CHAPTER THIRTY-FOUR

BINDING SPIRIT TO SPIRIT

Like all of the Jews of his time, Israel Baal Shem Tov believed that the sacred text of the Torah, the five books of Moses, were revealed to Moses and the Jewish people at Mount Sinai some 3,000 years before his time. This conviction was universally held by Jews and Christians until the nineteenth century, when biblical scholars began to notice a host of disparities in the biblical text. Why was it, they wondered, that the Pentateuch or Torah contained a number of different names for God; and multiple versions of the same narratives; and three distinct law codes that often repeated different versions of the same laws? It became apparent that the Torah was not a unitary text, that it contained a number of different documents composed by writers who had lived at different times and in different places. Parts of the Torah might actually go back to Moses, but most of it was probably composed long after the events depicted.

I was troubled and confused when I first encountered this theory, for it pointed toward what seemed to be a dangerous assumption, that the Torah had been composed by human beings rather than God. Yet, within a few years, I came to accept what was called "the documentary hypothesis." And the human origin of the Torah would explain the existence of so many elements in the Torah that seemed morally primitive: the command to destroy all the inhabitants of Canaan, the permissibility of owning slaves, the subservience of women. The list goes on and on.

Long before the formulation of the documentary hypothesis there were Jewish mystics who were distressed over certain contents of the Five Books of Moses. One anonymous kabbalist regarded the Torah of Moses as a document that was characterized by restrictions, prohibitions, and delimitations, meant to guide the Jewish people in the present world, directing them through a host of dangers and challenges. But, claimed this mystic, there exists a higher Torah, a Torah of freedom and unity, above and beyond the dualism of good and evil. This is the Torah of Emanation (*Atzilut*) or the Primordial Torah (*Torah Kedumah*) that existed even before the creation of the world and this loftier Torah will be revealed at the time of the messianic redemption, when it will replace the old lower Torah.[578]

Did this kabbalist actually believe he was able to experience the messianic Torah of freedom and unity? I think it possible. Nonetheless, as a traditionally observant Jew he would have been aware of his own limits, and in an unredeemed world he would have affirmed the contents of the lower Torah as fully applicable to his own life. But what exactly did this higher Torah contain? Moses de Leon, the principal author of the Zohar, believed the archetypal Torah was not the Five Books of Moses, but rather the Tree of Life, the primeval sefirotic map of the universe conceived within the divine mind.

The Baal Shem Tov was fully aware of the existence of this higher Torah as is evidenced by the following incident:

> One Simhat Torah night, the Baal Shem Tov danced joyously in the midst of his holy disciples, as he clasped a Torah scroll to his breast. After handing the Torah to one of his disciples, he continued to dance without it. Rabbi Yitzhak, another disciple, saw this and said, "Our holy master has now handed over the physical Torah and has taken to himself the spiritual Torah." Later, when the Baal Shem Tov heard this comment repeated, he said, "I'm surprised that Rabbi Yitzhak is on the level to perceive such things!"[579]

According to the Kabbalah, the souls of tzaddikim are rooted in the three highest sefirot, *Keter, Hokhmah*, and *Binah*. It would thus appear that the Baal Shem believed when he entered the ecstasy of No-thingness, he was returning to the ultimate origin of his soul, which was also the origin of existence itself.

I imagine he also thought this realm was the transcendent fount of all his highest spiritual teachings, and the root of his radical way of interpreting the Torah and other traditional teachings, for this Primordial Torah is a realm of pure compassion, as opposed to the lower Torah which contains so many harsh prohibitions. Yes, the Torah of Moses was necessary for a Jewish life in this lower world of contradictions and evil, but that Torah needed an infusion of love and compassion. In other words he was convinced that his insights were coming from the Primordial Torah, and that what he was doing in his interpretations of the lower Torah was a necessary healing of its harshness.

MY AWAKENING

I must have entered into the realm that the kabbalists called the Primordial Torah during my experiences with psychedelics. When the drug took effect, my ego slipped away and the field of consciousness that my "I" had occupied gradually became infinitely spacious and expansive. It became obvious that the little life I'd inhabited for some twenty-nine years had been extremely limited. Reality was so much vaster, mysterious, and full of wonder and awe than I could have known. It was an awakening from a tangled sleep-consciousness to the reality of an ineffable mystery beyond knowing. None of my encounters with psychedelics provided a new life direction, but they did force me to begin to look for such a direction. It was this quest that eventually brought me to the Baal Shem Tov, and later to the founding of a new kind of synagogue-community.

That awakening also took me far beyond my previously strict adherence to halakhah. I was living in an era that took for granted the universalist mindset of the European Enlightenment and the American promise of individual freedom. My studies of world religion and mysticism also brought a recognition that the founders of the great religions and the world's mystics had tapped into that realm. It was this truth, then, that I heard in my heart: *You are eternally connected to the depths of the universe. Open yourself to the reality of existence in the here and now. Free yourself from the straitjacket of your obsessive observance of Jewish law. Trust yourself. Learn from your ancestors, for what they had to teach was holy, but don't slavishly follow them. Study the teachings of the spiritual teachers of all the traditions. Find your own way to the Divine in accord with the contours of your own soul. Use your power of discernment to discover which aspects of the traditional Torah have continuing validity for you and which lack moral legitimacy or spiritual relevance demanded by this new age.*

This message became a sacred imperative, my own Torah as it were. It was in this way that Carl Jung became one of my mentors in linking my Jewish heritage with the Divinity I had experienced through psyche-delics. And sometime later I found another guide, as well, Martin Buber, who charted a post-halakhic Jewish path which he called "listening to the voice of the situation." God does not give us hard and fast rules for living, Buber wrote. Rather, the situations of our lives challenge us with questions, and we are tasked with finding the answers to those questions. As Buber told one of his disciples: "I do not accept any absolute formu-las for living. No preconceived code can see ahead to everything that can happen in a man's life. As we live, we grow and our beliefs change. They must change. So I think we should live with this constant discovery. We should be open to this adventure in heightened awareness of living. We should stake our whole existence on our willingness to explore and experience."[580]

It is no wonder, then, that Buber's notion of what occurred upon Sinai was radically different from the account of the epiphany found in the book of Exodus. Buber wrote that he believed what was revealed on the mountain was simply the overwhelming *presence* of the Divine. All of the narrative and legal contents of the Torah represented a kind of translation of that experience by human beings into human language and institutions.

I later discovered there was a radical Hasidic text paralleling Buber's view. Rabbi Mendel of Rymanov was born in 1745 while the Baal Shem Tov was still alive. Reb Mendel taught that at Sinai the Israelites heard nothing from the mouth of God other than the letter *aleph,* the first letter of the word *Anokhi,* which means "I," as in the beginning of the words that constitute the Ten Commandments: "*I* am Y-H-W-H, your Power, who brought you out of the land of Egypt." Gershom Scholem commented on this: "What sound is in the letter aleph? Just silence, at Sinai, just silence. To hear the aleph is to hear the silence, the preparation for all audible language, but which in itself conveys no specific meaning." In this way, Reb Mendel transformed the revelation on Sinai into a mystical revela-tion, pregnant with infinite meaning, but without specific meaning.[581]

As I wrote in Part Two, when I began studying the teachings of the Baal Shem I found how he affirmed the essence of the Torah exist-ing within the depths of the human psyche or soul: "Every human

being is a microcosm. Within each of us lie the secrets of the bondage
to Mitzrayim, the Passover, the Exodus, and the journey to Mt. Sinai. If
you attain wholeness, you carry within yourself Moses and Aaron—and
also Mitzrayim."[582] It is this understanding of the archetypal character of
Torah that has guided me now for so many years. What then does it mean
to wake up spiritually? Ralph Metzner writes, "[T]he teachings of transformation from many cultures and religions agree in pointing out the
sleeplike nature of our ordinary consciousness, and they share the popular belief that all of us are pursuing dreams—of honor, wealth, pleasure,
happiness. The teachers of spiritual transformation take the analogy one
step further and say that it is possible and desirable—even necessary—
to awaken from those dreams. For regardless of whether they are night-
mares or fantasies, these dreams that we seek or avoid are essentially
illusions, the transient creations of the imagination."[583]

Throughout this book we have seen how so many of the Baal Shem's
teachings have to do with awakening. Here, for instance, is a powerful
parable that illustrates his view of what it is like to live in the torpor of
ignorance:

> The village hall was filled with people, dancing to the
> vibrant music of the travelling band. As the night wore
> on, the rhythms became more rapid, and the villag-
> ers began to throw themselves into their dancing with
> abandon.
>
> Late in the evening, a deaf man entered the hall.
> He had always lived alone in the mountains, and only
> recently had come to dwell in the company of human
> community. Seeing the villagers whirling and leaping
> about, the deaf man wondered what was going on. He
> stood there for several minutes, watching the commo-
> tion. Then he noticed a man on an elevated stage fac-
> ing a group of others who were holding strange-looking
> thingamabobs which they were continually touching
> or blowing. The man on the stage was waving a stick up
> and down and back and forth. The deaf man saw that

whenever the movement of the stick became energetic, the people in the hall would move with greater intensity. And whenever the man slowed the movement of his stick, the dancers would slow down their pace as well.

Now he was dumbfounded. *What might be the relation between the movements of the man's stick and the movements of all the people in the room?* he wondered. *Their jumping cannot be affecting the motions of the man with the stick, for he is facing away from them, and cannot see them. The people must be imitating the stick! Somehow, these silly folk have lost their wits and have come under the power of that man and his stupid stick! They're all quite mad!* So the deaf man left the hall, disgusted by the villagers' stupidity. Yet his entire perception of what he had seen was false because he was unable to hear the music.

Now the universe we live in is like that hall. The marvelous panorama that is creation, and each of the wonders and miracles that take place in heaven and on earth—these are the work of an Order that transcends the visible world. But there are many who are stone deaf. They cannot hear the divine music that pulses through and harmonizes all creation; all they see is chaos.[584]

What an amazing parable! I must say, though, that I am not happy with the Baal Shem's use of deafness as a metaphor for spiritual unconsciousness, especially since I am hearing-impaired. Nevertheless, the point of the parable is crystal clear.

In another teaching, he offers a mindfulness practice that he believed would help his disciples stay awake: "Everything that you see or hear, and all the happenings that occur in your life come to awaken you.... They happen to you so that you may bring healing to them, elevating them toward the Divine."[585] Awakening is not a one-time happening. Throughout my life I have fallen asleep and have had to be woken up by someone close to me, or by circumstances that forced me to wake up. Although some of these arousals were painful, in the end I came to understand how necessary they'd been.

MESSAGES FROM THE SOUL

A passage from the Besht's disciple, Rabbi Menahem Nahum of Chernobyl, epitomizes what this journey of mine has attempted to convey:

> The teachings in our holy texts represent the life force
> and the intelligence of the sages of the past. As you
> study and speak the words of one of those teachers,
> you are infusing your own life-force and intelligence
> into that teacher's words. This is called the binding of
> spirit to spirit. It is in this way that you bring that sage
> back to life.... This teaching comes from the words of
> the Baal Shem Tov, whose soul lives in the hidden places
> beyond.[586]

To this profound truth let me add that it's been my experience when a student studies and speaks the words of the Baal Shem Tov, binding his spirit to that of the departed master, those words become enlivened in him. The Besht has guided me in deepening and refining my spirit, and I've felt summoned to share this liberating path with others. My goal in sharing this knowledge has been to witness to the power of the Baal Shem's path in awakening the potential of the human soul. From time to time I've wondered whether all of this introspective work was a self-indulgent exercise. But then I remembered that the kind of community-oriented work I engaged in as a rabbi required me to go deeper within to pursue my spiritual growth to serve my community. Continuing psychotherapy was also a necessity, and spiritual direction.

In his book, *Spirit Guides,* Hal Zina Bennett writes that throughout recorded history, and on every continent, there have been seekers who worked with spirits to assist them in living. These guides provided access to the inner world of the spiritual and imaginal realms, shifting perceptions from the world of the senses to the invisible reality of thought, emotion, and spirit. Bennett writes: "One of the insights we get after learning about spirit guides is that the boundaries of the self extend far beyond our immediate physical environment. We begin to experience new perceptions of the self. We see that we are linked with people who lived hundreds, even thousands of years ago. We begin to see that we emerge from, and are expressions of, a single consciousness that is limited by neither time nor space."[587]

Over the years, I became increasingly uncomfortable envisioning this inner capacity in anthropomorphic terms, as some kind of an entity separate from me. Instead, I began to see the phenomenon as a psychospiritual faculty within my unconscious. I came to refer to this aspect of my soul or psyche as the still, small voice within, or as my "inner guidance." I believe each of us possesses an intuitive capacity, a kind of inner compass that reaches beyond what can be known by other faculties of the mind. It is the root of our creativity, vision, and insight. It is this teleological image that guides what we will become as we work toward reaching potential. But the process is not automatic. We must choose to pay attention to the messages we receive from our souls and act on those insights. Every authentic wisdom teacher is by definition connected to the still small voice of their inner guidance, and like kabbalists before him, Israel Baal Shem Tov taught that our deepest insights derive from the highest sefirot within us.

"IN ALL YOUR WAYS KNOW GOD."

The Baal Shem often cited a verse from the book of Proverbs: *"In all your ways know God."* (3:6) For him this meant staying aware of the Divine in all of one's activities throughout the day. At this point in my life, I consider this my most important spiritual practice. And certainly, the most challenging. Most of my waking hours I live in a state of ordinary consciousness, but I often sense the Presence hovering just below the level of my awareness. The real practice is to consciously sense the divine dimension of existence as much as possible. This opens me to my origin in and my identity with the Ultimate, and through it I am able to perceive the present moment with greater clarity, wisdom, and non-attachment. I have also become better able to witness my thoughts, feelings, and patterns of reactivity without getting caught up in them. At times I find myself open to one of numerous states of spiritual awareness: wonder, radical amazement, gratitude, compassion, love, or a recognition of the world's holiness.

Of course, such transcendent moments don't last, and there are many times when I'm bothered by contradictory thoughts, or inner clashes that seem as if they can never be reconciled. When this happens, I breathe out "Yaaaaah . . .," while letting go of whatever has been blocking me. This form of surrender opens me to the miracle of consciousness itself, which I experience as the Divinity that holds all things together, a place of unity that lies beyond the opposites and contradictions of existence. I identify such consciousness with my neshamah, my soul, which is the link between my individual life and the *Hai Ha'olamim,* the Life of all worlds. I do not sense my soul as a static entity, but as a kind of everchanging movement. When I am open in this way, I can often experience contentment and peace, even in the midst of turmoil and confusion. And I sense the loosening of obsessive habits and patterns that have driven my life in the past. They are not gone, but I feel better able to make wise choices out of a sense of real freedom.

This expansion of consciousness is not constant. I am, after all, human. I experience passion and lust that can throw me off. I make errors in judgment. I sense that I have fallen from grace. But then I open again to the presence of the presence, and begin to pick myself up. In these states I often consult my inner guidance seeking help. At times I must offer others my apologies for having hurt them. With these tools I'm usually able to climb out of painful chasms that have temporarily trapped me. Without words I take up the thought: *These feelings are transient. They are not my true essence. I am here. I am alive. I am conscious. I am one with the web of love that links all things. I am grateful for this life.* Whatever difficulties I might encounter in the course of my day, I attempt to follow the Baal Shem's teaching about celebrating life and finding joy despite the trials I am undergoing.

This is the teaching that I receive from my favorite poem about the Baal Shem Tov, written by the modern Polish-American Yiddish poet, Zisha Landau (1889-1937). Landau grew up in the traditional Hasidic atmosphere in Europe, but later became disaffected from organized religion. Nonetheless, he was drawn to the spirituality that characterized the life and teachings of the founder of Hasidism, and especially the master's surrender to whatever God sent his way. This is "The Holy Baal Shem Tov," his most well-known poem:

The holy Baal Shem Tov walked through the fields,

in the early dawn he moved through the cold fields.
From the north the winds were blowing,
cold and icy the winds were blowing,
and his limbs began to freeze.
And then with frozen limbs
the holy Baal Shem Tov opened his lips
and loudly began to sing.
Thus were his opened lips
singing, singing, singing:
"How blessed is he who has been favored
once to be touched by Your winds.
How blessed am I to be worthy
to freeze in Your icy winds.
How blessed am I and how blessed and blessed,
how blessed and blessed and blessed."
And gratefully he drank in the frosty air,
and once more into deep reflection sank.

And little by little a lonely sun rose into the sky,
a sun so flaming and huge
that it became hot like the fires of hell.
From his face the sweat drops fell
and not a single breeze
was blowing in the burning meadow.
But suddenly the voice of the Baal Shem Tov
spread over the fiery field.
"For cold and for heat, for sun and for rain,
for day and for night, be You praised.
For all that You send to each of us,
praised be You, praised be You, praised.
And blessed am I that I am now burning,
in Your fires burning.
And if I am favored, and You have destined
that I now fall to Your earth, my thirst unquenched,
how blessed am I and how blessed and blessed,
and blessed and blessed and blessed."

CONCLUSION

In the early years of discipleship with the Baal Shem Tov, I found myself wanting to believe in and accept all of his teachings, even those that troubled me. Yet as I probed them in greater depth over the decades, I began to ask whether certain beliefs could actually be true, or perhaps whether they were true for me.

My sense of human failure had infected me during my formative years with early exposure to the Holocaust. I came to recognize that even though my life had been filled with joy, times of ecstasy, and moments of absolute transcendence, there was really no escape from the abysses human beings are forced to encounter. What the Besht gave me was a deep faith that human effort could alter and transform at least some of this darkness.

Like all great mystics, he knew that during moments of expanded awareness everything falls into place and becomes part of the great unity of existence. At rare but precious times I have experienced the grace of this realization, and have found that as I persist in deepening my practice of devekut, I'm able to gradually open to a place of greater freedom at my center. When one enters this realm, it is as if the great darkness is lifted and the shadows washed away forever. I have become convinced that this is the wellspring of the Baal Shem's vision. Poet Mary Oliver writes about it in a touching poem entitled "The Ponds": "Still, what I want in my life / is to be willing / to be dazzled – / to cast aside the weight of facts / and maybe even / to float a little / above this difficult world."

I do, too. And yet I have also descended at times into the hell of utter despair. It seems the Baal Shem may have come to believe that the dark abyss existed only on the phenomenal level which was external and superficial, and was thus illusory; it was like light masquerading as darkness. But I cannot accept such certainty. There is so much unredeemed pain and suffering in the world, and I do not believe it can be dismissed as illusion.

I'm not saying the Besht's faith is theologically unwarranted. After all, hundreds of thousands of Hasidim went to their deaths in the Nazi concentration camps holding to the triumphant faith that there was a better life awaiting them in the world to come, and that the messiah would eventually redeem the Jewish people and the world. Sometimes it seems that these pious people lived in an illusion. At other times, I have a sense that at the moments of their deaths they may have been transported in some way to the realm of the good. But after decades of heart-searching, I have come to the conclusion that holding such triumphant faith in the power of goodness is beyond my capabilities.

I've also come to understand that I don't have to accept everything the Besht believed, in order to consider him my most significant teacher. After all, he walked the earth over two and a half centuries ago. Living in the modern world, plagued by a range of brutality and suffering greater than anything he ever witnessed, it's impossible for me to hold on to the kind of faith he possessed—to believe that absolute meaning and goodness underlie the chaos of existence and will in the end prevail.

I don't think he expected his disciples to blindly mimic him. After all, he treasured the sheer variety of human beings as the gift of a Creator who loved diversity. He taught that the Divine lives at the core of every person, and it is thus incumbent upon each to discover the life at their center. Interpreting the phrase "Our God and God of our forbears . . .," the Besht stated that God must first be our God; only after we have experienced God's reality in our own way can we connect our experiences to those of our forebears. In one of his parables, he warns his disciples not to rely too heavily on their master. I would like to think that if he were alive today, he'd understand my difficulties, and would advise me to hold to my own experience and vision, even when it differed from his own.

TAKING REFUGE

I am now closer to ninety than eighty years old. I don't know how much longer I have on this earth, or what will happen to me—if anything—after my death. The imperatives of nature have been fashioned by something far greater than any human mind, and there's no use in raging against the dying of the light. At this time, I am merely trying to surrender to the God who ordained the inevitability of death.

There's a Buddhist practice called taking refuge in the Buddha. "This doesn't mean that we are worshipping the man who became enlightened," writes Tara Brach, but "honoring the Buddha nature that already exists within us.... Taking refuge in the truth of [the Buddha's] awakening can inspire us on our own path toward fearlessness.... By this, I am not trying to get rid of fear, but rather letting go into a refuge that is vast enough to hold my fear with love."[588] In like manner, the Baal Shem taught that "when you accept the things that frighten you in the world with total love, you are able to free yourself from those fears."[589] I haven't gotten there yet—I am still in love with life. But I am working on it.

"There is no place empty of the Presence"—even as that Presence is leading me into No-thingness.

THE WAY OF SERVICE

A GUIDE TO TRANSFORMATIVE SPIRITUAL PRACTICE
INSPIRED BY THE BAAL SHEM TOV

As I studied the Baal Shem Tov's teachings over the years, especially his statements regarding spiritual practice, I found direction for developing my own forms. I was particularly interested in approaches that would allow me to experience the luminous Divinity of the world, open to grace and gratitude, and lose myself in the vastness of existence. As I began to experiment, I integrated what I knew from other spiritual traditions with approaches I was learning from the Besht. Over time I found that these disciplines opened me to my soul (neshamah), i.e., the presence of the Divine within the self, and this deepened my recognition that there is no place devoid of the Divine.

These spiritual practices enabled me to realize that suffering as well as wonder, joy, and love can be a summons to transcendence and transformation. This resource, then, is a guide to such practices inspired by the vision and practices of the Baal Shem. I don't claim that what's presented here are the authentic forms pioneered by the master. They are "neo-Beshtian," that is, adaptations of his practices for contemporary people.

According to the Baal Shem, the overall purpose of spiritual practice has to do with serving the Divine:

> You must serve the blessed One with all of your strength. Remember that everything you engage in is a divine necessity, and can become a way of serving the One.... Wherever you are, whatever you are doing, you can bind your awareness to the blessed One, linking whatever you are doing with the whole of reality.... And why? In order that you serve the Divine through each and every one of your deeds.[590]

The language of serving might seem antiquated, a remnant of the old notion of fealty to a king or lord, but the Hebrew word *avodah* can be translated as "worship" as well as "service." And thus, avodah is a Jewish way of declaring that our self-serving needs and desires are not primary, and that finally there is Something That or Someone Who is greater than our egos. Our spiritual responsibility is to yield to and to align ourselves with that greater Reality.

> Your service should only be for the sake of the Highest One, and not for any personal gain that you yourself might receive. Don't even consider any of the possible benefits that you yourself might realize. Let it all be for the sake of Heaven![591]

Arthur Green and Barry Holtz write that Hasidism views all of Jewish life as "the way of service": "The core of 'service' as seen in Hasidism is the fulfillment of that desire, deeply implanted within each human soul, to return to its original state of oneness with God. Prayer, by its very nature pointing to the intimate relationship between God and soul, becomes the focal point of Hasidic religiosity."[592] I would phrase it somewhat differently: The overall aim of authentic Jewish spiritual practice is *service*—serving the Divine, our people, humanity, and the earth. I'm convinced that in the end this kind of devotion cannot but help to decenter our egos, elevating and transforming our own temporal lives.

There are three forms that such service takes in the Baal Shem's understanding of the nature of spiritual practice:

- Transcending the polarities of existential living and of the human self in exalted experiences of the underlying Oneness and mystery of reality.
- Integrating the higher states of consciousness into all our ordinary activities so that we come to appreciate the preciousness of each moment. This leads to experiencing ourselves and the world as the presence of the Divine.
- Deepening our moral compass to become more loving and compassionate people.

Serving a greater Reality is not easy, as we can see when we examine the Besht's early life. Our self-centered craving naturally vies with our higher longings for connection with the Divine. And for the Baal Shem this inner conflict must be resolved if the seeker is to reach spiritual wholeness. In my experience the moments of elevation and exaltation provided by my practices make the entire venture worthwhile.

The traditional Sabbath liturgy contains a prayer that asks for help in serving God: "And purify our hearts that we may serve you in truth." But how does one know whether one is actually serving the Divine *in truth*? I find that all I can do is try to remember this and when I forget, know that there will soon be another opportunity to carry out this kavanah. I well remember when I would *sh'vitz* (a Yiddish word meaning "sweat") over whether I did it right, but that time is long gone. Excessive worry was one of the reasons why I broke away from traditional Judaism.

Because the practices in this guide have largely come out of my own experimentation, I have tried not to frame them as prescriptive. My suggestion is that seekers experiment with the practices over a period of time to discover whether they feel engaging and uplifting, and offer the possibility of personal transformation. In sharing them, I do not want readers to think that they are the quintessential or only practices that can be drawn from the Baal Shem's teachings. It's evident that he experimented a great deal, and I want to encourage readers to feel free to do the same, perhaps with the ongoing help of a spiritual director.

Throughout, I use the term practice again and again, but in truth a more accurate term would be discipline, because there can be no transformative effects on one's attitudes or behavior without a commitment to regularity. I have to admit, though, that discipline is not a word I especially like. Nevertheless, I've come to see that the process of spiritual transformation demands a great deal of time and demands the disciplined cultivation of determination and persistence to deal with resistances to change and growth. You may want to choose a single practice to begin, and experiment with it for at least a month. Then evaluate whether it is working for you. Keeping a practice journal is a good way to chart your progress over time.

A DAILY PRACTICE OF DAVENING

Perhaps review the section beginning with "Devekut and Davening Practice"
in chapter 14 before reading this.

As far back in time as we can tell, human beings have yearned to
connect with a mystery greater than their personal or tribal identities.
These longings have taken the forms of celebration, worship, and prayer.
Going back 3,000 years, Judaism encompasses one of the oldest surviving
community-centered devotional traditions, and Hasidic spiritual praxis
was built out of that longstanding history. The public gatherings for daily
prayer, for weekly Sabbath services, and the annual cycle of holy days,
together with the family observances for Passover, Sukkot, Hanukkah,
and the rites of passage from birth to death all fostered this collective
sense of a people connecting to the God who blessed them with life
and the Torah. And because ritual is a shared religious activity, it gains
its momentum from people sharing this kind of transpersonal ideal in
community.

The Baal Shem's path intensified and deepened the ceremonial power
of common worship. Yet, what gave early Hasidic communal observance
its special intensity and meaning were the practices carried out by individuals on their own, like those introduced by the Besht. He was certainly
not the first to introduce such personal practices into Judaism, but traditional rituals can lose their power over time when carried out in a habitual way. Medieval kabbalists understood this and initiated many novel
rituals and practices which were performed by individual kabbalists. The
myriad of new Hasidic practices focused on the necessity for spiritual
awareness and intentionality. For the Besht, such practices went beyond
communal and family observance because he was teaching his disciples
ways to transform themselves and attain enlightenment.

EXPERIENCING DIVINITY

Rabbinic Judaism, the all-embracing Jewish religiosity that was practiced at the time of the Baal Shem Tov, focused on the sacred study of
the Talmud as the primary and optimal form of serving the divine will.
Those who were kabbalists added the study of the Zohar and other mystical works, together with spiritual practices introduced by Rabbi Isaac

Luria. These traditional ideals, however, underwent an immense change for Jews who came under the influence of the Besht, for even though he favored sacred study, he came to see the core Jewish practice as devekut. This could be achieved through ecstatic davening:

> The Baal Shem Tov's soul once told him that the reason
> he merited the revelation of lofty teachings had to do
> with his devotion to davening, and not because of his
> having studied a great deal of Talmud and Jewish law.
> The master davened constantly and with great depth.[593]

Davening is meant to open the heart and consciousness to an expanded vision of reality, which leads the seeker to exaltation and mystical unification. Devekut, again, means clinging or being attached to God. Other spiritual practices are meant to train the mind, heart, and body to engage with daily life in ways that would disclose the holiness of every moment.

SIX MORE FORMS OF NEO-BESHTIAN PRACTICE

The Baal Shem identified the four letters of the divine name Y-H-V-H with four aspects of the prayer experience: "Y" represents the word; "H" represents sound; "V" represents breath; and "H" represents thought. In other words, when davening and simultaneously engaging in all four of these activities, one enters into the EverPresent. These forms of Hasidic contemplative practice may also be discovered in Hindu, Buddhist, and Sufi forms of meditation. Let's briefly look at each.

Liturgical Words. Set liturgies are fundamental to most of the world's spiritual traditions. In Judaism, the traditional prayerbook and the book of Psalms (*Tehillim*) have been central to the act of prayer for millennia. The words of the traditional liturgy were also at the core of the Baal Shem's davening, yet it's clear that he wasn't exceedingly interested in the literal meanings of the prayers, which were couched in dualistic and anthropocentric modes of language. As we learned in Part One, he taught his disciples to use the words and letters of prayer of the siddur as instrumentalities to elevate the soul: "When you offer your prayers, invest all of your energy in the words of the prayer book. Sound out letter after letter in an intensive manner, and you will eventually forget your physical existence." I recommend Reb Zalman's book, *Davening: A Guide to Meaningful Jewish Prayer,* as well as Abraham Joshua Heschel's *Man's Quest for God: Studies in Prayer and Symbolism.*

Solitude. As we have learned, tales about the Baal Shem speak of his spending seven years alone in the mountains. Later on, wherever he would settle he would build a hut at a distance from his home where he would engage in davening and other spiritual work in seclusion. This set an example for future Hasidim, as well, but even more so for neo-Hasidism in our own day.

Silence. The Baal Shem's form of davening was loud, even boisterous, but there are a number of his teachings that reveal how he also treasured silence: "You can daven in such a way that no one who sees you will know you are engaged in spiritual service. You are not moving at all, but deep within your soul your heart is aflame and you are silently crying out because of the ecstasy you are experiencing." He also taught: "*Silence is a fence that guards wisdom.*' (*Avot 3*) When you are silent, you are able to bind yourself to the World of Pure Contemplation (*Olam Ha'ma'ha'sheh'vah*), which is Wisdom (*Hoch'mah*)."[594]

The Maggid of Medziritch was much more of a contemplative than his teacher, and there are later Hasidic teachings that demonstrate his influence on Hasidism, strongly emphasizing the importance of silence. Here, for instance, is a Hasidic practice that is quite similar to current understandings of meditation:

> Sit alone in silence and meditate on the exaltedness of the Divine. In such a state you enter the World of Wisdom (*Olam Ha'Hokh'mah*), which is the world of absolute rest and stillness, drawing these qualities into yourself. So when you wish to enter *devekut*—to bind yourself to the divine through God-consciousness—sit in absolute stillness, allowing your mind to engage in holy thoughts and awe.[595]

Chanting. I have found no evidence that the Baal Shem Tov engaged in *niggun* (melody) in his davening, although Rabbi Aubrey L. Glazer has made the case that the Besht was strongly influenced by Turkish Sufism, including Sufi chant and dancing.[596] And Moshe Idel suggests that the

Baal Shem's use of Abulafian chantlike vocalizations of Hebrew letters likely led the Hasidim in later years to the use of ecstatic sacred song during worship.

The use of music as a way of connecting to the Divine had not held such a high-ranking place in Jewish devotional life since the time when Levites sang the rites practiced in the ancient Temple in Jerusalem. The chanting of niggunim also has an analogue in Hindu kirtan, and ancient Sanskrit chants contain powerful renewing and transformative energy that help the seeker reconnect with the Divinity that dwells within. The Sufi practice of chanting the names of God is also similar to the Hasidic use of niggunim.

Mantra. Many Hasidic masters used repetitions of holy words and names of God to keep them mindful of God's presence. I have found no evidence that the Baal Shem himself made use of mantra; however, the Abulafian type of practice of vocalizing the letters that he employed has affinities with mantra. According to Yitzhak Buxbaum some of the Besht's students used a visual method of picturing the holy name *Y-H-W-H* before their eyes.[597]

Breathing. Both Hindu and Buddhist spiritual masters taught approaches to meditation that relied strongly on the process of breathing. Such techniques were not intrinsic to Jewish worship. However, Abraham Abulafia introduced breathing practices as part of his ecstatic mystical technology. It's not clear whether the Besht knew of this aspect of Abulafia's meditation. We do, however, have a Beshtian teaching that states: If our prayers are clear and pure, the holy breath we exhale blends with the divine breath that enters when we inhale, and through our breathing we can unite with our Source.[598] The Baal Shem recognized that "everything that breathes is breathing from the essence of Divinity." And we know that some of the Hasidic masters were aware of the power of conscious breathing to bring an individual into the orbit of the Divine.

DEVELOPING A PERSONAL PRACTICE

As a young man, I would daven the set prayers from a prayerbook in their prescribed order. This traditional approach to prayer (*tefillah*) is primarily language-based, requiring daveners to recite or chant the same prayer-texts three times a day—morning, afternoon, and evening. Many years later when I was in the process of returning to Judaism and wanted to daven, it seemed that the sheer volume of fixed liturgy employed in this kind of worship was simply too overburdening. I also experienced theological issues with the traditional liturgy. The dualistic images of God in the siddur did not represent a God I could worship. The Lord (*Adonai*) was depicted as a kind of magnified man. And Jews were assumed to be God's chosen people, a dangerous idea that I could no longer affirm. And after the Holocaust, I could no longer believe in the coming of a messiah or a messianic era. Despite all the problems I had with traditional prayer language, however, as a synagogue rabbi I knew that public services would require liturgy; so I undertook a process of revision.

This led me to six more practices, as described in the next section. Each is independent of the others and may be practiced alone. However, the first four form a morning devotional sequence, one flowing into the next. Thus, Niggun Chanting can open the heart to Yah Breathing Meditation, which in turn can prepare one for the Unitive Love Practice. This, in turn, readies the davener for the practice of Sacred Study. In my experience, this all takes approximately thirty to forty minutes, most days, but this will vary with each person. The fifth practice, which I call Living in the Presence, follows on the heels of the preceding four, so that the regular activities of the day—grooming, dressing, eating breakfast, conversation with people, engaging in business, etc.—can be carried out in a spiritually conscious manner.

PRACTICE 1: NIGGUN CHANTING

Nothing matches a Hasidic niggun for unlocking my heart to the holy. The melodies have a way of massaging my soul and opening me to whispers of the Divine. Most of these melodies can be categorized as either joyous niggunim (*niggunei simha*), meant for loud singing, clapping, and dancing; table songs (*tisch niggunim*) sung at the Shabbat or holy day table, or contemplative niggunim (*niggunei devekut*), that draw one toward union with God. I find the two latter types of niggunim most appropriate and effective for personal devotional practice.

I'm familiar with numerous Hasidic niggunim, and when I'm engaging in niggun practice on my own I might begin with a traditional melody that comes to mind. Most days, however, I put on my headphones and listen to a niggun recording. Sometimes I simply sit, listening in silence, absorbing the melody as it takes me higher. Then I continue chanting after the recording has ended.

The key to deep niggun practice is twofold. First is the *intentionality* that one brings to the chanting, that is, the sincere longing to link oneself to one's soul and to the Divine. And second, *letting go,* yielding, giving oneself as fully as possible to the melody. There are moments, now, when I find myself clapping or dancing with my arms and hands as I sit in my recliner. On occasion, moved by the niggun, I will get up and dance. Many niggunim have a melancholy aspect that connects me with suffering—my own or that of others—and at times I am moved to tears. The chanting of Hasidic melodies can be an extraordinary entranceway into contemplative silence, and after singing, I will inevitably move into meditation. I find that the niggun I have been chanting helps to shape the kind of silence that I enter.

Although I own many recordings of niggunim, two of my favorite come from a Bratslaver Hasid, Alon Michael, and I suggest that aspiring niggun chanters acquire them. The CDs are titled *Meditations of the Heart, Volumes I* and *II.* You might wish to listen to the entire album or both albums before choosing the melodies you will use in your spiritual practice.

Original Hasidic niggunim had no words. Klezmer clarinetist Chilik Frank has recorded two albums of traditional niggunim without words. The first is titled *Be Mindful of My Soul* and the second, *Tikkun Chatzos.* Both bear the Daberi Shir label. Finally, Frank London and Lorin Sklamberg of the Klezmatics recorded an album entitled *Niggunim* on the Tsadik label. I suggest tracks 1, 3, 5, 6, 7, and 9. They have a second CD titled *Tsuker-zis* on the same label. The best cuts for devotional chanting are 1, 2, 3, 4, and 9.

PRACTICE 2: YAH BREATH MEDITATION

We ordinarily understand ourselves to be separate beings with our own special and separate identities. But the Baal Shem Tov taught, we are each "limbs of the Shekhinah," manifestations of the mysterious oneness of the universe, able to connect with the deeper realms of the spirit, the origin of existence. It is possible, the master taught, to pierce the veil of ordinary awareness and enter into expanded consciousness, the mystery and unity at the core of the self, where the neshamah is one with the Divine. Afterwards, when one returns to the physical world, to realize that everything one sees, everything one experiences is truly Divinity clothed in physical garments.

We are told in *In Praise of the Baal Shem Tov* that the Besht once longed to make a pilgrimage to the Land of Israel, and that he actually undertook such a journey with his daughter, Udel. But events transpired that made this aspiration impossible. It may be that this teaching about worship came out of his failed attempt—a realization that because the Divine Presence inhabits every nook and cranny of this world, it is truly possible to offer prayer in every land:

> Remember this when you are praying in a country out-side of the land of Israel: The essence of all devotional practices lies in the faith and conviction that the Holy One fills the entire universe with divine splendor. And through your own experience of this radiance you are elevating and exalting the presence of the Shekhinah in the world.

And again: "Meditate on God and how the divine splendor fills the earth, and know that wherever you are you are always living in the presence of the Shekhinah.... And just as you are able to see material objects, so you are able to see the Shekhinah, and recognize that you exist within her very presence."[599]

I understand the second sentence above in the following way: Just as you are able to *experience* the presence of material objects, so you are actually able to *experience* the presence the Shekhinah, for when you enter a deeply ecstatic state, you can then recognize that your conscious-ness, and everything you are aware of, are part of the Shekhinah, and you yourself are an aspect of her very presence.

As I explained in chapter 14, I use the holy name Yah in my breathing meditation. Yah is a shortened form of the Tetragrammaton, the four-let-ter name of God, *Y-H-W-H*—considered the holiest name of God. In Rabbinic Judaism, Y-H-W-H is understood to be divine love.

Like niggun practice, Yah Breathing Meditation is, in essence, a sur-render practice. Each exhalation is a letting go into the Divine. Whatever burdens one is carrying, whatever noise the mind is churning up, what-ever thoughts come up—all of these find release when given over to the underlying Oneness of existence. The neshamah can then experience the preciousness and holiness of each moment. It opens the heart to expe-rience existence, life, energy, and consciousness as veritable miracles. Deeply engaged in meditation, I come to realize that, as the Besht taught, there is no time or place devoid of the Divine.

I have experienced transcendental periods of bliss when everything radiates Divinity. I cannot distinguish myself from creation as a whole. I am enfolded by great love. There is an openness to my inner depths and to the vastness of the cosmos. A sense of the ultimate mystery and unity. A loss of self-concern. An inexpressible joy. An unearthly freedom.

Most meditation periods, however, are not this ecstatic. Still, I can often feel transported into a higher octave, as it were, part of the song of creation. There are also days when the practice just seems like a rote exercise. If this continues day after day, I stop the practice entirely and give myself a rest.

The Baal Shem taught that joy and delight are essential to life. Nonetheless, he was clear that attaining personal pleasure should not be the chief purpose of our practice. Desiring to "become high" merely reifies the ego, and authentic spiritual discipline is about de-centering the ego and making Spirit our center. Meditation and worship should contribute in some small or large way to transforming ourselves so that we become vehicles of the Divine.

The keys to Yah Breathing meditation are intentionality, passion, and surrender. Without these our practices lapse into mere form. As we have learned, the Baal Shem compared authentic worship with making love to one's life-partner. Davening, then, is making love to the Shekhinah. It is wholehearted surrender to the holy Oneness that allows this kind of meditation to take wings. Distracting thoughts will come. Any med-itator will tell you that one of the great challenges they face is what the Baal Shem calls "alien thoughts" (*ma'ha'sh'vot zar'ot*), those mental dis-turbances that inevitably enter one's consciousness during practice. Over time, I've learned to recognize, distinguish, and disempower these reactive patterns, so that they began to lose their power to affect my emotions and thoughts in negative ways.

The Baal Shem taught me that the "alien thoughts" arising during my practice were actually aspects of the Divine, so they should not disturb me. Similarly, in Buddhist Vipasana/Insight meditation, practitioners are told to pay attention to the thoughts, feelings, and sensations that arise, and not to try to push them away. At the same time, they are told to stay centered on the object of meditation, such as one's breathing. This approach accustoms a meditator to the virtue of non-attachment, gives direct experience of the transient character of all mental formations, and promotes greater inner freedom. I have found that when I am beset by negative thought patterns, Yah Breathing Meditation can have an immediate salutary effect. It breaks up the negativity, and restores my sense of the underlying oneness of Existence.

Here I offer a guided visualization that introduces Yah Breathing Meditation. You might like to record it for yourself and then play it back as a gateway into meditation. If you do this, be sure to speak slowly and distinctly. And when you see a series of dots like these: . . . , pause for a few moments. When you observe a longer series of dots . . . . . . , pause for a longer period of time.

> *Please close your eyes . . .*
> *Be aware of your breathing . . .*
> *Notice how your breath flows in and out of your nostrils*
> *without any need on your part to exert your will . . .*
> *Take a few moments now to simply breathe in this way,*
> *allowing yourself to be breathed . . . . . .*
> *Now, as you exhale, slowly breathe out the sacred name,*
> *Yaaaaaah . . .*
> *Yaaaaaah . . . Source of all reality . . .*
> *Yaaaaaah . . . Silent core of being . . .*
> *Yaaaaaah . . . Hidden Oneness . . .*
> *Yaaaaaah . . . Mystery of mysteries . . .*
> *Yaaaaaah . . . Letting go, letting go fully . . .*
> *Yaaaaaah . . . You are present . . .*

Yaaaaaah . . . You are alive . . .

Yaaaaaah . . . You are conscious . . .

Yaaaaaah . . . You are connected to everything . . .

Yaaaaaah . . . This moment is divine . . .

Yaaaaaah . . . You are part of it all . . .

Yaaaaaah . . . What a miracle . . .

Yaaaaaah . . . Whatever you are perceiving . . .

Yaaaaaah . . . Whatever you are thinking . . .

Yaaaaaah . . . Whatever you are feeling . . .

Are there distracting thoughts? . . . Yaaaaaah . . .

Do not attempt to banish them . . . Yaaaaaah . . .

They are expressions of the Divine . . . Yaaaaaah . . .

Just allow them to come and go . . . Yaaaaaah . . .

To ebb and flow . . . Yaaaaaah . . .

Yah-ah-ah-ah-ah-ah . . . Yaaaaaah . . .

(Pause here and simply enter the silence for as long as you wish.)

You are about to leave your meditation . . .
When you open your eyes, do not abandon your contem-
plative state. "No place devoid of the Divine." . . .
Whoever or whatever your eyes fall on in the world about
you is in some way divine . . .
If you are meditating with others, look into their eyes . . .
Smile . . . Everything is in God . . .

Next, I have outlined a step-by-step method for learning the steps to practicing Yah Breathing Meditation. I suggest you read through the entire sequence, first, to get a sense of the whole process. I advise you to take one new step at a time, experiencing it for several minutes. Each time you wish to meditate, repeat all the steps you have learned and add the newest step to your repertoire.

1. Sitting in a comfortable position with your eyes closed, listen to and/or chant a niggun.
2. When you complete the niggun, be aware of your breathing. Notice how your breath flows in and out of your nostrils without

any need on your part to exert your will. Spend some time breathing with this kind of awareness.

3. As you exhale, slowly breathe out the sacred name, "Yah." *Yaaaaaah*... Let yourself go fully into this holy name...

4. As you continue your Yah breathing, notice that you are *present*, you are *alive,* you are *conscious,* and you are *connected* to everything. What a miracle!

5. As you breathe out "*Yaaaaaah*," pay attention to the subtle energy field in your body that is giving vibrant life to every organ and every cell within you. This is the energy that is enlivening you. This is Yah.

6. When distracting thoughts, sensations, or feelings arise within you, don't try to push them away ... Try not to fall into them either. Rather, step back and pay attention to them as if you are a witness watching them...

7. When you become aware that you are lost in a thought, simply let it go and return to your Yah breathing and the consciousness that God is present in this present moment...

8. Come out of the meditation slowly. Don't abandon your contemplative state when you open your eyes. Whatever your eyes fall on in the world about you is in some way divine. If you are meditating with others, look into their eyes. Smile.

You can meditate this way for as little as five minutes, or up to a half hour or even longer. You might wish to begin with a short time span and increase the time as you become used to the practice.

PRACTICE 3: UNITIVE LOVE PRACTICE

For the background of Unitive Love Practice, see chapter 16, "Steeped in Love and Compassion."

The great sixteenth-century kabbalist Isaac Luria instituted a ritual at the beginning of the morning prayer service during which his fellow worshippers took upon themselves the mitzvah of loving their fellow human beings as themselves. In this way the entire service became dedicated to opening the heart to the love of others in one's community.

When I was attempting to fashion a contemplative practice of love and compassion, I was also aware of a Buddhist practice called *metta* or loving-kindness meditation. In metta, a person directs loving-kindness toward themselves, and then, in a widening circle, toward others. My friend and teacher, Sylvia Boorstein, describes the long-term results:

> *Metta* practice is transformative. The direct experience of the pleasure—indeed, the joy—of benevolence, over time, lessens the habitual self-centered, defensive actions of the mind and strengthens the habit of friendly acceptance.
>
> Responsive behavior—motivated by kindness—replaces reactive behavior. Benevolent, decisive, strong responses are possible. We become peaceful, passionate people.[600]

Sylvia associates metta with the Shema: *"V'ahavta....* And you shall love—the Lord your God with all your heart, with all your soul, and with all your strength" is, I think, the metta practice of Judaism."[601] Yes, I thought, I could adapt metta practice to a Jewish context, associating it with the Shema.

The Baal Shem Tov taught that because all of God's creations are divine, the love of God's creations *is* the love of God. Likewise, Boorstein writes: "I don't think it's possible to love God with all your heart and not love everything else. Complete loving mandates and rejoices in complete acceptance. I learned that doing Buddhist *metta* (lovingkindness) meditation."[602] And so I decided to add Rav Kook's wonderful teaching after the V'Ahavta: "Let love fill your heart and flow out to everyone and everything." Inspired by metta, I added specific rubrics to apply Rav Kook's words to actual people and entities.

Let me briefly describe the elements in Unitive Love Practice. I begin with Niggun Practice, and follow this with a period of Yah Breathing Meditation. Then I rise and face the window in my study. During the ritual I make use of bodily postures and gestures, which I find enhances the experience. Closing my eyes, I take a few moments to receive God's love into my heart. Then I connect with the divine unity through the chanting of the Shema, and pour out my love to God. After this, I direct my love toward myself, toward people close to me, toward those who are sick or in mourning, to those with whom I am having difficulties, and toward places on the globe where there have been natural disasters or outbreaks of violence or war. Finally, I direct my love toward the people of Israel and Palestine and to all people who are suffering from violence, war, trauma, or sickness. I have engaged in this practice for almost twenty-five years. It has refined my attitude toward violence and war and helped open my heart to suffering. I have also found that it has enabled me to learn to listen better to differing points of view.

Unitive Love Practice is an unhurried practice, preferably carried out with eyes closed, but it may be practiced either standing or sitting. I've memorized the sequence and the liturgical texts employed, but those who wish to experiment with it might choose to record it and then play the recording back while engaging in the practice. If you are unfamiliar or uncomfortable with the transliterated Hebrew, feel free to record the English passages alone, and read the text of the meditation slowly as you record it.

Please close your eyes . . .
Notice your breathing . . . Breathing in . . .
Breathing out . . . As you breathe, begin to let go . . . .
Now take a few moments to receive God's love into your
heart, and lift your arms to the heavens . . .
Lift your hands toward the Holy, and bless the EverPresent!
S'u y'day'khem kodesh, U'va'rekhu et HaVaYaH!

(Pause for a few moments, and then spread your arms out wide—and with your palms open heavenwards to receive God's love, chant the following words. As you do, imagine divine love pouring through you, entering every pore of your body, giving you life and consciousness.)

With a deep love You have loved us, unfathomable power
that we are,
embracing us with great compassion . . .
Ahavah rabbah ahav'ta'nu HaVaYaH Elo'hey'nu,
Chemla g'dolah vi-tay'ra cha'mahl't ah'lay'nu.

(Now, recite the following words, and as you do, imagine you are one with the Oneness of existence, and through your spiritual power, you are able to bring greater unity to the world.)

O hear Israel:
the EverPresent, our only Power, the EverPresent alone!
Shema Yisrael: HaVaYah Eloheynu, HaVaYah echad...

(Once again, take a long moment of silence with eyes closed. Then lower your arms and place your hands over your heart, preparing to return your love to the EverPresent. Recite the following words and as you do, offer your love, offer yourself to the Oneness that is wholly One.)

Love the EverPresent, your own godliness,
with all of your heart,
with all of your soul,
and with all of your passion.
Va'hahvtah et Yah Elo'heh'chah
b'chol l'vahv'vecha...
u'v'chol nahf'sheh'chah...
uv'chol m'oh'decha.

(Now say or chant the following words of Rav Kook.)

Let love fill your heart and flow out to everyone and everything.
Ha'ahavah tzrikha li'hi'yot m'lay'ah ba'lev la'khol.

Let the EverPresent love of the Holy Oneness enter your heart . . . Feel yourself embraced by love . . . Call to mind someone you love dearly, perhaps a friend . . .

Imagine that you are sending love to that person . . . Visualize a member of your family . . . Imagine that you are sending love to that person . . . Now, bring to awareness someone who is ill . . . Imagine that you are sending love to that person . . .

This may be somewhat more difficult: Envision someone toward whom you have negative feelings . . . If you are able, offer loving-kindness to this person . . .

If you will, visualize the people of Israel . . . And the people of Palestine . . . Imagine that you are sending love to Israel and Palestine . . .

And now the people of another area of the globe where people are suffering . . .
And now, all the people of the United States . . . Imagine that you are sending love to the people of the United States . . .

(Take a few minutes of silence.)

Now open your eyes, sit down, and conclude the ritual with the last verse of the Adon Olam hymn:

Into Your hand I entrust my spirit, when I lie down and when I rise.

And with my spirit my body, too, You are with me, I will not fear.

B'yahd'khah ahf'keed ru'khi, b'ait ee-shan v'ah'ee'rah.

V'eem ru'khee g'vee'ah'tee, Havayah lee v'lo ee'rah.

(If you have been recording the practice, you can end the recording here.)

* * *

The Shema is the central affirmation recited in both the morning and evening daily prayer services, and it is at the core of Unitive Love Practice. When traditional Jews are about to chant the Shema, they typically close their eyes, placing a hand over them in order to concentrate all their energy on the meaning of the words. This also helps to block out any possible interruption. The Baal Shem Tov offered his disciples a powerful way to concentrate on the spiritual meaning of the word "One" during the recitation:

Shema Yisrael: HaVaYah Eloheynu, HaVaYah echad . . .

O hear Israel: the EverPresent, our only Power, the EverPresent alone!

The meaning of the word One has to do with the practice of unification. While chanting the word One, hold the intention that there is nothing in the world except the holy blessed One, for the divine splendor truly fills the earth. There is truly no place at all where the blessed One is not present. Consider yourself to be nothing at all, for only the soul within you is real, and your soul is part of God beyond.[603]

Just a final personal word about love and compassion: Refining these virtues takes far more than Unitive Love Practice. Besides the suggestions thus far offered, you may find these resources helpful:

Yitzhak Buxbaum, *An Open Heart: The Mystic Path of Loving People,* The Jewish Spirit Booklet Series, #2, 1997.
Yitzhak Buxbaum, *The Light and Fire of the Ba'al Shem Tov,* Continuum, 2005.
Heszel Klepfisz, *Culture of Compassion: The Spirit of Polish Jewry from Hasidism to the Holocaust,* Ktav Publishing, 1983.
Zelig Pliskin, *Love Your Neighbor,* published by Rabbi Zelig Pliskin, 1742 E. 7th St., Brooklyn, NY, 11223.
Rami Shapiro, *The Sacred Art of Lovingkindness,* Skylight Paths Publishing, 2006.

PRACTICE 4: SACRED STUDY

For an introduction to Sacred Study Practice, please see chapter 12, "What the Archives Reveal."

When the Baal Shem Tov was teaching his students, he was in an exalted frame of mind, and this opened him to the words of the Shekhinah that came pouring out. Often, he linked his intuition with fresh insights into sacred texts. For this reason, I follow my davening practice with sacred study, and in this way bring the inspiration of my davening practice to the study of the Baal Shem's wisdom.

The master had words for his disciples regarding how they too could make a sacred text come alive. He cited the following text from the Talmud to his students:

> The Talmud teaches that when one is engaged in the study of the laws sacrificial offerings, it is as if he is actually bringing those offerings himself to the ancient temple in Jerusalem. (*Talmud Menahot 110a*) And then the Baal Shem asked them: "How can a mere act of study be transformed into an actual physical deed?" the students were silent. Then the master answered his own question: "Before you study a holy teaching, the living reality within the text is hidden, clothed in the words of the Torah. But when you as a student engage with those words, investing your own awareness in the teachings, you disrobe those words of their physical garments, and bring the words on the page to life. In this way you reveal their truths and you gain a new understanding of an aspect of the Torah's wisdom. Through the awe and love that you infuse into the ancient words you can restore their original vitality. And this is the way that the study of the laws of offerings become actual offerings."[604]

> And what is it that inspires love and awe in the student?

> As you begin to study, say to yourself: Hasn't the Divine contracted itself and entered into this portion of Torah that I am learning? And then, as you realize that you are actually studying in the presence of the Divine, you will learn with joy, with awe, and with the love of God.[605]

It was in this vein that the nineteenth-century Hasidic rebbe Tzvi Elimelech of Dinov cited the following teaching of the Baal Shem: "The purpose of studying Torah for its own sake is to bind one's consciousness to the One hidden within it."[606] This is how the entire process of studying Torah becomes a form of personal healing, as another Beshtian source cited by Rebbe Yitzhak Meir Alter of Ger declares:

> In the Torah we read: *"Y-H-W-H spoke all of these words to the entire community on the mountain from the midst of the fire, the cloud, and the darkness. It was a great Voice that did not stop."* (Deuteronomy 5:22-24) Because the Voice does not stop, every Jew throughout the generations receives the healing (*tikkun*) that he or she needs time after time from every letter of the Torah.[607]

The following approach to sacred study is phrased in the singular, because that has been my way of engaging with the Besht's wisdom. However, it can easily be adapted to study with a companion or for group learning. There are two sets of questions, one having to do with investigating the historical meaning of the text under consideration, the other on the personal meaning of the teaching. The process may be undertaken during a single study session, or in two. You will likely not be able to address all of these questions to each text you encounter. In fact, you may wish to settle on only those particular questions that really draw your attention.

First, investigate the meaning of the teaching.

1. Close your eyes, take a deep breath, and as you exhale breathe into the Holy Oneness, the source of all wisdom and holiness.

2. This leads into reciting the blessing (*b'rakhah*) for study. Here are two versions of this blessing, the first traditional, and the second, a contemporary adaptation:

Baruch atah Adonai Elo'hay'nu Melech Ha'olam, asher kid'sha'nu b'mitz'vo'tav, v'tzee'va'nu la'ah'sok b'div'ray Torah.

Blessed are You, Lord our God, Ruler of the universe, who made us holy through Your mitzvot, and commanded us to engage with words of Torah.

Baruch atah b'havah'yah ku'lah v'sod om'kah,

*ha'po'tay'akh li'bay-nu l'mitzvot k'do'shoat, ha'm'or'ray'nu
la'ah'sok b'divray Torah.*

Blessed be this moment within the whole of Existence,
opening our hearts to holy mitzvot, and awakening us to
engage with words of Torah.

3. Read the teaching aloud. If you are reading it in Hebrew, look
   up words that you don't recognize in a Hebrew dictionary. You
   might also wish to look up citations from the Bible and other traditional sources, and any abbreviations that appear in the text.
   Now re-read the text aloud once more, and translate it into good
   English.

4. Reflect on the historical context and meaning of the teaching as
   best you can. You can do this either aloud or in writing.

5. Now, re-reading the text aloud, try as best you can to identify the
   underlying spiritual question that the Baal Shem Tov seems to
   be addressing.

6. What insight does the Baal Shem provide as an answer to the
   question he is posing?

7. What foundational spiritual or moral values underlie this
   answer?

8. Where do you find divinity in this teaching?

9. In what way do you think the Besht points toward individual
   spiritual or moral transformation?

10. From what you know about the Baal Shem Tov, what does this
    seem to reveal about his personal life and/or his inner spiritual
    process?

11. Once again re-read the text aloud; now close your eyes and let
    your mind reflect on it in silence for three or four minutes.

12. What stands out for you in this teaching?

Next, personalize the teaching.

1. Once again, close your eyes, take a deep breath, and as you
   exhale breathe into the Holy Oneness, the source of all wisdom
   and holiness.

2. Now imagine that you are in the presence of the Baal Shem.

Re-word the teaching in the second person singular—as if he is speaking directly to you. Begin with your own name.

3. How do you personally respond to this insight?

4. Can you imagine a situation in which this might be relevant to your life? If not, have you ever been in a situation in which his wisdom could have provided you with guidance?

5. Is there some action-directive or spiritual practice that comes out of this for you?

6. What hope or prayer comes out of this teaching for you?

7. Now, once more, close your eyes, take a deep breath, and as you exhale breathe into the Holy Oneness, the source of all wisdom and holiness.

What follows is an example of interpreting a Beshtian text. Almost at random I have chosen a Baal Shem text that points to certain virtues of the tzaddik. The teaching comes from Rebbe Chaim Ephraim of Sudilkov, the grandson of the master. You will notice that I have focused on only some of the questions detailed above, in my answers, which appear in italics after the questions.

First, the text:

> Tzaddikim are able to elevate everything. They make it possible for their disciples to refine their character traits and their ways of speaking with others. There are some tzaddikim who can elevate individuals through their devotion to sacred study and prayer. But there are other tzaddikim who are actually able to elevate people through ordinary conversation. For even though the mundane remarks of a tzaddik may on the surface seem pointless, they always have a deeper purpose. I heard this directly from my grandfather, the Baal Shem Tov, but few people are really able to attain this degree of understanding.[608]

1. Explain the historical meaning of the teaching as best you can. *We don't really know who the Baal Shem's human teachers were, but this teaching shows what it was that he valued in those teachers.*

We do know something about his relationship with his spirit guide, Ahiyah the Shilonite, and possibly this provides a sense of what he valued in that teacher. We have a text in In Praise of the Baal Shem Tov *that tells us that when he was young, the Besht didn't know how to speak with people, and Ahiyah gave him a practice that taught him how to do so. It's also important to note that the Baal Shem recognized the legitimate differences between tzaddikim, even though they all share certain essential characteristics.*

2. Try to identify the underlying spiritual question that the Besht seems to be addressing.

   How do different tzaddikim benefit their disciples' moral growth and ways of speaking with people?

3. What insight does the Besht provide as an answer to the question he is posing?

   He says that the true tzaddik is able to elevate his student spiritually, and that there are a variety of ways in which different tzaddikim are able to do this.

4. What foundational religious or moral values underlie this answer?

   At the core of this teaching is a certainty that seekers require teachers, and that an individual cannot refine their character traits and way of speaking with others on their own. Also this: As a tzaddik, one needs to be able to tailor one's guidance to the specific needs of each disciple. Each disciple needs to find the kind of teacher whose teaching method will be most effective for them.

5. Where do you find the Divinity in this teaching?

   In the notion that the tzaddik has the ability to elevate his disciples. This points toward the masters' purpose, which is raising his student's consciousness and deepening his conscience, helping him refine his way of being in relation to others, and in these ways bringing him closer to the Divine.

6. In what way does this point toward individual spiritual or moral transformation?

   The entire teaching is about the master's purpose and ability to help his disciples in the process of moral transformation so that they will become more sensitive to people.

Now, personalize it. You might wish to engage with these questions during a subsequent study session.

1. Imagine that you are the Besht. Re-word the question underlying the teaching and the answer given in the second person singular, i.e., as if the Besht is speaking to you. Begin with your own name.

   Burt, how has the Baal Shem Tov enabled you to refine your charac-ter and your ways of speaking with others? Well, there are particu-lar values in the teachings and some of the stories about him that have meant a great deal to me, and whose messages I have inter-nalized. Ethically, the most important of these have to do with love, compassion, and humility. But the Baal Shem was also a spiritual seeker who recognized his own deficiencies and worked to trans-form himself, and this proved to be extremely important for me as a model motivating my own growth.

2. Can you imagine a real-life situation in which the Besht's teach-ing might be relevant? If not, have you ever been in a situation in which the Besht's wisdom could have provided you with guidance?

   Definitely. I think back to many situations when I was overly harsh and judgmental. What comes to mind is the severe way that I con-ducted myself as a teacher of children when in my twenties and thirties. This was long before I encountered the Baal Shem Tov, and I was already involved in the process of change when I began study-ing his path. As I absorbed his insights, I was able to refine the ways I taught my students in deep and important ways.

3. Is there some action or action-directive or spiritual practice that comes out of this teaching for you?

   Given the fact that he lived in the eighteenth century, the examples he provides don't really apply to me. But in addition to being able to refine my character and ways of speaking with others, I have also felt that the Besht's life and teachings have elevated me toward God. I've developed a great deal of love and compassion for people, and have worked to become a more humble and joyous person. I have also learned how talents that I chose to nurture enable me to help congregants and spiritual directees on their own paths.

4. What hope, prayer, or form of gratitude comes out of this for
you?
*Really, gratitude! I think of Rumi's words: "Whoever travels without
a guide needs two hundred years for a two-day journey."*

* * *

Here are resources that will help you as you study the Baal Shem's
teachings in greater detail and depth. At the beginning of the chapter,
"The Disciples' Testimonies," I offered the major Hebrew works containing the teachings. For those who are unable to study the original
Hebrew texts, there are a number of English translations that I can also
recommend.

I begin with Martin Buber's translations of texts from "The Testament
of Rabbi Israel Baal Shem," (in Hebrew, *Tzi'va'aht Ha'Ri'vash*). This is a
collection of short teachings pertaining to problems of davening in the
Hasidic manner. The subjects treated include communion with God,
intentionality in prayer, sacred study, joy, and sorrow. Modern scholars
believe that the homilies in this work come from the school of the Maggid
of Medziritch, but there are some which are specifically identified as having been taught by the Besht. Buber translated those that he believed
came from the Baal Shem, and his versions represent a good introduction
to the master's teachings on worship. The collection is called, "The Baal-
Shem-Tov's Instruction in Intercourse with God," and is found in Buber's
book, *Hasidism and Modern Man*. While the translations are somewhat
stilted, the discerning student will appreciate Buber's achievement.

David Sears' *The Path of the Baal Shem Tov: Early Chasidic Teachings
and Customs* offers an excellent and divergent collection of the Besht's
wisdom on a wide range of themes. The translations are generally excellent. The book was published by Jason Aronson in 1997.

Rabbi Yehoshua Starrett has translated selections from the great
anthology of Baal Shem teachings, *Keser Shem Tov: Mystical Teachings on
the Torah*. Rabbi Starrett has also provided extremely useful commentaries on difficult concepts in those teachings. The volume is available from
BST Publishing in Cleveland, Ohio.

The tractate *Ethics of the Fathers* (*Pirkei Avot*) is the most popular
treatise in the Mishnah. The Besht's teachings on the aphorisms in this

collection can be found in *The Baal Shem Tov on Pirkey Avoth,* gathered and arranged by Isaiah Aryeh and Joshua Dvorkes, and translated into English by Charles Wengrov. The book was published in 1974 by Jerusalem Academy Publications and Feldheim Publishers in Jerusalem.

It does not appear that the Besht offered teachings each week connected to the annual cycle of readings from the Torah. Nevertheless, traditional scholars have anthologized large numbers of his teachings arranging them according to annual Torah reading cycle. BST Publishing offers Rabbi Eliezer Shore's selection of those teachings in two volumes: *Genesis and Exodus,* and *Leviticus, Numbers, and Deuteronomy.*

Finally, the most complete collection of the Baal Shem's teachings on prayer, sacred study, and the spiritual life can be found in Menahem Kallus' *Pillar of Prayer,* published by Fons Vitae. The academic translations are accurate and exact, though somewhat difficult. The book has the added advantage of including all of the original Hebrew texts.

PRACTICE 5: LIVING IN THE PRESENCE

In an exquisite passage of his essay on piety, Abraham Joshua Heschel writes,

> The pious man is possessed by his awareness of the presence and nearness of God. Everywhere and at all times he lives as in His sight, whether he remains always heedful of His proximity or not. He feels embraced by God's mercy as by a vast encircling space. Awareness of God is as close to him as the throbbing of his own heart, often deep and calm but at times overwhelming, intoxicating, setting the soul afire. The momentous reality of God stands there as peace, power and endless tranquility, as an inexhaustible source of help, as boundless compassion, as an open gate awaiting prayer. It sometimes happens that the life of a pious man becomes so involved in God that his heart overflows as though it were a cup in the hand of God.[609]

As we've seen, this is called devekut, being bound to the Divine. This is the term the Baal Shem Tov uses for intense connection with God during ecstatic prayer, for he believed one should always be aware of God, whatever one was engaged in doing and whatever state one was in. As he says in *Toledot Ya'akov Yosef, Vaye'rah,* "When you are involved in any activity, bring your most spacious state of consciousness into relation with whatever you are doing. In this way you integrate your awareness with whatever you are doing, continually remembering that you are living in the Presence. This is called the unification of the blessed Holy One and the Shekhinah." And then, in *Tsi'va'at Harivash 3:*

> Perhaps you are speaking with someone about an ordinary matter, or you are travelling to some distant destination, and because of these activities you aren't able to study Torah. Does this mean that you should feel bad because you are doing something without the intrinsic holiness of sacred study? Not at all! For wherever you are, whatever you are doing, you can bind your awareness to the blessed One, linking whatever you are doing with the Whole of reality. God ordains everything, and it is God who wants you to travel, or to hold a conversation with a particular person, or to engage in whatever action you happen to be doing. And why? In order that you serve the Divine through each and every one of your acts.

The essence of piety for the Besht is accustoming one's consciousness to the realization of the potential holiness and Divinity of all of one's actions. As I have discovered, this can have a profound effect in sensitizing the conscience to the necessity of spiritual and moral living. This practice not only elevates our deeds, it ennobles us as individuals, for through its effects it can enable us to realize our potential as human beings who have the ability to elevate all reality.

The Baal Shem identified this practice with the true meaning of the Hebrew word *emunah,* which means faith. To him, faith is staying aware at all times that one is a part of the Shekhinah. The Hebrew word for a nursing mother is *omenet,* which derives from the same root as emunah (Alef-Mem-Nun). Omenet could be translated as "she who nurses a child." We are not independent individuals, but minute yet significant parts of the Shekhinah, being nursed by her.

Here is a teaching of the Besht's in which he attributes his understanding of the word emunah to the founder of the Jewish path:

> Our forefather Abraham has been the model for all those who have sought to anchor their lives in faith, as we have been taught in the Torah: "And Abraham had faith in the EverPresent, and the EverPresent deemed this faith as righteous merit." (Genesis 15) It was through his faith that Abraham was able to bind his "I"—his sense of individual selfhood—to the most expansive awareness, that which is known as No-thingness. And it was with the aid of such faith that Abraham was able to nullify all of the evil occurrences that came from the Divine.[610]

What does that last line mean? My understanding derives from my experience. In high states of awareness, when I experience wholeness, I realize that all the things and events that occur in my ordinary life, good or bad, are impermanent and unreal, and at death my "I" will dissolve into No-thingness.

I think Heschel's poetic way of describing the virtues of the pious person must have come from his own direct experience, for he grew up in an atmosphere in which this ideal was cherished and nurtured. I too have had spacious experiences of wonder, awe, radical amazement, and the majesty of existence. Such occurrences still surprise me and take my breath away. But how can I accustom myself to daily living in a way that enables me to sense the Divine Presence in the most ordinary activities? How can I engage in such a practice each day?

What helped me to develop and deepen this form of devekut was Thomas Kelly's book, *A Testament of Devotion*. Kelly was a beloved instructor in a number of Quaker colleges. He was serious about the Christian practice of the Presence and treated it like a discipline of love. In a short number of years, he was completely transformed spiritually by his engagement with the practice. Reading his book, I found what I needed. He writes that a person can conduct his mental life on more than one plane at the same time. At one level he may be involved with the world—thinking, discussing, seeing, calculating—but deep within at a more profound level, he can dwell in the presence of the Holy One in prayer and adoration and song. And whatever is occurring in his life on the external level can be brought "down into the Light, holding them in the Presence, reseeing them and the whole world of men and things in a new and overturning way, and responding to them in spontaneous, incisive and simple ways of love and faith. Facts remain facts, when brought into the Presence in the deeper level, but their value, their significance, is wholly realigned. Much apparent wheat becomes utter chaff, and some chaff becomes wheat."[61]

How does one take up such a practice? In the early weeks, Kelly writes, begin with simple, whispered words. Formulate them spontaneously: "Yours alone, Yours alone," or make use of a line from the Psalms, such as "My soul longs for You, O God." Repeat them inwardly, again and again. Kelly is realistic, informing readers that it will take weeks, months, perhaps years before the discipline becomes stable. There will be many lapses and the practice will require constant vigilance and effort and reassertions of the will. In working with his instructions, I discovered that he was right about this.

For a time, I experimented by using a name of God or a phrase from the Psalms as a constant mantra. I also tried speaking conversationally with God throughout the day. And I attempted to visualize one or another Hebrew name of the Divine in my mind's eye, a practice used by many kabbalists before the Besht. Whatever the method, however, the same problem would occur. My practice would be interrupted by a telephone call, or an encounter with someone, or a work activity, and I would forget to return to the practice afterwards. It seemed that to be aware of God's presence would mean somehow shutting the world out. Nonetheless, using Kelly's suggestions, I kept experimenting.

I began to use the phrase, "This is God . . ." Whenever I was thrown off by something in the external world I would pause, let go of what was on my mind, silently whisper "This is God," and then briefly move into a contemplative state. I later experimented with a different approach— stopping whatever I was doing for a moment, closing my eyes, and exhaling, "Yaaaaaaah . . ." As I did this I let go completely, surrendering to God.

And if I remembered, I would smile. Sometimes I wore a leather band around my wrist which I called my "God bracelet." Every time I would see it or feel its presence, I was reminded of my practice. (For some people, a *kippah* or the tassels on a *tallit* can be such reminders.)

Over the years I was able to develop and deepen my practice. When I'm reminded of the need to live this moment in the Presence, I breathe out "Yaaaaah...," letting go of thoughts or concerns that have been occupying my mind, surrendering to the present moment. At the same time, I recognize that everything in my field of awareness is divine and part of the Shekhinah: *I am Divine; everything around me is Divine; the cosmos of which I am a small part is Divine.*

As Kelly had forewarned it took several years to truly integrate the practice into my daily life. Yet because living in the Presence meant so much to me, I poured a lot of energy into remembering and practicing the form. Through strengthening my will, and through persistence I learned to enter into the Presence many times during the day, and this was enough to alter my way of living. Charles Duhigg, the author of *The Power of Habit,* wrote, "This is the real power of habit: the insight that your habits are what you choose them to be.... There's nothing you can't do if you get the habits right."

One issue that I frequently faced was what I call "neutral" time. So much of one's day must be given over to carrying out everyday tasks and responsibilities. These activities can become repetitive, boring, and meaningless. But living in the Presence has helped me resolve this problem. I have come to see that I can reframe these mandatory tasks as occasions to open my awareness and tune in to the Divine Presence, making them opportunities for living in the Presence, rather than burdens. I also found that undertaking Yah Breath Meditation in the morning helped anchor and deepen my practice of living in the Presence throughout the day.

Like Kelly—and the Besht—I have found this to be especially valuable in dealing with the daily problems, struggles, disappointments, and times of suffering which I meet. It allows me to put whatever occurs in life into a larger perspective, and prompts me to reframe what appears to be negative in a positive light. Everything, good or bad, is in some way a manifestation of the Divine, part of the wholeness of existence. It's all part of the human journey through life. I have to admit that I was never able to give myself *continually* to the practice, but I did learn to punctuate the day from morning through the evening with moments during which I actually experienced the Presence.

PRACTICE SIX: SPIRITUAL DIRECTION

As important and effective as spiritual practices can be, they alone cannot bring a true and lasting transformation of life. Our instincts and conditioning, and the traumatic experiences we bring to the process of change and growth, require a commitment to ongoing inner work. Psychotherapy might be necessary, and work with a spiritual director can be essential in the struggle to become a *mensch,* a human being guided by and committed to moral and spiritual principles. We have seen these kinds of inner struggles and work that the Besht undertook in order to become more whole, and his efforts resulted in the kind of compassion that he embodied.

We also witness this kind of growth process in the diaries of Etty Hillesum, a young assimilated Jewish woman who lived in Holland during the Nazi occupation. In *An Interrupted Life: The Diaries of Etty Hillesum,* we witness her self-preoccupation, along with the contradictory emotions, impulses, and reflections she experienced as she struggled to refine her character and to become whole. Working with a Jungian psychologist who challenged her, Etty discovered the Divinity at her core and uncovered her potential for compassion and selfless action. As a result, Etty's conscience required her to voluntarily enter the Nazi internment camp near Amsterdam so that she could give herself to supporting and sustaining fellow Jews confined there. Within a short time, Etty Hillesum was transferred to Auschwitz where she died.

What is spiritual direction (*Hash'pa'ah Ru'hanit*)? It has been defined a number of ways. Most of all, it is a discipline of receiving guidance in order to transform one's life and live in more conscious and holy ways. It can come from three different sources: Studying traditional wisdom teachings of the past, working with spiritual directors trained to help individuals in their quest for wisdom, and perceiving the still small voice of one's soul.

In the earliest parts of the Bible, spiritual direction comes directly from God. According to the Torah, Abraham, the founder of the Jewish path, heard a voice speaking to him: *"Go forth from your land, from the place of your birth, and from the house of your father, to the land that I will show you."* (Exodus 12:1) How might the Baal Shem Tov have understood this voice and its origin? Since he believed that the Divine inhabits the psyche, I think he would have recognized the command as having come out of the depths of Abraham himself, perhaps from the kabbalistic realm of *Hokhma* (Wisdom) or *Binah* (Understanding). Rabbi Lawrence Kushner sees Hokhma as intuition, and Binah as insight. The Baal Shem testified that in an expanded state of awareness, when he was in touch with the higher realms, he was able to channel the wisdom of the Shekhinah speaking through him. This often happened while he was teaching, although it is clear that it occurred during mystical experiences as well.

When the Besht was in an ordinary state of awareness, however, he was often directed by Ahiyah of Shiloh. It was this mentor who inducted him into the spiritual life and guided him through many changes and transformations. Later Hasidic traditions also mention other spirit guides and teachers who aided the Besht in spiritual formation, including the biblical prophet Elijah.

From a Jungian point of view, Ahiyah of Shiloh would be considered an archetypal representation of the archetype of the Self, the deepest aspect of the Baal Shem Tov. Ahiyah fits the Jungian archetype of the Wise Old Man, a psychic visage representing the enlightened wholeness that the Baal Shem was slowly becoming. Spirit guides like Ahiyah are found in many religious traditions and have their origin in the ancient shamanistic cultures. In my own life I have had a number of different inner spirit guides who have provided me with the wisdom I needed at the time.

Reb Zalman has traced how the Hasidic rebbe took on the function of the spiritual director in Hasidism. The one-on-one meetings between a Hasid and his rebbe "is a spiritual treatment whereby a trained rebbe, who stands in a direct contractual relationship with his Hasid, listens to his problems and advises him to engage in actions which are designed not only to relieve his suffering, but also to align him with God's will for him."[612] This vocation of the tzaddik has its roots in the life and practice of the Baal Shem Tov himself. There's a trove of tales in which he offers wise guidance to individuals. His clairvoyant abilities are often highlighted; he is able to discern what is going on in the soul of the seeker and offer exceedingly wise counsel.

We can see in many of his teachings the Besht addressing unvoiced issues troubling his disciples. In one tale, we read that every evening after communal prayers the Besht would go to his study where two lit candles were set in front of him. All who needed his counsel were then admitted, and he spoke with them long into the night. One evening after the gathering had ended one of the men told the others how much good the words the master had directed to him had been. But another disciple disputed this. "You are wrong," he declared, "the master was talking intimately to me." Then one after another stated that the Baal Shem had spoken only to them. Each man shared what he had experienced. When the last disciple had spoken, they all fell silent.

In the last twenty-five years a large number of Jews have been trained in the contemporary practice Jewish spiritual direction. These *mash'pi'im/ot* (spiritual directors) work with directees in person, and many of them now work also with directees via Zoom. For me, spiritual direction has taken the place of halakhah as the way to make spiritually-informed decisions about the crucial issues I face. I respect the halakhah because it provides me with the broad outlines of an authentic Jewish religious lifestyle; however, it represents a body of prescriptions and strictures meant to fashion a fixed collective religious lifestyle. And even though the neo-Beshtian forms of spiritual practice have become foundational to my life, I do not feel completely bound to them either.

I have worked with my spiritual director for more than twenty years, and I listen carefully to her counsel. In the end, though, I trust the still, small voice within my depths the most, and attempt to align my life with its wisdom. Through journal writing I also deal with issues having to do with my spiritual journey, including taming the ego. And I know first-hand how spiritual guidance is available to those who pay attention to messages that emanate from the unconscious. Sometimes an insight will occur during sacred study, prayer, or reflection. At other times our dreams point us toward wisdom. The wisest spiritual directors point directees toward the well of wisdom that lies within the neshamah. Whatever the form, spiritual direction enables one to perceive the divine dimension of experience, whether ordinary or extraordinary. This brings us close to the Baal Shem's recognition that there is no situation devoid of the Divine.

I've developed my own step-by-step process for working with difficulties that I meet in daily life. This way of dealing with problems has often enabled me to tap into the wisdom of my soul and to either solve the conflicts or issues that I'm facing, or learn to accept what I cannot alter. Here are the steps I take:

1. Consider the pros and cons of different possibilities, decisions or courses of action.
2. Pose the problem or issue as a prayer to God or to the Spirit in written form in your journal.
3. Turn your concern over to the Spirit and put all thoughts of it aside.
4. Sleep on it and/or yield to the Spirit in meditation.
5. Come back to the problem or issue with fresh eyes. Read what you originally wrote in your journal. Write down whatever comes up without thinking or censoring.
6. Discern where the counsel came from by asking: How does this answer make me feel? Do I experience relief or joy? What might the fruits of this decision be? Do I think that this course of action will eventually lead to greater freedom, love, connection, humility, peacefulness, balance, equanimity, non-attachment? Or will it lead to fear, pride, anxiety, egoic attachment to specific results?
7. Ask yourself: Do I have a sense that my question has been answered? Do I recognize this as the right course of action for me at this time?
8. Now, begin to act on what you discerned. What can you do today to start making this come alive?

The contemporary approach to spiritual direction as a counseling practice was pioneered in the Catholic world. Like me, the first modern Jewish spiritual directors received their training in Catholic institutions. I benefited immensely from studies at Mercy Center in Burlingame, California, in the early 1990s. I received certification from Mercy Center, and later directly from Reb Zalman Schachter-Shalomi.

If you are interested in experiencing the kind of spiritual support that a relationship with a spiritual director might provide, you will find information on the website of Spiritual Directors International. You can also ask an ordained rabbi, minister, or vowed religious leader for names of spiritual directors that they would recommend. And to learn more about Jewish spiritual direction, you may find the following books helpful.

Rabbi Howard Avruhm Addison and Barbara Eve Beitman, *Jewish Spiritual Direction*, Jewish Lights Publishing.

Rabbi Goldie Milgram, editor, *Seeking and Soaring: Jewish Approaches to Spiritual Direction*, Reclaiming Judaism Press, 2009.

Carol Ochs and Kerry M. Olitzky, *Jewish Spiritual Guidance*, Jossey-Bass, 1997.

Zalman M. Schachter-Shalomi, *Spiritual Intimacy: A Study of Counseling in Hasidism*, Jason Aronson, 1991.

AFTERWORD

When Burt asked me to look at his early writings about the Baal Shem Tov I was gratified to contribute to what seemed like important work. Although I don't maintain a religious practice, I felt attuned to this strand of Jewish spiritual engagement. It felt personally affirming for me to delve, alongside Burt, into such subjects as how a transcendent soul like the Baal Shem's inhabits a mortal's life; the value of legends and miracle stories in establishing the presence of a metaphysical reality; and how, in our age of radical individualism, a kind of skeptical discipleship may be established. My dialogue with Burt over how to organize his ever-evolving material, and how to sustain his personal voice and narrative amongst the other stories he was committed to tell, has through these many years kept alive in me evocative questions of heritage, influence, and selfhood.

My involvement in this project, though, required a mysterious turn of events. I grew up knowing I was Jewish, yet without a clue as to what that meant. For three summers I went to a camp where Shabbat services were held, and I learned to sing *Adon Olam*; but I received no real Jewish education, nor did I experience discrimination as a Jew. Not until I was in my thirties did I have a sudden awakening to the knowledge that my heritage was significant. Then I began to explore.

Early on I came upon Elie Wiesel's *Souls on Fire*, Martin Buber's *Legends of the Baal Shem,* and writings by Maurice Friedman, whose workshop on Hasidic lore I was also able to attend. I was greatly taken by the stories of wonder and the quirky insights, stirring a spiritual imagination I didn't know I had. And then I met Rabbi Burt Jacobson. In courses and workshops I serendipitously enrolled in, he introduced me to the power of Hasidic niggun and dance, and to the history of the Baal Shem's renewal movements—both in the past and the present.

Since that initiation, I've had surprising, even perplexing, experiences that have been best understood in the context of this "Baal Shem work" that Burt has implicated me in. There were, for instance, improbable events beyond coincidence; journeys seemingly outside chronological time and everyday awareness; stories inspired by a subconscious Hasidic sensibility calling on me to write them. Here is one such, excerpted from a piece called *My Tribe: A Mosaic.*

"While on a European trip, I was passing through Munich, for convenience only, when I discovered on a train's map that the Dachau memorial lay on the city's outskirts. I was impelled to visit. I took it all in with no special thought or feeling occurring; but the next day I wrote a poem:

Dachau 1977

Such trees, shapely and lithe,
Autumnal now
With seasoned grace and brilliance
They watch over
Stand at parade rest on
Root for nourishment below
This concrete world.
Past the museum
Pronouncements, memoranda, stills of death
Of death before death
Unguided we intrude where only ghosts survive
Emptiness speaks:
Spectral barking of commandants and dogs
Moans
    Snapping bones
           Paddling clogs.
Dumb, numb
We listen for a small girl's voice
Asking to have a candle lit
Directing where she'd been struck down
For wanting too much soup.
None sounds.
But was it she who yesterday
Dressed well-to-do, with skates a-dangle from her arm
Asked two marks so her friend and she could swim?
Perhaps not just a spoiled young Fraulein taught to charm,

Was it she we refused, was it She?
In the cold mist the trees stand clear,
Another spring, another summer gone.
Two heaps of messianic ash lie next the Krematorium
One of peace,
One of war.
In this our world
We trust not even winter to follow full,
Except for the trees.

The story that told itself to me was this: my soul, in my mother's womb in 1943, was in communication with a young girl who died in Dachau. Knowing her circumstances and her fate gave rise to an inborn anxiety that underlay, and gave the lie to, my sedate upbringing. Though raised with virtually no education about the special case of being a Jew, I knew.

I know.

I am appreciative of the opportunity to have participated in the wide-ranging exploratory process that resulted in this manuscript. I hope others will be similarly stimulated by Burt's mindful and mind-blowing adventures into the very heart of "spiritual life" in the twenty-first century. It may be the story of just one individual, but one deeply rooted in tradition, recent history, and contemporary understanding. Burt, my friend, it is quite a trip you have taken.

RICHARD STONE

ACKNOWLEDGMENTS

First of all, my gratitude goes to the Holy Oneness that birthed the world and everything in it, without whose inherent creativity there could be no human creativity.

My enduring thanks goes to the Baal Shem Tov, whose vision made it possible to renew Judaism in the eighteenth century. This book is the result of my fifty-year encounter with the Baal Shem. Its length and contents testify to the all of the people and sources that I have depended on throughout these many decades.

I wish to thank three of my spiritual directors, Rev. Ted Pecot, Brother Donald Bisson, and Janice Farrell. Their insights over the years have enabled me to break though the many obstacles that I have had to face since the 1980s and to incorporate the Besht's insights into the ways that I live my life.

I am thankful for my studies of a number of modern neo-Hasidic thinkers who articulated the Besht's insights in contemporary terms, either in person or through their writing. These have included Abraham Joshua Heschel, Martin Buber, Zalman Schachter-Shalomi, and Arthur Green.

And my teachers in the craft of writing: Richard Stone, Susan Schacht, Lynn Feinerman, and my wife, Diane.

And my gratitude certainly extends to the academic scholars, both those who have focused on Hasidism, and those who have been concerned with elucidating the shared and universal foundations of religion. I could have hardly synthesized the comprehensive portrait of the founder offered in this book without having incorporating their erudition. It is an old Jewish practice to name one's teachers, and I have tried to act in accord with this custom by naming the most important of these researchers throughout the book. Special thanks go to historian Dr. Barbara Epstein, who helped me enormously in developing the methodology that I have employed in my reconstruction of the Baal Shem Tov.

I also owe a debt of gratitude to all those throughout the years with whom I shared my emerging findings, both at Kehilla Community Synagogue and in the wider Jewish Renewal movement. My closest partners in this dialogue have been Barry Barkan, Rabbi Ronnie Serr, Rabbi Cynthia Hoffman, and more recently, Zvika Krieger.

And to those who read parts of the emerging manuscript and offered me critical feedback: Rabbi Cynthia Hoffman, Stuart Jacobson, Kenneth Cohen, Joel Elliot, David Levine, Rabbi Tirzah Firestone, Rabbi Wayne Dosick, and Adam Horowitz. And a special thanks to Jacob Picheny, who read through the entire manuscript and helped me to clarify my thinking. I want to apologize to any other colleagues and friends who have in any way contributed to this book, but whom I have unknowingly left out.

And special thanks to Jon M. Sweeney, my editor at Monkfish Book Publishing who streamlined the text and made numerous suggestions that bettered the text. I also want to thank both Jon and my publisher Paul Cohen for their enthusiasm for my manuscipt.

I have dedicated this book to my precious wife, Diane Elliot. Diane is a dancer, singer, somatic practitioner, spiritual director, and rabbi. We have taught classes on the Baal Shem Tov together in which she was able to transform his ideas and experiences into somatic forms of embodied Hasidism. Diane has been at my side for more than twenty years, offering her support and many talents to the gradual unfolding of this book. I value her love and support beyond measure. When we became engaged, I wrote the following lines in my beloved's honor.

> *Finding you has been a re-discovery,*
> *a recovery of that country*
> *that place other than my self,*
> *and yet my true Home.*
>
> *I promise to remember, to never forget*
> *the bright joy of what we have created,*
> *the luminous truth that has graced our union.*
>
> *I am larger now, and I grow by the moment.*
> *There are hours when I forget my self,*
> *and there is only one in two forms.*
>
> *There is only One.*

NOTES

1   Abraham Joshua Heschel, *The Earth Is the Lord's: The Inner World of the Jew in Eastern Europe* (NY: Farrar, Straus and Giroux, 1949), 107.

2   Abraham Joshua Heschel, *Moral Grandeur and Spiritual Audacity,* ed. Susannah Heschel (NY: Farrar, Straus and Giroux, 1996), 34.

3   *Keter Shem Tov,* 16a.

4   Gershom Scholem, *Major Trends in Jewish Mysticism* (NY: Schocken Books, 1941), 15.

5   Will Herberg, *Judaism and Modern Man* (NY: Farrar, Straus and Young, 1951), 124.

6   Abraham Joshua Heschel, *A Passion for Truth* (Farrar, Straus and Giroux, 1973), 300-1.

7   Ibid, 256.

8   Laurence Heller and Aline LaPierre, *Healing Developmental Trauma* (Berkeley, CA: North Atlantic Books, 2012), 28.

9   Heschel, *A Passion for Truth*, xiv.

10   Ibid, 4.

11   Ibid, 8.

12   Ibid, xiv.

13   Ibid, 37, 130.

14   Ibid, 6.

15   Ibid, 25.

16   Ibid, 66.

17   Abraham Joshua Heschel, "Hasidism as a New Approach to Torah," *Moral Grandeur and Spiritual Audacity*, 34.

18   *The Zohar,* Vol. 1, Daniel C. Matt, translator, Pritzker Edition (Stanford, CA: Stanford University Press, 2004), 75-76. I have made a number of alterations in Matt's translation.

19   Gershom G. Scholem, *Major Trends in Jewish Mysticism*, 254.

20   According to Luria, though, the first three of these vessels, known as *Keter* (Crown), *Chochmah* (Wisdom) and *Binah* (Understanding), however, were close to the Infinite itself. They did not fracture like the lower vessels, and they held on to the light of the Infinite.

21   Ram Dass, *Be Here Now* (Lama Foundation, 1971), 84, 77.

22   Heschel, *A Passion for Truth*, 19, 33.

23   *Tzvi LaZaddik,* Introduction, Note 2; Joshua Joseph Kornbleit, *Me'ir Einei Yisrael.* Heschel cites this parable on p. 5 of *A Passion for Truth.*

24   Approbation of R. Yehuda Segal Rosner to *Sefer Rabbenu Yisrael Baal Shem Tov.*

25   *Talmud Shabbat* 88a.

26   Abraham Joshua Heschel, *God in Search of Man* (New York: Harper and Row, 1955), 131.

27   Abraham Joshua Heschel, *Man Is Not Alone* (New York: Noonday Press, 1951), 149.

28   Simon Dubnow, *Toledot HaHasidut,* p. 41. Translation by Saadya Sternberg in Immanuel Etkes, *The Besht: Magician, Mystic, and Leader* (Boston: Brandeis University Press, 2005), 205.

29   Martin Buber, *Tales of the Hasidim: The Early Masters* (New York: Schocken Books, 1947), 1.

30   *In Praise of the Baal Shem Tov: The Earliest Collection of Legends About the Founder of Hasidism,* by Dan Ben-Amos and Jerome R. Mintz (Bloomington, IN: Indiana University Press, 1970), 107.

31   Simon Dubnow, "The Beginnings: The Baal Shem Tov (Besht) and the Center in Podolia," in *Essential Papers on Hasidism: Origins to Present,* ed. Gershon David Hundert (New York: New York University Press, 1991), 25-57.

32   Dubnow, *Essential Papers on Hasidism*, 25-26.

33   Etkes, *The Besht*, 214.

34   The chronology came from Eliach's 1973 dissertation (unpublished), Jewish Hasidim, Russian Sectarian Non-conformists in the Ukraine, 1700-1760.

35   *In Praise of the Baal Shem Tov* does not provide Eliezer with a last name, but Reb Zalman Schachter-Shalomi informed me that there is a later source that claims it was "Talismacher."

36   Moshe Idel, "R.Israel Baal Shem Tov 'In the State of Walachia,' pp. 69-103, in Glenn Dynner, *Holy Dissent: Jewish and Christian Mystics in Eastern Europe* (Detroit: Wayne State University Press, 2011).

37   Dubnow, *Essential Papers on Hasidim*, 21.

38   Ibid, 29.

39   Ibid, 30.

40   Ibid, 35.

41   Dubnow, *History of the Jews in Russia and Poland, Vol. 1* (Philadelphia: Jewish Publication Society of America, 1916), 225-27.

42   Ibid, 226-27.

43   Dubnow, *Essential Papers on Hasidim*, 90.

44   Ibid, 96.

45   Joseph Campbell, *The Hero with a Thousand Faces* (Princeton: Princeton University Press, 1949), 30.

46   Ibid, 19-20.

47   Ibid, 55, 71.

48   Ibid, 16.

49   Ibid, 345.

50   Moshe Idel, *Ben: Sonship and Jewish Mysticism* (New York: Continuum, 2007), 540.

51   Campbell, *The Hero with a Thousand Faces*, 39.

52   Aryeh Wineman, *Mystic Tales from the Zohar* (Princeton: Princeton University Press, 1998), 95.

53   Ibid, 93.

54   Rachel Elior, *The Mystical Origins of Hasidism* (Liverpool, UK: The Littman Library of Jewish Civilization, 2006), 70; *Degel Machaneh Efrayim*, 282.

55   *The Essential Jung*, ed. Anthony Storr (New York; MJF Books, 1983), 142.

56   Frieda Fordham, *An Introduction to Jung's Psychology* (New York: Penguin Books, 1959), 44.

57   Ibid, 44.

58   *The Essential Jung*, 77-78.

59   Leo D. Lefebure, *The Buddha and the Christ: Explorations in Buddhist and Christian Dialogue* (Maryknoll, NY: Orbis, 1993), 29.

60   Elie Wiesel, *Souls on Fire* (New York: Random House, 1972), 27, 37.

61   *Meir Einei Yisrael: Sefer Baal Shem Tov*, published by Machon Da'at Yoseph in 1991. A recent Google search for information about the editor of the volume, Yehoshuah Yosef Kornblit, yielded no information, but I would imagine that he is or was a Hasid living somewhere in Israel, where the book was published.

62   *Torat HaBaal Shem Tov: Me'ir Einei Yisrael* was published by Machon Da'at Yosef, Jerusalem, 5751/1991, 11.

63   Ibid, *Shivhei HaBesht*, #36. Unless indicated otherwise, translations are my own.

64   Ibid, *Ginzei Yisrael*.

65 *Sippurei Baal Shem Tov; Admorei Beltz* I:332; *Me'ir Einei Yisrael* 52.

66 *Sefer HaDorot HeHadash,* Lublin, 1927, 5.

67 *Hovat Hatalmidim* 1:2 and *Likutei D'varim* IV:1322.

68 *Shivhei HaBesht.*

69 *Hayom Yom.*

70 Ibid.

71 *Ma'or v'Shemesh* 1:38a.

72 *Tiferet Sh'lomo, Vayeshev.*

73 *Meir Einei Yisrael,* 105-6.

74 Yitzhak Buxbaum, *The Light and Fire of the Baal Shem Tov* (New York: Continuum, 2006), 144-5.

75 Moshe Idel, *Hasidism: Between Ecstasy and Magic* (Albany, NY: State University of New York Press, 1995), ch. 5.

76 *Heikhel HaB'rakha, Parashat V'et'hanan.*

77 Moshe Idel, YouTube: http://www.youtube.com/watch?v=2qMI8RKtHgs&feature=related.

78 *Sefer Baal Shem Tov, B'raishit* 106.

79 *Niflaot Sippurim.*

80 *Shiv'hei HaBesht, ibid.,* #69.

81 I. Biderman, *Mayer Balaban: Historian of Polish Judaism* (New York: Biderman Book Committee, 1976), 204-5.

82 Abraham Joshua Heschel, *The Circle of the Besht: Studies in Hasidism*, ed. Samuel H. Dresner (Chicago: University of Chicago Press, 1985), xli.

83 Buxbaum, *The Light and Fire of the Baal Shem Tov,* 4.

84 Walter Brueggemann, *David's Truth in Israel's Imagination and Memory* (Minneapolis: Fortress Press, 2002), 1.

85 Shaul Magid, "Defining Christianity and Judaism from the Perspective of Religious Anarchy: Martin Buber on Jesus and the Baal Shem Tov," in Sam Berrin Shonkoff, *Martin Buber: His Intellectual and Scholarly Legacy* (Boston: Brill, Leiden, 2018).

86 All the citations by Wiesel relating to Hasidism come from the first chapter of *Souls on Fire: Portraits and Legends of Hasidic Masters* (New York: Random House, 1972).

87 Dubnow, *Essential Papers on Hasidism,* 25-26.

88 Gershom Scholem, *Devarim B'Go,* Am Ovair, 295.

89 Louis I. Newman, *The Hasidic Anthology* (New York: Jason Aronson, 1987), lxxii.

90 *Time,* August 15, 1988, 37.

91 David B. Gowler, *What Are They Saying About the Historical Jesus?* (New York: Paulist Press, 2007), vii.

92 John Dominic Crossan, *The Historical Jesus: The Life of a Mediterranean Jesus Peasant* (New York: HarperOne, 1993), 421-22.

93 Cited by David B. Gowler in *What Are They Saying About the Historical Jesus*, 29.

94 Daniel C. Matt, *God and the Big Bang* (Woodstock, VT; Jewish Lights, 1996), 156.

95 Geza Vermes, *The Religion of Jesus the Jew* (Minneapolis: Fortress Press, 1993), 5. Before either Matt or Vermes, the eminent Reform theologian, Kaufman Kohler (1843-1926) held that Jesus had been inspired by the Hasidim, whom he defined as a virtuous and ascetic group that served as the *avant guard* of the Pharisees. He also postulated that it was the Hasidim who invented the synagogue. Israeli historian Shmuel Safrai also believed that Jesus had been a Hasid.

96 *Hayom Yom,* 78.

97 "Typologies of Leadership and the Hasidic *Zaddiq*," and "The Zaddiq as *Axis* Mundi in Later Judaism," in Arthur Green, *The Heart of the Matter: Studies in Jewish Mysticism and Theology* (Philadelphia: Jewish Publication Society, 2015).

98 Yaffa Eliach, "The Russian Dissenting Sects and Their Influence on Israel Baal Shem Tov, Founder of Hassidism," in *Proceedings of the American Academy for Jewish Research* 36 (1968), 57-83.

99 Moshe Rosman, *Founder of Hasidism: A Quest for the Historical Baal Shem Tov* (Berkeley, CA: University of California Press, 1996), 59.

100 Torsten Ysander, *Studien zum B'estschen Hasidismus,* Uppsala University, 1933.

101 Raphael Patai, *The Jewish Mind* (New York: Charles Scribner's Sons, 1977), 185.

102 Besides Raphael Patai's book, see Joseph P. Schultz, *Judaism and the Gentile Faiths: Comparative Studies in Religion,* Farleigh Dickinson, 1981; Efraim Shmueli, *Seven Jewish Cultures: A Reinterpretation of Jewish History and Thought,* Cambridge University Press, 2008; Glenn Dynner, ed., *Holy Dissent: Jewish and Christian Mystics in Eastern Europe,* Wayne State University Press, 2011; Thomas Block, *Shalom/Salaam: A Story of Mystical Fraternity,* Fons Vitae, 2010.

103 Idel, *Ben: Sonship and Jewish Mysticism,* 570.

104 Stanislaw Vincenz, "An Encounter with the Hasidim," in *Four Decades of*

Polish Essays, ed. by Jan Kott (Evanston, IL: Northwestern University Press, 1990), 37-53.

105   Heschel, *Moral Grandeur and Spiritual Audacity*, 237.

106   Rabbi David Zaslow, *Jesus: First-Century Rabbi* (Brewster, MA: Paraclete Press, 2014), vii.

107   Rosman, *Founder of Hasidism*, 211.

108   Rosman tells this story in the introduction to the 2nd edition of *Founder of Hasidism: A Quest for the Historical Baal Shem Tov,* published by the Littman Library of Jewish Civilization, in 2013.

109   Ibid, 210.

110   Ibid, 4, 6, 7.

111   Arthur Green, "Review of Rosman's Founder of Hasidism," in *History of Religions,* 40:42 (November 2000), 185-87.

112   Etkes, *The Besht*, 5.

113   Rosman, *Founder of Hasidism*, 183.

114   Etkes, *The Besht*, 304.

115   Ibid, 249, 190.

116   Ibid, xli.

117   Roman A. Foxbrunner, *Habad: The Hasidism of R. Shneur Zalman of Lyady* (New York: Jason Aronson, 1993), 10-11.

118   Translation from Etkes's book. Source: Gedaliah Nigal, *Gedolim Ma'asei Tzaddikim,* 23.

119   Etkes, *The Besht,* 106-7.

120   Moshe Idel, *Vocal Rites and Broken Theologies: Cleaving to Vocables in R. Israel Ba'al Shem Tov's Mysticism* (New York: Herder & Herder, 2020), 148.

121   Idel, *Hasidism,* 225.

122   Mary Blye Howe, *Sitting with Sufis* (Brewster, MA: Paraclete Press, 2005), 9-11.

123   Jiri Langer, *Nine Gates to the Chassidic Mysteries* (New York: David McKay Co., 1961), 6-7.

124   A. S. Halkin, "The Great Fusion," in *Great Ages and Ideas of the Jewish People,* ed. Leo Schwarz (New York: Random House, 1956), 219.

125   Thomas Block, *Shalom/Salaam: A Story of Mystical Fraternity* (Louisville, KY: Fons Vitae, 2010), 183.

126   Harvey J. Hames, "A Seal Within a Seal: The Imprint of Sufism in Abraham Abulafia's Teachings," in *Medieval Encounters* 12.2, 2006, 169.

127   Block, *Shalom/Salaam,* 183.

128 Moshe Idel, "Universalization and Integration: Two Conceptions of Mystical Union in Jewish Mysticism," in *Mystical Union in Judaism, Christianity and Islam,* eds. Moshe Idel and Bernard McGinn (New York: Continuum, 1996), 160.

129 Idel, *Studies in Ecstatic Kabbalah,* 133.

130 Eric Geoffroy, "Approaching Sufism," in *Love and Wisdom,* eds. Louis Michon and Roger Gaetani (New York: World Wisdom, Inc., 2006), 59-60.

131 Block, *Shalom/Salaam,* 206.

132 Paul Fenton, *Cambridge Companion to Medieval Jewish Philosophy,* eds. Daniel H. Frank and Oliver Leaman (New York: Cambridge University Press, 2006), part II, ch. 10.

133 For another attempt to show the possibility of Sufi influence on the Baal Shem Tov and Hasidism, see Aubrey L. Glazer's "Imaginal Journeying to Istanbul" in Menahem Kallus' *Pillar of Prayer* (Louisville, KY: Fons Vitae, 2011).

134 Elior, *The Mystical Origins of Hasidism,* 204-5.

135 Ibid, 26. See also Hayden White, *The Content of the Form* (Baltimore: Johns Hopkins University Press, 1987). Interested readers might like to read Adam Timmons' review of Herman Paul's book, *Hayden White* at history. ac.uk/reviews. Also, Paul Sutermeister's essay, "Hayden White, History as Narrative: A Constructive Approach to Historiography," which can be found at http://www.grin.com/en/e-book/109135/hayden-white-history-as-narrative-a-constructive-approach-to-historiography.

136 See Robbie Davis-Floyd and P. Sven Arvidson, eds., *Intuition: The Inside Story* (NY: Routledge, 1997); and Bernard Bailyn, "History and the Creative Imagination," in *Sometimes an Art* (NY: Alfred A Knopf, 2015); also, Giorgio Parisi, *In a Flight of Startlings: The Wonders of Complex Systems* (NY: Penguin Press, 2023).

137 Wiesel, *Souls on Fire,* 7.

138 Maurice Friedman, *Martin Buber's Life and Work, Vol. 3* (Detroit: Wayne State University Press, 1988), 59-60.

139 Buber, *Tales of the Hasidim: Early Masters,* 42.

140 *Keter Shem Tov, Hosafot—Im'rot Kodesh.*

141 Ben-Amos and Mintz, *In Praise of the Baal Shem Tov,* #47.

142 Samuel Dresner, *The Zaddik* (New York: Schocken Books, 1974), 46.

143 Wiesel, *Souls on Fire,* 32.

144 *Midrash She'mot Rabbah* 2:9.

145 *Keter Shem Tov* 144; *B'er Ha'Hasidut* 243:2. Some of the teachings in *Sefer Keter Shem Tov* come from the Baal Shem's chief disciples, R. Dov Baer of Medziritch, but in my judgement this text comes from the Besht.

146 Jacob Neusner, *Torah from Our Sages: Pirkei Avot* (Dallas: Rossel Books, 1984), 62.

147 Respectively: *Tz'va'at Ha'Rivash* 99; *Avodat Yisrael, Likkutim, Ta'anit; Div'rei Moshe, Parashat Va'yeh'ra; Degel Mahaneh Efrayim, Parashat Metzorah.*

148 The first of these four teachings comes from the book, *The Testament of the Besht,* and may have actually been formulated by Dov Baer, the Maggid of Medziritch—the Baal Shem's foremost disciple—or by one of the Maggid's own disciples. The second teaching was reported by R. Yisrael of Koznitz (1740-1814), who did not study directly with the Besht. The third text comes from one of the Besht's own students, R. Moshe Shoham of Dolyna. And the last teaching was recorded by the Baal Shem's grandson, R. Chaim Ephraim of Sudilkov.

149 *Heikhel HaB'rakha, Parashat V'et'hanan.*

150 My version of the story is an elaboration of sources found in *Keter Shem Tov* 144 and *B'er HaHasidut* 243:2.

151 *Degel Mahaneh Efrayim* 13.

152 Philip Zaleski, foreword to *The Best Spiritual Writing: 2013* (New York: Penguin Books, 2012).

153 See Moshe Rosman, *Founder of Hasidism,* 146.

154 Zalman Schachter-Shalomi and Netanel Miles-Yepez, *A Heart Afire: Stories and Teachings of the Early Hasidic Masters* (Philadelphia: Jewish Publication Society, 2009), xxiv.

155 Wiesel, *Souls on Fire,* x.

156 Buber, *Tales of the Hasidim: Early Masters,* 35.

157 Raphael Patai, *The Jewish Mind* (New York: Charles Scribner's Sons, 1977), 191.

158 *Shivhei HaBesht* #105. All references to specific narratives in *Shivhei HaBesht* employ the numbering system used by the authors of the English translation.

159 *Shivhei HaBesht,* #231.

160 Estelle Frankel, *Sacred Therapy* (Boston: Shambhala, 2003), 64-65.

161 Ibid.

162 *Shivhei HaBesht,* #43.

163 See, for instance, Yehoshuah Yosef Kornbleit, *Me'ir Einei Yisrael,* Machon Da'at Yosef, 258-264.

164 See *Tzafnat Pane'ah, Yitro*; *Degel Mahane Efrayim, VaYehi*, also Eliezer Steinmann, *B'er HaHasidut: Sefer Baal Shem Tov*, Machon L'ho'ts'at Kabbalah, Maha'shavah, Hasidut, 109-110, and the sources in *Me'ir Einei Yisrael* under the heading *Anavah V'ga'avah*, 160-70; *Degel Mahaneh Efrayim, B'hu'kotai*; *Tzafnat Pane'ah, Yitro*.

165 *Toledot Ya'akov Yosef, Tzav*.

166 *Toledot Ya'akov Yosef, Hukat*.

167 *Toldot Ya'akov Yosef, Bereshit*.

168 *Keter Shem Tov* 70.

169 *Degel Mahaneh Efrayim* 1:126.

170 *Ben Porat Yosef*, 27a.

171 See *Me'ir Einei Yisrael*, 112-116, and also Eliezer Steinmann, *B'er HaHasidut: Sefer Baal Shem Tov*, 123-24.

172 *Shivhei HaBesht*, #88.

173 Ben-Amos and Mintz, *In Praise of the Baal Shem Tov*, 112.

174 *Degel Mahaneh Efraim, Purim*.

175 *Hanhagot Yesharot* 14b.

176 *Hanhagot Yesharot*, 14b; *Sefer Baal Shem Tov, Metzorah* 12.

177 *Kovetz Or Haganuz*.

178 *Tzaf'nat Pa'nei'ah, Parashat B'shalah*; *Siftei Tzaddikim, Parashat B'ha'a lot'khah*.

179 *Toledot Ya'akov Yosef, Parashat Ekev*.

180 James F. Masterson, *Search for the Real Self: Unmasking the Personality Disorders of Our Age* (New York: The Free Press, 1990).

181 *Toledot Ya'akov Yosef, Tzav*.

182 *Tzi'va'at HaRivash* 8a.

183 *Toledot Ya'akov Yosef, Tzav*.

184 *Likkutei Torah Mei'ha'Rav, z"l, Va'yik'rah* 51:3.

185 Solomon Schechter, *Studies in Judaism* (New York: Atheneum, 1970), 127.

186 Buber, *Tales of the Hasidim: Early Masters*, 71.

187 Ken Wilber, "Spiritual Diary," in *Tikkun*, September/October 1998, 39-40.

188 Campbell, *The Hero with a Thousand Faces*, 25-29.

189 Hebrew: *Ha'rah hu kisei el ha'tov*, which literally means, "Evil is the throne of the good."

190 Campbell, *The Hero with a Thousand Faces*, 148.

191 Israel Regardie, "A Jewish Mystical Movement," in J. Marvin Spiegelman and Abraham Jacobson, *A Modern Jew in Search of a Soul* (Phoenix, AZ: Falcon Press, 1986), 43.

192   Gershon David Hundert, *Jews in Poland-Lithuania in the Eighteenth Century* (Berkeley, CA: University of California Press, 2004), 142-43.

193   Michael Harner, *The Way of the Shaman* (San Francisco: HarperSanFrancisco, 1980), 42-43.

194   Buxbaum, *The Light and Fire of the Baal Shem Tov*, 101.

195   "The Varieties of Mind-Enhancing Practices," in *Spiritual Growth with Entheogens,* ed. Thomas B. Roberts (Rochester, VT: Park Street Press, 2012), xxi-xxii.

196   Scholem, *Major Trends in Jewish Mysticism*, 134, 137.

197   *Sha'aray Tzedek.*

198   Idel, *Vocal Rites and Broken Theologies*, 186.

199   *Keter Shem Tov,* 56ab; and Idel, *ibid.,* 36, and n. 9 on 305.

200   *Keter Shem Tov,* 1.

201   *Keter Shem Tov* II: 4d.

202   *Likutim Y'karim* 14a and *Sefer Baal Shem Tov, V'et'hanan.*

203   Lawrence Kushner, *Eyes Remade for Wonder* (Woodstock, VT: Jewish Lights Publishing, 1998), 178.

204   Etkes, *The Besht*, 136-37; 127-28.

205   *Shiv'hei HaBesht,* #34.

206   Buxbaum, *The Light and Fire of the Baal Shem Tov*, 128.

207   *Keter Shem Tov,* 18b.

208   Menachem Kallus, trans. *Pillar of Prayer* (Louisville, KY: Fons Vitae, 2011), 134-35, #101.5. The passage comes from *Amtachat Binyamin* on Eccl. 2:10.

209   Ibid, 54, n. 292.

210   Mosheh Aaron Krassen, "Rabbi Israel Baal Shem Tov, Prophet of a New Paradigm," in Kallus' *Pillar of Prayer*, xiv-xxv.

211   Andrew Newberg and Mark Robert Waldman, *How Enlightenment Changes Your Brain: The New Science of Transformation* (New York: Avery, 2016), 34.

212   Many different versions of this parable exist. This version is based on *Ben Porat Yosef* 70c and 111; *Sefer Baal Shem Tov, Vayelech,* note 3 and *Noah,* note 83; *B'er HaHasidut* 246:9.

213   *Sh'mu'ah Tovah* 71b. See also Rivka Schatz, *Hasidism as Mysticism* (Princeton: Princeton University Press, 1993), 173.

214   Ralph Metzner, *The Unfolding Self: Varieties of Transformative Experience* (San Rafael, CA: Origin Press, 1986), 159-60.

215   *Keter Shem Tov* 192-93.

216   Metzner, *The Unfolding Self,* 162.

217   Newberg and Waldman, *How Enlightenment Changes Your Brain,* 51.

218   Ibid, 51.

219   Ibid, 29-30.

220   *Tz'va'at HaRivash* 41.

221   Schechter, *Studies in Judaism,* 147.

222   *Me'or Einayim, Yitro.*

223   Deepak Chopra, *How to Know God* (New York: Harmony Books, 2000), 93.

224   Robert Gass, *Chanting: Discovering Spirit in Sound* (New York: Broadway Books, 1999), 59.

225   *Ish Ha'pele,* 69. See Yitzhak Buxbaum, *Jewish Spiritual Practices,* 481. Chapter 24 of that book will be extremely helpful for seekers who wish to work with song and dance.

226   *Ben Porat Yosef* 29c.

227   *Tze'va'at HaRivash* 22b.

228   Buxbaum, *Jewish Spiritual Practices,* 160.

229   *Bereishit Rabbah* 4:11.

230   *Sefer Chasidim,* condensed, translated, and annotated by Avraham Yehudah Finkel (New York: Jason Aronson, 1997), 65, 66, and 62.

231   Bernard D. Weinryb, *The Jews of Poland* (Philadelphia: Jewish Publication Society of America, 1973), 277.

232   Mendel Piekarz, "Hasidism as a Socio-religious Movement on the Evidence of *Devekut,*" in Ada Rapaport-Albert, *Hasidism Reappraised* (The Littman Library of Jewish Civilization, 1966), 228.

233   My version. See also Buber in *Tales of the Hasidim: Early Masters,* 70.

234   *Amtahat Benyamin,* 1-2.

235   *Shivhei HaBesht,* 82.

236   Dresner, *The Zaddik,* 232.

237   *Toldedot Ya'akov Yosef,* 147a.

238   Dresner, *The Zaddik,* 235.

239   *Toledot Ya'akov Yosef, Kedoshim* 102c. See also *Tikkunei Zohar* 19.

240   *Tzaf'nat Panei'ah* 49c.

241   *Meir Einayim, Yitro.*

242   *Rishpei Esh* 111; Heschel, *Man is Not Alone,* 12.

243   *Tza'va'at Ha'Rivash* 127.

244   *Devarim Hemadim Avot,* chapter 1.

245   *Toledot Ya'akov Yoseph* 47c.

246   *Toledot Ya'akov Yosef* 137c.

247 Idel, *Vocal Rites and Broken Theologies*, appendices C and E; 220, 264.

248 Joseph Dan, *The Heart and the Fountain* (New York: Oxford University Press, 2002), 196.

249 Raphael Mahler, *A History of Modern Jewry: 1780-1815* (London: Valentine, Mitchell, 1971), 457.

250 Smith, *The World's Religions*, 102-3.

251 *Keter Shem Tov* 16a.

252 *Tzi'va'at HaRivash* 5b.

253 *Tzaf'nhat Pa'nay'akh, Yit'ro*.

254 *Tzi'va'at HaRivash* 130.

255 *Sefer Baal Shem Tov, Bereshit*.

256 *Tiferet Shlomo, Toledot*.

257 Etkes, *The Besht*, 110.

258 Heschel, *A Passion for Truth*, 73-74; also see the sources in Steinmann, *B'er HaHasidut*, 123-24.

259 *Toldot Ya'akov Yosef*, Devarim, 175c.

260 *T'shu'ot Hain, Va'era*.

261 Steinmann, *B'er HaHasidut*, 123.

262 Charlene Spretnek, *States of Grace: The Recovery of Meaning in the Postmodern Age* (San Francisco: HarperSanFrancisco, 1991), 76.

263 Ibid, 113.

264 Ibid, 78.

265 Philip Novak, *The World's Wisdom* (Edison, NJ: Castle Books, 1994), 74.

266 Wayne Teasdale, *The Mystic Heart* (Novato, CA: New World Library, 1999), 102.

267 My versions are free renderings of Lucy S. Dawidowitz's translations, found in *The Golden Tradition: Jewish Life and Thought in Eastern Europe* (Boston: Beacon Press, 1967), chapter 14, translated from *Gdolim fun undzer tsayt*, NY, 1927.

268 Immanuel Etkes, "Rabbi Israel Salanter and His Psychology of *Musar*," in Arthur Green, ed., *Jewish Spirituality from the Sixteenth-Century Revival to the Present* (New York: Crossroad, 1987), ch. 7.

269 *Tzaf'nhat Pa'anei'ah, B'shalah* 5.

270 *Ben Porat Yoseph* 82b.

271 Etkes, in *Jewish Spirituality from the Sixteenth-Century Revival to the Present*, 219; taken from *Sefer Or Yisra'el*, 112.

272 *Talmud, Tractate Ta'anit* 22a.

273 *Keter Shem Tov* 272.

274 *Degel Mahaneh Efrayim, Parashat Tei'tzei.*

275 Heschel, *A Passion for Truth,* 46.

276 *Midrash Pinhas 38b.*

277 *Leket Imrey Peninim* 208b.

278 *Sippurei Chasidism, Shir HaShirim.*

279 *Sefer Milin Y'karin* 18a.

280 *Me'or Ei'nayim, V'et'hanan* 104.

281 Green, *Radical Judaism,* 75, 176.

282 *Hayom Yom,* 78.

283 *Ner Mitzvah* 13b.

284 *Toledot Ya'akov Yoseph, Ekev.*

285 Heszel Klepfisz, *Culture of Compassion: The Spirit of Polish Jewry from Hasidism to the Holocaust* (New York: KTAV Publishing House, 1983), 42.

286 Diane Ackerman, "The Thisness of What Is," *Shambhala Sun,* March 2008.

287 *Or Haganuz L'tzaddikim, Parashat Balak;* Mosheh Aaron Krassen, "Introduction—Rabbi Israel Baal Shem Tov: Prophet of a New Paradigm," in Menachem Kallus, *Pillar of Prayer,* xx.

288 Hillel Zeitlin, *Hasidic Spirituality for a New Era,* edited and translated by Arthur Green (New York: Paulist Press, 2012). 34.

289 Buber, *Tales of the Hasidim: The Early Masters,* 69.

290 I have revised the English translation of this poem found in *Poems of Yehoash,* selected and translated by Isidore Goldstick, Canadian Yehoash Committee, 1952, 74.

291 Rav Avraham Yitzhak Kook, "Universal Love," trans. Burt Jacobson, *Agada Magazine,* II:3, Winter, 1984, 26-30.

292 Phillip Bennet, *Let Yourself Be Loved* (New York: Paulist Press, 1997), 53.

293 Sylvia Boorstein, *That's Funny, You Don't Look Buddhist* (New York: HarperOne, 1998), 129.

294 Ibid, 128, 130.

295 See Elizabeth Svoboda, *What Makes a Hero: The Surprising Science of Selflessnes* (New York: Current/Penguin Books, 2013), chapter 4.

296 Roger Walsh, *The World of Shamanism* (Woodbury, MN: Llewellyn Publications, 2007), 37.

297 This is my rendering. See also *In Praise of the Baal Shem Tov,* #19-20.

298 *Keter Shem Tov,* 1.

299 Michael Harner, *The Way of the Shaman* (San Francisco: HarperSanFrancisco, 1990), 20-21.

300 Neville Drury, *The Elements of Shamanism* (Rockport, MA: Element Books, 1994), 101.

301 *Shivhei HaBesht,* #15 (abbreviated).

302 Karl Erich Grozinger, "The Source Value of the Basic Recensions of *Shivhei haBesht,*" in Ada Rappaport-Albert, ed., *Hasidism Reappraised* (New York: The Littman Library of Jewish Civilization, 1996), 354-63.

303 "Demuto Hahistorit Shel R' Yisroel Baal Shem Tov," in *Devarim B'Go,* Vol. 2, 287-324, Tel Aviv, 1982.

304 Simon Dubnow, *Toldot HaHasidut,* Ho'tza'at D'vir, Tel Aviv, 1930, 50.

305 Rosman, *Founder of Hasidism,* 13.

306 Walsh, *The World of Shamanism,* 223, 234.

307 Dean Radin, *The Conscious Universe* (New York: HarperOne, 1997), xiv-xv. Another book that I found useful was Maureen Caudill's *Impossible Realities.*

308 Etkes, *The Besht,* 243.

309 Hundert, *Jews in Poland-Lithuania in the Eighteenth Century,* 142.

310 Moshe Idel, *Ascensions on High in Jewish Mysticism* (New York: Central European University Press, 2005), 149-50.

311 Yohanan Petrovsky-Shtern, "You Will Find It in the Pharmacy," in Glenn Dynner, ed., *Holy Dissent: Jewish and Christian Mystics in Eastern Europe* (Detroit: Wayne State University Press, 2011), 32.

312 Antony Polonsky, *The Jews in Poland and Russia, Vol. I* (New York: The Littman Library of Jewish Civilization, 2009), 14.

313 Nathan Hanover, *Abyss of Despair: The Famous 17th Century Chronicle Depicting Jewish Life in Russia and Poland During the Chmielnicki Massacres of 1648-1649* (New York: Routledge, 1983), xiii-xiv.

314 William Helmreich, in Hanover, *op cit.,* xiii.

315 Rachel Elior, *The Mystical Origins of Hasidism* (New York: Routledge, 2006), 5-6.

316 Hundert, *Jews in Poland-Lithuania in the Eighteenth Century,* 183-84.

317 Ibid, 184f.

318 Nehemia Polen, *The Holy Fire: The Teachings of Rabbi Kalonymus Kalman Shapira, the Rebbe of the Warsaw Ghetto* (New York: Jason Aronson, 1994), xvii, 20.

319 Dresner, *The Zaddik,* 28-29.

320 *Toledot Ya'akov Yosef* 209b.

321 Dresner, *The Zaddik,* 30-31.

322 Ibid, 89.

323   Ibid, 116-17.

324   Ibid, 125.

325   Ibid, 128, 241-2.

326   Heschel, in Dresner, *The Zaddik,* 8.

327   Rabbi Tirzah Firestone, *Wounds into Wisdom: Healing Intergenerational Jewish Trauma* (Rhinebeck, NY: Monkfish Book Publishing, 2019), 15, 105.

328   Ibid, 167.

329   Ibid, 80.

330   Ibid, 63-64, 52.

331   Ibid, 153.

332   Ibid, 123.

333   Ibid, 105.

334   Ibid,152.

335   Thomas Hübl, "Lean into Wisdom," *Spirituality and Health Magazine,* September/October, 2020, 54.

336   *Ben Porat Yosef.*

337   See Benzion Dinur, "The Origins of Hasidism and Its Social and Messianic Foundations," in *Essential Papers on Hasidism,* ch. 4.

338   *M'or Einayim, Pinhas.*

339   *Teshuot Hen B'likutim, Parashat Vva'yehi; Sefer Baal Shem Tov I,* #13, 240.

340   *Sefer Baal Shem Tov, Vayerah,* 14.

341   Smith, *The World's Religions,* 101.

342   Sylvia Boorstein, "The Buddha's Four Noble Truths," in *Lion's Roar,* September 1, 2002.

343   From the *Dhammapada,* trans. Thomas Byrom, in Jack Kornfield, ed., *Teachings of the Buddha* (Boston: Shambhala, 2007), 65.

344   Adapted from the *Digha Nikaya,* trans. Maurice Walshe, in Jack Kornfield, *op. cit,* 7.

345   Frankel, *Sacred Therapy,* 83-84.

346   *K'tonet Passim,* 46a.

347   *Nofet Tzufim* 50:69; *M'vaser Tzedek, B'har.*

348   *Igeret D'Kalah, Korach.*

349   *B'er Hahasidut: Sefer HaBesht,* 123.

350   *Ketonet Passim* 27a.

351   See Burt Jacobson, "Fear, Loss, and the Power of Yielding," in Goldie Milgram, ed., *Seeking and Soaring: Jewish Approaches to Spiritual Direction* (New Rochelle, NY: Reclaiming Judaism Press, 2009), 244-56.

352   *Devarim Hehmadim Avot,* ch. 1.

353 Wiesel, *Souls on Fire*, 36-7.

354 The interview is entitled, "Falling in Love with Death." Beyondawakeningseries.com, July 5, 2015.

355 *B'er Hahasidut: Sefer HaBesht*, 142.

356 Ibid, 122.

357 The entire text comes from *Sefer Ginzei Yosef,* authored by R. Yosef Bloch of Stanov and published in 1792. It is found in *Sefer Baal Shem Tov, B'raishit* 88.

358 *Yativ Panim* 1:119.

359 *Ketonet Passim* 27a.

360 *Degel Mahaneh Efrayim, Yitro* and *B'shalah.*

361 *Ginzei Yisrael, Rosh Hashanah* 15; *Tzaf'nat Pa'neah* 76b.

362 Personal email with the author.

363 The Dalai Lama and Desmond Tutu, *The Book of Joy* (New York: Random House, 2016), 283-84.

364 Wiesel, *Souls on Fire,* 38.

365 Heschel, *A Passion for Truth*, 52.

366 *Shivhei HaBesht,* 61.

367 *Likutei Yekarim 2b.*

368 Chaim Bloch, *Priester der Liebe,* Vienna, 1930, 36ff.

369 Verena Kast, *Joy, Inspiration and Hope* (College Station, TX: Texas A&M Press, 1991), x.

370 Martin Buber, *Meetings* (La Salle, IL: Open Court Publishing, 1973), 39. Buber remembered that it was his father who took him to the Hasidic synagogue, but Prof. Sam Shonkoff told me it was his grandfather. See https://www.academia.edu/40906445/_Martin_Buber_in_A_New_Hasidism_Roots_ed_Arthur_Green_and_Ariel_Mayse.

371 *Tsi'vat HaRivash* 20.

372 Buber, *Hasidism and Modern Man,* 51.

373 Maurice Friedman, *Martin Buber's Life and Work: The Early Years* (Detroit: Wayne State University Press, 1988), 179.

374 Buber, *The Origin and Meaning of Hasidism,* ed. and trans. Maurice Friedman (Atlantic Highlands, NJ: Humanities Press International, 1988), 25-26.

375 Ibid, 41.

376 Ibid, 55-56. I have substituted the phrase "intentional holiness" for Friedman's use of the word "consecration."

377 Martin Buber, *Two Types of Faith* (New York: Harper Torchbooks, 1961), 56ff, 63ff, 136f.

378 Ibid, 11.

379 Shaul Magid, "Defining Christianity and Judaism from the Perspective of Religious Anarchy: Martin Buber on Jesus and the Baal Shem Tov," in Sam Berrin Shonkoff, *Martin Buber: His Intellectual and Scholarly Legacy* (Boston: Brill, 2018), 38.

380 See David B. Gowler, *What Are They Saying About the Historical Jesus?*, ch. 3; see also Richard Maurice Bucke, *Cosmic Consciousness* (New York: E.P. Dutton, 1901), 103ff.

381 Stephen Mitchell, *The Gospel According to Jesus* (New York: HarperCollins, 1991), 9-10.

382 Arthur Green, from a review of Moshe Rosman's *Founder of Hasidism: A Quest for the Historical Baal Shem Tov,* in *History of Religions,* November 2000, 40:2, 185-87.

383 Wiesel, *Souls on Fire*, 15.

384 There are a number of versions of this story. This rendition is based on Buber's version in *Tales of the Hasidim: The Early Masters*, 99-100.

385 Idel, *Hasidism*, 173.

386 Krassen, "Rabbi Israel Baal Shem Tov: Prophet of a New Paradigm," in Kalus, *Pillar of Prayer*, xvii.

387 Buber, *Tales of the Hasidim: The Early Masters*, 100.

388 Smith, *The World's Religions*, 135.

389 Arthur Green, "From Circle to Court: The Maggid of Mezritsh and Hasidism's First Opponents" in *Hasidism: A New History,* ed. Biale, 77-8.

390 Rivka Horwitz, *Buber's Way to "I and Thou"* (Philadelphia: Jewish Publication Society, 1988), 19-20.

391 Scholem, *The Messianic Idea in Judaism*, 203ff.

392 Ibid, 210. See also the study of the Baal Shem's form of devekut in Roman A. Foxbrunner's *Habad,* Jason Aronson, 1993, ch. 1; also Miles Krassen's *Uniter of Heaven and Earth* (Albany: State University of New York Press, 1999), ch. 2; and the index to Rachel Elior's *The Mystical Origins of Hasidism*.

393 *Toledot Ya'akov Yosef, Parashat Vaye'rah*; a Hebrew collection of the Besht's teachings on devekut can be found in *Sefer Meir Einei Yisrael,* by Yehoshuah Yosef Kornbleit, published by Machon Da'at Yosef. For a collection of the Besht's teachings on devekut in English see David Sears, *The Path of the Baal Shem Tov* (Northvale, NJ: Jason Aronson, 1997), 26-36.

394 *Keter Shem Tov,* 200.

395 Etkes, *The Besht*, 143-44.

396 *Sefer Baal Shem Tov, Parashat Toledot.*

397 Idel, *Hasidism*, 204.

398 Buber, *Tales of the Hasidim: Early Masters*, 1.

399 Martin Buber, *Between Man and Man*, cited from Aubrey Hodes, *Martin Buber: An Intimate Portrait* (New York: Viking Compass, 1971), 11.

400 I found this anecdote in Alan Unterman's *The Wisdom of the Jewish Mystics* (Norfolk, CT: New Directions, 1976), 58.

401 Martin Buber, *The Legend of the Baal-Shem* (New York: Schocken Books, 1969), 19.

402 Hodes, *Martin Buber*, 222.

403 Gary Snyder, *Turtle Island* (New York: New Directions, 1974), 103.

404 C. G. Jung, *The Undiscovered Self* (Princeton: Princeton University Press, 2010), 46.

405 Scholem, *Major Trends in Jewish Mysticism*, 340-41.

406 Sanford L. Drob, *Kabbalistic Visions: C.G. Jung and Jewish Mysticism* (New York: Routledge, 2010), v.

407 Sanford Drob, "Jung's Kabbalistic Visions," in *Journal of Jungian Theory and Practice*, Vol. 7, No. 1, 2005.

408 *Or HaEmet* 36c-d; see also Idel, *Hasidism*, 235.

409 C. G. Jung, *The Archetypes of the Collective Unconscious* 9:1, in Collected Works (Princeton: Princeton University Press, 1968).

410 Gershom Scholem, "The Meaning of the Torah in Jewish Mysticism," in *Kabbalah and Its Symbolism* (New York: Schocken Books, 1969), 50.

411 *Or Ha'Ganuz LaTzaddikim, Va'yik'rah.*

412 *Toledot Ya'akov Yosef, Lech L'khah* 19a.

413 *Ben Porat Yosef, Toledot/Sefer Baal Shem Tov, B'raishit.*

414 It is not clear, however, whether the Besht believed these events were part of a biological inheritance, or were instilled in the consciousness of Jewish children through their education and home and community observances.

415 In this and other teachings I don't translate the word *Mitzrayim,* the ancient Hebrew word for Egypt, so as not to demonize the contemporary nation of Egypt. Jewish writers often understand the word Mitzrayim to be related to the Hebrew word *tza'ar,* which means the narrow place, the land of distress.

416 *Degel Mahaneh Efrayim, Masai.*

417 *B'er Hahasidut: Sefer HaBesht,* 99; *Toldot Ya'akov Yosef, Sh'mini,* 88a.

418 *B'er HaHasidut: Sefer Baal Shem Tov* 113.

419 *Otzar HaHayim, Behar* 264b.

420 *Toldot Ya'akov Yosef,* Pekudei 75a.

421 *Otzar HaHayim, Behar* 264b.

422 Frankel, *Sacred Therapy,* 104-5.

423 *B'er HaHasidut: Sefer Baal Shem Tov* 124; *Teshuot Hen,* Vaera; *Degel Mahane Efrayim,* Balak.

424 *Otzar HaHayim, Behar* 264b.

425 C. G. Jung, *Letters, Vol. I: 1906-1950,* ed. Gerhard Adler and Aniela Jaffé, trans. R.F.C. Hull (Princeton, Bollingen, 1992), x.

426 David Maybury-Lewis, *Millennium: Tribal Wisdom and the Modern World* (NY: Viking Penguin, 1992), x.

427 Jung, *Modern Man in Search of a Soul,* ch. 11.

428 Jolande Jacobi, *The Way of Individuation* (New York: New American Library, 1967), 91.

429 Many different versions of this parable are found in the works of the Besht's disciples. The rendering above is an imaginative reconstruction based on the following texts: *Ben Porat Yosef* 70c and 111; *Sefer Baal Shem Tov, Vayelech,* note 3 and *Noah,* note 83; *B'er HaHasidut* 246:9.

430 Erich Neumann, *The Roots of Jewish Consciousness, Vol. 2: Hasidism,* ed. Ann Conrad Lammers (NY: Routledge, 2019), 136.

431 Jung, *Modern Man in Search of a Soul.* 130.

432 Jung, *Collected Works, Vol, 17.* "The Development of Personality," 115.

433 Jacobi, *The Way of Individuation,* 107.

434 Idel, *Ben: Sonship and Jewish Mysticism,* ch. 6.

435 *Sh'mu'ah Tovah* 71b. See also Rivka Schatz, *Hasidism as Mysticism,* 173.

436 Idel, *Vocal Rites and Broken Theologies,* 122.

437 Idel, *Hasidism,* 204, 192.

438 Erich Neumann, "Mystical Man," in Joseph Campbell, *The Mystic Vision* (Princeton: Princeton University Press, 1968), 405.

439 *B'er HaHasidut: Sefer HaBesht,* 309.

440 This teaching comes from Alan Unterman's *The Wisdom of the Jewish Mystics* (New York: New Directions, 1976).

441 Cited in *Mystic Journey: Getting to the Heart of Your Soul's Story* by Robert Atkinson (New York: Cosimo Books, 2012), 48.

442 Hillel Zeitlin, *Hasidic Spirituality for a New Era* (NY: Paulist Press, 2012), 98.

443 Reuven Kruger, "Hasidism, Jung, and the Jewish Spiritual Crisis," in *The Jewish Review of Books, Vol. 12, Num. 4, Winter* 2022.

444 Neumann, *"Mystical Man,"* in *The Mystic Vision,* 412.

445 Neumann, *The Roots of Jewish Consciousness, Vol. II: Hasidism,* 46.

446 Green, *Seek My Face, Speak My Name,* 8.

447 Elior, *Jewish Mysticism,* 133, 67.

448 Elior, *The Mystical Origins of Hasidism,* 74, 185.

449 *Maggid Devarav L'ya'akov,* 240.

450 David Gelernter, *Judaism: A Way of Being* (New Haven, CT: Yale University Press, 2009), chapter 2.

451 Gelernter, *Judaism,* 53.

452 Elior, *Jewish Mysticism,* 66-67.

453 Cited by Immanuel Etkes, *The Besht,* 136.

454 Rachel Elior, "The Origins of Hasidism," in *Scripta Judaica Cracoviensia,* Vol. 10, 2012, 85-109.

455 Huston Smith, *Forgotten Truth* (New York: HarperCollins, 1976), 1-5.

456 Arthur Green and Barry W. Holtz, *Your Word Is Fire* (New York: Schocken Books, 1987), 56.

457 Menaham Kallus, *Pillar of Prayer* (Louisville: Fons Vitae, 2011), #148.13; This is further proof for my argument later on in this chapter that the Besht affirmed both a non-dualistic and a dualistic understanding of reality, depending on the current state of consciousness of the mystic.

458 Here I disagree with Elior. Although there are a few teachings of the Besht that seem to indicate that "the physical world turns out to be an illusion without substance," the vast majority of his utterances show that he accepted the physical world as real. Most of the early teachings that focus on the illusory character of the physical world derive from the teachings of the Besht's disciple, Dov Baer, the Maggid of Medziritch.

459 When the Baal Shem used the phrase the "World of Thought," he was not referring to analytical thought at all, but rather to the vast nondualistic awareness of existence when it is grasped from a divine perspective, i.e., the sefirah of Hokhmah.

460 This translation comes from Stephen Mitchell's, *The Enlightened Heart* (New York: HarperPerennial, 1989), 13.

461 Mitchell, *The Enlightened Heart,* 4.

462 James N. Judd, *Two Ways of Light: Kabbalah and Vedanta* (Xlibris, 2000), 15.

463 Ibid, 86.

464 Ibid, 86-7.

465 Joseph P. Schultz, *Judaism and the Gentile Faiths: Comparative Studies of Religion* (Teaneck, NJ: Fairleigh Dickonson, 1981), 82-83.

466 *Tzaf'nat Pa'nei'akh, Bo.*

467 *K'tonet Passim* 11b.

468 *Toledot Ya'akov Yosef, Vayashev; Toledot Ya'akov Yosef,* 157d.

469 Solomon Schechter, *Studies in Judaism* (New York: Atheneum, 1970), 167.

470 There are scholars, though, who take a more radical view of this issue. Gedaliah Nigal of Bar Ilan University in Tel Aviv believes that R. Jacob Joseph and the Maggid actually put forward two quite different interpretations of the Besht's spiritual philosophy. Historian Moshe Rosman apparently agrees with Nigal. See Moshe Rosman, 138.

471 Arthur Green, with Ebn Leader, Ariel Mayse and Or Rose, *Around the Maggid's Table: Torah Interpretations by the Founders of Hasidism* (Woodstock, VT: Jewish Lights, 2013), 3-4.

472 Joanna Macy, *World as Lover, World as Self* (Berkeley, CA: Parallax Press, 1991), 8.

473 Alan Lightman, *A Sense of the Mysterious* (New York: Vintage Books, 2005), 42.

474 Richard Elliot Friedman, *The Disappearance of God: A Divine Master* (New York: Little, Brown, 1995), 165.

475 Stuart A. Kauffman, *Reinventing the Sacred* (New York: Basic Books, 2008), 284, 287-88.

476 *Likkutei Diburim* 1322.

477 Brian Swimme, *The Universe is a Green Dragon* (Santa Fe, NM: Bear & Company, 1984), 25-26.

478 Ibid, 18.

479 Ibid, 36.

480 Brian Swimme, *The Hidden Heart of the Cosmos* (Maryknoll, NY: Orbis Books, 1996), 109.

481 Ibid, 97.

482 Ibid, 100.

483 Richard Maurice Bucke, *Cosmic Consciousness,* no page numbers listed.

484 Ibid, 3.

485 Michael Robinson, *Worshiping Walt: The Whitman Disciples* (Princeton: Princeton University Press, 2008), x.

486 Ibid, 229-30.

487 Bucke, *Cosmic Consciousness,* 123.

488 Pierre Hadot, *Plotinus: The Simplicity of Vision* (Chicago: University of Chicago Press, 1993), 55.

489 Plotinus, *The Enneads* 7.3.2.

490 *Der Jude sein Judentum,* 273, cited by Gershon Scholem in "Martin Buber's

Conception of Judaism," in *On Jews and Judaism in Crisis* (New York: Schocken Books, 1976), 144.

491 Huxley, *The Perennial Philosophy*, 5.

492 *Or HaMeir, Parashat Pekudei.*

493 Buxbaum, *The Light and Fire of the Baal Shem Tov*, 101. Buxbaum provides the following footnote for his sources: Glitzenstein, *Sefer Ha'Toldot*: Rabbi Yisrael Baal Shem Tov, vol. 2, 631. Horodetzky, *Rabbi Yisrael Baal Shem Tov: Hayav, V'Torato*, 14, quoting *Keter Shem Tov. Midrah Rivash Tov*, 52, quoting *Likkutei Yekarim*.

494 *Or HaMeir, Parashat Pekudei.*

495 Buber, *Tales of the Hasidim: Early Masters*, 52. The phrase "coming world" is a translation of the Hebrew *Olam HaBah,* also translated as "The World to Come."

496 *Toldot Ya'akov Yosef, Bereshit.*

497 *Or HaHokhmah Va'yakel, Ki Tissa #15.*

498 *Toledot Ya'akov Yosef, B'rai'sheet* 12b.

499 *Toledot, Va'era* 44b.

500 *Toledot Ya'akov Yosef, Vayera* 2a. See also note #1027 in Kallus' *Pillar of Prayer.*

501 *Toledot Ya'akov Yosef, Parashat Vaye'rah*; a Hebrew collection of the Besht's teachings on devekut can be found in *Sefer Meir Einei Yisrael,* by Yehoshuah Yosef Kornbleit, published by Machon Da'at Yosef.

502 Buxbaum, *The Light and Fire of the Baal Shem Tov,* 223-24.

503 Karen Bouris, ed. "The Four Aspects of Love," by Thich Nhat Hanh, *Spirituality and Health Magazine,* July 16, 2012.

504 *Or HaMeir, Parashat Pekudei.*

505 Smith, *The Religions of Man,* 129, 130.

506 Ibid, 2.

507 Heschel, *A Passion for Truth,* 24.

508 *B'er HaHasidut: Sefer HaBesht* 171.

509 Smith, *The Religions of Man,* 272.

510 Ibid, 278.

511 *B'er HaHasidut: Sefer HaBesht* 108.

512 *Sha'ar Ha'otiot Hash'ga'hah P'ratit, Ot Gimel.*

513 Heschel, *God in Search of Man,* 107.

514 Heschel, *Man Is Not Alone,* 40-44.

515 Ibid, 55-56.

516 Moshe Idel, *Old Worlds, New Mirrors: On Jewish Mysticism and*

Twentieth-Century Thought (Philadelphia: University of Pennsylvania Press, 2010), ch. 12.

517 Heschel, *God in Search of Man,* 119.

518 *Between God and Man: an Interpretation of Judaism,* selected, edited and introduced by Fritz A. Rothschild (New York: The Free Press, 1959), 150.

519 Heschel, *A Passion for Truth,* 307.

520 Henry Rosemont and Huston Smith, *Is There a Universal Grammar of Religion?* (LaSalle, IL: Open Court, 2008), 73, 83.

521 Don Lattin, *The Harvard Psychedelic Club* (New York: HarperOne, 2010), 207.

522 From the foreword to Heard's book, *The Gospel According to Gamaliel* (Eugene, OR: Wipf & Stock, 1945), xiii.

523 Aldous Huxley, *Eyeless in Gaza* (London: Chatto and Windus, 1936), 156.

524 Aldous Huxley, *The Perennial Philosophy,* (London: Chatto and Windus, 1948), 1.

525 *Ba'er HaHasidut,* 309.

526 Huxley, *The Perennial Philosophy,* 11-12.

527 *Bhagavad-Gita: The Song of God,* trans. Swami Prabhavananda and Christopher Isherwood. Introduction by Aldous Huxley (New York: New American Library, 1944), 13.

528 David Brooks, "The Way to Heal These Great Divides is One Person at a Time" in *AARP Bulletin,* November 2023, 40.

529 Robert N. Bellah, et. al., *Habits of the Heart: Individualism and Commitment in American Life* (Berkeley, CA: University of California Press, 1985), ch. 1.

530 From the book *Grace and Grit* by Ken Wilber and Treya Killam Wilber (Boston: Shambhala, 1991), 77-88.

531 Ken Wilber, *The Eye of the Spirit* (Boston: Shambhala, 1997), 44, 39.

532 Ken Wilber, *Grace and Grit,* 77-78.

533 Philip Goldberg, *American Veda: From Emerson and the Beatles to Yoga and Meditation—How Indian Spirituality Changed the West* (NY: Three Rivers Press, 2010), 345.

534 Wayne Teasdale, *The Mystic Heart: Discovering a Universal Spirituality in the World's Religions* (New York: New World Library, 2001), 236.

535 Zalman Schachter-Shalomi, *Jewish with Feeling: A Guide to Meaningful Jewish Practice* (New York: Riverhead Books, 2005), 184.

536 Ibid, 186-87.

537 Zalman Schachter-Shalomi, "The Future of Neo-Hasidism," in Shaul

Magid, *American Post-Judaism* (Bloomington, IN: Indiana University Press, 2013), 39.

538　This legend comes from Martin Buber's early work, *The Legend of the Baal-Shem*. I've simplified Buber's more elaborate version.

539　A.H. Maslow, *Religions, Values and Peak-Experiences* (New York: Penguin Compass, 1970), 49.

540　See Algis Valiunas, "Abraham Maslow and the All-American Self," *The New Atlantis*, Number 33, Fall 2011, 93-110.

541　Maslow, *Religions, Values and Peak-Experiences*, appendix G, "B-Values as Descriptions of Perception in Peak-Experiences."

542　Ibid, 64-65, 95.

543　Ibid, 26-27. Maslow lists Richard Maurice Bucke's *Cosmic Consciousness* in his bibliography.

544　Ibid, 113.

545　Schachter-Shalomi, *My Life in Jewish Renewal*, 166.

546　Maslow, *Religions, Values and Peak-Experiences*, 27.

547　Schachter-Shalomi, *My Life in Jewish Renewal*, 167-68.

548　Mary Barnard, "The God in the Flowerpot," *The American Scholar* 32, 4 (Autumn 1963): 584.

549　Dan Merkur, *The Mystery of Manna: The Psychedelic Sacrament of the Bible* (Rochester, VT: Park Street Press, Rochester, 2000).

550　Benny Shannon, "Biblical Entheogens: A Speculative Hypothesis," in *Time and Mind*, Volume 1:1, March 2008, 51–74.

551　Rick Strassman, M.D., *DMT and the Soul of Prophecy: A New Science of Spiritual Revelation in the Hebrew Bible* (Rochester, VT: Park Street Press, 2014).

552　Their article "Cannabis and Frankincense at the Judahite Shrine of Arad" appeared in *Tel Aviv: Journal of the Institute of Archeology of Tel Aviv University*, Vol. 47:1, 2020; Madison Margolin, "Ecstatic Excavations: A Conversation on Jewish Psychedelia with Natalie Lyla Ginsberg," at AyinPress.org.

553　Sharon Packer, "Jewish Mystical Movements and the European Ergot Epidemics," in *The Israel Journal of Psychiatry and Related Sciences*, 1998, 35:3, 231.

554　Ibid, 234.

555　Yaffa Eliach, "The Russian Dissenting Sects and Their Influence on Israel Baal Shem Tov, Founder of Hassidism," Proceedings of the American Academy for Jewish Research, Vol. 36 (1968), 57-83. Unfortunately, Eliach's references to the pipe stories of the Besht are cited from an edition of *Shivhei HaBesht* that I have not been able to locate.

556 Kenneth Cohen, *Honoring the Medicine* (New York: Random House, 2003), 274, 276.

557 Louis Jacobs, "Tobacco and the Hasidim," *Polin* 11, 1998, 26.

558 Solomon Maimon, "On a Secret Society, and Therefore a Long Chapter," in Gershon David Hundert, ed., *Essential Papers on Hasidism* (New York: New York University Press, 1991), 17.

559 Reb Zalman Schachter, *Fragments of a Future Scroll* (Germantown, PA: Leaves of Grass Press, 1975), 10.

560 Ibid, 153.

561 Ibid, 154, 97.

562 William Novak, "A Conversation with Arthur Green," in *Kerem*, Spring 1995, 41.

563 Itzik Lodger, "Psychedelics and Kabbalah," in James A. Sleeper and Alan L. Mintz, eds., *The New Jews* (New York: Vintage Books, 1971), 177.

564 Ibid.

565 Ibid.

566 Michael Pollan, *How to Change Your Mind* (New York: Penguin Press, 2018), 136-37.

567 Michael Pollan, quoted in Mandy Oaklander's "This Will Change Your Mind About Psychedelic Drugs," *Time* magazine, May 16, 2018.

568 From "Can Psychedelics Heal the Jewish People: This Rabbi Is Exploring That Question," JWeekly.com, August 20, 2019.

569 Madison Margolin, "Ecstatic Excavations: A Conversation on Jewish Psychedelia," March 11, 2022, Ayinpress.org.

570 Barry Barkan, "You Are Building It and They Are Coming," in Victor Gross, Reuven Goldfarb, Yehudit Goldfarb, Nadya Gross, and Miriam Stampfer, *Ancient Roots, Radical Practices, and Contemporary Visions,* (Berkeley, CA: The Aquarian Minyan, 1999), 75.

571 Ibid.

572 *Sippurei Chasidism, Shir HaShirim.*

573 Arthur Waskow, *These Holy Sparks: The Rebirth of the Jewish People* (New York: Harper & Row, 1983), 8-9.

574 Burt Jacobson, "Blueprint for a Havurah," in *The First Jewish Catalog* (Philadelphia: The Jewish Publication Society, 1973), 281.

575 Rabbi Shefa Gold, "Love at the Center," at rabbishefagold.com.

576 *Me'or Einayim, Pinchas.*

577 Michael Lerner, *Revolutionary Love: A Political Manifesto to Heal and Transform the World* (Berkeley, CA: University of California Press, 2019), 1-2.

578 This kabbalist was the anonymous author of the *Raya Mehemna* and the *Tikkunim,* which are part of the Zohar. See Gershom Scholem, *On the Kabbalah and Its Symbolism* (New York: Schocken Books, 1969), 68ff.

579 *Kol Sippurei Baal Shem Tov,* vol. 1, 207. Translation by Yitzhak Buxbaum, *Jewish Tales of Mystic Joy,* 24.

580 Hodes, *Martin Buber,* 56.

581 See sefaria.org, "What Was Said at Sinai," by Jeff Schulman.

582 *B'er Hahasidut: Sefer HaBesht,* 99.

583 Ralph Metzner, *The Unfolding Self: Varieties of Transformative Experience* (Novato, CA: Origin Press, 1986), 24.

584 This is my own rendering of the parable. Hebrew versions can be found in *B'er HaHasidut,* 246, and in *Degel Mahaneh Ephraim, Sh'mot* 20:15.

585 *Sefer Baal Shem Tov, B'rei'shit.*

586 *Me'or Eyna'im, Yis'mah Lev, Mesehet Shabbat.*

587 Hal Zina Bennett, *Spirit Guides: Companions and Mentors for Your Inner Journey* (Tenacity Press, 1997).

588 Tara Branch, "Taking Refuge in the Buddha," July 10, 2013, blog post at TaraBranch.com.

589 *Ben Porat Yosef* 50a.

590 *Tsi'va'at Harivash* 3.

591 *Tsi'va'at Ha'Rivash* 95.

592 Green and Holtz, *Your Word Is Fire: The Hasidic Masters Contemplative Prayer* (NY: Schocken Books, 1987).

593 *Tsi'va'at HaRivash* 41.

594 *Sefer Ba'al Shem Tov, Parashat Bereishit; Keter Shem Tov* 225.

595 *Or Ha'ganuz La'Tzaddikim.*

596 See "Imaginal Journeying to Istanbul," in Menachem Kallus, *Pillar of Prayer.*

597 See Buxbaum, *Jewish Spiritual Practices,* ch. 21.

598 *Likkutim Yekarim* 15b. See Yitzhak Buxbaum, *Jewish Spiritual Practices,* 110.

599 *Keter Shem Tov* 80.

600 Boorstein, *That's Funny, You Don't Look Jewish,* 129.

601 Ibid, 130.

602 Ibid, 128.

603 *Keter Shem Tov, II: 163.*

604 *Keter Shem Tov,* 36.

605   *Ts'va'aht HaRivash* 19.

606   *Avodah U'moreh Derekh* 8:16.

607   *Hidushei HaRim, Yitro.*

608   *Degel Mahaneh Efrayim, Parashat Metzorah.*

609   Though originally published in 1943, "An Analysis of Piety" forms the final chapter of Heschel's *Man Is Not Alone*, 277-78.

610   *Toledot Ya'akov Yosef, Hayyei Sarah.*

611   Thomas R. Kelly, *A Testament of Devotion* (New York: Harper & Row, 1941), 56-57.

612   Zalman Schachter-Shalomi, *Spiritual Intimacy: A Study of Counseling in Hasidism* (New York: Jason Aronson, 1991), 4.

INDEX

Printed in the USA
CPSIA information can be obtained
at www.ICGtesting.com
JSHW021120201024
71907JS00002B/2